More Than Just a Textbook

*Log on to **tx.gr4math.com** to...*

Access your book from home

- **Online Student Edition**
- **Student Workbooks**

See mathematical concepts come to life

- **Personal Tutor**
- **Concepts in Motion**

Practice what you've learned

- **Chapter Readiness**
- **Extra Examples**
- **Self-Check Quizzes**
- **Vocabulary Review**
- **Chapter Tests**
- **Test Practice**

Try these other activities

- **Cross-Curricular Features**
- **Game Time**

Macmillan McGraw-Hill

TEXAS Mathematics

4

Authors

Altieri • Balka • Day • Gonsalves • Grace • Krulik
Malloy • Molix-Bailey • Moseley • Mowry • Myren
Price • Reynosa • Santa Cruz • Silbey • Vielhaber

Mc Graw Hill Macmillan McGraw-Hill

About the Cover

Texas Focus The Rio Grande River is 1,900 miles long. It is the largest river in Texas and one of the longest in the United States. In fact, *Rio Grande* means *big river* in Spanish. The river creates the border between the United States and Mexico. The Rio Grande River is known as an excellent place for trout fishing, rafting, and canoeing. Wildlife such as deer, elk, beaver, muskrat, raccoons, eagles, and falcons are frequently sighted by boaters.

Mathematics Focus This year you will learn about fractions. Of the animals shown on the cover, $\frac{3}{4}$ are raccoons. One-fourth of the animals are trout. Are there more raccoons or trout? What other fractions are represented on the cover?

Mc Graw Hill **Macmillan McGraw-Hill**

The McGraw·Hill Companies

Send all inquiries to:
Macmillan/McGraw-Hill
8787 Orion Place
Columbus, OH 43240-4027

ISBN: 978-0-02-105756-6
MHID: 0-02-105756-7

Printed in the United States of America.

3 4 5 6 7 8 9 10 027/055 16 15 14 13 12 11 10 09 08

Contents in Brief

Authors

Mary Behr Altieri
Putnam/Northern Westchester BOCES
Yorktown Heights, New York

Don S. Balka
Professor Emeritus
Saint Mary's College
Notre Dame, Indiana

Roger Day, Ph.D.
Mathematics Department Chair
Pontiac Township High School
Pontiac, Illinois

Philip D. Gonsalves
Mathematics Coordinator
Alameda County Office of Education and California State University East Bay
Hayward, California

Ellen C. Grace
Consultant
Albuquerque, New Mexico

Stephen Krulik
Mathematics Consultant
Cherry Hill, New Jersey

Carol E. Malloy
Assistant Professor of Mathematics Education
University of North Carolina at Chapel Hill
Chapel Hill, North Carolina

Rhonda J. Molix-Bailey
Mathematics Consultant
Mathematics by Design
Desoto, Texas

Lois Gordon Moseley
Staff Developer
NUMBERS: Mathematics Professional Development
Houston, Texas

Brian Mowry
Independent Math Educational Consultant/Part-Time Pre-K Instructional Specialist
Austin Independent School District
Austin, Texas

Math Online Meet the Authors at tx.gr4math.com

Christina L. Myren
Consultant Teacher
Conejo Valley Unified School District
Thousand Oaks, California

Jack Price
Professor Emeritus
California State Polytechnic University
Pomona, California

Mary Esther Reynosa
Instructional Specialist for Elementary Mathematics
Northside Independent School District
San Antonio, Texas

Rafaela M. Santa Cruz
SDSU/CGU Doctoral Program in Education
San Diego State University
San Diego, California

Robyn Silbey
Math Content Coach
Montgomery County Public Schools
Gaithersburg, Maryland

Kathleen Vielhaber
Mathematics Consultant
St. Louis, Missouri

Consulting and Contributing Authors

Margaret Kilgo
Consulting Author and Educational Consultant
Kilgo Consulting, Inc.
Austin, Texas

Donna J. Long
Mathematics Consultant
Indianapolis, Indiana

FOLDABLES™ **Dinah Zike**
Educational Consultant
Dinah-Might Activities, Inc.
San Antonio, Texas

Texas Mathematics Advisory Board

Macmillan/McGraw-Hill wishes to thank the following professionals for their invaluable feedback during the development of the program. They reviewed a variety of instructional materials at different stages of development.

Julie Acosta
Math Coordinator
McAllen ISD
McAllen, Texas

Tita Alarcon
Elementary Curriculum Specialist
Plano ISD
Plano, Texas

Monica Arriaga
Instructional Specialist
Ryan Elementary
Laredo ISD
Laredo, Texas

Susie Bellah
Kindergarten Teacher
Lakeland Elementary
Humble ISD
Humble, Texas

Elizabeth Firmin Birdwell
Director of Curriculum and Instruction, PK–12
Duncanville ISD
Duncanville, Texas

Brooke Borer
Elementary Math Specialist
Northside ISD
San Antonio, Texas

Wendy Buchanan
3rd Grade Teacher
The Classical Center at Vial
Garland ISD
Garland, Texas

Ida Burkhart
5th Grade Teacher
R. L. Martin Elementary
Brownsville ISD
Brownsville, Texas

Carol S. Carter
PK-8 Math/Science Coordinator
Corsicana ISD
Corsicana, Texas

Patricia Delgado
Mathematics Strategist
Mercedes ISD
Mercedes, Texas

Sheila Q. Delony
3rd Grade Teacher
Maedgen Elementary
Lubbock ISD
Lubbock, Texas

Lorrie Drennon
Teacher/Curriculum Coordinator
Mildred ISD
Mildred, Texas

Carolyn Elender
District Math Instructional Specialist
Pasadena ISD
Pasadena, Texas

Anna Dahinden Flynn
5th Grade Teacher
Coulson Tough K-6 Flex School
Conroe ISD
The Woodlands, Texas

Irene C. Garcia
District Elementary Math Specialist
Midland ISD
Midland, Texas

Lucy Gijon
3rd Grade Bilingual Teacher
Vista Hills Elementary
Ysleta ISD
El Paso, Texas

Gail Brown Guthrie
Teacher
Huppertz Elementary School
San Antonio ISD
San Antonio, Texas

Ellen Hatley
Instructional Teacher for Elementary Mathematics
Northside ISD
San Antonio, Texas

Jennifer Houghton
Math Instruction Specialist
Palm Elementary
Austin ISD
Austin, Texas

Ty G. Jones
Accelerated Mathematics Instruction Specialist
Lancaster ISD
Lancaster, Texas

Frieda Lamprecht
Elementary Curriculum Specialist
Austin ISD
Austin, Texas

Leigh Ann Mewhirter
1st Grade Teacher
University Park Elementary
Highland Park ISD
Dallas, Texas

Susan Murphy
Assistant Principal
Christie Elementary
Frisco ISD
Frisco, Texas

Virginia A. Nwuba
Math Specialist
Tinsley Elementary School
Houston ISD
Houston, Texas

Cindy Pearson
5th Grade Teacher
John D. Spicer Elementary
Birdville ISD
Haltom City, Texas

Julia C. Perez
Elementary Math Content Specialist
Houston ISD
South Region
Houston, Texas

Lacy Prince
3rd Grade Vanguard Teacher
Pleasantville Elementary
Houston ISD
Houston, Texas

Dr. Karen Rhynard
Math Coordinator
Round Rock ISD
Round Rock, Texas

Jesusita I. Rios
District Bilingual Elementary Specialist
Edgewood ISD
San Antonio, Texas

Caroline Soderstrom
Elementary Teacher
O'Shea Keleher Elementary
Socorro ISD
El Paso, Texas

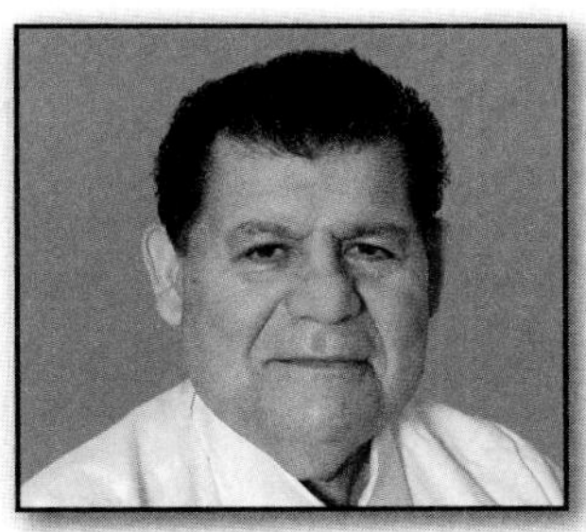

Dr. Jose Solis
Mathematics Dean K–12
Laredo ISD
Laredo, Texas

Alice B. Watkins
Math Specialist
DeZavala Elementary
Midland ISD
Midland, Texas

Maria L. Zsohar
Math Specialist
Richardson ISD
Richardson, Texas

Judy Rogers
Math Specialist, Instructional Division
Lubbock ISD
Lubbock, Texas

Consultants and Reviewers

Macmillan/McGraw-Hill wishes to thank the following professionals for their feedback. They were instrumental in providing valuable input toward the development of this program in these specific areas.

Mathematical Content

Gerald Kulm
Curtis D. Robert Professor
Texas A & M University
College Station, Texas

Leo Armando Ramirez, Sr.
Consultant/Author
Retired (McAllen High School)
McAllen, Texas

Assessment

Jane D. Gawronski
Director of Assessment and Outreach
San Diego State University
San Diego, California

Cognitive Guided Instruction

Susan B. Empson
Associate Professor of Mathematics and Science Education
University of Texas at Austin
Austin, Texas

English Learners

Cheryl Avalos
Mathematics Consultant
Los Angeles County Office of Education, Retired
Hacienda Heights, California

Kathryn Heinze
Graduate School of Education
Hamline University
St. Paul, Minnesota

Family Involvement

Paul Giganti, Jr.
Mathematics Education Consultant
Albany, California

Literature

David M. Schwartz
Children's Author, Speaker, Storyteller
Oakland, California

Problem Solving

Lydia Aranda
First Grade Teacher
Herff Elementary School
San Antonio, Texas

Susie Bellah
Teacher
Lakeland Elementary
Humble, Texas

Elizabeth Firmin Birdwell
Director of Curriculum and Instruction
Duncanville ISD
Duncanville, Texas

Brooke Borer
Elementary Math Specialist
Northside Independent School District
San Antonio, Texas

Anna Dahinden Flynn
5th Grade Math Teacher
Coulson Tough School
Spring, Texas

Ellen D. Hatley
Instructional Teacher for Elementary Mathematics
Northside ISD
San Antonio, Texas

June Ann Hurt
First Grade Teacher
Gifted and Talented
Lamkin Elementary
Cypress, Texas

Jacqueline E. Navarro
Grade Level Chair, 1st Grade
Miguel Carrillo Elementary
San Antonio, Texas

Virginia A. Nwuba
Math Specialist
Tinsley Elementary School
HISD
Houston, Texas

Vertical Alignment

Berchie Holliday
National Educational Consultant
Silver Spring, Maryland

Deborah A. Hutchens, Ed.D.
Principal
Norfolk Highlands Elementary
Chesapeake, Virginia

Texas Reviewers

Each Texas reviewer reviewed at least two chapters of the Student Edition, giving feedback and suggestions for improving the effectiveness of the mathematics instruction.

Adelina Bazan-Alaniz
Coordinator for Mathematics
Mission C.I.S.D
Mission, Texas

Sangeeta Bhattacharya
ESL Lead Teacher
Klentzman Intermediate School
Houston, Texas

Lisa Bolte
Math Specialist
Southwest ISD
San Antonio, Texas

Adriana Cantu
4th Grade Teacher
O'Shea Keleher Elementary
El Paso, Texas

Carol S. Carter
Elementary Math/Science Coordinator
Corsicana ISD
Corsicana, Texas

William J. Comley
First Grade Teacher
Western Hills Primary
Fort Worth, Texas

Mercy Cosper
First Grade Teacher
Pershing Park Elementary
Killeen, Texas

Sheila Delony, M.Ed.
3rd Grade Teacher
Maedgen Elementary
Lubbock, Texas

Irene C. Garcia
Elementary Math Specialist
Administration Office
Midland, Texas

Sylvia Hill, Ph.D.
Math Teacher
The Rice School/LaEscuela Rice
Houston, Texas

Juanita Hutto
Math Skills Specialist
Sammons Elementary
Houston, Texas

Ty G. Jones
AMI Specialist
Lancaster ISD
Lancaster, Texas

Tekeisha Lee
Special Education Teacher
Classical Center at Vial Elementary
Garland, Texas

Elizabeth T. Martinez
Bilingual Teacher
Lantrip Elementary
Houston, Texas

Rashad Javed Rana
Math Coordinator
Donna ISD
Donna, Texas

Judy Rehms-Rogers
Math Specialist
Math Department, Instructional Division
Lubbock ISD
Lubbock, Texas

Delinda Martinez Sanchelli
ESL Lead Teacher
Klentzman Intermediate
Houston, Texas

Velma Sanchez
Teacher
Franklin Elementary
PSJA ISD
Alamo, Texas

Barbara J. Savage
1st Grade Teacher
University Park Elementary
Dallas, Texas

Stacey L. Shapiro
Teacher
Zilker Elementary
Austin, Texas

Mary J. Wick
Second Grade Teacher
Hanby Elementary School
Mesquite, Texas

Maria L. Zsohar
Math Support Teacher
Forest Lane Academy
Dallas, Texas

Contents

Start Smart

Use Place Value to Represent Whole Numbers

Texas Test Practice

- 25, 31, 39, 49, 50, 51

H.O.T. Problems
Higher Order Thinking
19, 25, 30, 34, 39

WRITING IN MATH 19, 21, 25, 27, 30, 31, 34, 39, 41, 49

Chapter 2 Add and Subtract to Solve Problems

Texas Test Practice

- 61, 67, 69, 83, 89, 90, 91

H.O.T. Problems
Higher Order Thinking
57, 61, 67, 74, 82

WRITING IN MATH 57, 61, 63, 67, 68, 69, 71, 74, 77, 82, 89

CHAPTER 3 Organize, Display, and Interpret Data

Texas Test Practice
- 103, 119, 129, 130, 131

H.O.T. Problems
Higher Order Thinking
97, 102, 106, 119, 122

WRITING IN MATH 97, 99, 102, 103, 106, 109, 111, 115, 119, 122, 129

Apply Multiplication and Division Facts

Texas Test Practice

- 143, 147, 153, 159, 169, 177, 178, 179

H.O.T. Problems
Higher Order Thinking
139, 143, 147, 152, 159, 164, 169

WRITING IN ▸MATH 136, 139, 143, 147, 149, 152, 153, 159, 161, 164, 169, 177

Describe Algebraic Patterns

Texas Test Practice

H.O.T. Problems
Higher Order Thinking

Chapter 6 Multiply Whole Numbers

Divide by One-Digit Numbers

Texas Test Practice

H.O.T. Problems
Higher Order Thinking

WRITING IN MATH

Identify and Describe Geometric Figures

CHAPTER 9 Understand and Develop Spatial Reasoning

Texas Test Practice

H.O.T. Problems
Higher Order Thinking

Contents

CHAPTER 10 Measure Length, Perimeter, Area, and Temperature

Texas Test Practice

H.O.T. Problems
Higher Order Thinking

WRITING IN MATH

Measure Capacity, Weight/ Mass, and Volume

Texas Test Practice

H.O.T. Problems
Higher Order Thinking

WRITING IN MATH

Chapter 12 Describe and Compare Fractions

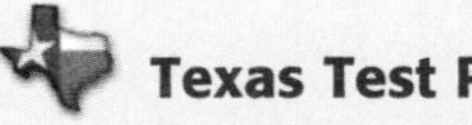

Texas Test Practice

CHAPTER 13 Use Place Value to Represent Decimals

Chapter 14 Add and Subtract Decimals

Texas Test Practice

H.O.T. Problems
Higher Order Thinking

WRITING IN MATH

Get Ready for the Texas Test

End-of-Year Projects

Student Handbook

Texas Essential Knowledge and Skills for Mathematics Grade 4

The lessons in which the TEKS is the primary focus are indicated in bold.

Texas Essential Knowledge and Skills (TEKS)	Student Edition Lesson(s)
(4.1) Number, operation, and quantitative reasoning. The student uses place value to represent whole numbers and decimals.	
The student is expected to:	
(A) use place value to read, write, compare, and order whole numbers through 999,999,999; and	**1-1, Explore 1-2, 1-2, 1-4, 1-5**
(B) use place value to read, write, compare, and order decimals involving tenths and hundredths, including money, using concrete objects and pictorial models.	**13-1, 13-5,** 13-8, **14-1,** Project 2
(4.2) Number, operation, and quantitative reasoning. The student describes and compares fractional parts of whole objects or sets of objects.	**12-1, 12-2**
The student is expected to:	
(A) use concrete objects and pictorial models to generate equivalent fractions;	**Explore 12-4, 12-4**
(B) model fraction quantities greater than one using concrete objects and pictorial models;	**12-6**
(C) compare and order fractions using concrete objects and pictorial models; and	**12-5**
(D) relate decimals to fractions that name tenths and hundredths using concrete objects and pictorial models.	**Explore 13-1,** 13-1, **13-2, 13-7, 13-8**
(4.3) Number, operation, and quantitative reasoning. The student adds and subtracts to solve meaningful problems involving whole numbers and decimals.	
The student is expected to:	
(A) use addition and subtraction to solve problems involving whole numbers; and	**2-1, 2-4, Explore 2-5, 2-5, 2-7, 5-2,** Project 2, Project 3
(B) add and subtract decimals to the hundredths place using concrete objects and pictorial models.	**14-2, Explore 14-4, 14-4, Explore 14-6, 14-6,** Project 2
(4.4) Number, operation, and quantitative reasoning. The student multiplies and divides to solve meaningful problems involving whole numbers.	
The student is expected to:	
(A) model factors and products using arrays and area models;	4-1, **4-3, 4-5, 4-6,** Explore 6-8
(B) represent multiplication and division situations in picture, word, and number form;	**Explore 4-1,** 4-1, **4-3, 4-5, 4-6, 4-9,** Explore 6-8, **Explore 7-1, 7-1**
(C) recall and apply multiplication facts through 12 $\times$ 12;	4-3, 4-5, 4-6, **4-9,** 7-2, 7-4
(D) use multiplication to solve problems (no more than two digits times two digits without technology); and	**4-8, 6-4, 6-6, 6-7, Explore 6-8, 6-8,** Project 2, Project 4
(E) use division to solve problems (no more than one-digit divisors and three-digit dividends without technology).	**Explore 7-1, 7-1, 7-2, 7-5, 7-7, 7-8, 7-9**

Texas Essential Knowledge and Skills (TEKS)	Student Edition Lesson(s)
(4.5) Number, operation, and quantitative reasoning. The student estimates to determine reasonable results.	
The student is expected to:	
(A) round whole numbers to the nearest ten, hundred, or thousand to approximate reasonable results in problem situations; and	**1-6, 2-2,** 14-1
(B) use strategies including rounding and compatible numbers to estimate solutions to multiplication and division problems.	**6-3, 7-4,** 7-5, 7-7, 7-8, 7-9, Project 4
(4.6) Patterns, relationships, and algebraic thinking. The student uses patterns in multiplication and division.	
The student is expected to:	
(A) use patterns and relationships to develop strategies to remember basic multiplication and division facts (such as the patterns in related multiplication and division number sentences (fact families) such as $9 \times 9 = 81$ and $81 \div 9 = 9$); and	**4-1, 4-2,** 4-3, 4-5, 4-6, 4-9
(B) use patterns to multiply by 10 and 100.	**6-1,** 7-2, 7-4
(4.7) Patterns, relationships, and algebraic thinking. The student uses organizational structures to analyze and describe patterns and relationships.	5-4, **5-5, 5-8**
The student is expected to describe the relationship between two sets of related data such as ordered pairs in a table.	
(4.8) Geometry and spatial reasoning. The student identifies and describes attributes of geometric figures using formal geometric language.	
The student is expected to:	
(A) identify and describe right, acute, and obtuse angles;	**8-4,** 8-5,
(B) identify and describe parallel and intersecting (including perpendicular) lines using concrete objects and pictorial models; and	**Explore 9-2, 9-2**
(C) use essential attributes to define two- and three-dimensional geometric figures.	**8-1, 8-2, 8-5, 8-6**
(4.9) Geometry and spatial reasoning. The student connects transformations to congruence and symmetry.	
The student is expected to:	
(A) demonstrate translations, reflections, and rotations using concrete models;	**Explore 9-5, 9-5,** 9-7
(B) use translations, reflections, and rotations to verify that two shapes are congruent; and	**9-7**
(C) use reflections to verify that a shape has symmetry.	**9-8**

Texas Essential Knowledge and Skills (TEKS)	Student Edition Lesson(s)
(4.10) Geometry and spatial reasoning. The student recognizes the connection between numbers and their properties and points on a line.	**9-1,** 12-4, 12-5, 12-6, **13-4, 13-5**
The student is expected to locate and name points on a number line using whole numbers, fractions such as halves and fourths, and decimals such as tenths.	
(4.11) Measurement. The student applies measurement concepts. The student is expected to estimate and measure to solve problems involving length (including perimeter) and area. The student uses measurement tools to measure capacity/volume and weight/mass.	
The student is expected to:	
(A) estimate and use measurement tools to determine length (including perimeter), area, capacity and weight/mass using standard units SI (metric) and customary;	**Explore 10-1, 10-1, Explore 10-4, 10-4, 10-5, 10-6, Extend 10-6, Explore 11-1, 11-1, 11-3, Explore 11-4, 11-4, 11-7,** Project 3, Project 4
(B) perform simple conversions between different units of length, between different units of capacity, and between different units of weight within the customary measurement system;	**10-2, 11-2, 11-6,** Project 3
(C) use concrete models of standard cubic units to measure volume;	**11-8**
(D) estimate volume in cubic units; and	**11-8**
(E) explain the difference between weight and mass.	11-7
(4.12) Measurement. The student applies measurement concepts. The student measures time and temperature (in degrees Fahrenheit and Celsius).	
The student is expected to:	
(A) use a thermometer to measure temperature and changes in temperature; and	**10-8**
(B) use tools such as a clock with gears or a stopwatch to solve problems involving elapsed time.	**11-10,** Project 4
(4.13) Probability and statistics. The student solves problems by collecting, organizing, displaying, and interpreting sets of data.	Project 2, Project 3
The student is expected to:	
(A) use concrete objects or pictures to make generalizations about determining all possible combinations of a given set of data or of objects in a problem situation; and	**3-1, Explore 3-6, 3-6, 3-7,** Project 4
(B) interpret bar graphs.	**3-3, 3-4, Extend 3-4**

Texas Essential Knowledge and Skills (TEKS)	Student Edition Lesson(s)
(4.14) Underlying processes and mathematical tools. The student applies Grade 4 mathematics to solve problems connected to everyday experiences and activities in and outside of school.	
The student is expected to:	
(A) identify the mathematics in everyday situations;	Throughout the text; for example, Cross-Curricular Problem Solving features in Chapters 1-14. Explore 3-6, Project 1, Project 2, Project 3, Project 4
(B) solve problems that incorporate understanding the problem, making a plan, carrying out the plan, and evaluating the solution for reasonableness;	**1-3, 1-7,** 2-3, **2-6,** 3-2, **3-5,** 4-4, **4-7,** 5-3, **5-7,** 6-2, **6-5,** 7-3, **7-6,** 8-3, **8-7,** 9-3, **9-6,** 10-3, **10-7,** 11-5, **11-9,** 12-3, **12-7,** 13-3, **13-6,** 14-3, **14-5,** Project 1
(C) select or develop an appropriate problem-solving plan or strategy, including drawing a picture, looking for a pattern, systematic guessing and checking, acting it out, making a table, working a simpler problem, or working backwards to solve a problem; and	1-3, 1-7, **2-3,** 2-6, **3-2,** 3-5, **4-4,** 4-7, 5-3, 5-7, **6-2,** 6-5, **7-3,** 7-6, **8-3,** 8-7, **9-3,** 9-6, **10-3,** 10-7, **11-5,** 11-9, **12-3,** 12-7, **13-3,** 13-6, **14-3,** 14-5
(D) use tools such as real objects, manipulatives, and technology to solve problems.	Explore 1-2, **Extend 2-4, Extend 3-7,** 6-4, 6-6, **Extend 7-7, Extend 9-7,** Project 2
(4.15) Underlying processes and mathematical tools. The student communicates about Grade 4 mathematics using informal language.	
The student is expected to:	
(A) explain and record observations using objects, words, pictures, numbers, and technology; and	Extend 2-4, 3-1, Extend 3-4, 3-7, **5-1, Explore 5-2, 5-6,** Explore 7-1, 7-9, Project 2, Project 3, Project 4
(B) relate informal language to mathematical language and symbols.	3-6, 5-2, Project 1
(4.16) Underlying processes and mathematical tools. The student uses logical reasoning.	
The student is expected to:	
(A) make generalizations from patterns or sets of examples and nonexamples; and	**5-4,** 8-1, Project 2, Project 3
(B) justify why an answer is reasonable and explain the solution process.	Throughout the text; for example, Project 1, Project 2, Project 4

CHAPTER 1

Let's Get Started

Use the Scavenger Hunt below to learn where things are located in each chapter.

1. What is the title of Chapter 1?
2. What is the Main Idea of Lesson 1-1?
3. How do you know which words are vocabulary words?
4. What are the vocabulary words for Lesson 1-1?
5. On what page will you find directions for making a Foldable to help organize information about place value and number sense?
6. How many Examples are presented in Lesson 1-4?
7. What is the Web address where you could find extra examples?
8. On page 29, there is a Remember tip box. How does the Remember tip help you?
9. How many exercises are there in Lesson 1-5?
10. Suppose you need more practice on a concept. Where can you go for Extra Practice?
11. Suppose you are doing your homework on page 38 and you get stuck on Exercise 16. Where could you find help?
12. What is the web address that would allow you to take a self-check quiz to be sure you understand the lesson?
13. On what pages will you find the Chapter 1 Study Guide and Review?
14. Suppose you cannot figure out how to do Exercise 36 in the Study Guide and Review on page 48. Where could you find help?

MATH? SYMBOLS!

Start Smart

Let's Review!

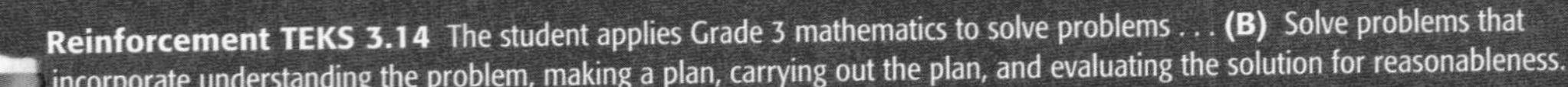
Reinforcement TEKS 3.14 The student applies Grade 3 mathematics to solve problems . . . **(B)** Solve problems that incorporate understanding the problem, making a plan, carrying out the plan, and evaluating the solution for reasonableness.

START SMART 1

Underlying Processes and Mathematical Tools

Touring Texas

Texas has great places to stop along its highways. One place is the Cadillac Ranch in Amarillo.

The table shows some of the cars used in the sculpture. Was more than $1,000 paid for the four cars in the table?

Cadillac Ranch

Model	Cost
1949 Club Coupe	$700
1956 Series 62 Sedan	$100
1959 Coupe de Ville	$100
1962 Sedan de Ville	$300

You can use the *four-step plan* to solve math problems. The four steps are Understand, Plan, Solve, and Check.

Understand

- **Read the problem carefully.**
- **What facts do you know?**
- **What do you need to find?**

The table lists the amount of each car. You need to find out if more than $1,000 was spent for the four cars.

Plan

- **Think about how the facts relate to each other.**
- **Plan a strategy to solve the problem.**

Add all the dollar amounts together and compare the sum to 1,000.
$700 + 100 + 100 + 300$

Solve

- **Use your plan to solve the problem.**
- **What is the solution?**

$700 + 100 + 100 + 300 = 1{,}200$
$\$1{,}200 > \$1{,}000$

So, more than $1,000 was spent on the four cars in the table.

Did you Know
The Cadillac brand was formed by Henry Ford and was named after the French founder of the city of Detroit.

Check

- **Look back at the problem.**
- **Does your answer make sense?**
- **If not, solve the problem another way.**

To check the answer, you can subtract.
$1{,}200 - 100 - 100 - 300 = 700$
Since the result is 700, you know the answer makes sense.

CHECK What You Know

1. List and describe the four steps of the *four-step plan*.

2. WRITING IN ▶MATH The table shows other sculptures found in Texas. Write a real-world problem using the table. Ask a classmate to solve the problem using the *four-step plan*.

Texas Sculpture

Sculpture	Height (ft)
World's 3rd Largest Fire Hydrant	24
Sam Houston Statue	67
Dinosaur Valley State Park T-Rex	45
World's Largest Pair of Boots	40

Source: roadsideamerica.com

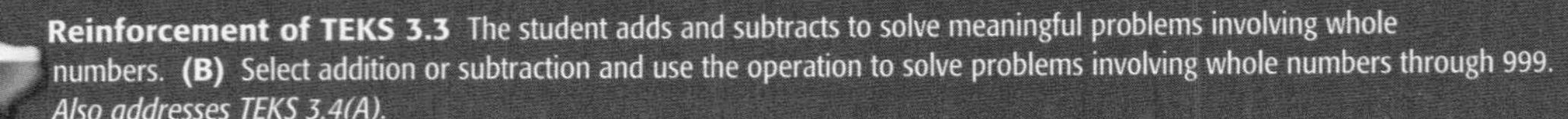

Reinforcement of TEKS 3.3 The student adds and subtracts to solve meaningful problems involving whole numbers. (B) Select addition or subtraction and use the operation to solve problems involving whole numbers through 999.
Also addresses TEKS 3.4(A).

Number, Operation, and Quantitative Reasoning

Animal Math

The Texas horned lizard is the state reptile. These reptiles can be found throughout much of Texas.

CHECK What You Know — Addition and Subtraction

1. Suppose a Texas horned lizard lays 37 eggs the first year and 23 eggs the second year. How many more eggs would it need to lay to have laid 100 eggs?

2. The Texas horned lizard became a threatened species in 1977. Then, 16 years later the lizard became the state reptile for Texas. What year did the Texas horned lizard become the state reptile for Texas?

Adult Texas Horned Lizard

Type	Length (mm)
Female	114
Male	94

For Exercises 3–4, use the table. It shows the average length of adult Texas horned lizards.

3. What will be the total length of two male Texas horned lizards?

4. Find the difference in length between a male horned lizard and a female horned lizard.

CHECK What You Know Multiplication and Division

Did you Know

The Texas horned lizard has the ability to spray a stream of blood out of the corners of its eyes up to 3 feet to defend itself.

Another animal found in the state is the Texas longhorn. The longhorn is the state mammal. When large groups of longhorns are moved from one location to another, it is called a cattle drive.

5. How many feet tall is a Texas longhorn?

6. How many inches long are the horns from tip to tip?

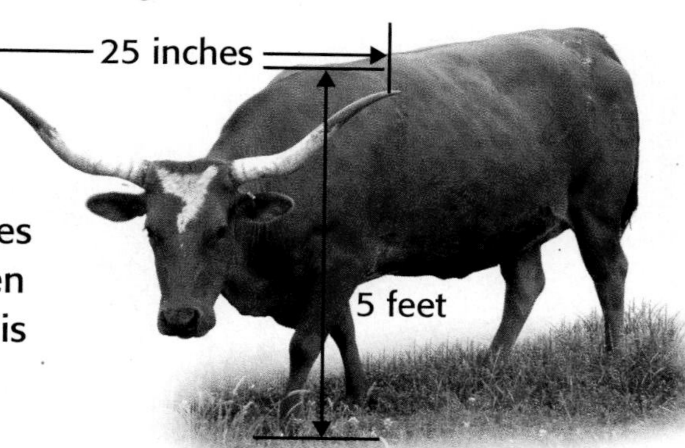

7. Most Texas longhorn calves when born weigh between 40 and 60 pounds. What is the most that 3 calves could weigh?

8. The Perry family is on a cattle drive. For 7 days, the family will drive Texas longhorns 8 miles for each day. Will the family drive the cattle more than 60 miles? How do you know?

9. On the cattle drive, there are 121 longhorns and 11 ranchers. How many longhorns are there for each rancher to watch if they each watch the same number of longhorns?

10. On the cattle drive, the longhorns move at a rate of 2 miles per hour. The drive travels 2 hours before lunch and 3 hours after lunch. How many miles are covered for the day?

11. WRITING IN ▸MATH The table shows information about longhorns. Use the table to write a real-world multiplication or division problem about the Texas longhorn. Ask a classmate to solve the problem.

Texas Longhorns

Gender	Weight	Length of Horns (in.)
Cow	600–1,400	40–65
Bull	1,400–2,200	40–65

Reinforcement of TEKS 3.6 The student uses patterns to solve problems. **(A)** Identify and extend whole numbers and geometric patterns to make predictions and solve problems. *Also addresses TEKS 3.7(A).*

Patterns, Relationships, and Algebraic Thinking

The Austin City Limits Music Festival is one of the largest music festivals in the United States. The festival lasts for 3 days and has over 125 performers, one of which is an elementary school choir from Austin.

CHECK What You Know Patterns

A pattern is a series of numbers or figures that follow a rule. Finding a pattern can be a useful problem-solving strategy.

For Exercises 1 and 2, use the table of the cost of T-shirts.

1. How much would 4 music T-shirts cost?

2. Find the total cost of 8 music T-shirts.

3. A taco costs $3. Two tacos cost $6. Three tacos cost $9. If the pattern continues, how much will 5 tacos cost?

4. Refer to Exercise 3. Find the cost of 10 tacos.

Cost of T-Shirts

Number of T-shirts	Cost ($)
1	$12
2	$24
3	$36

Relationships

Did you Know
The idea for the music festival originated from a television show.

At the music festival, there are 8 stages. On the first day of the festival, 40 bands are scheduled to play. How many bands will play on each stage if each stage has the same number of bands?

One way to find the answer is by using a division equation.
$40 \div 8 = \blacksquare$
Another way is by using a multiplication equation.
$8 \times \blacksquare = 40$
By knowing the multiplication facts for 8, you know that $8 \times 5 = 40$, and since division is related to multiplication you know $40 \div 8 = 5$.

Choose the statement that describes each situation. Then solve.
A Multiply by 5. **B** Divide by 5. **C** Subtract 5. **D** Add 5.

5. The table shows the number of bands that performed during each set because of the 5 different stages.

Total Bands Performing			
Stage set	1	2	3
Total bands	5	10	15

What is one way to find the number of bands that performed during the fourth set?

6. Julia has 15 tickets to the music festival. She gives 5 tickets away at a time. How many groups of tickets will she give away if she gives all of them away?

7. Thom bought 5 CDs. Each CD was \$12. How much did he spend altogether?

8. **WRITING IN MATH** Write a real-world problem that involves multiplication. What multiplication equation would you use to solve the problem? Have a classmate solve.

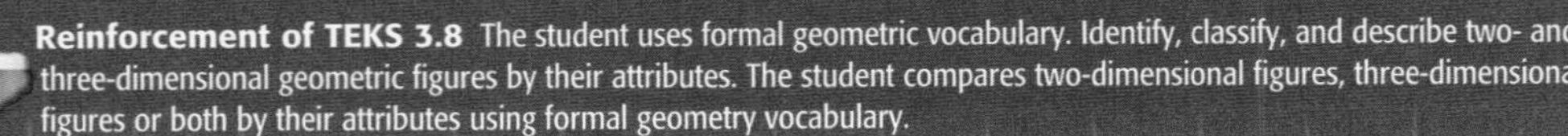

START 4 SMART

Geometry and Spatial Reasoning

Artistic Shapes

The Modern Art Museum of Fort Worth is the oldest art museum in Texas.

Three-Dimensional Figures

Three-dimensional figures are commonly found in architecture as shown above.

Three-dimensional figures have length, width, and height. A flat side is called a *face*. An *edge* is the line segment where two faces meet. The point where three or more edges meet is a *vertex*.

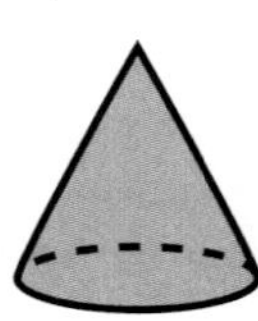

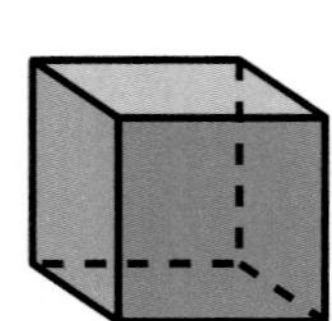

rectangular prism cone cube

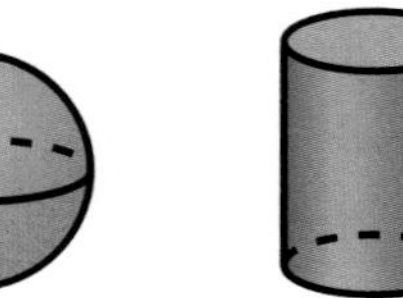
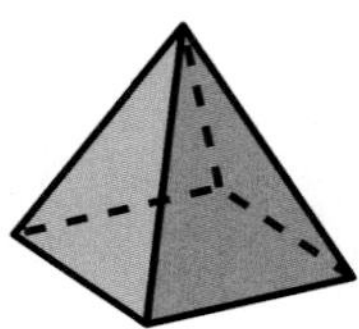

sphere cylinder (square) pyramid

1. Which two three-dimensional figures have 6 faces?
2. Which three-dimensional figure has 5 vertices?
3. What three-dimensional figure does a basketball represent?

CHECK What You Know Two-Dimensional Figures

A two-dimensional figure has length and width. Two-dimensional figures are all around us. Just take a look at these traffic signs.

stop sign

yield sign

speed limit

railroad sign

4. Which sign is an example of an octagon?
5. Which sign(s) contain right angles?
6. Explain the difference between an isosceles triangle and an equilateral triangle. Is a yield sign an equilateral or isosceles triangle?

CHECK What You Know

7. The quilt at the right has several two-dimensional figures in the design. Name two figures in the quilt.

8. Look for three-dimensional and two-dimensional figures in your classroom. Draw and label each figure.

9. WRITING IN MATH Describe a three-dimensional figure. Then exchange papers with a classmate to see if he or she can guess the figure.

Did you Know?

The Modern Art Museum of Fort Worth opened a new building in 2002. The building was designed by Japanese architect Tadao Ando.

Reinforcement of TEKS 3.11 The student directly compares the attributes of length, area, weight/mass, and capacity, and uses comparative language to solve problems and answer questions. The student selects and uses standard units to describe length, area, capacity/volume, and weight/mass. *Also addresses TEKS 3.11(D), 3.11(E).*

START 5 SMART

Measurement

The King of Cotton

Cotton is the most important fiber in the world. In the United States, Texas leads the nation in cotton production. It creates about $1.6 billion for Texas farmers.

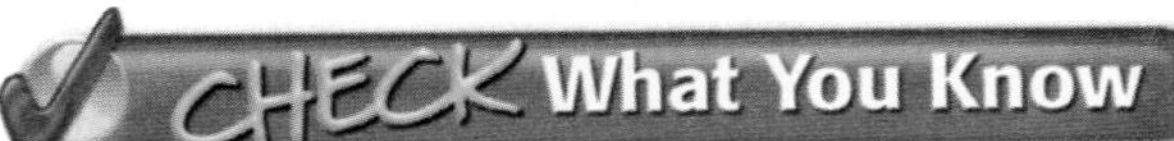

Weight

Weight is a measurement of how much an object weighs. Weight can be measured in ounces and pounds.

16 ounces (oz) = 1 pound (lb)

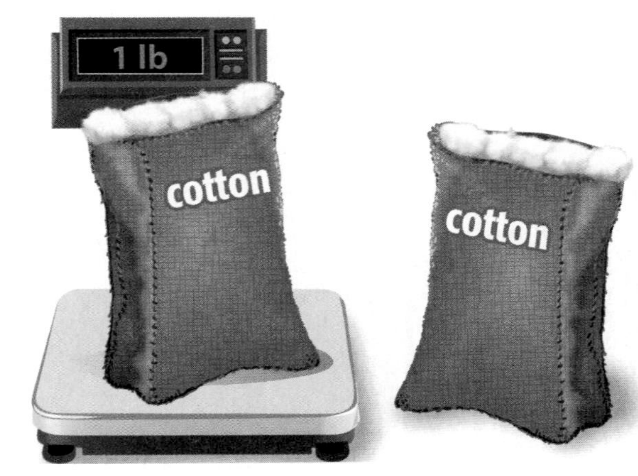

1. What is the total weight of the bags of cotton shown if each bag weighs the same amount?

2. Choose the best estimate for the weight of 100 cotton balls.

   A 1 ounce
   B 1 pound
   C 10 pounds
   D 100 ounces

Another important crop for Texas is strawberries. Each year about 100,000 people travel to the Poteet Strawberry Festival. At the festival, strawberries are used to make a variety of beverages.

Capacity

Capacity is the amount a container can hold. The most common units are fluid ounces, cups, pints, quarts, and gallons.

8 fluid ounces (fl oz) = 1 cup (c)
2 cups = 1 pint (pt)
2 pints = 1 quart (qt)
4 quarts = 1 gallon (gal)

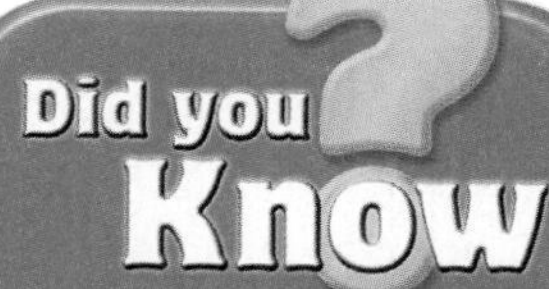

Capacity

Did you Know?

Texas produces between 4 and 7 million bales of cotton annually. A bale weighs about 500 pounds.

Write the unit you measure the capacity of each.

3. a strawberry-banana smoothie

4. a bath tub

5. Choose the best estimate for a bowl for cereal.

A 12 fluid ounces
B 4 pints
C 120 fluid ounces
D 4 gallons

6. **WRITING IN MATH** Find two objects in your classroom that weigh more than one ounce. Find two objects that weigh less than one ounce. Explain your reasoning for each choice.

START 6 SMART

Probability and Statistics

Hello Sports Fans!

Football is a popular sport. There are four professional teams in Texas, including two arena football teams.

Pictographs

A pictograph shows data by using pictures. The pictograph shows the number of games a professional football team played each month during a regular season of the National Football League.

1. What does each represent?
2. How many games did the team play in November? December?
3. During which month were fewer than four games played?

CHECK What You Know Bar Graphs

A bar graph compares data by using bars of different lengths. The bar graph below shows the number of Texas professional sports teams divided by sport.

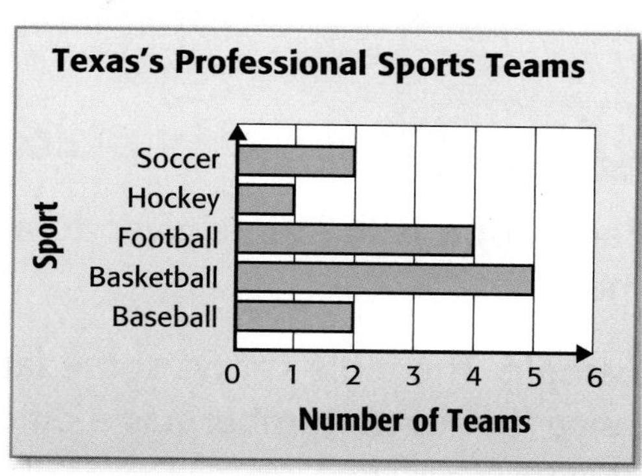

4. Which sport has the fewest teams? the greatest?

5. Which two sports have two teams each? Explain your answer.

6. Which sport has two times the number of teams as soccer? Prove your answer.

7. What is the difference between the greatest and least number of teams?

8. What is the total number of teams?

9. **Collect and Record Data** Take a survey to find your classmates' favorite sports. Make a bar graph to show the results. Follow these steps.

- Ask each student to name his or her favorite sport.
- Make a tally chart showing how many students like each sport.
- Make a bar graph from the tally chart.
- Write a title for the graph. Label each column.

Arena football was invented during an indoor soccer game when its rules were written on an envelope.

10. WRITING IN MATH Write a sentence that describes what your graph shows.

Use Place Value to Represent Whole Numbers

BIG Idea What is place value?

Place value is the value given to a digit by its position in a number.

Example The table shows some facts about the honeybee. Notice that each number has a different value.

Honeybee Facts
• Travels 15 miles per hour
• Makes 154 trips to make one tablespoon of honey
• Wing stroke of 11,400 times per minute

Source: honey.com

What will I learn in this chapter?

- Read and write whole numbers to millions.
- Compare and order whole numbers.
- Round whole numbers.
- Use the *four-step plan* to solve problems.

Key Vocabulary

place value

standard form

expanded form

is greater than (>)

is less than (<)

Student Study Tools at tx.gr4math.com

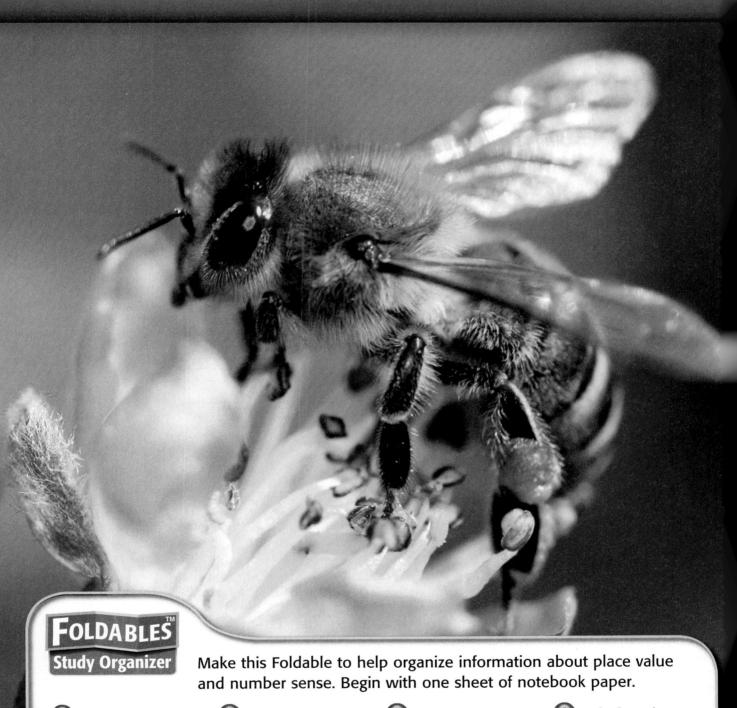

FOLDABLES™
Study Organizer

Make this Foldable to help organize information about place value and number sense. Begin with one sheet of notebook paper.

1. **Fold** a sheet of paper. Leave a two-inch tab at the top.

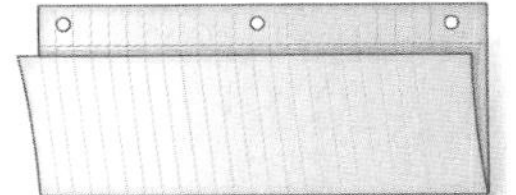

2. **Fold** the right side and the left side to make three equal sections.

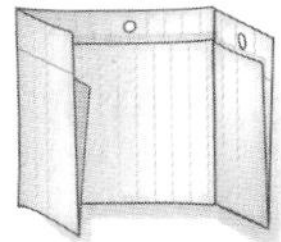

3. **Unfold** the sides. Then cut along the creases as shown.

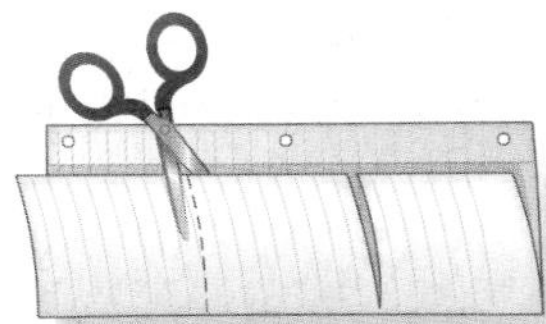

4. **Label** as shown. Take notes as you move through the chapter.

Place Value and Number Sense
Place Value through Hundred Thousands
Place Value through Millions
Compare, Order, and Round Whole Numbers

ARE YOU READY for Chapter 1?

You have two ways to check prerequisite skills for this chapter.

Option 2

Math Online Take the Chapter Readiness Quiz at tx.gr4math.com.

Option 1

Complete the Quick Check below.

QUICK Check

Write each number in word form and expanded form. (Prior grade)

1.

Ones		
hundreds	tens	ones
	6	4

2.

Ones		
hundreds	tens	ones
9	9	5

3. 79 **4.** 30 **5.** 90 **6.** 165

7. 347 **8.** 692 **9.** 1,840 **10.** 4,505

11. Write 300 + 20 + 1 in standard form and word form.

Compare. Use >, <, or =. (Prior grade)

12. 40 ● 4 **13.** 59 ● 59 **14.** 888 ● 898 **15.** 682 ● 700

16. Nora earned $425. She wants to buy a video game system that costs $375. Does she have enough money? Explain.

Round to the nearest ten. (Prior grade)

17. 26 **18.** 4 **19.** 18 **20.** 75

21. 152 **22.** 175 **23.** 347 **24.** 508

25. **Measurement** Galveston is 48 miles from Houston. Would it be reasonable to say that Galveston is about 50 miles from Houston? Explain.

Place Value Through Hundred Thousands

GET READY to Learn

The average lead pencil can draw a line that is almost 184,800 feet (about 35 miles) long. Do you know the value of each digit in 184,800?

MAIN IDEA

I will read and write whole numbers to hundred thousands.

 **Targeted TEKS 4.1** The student uses place value to represent whole numbers and decimals. **(A) Use place value to read, write,** compare, and order **whole numbers through 999,999,999.**

New Vocabulary

digit
place value
period
standard form
word form
expanded form

A **digit** is any of the symbols used to write numbers 0, 1, 2, 3, 4, 5, 6, 7, 8, 9. A **place-value** chart shows the value of the digits in a number. Each group of three digits is called a **period**. Each period is separated by a comma.

Period			Period		
Thousands			**Ones**		
hundreds	tens	ones	hundreds	tens	ones
1	8	4,	8	0	0

EXAMPLE Identify Value of Digits

1 **Write the value of the underlined digit in 184,800.**

Step 1 Write the number in a place-value chart.

Thousands			**Ones**		
hundreds	tens	ones	hundreds	tens	ones
1	8	(4),	8	0	0

Step 2 Identify the column where the 4 is located. Circle it.

Step 3 Replace all the digits that are to the right of the 4 with zeros.

The underlined digit has a value of 4,000. This is because the 4 is in the thousands place.

KEY CONCEPT — Read and Write Numbers

Words	Examples
Standard form is the usual way to write a number using digits.	3,563
Word form is the way you read or say a number.	three thousand, five hundred sixty-three
Expanded form shows the value of each digit.	3,000 + 500 + 60 + 3

Remember

When reading whole numbers in word form, the word *and* is not used.

EXAMPLE Read and Write Numbers

2 **Write 628,371 in word form and in expanded form.**

Thousands			Ones		
hundreds	tens	ones	hundreds	tens	ones
6	2	8,	3	7	1

Word form: six hundred twenty-eight thousand, three hundred seventy-one

Expanded form: 600,000 + 20,000 + 8,000 + 300 + 70 + 1

Online **Personal Tutor at** tx.gr4math.com

CHECK What You Know

Write the value of the underlined digit. See Example 1 (p. 17)

1. 32,0$\underline{8}$6 **2.** 78,$\underline{3}$87 **3.** 1$\underline{0}$9,378 **4.** $\underline{5}$90,320

Write each number in word form and in expanded form. See Example 2 (p. 18)

5. 5,789 **6.** 18,046 **7.** 49,909 **8.** 270,006

9. Write *one hundred thousand, two hundred fifty-six* in standard form and expanded form. See Example 2 (p. 18)

10. China has 555,200 fast food restaurants. Write 555,200 in word form.

11. Talk About It Do 800,600 and 860,000 represent the same values? Explain.

Math Online **Extra Examples at** tx.gr4math.com

Practice and Problem Solving

EXTRA PRACTICE See page R2.

Write the value of the underlined digit. See Example 1 (p. 17)

12. 59,833 **13.** 72,134 **14.** 93,743 **15.** 174,305

16. 593,802 **17.** 826,193 **18.** 830,259 **19.** 926,794

Write each number in word form and in expanded form. See Example 2 (p. 18)

20. 5,050 **21.** 3,791 **22.** 57,402 **23.** 89,074

24. 243,895 **25.** 485,830 **26.** 649,320 **27.** 784,132

Write each number in standard form and in expanded form. See Example 2 (p. 18)

28. twenty-five thousand, four hundred eight

29. forty thousand, eight hundred eleven

30. seven hundred sixty-one thousand, three hundred fifty-six

Write each number in word form and in standard form.

31. 7,000 + 600 + 30 + 5 **32.** 20,000 + 900 + 70 + 6 **33.** 60,000 + 80 + 4

Real-World PROBLEM SOLVING

Science The photo shows an African elephant.

34. African elephants can weigh up to 14,432 pounds. What is the value of the underlined digit?

35. Write 14,432 in expanded form.

36. A zookeeper weighed a newborn African elephant. He was 232 pounds. After one year, the elephant had gained 1,000 pounds. Write the elephant's new weight in standard form and word form.

H.O.T. Problems

37. **OPEN ENDED** Write a six-digit number that has a 9 in the hundreds place and a 6 in the hundred thousands place.

38. **WRITING IN ▸MATH** Explain how the value of the 4 in 694,213 will change if you move it to the tens place.

Explore

Math Activity for 1-2

How Big is One Million?

You can use models to help understand the value of 1,000,000.

MAIN IDEA

I will explore the concept of a million.

Targeted TEKS 4.1 The student uses place value to represent whole numbers and decimals. (A) **Use place value to read, write,** compare, and order **whole numbers through 999,999,999.** *Also addresses TEKS 4.14(D).*

You Will Need
thousand cube sheet
scissors
tape

ACTIVITY **Model 1,000,000.**

Step 1 **Model 1,000.**

Cut out a thousand cube model. Fold the edges where the sides meet and form a cube. This shows 1,000.

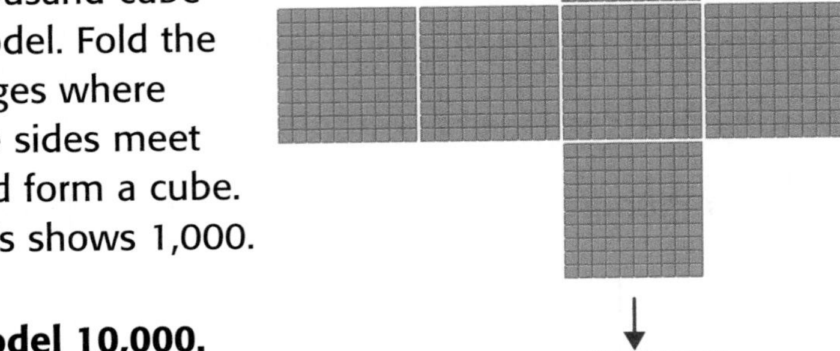

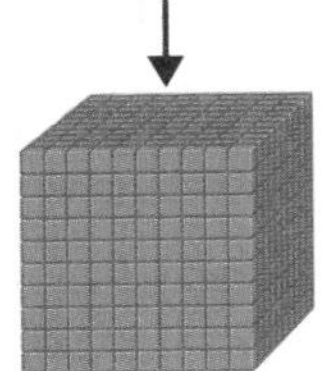

Step 2 **Model 10,000.**

Work with your classmates. Use 10 of the cubes to show 10,000.

Step 3 **Model 100,000.**

Make more cubes to build a model of 100,000.

Step 4 **Create 1,000,000.**

Suppose you were to build a model of 1,000,000. How many more 100,000 models would you need? (*Hint:* There are ten 100,000s in 1,000,000.)

Animation
tx.gr4math.com

Hands-On Activity

Think About It

1. How did you build a model of 10,000?
2. Describe what your model of 1,000,000 looks like.
3. How are the models you built and drew like the models for ones, tens, and hundreds?
4. What number patterns did you see as you built and drew these models?

CHECK What You Know

Write the number shown by each model.

5. 

6. 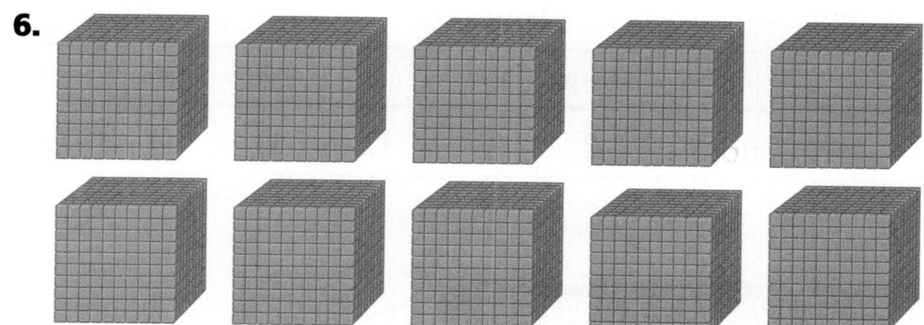

7. The model at the right shows 1,000. How many tens are in 1,000?
8. How many thousands are in 1,000,000?
9. Explain how to determine how long it would take to count to one million.
10. WRITING IN ►MATH How many hundreds are there in 1,000,000? Explain your answer.

1-2 Place Value Through Millions

GET READY to Learn

Baseball is one of America's favorite sports. The graph shows how many fans attended games for three teams during recent years. The attendance numbers are in the millions.

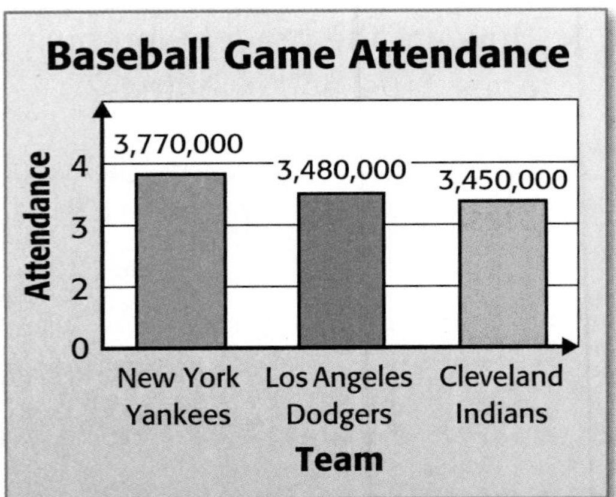

MAIN IDEA

I will read and write whole numbers through the millions.

Targeted TEKS 4.1 The student uses place value to represent whole numbers and decimals. (A) **Use place value to read, write,** compare, and order **whole numbers through 999,999,999.**

A place-value chart can be used to read and write numbers in the millions. The place-value chart below shows the value of each digit in 3,480,000, the attendance at the Los Angeles Dodgers baseball games.

Millions (Period)			Thousands (Period)			Ones (Period)		
		ones	hundreds	tens	ones	hundreds	tens	ones
		3	4	8	0	0	0	0

Real-World EXAMPLE — Read and Write Numbers

1 **SCIENCE The human eye blinks an average of 5,500,000 times a year. Write 5,500,000 in three ways.**

Standard form: 5,500,000

Word form: five million, five hundred thousand

Expanded form: 5,000,000 + 500,000

Real-World EXAMPLE

2 **CARS United States citizens own *one hundred thirty-five million, seven hundred thousand* cars. Write this number in standard form and in expanded form.**

One hundred thirty-five million, seven hundred thousand is written in the place-value chart below.

Millions			Thousands			Ones		
hundreds	tens	ones	hundreds	tens	ones	hundreds	tens	ones
1	3	5	7	0	0	0	0	0

Standard form: 135,700,000

Expanded form: 100,000,000 + 30,000,000 + 5,000,000 + 700,000

Online Personal Tutor at tx.gr4math.com

CHECK What You Know

Write the value of the underlined digit. See Examples 1 and 2 (pp. 22–23)

1. 469,9$\underline{9}$9 **2.** $\underline{1}$,040,710 **3.** 35,0$\underline{9}$8,098 **4.** $\underline{8}$3,023,215

Write each number in word form and in expanded form. See Example 1 (p. 22)

5. 2,007 **6.** 43,980 **7.** 302,806 **8.** 38,000,875

Write each number in standard form and in expanded form. See Example 2 (p. 23)

9. nine hundred thousand, five hundred fifty-two

10. two hundred forty-six million, nine hundred thousand, eighteen

11. On Sunday, 2,617,000 newspapers were sold. Write the number of newspapers sold in word form and expanded form.

12. Talk About It Explain how to find the value of the underlined digit in the number 26,0$\underline{5}$7,928.

Practice and Problem Solving

EXTRA PRACTICE
See page R2.

Write the value of the underlined digit. See Examples 1 and 2 (pp. 22–23)

13. 132,685 **14.** 309,573 **15.** 2,309,841 **16.** 7,824,015

17. 40,245,854 **18.** 68,210,397 **19.** 73,581,209 **20.** 97,530,284

Write each number in word form and in expanded form. See Example 1 (p. 22)

21. 29,205 **22.** 82,009 **23.** 901,452 **24.** 200,013

25. 30,842,085 **26.** 63,930,053 **27.** 319,999,990 **28.** 800,493,301

Write each number in standard form and in expanded form. See Example 2 (p. 23)

29. two hundred thirty-eight thousand, three hundred seventy

30. four million, ninety-four thousand, two hundred fifteen

31. eighty three million, twenty-three thousand, seven

32. three hundred four million, eight hundred thousand, four hundred

Write the following numbers in word form and in standard form.

33. 200,000 + 60,000 + 3,000 + 200 + 70 + 3

34. 1,000,000 + 900,000 + 50,000 + 6,000 + 200 + 20 + 5

35. As of 2005, the population of Houston was 2,016,582. Write Houston's population in word form.

36. **Measurement** The land area for California is 400,000 + 3,000 + 900 + 70 square kilometers. Write the area in word form.

Real-World PROBLEM SOLVING

Planets The Sun and Earth are shown.

37. The distance from Earth to the Sun is 92,955,793 miles. Write this number in word form and expanded form.

38. The amount of time that U.S. astronauts have spent in space is about 13,507,804 minutes. Is this number read as *thirteen million, fifty-seven thousand, eight hundred four*? Explain.

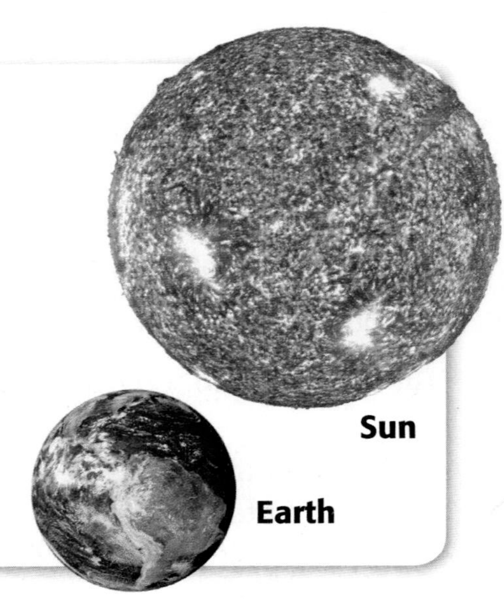

H.O.T. Problems

39. OPEN ENDED Write an eight-digit number that has a 7 in the ten millions place and a number in the thousands place with a value of 2,000.

40. CHALLENGE Write the number with the smallest value using the digits 1 through 9. Use each digit only once.

41. NUMBER SENSE Is the following statement *true* or *false*? Explain your answer.

1,000 thousands = 1,000,000

42. WRITING IN ▸MATH Explain how you know what number is missing in 3,947 = 3,000 + ■ + 40 + 7.

TEST Practice

43. Which number below is the word form of 57,302? **(Lesson 1-1)**

A five thousand, three hundred two

B fifty-seven thousand, three hundred twenty

C fifty-seven thousand, three hundred two

D five hundred thousand, three hundred two

44. Yosemite National Park hosts three million, three hundred seventy thousand visitors each year. What is another way to write this number? **(Lesson 1-2)**

F 3,307,000

G 3,370,000

H 30,307,000

J 30,370,000

Spiral Review

Write the value of the underlined digit. **(Lesson 1-1)**

45. 130,498

46. 152,004

47. 630,182

Write each number in standard form and in expanded form. **(Lesson 1-2)**

48. four million, six hundred thirty-seven thousand, five hundred four

49. seventeen million, twenty thousand, four hundred fifty-eight

1-3 Problem-Solving Skill

MAIN IDEA I will solve problems using a four-step plan.

Targeted TEKS 4.14 The student applies Grade 4 mathematics to solve problems connected to everyday experiences and activities in and outside of school. **(B) Solve problems that incorporate understanding the problem, making a plan, carrying out the plan, and evaluating the solution for reasonableness.** *Also addresses TEKS 4.14(C).*

There are six girls in Dina's scout troop. They are planning a trip to the local amusement park. Admission for children is $12. What is the total cost of admission for everyone to go?

Understand

What facts do you know?

- There are six scouts who want to go.
- The price of admission is $12 for each girl.

What do you need to find?

- The total cost of admission for all the girls.

Plan

To find the total cost, you can use addition. There are 6 girls, and it will cost $12 each. So, add 12 six times.

Solve

$12 + $12 + $12 + $12 + $12 + $12 = $72

So, the troop needs $72 to go to the amusement park.

Check

Look back at the problem. One way to check the answer is to use a drawing.

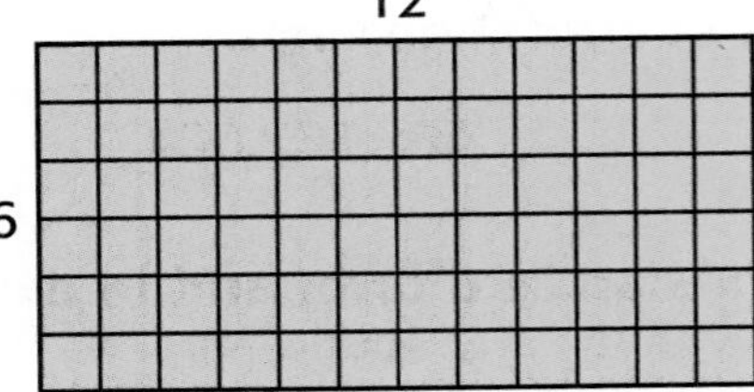

There are 72 squares, so the answer is correct.

ANALYZE the Skill

Refer to the problem on the previous page.

1. Explain why multiplication was used to solve the problem.

2. In the problem, the price for an adult admission was not included. Suppose the price of an adult ticket is $8 more than a child's ticket. Find the total cost of three adult tickets. Explain.

3. Refer to Exercise 2. Draw a model to check. Explain how the model shows that your answer is correct.

4. If three adults were to go on the trip with the scouts, how much would admission cost for everyone to go? Explain how you found your answer.

PRACTICE the Skill

EXTRA PRACTICE
See page R2.

Solve. Use the *four-step plan*.

5. A class is playing a game. Each correct answer is worth 5 points. Team 1 has 55 total points. Team 2 has answered 12 questions correctly. Who has answered more questions correctly?

6. Rosa is downloading music. It takes about 3 minutes to download one song. If she downloads an album with 10 songs, about how long will it take her to download the album?

7. Casey's mom is the baseball coach for his team. She spent $50 on 10 baseballs. How much would 1 baseball cost?

8. William can make 4 bracelets in an hour. With Daisy's help, they can make twice as many in an hour. If they work for 2 hours, how many bracelets can they make?

9. The opening phrase of the Gettysburg Address is shown. A score is 20 years. How many years would be in four score and seven years?

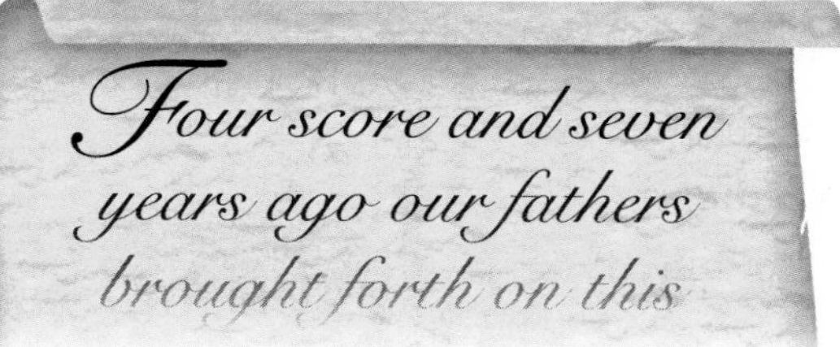
Four score and seven
years ago our fathers
brought forth on this

10. Scott spends 1 hour a day in math class. How many hours does he spend in math class in four weeks in which there are no days off?

11. Karl Freidrich Benz invented the first gasoline-powered automobile in 1885. Estimate how many years ago this automobile was invented.

12. **WRITING IN MATH** Select one problem from Exercises 5–11. Explain how you used the *four-step plan* to solve the problem.

1-4 Compare Whole Numbers

MAIN IDEA

I will compare whole numbers.

Targeted TEKS 4.1 The student uses place value to represent whole numbers and decimals. **(A) Use place value to** read, write, **compare,** and order **whole numbers through 999,999,999.**

New Vocabulary

is greater than (>)
is less than (<)
is equal to (=)

GET READY to Learn

A first-year police officer earns $41,793 in one year. A first-year firefighter earns $41,294 in one year. Which occupation pays more for the first year?

You can use a number line to compare numbers. The symbols below are used to show relationships of numbers.

is greater than	is less than	is equal to
>	<	=

Real-World EXAMPLE Use a Number Line

1 JOBS Which occupation pays more for the first year: police officer or firefighter?

On a number line, numbers to the right are greater than numbers to the left.

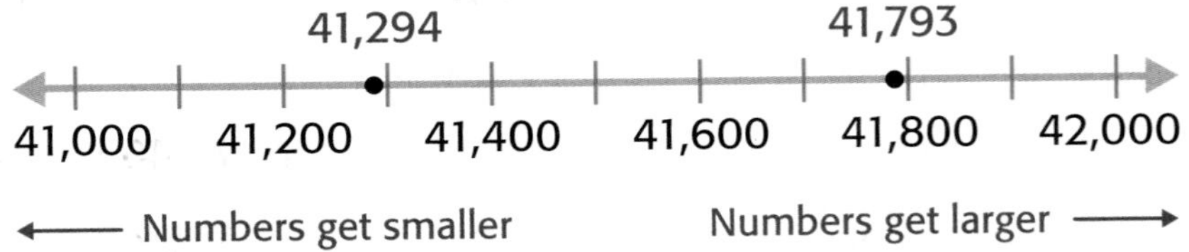

41,793 is to the right of 41,294.

So, 41,793 is greater than 41,294.

Therefore, $41,793 > 41,294$.

So, police officers earn more money than firefighters.

To compare numbers, you can also use place value.

Real-World EXAMPLE Use Place Value

2 **DATA The table shows the two most popular last names in the United States. Which name is more popular?**

Last Name	Number of People
Miller	1,253,913
Jones	1,836,509

Source: *Top 10 of Everything*

Remember

Before comparing numbers, always line up the ones place.

Step 1 Line up the numbers so that the digits in the ones place align.
1,253,913
1,836,509

Step 2 Begin at the greatest place. Compare the digits.
1,253,913
1,836,509
Since $1 = 1$, go to the next place.

Step 3 Compare the digits in the next place on the right.
1,253,913
1,836,509
$8 > 2$

So, 1,836,509 is greater. Therefore, the more popular last name is Jones.

Online **Personal Tutor at** tx.gr4math.com

CHECK What You Know

Compare. Use $>$, $<$, or $=$. See Examples 1 and 2 (pp. 28–29)

1. 1,798 ● 1,789

2. 7,440 ● 7,436

3. 25,409 ● 26,409

4. 50,402 ● 50,406

5. 655,543 ● 556,543

6. 10,027,301 ● 10,207,301

7. Jun collects stamps and baseball cards. He has 1,834 stamps and 1,286 baseball cards. Does he have more stamps or more baseball cards?

8. Talk About It Explain why any five-digit number is less than any six-digit number.

Practice and Problem Solving

EXTRA PRACTICE See page R3.

Compare. Use >, <, or =. See Examples 1 and 2 (pp. 28–29)

9. 3,030 ● 3,030

10. 5,980 ● 5,090

11. 6,789 ● 6,798

12. 9,623 ● 9,623

13. 23,001 ● 23,010

14. 18,041 ● 18,040

15. 76,101 ● 77,000

16. 12,683 ● 12,638

17. 304,999 ● 305,049

18. 701,010 ● 701,010

19. 2,999,214 ● 2,999,214

Copy and complete to make the number sentence true.

20. 658,431 < ■00,000

21. 1,342,646 > 1,■89,035

22. Delaney received 1,127 e-mails in a year. Patricia received 1,132 e-mails in a year. Who received more e-mails?

23. Hassan read 2,365 pages during the school year. Anjelita read 2,382 pages during the school year. Who read more pages during the school year?

Real-World PROBLEM SOLVING

Technology The table shows the top four online languages.

Top Online Languages

Language	Internet Users
Chinese	105,736,236
English	286,642,757
Japanese	66,763,838
Spanish	55,887,063

24. Which language is used most on the Internet?

25. Which language is used less on the Internet, Japanese or Spanish?

H.O.T. Problems

26. OPEN ENDED Write a seven-digit number that is greater than 8,458,942.

27. WHICH ONE DOESN'T BELONG? Which number does not belong? Explain.

10,000 | 10 hundreds | ten thousand | 100 hundreds

NUMBER SENSE Compare. Use >, <, or =.

28. 3 thousands ● 3,200

29. 1,000,000 ● 1,000 thousands

30. **WRITING IN MATH** Explain how to compare numbers using place value.

CHAPTER 1

Mid-Chapter Check

Lessons 1-1 through 1-4

Write each number in word form and in expanded form. (Lesson 1-1)

1. 2,384

2. 917,022

Write each number in standard form and in expanded form. (Lesson 1-2)

3. nineteen thousand, two hundred six

4. two hundred seventy-two

5. There are 3 schools. Each school has 297 students. How many students are in all three schools? Write in standard form and word form. (Lesson 1-2)

6. **TEST PRACTICE** Which of these is 7,402,644? (Lesson 1-2)

A seven million, forty-two thousand, six hundred four

B seven thousand, four hundred two

C seven million, four hundred two thousand, six hundred forty-four

D seven million, two hundred four thousand, six hundred four

7. Erika is writing the greatest number possible using the digits shown.

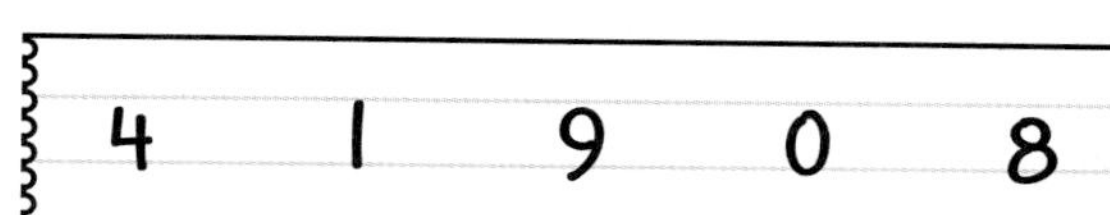

What would be the number in expanded form? (Lesson 1-2)

8. What is 20,000,000 + 8,000,000 + 300,000 + 6,000 + 30 + 7 in standard form and in word form? (Lesson 1-2)

Compare. Use >, <, and =. (Lesson 1-4)

9. 2,481 ● 2,814

10. 200 + 70 + 8 ● 700 + 80 + 2

Algebra Find the value of ■. (Lesson 1-4)

11. 5,000 + ■ + 9 = 5,709

12. 40,000 + 6,000 + ■ = 46,009

13. Rolando traveled 2,643 miles by air. Ramiro traveled 2,643 miles by car. Who traveled farther? Explain. (Lesson 1-4)

14. **TEST PRACTICE** Which sentence below is correct? (Lesson 1-4)

F 38,521 < 37,125

G 65,349 > 65,400

H 90,502 > 90,205

J 12,754 < 12,574

15. On Monday, Dylan used a pedometer to record 15,725 steps. On Tuesday, he took 15,806 steps. On which day did he take more steps? (Lesson 1-4)

16. **WRITING IN MATH** Explain how to find the number missing in the following expanded form sentence.
8,000,000 + 5,000 + 90 + 3 = 8,■05,093

1-5 Order Whole Numbers

GET READY to Learn

Having a dog is very popular. The table shows the number of Yorkshire Terriers, Beagles, and German Shepherds in the United States. Which of these three dogs is most popular? least popular?

Dog Breeds in the U.S.	
Dog	**Number**
Yorkshire Terrier	47,238
Beagle	42,592
German Shepherd	45,868

Source: American Kennel Club

MAIN IDEA

I will order whole numbers through the millions.

Targeted TEKS 4.1 The student uses place value to represent whole numbers and decimals. **(A) Use place value to** read, write, compare, and **order whole numbers through 999,999,999.**

To order numbers, you can use a number line or place value.

Real-World EXAMPLE Use a Number Line

1 **DOGS Order the dog breeds in the table above from most popular to least popular.**

Graph each number on a number line.

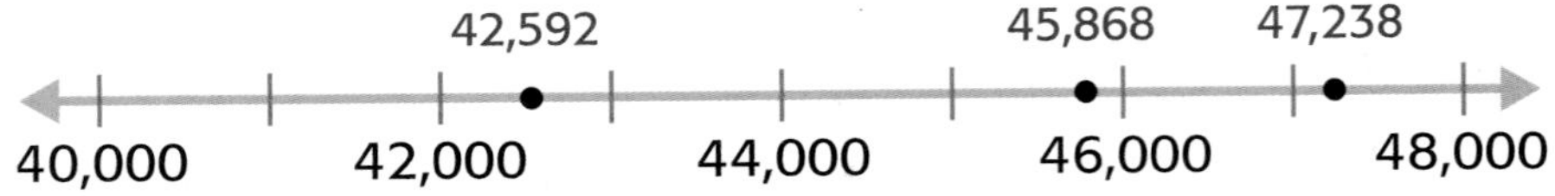

47,238 is farthest to the right.

45,868 is between 42,592 and 47,238.

42,592 is the farthest to the left.

The order is Yorkshire Terrier, German Shepherd, Beagle.

Real-World EXAMPLE Use Place Value

2 **OIL The table shows the number of barrels of oil used each day in different countries. Use place value to order the data from greatest to least.**

Oil Usage	
Country	**Barrels per Day**
Brazil	2,199,000
Canada	2,200,000
India	2,130,000
United States	19,650,000

Source: *CIA World Fact Book* (2005)

Remember

When ordering numbers, you can use number lines or place value.

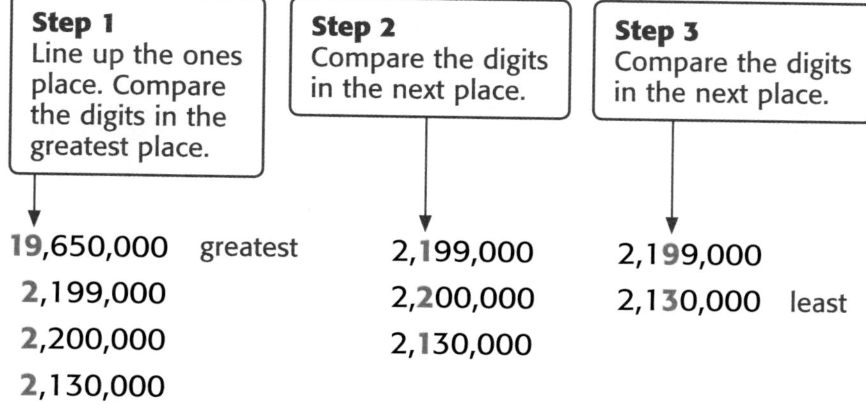

Step 1
Line up the ones place. Compare the digits in the greatest place.
Step 2
Compare the digits in the next place.
Step 3
Compare the digits in the next place.
19,650,000 greatest
2,199,000
2,200,000
2,130,000
2,199,000
2,200,000
2,130,000
2,199,000
2,130,000 least

The numbers ordered from greatest to least are 19,650,000; 2,200,000; 2,199,000; and 2,130,000.

So, the order is the United States, Canada, Brazil, and India.

CHECK What You Know

Order the numbers from greatest to least. See Examples 1 and 2 (pp. 32–33)

1. 3,456; 4,356; 3,465; 6,543

2. 52,482; 50,023; 56,028; 63,340

3. 87,035; 80,562; 78,035; 79,003

4. 145,099; 154,032; 145,004; 159,023

5. **Measurement** Order the surface areas of the lakes shown in the table from greatest to least surface area.

6. Talk About It When ordering whole numbers, explain what you do when the digits in the same place have the same value.

Texas Lakes	
Lake	**Surface Area (acres)**
Caddo Lake	26,800
Lake Texoma	74,686
Houston Lake	11,854
Lake Conroe	21,000
Falcon Lake	83,654

Source: worldatlas.com

Practice and Problem Solving

EXTRA PRACTICE See page R3.

Order the numbers from greatest to least. See Examples 1 and 2 (pp. 32–33)

7. 2,004; 1,906; 2,006; 1,507

8. 3,521; 3,512; 1,243; 3,306

9. 79,920; 82,234; 97,902; 90,125

10. 12,378; 12,783; 12,873

11. 138,023; 138,032; 139,006; 183,487

12. 258,103; 248,034; 285,091; 248,934

13. 6,052,264; 6,025,264; 6,052,462

14. 12,345,678; 1,234,567; 123,456,789

15. Rank the following cities in Texas from least to greatest population.

Texas Population	
City	**Population**
Abilene	114,757
Waco	120,465
Denton	104,153
Carrolton	118,870

Source: U.S. Census Bureau

16. Order the cars from most expensive to least expensive.

Most Expensive Cars	
Car	**Price**
Bugatti Veyron 16.4	$1,192,057
Leblanc Mirabeau	$645,084
Pagani Zonda Roadster	$667,321
Saleen S7	$555,000

Source: Forbes

Real-World PROBLEM SOLVING

Data File Texas is the second largest and second most populous state in the U.S. The table shows the size and population of Texas and three other states.

17. Order the states from greatest to least based on their size.

18. Order the state populations from least to greatest.

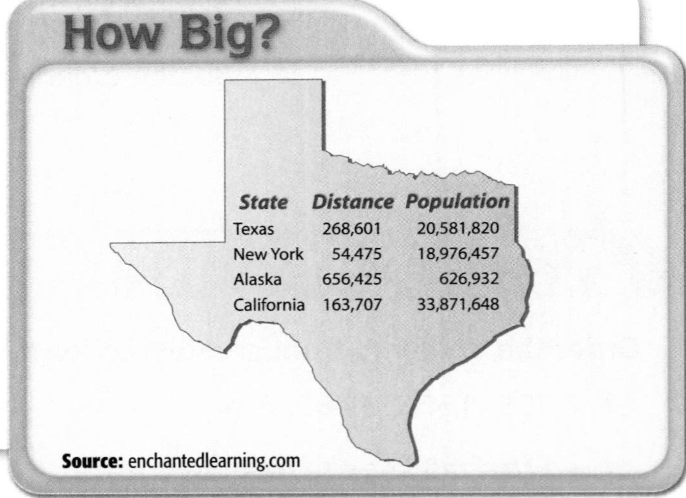

State	Distance	Population
Texas	268,601	20,581,820
New York	54,475	18,976,457
Alaska	656,425	626,932
California	163,707	33,871,648

Source: enchantedlearning.com

H.O.T. Problems

19. OPEN ENDED Write three numbers that are greater than 750,000 but less than 760,000.

20. NUMBER SENSE Use the digits 2, 3, 4, and 9 to create four numbers. Order them from least to greatest.

21. WRITING IN MATH Write a real-word problem in which you would order three numbers from least to greatest.

Greater Number Game

Compare Whole Numbers

Get Ready!

Players: 2 players

You will need: 40 index cards

Get Set!

Each player gets 20 index cards. Separate the cards into 2 piles of 10. On each card in the first pile, write a number in standard form that has no more than 4 digits. Next, write the expanded form of each number on one of the cards in the second pile.

Go!

- Combine both sets of cards.
- Shuffle and deal the cards.
- Place your cards face down. Turn over the top card at the same time as your partner.
- The person who turns over the greater number takes both cards. If the cards are equal, keep turning over cards until a player can take the cards.
- Play until one person has all the cards.

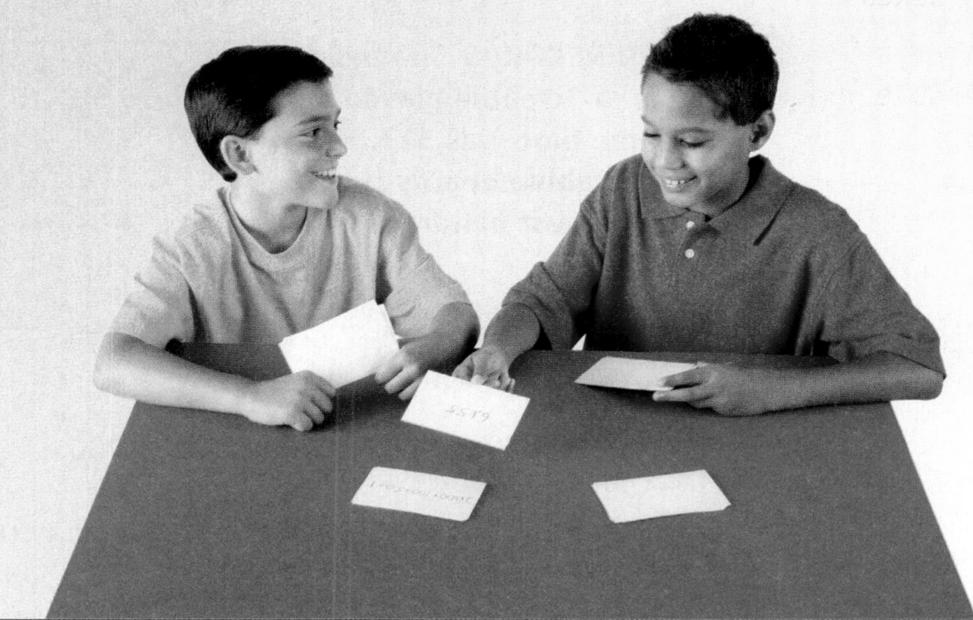

1-6 Round Whole Numbers

MAIN IDEA

I will round whole numbers through the thousands.

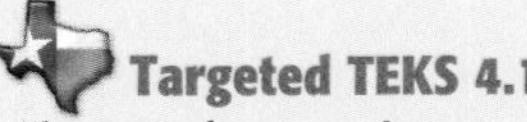

Targeted TEKS 4.1 The student estimates to determine reasonable results. (A) **Round whole numbers to the nearest ten, hundred, or thousand to approximate reasonable results in problem situations.**

New Vocabulary

rounding (or round)

GET READY to Learn

A certain tractor weighed 528 pounds. About how much does it weigh?

When you do not need an exact answer, you can estimate by **rounding**. You can use a number line to round.

Real-World EXAMPLES Round Whole Numbers

1 MEASUREMENT **To the nearest ten, how much does the tractor weigh?**

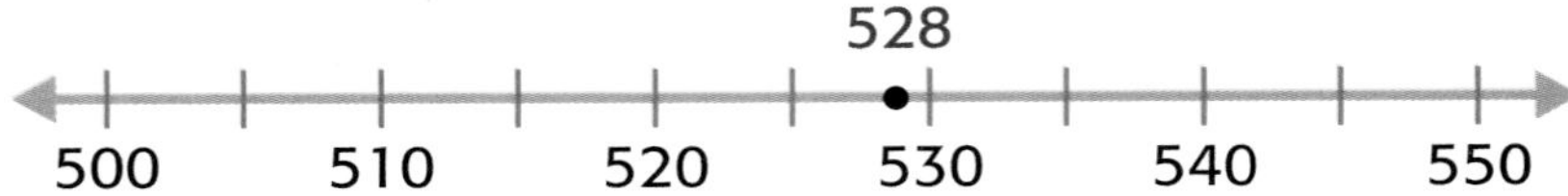

On the number line, 528 is closer to 530 than 520. So, round 528 to 530.

2 WORLD RECORDS **The most games of Scrabble played at the same time was 521. How many Scrabble boards is this to the nearest hundred?**

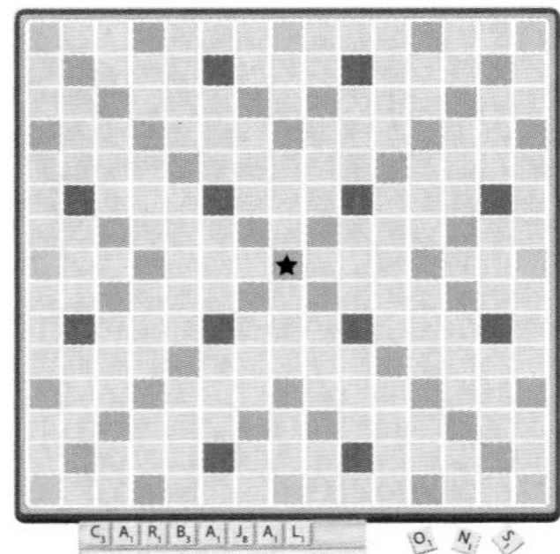

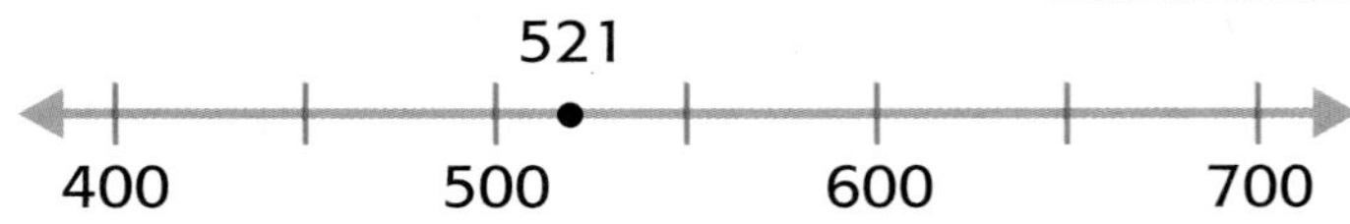

On the number line, 521 is closer to 500 than 600. So, round 521 to 500.

Real-World EXAMPLES Round Whole Numbers

3 **El Paso, Texas, is 516 miles from Needles, California, and 571 miles from Dallas, Texas. About how far away is each city to the nearest ten? Which city is closer to El Paso?**

516 is closer to 520 than 510. So, Needles is about 520 miles from El Paso.
571 is closer to 570 than 580. So, Dallas is about 570 miles from El Paso.

El Paso is closer to Needles, California.

4 **RIVERS The Rio Grande is 1,270 miles long and is the longest river in Texas. How many miles is this to the nearest thousand?**

You need to round 1,270 to the nearest thousand.

1,270 is about 1,000. 1,270 is closer to 1,000 than 2,000.

To the nearest thousand, 1,270 is rounded to 1,000.

Remember
Check your answer to make sure it is reasonable.

Check

The number line shows that the answer is correct.

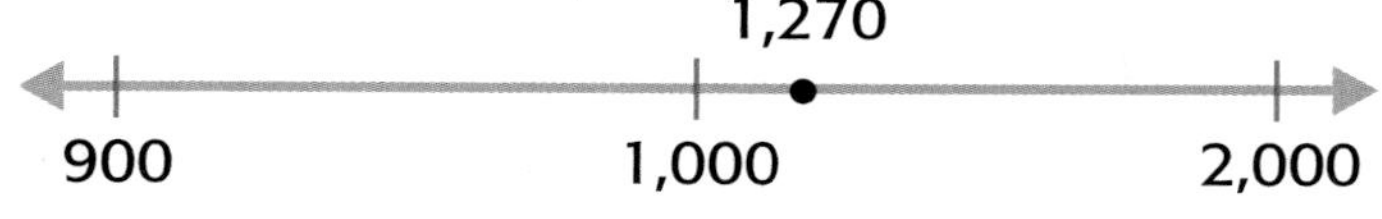

Personal Tutor at tx.gr4math.com

CHECK What You Know

Round each number to the given place-value position. See Examples 1–4 (pp. 36–37)

1. 927; ten

2. 934; hundred

3. 4,282; ten

4. 332; hundred

5. 3,205; thousand

6. 9,385; thousand

7. A house made out of playing cards used 1,800 cards. To the nearest thousand, how many cards were used?

8. Talk About It Write the least number that you can round to the thousands place to get 8,000. Explain.

Practice and Problem Solving

See page R3.

Round each number to the given place-value position. See Examples 1–4 (pp. 36–37)

9. 568; ten

10. 396; ten

11. 297; hundred

12. 8,245; hundred

13. 4,752; thousand

14. 3,580; thousand

15. 9,158; thousand

16. 1,675; thousand

17. 690; hundred

18. 5,230; thousand

19. 36; ten

20. 985; ten

21. **Measurement** The United States' highest peak is Mount McKinley. It is 6,194 feet high. Is this about 6,000 feet high? Explain.

22. **Measurement** The highest point in Texas is Guadalupe Peak. It is 8,749 feet high. Is this about 8,000 feet high? Explain.

23. The library checked out about 3,000 books last week. If they check out 2,256 books this week, is this about the same amount?

24. Mr. Cantora's classes use 4,765 sheets of paper in a year. If he buys 5,000 sheets of paper will he have enough paper for the year? Explain.

Real-World PROBLEM SOLVING

Arts The graphic shows the number of cars that make up the longest model train in the world.

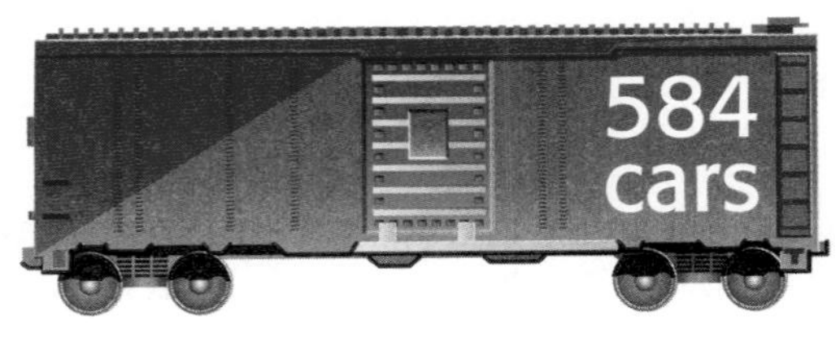

25. Round this number to the nearest hundred.

26. To which place would this number be rounded if the rounded number was 580?

H.O.T. Problems

27. OPEN ENDED Write five numbers that would round to 50,000.

28. FIND THE ERROR Amanda and Jamal round 83,275,925 to the hundred thousands place. Who is correct? Explain.

Amanda
80,000,000

Jamal
83,300,000

29. WRITING IN MATH Create a real-world problem that involves rounding a number and results in an answer of 670,000.

TEST Practice

30. Which shows the correct order from least to greatest? **(Lesson 1-5)**

A 1,245; 2,451; 5,412; 4,152

B 2,124; 4,215; 4,512; 5,214

C 5,214; 4,512; 4,215; 2,124

D 2,512; 2,215; 4,124; 4,421

31. Yuma, Arizona, is the sunniest place in the world. Round Yuma's average hours of sunlight each year to the nearest thousand. **(Lesson 1-6)**

Top Two Sunniest Places	
Location	**Hours of Sunlight Each Year**
Yuma, Arizona	4,127
Phoenix, Arizona	4,041

F 4,000 **H** 4,200

G 4,100 **J** 5,000

Spiral Review

Order the numbers from greatest to least. **(Lesson 1-5)**

32. 685; 700; 660

33. 1,363; 1,468; 1,333

34. 12,009; 12,090; 12,900

Compare. Use >, <, or =. **(Lesson 1-4)**

35. 163 ● 165

36. 16,094 ● 16,090

37. 1,866 ● 1,866

38. The tallest mountain in the United States is 20,320 feet tall. Round this number to the nearest thousand. **(Lesson 1-3)**

Problem-Solving Investigation

MAIN IDEA I will choose the best strategy to solve a problem.

Targeted TEKS 4.14 The student applies Grade 4 mathematics to solve problems connected to everyday experiences and activities in and outside of school. (B) **Solve problems that incorporate understanding the problem, making a plan, carrying out the plan, and evaluating the solution of reasonableness.** *Also addresses TEKS 4.14(C).*

P.S.I. TEAM +

TORY: My family is going on vacation to Mexico. Before we go, we have to trade our dollars for Mexican pesos. For every dollar we will get about 11 pesos.

YOUR MISSION: Find about how many pesos Tory's family will get for $8.

Understand

You know that one dollar is about 11 pesos.

You need to find about how many pesos they will get for $8.

Plan

For every 1 dollar, they get 11 pesos. Make a table to solve the problem.

Solve

Dollars	$1	$2	$3	$4	$5	$6	$7	$8
Pesos	11	22	33	44	55	66	77	88

+11 +11 +11 +11 +11 +11 +11

The pattern is to add 11.

The family can expect to get about 88 pesos for $8.

Check

There is a second pattern in the table. When the digit in the dollar row is changed to pesos, the dollar digit is repeated twice. For example, $5 is 55 pesos. $8 is 88 pesos follows this pattern.

So, the answer is correct.

Mixed Problem Solving

See page R4.

Use the *four-step plan* to solve.

1. **Measurement** A black bear weighs 25 pounds more than a gorilla. Use the information in the table to find how much a black bear weighs.

Large Animal Weights	
Animal	**Weight (pounds)**
Gorilla	400
Black bear	■
Lion	440

2. A robin can fly 20 miles in one hour. An eagle can fly 40 miles in one hour. How many hours would it take for a robin to fly as far as an eagle flies in 3 hours?

3. Jade has 3 sticker sheets with 6 stickers on each sheet. How many stickers does she have in all?

4. A watch costs $34. A pair of sunglasses costs $6. How much change could you expect to receive if you bought one of each item above and paid with a $50 bill?

5. A video game store buys used video games for $10 each. Vivian wants a new video game for $77. How many used games must she sell to buy the new game?

6. Lee wants a motorized scooter. He earns $8 a week, and already has $11. How many weeks will he have to save all of his money to buy the scooter?

7. Leticia earns $20 each time she babysits. How many times will she need to babysit to earn $120?

8. Turi burns about 350 calories for every hour he skis. The last time he skied, he burned 1,200 calories. Did he ski over 3 hours? Explain.

9. Jack's basketball games are 4 quarters that are each 8 minutes long. Is it possible for Jack to play 35 minutes in a game? How do you know?

10. Xavier saved three $10 bills, six $5 bills, and twelve $1 bills. Does he have enough money to buy this digital music player?

11. **WRITING IN MATH** Refer to Exercise 10. Suppose Xavier has 5 bills, and the total is $37. Explain the steps you would take to find which bills he has.

Problem Solving in Science

CREATURES Under the SEA

Earth's oceans are filled with many different sea creatures. Of these creatures in the ocean, marine mammals such as whales, dolphins, seals, and sea lions are the most skilled divers. Both sperm whales and elephant seals can stay underwater for almost two hours. That's a long time to hold your breath!

Protected Species of Pacific Coast Marine Mammals

Species	Estimated Population
California sea lion	111,016
Central common dolphin	406,100
Gray whale	20,869
Hawaiian monk seal	1,300
Northern common dolphin	476,300
Northern fur seal	988,000
Pacific harbor seal	131,826
Spinner dolphin	631,000
Spotted dolphin	731,000
Steller sea lion	116,000

Source: National Biological Service

Targeted TEKS 4.14 The student applies Grade 4 mathematics to solve problems connected to everyday experiences and activities in and outside of school. (A) **Identify the mathematics in everyday situations.**

Real-World Math

Use the information on page 42 to solve each problem.

1. Which marine mammal species has the greatest population? Write in expanded and word forms.

2. There are about 20,000 blue whales. Your friend tells you that there are more blue whales than gray whales. Is your friend right? Explain.

3. A humpback whale can eat up to 9,000 pounds of food a day. Is this more or less than a blue whale eats? How much more or less?

4. A sea lion can dive 400 feet. Some seals can dive 5,314 feet. Dolphins can dive up to 1,000 feet. List these dives from greatest to least.

5. You are told that there are about 132,000 Pacific harbor seals. Is this true when you round to the nearest ten thousand? Explain.

6. Which animal populations, when rounded to the nearest thousand, have a one in the thousands place?

Did You Know?

A blue whale eats about 7,500 pounds of food per day.

Study Guide and Review

FOLDABLES™ Study Organizer GET READY to Study

Be sure the following Key Vocabulary words and Key Concepts are written in your Foldable.

Place Value and Number Sense
Place Value through Hundred Thousands
Place Value through Millions
Compare, Order, and Round Whole Numbers

BIG Ideas

Place Value

- A **place-value** chart shows the value of the digits in a number. (pp. 17–19)

Thousands			Ones		
hundreds	tens	ones	hundreds	tens	ones
	4	7,	2	1	4

Read and Write Numbers (pp. 17–19)

- Standard form: 21,833
- Word form: twenty-one thousand, eight hundred thirty-three
- Expanded form: 20,000 + 1,000 + 800 + 30 + 3

Compare Numbers (pp. 28–30)

- To compare numbers, use **is greater than** $(>)$, **is less than** $(<)$, or **equal to** $(=)$.

$123 > 122$ $478 < 874$ $925 = 925$

Key Vocabulary

is equal to (p. 28)
is greater than $(>)$ (p. 28)
is less than $(<)$ (p. 28)
place value (p. 17)
rounding (p. 36)

Vocabulary Check

Choose the vocabulary word that completes each sentence.

1. When you do not need an exact answer, you can estimate by ___?___.
2. To help you read and write numbers, you can use ___?___.
3. The symbol = is used to show that one amount ___?___ another.
4. The ___?___ of the 7 in 7,495 is the thousands.
5. The symbol $>$ is used to show that a number is ___?___ another number.
6. The symbol $<$ is used to show that a number is ___?___ another number.

Lesson-by-Lesson Review

1-1 Place Value Through Hundred Thousands (pp. 17–19)

Example 1
Write 5,789 in three different ways.

Thousands			Ones		
hundreds	tens	ones	hundreds	tens	ones
		5,	7	8	9

Standard form: 5,789

Word form: five thousand, seven hundred eighty-nine

Expanded form: 5,000 + 700 + 80 + 9

Write each number in word form and in expanded form.

7. 18,045
8. 94,804
9. Write *four hundred thirty thousand, two hundred fifty-six* in standard form and in expanded form.

Write the value of the underlined digit.

10. 1<u>9</u>0,843
11. 84,<u>2</u>99
12. The Petrified Forest National Park in northeast Arizona is 93,533 acres. Write this number in word form and in expanded form.

1-2 Place Value Through Millions (pp. 22–25)

Example 2
Write *nine million, three hundred seventy-two thousand, five hundred* in standard form and expanded form.

Standard form: 9,372,500

Word form: nine million, three hundred seventy-two thousand, five hundred

Expanded form: 9,000,000 + 300,000 + 70,000 + 2,000 + 500

Write each number in standard form and in expanded form.

13. two thousand, six hundred ninety-seven
14. nine million, four hundred six thousand, two hundred seventy-one
15. León has a baseball card collection of 4,826 cards. He sells 215 cards to another collector. How many cards does he have left? Write in word form and in expanded form.

Problem-Solving Skill: The Four-Step Plan (pp. 26–27)

Example 3
Dorota saves $2 each week. How much will she save after 2 months?

Understand Dorota saves $2 each week. You need to find out how much money will she save after 2 months.

Plan There are 4 weeks in 1 month. Use repeated addition to find out how much money she has saved after 2 months.

Solve First, find out how much she saved in one month.

$2	1 week
$2	1 week
$2	1 week
+ $2	1 week
$8	

Now, find the amount saved in two months.

$8	1 month
+ $8	1 month
$16	

So, Dorota will save $16 after 2 months.

Check Count by twos 8 times.
2, 4, 6, 8, 10, 12, 14, 16

So, the answer is correct.

Solve. Use the *four-step plan*.

16. Cynthia earns 5 points at the library for each book she reads. She wants to earn 75 points in order to win the grand prize. How many books does she need to read?

17. Rafael has $72. He wants to buy the bike shown. How much more money does he need?

18. Kristina earned $22 dollars babysitting. She owes her mom $17. How much will Kristina have left after she pays her mom?

19. Trent has to read a book for class by Friday. It is Tuesday and he has 60 pages left to read. If he reads 20 pages a night for the next 3 nights, will he finish the book? Explain.

20. Presta's family is going to the mountains 280 miles away. The family's car can go 25 miles on a gallon of gas, and the gas tank holds 10 gallons. Can they travel to the mountains without stopping to fill up the gas tank? Explain.

1-4 Compare Whole Numbers (pp. 28–30)

Example 4

Compare 1,278 ● 1,500.
Use >, <, or =.

1,278

1,000 1,500 2,000

1,500 is to the right of 1,278.
So, 1,500 is greater than 1,278.
Therefore, 1,500 > 1,278.

Compare. Use <, >, or =.

21. 25,689 ● 25,679

22. 54,820 ● 58,240

23. 109,050 ● 109,050

24. 234,461 ● 234,641

25. Ela ate 2,142 calories on Monday. On the same day her brother ate 2,111 calories. Who had more calories on Monday?

1-5 Order Whole Numbers (pp. 32–35)

Example 5

Order 54,282; 65,820; and 52,466 from greatest to least.

First, line up the ones place. Compare the digits in the greatest place.

54,282
65,820 ← greatest
52,466

Then, compare the digits in the next place.

54,282
52,466

4 > 2. So, 54,282 is the next greatest number.

The numbers ordered from greatest to least are 65,820; 54,282; and 52,466.

Order the numbers from greatest to least.

26. 12,378; 12,784; 12,837

27. 138,023; 138,032; 139,006

28. 456,980; 612,701; 611,036

29. The table shows the population of the three states with the largest land area. Order these states from greatest to least population.

State	Population
Alaska	626,932
California	33,871,648
Texas	20,851,820

Source: enchantedlearning.com

1-6 Round Whole Numbers (pp. 36–39)

Example 6
Round 587 to the nearest ten.

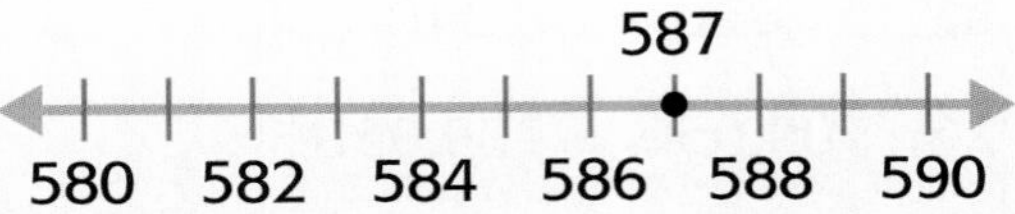

On the number line, 587 is closer to 590 than 580. Therefore, round 587 to 590.

Round each number to the given place-value position.

30. 874; hundred

31. 2,025; thousands

32. 589; hundred

33. Death Valley, California, is 282 feet below sea level. To the nearest hundred, about how many feet below sea level is Death Valley?

1-7 Problem-Solving Investigation: Choose a Strategy (pp. 40–41)

Example 7
Each time Esteban goes to the grocery store for his grandmother, she gives him $4. He has $12. How many times has Esteban gone to the grocery store?

Esteban has $12, and he gets $4 each time he goes to the store. You need to find how many times he has gone to the store. Use addition.

$4	1 trip
$4	1 trip
+ $4	1 trip
$12	

So, Esteban has gone to the store for his grandmother 3 times.

Use the *four-step plan* to solve.

34. Lindsay earns $5 for every A she gets on her report card and $3 for every B. On her last report card, she received a total of $19 for 5 subjects. How many As and Bs did she get?

35. Precious spends 35 hours in school every five-day week. How many five-day weeks will she have been in school if she has been in school for 175 hours?

36. In 1916, Jeannette Rankin of Montana became the first woman elected to Congress. Use rounding to estimate how many years ago the first woman was elected to Congress.

CHAPTER 1

Chapter Test

For Exercises 1 and 2, tell whether each statement is *true* or *false*.

1. The four steps of the *four-step plan* in order are Plan, Understand, Solve, Check.

2. The standard form of nine hundred seventy is 970.

Write the value of the underlined digit.

3. 1$\underline{8}$,765 **4.** $\underline{3}$01,936

5. Students voted on their favorite frozen yogurt flavors. The results are shown. Order the results from most favorite to least favorite.

Flavor	Number of Students
Vanilla	410
Chocolate	240
Strawberry	99
Chocolate chip	401

6. **TEST PRACTICE** Which of these is 7,201,446?

A seven thousand, two hundred one, four hundred forty-six

B seven million, two hundred one thousand, four hundred forty-six

C seven hundred two thousand, one hundred forty-six

D seven million, two hundred ten thousand, four hundred forty-six

Order the numbers from greatest to least.

7. 1,002; 1,037; 1,200; 1,102

8. 7,613; 7,702; 8,045; 7,499

9. A computer costs $1,295. Round this price to the nearest hundred.

Compare. Use $<$, $>$, or $=$.

10. 6,782 ● 6,702 **11.** 2,487 ● 2,784

12. **TEST PRACTICE** What is 7,620 rounded to the nearest thousand?

F 7,600

G 7,620

H 7,700

J 8,000

13. Sora earned a score of 98 on a test. Ryan earned a score of 89. Who earned a higher score?

Write each number in word form.

14. 3,476 **15.** 97,602

16. **WRITING IN MATH** Andrew rounded 7,963 to the nearest thousand. Is his answer correct? Explain.

7,000

Texas Test Practice

Cumulative, Chapter 1

The population of Devon's hometown is four hundred sixty-one thousand, eight hundred five. What is this number in standard form?

A 461,580 **C** 416,805

B 461,805 **D** 461,850

Read the Test Question

You need to determine what the number is in standard form.

Solve the Test Question

Make a place-value chart to help you find the standard form of the number.

Thousands			Ones		
hundreds	tens	ones	hundreds	tens	ones
4	6	1,	8	0	5

As you read the numbers, listen to the place value. Find the number that has the place values listed in the problem statement.

The answer is B.

Online Personal Tutor at tx.gr4math.com

TEST-TAKING TIP

You can use place value to help you read and write numbers in the millions.

Choose the best answer.

1. **What is the standard form for sixteen million, three hundred twenty-seven thousand, four hundred three?**

   A 16,723,043 **C** 16,327,403

   B 16,372,430 **D** 16,237,340

2. **What is the standard form for eight million, four hundred fifty-six thousand, two hundred eleven?**

   F 8,456,201 **H** 8,465,211

   G 80,456,211 **J** 8,456,211

Get Ready for the Texas Test
For test-taking strategies and more practice, see pages TX1–TX21.

3. Which of the following has the least value?

A 2,562,871 **C** 1,110,335

B 1,010,884 **D** 2,411,123

4. What is $4,775,000 rounded to the nearest million?

F $4,800,000 **H** $4,900,000

G $4,000,000 **J** $5,000,000

5. The table shows the number of coupons mailed out by four large grocery store chains.

Grocery Store Coupons	
Store	**Number of Coupons**
Fast Mart	35,411
Saver Center	35,408
Gardens	35,416
Big Value	35,420

Which store mailed out the most coupons?

A Big Value **C** Gardens

B Fast Mart **D** Saver Center

6. Which is the value of the digit 7 in 273,158?

F 70 **H** 7,000

G 700 **J** 70,000

7. Shen bought a new car for thirty-two thousand, six hundred fifty-four dollars. What is this number rounded to the nearest thousand?

A $32,000 **C** $32,700

B $32,600 **D** $33,000

8. GRIDDABLE What is 184 rounded to the nearest hundred?

9. Which point on the number line represents 22?

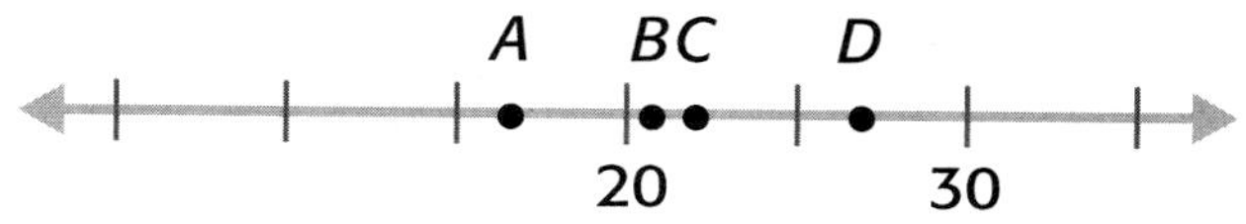

F point *A* **H** point *C*

G point *B* **J** point *D*

10. Which symbol makes the following true?

43,872,195 ■ 48,872,211

A > **C** =

B < **D** +

CHAPTER 2

Add and Subtract to Solve Problems

BIG Idea What is addition? What is subtraction?

Addition is an operation on two or more numbers that tells how many in all. Subtraction is an operation on two numbers that tells how many are left when some are taken away.

Example Celeste and her parents are painting a fence. The fence has three sides. To find the total length of the fence, use addition.

$$\begin{array}{r} \scriptstyle 1 \\ 25 \\ 30 \\ +\ 25 \\ \hline 80 \end{array}$$

25 ft 25 ft 30 ft

The total length of the fence is 80 feet.

What will I learn in this chapter?

- Use addition properties and subtraction rules.
- Estimate sums and differences.
- Use the *act it out* strategy to solve problems.
- Add and subtract whole numbers, including multi-digit numbers.

Key Vocabulary

Commutative Property of Addition

Associative Property of Addition

estimate

Student Study Tools at tx.gr4math.com

FOLDABLES™
Study Organizer

Make this Foldable to help you organize information about addition and subtraction. Begin with one sheet of 11″ × 17″ paper.

1. **Fold** lengthwise about 3″ from the bottom.

2. **Fold** the paper in thirds.

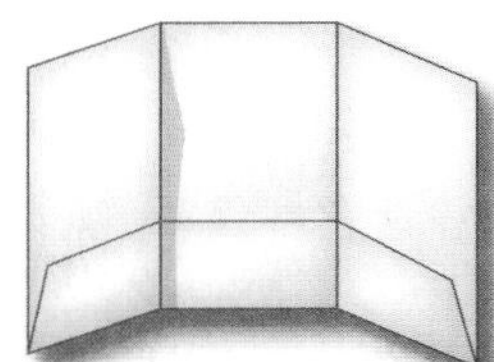

3. **Open** and staple to form 3 pockets.

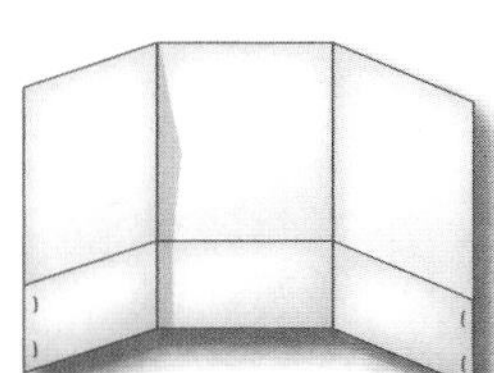

4. **Label** as shown. Place 2 index cards in each pocket.

ARE YOU READY for Chapter 2?

You have two ways to check prerequisite skills for this chapter.

Option 2

Math Online Take the Chapter Readiness Quiz at tx.gr4math.com.

Option 1

Complete the Quick Check below.

QUICK Check

Estimate. Round to the tens place. (Lesson 1-6)

1. 65 + 23

2. 58 + 31

3. \$64 − \$21

4. 98 − 22

5. \$60 + \$29

6. 88 − 26

7. Kavel wants to buy a pair of swimming goggles and a snorkel. Kavel has \$22. About how much more money does he need to buy the items?

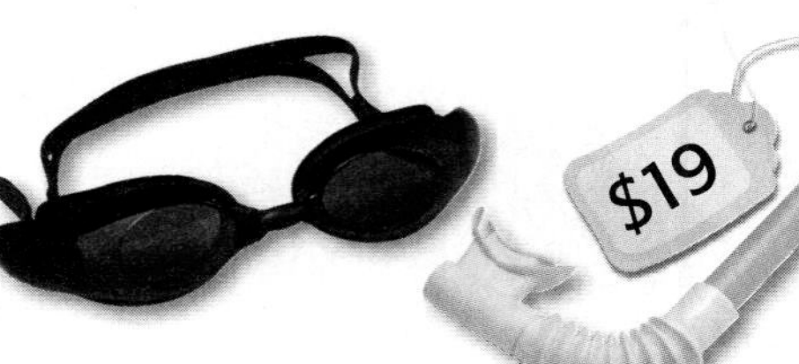

Add. (Prior grade)

8. 24 + 47

9. 36 + 57

10. 67 + 24

11. \$56 + \$25

12. 46 + 78

13. \$89 + \$53

14. Zita read an 82-page book. Then she read a 69-page book. How many pages did she read in all?

Subtract. (Prior grade)

15. 26 − 9

16. \$31 − \$ 7

17. 47 − 19

18. 42 − 19

19. 64 − 27

20. \$73 − \$45

21. Minho took 34 pictures on Monday and some more on Tuesday. He took 71 pictures in all. How many did Minho take on Tuesday?

2-1 Addition Properties and Subtraction Rules

MAIN IDEA

I will use addition properties and subtraction rules to add and subtract.

Targeted TEKS 4.3 The student adds and subtracts to solve meaningful problems involving whole numbers and decimals. (A) **Use addition and subtraction to solve problems involving whole numbers.**

New Vocabulary

Commutative Property of Addition

Associative Property of Addition

GET READY to Learn

Carlos is buying the items shown. Does the order in which the cashier scans the items change the total cost?

The following properties apply to addition.

KEY CONCEPT — **Addition Properties**

Words **Commutative Property of Addition** The order in which numbers are added does not change the sum.

Examples $4 + 1 = 5 \qquad 1 + 4 = 5$

Words **Associative Property of Addition** The way in which numbers are grouped when added does not change the sum.

Examples $(5 + 2) + 3$ → $7 + 3$ → 10 $\qquad 5 + (2 + 3)$ → $5 + 5$ → 10

Parentheses ( ) show which numbers are added first.

Words **Identity Property of Addition** The sum of any number and 0 is the number.

Examples $8 + 0 = 8 \qquad 0 + 8 = 8$

Real-World EXAMPLE Use Addition Properties

1 **Does the order in which the camping supplies are scanned change the total cost?**

The Associative Property tells us the order in which numbers are added does not change the sum.

$$(\$20 + \$15) + \$10 = \$20 + (\$15 + \$10)$$
$$(\$35 + \$10) = \$20 + \$25$$
$$\$45 = \$45$$

EXAMPLE Use Addition Properties

2 ALGEBRA Complete 0 + ■ = 6. Identify the property used.

Zero is added to a number, and the sum is 6. So, the missing number is 6. 0 + 6 = 6.

This is the Identity Property of Addition.

Online **Personal Tutor at** tx.gr4math.com

> **Remember**
>
> Use parentheses ( ) to show the two numbers you are adding first.

The following rules apply to subtraction.

KEY CONCEPT — Subtraction Rules

Words	When you subtract 0 from any number, the result is the number.
Examples	6 − 0 = 6 4 − 0 = 4
Words	When you subtract any number from itself, the result is 0.
Examples	6 − 6 = 0 5 − 5 = 0

EXAMPLE Use Subtraction Rules

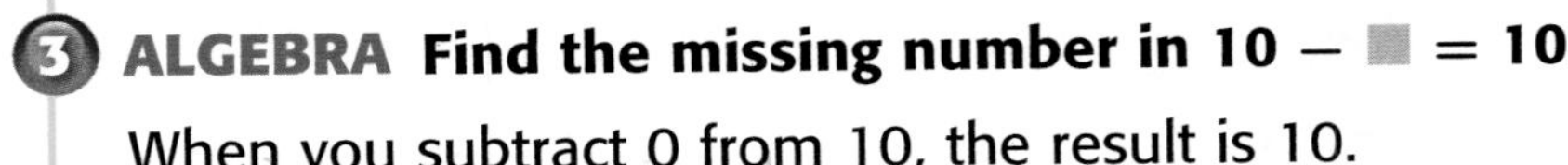

3 ALGEBRA Find the missing number in 10 − ■ = 10.

When you subtract 0 from 10, the result is 10.

10 − 0 = 10 So, the missing number is 0.

CHECK What You Know

Copy and complete each number sentence. Identify the property or rule. See Examples 1–3 (pp. 55–56)

1. 19 − ■ = 19

2. (5 + ■) + 2 = 5 + (9 + 2)

3. 74 + 68 = ■ + 74

Add mentally. See Example 1 (p. 55)

4. 12 + 13 + 28

5. 21 + 16 + 19

6. 24 + 17 + 36

7. Talk About It Which subtraction rule is like the opposite of the Identity Property of Addition? Explain your reasoning.

Practice and Problem Solving

Copy and complete each number sentence. Identify the property or rule. See Examples 1–3 (pp. 55–56)

8. $(\blacksquare + 8) + 7 = 9 + (8 + 7)$

9. $4 + 3 + 1 = 3 + 1 + \blacksquare$

10. $\blacksquare + 0 = 9$

11. $5 - \blacksquare = 0$

12. $7 + (1 + 8) = (7 + \blacksquare) + 8$

13. $15 - \blacksquare = 15$

Add mentally. See Example 1 (p. 55)

14. $17 + 24 + 13$

15. $35 + 22 + 15$

16. $13 + 11 + 27$

17. $22 + 16 + 28$

18. $14 + 33 + 26$

19. $31 + 22 + 29$

20. **Measurement** There are 24 minutes left in Asia's class. Then she has 2 more classes before lunch that are each 35 minutes. How many minutes does Asia have before lunch?

21. **Measurement** Paco has 75 minutes before baseball practice. He cleans his room for 40 minutes and reads for 30 minutes. Can he do both of these activities before practice? Explain.

Write a number sentence. Then identify the property or rule used.

22. Susan ate 1 hot dog and 2 apples. Amelia ate 2 hot dogs and 1 apple. Who ate more food items?

23. Carla has 4 triangles, 3 squares, and 5 circles. Ethan has 3 circles, 4 squares, and 5 triangles. Who has more shapes?

H.O.T. Problems

24. **OPEN ENDED** Copy and complete the number sentence $(23 + \blacksquare) + 19 = 23 + (\blacksquare + 19)$. Can any number complete the number sentence? Explain.

25. **FIND THE ERROR** Trey and Mika are showing an example of the Identity Property of Addition. Who is correct? Explain.

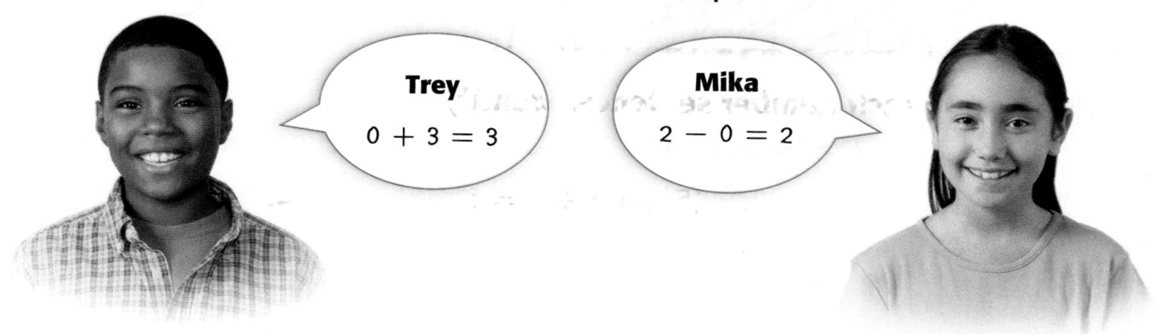

26. **WRITING IN ▶MATH** Explain how you could group $775 + 639 + 225$ to find the sum mentally.

2-2

Estimate Sums and Differences

MAIN IDEA

I will estimate sums and differences of numbers.

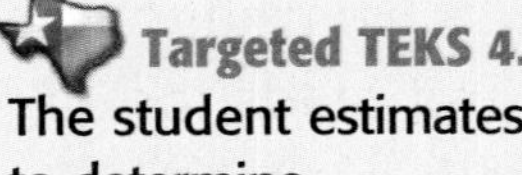

Targeted TEKS 4.5 The student estimates to determine reasonable results. (A) **Round whole numbers to the nearest ten, hundred, or thousand to approximate reasonable results in problem situations.**

New Vocabulary

estimate

GET READY to Learn

Natalie has been saving her money so that she can buy snowboarding equipment. She wants to buy the items shown. About how much money does she need?

Sometimes you do not need an exact answer. When the word *about* is used in a problem, you can find an estimate. An **estimate** is an answer close to the exact answer.

Real-World EXAMPLE Estimate Sums

1 MONEY **About how much money does Natalie need to buy a snowboard and boots? Round to the tens place.**

Round each amount to the nearest tens place. Then add.

$119	rounds to →	$120
+$ 67	rounds to →	+$ 70
		$190

So, Natalie needs to save about $190.

When estimating, you can also round to the nearest hundred or thousand.

EXAMPLE Estimate Sums

Remember

Use place value to help you round whole numbers.

2 **Estimate 2,342 + 637. Round to the hundreds place.**

Round to the nearest hundreds place. Then add.

2,342	rounds to →	2,300
+ 637	rounds to →	+ 600
		2,900

So, 2,342 + 637 is about 2,900.

EXAMPLE Estimate Differences

3 **Estimate $75 − $32. Round to the tens place.**

Round each amount to the nearest ten dollars. Then subtract.

$75	rounds to →	$80
− $32	rounds to →	−$30
		$50

So, $75 − $32 is about $50.

Real-World EXAMPLE Estimate Differences

4 **MEASUREMENT The table shows populations for two cities in Texas. About how many more people live in Alice than in El Campo?**

City Populations

City	Population
Alice	19,010
El Campo	10,945

Round each population to the nearest thousand. Then subtract.

19,010	rounds to →	19,000
− 10,945	rounds to →	− 11,000
		8,000

So, Alice has about 8,000 more people.

Online Personal Tutor at tx.gr4math.com

CHECK What You Know

Estimate. Round to the indicated place value. **See Examples 1–4 (pp. 58–59)**

1. 312 + 27; tens
2. 1,561 + 305; hundreds
3. $21 + $73; tens
4. 383 − 122; hundreds
5. $74 − $52; tens
6. 37,215 − 6,972; thousands
7. The Davis family will buy the camping equipment shown. About how much will the equipment cost?

Camping Equipment

Item	Cost
Family-size tent	$399
Camping stove	$179

8. **Talk About It** Estimate 829 + 1,560 to the nearest hundred and the nearest thousand. Compare both estimates to the actual sum. What do you notice?

Practice and Problem Solving

EXTRA PRACTICE See page R4.

Estimate. Round to the indicated place value. See Examples 1–4 (pp. 58–59)

9. $455 + $22; tens

10. 624 + 53; tens

11. 2,647 + 256; hundreds

12. $772 − $593; hundreds

13. $63 + $27; tens

14. $35 + $42; tens

15. 985 − 639; tens

16. $34 − $23; tens

17. $68 − $33; tens

18. $20,425 + $47,236; thousands

19. 27,629 − 5,364; thousands

20. $48,986 − $7,664; thousands

Solve. Round to the nearest thousand.

21. The largest NBA arena can seat 22,076 people. Suppose two games are sold out. About how many people will attend the two games?

22. Luz is going to buy a car that costs $18,460 new and $15,788 used. About how much money would Luz save if she bought the car used?

23. **Measurement** A mountain climber is climbing Mt. Everest. It is 29,035 feet tall. About how many feet will the climber have traveled after going up and down the mountain?

24. Jupiter and Saturn are the two largest planets in our solar system. Jupiter is 88,846 miles across and Saturn is 74,898 miles across. What is the approximate difference in the distance across these two planets?

Real-World PROBLEM SOLVING

Architecture This table shows the tallest buildings in the world. Round to the nearest hundred.

25. About how much taller is the Sears Tower than the Jin Mao Building?

26. Estimate the difference between the height of the Taipai 101 Building and the Empire State Building.

27. About how much taller is Petronas Towers than the Empire State Building?

Tallest Buildings in the World

Building	Location	Height (ft)
Taipai 101	Taiwan	1,669
Petronas Towers	Malaysia	1,482
Sears Tower	United States	1,450
Jin Mao Building	China	1,381
CITIC Plaza	China	1,282
Shun Hing Square	China	1,259
Empire State Building	United States	1,250

Source: *The Ultimate Book of Lists*

Math Online **Self-Check Quiz** tx.gr4math.com

H.O.T. Problems

28. OPEN ENDED Write two numbers that when rounded to the thousands place have an estimated sum of 10,000.

29. NUMBER SENSE If both addends are rounded down, will the sum of the numbers be greater or less than the actual sum? Explain.

30. WRITING IN ▸MATH When rounding to estimate the sum or difference of numbers, explain a situation where less exact answers would be better than more exact answers.

TEST Practice

31. What number completes the number sentence below? **(Lesson 2-1)**

(24 + ■) + 18 = 24 + (36 + 18)

A 18 **C** 36

B 24 **D** 38

32. The Casey family traveled last week. They drove 182 miles on Friday, 138 miles on Saturday, and 119 miles on Sunday. Approximately how many miles did they travel? **(Lesson 2-2)**

F 200 miles **H** 320 miles

G 300 miles **J** 400 miles

Spiral Review

Algebra Copy and complete each number sentence. Identify the property or rule. (Lesson 2-1)

33. 35 − ■ = 35

34. (57 + ■) + 36 = 57 + (25 + 36)

Round each number to the given place-value position. (Lesson 1-6)

35. 354; ten

36. 4,396; thousand

37. 257,468; hundred

Compare. Use >, <, or =. (Lesson 1-4)

38. 8,650 ● 8,623

39. 44,068 ● 44,086

40. 248,632 ● 284,632

41. Jameson's basketball team scored a total of 58 points. Jameson scored 18 points, and his sister scored 12 points. How many points did the rest of the team score? **(Lesson 1-3)**

42. Teresa's cell phone bill is $32 each month. About how much money does she spend on cell phone service every two months? **(Lesson 1-3)**

Problem-Solving Strategy

MAIN IDEA I will solve a problem by acting it out.

Targeted TEKS 4.14 The student applies Grade 4 mathematics to solve problems connected to everyday experiences and activities in and outside of school. (C) **Select or develop an appropriate problem-solving plan or strategy,...to solve problems.** *Also addresses TEKS 4.14(B).*

Sonoda has 6 coins in his bank. The coins equal 65¢. What combination of coins does he have in his bank?

Understand

What facts do you know?

- Sonoda has 6 coins.
- The value of the 6 coins is 65¢.

What do you need to find?

- Find the coins Sonoda has in his bank.

Plan

You can use play money to act out different combinations of 65¢.

Solve

One way to make 65¢ is with 2 quarters, 1 dime, and 1 nickel. But, that is only 4 coins. You need 2 more coins.

Take 1 quarter and exchange it for 2 dimes and 1 nickel. The value stays the same, and the number of coins increases to 6.

=

So, Sonoda has 1 quarter, 3 dimes, and 2 nickels.

Check

Look back at the problem.

1 quarter + 3 dimes + 2 nickels
= 25¢ + 10¢ + 10¢ + 10¢ + 5¢ + 5¢
= 25¢ + 30¢ + 10¢
= 65¢

So, the answer is correct.

ANALYZE the Strategy

Refer to the problem on the previous page.

1. If Sonoda has a few coins that total 55¢, what is the least amount of coins he can have?

2. Suppose Sonoda had 60¢ in his bank. What 5 coins would he have?

3. Suppose Sonoda found 3 coins on the sidewalk. The coins total $1. What coins did Sonoda find? Explain.

4. Describe another strategy you could use to solve this problem.

PRACTICE the Strategy

EXTRA PRACTICE
See page R5.

Solve. Use the *act it out* strategy.

5. Angelo's father is 30 years old. This is 10 years older than twice Angelo's age. How old is Angelo?

6. Ellen needs to visit 3 Web sites for a homework assignment. In how many different ways can she visit the Web sites?

7. List five different money combinations that equal 34¢.

8. There are five people at a party, and each person has shaken hands with every other person. How many handshakes took place among the five people?

9. **Geometry** Can 12 toothpicks be used to form 4 squares that are the same size and same shape?

10. Berta, Maya, and Zach are in different checkout lines at a store. Berta has 3 more people in front of her than are in front of Maya. There are 2 times as many people in front of Zach as there are in front of Maya. The total number of people in front of the girls is 11. How many people are in front of each person?

11. **Geometry** How many rectangles can you make using all of the squares shown below?

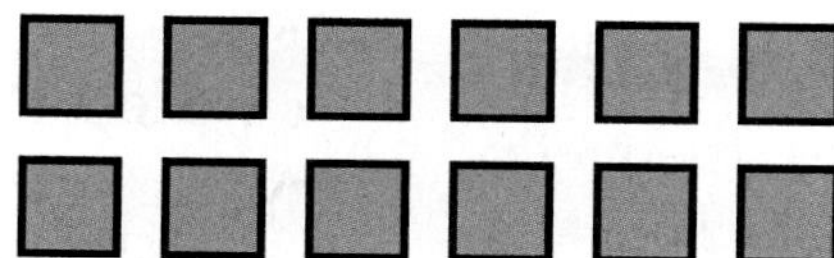

12. Dane needs to set up tables for his nine family members and himself to eat dinner. The square tables will seat one person on each side. Explain how Dane can arrange six square tables in a rectangle so that there is one seat for each person with no extra seats.

13. **WRITING IN ▶MATH** When should the *act it out* strategy be used to solve a problem? Explain.

2-4 Add Whole Numbers

MAIN IDEA

I will add numbers, including multidigit numbers.

Targeted TEKS 4.3 The student adds and subtracts to solve meaningful problems involving whole numbers and decimals. (A) **Use addition** and subtraction **to solve problems involving whole numbers.**

GET READY to Learn

Hands-On Mini Activity

The model shows 135 + 127.

1. Estimate 135 + 127.
2. To find 135 + 127, is it necessary to regroup the ones? How do you know?
3. Is it necessary to regroup the tens? How do you know?

Hundreds	Tens	Ones
1	3	5
+ 1	2	7

When you add whole numbers, it may be necessary to regroup.

Vocabulary Link

prefixes The prefix *re-* means *again*. Example: *regroup* means *to group again.*

EXAMPLE Add Whole Numbers

1 Find 6,824 + 349.

Estimate

$$\begin{array}{r} 6{,}824 \\ +\ 349 \\ \hline \end{array} \rightarrow \begin{array}{r} 6{,}800 \\ +\ 300 \\ \hline 7{,}100 \end{array}$$

Step 1 Add ones.

$$\begin{array}{r} ^{1}\ \\ 6{,}824 \\ +\ 349 \\ \hline 3 \end{array}$$

4 + 9 = 13
Regroup 13 ones as 1 ten and 3 ones.

Step 2 Add tens.

$$\begin{array}{r} ^{1}\ \\ 6{,}824 \\ +\ 349 \\ \hline 73 \end{array}$$

1 + 2 + 4 = 7

Step 3 Add hundreds.

$$\begin{array}{r} ^{1\ \ 1}\ \\ 6{,}824 \\ +\ 349 \\ \hline 173 \end{array}$$

8 + 3 = 11
Regroup 11 hundreds as 1 thousand and 1 hundred.

Step 4 Add thousands.

$$\begin{array}{r} ^{1\ \ 1}\ \\ 6{,}824 \\ +\ 349 \\ \hline 7{,}173 \end{array}$$

6 + 1 = 7

Check for reasonableness

The estimate is 7,100. Since 7,173 is close to the estimate, the answer is reasonable. ✓

Real-World EXAMPLE — Add Multi-Digit Numbers

2 **TICKETS** **Weekend ticket sales for a school play are shown in the table. What was the total?**

Ticket Sales	
Day	**Amount**
Saturday	$273
Sunday	$97

Estimate $273 → $270
+ $97 → + $100
$370

Step 1 Add ones.

```
   11
 $273
+$ 97
    0
```

3 + 7 = 10
Regroup 10 ones as 1 ten and 0 ones.

Step 2 Add tens.

```
  111
 $273
+$ 97
   70
```

1 + 7 + 9 = 17
Regroup 17 tens as 1 hundred and 7 tens.

Step 3 Add hundreds.

```
  111
 $273
+$ 97
 $370
```

1 + 2 = 3

Step 4 Place $ sign.

```
   1
 $273
+$ 97
 $370
```

Place $ in front.

So, the total ticket sales were $371.

Check for reasonableness

The estimate is $370. Since $371 is close to the estimate, the answer is reasonable. ✓

Online Personal Tutor at tx.gr4math.com

Find each sum. Check your work by estimating. See Examples 1 and 2 (pp. 64–65)

1. 397 + 84

2. 1,592 + 429

3. \$2,971 + \$ 864

4. \$29,380 + \$ 8,253

5. Mr. Russo's class is collecting bottles to recycle. The class collected 178 bottles in March and 236 bottles in April. How many bottles were collected?

6. Talk About It Explain why it is important to line up digits in numbers when you add.

Practice and Problem Solving

Find each sum. Check your work by estimating. See Examples 1 and 2 (pp. 64–65)

7. 364 + 58

8. 290 + 693

9. 6,742 + 975

10. 8,346 + 7,208

11. \$23,824 + \$ 7,346

12. 82,828 + 4,789

13. \$37,178 + \$82,370

14. \$693,782 + \$ 47,816

15. There are 4,585 students who rode the bus to school today. There were 3,369 students who came to school another way. How many students were there in all at school?

16. Becky wants to buy a new bike that costs \$150 and a pair of roller blades that costs \$30. She made \$200 babysitting her younger brother. If she buys a book that is \$15, will she have enough money?

Real-World PROBLEM SOLVING

Data File The table shows the miles of roads for various counties in Texas.

17. How many miles of roads are in Lubbock and Montgomery Counties?

18. How many miles of roads are in Maverick, Harris, and Williamson Counties?

19. Which has more miles of roads, Cameron and Harris Counties or the total of the rest of the counties combined?

Texas Roads

County	Miles of Roads
Cameron	2,199
Harris	13,380
Hidalgo	4,396
Lubbock	3,516
Maverick	445
Montgomery	6,004
Williamson	4,404

Source: www.state.tx.us

H.O.T. Problems

20. OPEN ENDED Write two 5-digit addends that would give an estimate of 60,000.

21. WRITING IN ▶MATH Explain why an addition problem that has 4-digit addends could have a 5-digit sum.

TEST Practice

22. Jackson is buying a new board game. It costs $26. If he has 2 ten-dollar bills and 5 one-dollar bills, which of the following statements is true? (Lesson 2-3)

A He will have less than $5 left over.

B He does not have enough money.

C He has the exact amount of money.

D He will have more than $5 left over.

23. There are 17 extra chairs in the library and 45 extra chairs in the cafeteria. Which number sentence shows how to find the total number of extra chairs? (Lesson 2-4)

F $17 + 45$

G $17 - 45$

H 17×45

J $17 \div 45$

Spiral Review

24. The school collected 189 cans of corn, 500 cans of soup, 168 cans of beans, and 269 jars of spaghetti sauce in its food drive. How many items did the school collect? (Lesson 2-3)

Estimate. Round to the indicated place value. (Lesson 2-2)

25. 137 + 192; tens

26. 489 + 1,963; hundreds

Add mentally. (Lesson 2-1)

27. 10 + 25 + 18

28. 26 + 14 + 3

29. 15 + 12 + 30

Round each number to the given place-value position. (Lesson 1-6)

30. 987; ten

31. 2,159; hundred

32. 78,368; thousand

Technology Activity for 2-4

Explore Composing and Decomposing Numbers

Tech Link

You can use the *Math Tool Chest* to model composing and decomposing numbers.

MAIN IDEA

I will use technology to have base-ten models explore composing and decomposing numbers.

Targeted TEKS 4.14 The student applies Grade 4 mathematics to solve problems connected to everyday experiences and activities in and outside of school. **(D) Use tools such** as real objects, manipulatives, **and technology to solve problems.** *Also addresses TEKS 4.15(A).*

EXAMPLE

1 **Angela has 58 books in her classroom library. Each book is either non-fiction or fiction. How many of each type might the library have?**

Click on place-value tool from the *Math Tool Chest.*

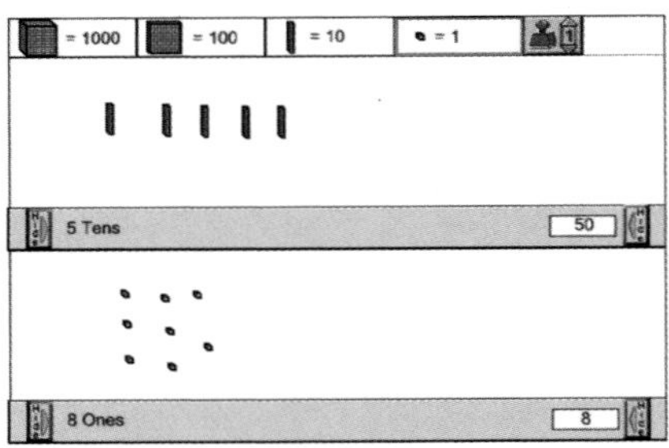

- In A, start with tens and stamp out 50.
- In B, use ones and stamp out 8.
- Click on sum.
- This shows that $50 + 8 = 58$.
- Explore different ways to make 58.

CHECK What You Know

Use the *Math Tool Chest* to explore different ways to compose and decompose each amount. Name two different ways.

1. There are 895 students in the 4th grade at South Elementary. How might this population be divided between boys and girls?

2. Mitchell and Vara have a total of 29 rocks. They do not have the same number of rocks. What number of rocks might each person have?

3. **WRITING IN MATH** Describe how different combinations of numbers can have the same sum.

CHAPTER 2

Mid-Chapter Check

Lessons 2-1 through 2-4

Algebra Copy and complete each number sentence. Identify the property or rule. (Lesson 2-1)

1. 136 + 0 = ■

2. (4 + ■)+ 7 = 4 + (2 + 7)

3. 58 + 98 = ■ + 58

Write a number sentence. Then identify the property or rule. (Lesson 2-1)

4. Andrea's pencil box has 3 pencils, 2 pencil-top erasers, and 1 red pen. Max's pencil box has 2 pencils, 1 pencil-top eraser, and 3 red pens. Whose pencil box contains more items? Explain.

5. **TEST PRACTICE** What number completes the number sentence below? (Lesson 2-1)

   (21 + ■) + 12 = 21 + (17 + 12)

   A 11 **C** 17

   B 12 **D** 21

Estimate. Round to the indicated place value. (Lesson 2-2)

6. \$22 + \$63; tens

7. 567 − 203; hundreds

8. 5,825 − 551; hundreds

9. **TEST PRACTICE** About how many miles did a soccer team travel during the weekend? (Lesson 2-2)

Distance Traveled	
Day	**Distance (miles)**
Friday	146
Saturday	175
Sunday	206

   F 400 miles **H** 600 miles

   G 500 miles **J** 700 miles

Tell whether an estimate or exact answer is needed. Then solve. (Lesson 2-3)

10. Alejandra needs to make a fence in her yard for her puppy. She wants it to be square. One side measures 20 feet. How much fence should she buy?

Find each sum. Check for reasonableness. (Lesson 2-4)

11. 28,180 + 7,233

12. 63,456 + 37,425

13. Gina's brother is starting college in the fall. The cost of tuition for one year will be \$5,491. All the other expenses for the year will cost \$10,065. What will the total cost of one year of college be for Gina's brother? (Lesson 2-4)

14. **WRITING IN MATH** Explain how you could add 175 + 139 + 225 mentally. (Lesson 2-1)

Math Activity for 2-5
Subtract Whole Numbers

When subtracting whole numbers, you may need to regroup.

MAIN IDEA
I will explore how to subtract whole numbers

Targeted TEKS 4.3 The student adds and subtracts to solve meaningful problems. (A) **Use** addition and **subtraction to solve problems involving whole numbers.**

You Will Need
base-ten blocks

ACTIVITY **Use models to find 421 − 241.**

Step 1 **Model 421.**
Use base-ten blocks to model 421.

Hundreds	Tens	Ones
4 hundreds flats	2 tens rods	1 one (crossed out)

Step 2 **Subtract the ones.**
Subtract.

$$\begin{array}{r} 421 \\ -\ 241 \\ \hline 0 \end{array}$$

Step 3 **Subtract the tens.**
Since you cannot take 4 tens from 2 tens, you need to regroup. Regroup one hundreds flat as 10 tens. You now have 12 tens.

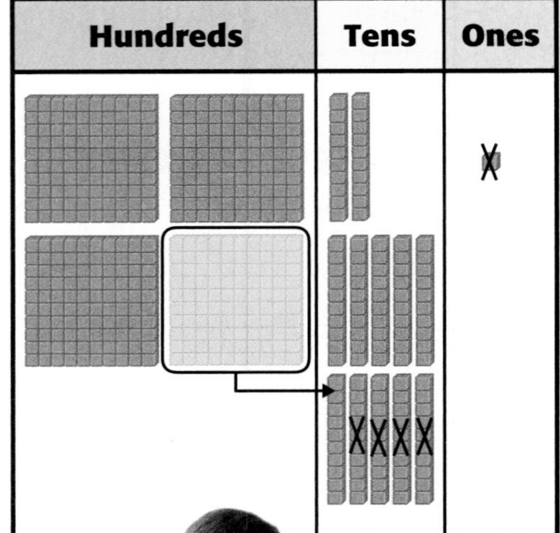

$$\begin{array}{r} \overset{3}{\cancel{4}}\overset{12}{\cancel{2}}1 \\ -\ 241 \\ \hline 80 \end{array}$$

Animation
tx.gr4math.com

Hands-On Activity

Step 4 **Subtract the hundreds.**

Take 2 hundreds flats away from the 3 hundreds flats.

$$\begin{array}{r} \overset{3\ 12}{\cancel{4}\cancel{2}1} \\ -\ 241 \\ \hline 180 \end{array}$$

421 ← **minuend**
− 241 ← **subtrahend**
180 ← **difference**

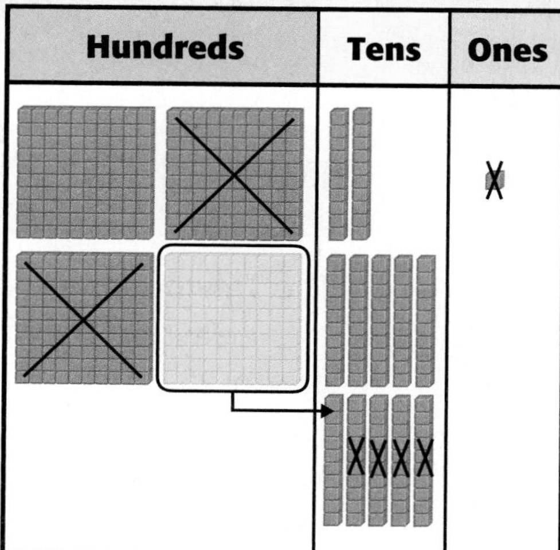

Check

You can use addition to check your subtraction.

$$\begin{array}{r} 421 \\ -\ 241 \\ \hline 180 \end{array} \rightarrow \begin{array}{r} 180 \\ +\ 241 \\ \hline 421 \end{array}$$

So, the answer is correct. ✓

Think About It

1. How did you subtract 241 from 421 using base-ten blocks?
2. Describe how you regrouped the tens place.

CHECK What You Know

Subtract. Check by adding.

3. 357 − 98

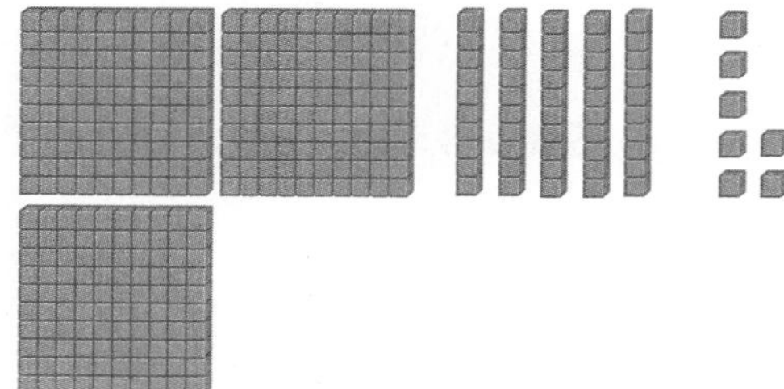

4. 679 − 345

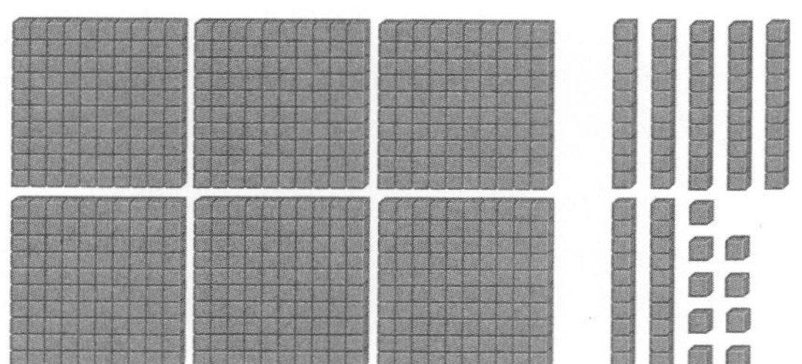

5. 287 − 195
6. 525 − 385
7. 632 − 248
8. 727 − 469
9. 861 − 593
10. 948 − 729
11. **WRITING IN ▸MATH** Why is it important to line up the digits in each place-value position when subtracting?

2-5 Subtract Whole Numbers

MAIN IDEA

I will subtract multidigit numbers.

Targeted TEKS 4.3 The student adds and subtracts to solve meaningful problems involving whole numbers and decimals. **(A) Use** addition and **subtraction to solve problems involving whole numbers.**

GET READY to Learn

The Trevino family is moving to a new city. They have driven 957 miles out of the 3,214 miles that they need to travel. How many more miles do they need to drive?

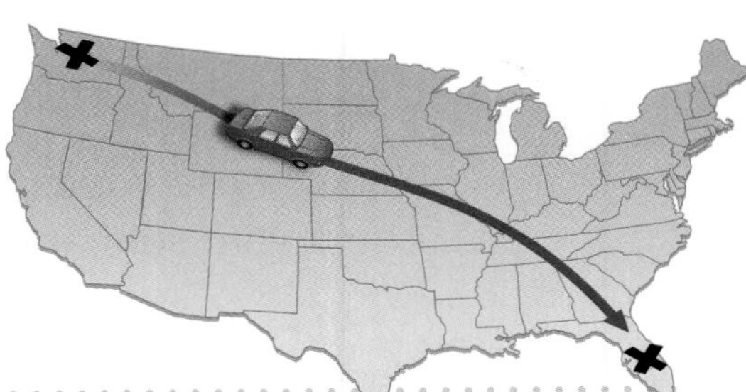

Subtraction of whole numbers is similar to addition of whole numbers in that you may need to regroup.

Real-World EXAMPLE Subtract Whole Numbers

1 **MEASUREMENT Find 3,214 − 957 to find how many miles the Trevino family needs to travel.**

Estimate

3,214	→	3,200
− 957	→	− 1,000
		2,200

Step 1 Subtract ones.

```
   0 14
  3,214
 −  957
      7
```

Regroup a ten as 10 ones.

Step 2 Subtract tens.

```
   10
  1 0 14
  3,214
 −  957
     57
```

Regroup a hundred as 10 tens.

Step 3 Subtract hundreds.

```
  11 10
  2 1 0 14
  3,214
 −  957
    257
```

Regroup a thousand as 10 hundreds.

Step 4 Subtract thousands.

```
  11 10
  2 1 0 14
  3,214
 −  957
  2,257
```

Check You can use addition to check your subtraction.

```
 3,214        2,257
 − 957        + 957
 2,257   →    3,214
```

The answer is correct and close to the estimate. ✓

Real-World EXAMPLE Subtract Money

2 **MONEY** **Tamara has $85 in her bank account. She buys a stuffed animal for $12. How much money is left?**

Estimate

$$\begin{array}{r} \$85 \\ -\ \$12 \\ \hline \end{array} \rightarrow \begin{array}{r} \$80 \\ -\ \$10 \\ \hline \$70 \end{array}$$

Step 1 Subtract the ones place.

$$\begin{array}{r} \$85 \\ -\ \$12 \\ \hline 3 \end{array}$$

Step 2 Subtract the tens place.

$$\begin{array}{r} \$85 \\ -\ \$12 \\ \hline \$73 \end{array}$$

Check

$$\begin{array}{r} \$85 \\ -\ \$12 \\ \hline \$73 \end{array} \rightarrow \begin{array}{r} \$73 \\ +\ \$12 \\ \hline \$85 \end{array}$$

The answer is correct and close to the estimate. ✓

Personal Tutor at tx.gr4math.com

CHECK What You Know

Subtract. Use addition or estimation to check. See Examples 1 and 2 (pp. 72–73)

1. $\begin{array}{r} 526 \\ -\ 403 \\ \hline \end{array}$

2. $\begin{array}{r} \$937 \\ -\ \$729 \\ \hline \end{array}$

3. $\begin{array}{r} 2,962 \\ -\ 845 \\ \hline \end{array}$

4. $\begin{array}{r} \$47 \\ -\ \$22 \\ \hline \end{array}$

5. Kerri had $95 in her bank account. She bought her mom a bottle of perfume for her birthday for $25. How much money does she have left?

6. **Talk About It** Explain how to check the answer to a subtraction problem by using addition.

Practice and Problem Solving

EXTRA PRACTICE
See page R5.

Subtract. Use addition or estimation to check. See Examples 1 and 2 (pp. 72–73)

7. 479 − 292

8. \$924 − \$837

9. \$524 − \$246

10. \$986 − \$339

11. 4,273 − 365

12. 8,845 − 627

13. \$5,751 − \$4,824

14. \$64,779 − \$42,788

15. \$832 − \$570

16. 39,536 − 18,698

17. Ramon is buying a DVD that costs \$14, a book that costs \$15, and pays \$2 in tax. If he hands the cashier \$40, how much change will he get back?

18. Mount Everest is 29,035 feet tall. From base camp at 17,600 feet, a climber hiked 2,300 feet. How much farther does the climber have before reaching the top of the mountain?

Real-World PROBLEM SOLVING

History This table shows information about former Presidents of the United States.

19. Who was older when he became President, John Adams or Harry S. Truman?

20. Who was the youngest person on this list to become President? How old was he?

21. How old was Ronald Reagan when John F. Kennedy died?

United States Presidents

President	Born	Year became President	Death
John Adams	1732	1797	1801
James K. Polk	1795	1845	1849
Harry S. Truman	1884	1945	1972
John F. Kennedy	1917	1961	1963
Ronald Reagan	1911	1981	2004

Source: whitehouse.gov/history/presidents

H.O.T. Problems

22. WHICH ONE DOESN'T BELONG? Which subtraction problem does not require regrouping? Explain.

67,457 − 40,724

70,639 − 39,607

89,584 − 57,372

95,947 − 26,377

23. WRITING IN MATH Write a real-world problem that involves subtraction and regrouping to solve. The numbers used in the problem must have at least three digits.

Math Online Self-Check Quiz at tx.gr4math.com

Make a Big Difference

Subtract Multi-Digit Numbers

Get Ready!

Players: 2 players

You will need: paper and pencil, 0–9 spinner

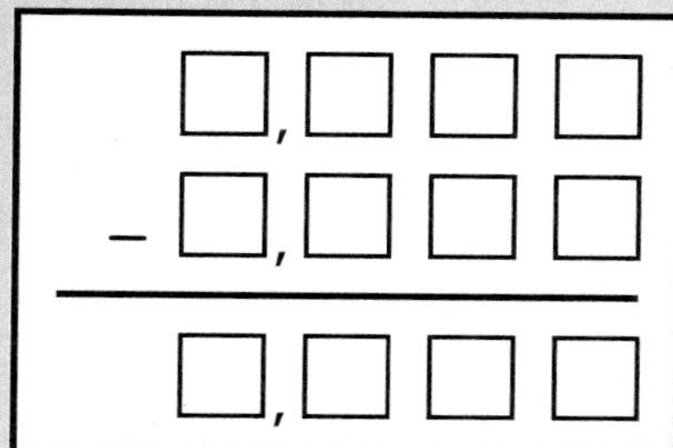

Get Set!

Make a game sheet like the one shown. Divide a spinner into ten equal sections. Label 0–9.

Go!

- Player 1 spins the spinner. Both players write that digit in a box of their choice on their game sheets.
- Continue until all eight boxes are filled. Then find the difference.
- Compare the differences. The player with the greatest difference scores 1 point.
- If the differences are equal, both players score 1 point.
- Continue playing until one player scores 5 points.

2-6 Problem-Solving Investigation

MAIN IDEA I will choose the best strategy to solve a problem.

Targeted TEKS 4.14 The student applies Grade 4 mathematics to solve problems connected to everyday experiences and activities in and outside of school. **(B) Solve problems that incorporate understanding the problem, making a plan, and evaluating the solution for reasonableness.** *Also addresses TEKS 4.14(C).*

P.S.I. TEAM +

MARCO: **I am downloading music. So far, I have downloaded 4 albums. Each album has 14 songs.**

YOUR MISSION: **Find how many songs Marco has downloaded.**

Understand Marco has downloaded 4 albums, and each album has 14 songs. Find how many songs Marco has downloaded.

Plan You can organize the information in a table and use repeated addition to find how many songs Marco has downloaded..

Solve Start with 14, the number of songs on the first album. Then continue to add 14 for each additional album.

$$\begin{array}{r} 14 \\ +\ 14 \\ \hline 28 \end{array}$$

14 ← first album; + 14 ← second album

$$\begin{array}{r} {}^{1} \\ 28 \\ +\ 14 \\ \hline 42 \end{array}$$

+ 14 ← third album

$$\begin{array}{r} 42 \\ +\ 14 \\ \hline 56 \end{array}$$

+ 14 ← fourth album

Albums	Songs
1	14
2	28
3	42
4	56

So, he downloaded a total of 56 songs.

Check Look back at the problem. 56 − 14 = 42, 42 − 14 = 28, 28 − 14 = 14, and 14 − 14 = 0. The answer is correct.

Mixed Problem Solving

See page R6.

Use any strategy to solve each problem.

1. Mrs. Thomas had $85. She bought a toaster. She now has $43. How much was the toaster?

2. **Measurement** The Nile River is 4,145 miles long. The Mississippi River is 405 miles shorter than the Nile River. How long is the Mississippi River?

3. Rosana has $9 left over after buying a movie ticket. If she buys a soft pretzel, what other item can she buy?

Movie Palace	
Item	**Cost**
Small soda	$4
Large soda	$6
Soft pretzel	$5
Medium popcorn	$6

4. Alonso has 139 comic books. Maggie has 72 comic books. Do they have a total of about 200 comic books? Explain.

5. A piñata is $36, and party decorations are $18. A gift is $28. About how much is spent altogether?

6. Prem is thinking of three numbers from 1 to 10. The sum of the numbers is 14. Find the numbers.

7. Marcel earns $5 a week for doing his chores. About how many weeks will he have to save his money in order to buy the sports equipment below?

8. Greta earns $5 each week walking dogs. Her portion of the family cell phone bill each month is $15. How much does she have left after paying her cell phone bill for a month that has four weeks?

9. There are 58 third graders and 62 fourth graders going on a field trip. Each bus can carry 40 people. How many buses are needed?

10. **Measurement** About how much farther does the willow warbler migrate than the barn swallow?

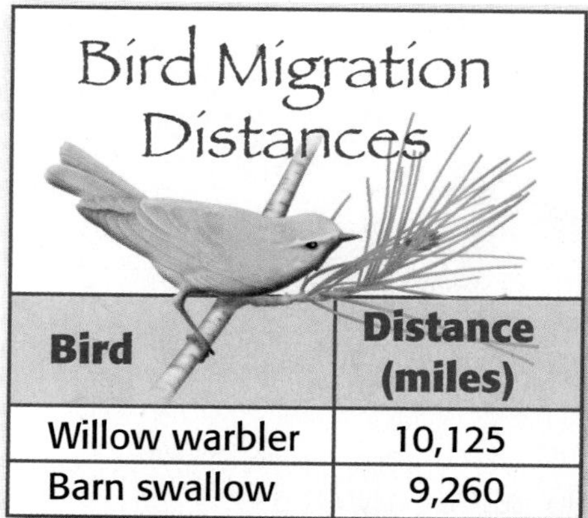

Bird Migration Distances

Bird	Distance (miles)
Willow warbler	10,125
Barn swallow	9,260

11. **WRITING IN MATH** Juan bowls 132 in his first game. He bowls 148 in his second game. The answer is 280. What is the question?

Problem Solving in Science

Ready, Set, Click!

The first photographers had difficult jobs. They carried separate pieces of film in large metal containers. Each container was 12 inches wide and 16 inches long.

Taking a picture was first a chemical process. Today, taking a picture is a digital process, too. Digital cameras take pictures like a television records images.

There are now many different types of cameras that are affordable. Some cameras that scientists have invented are used only once. There are many different kinds of these cameras, including digital disposable cameras.

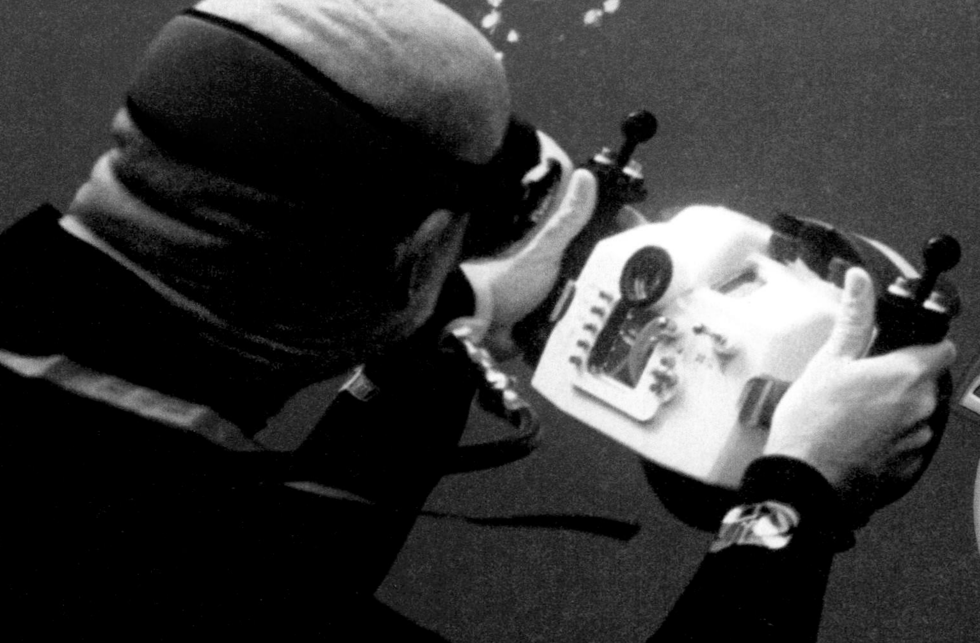

Did You Know?

The digital camera revolution started in 1981.

Targeted TEKS 4.14 The student applies Grade 4 mathematics to solve problems connected to everyday experiences and activities in and outside of school. (A) **Identify the mathematics in everyday situations.**

Real-World Math

Use the information on pages 78 and 79 to solve each problem.

1. Hanna paid $35 for disposable cameras. If she purchased 4 cameras, which ones did she buy?

2. Cesar buys two digital cameras, three outdoor cameras, and three flash cameras. How much money does Cesar spend?

3. Suppose you buy an outdoor disposable camera and a flash disposable camera. If you pay with $30, how much change will you get?

4. Which two cameras cost the same as one underwater camera?

5. If you buy 2 packages of underwater cameras, you get a $3 discount. How much money will you spend?

6. What two packages of cameras can you buy with $65?

7. Emily has $30. Identify two ways she can spend her money on individual cameras without having any change.

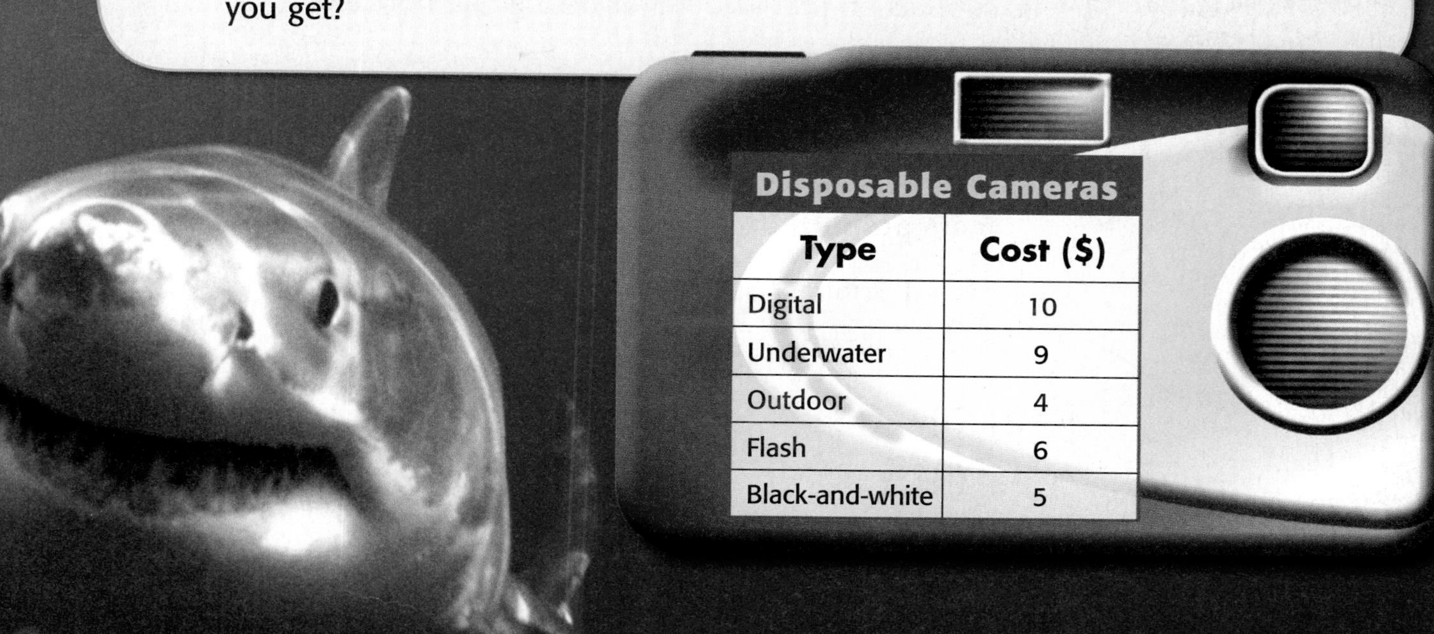

Disposable Cameras

Type	Cost ($)
Digital	10
Underwater	9
Outdoor	4
Flash	6
Black-and-white	5

2-7 Subtract Across Zeros

MAIN IDEA

I will subtract multi-digit numbers, when some digits are zero.

Targeted TEKS 4.3 The student adds and subtracts to solve meaningful problems involving whole numbers and decimals. (A) **Use** addition and **subtraction to solve problems involving whole numbers.** *Also addresses TEKS 4.1(A).*

GET READY to Learn

The bar graph shows the number of movies produced by five countries. What is the difference in the greatest and least number of movies produced?

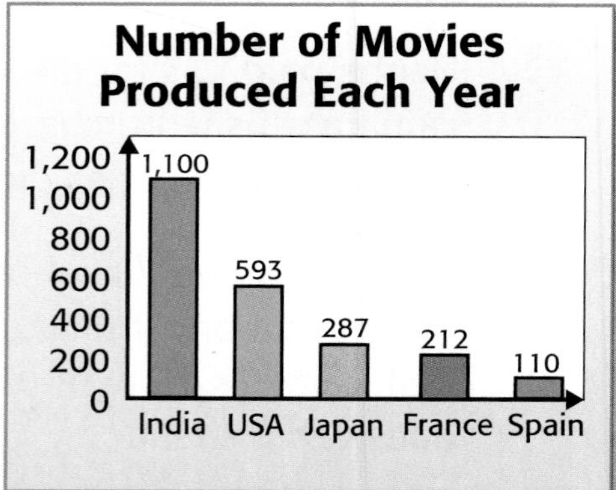

Source: *The Top 10 of Everything 2006*

Subtraction that involves digits that are zeros has the same steps as subtraction that involves digits that are not zeros.

Real-World EXAMPLE Subtract Across Zeros

1 **MOVIES** **Refer to the graph. How many more movies does India produce than Spain?**

Step 1 Subtract ones.

$$\begin{array}{r} 1{,}100 \\ -110 \\ \hline 0 \end{array}$$

$0 - 0 = 0$

Step 2 Subtract tens.

$$\begin{array}{r} 0\,10 \\ 1{,}\not{1}\not{0}0 \\ -110 \\ \hline 90 \end{array}$$

Regroup 1 hundred as 10 tens. $10 - 1 = 9$

Step 3 Subtract hundreds.

$$\begin{array}{r} 10 \\ 0\,\not{0}10 \\ \not{1}{,}\not{1}\not{0}0 \\ -110 \\ \hline 990 \end{array}$$

Regroup 1 thousand as 10 hundreds. $10 - 1 = 9$

Step 4 Subtract thousands.

$$\begin{array}{r} 10 \\ 0\,\not{0}10 \\ \not{1}{,}\not{1}\not{0}0 \\ -110 \\ \hline 990 \end{array}$$

$0 - 0 = 0$

So, India produces 990 more movies a year than Spain.

Check $990 + 110 = 1{,}100$. So, the answer is correct. ✔

Subtract Across Zeros

2 MONEY Lucy's dad spent $100. He bought a radio and a video game. The cost of the radio was $48. What was the cost of the video game?

Remember

When you subtract, start at the place farthest to the right.

Step 1 Subtract ones.

```
     9
   0 10 10
   $1 0 0
 − $  4 8
 --------
        2
```

Regroup 1 hundred as 10 tens. Regroup one of the tens as 10 ones. 10 − 8 = 2

Step 2 Subtract tens.

```
     9
   0 10 10
   $1 0 0
 − $  4 8
 --------
      5 2
```

9 − 4 = 5

Step 3 Subtract hundreds.

```
     9
   0 10 10
   $1 0 0
 − $  4 8
 --------
   $  5 2
```

0 − 0 = 0

So, the cost of the video game was $52.

Online Personal Tutor at tx.gr4math.com

Subtract. Use addition to check. See Examples 1 and 2 (pp. 80–81)

1. 309 − 57
2. 608 − 45
3. $707 − $535
4. 903 − 791
5. 2,006 − 536
6. $8,005 − $4,423
7. On Saturday, there were 1,000 balloons at a hot air balloon festival. On Sunday, there were 150 balloons. How many more balloons were there on Saturday than on Sunday?
8. **Talk About It** Look at the problem below. Explain where you would start regrouping to find the difference.

   66,000 − 23,475

Practice and Problem Solving

EXTRA PRACTICE
See page R6.

Subtract. Use addition to check. See Examples 1 and 2 (pp. 80–81)

9. 408 − 36

10. 805 − 75

11. 604 − 492

12. \$502 − \$130

13. \$708 − \$222

14. 809 − 566

15. \$8,001 − \$6,930

16. 9,006 − 7,474

17. 8,007 − 4,836

18. \$93 − \$52

19. 30,070 − 14,021

20. Ava guessed that there were 1,007 marbles in a jar for a contest. There were actually 972 marbles in the jar. How far off was Ava's guess?

21. **Measurement** Oscar hiked one and a half miles or 7,920 feet. If Sato hiked two miles or 10,560 feet, how many more feet did Sato hike?

Real-World PROBLEM SOLVING

Travel The length of paved and unpaved roads in four countries is shown.

Countries' Roads	
Country	**Length (miles)**
France	555,506
Australia	504,307
Spain	412,463
Russia	330,814

22. How many more miles of road does Australia have than Spain?

23. Which two countries have the greatest difference in miles of roads? France and Australia, Australia and Spain, or Spain and Russia?

H.O.T. Problems

24. **OPEN ENDED** Identify a number that results in a 3-digit number when 35,475 is subtracted from it.

25. **FIND THE ERROR** Jim and Sabrina are solving the subtraction problem shown. Who is correct? Explain.

26. **WRITING IN MATH** Explain how you would regroup to subtract 3,406 from 5,000.

27. There were 4,668 people at the fair on Saturday and 3,816 people on Sunday. How many more people were at the fair on Saturday? (Lesson 2-5)

A 842 **C** 942

B 852 **D** 952

28. There were 34,007 visitors at the amusement park last week. There were 21,829 visitors this week. How many fewer visitors were there this week? (Lesson 2-7)

F 12,178 **H** 13,108

G 12,912 **J** 13,112

Spiral Review

Solve. (Lesson 2-6)

29. Measurement On Friday, Nida drove 178 miles. On Saturday, she drove 129 miles. On Sunday, she drove 205 miles. How many miles did she drive in the three days?

30. Henri is going to buy a football that costs $10, a shirt that costs $8, and a hat that costs $6. If he has $30, about how much change can he expect to get back?

Subtract. Use addition or estimation to check. (Lesson 2-5)

31. $\begin{array}{r} 952 \\ -\ 624 \\ \hline \end{array}$

32. $\begin{array}{r} \$8,961 \\ -\ \$1,258 \\ \hline \end{array}$

33. $\begin{array}{r} 19,034 \\ -\ 1,617 \\ \hline \end{array}$

Find each sum. Check your work by estimating. (Lesson 2-4)

34. $\begin{array}{r} 6,922 \\ +\ 24,367 \\ \hline \end{array}$

35. $\begin{array}{r} \$8,738 \\ +\ \$2,253 \\ \hline \end{array}$

36. $\begin{array}{r} 36,640 \\ +\ 14,255 \\ \hline \end{array}$

For Exercises 37–39, use the table shown. (Lesson 1-3)

37. What is the difference between the lakes with the greatest and least area?

38. Which two lakes have the least difference in area?

39. Is the combined area of Lake Erie and Lake Michigan greater than the area of Lake Superior? Explain.

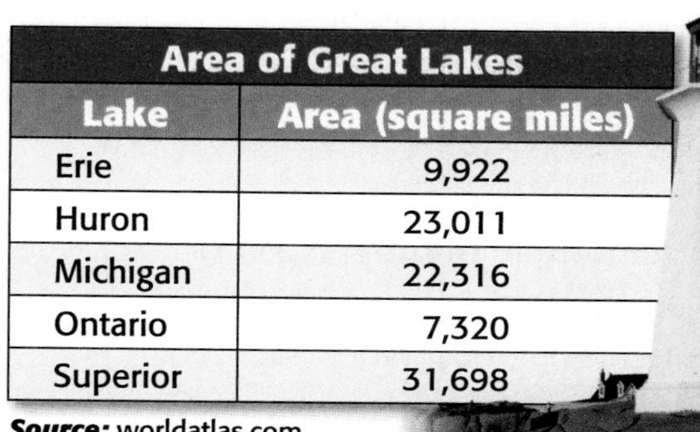

Area of Great Lakes

Lake	Area (square miles)
Erie	9,922
Huron	23,011
Michigan	22,316
Ontario	7,320
Superior	31,698

Source: worldatlas.com

CHAPTER 2

Study Guide and Review

FOLDABLES Study Organizer GET READY to Study

Be sure the following Key Vocabulary words and Key Concepts are written in your Foldable.

BIG Ideas

Addition Properties and Rules (p. 55)

- Addition properties and subtraction rules can help you to add and subtract.

Estimate Sums and Differences (p. 58)

3,678	rounds to	4,000
+ 1,295	rounds to	+ 1,000
		5,000

7,418	rounds to	7,000
− 2,557	rounds to	− 3,000
		4,000

Add and Subtract Whole Numbers (p. 64, p. 72)

- To add or subtract whole numbers, add or subtract each place, starting with the place farthest to the right. Regroup when needed.

$$\begin{array}{r} {}^{1\,1} \\ 3{,}752 \\ +\ \ 481 \\ \hline 4{,}233 \end{array} \qquad \begin{array}{r} {}^{8\,13} \\ \not{9}{,}\not{3}68 \\ -\ \ 827 \\ \hline 8{,}541 \end{array}$$

Key Vocabulary

Associative Property of Addition (p. 55)
Commutative Property of Addition (p. 55)
estimate (p. 58)

Vocabulary Check

Complete each sentence with the correct vocabulary word.

1. The number sentence $3 + 7 = 7 + 3$ represents the ___?___ .
2. If you do not need an exact answer, you can ___?___ .
3. The ___?___ says you can change the grouping without changing the sum.
4. The ___?___ says the order in which numbers are added does not change the sum.
5. When the word *about* is used in a problem, you should find a(n) ___?___ .

Math Online Vocabulary Review at tx.gr4math.com

Lesson-by-Lesson Review

2-1 Addition Properties and Subtraction Rules (pp. 55–57)

Example 1
Complete 4 + ■ = 6 + 4. Identify the property or rule.

The right side of the sentence shows 6 + 4. The left side shows a 4. So, the missing number is 6.

$$4 + 6 = 6 + 4$$

This is the Commutative Property of Addition.

Copy and complete each number sentence. Identify the property or rule.

6. ■ + 0 = 11 **7.** 12 − ■ = 12

8. (■ + 9) + 2 = 9 + (9 + 2)

9. 5 + 4 + 3 = 4 + 3 + ■

10. Lamont has 3 pencils and 2 pens. Aida has 2 pencils and 3 pens. Who has more writing utensils? Identify the property used.

2-2 Estimate Sums and Differences (pp. 58–61)

Example 2
Estimate 1,352 + 487. Round to the hundreds place.

Round. Then add.

1,352	rounds to →	1,400
+ 487	rounds to →	+ 500
		1,900

So, 1,352 + 487 is about 1,900.

Example 3
Estimate $53 – $27. Round to the tens place.

Round. Then subtract.

$53	rounds to →	$50
− $27	rounds to →	− $30
		$20

So, $53 − $27 is about $20.

Estimate. Round to the indicated place value.

11. $519 + $368; tens

12. 3,436 + 597; hundreds

13. 8,728 − 6,493; thousands

14. $17 − $12; tens

15. Neka wants to buy a book that costs $32 and a bookmark that costs $3. Approximately how much will these items cost?

16. Derek is 3,285 days old. Tionna is 4,015 days old. About how much older is Tionna?

2-3 Problem-Solving Strategy: Act It Out (pp. 62–63)

Example 4
Jenelle and her sister are going to build a bookcase. They will need $9 for nails, $18 for tools, and $38 for wood. How much money do they need to build the bookcase?

Understand

What facts do you know?
- Nails cost $9.
- Tools cost $18.
- Wood costs $38.

What do you need to find?
- Find how much money they need to build the bookcase.

Plan Since the question asks how much money is needed, you can use play money to act it out. Then add the amounts together.

Solve

$$\begin{array}{r} \$9 \\ \$18 \\ + \$38 \\ \hline \$65 \end{array}$$

So, about $65 is needed to build the bookcase.

Check Look back at the problem.
Estimate

$$\begin{array}{rcr} \$9 & \longrightarrow & \$10 \\ \$18 & \longrightarrow & \$20 \\ + \$38 & \longrightarrow & + \$40 \\ \hline \$65 & & \$70 \end{array}$$

Since $70 is close to $65, it makes sense.

17. There are 365 days in a year. Tess's younger brother is 3 years old. How many days old is he?

18. Benton needs to buy the items shown. He has $20. Does Benton have enough money?

19. Admission to a water park is $21 for adults and $14 for children. How much will admission cost for two adults and three children?

20. Rebeca will go to the park when her chores are complete. How many minutes before she will go to the park?

List of Chores

Chore	Time (min)
Clean room	45
Dust	15
Sweep	25

21. Chet has $7 in change after buying skates for $62 and a helmet for $22. How much money did he have?

2-4 Add Whole Numbers (pp. 64–67)

Example 5
Find 714 + 249.

Step 1 Add ones.

```
   1
  714
+ 249
    3
```

4 + 9 = 13
Regroup 13 ones as 1 ten and 3 ones.

Step 2 Add tens.

```
   1
  714
+ 249
   63
```

1 + 1 + 4 = 6

Step 3 Add hundreds.

```
   1
  714
+ 249
  963
```

7 + 2 = 9

Find each sum. Check your work by estimating.

22. 564 + 308

23. 2,875 + 496

24. $4,691 + $ 872

25. $6,467 + $5,237

26. 61,248 + 47,229

27. 82,267 + 21,037

28. Measurement Rick drove 12,363 miles in his new car the first year he owned it. He drove 15,934 miles in his car the second year he owned it. How many miles did Rick drive these two years?

2-5 Subtract Whole Numbers (pp. 72–75)

Example 6
Find 4,274 – 857.

Step 1 Subtract ones.

```
       6 14
  4, 2 7 4
  –  8 5 7
         7
```

Regroup 1 ten as 10 ones.

Step 2 Subtract each place.

```
  3 12 6 14
  4, 2 7 4
  –  8 5 7
  3, 4 1 7
```

Regroup if necessary.

Subtract. Use addition or estimation to check.

29. 478 – 293

30. 872 – 694

31. 5,524 – 2,346

32. $54,751 – $43,226

33. 7,367 – 2,128

34. 73,979 – 63,485

35. Measurement A moose weighs 1,820 pounds. A camel weighs 1,521 pounds. How much more does a moose weigh than a camel?

2-6 Problem-Solving Investigation: Choose a Strategy (pp. 76–77)

Example 7
Naomi had $125. She bought rollerblades. She now has $19. How much were the rollerblades?

Understand Naomi had $125. She now has $19. You need to find the cost of the rollerblades.

Plan Solve $125 – $19 to find the cost of the rollerblades.

Solve

```
   115
  $125
– $ 19
  $106
```

So, the cost was $106.

Check $19 + $106 = $125.
So, the answer is correct.

Use any strategy to solve.

36. Jase earned $125 last month for delivering newspapers. He will earn $185 this month. How much money will Jase earn from delivering newspapers for the two months?

37. Measurement A cheetah can run up to 71 miles per hour. A horse can run up to 45 miles per hour. Suppose both animals ran at these speeds for two hours. How much farther would a cheetah have run?

38. Measurement The highest elevation in the United States is 20,320 feet. The second highest elevation is 14,494. What is the difference in these heights?

2-7 Subtract Across Zeros (pp. 80–83)

Example 8
Find 2,005 – 593.

Step 1 Subtract ones.

```
  2,005
–   593
      2
```

5 – 3 = 2

Step 2 Subtract each place.

```
     9
  1 10 10
  2, 0 0 5
–   5 9 3
  1, 4 1 2
```

Regroup.

Subtract. Use addition to check.

39. 300 – 206

40. $800 – $392

41. 4,008 – 642

42. $9,004 – $ 531

43. 8,000 – 3,836

44. $1,300 – $1,195

45. Mr. Acosta had $2,003 in his bank account. He bought a laptop computer for $1,299. How much money does he have left?

CHAPTER 2

Chapter Test

For Exercises 1–3, tell whether each statement is *true* or *false*.

1. Always start with the ones place when subtracting.
2. When asked to find the sum, you are to subtract.
3. To *regroup* means to *add again*.

Copy and complete each number sentence. Identify the property or rule.

4. ■ + 73 + 79 = 73 + 79 + 65
5. ■ − 389 = 0
6. 2 + (3 + 9) = (2 + ■) + 9
7. **TEST PRACTICE** What number completes the number sentence below?

   23 + ■ = 17 + 23

   A 17 **C** 36

   B 23 **D** 38

Estimate. Round to the indicated place value.

8. 5,364 + 482; hundreds
9. 89,325 − 80,236; ten thousands

Use the *act it out* strategy to solve.

10. Mr. Murphy had $192. He bought a watch. Now he has $76. How much was the watch?

11. **TEST PRACTICE** What is the sum of 212,048 and 37,251?

    F 249,299

    G 289,299

    H 289,399

    J 299,289

Subtract. Use addition or estimation to check.

12. $\begin{array}{r} 612 \\ -\ 430 \\ \hline \end{array}$
13. $\begin{array}{r} 8,547 \\ -6,391 \\ \hline \end{array}$
14. $\begin{array}{r} 4,005 \\ -\ 273 \\ \hline \end{array}$
15. $\begin{array}{r} 6,007 \\ -\ 317 \\ \hline \end{array}$
16. Ivana had $87 in her bank account. She bought her sister a doll for her birthday for $15. How much money does she have left in her account?
17. **Measurement** The lengths of the longest rivers in the world are shown in the table.

World's Longest Rivers	
River	**Length (miles)**
Nile	4,145
Amazon	4,000
Mississippi-Missouri	3,740

Source: *The Top 10 of Everything*

Find the difference in length of the Nile and the Mississippi-Missouri Rivers.

18. **WRITING IN MATH** Explain how you would regroup to subtract 2,317 from 4,000.

CHAPTER 2

Texas Test Practice

Cumulative, Chapters 1–2

Roger has $40. He buys a CD for $12.88 and a poster for $8.95. Which of the following is the best estimate of how much money Roger has left?

A $18 **C** $20

B $19 **D** $22

TEST-TAKING TIP

You can round numbers to find the sum or difference mentally.

Read the Test Question

You need to estimate the cost of each item and then mentally subtract.

Solve the Test Question

$12.88 rounded to the nearest dollar is $13.
$8.95 rounded to the nearest dollar is $9.
The estimate of both items is $9 + $13, or $22.

THINK $40 – $22 = $18

So, the answer is A.

Online **Personal Tutor at** tx.gr4math.com

Choose the best answer.

1. **Melinda buys a binder for $3. She hands the clerk $10. How much change should she receive?**

A $5 **C** $7

B $6 **D** $8

2. **Silvio had deposits to his savings account of $20, $9, and $31. How much did he deposit in all?**

F $50 **H** $70

G $60 **J** $80

Get Ready for the Texas Test
For test-taking strategies and more practice, see pages TX1–TX21.

3. GRIDDABLE The local zoo had 1,842 visitors on Friday and 2,236 visitors on Saturday. How many visitors did the zoo have on the two days?

4. Which number is 10,000 more than 312,884?

A 302,884 **B** 319,884 **C** 324,882 **D** 322,884

5. On Saturday, a clothing store had 218 customers. On Sunday, the store had 24 fewer customers. How many customers did the store have on Sunday?

F 188 **G** 194 **H** 236 **J** 242

6. Which point on the number line represents 8?

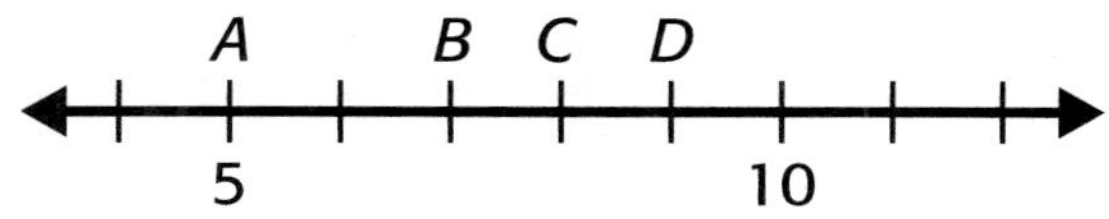

A point *A* **B** point *B* **C** point *C* **D** point *D*

7. A local hobby store owner said his shop sold 15,871 kites since the store opened 25 years ago. What is the number rounded to the nearest thousand?

F 15,000 **G** 15,800 **H** 15,900 **J** 16,000

8. Which of the following is another way to write *nine million, three hundred thirty-one thousand, one-hundred eight*?

A 9,313,180 **B** 9,331,108 **C** 9,331,180 **D** 90,331,108

9. Which is the value of the digit 5 in 805,312?

F 50 **G** 500 **H** 5,000 **J** 50,000

10. Which symbol makes the following true?

76,153 ■ 76,149

A > **B** < **C** = **D** +

CHAPTER 3 Organize, Display, and Interpret Data

BIG Idea What are data and graphs?

Data is a set of information. When data is displayed in a **graph**, it is easier to read and interpret.

Example The graph shows the number of children in the United States. About 36 million children are 5 to 13 years old.

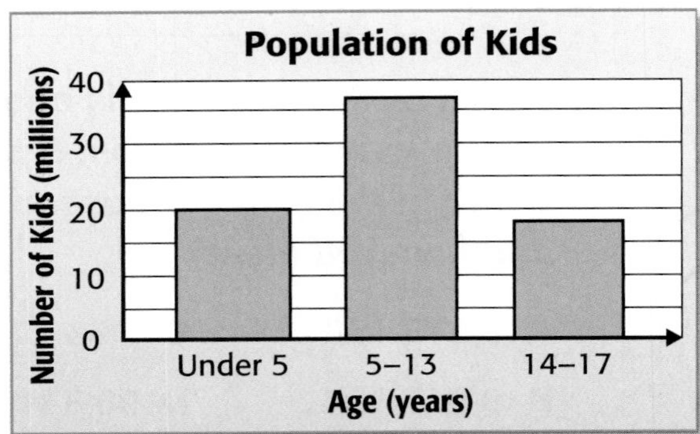

What will I learn in this chapter?

- Collect and represent data on a number line, and in graphs, tables, and charts.
- Read and interpret data.
- Determine all possible outcomes of a situation.
- Solve problems by making a table.

Key Vocabulary

data
survey
bar graph
probability
tree diagram

Student Study Tools at tx.gr4math.com

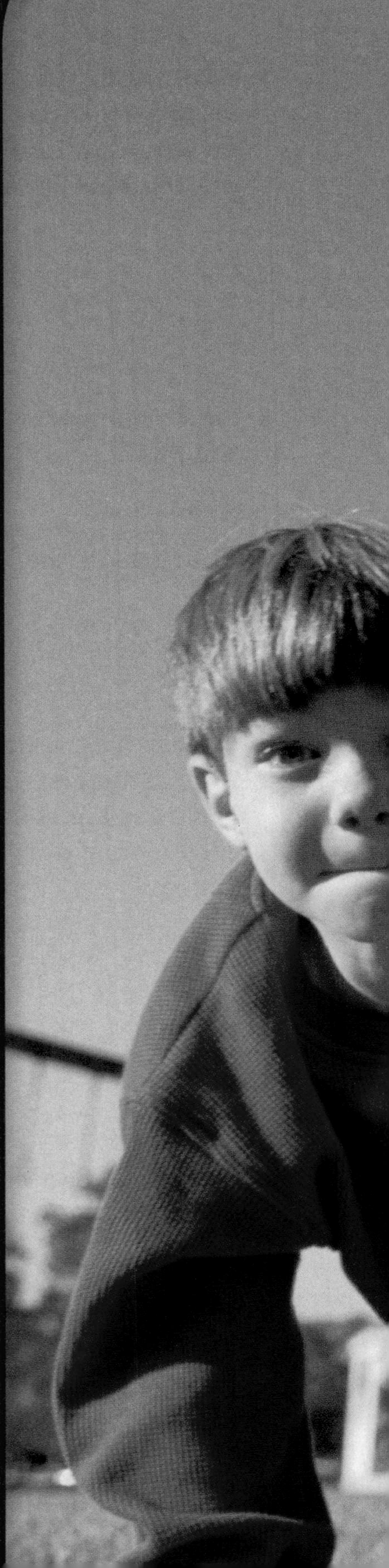

FOLDABLES™ Study Organizer

Make this Foldable to help you organize information about data and graphs. Begin with three sheets of $8\frac{1}{2}'' \times 11''$ paper.

1. **Stack** the paper about 3 inches apart.
2. **Roll** up the bottom so all tabs are the same size.
3. **Crease** and staple along the fold as shown.
4. **Label.** Take notes as you move through the chapter.

ARE YOU READY for Chapter 3?

You have two ways to check prerequisite skills for this chapter.

Option 2

Math Online Take the Chapter Readiness Quiz at tx.gr4math.com.

Option 1

Complete the Quick Check below.

QUICK Check

Make a tally chart for each situation. (Prior grade)

1. Sondra took a survey to find out her friends' favorite colors.

Favorite Colors		
red	yellow	green
blue	pink	red
green	blue	pink
red	blue	blue

2. Mr. Bailey recorded the ages of the students on the basketball team.

Ages of Basketball Players		
10	11	9
9	10	11
10	9	10
10	10	10

Write the fraction that represents the shaded area. (Prior grade)

3. 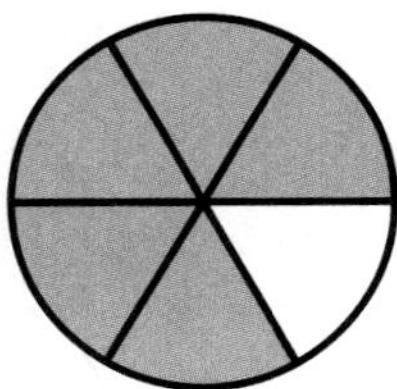

4. 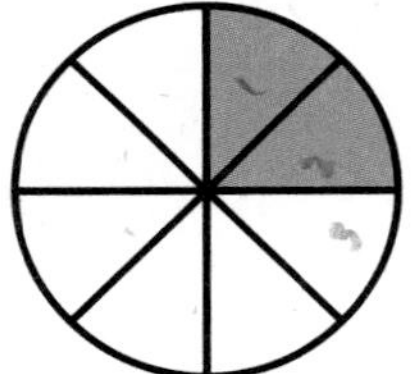

5. 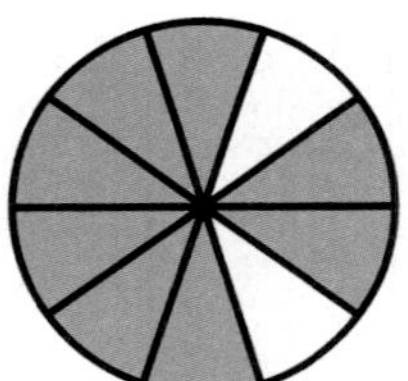

6. Mora has three Labrador puppies. Write a fraction that represents the number of black Labrador puppies.

7. What fraction of the Labrador puppies is yellow?

3-1 Collect and Organize Data

MAIN IDEA

I will take a survey, and collect and organize data.

Targeted TEKS 4.13 **The student solves problems by collecting, organizing, displaying, and interpreting sets of data.** *Also addresses TEKS 4.15(A).*

New Vocabulary

survey
data
tally chart
frequency table

GET READY to Learn

Ms. Alvarez asked each of her students, "What is your favorite after-school activity?" The results are shown.

Playing a Sport	Reading	Watching T.V.
Staci	Alita	Julian
Eric	Sue	Chen
Melisa	Omar	Sarita
Kensey	Nicolas	
Alano		

Ms. Alvarez took a survey. A **survey** is a way to collect **data** or information that answers a question. You can use a **tally chart** or a **frequency table** to record data.

Real-World EXAMPLE Organize Data

1 SCHOOL **Look at the data Ms. Alvarez collected. Organize the data in a tally chart and a frequency table.**

Step 1 Draw a table with two columns. Include a title.

Step 2 List each activity in the first column.

Step 3 Use tally marks or numbers to record the results.

Tally Chart

Favorite After School Activities	
Activity	**Tally**
Playing a sport	𝍸
Reading	IIII
Watching T.V.	III

Each tally mark represents a student.

Frequency Table

Favorite After School Activities	
Activity	**Frequency**
Playing a sport	5
Reading	4
Watching T.V.	3

Numbers are used to record the results.

You can take a survey and collect and represent data on charts and tables.

Hands-On Mini Activity

Step 1 Formulate or create a survey question you can ask your classmates. An example is shown.

What type of pet is your favorite?

a) Dog b) Cat

c) Fish d) I do not like pets.

Remember

The tally marks used to represent a value of 5 are ~~IIII~~, not IIIII.

Step 2 Create a tally chart to record your results.

Step 3 Ask the question to each of your classmates. Organize the data as you collect it.

Step 4 Use the information on your tally chart to create a frequency table.

Analyze the data.

1. Write two sentences that describe your survey results.
2. Were the survey results what you expected? Explain.

CHECK What You Know

1. The data shows the ways Mrs. Jackson's students travel to school. Organize the data in a tally chart. See Example 1 (p. 95)

How Do You Travel to School?	
Method	**Frequency**
Bicycle	3
Bus	6
Car	9
Walk	5

2. Mary lists all of the fish in her fish tank. Organize the data below in a frequency table. See Example 1 (p. 95)

Mary's Fish Tank	
angelfish	damsel
angelfish	damsel
angelfish	damsel
clown fish	eel
clown fish	eel

3. Refer to Exercise 1. What is the most popular way to travel to school? What is the least popular? See Example 1 (p. 95)

4. Talk About It What are three different questions that you could use to conduct a survey?

Practice and Problem Solving

Organize each set of data in a tally chart. See Example 1 (p. 95)

5. Mr. Ortega records the type of pizza that his science club members like.

Favorite Type of Pizza		
cheese	cheese	sausage
cheese	pepperoni	sausage
cheese	pepperoni	
cheese	pepperoni	

6. Elisa took a survey to find out which movie to rent for her party.

Type of Movie	
action	comedy
action	comedy
action	comedy
animated	comedy

Organize each set of data in a frequency table. See Example 1 (p. 95)

7. **Measurement** Damián recorded the temperatures in one week.

Weekly Temperatures	
Temperature (°F)	**Days**
70–75	||
76–80	|||
81–85	|
86–90	|

8. A survey was taken to see how students spend their time at recess.

Recess Activities		
kickball	drawing	swing
kickball	drawing	swing
kickball	swing	tag
kickball	swing	tag
drawing	swing	tag

For Exercises 9–12, use the tally chart that shows items sold at a school store.

Items Sold at School Store	
Item	**Tally**
Eraser	卌
Bottle of glue	
Pencil	卌 |||
Scissors	|

9. Which item was the top seller? How many were sold?

10. Which item sold once?

11. How many items were sold altogether?

12. Organize the data in a frequency table.

H.O.T. Problems

13. **OPEN ENDED** Explain how a frequency table differs from a tally chart. How are they alike?

14. **WRITING IN ▶MATH** Suppose you are collecting and organizing data about the population of your city. Would it be better to use a frequency table or a tally chart? Explain.

3-2 Problem-Solving Strategy

MAIN IDEA I will solve problems by making a table.

Targeted TEKS 4.14 The student applies Grade 4 mathematics to solve problems connected to everyday experiences and activities in and outside of school. (C) **Select or develop an appropriate problem-solving plan or strategy, including . . . making a table, . . . to solve a problem.** *Also addresses TEKS 4.14(B).*

The music club at Steven's school is going to a concert. There are 2 teachers going to the concert for every 9 students going. If there are 16 teachers going, how many students are going to the concert?

Understand

What facts do you know?

- There are 2 teachers going for every 9 students going to the concert.
- The total number of teachers going is 16.

What do you need to find?

- Find how many students are going to the concert.

Plan

You can make a table to solve the problem.

Solve

Make a table to show that there are 2 teachers going for every 9 students going.

+2 +2 +2 +2 +2 +2 +2

Teachers	2	4	6	8	10	12	14	16
Students	9	18	27	36	45	54	63	72

+9 +9 +9 +9 +9 +9 +9

So, 72 students are going to the concert.

Check

Divide the total number of teachers by the number of teachers per group.

$16 \div 2 = 8$

There are 8 groups. There are 9 students in each group. So, there are $8 \times 9 = 72$ students going altogether. The answer is correct.

ANALYZE the Strategy

Refer to the problem on the previous page.

1. Explain how a table was used to find the number of students going to the concert.

2. What pattern is shown on the table?

3. Suppose 1 teacher was going for every 3 students. How many teachers would be going on the trip?

4. Refer to Exercise 3. Check your answer. How do you know that it is correct?

PRACTICE the Strategy

EXTRA PRACTICE
See page R7.

Solve. Use the *make a table* strategy.

5. **Algebra** Kenya's school day is 6 hours long. Copy and complete the table to find if her school day is more or less than 300 minutes.

Hours	1	2	3	4	5	6
Minutes	60	120	■	■	■	■

6. Malik buys a $2 lunch every day at school. How many lunches can Malik purchase for $17?

7. Martín sold some of his old toys on the Internet. The cost of shipping each item is shown. If he paid $32 in shipping, how many of his toys did he ship?

8. Jenna scored 24 points in her last basketball game. She made 2 baskets for every 5 shots she took. If one basket is equal to 2 points, how many shots did she take for the entire game?

9. Elki received her first paycheck from a job. She earns $150 every 2 weeks. How many weeks will it take her to earn more than $1,000?

10. The state sales tax is $7 for every $100 spent on certain items. Takara's mother spends $21 in tax at the grocery store. What was the total cost of all the items she purchased?

11. **Algebra** Don spends 40 minutes on homework every night. How many minutes of homework does he complete in a week?

Day	Time Spent on Homework (min)
Monday	40
Tuesday	80
Wednesday	120
Thursday	■
Friday	■

12. **WRITING IN MATH** Explain why the *make a table* strategy is a good problem-solving strategy to use for Exercise 10.

3-3 Bar Graphs

GET READY to Learn

Mrs. Smith's class completed a measurement activity in which each student measured another student's height in inches. What was the most common height?

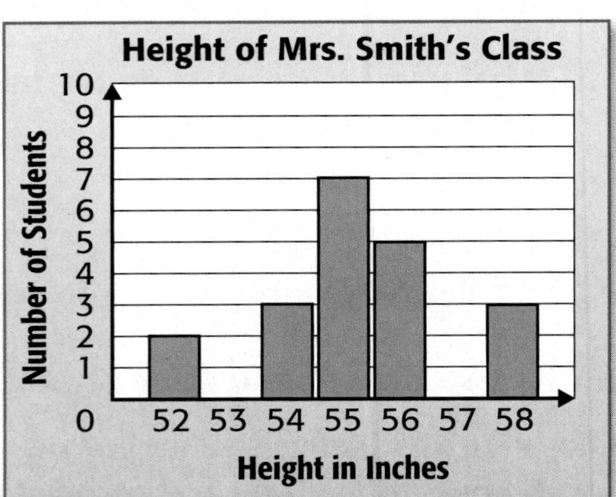

MAIN IDEA

I will interpret a bar graph.

Targeted TEKS 4.13 The student solves problems by collecting, organizing, displaying, and interpreting sets of data. (B) **Interpret bar graphs.**

New Vocabulary

bar graph

A **bar graph** is used to compare data by using bars of different heights to represent values.

EXAMPLE Interpret a Bar Graph

1 What was the most common height?

The tallest bar represents the most common height.

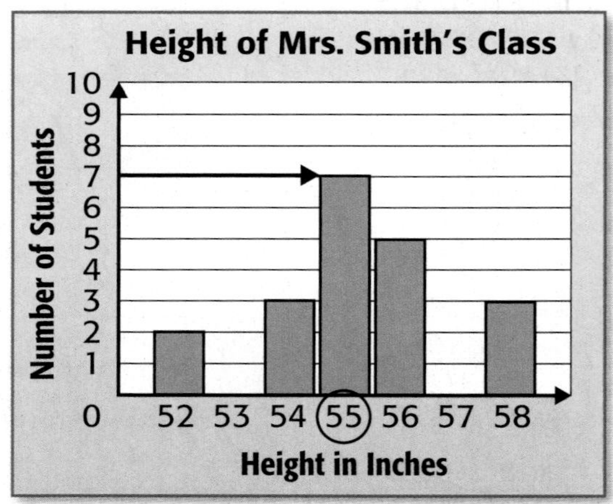

So, the most common height was 55 inches tall.

Online Personal Tutor at tx.gr4math.com

EXAMPLE Interpret a Bar Graph

2 **The bar graph shows the land area of four cities in Texas. Write a statement that describes the data.**

To write a statement that describes the data in a bar graph, you need to compare the lengths of the bars in the graph.

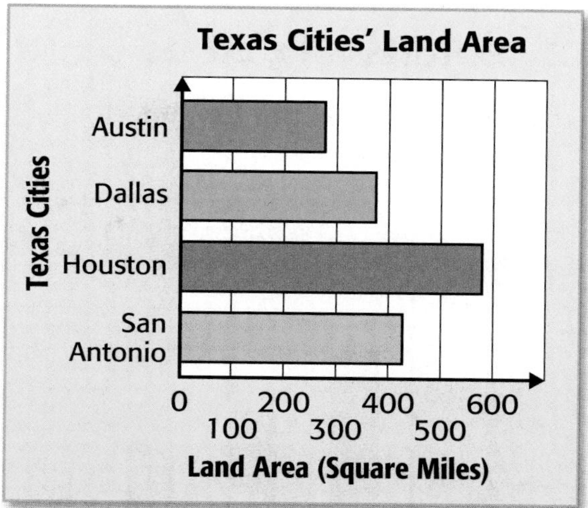

The bar for Houston is the longest. So, you can write that Houston has the largest land area of the four cities shown.

CHECK What You Know

For Exercises 1–4, use the graph shown. See Examples 1–2 (pp. 100–101)

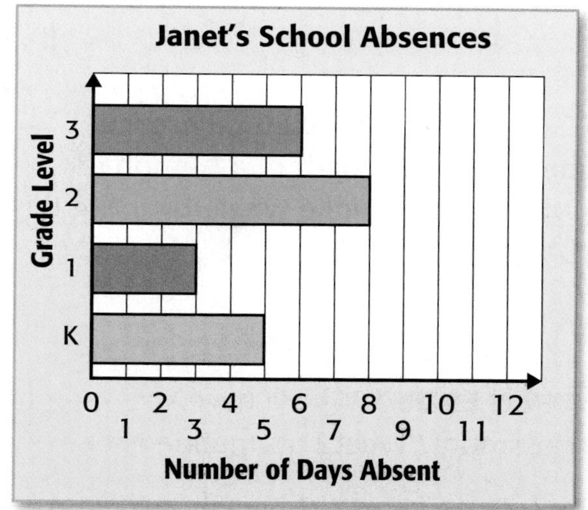

1. During which grade was Janet absent the most days?
2. What grade was Janet in when she was absent for 3 days?
3. How many more days was Janet absent in second grade than in third grade?
4. How many days has Janet been absent since she finished the first grade?
5. Write a statement that describes the data in the graph.
6. **Talk About It** Refer back to Exercise 4. How did you find the answer?

Practice and Problem Solving

For Exercises 7–14, use the graphs shown. See Examples 1–2 (pp. 100–101)

The graph shows the lengths of certain whales.

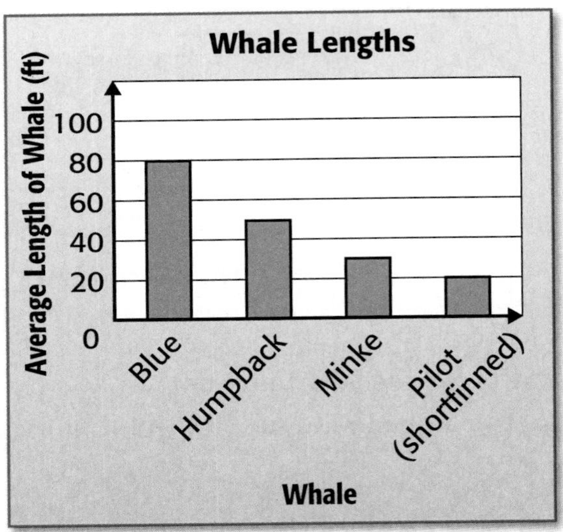

7. Which type of whale is the shortest?

8. Which whale is about 50 feet long?

9. Why is the scale set in intervals of 20 feet?

10. Can you find the exact difference between the length of a humpback whale and a minke whale by using this bar graph? Explain.

The graph shows the states with the most tornadoes for 2005.

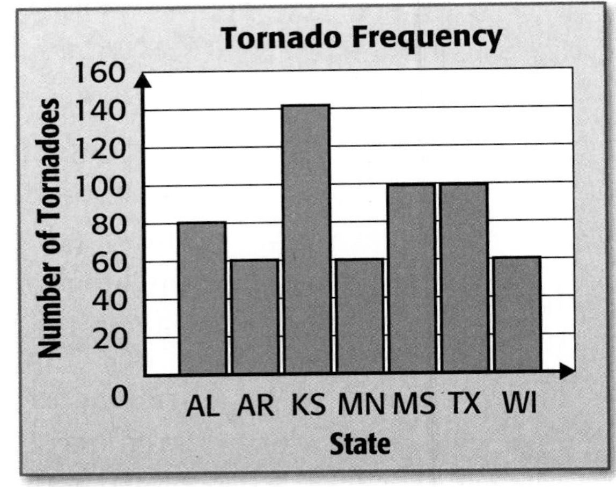

11. Which states appear to have had the same number of tornadoes in 2005?

12. About how many more tornadoes were in Texas than in Alabama?

13. About how many more tornadoes were in Kansas than in Wisconsin?

14. Which two states had a combined total of about 220 tornadoes? Explain how you found your answer.

H.O.T. Problems

15. **OPEN ENDED** Where have you seen bar graphs used outside of the classroom? What information was being described?

16. **NUMBER SENSE** Why is it sometimes necessary to estimate when reading a bar graph?

17. **WRITING IN MATH** Refer to the graph used for Exercises 11–14. Would this graph be easier to read if the scale was changed to intervals of 100? Explain.

CHAPTER 3

Mid-Chapter Check

Lessons 3-1 through 3-3

1. Organize the set of data in a tally chart and in a frequency table. (Lesson 3-1)

Sandwiches for a Picnic		
Peanut butter	Ham	Turkey
Turkey	Turkey	Peanut butter
Ham	Ham	Ham

For Exercises 2 and 3, use the tally chart below. (Lesson 3-1)

Where Do You Read?	
Place	**Tally**
Outside	𝍸 I
Bedroom	𝍸 II
Library	𝍸
Living room	III

2. Where do most students like to read?

3. How many students read in their bedroom or at the library?

Solve. Use the *make a table* strategy.
(Lesson 3-2)

4. One stamp costs 39¢. If Miguel spends $1.95 on stamps, how many stamps did he buy?

5. It costs $32 for 2 admissions to a museum. Ebony and her father invite 10 friends for opening night. At this rate, how much would it cost for everyone to go to the museum?

6. **TEST PRACTICE** Which vegetable is the class's least favorite?
(Lesson 3-3)

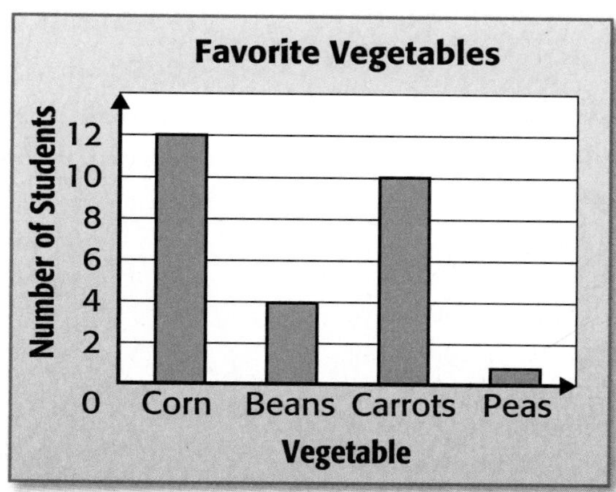

A Corn　　**C** Beans
B Carrots　　**D** Peas

7. **TEST PRACTICE** About how much farther did Greg travel than Joy?
(Lesson 3-3)

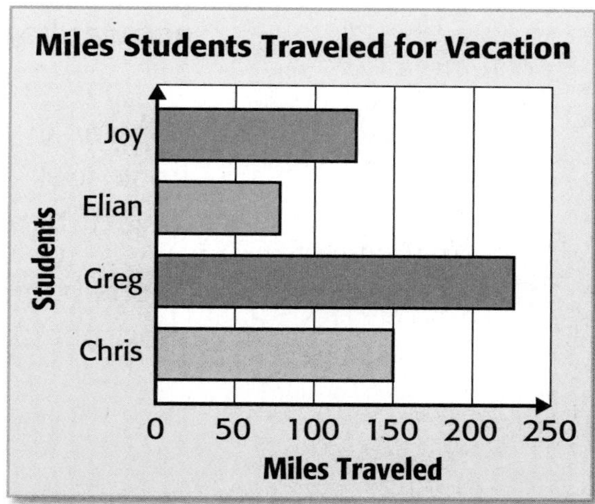

F 50 miles　　**H** 200 miles
G 100 miles　　**J** 300 miles

8. **WRITING IN MATH** In the graph above, Elian traveled about 75 miles. Explain how you can tell that this is correct.

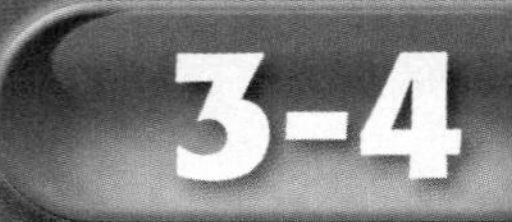

Bar and Double Bar Graphs

GET READY to Learn

The graph shows the amount of time four astronauts spent in space during a single mission. You can use the graph to compare the time spent in space.

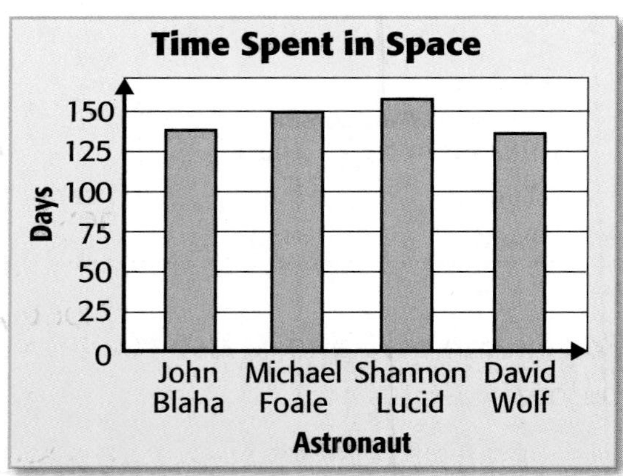

Source: *Time for Kids*

MAIN IDEA

I will interpret bar graphs to answer questions.

Targeted TEKS 4.13 The student solves problems by collecting, organizing, displaying, and interpreting sets of data. (B) **Interpret bar graphs.**

New Vocabulary

double bar graph

A bar graph allows you to compare data easily.

Real-World EXAMPLES Read Bar Graphs

BOOKS The bar graph shows the number of books checked out of a school library.

1 What is the most popular book?

To find the most popular kind of book, look for the longest bar.

Sports books are most popular.

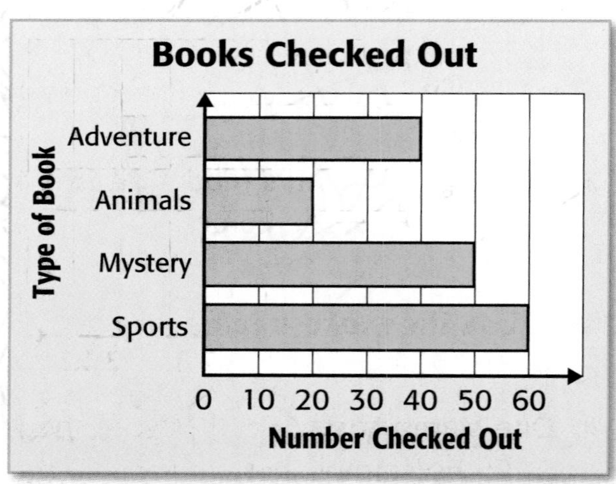

2 How many sports and animal books were checked out?

60 sports books and 20 animal books were checked out.

$60 + 20 = 80$

So, there were 80 sports and animal books checked out.

A **double bar graph** displays two sets of related data using bars of different colors and heights.

Read Double Bar Graphs

Remember

When reading a double bar graph, always look at the scale and the key.

3 SCHOOL **Students are selling magazines for a fundraiser. About how many students will sell magazines in the second grade?**

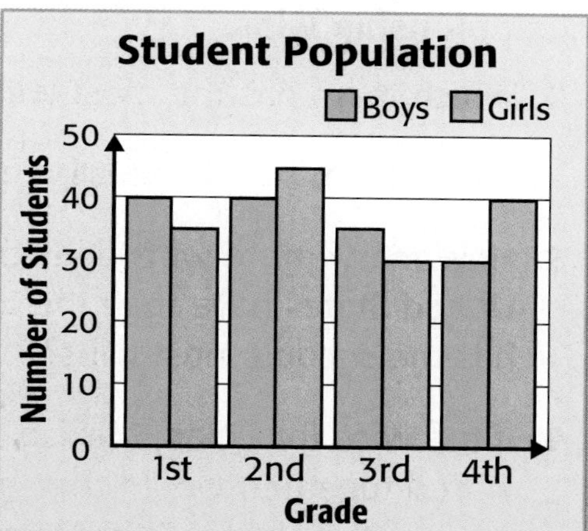

There are about 40 boys and about 45 girls in the second grade.

$40 + 45 = 85$

So, about 85 students will sell magazines in second grade.

Online **Personal Tutor at** tx.gr4math.com

CHECK What You Know

For Exercises 1–4, use the graphs shown. See Examples 1–3 (pp. 104–105)

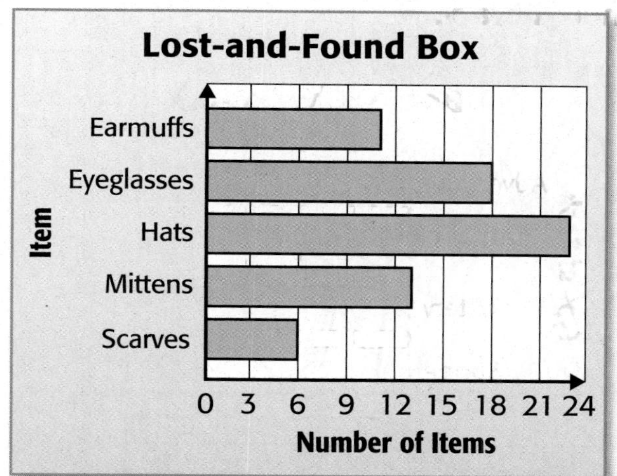

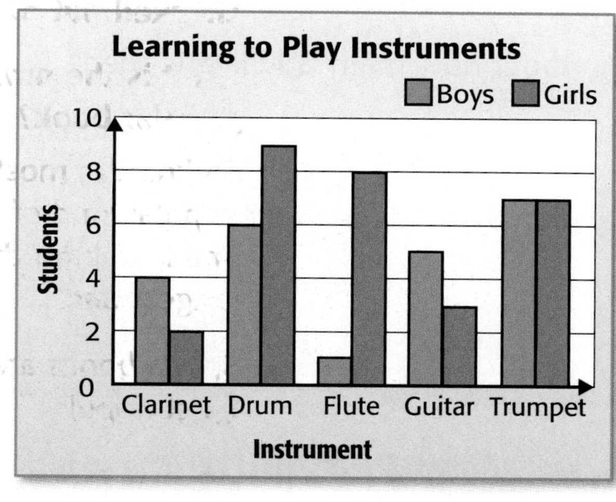

1. What is the most common item in the lost-and-found box?
2. How many more eyeglasses are in the box than scarves?
3. What is the least popular instrument for boys?
4. What is the total number of students surveyed?
5. Talk About It Describe when you would use a bar graph and a double bar graph to display sets of data.

Practice and Problem Solving

For Exercises 6–9, use the bar graph that shows the number of Little League Championship wins. See Examples 1–2 (p. 104)

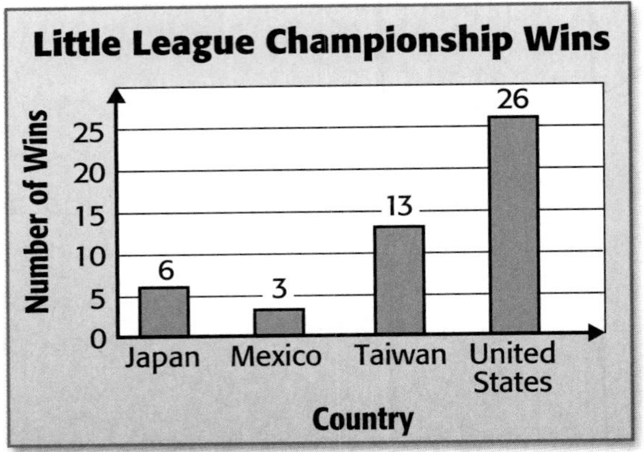

Source: *Scholastic Book of World Records*

6. Which team has the most wins?
7. Which team has the least wins?
8. How many more wins does the United States have than the team that has the second most wins?
9. If the wins for Japan, Mexico, and Taiwan were added together, would they have as many wins as the United States? Explain.

For Exercises 10–13, use the double bar graph that shows the number of tickets sold for a high school play. See Example 3 (p. 105)

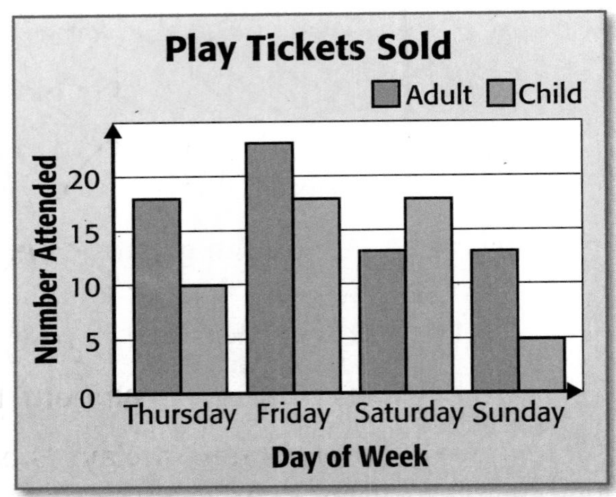

10. Which day had the highest total attendance?
11. Did more adults or children attend on Friday?
12. About how many adults attended?
13. Suppose adult tickets cost $4 and children tickets cost $2. On which day was more than $100 made in ticket sales?

H.O.T. Problems

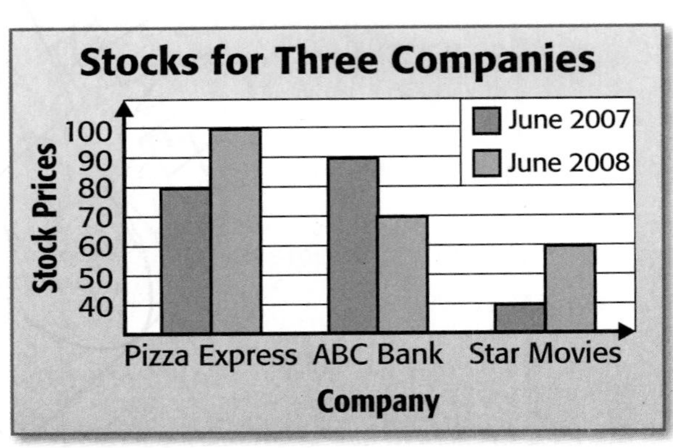

14. **WRITING IN MATH** The graph shows the value of stocks for three companies. Write 2 sentences that describe the data.
15. **OPEN ENDED** Describe a set of data that could not be shown in a double bar graph.

Math Online Self-Check Quiz at tx.gr4math.com

Graph Race

Create a Bar Graph

Get Ready!

Players: 2 players

You will need: 0–5 number cube, grid paper

Get Set!

Draw a bar graph on grid paper as shown.

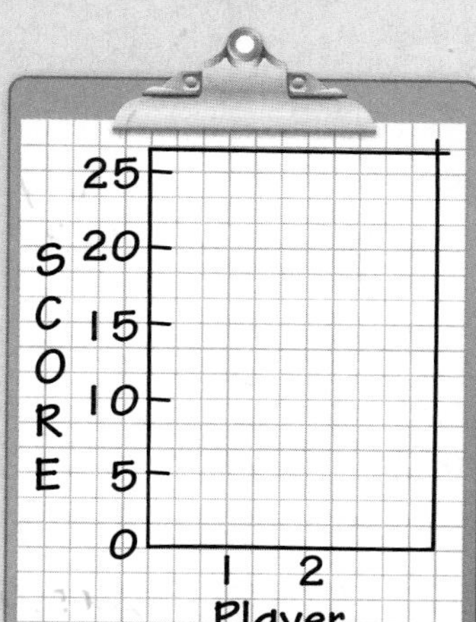

Go!

- Roll, the greatest number goes first.
- Player 1 rolls the number cube and graphs the number on the bar graph.
- Player 2 rolls the number cube and graphs the number on the bar graph.
- Player 1 rolls the number cube again and adds the result to his or her previous amount. If a 0 is rolled, it is player 2's turn.
- Play continues until a player's bar goes over 25. That player wins.

Extend

Statistics Activity for 3-4
Make Double Bar Graphs

Double bar graphs are used to compare two sets of related data.

MAIN IDEA

I will display data in double bar graph.

Targeted TEKS 4.13 The student solves problems by collecting, organizing, displaying, and interpreting sets of data. *Also addresses TEKS 4.15(A).*

You Will Need
colored pencils
graph paper

ACTIVITY

Step 1 **Collect data.**

Create a frequency table that shows the number of minutes you and a partner spend studying or doing homework each day over the span of a school week.

Time Spent Studying/Homework		
Day	**Student 1**	**Student 2**
Mon.		
Tues.		
Wed.		
Thurs.		
Fri.		

Step 2 **Create a graph.**

Draw two axes and label them. Write a title at the top. Choose a color for each set of data and make a **key**.

Animation
tx.gr4math.com

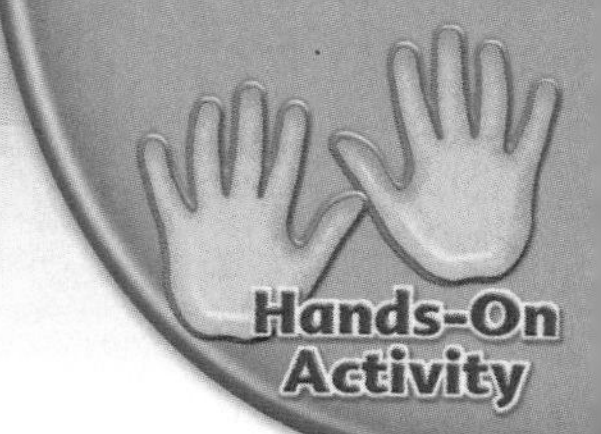

Step 3 **Choose a scale.**

The scale should include the least and the greatest number from your data.

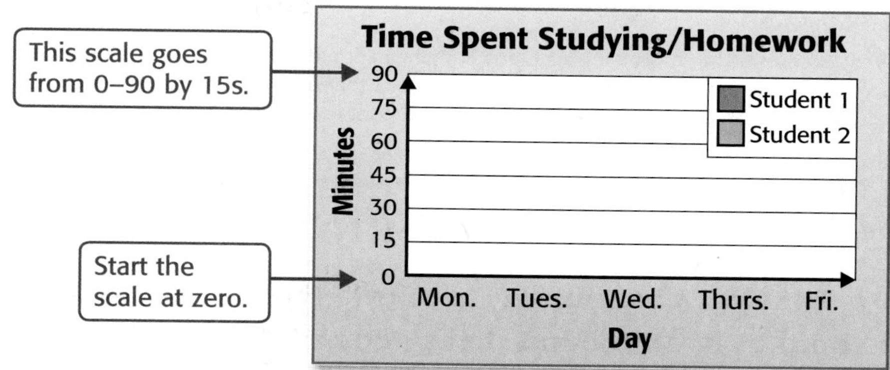

Step 4 **Draw bars.**

Draw the bars for your data on the graph. Then draw the bars for your partner's data on the graph.

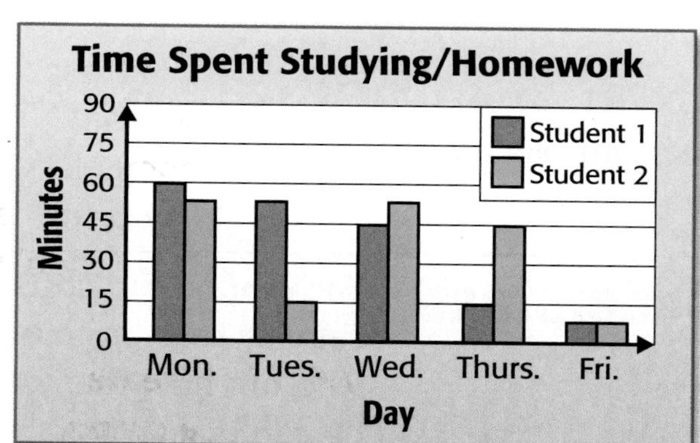

Think About It

1. Tell how you can use a double bar graph to compare data.
2. Explain how you choose a scale and intervals.

CHECK What You Know

Represent each set of data in a double bar graph.

3.

Books Read		
Month	**Miki**	**Alicia**
May	3	2
June	5	6
July	4	5
August	6	4

4.

Allowance		
Age	**Morgan**	**Eli**
7	$2	$0
8	$3	$1
9	$4	$3
10	$5	$5

5. **WRITING IN ►MATH** Look at Exercises 3 and 4. Write a comparison sentence that describes the data.

3-5 Problem-Solving Investigation

MAIN IDEA I will choose the best strategy to solve a problem.

Targeted TEKS 4.14 The student applies Grade 4 mathematics to solve problems connected to everyday experiences and activities in and outside of school. **(B) Solve problems that incorporate understanding the problem, making a plan, carrying out the plan, and evaluating the solution for reasonableness.** *Also addresses TEKS 4.14(C).*

P.S.I. TEAM +

TAO: I take the subway to get to school and back. Each round trip costs $2. My subway card has a value of $11.

YOUR MISSION: Find how many round trips Tao can make with $11.

Understand Each round trip costs $2. Tao's subway card has a value of $11. Find out how many round trips he can make.

Plan Organize the data in a table to solve the problem.

Solve For each round trip, the total cost increases by $2.

Trips	1	2	3	4	5	6
Cost	$2	$4	$6	$8	$10	$12

+2 +2 +2 +2 +2

Tao's card has a value of $11. He cannot make a sixth trip because after making 5 trips he has only $1 left. This is not enough for another trip. So, he can make 5 trips to school and back.

Check Use a set of play money that is in piles of $2. Add the money until you have more than $11.

Mixed Problem Solving

See page R8.

Use any strategy to solve.

1. Mrs. Vargas is making costumes for a play. She needs 4 buttons for each costume. Copy and complete the table to find how many buttons she will need for 14 costumes.

Costumes	Buttons
1	4
2	8
4	16
6	24
8	32
10	40
12	■
14	■

2. It costs $12 for 2 admissions to miniature golf. Marcus wants to invite 9 friends. At this rate, how much would it cost for 10 people?

3. **Measurement** The Castros drove 64 miles to a water park. The Baxters drove 81 miles. The Klines drove 19 miles. How much farther did the Castros have to drive than the Klines?

4. Ricardo has to mail 27 party invitations. The invitations come in packs of 8 that cost $3. How much will he spend on invitations?

5. Pete spends 30 minutes a night reading. About how many hours does he spend reading each month?

6. Tomas has $49. He wants to buy as many video games as he can. How many can he get at the yard sale?

7. Dawn mows the lawn the first and second weeks of the month. Ana mows the lawn the third and fourth weeks. Each person gets paid $6 for each mow. There are 19 weeks in which the lawn needs mowed. Who will make more money?

8. Paz is making granola bars for her scout meeting. There are 8 girls in her troop. If she makes 2 dozen granola bars, how many will each girl get?

9. During a basketball game, Faith and Brandy each scored 4 points. Maria and Jo each scored 7 points. Dena scored 12 points. Find the total points scored by this team.

10. **WRITING IN MATH** Explain when to use the *make a table* strategy to solve a word problem.

Problem Solving in Science

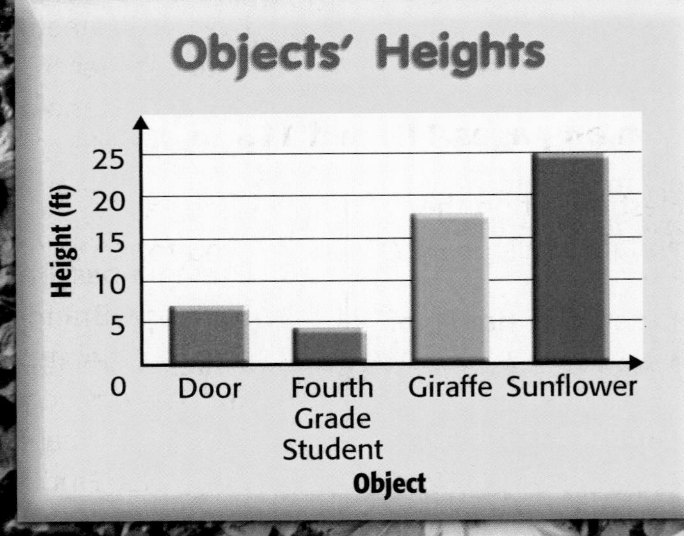

Targeted TEKS 4.14 The student applies Grade 4 mathematics to solve problems connected to everyday experiences and activities in and outside of school. **(A) Identify the mathematics in everyday situations.**

Sunflowers are giants in the plant world. The tallest sunflower grew to a total height of 25 feet 5 inches. The size of the largest sunflower head is 32 inches across. This is almost three feet across!

Sunflowers can be used for decoration, but they are also an important source of food.

Sunflower oil is a valued and healthy vegetable oil. In addition, sunflower seeds are enjoyed as a healthy, tasty snack and nutritious ingredient in many foods.

Did You Know?

The shortest sunflower on record measured just over 2 inches tall.

Real-World Math

Use the information on pages 112 and 113 to solve each problem.

1. What is the tallest object on the bar graph? How tall is this object?
2. What is the difference in height of a sunflower and a giraffe?
3. What is the shortest object on the bar graph? How tall is this object?
4. Look at Exercise 3. Explain how you found the answer.
5. What is the difference between the tallest and shortest objects on the bar graph?
6. The height of how many fourth grade students equals the height of a sunflower?

Math Activity for 3-6

Possible Combinations

Possible **outcomes** are all of the combinations that could occur from an experiment.

MAIN IDEA

I will determine the possible combinations of outcomes.

Targeted TEKS 4.13 The student solves problems by collecting, organizing, displaying, and interpreting sets of data. (A) **Use concrete objects or pictures to make generalizations about determining all possible combinations of a given set of data or objects in a problem situation.** *Also addresses TEKS 4.15(A).*

You Will Need
number cubes labeled 0–5

ACTIVITY

1 Roll 0–5 number cubes to create multi-digit numbers.

Step 1 **Roll two 0–5 number cubes.**

Step 2 **Create two-digit numbers.**

Use each digit rolled only once to make as many two-digit numbers as possible. Record the numbers you made.

35 53

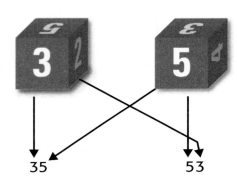

Step 3 **Create three-digit numbers.**

Roll a third 0–5 number cube. If you roll a digit you already rolled, roll again. Use the two digits you rolled in Step 1 and the digit you have just rolled to make as many three-digit numbers as possible. Remember to use each digit only once. Record the numbers you made.

Step 4 **Create four-digit numbers.**

Roll a fourth 0–5 number cube to go with the three digits you previously rolled. If you roll a digit you already have, roll again. Use the fourth digit to create as many numbers as possible.

Hands-On Activity

Think About It

1. How many two-digit numbers can be made with two digits, if each digit is used only once?

2. How many three-digit numbers can be made with three digits, if each digit is used only once?

3. How many four-digit numbers can be made with four digits, if each digit is used only once?

4. Describe the strategy you used to find the numbers you made.

Determine all the possible outcomes for each situation.

5. What are all the possible outcomes if the spinner is spun twice?

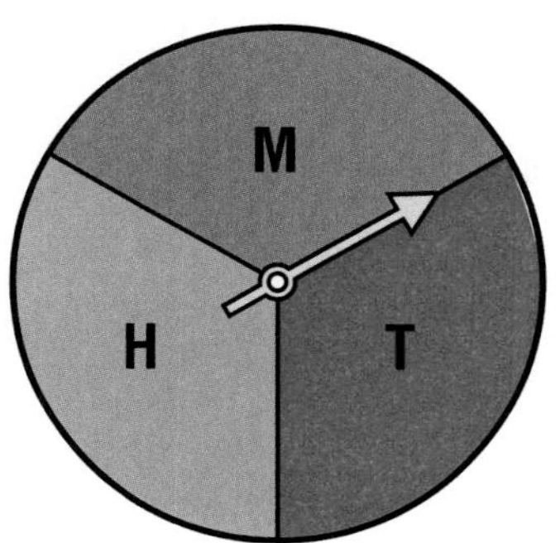

6. Describe an outcome that is not possible if 2 connecting cubes are chosen from the bag at a time.

7. What are all the possible combinations if the coin is flipped twice?

8. What are all the possible combinations if two counters are each flipped once?

9. **WRITING IN ▸MATH** Create an experiment using 2 spinners. What are all the possible combinations for that experiment? How did you find all the possible outcomes? What generalizations can you make?

3-6 Determine Possible Combinations

GET READY to Learn

In a basketball game, Samantha went to the freethrow line twice. Each time she shot the ball twice. What are all the possible combinations of her free throws?

MAIN IDEA

I will use pictures to find all the possible outcomes in a problem situation.

Targeted TEKS 4.13 The student solves problems by collecting, organizing, displaying, and interpreting data. **(A) Use concrete objects or pictures to make generalizations about determining all possible combinations of a given set of data or objects in a problem situation.** *Also addresses 4.15(B).*

New Vocabulary

tree diagram

Pictures can help you find all the possible outcomes of a situation.

EXAMPLE Determine Combinations

1 How many possible combinations does Samantha have for her two free throws?

One way to find the possible combinations is by creating a grid.

	Shot 1	Shot 2
1st Time	Make Miss Make Miss	Make Miss Miss Make
2nd Time	Make Miss Make Miss	Make Miss Miss Make

These are Samantha's possible combinations.

So, there are eight possible combinations.

Online Personal Tutor at tx.gr4math.com

Another way to find the possible outcomes is by using a **tree diagram**. A tree diagram uses "branches" to show all the possible combinations.

EXAMPLE Possible Combinations

2 **A student is spinning two spinners. How many possible combinations are there?**

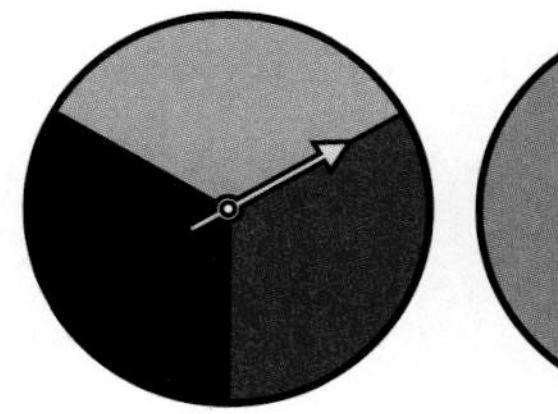

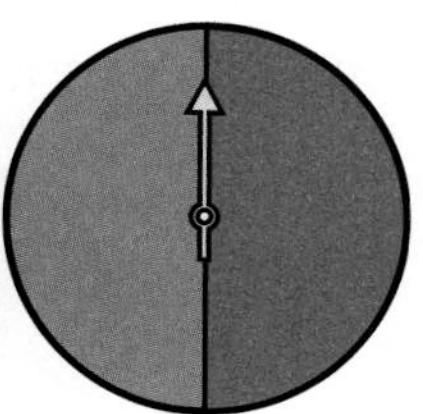

A tree diagram can be used to find all the possible combinations for spinning both spinners.

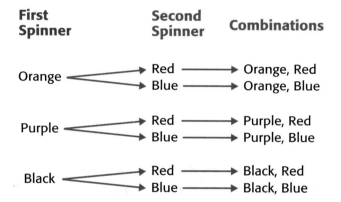

First Spinner	Second Spinner	Combinations
Orange	→ Red	→ Orange, Red
	→ Blue	→ Orange, Blue
Purple	→ Red	→ Purple, Red
	→ Blue	→ Purple, Blue
Black	→ Red	→ Black, Red
	→ Blue	→ Black, Blue

So, there are 6 possible combinations.

CHECK What You Know

1. Draw a grid to find the number of possible combinations if the spinner is spun twice. See Example 1 (p. 116)

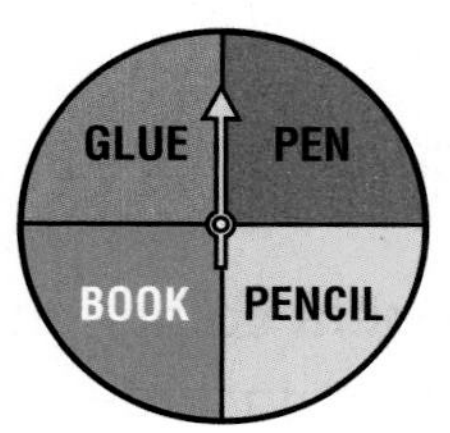

2. Draw a tree diagram to find the number of possible combinations if the coin is tossed and the spinner is spun. See Example 2 (p. 117)

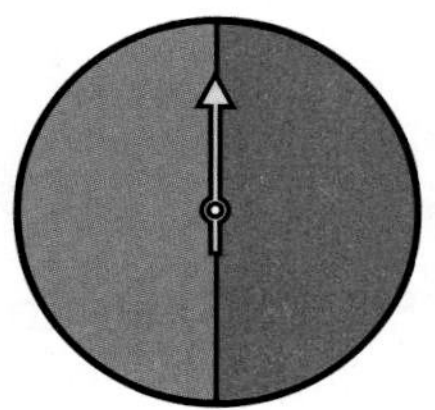

3. Talk About It In Exercise 2, what generalization can be made about determining all possible combinations?

Practice and Problem Solving

See page R8.

Draw a grid to find the number of possible combinations for each situation. See Example 1 (p. 116)

4. How many combinations are possible if the spinner is spun twice?

5. How many combinations are possible if the 5–10 number cube is rolled twice?

Draw a tree diagram to find the number of possible combinations for each situation. See Example 2 (p. 117)

6. How many combinations are possible if the spinners are spun?

7. How many combinations are possible if the 0–5 number cube is rolled twice?

Real-World PROBLEM SOLVING

Data File The state shell of Texas, the Lightning Whelk, is found on the shorelines of the Gulf Coast.

8. Make a tree diagram to show all the two-shell combinations that are possible from the shells listed in the table if each shell is used once.

9. After you take out shell combinations that are the same, how many combinations are left?

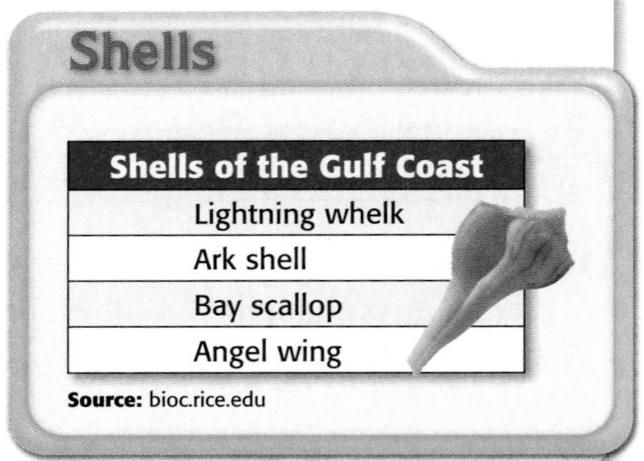

Shells

Shells of the Gulf Coast
Lightning whelk
Ark shell
Bay scallop
Angel wing

Source: bioc.rice.edu

H.O.T. Problems

10. OPEN ENDED Create two spinners with at least three different colors on each spinner. The possible combinations of the spinners must include red more often than any other color.

11. WRITING IN MATH In Exercise 10, what generalization can you make about determining all possible combinations?

TEST Practice

12. About how many more moons does Saturn have than Uranus? (Lesson 3-4)

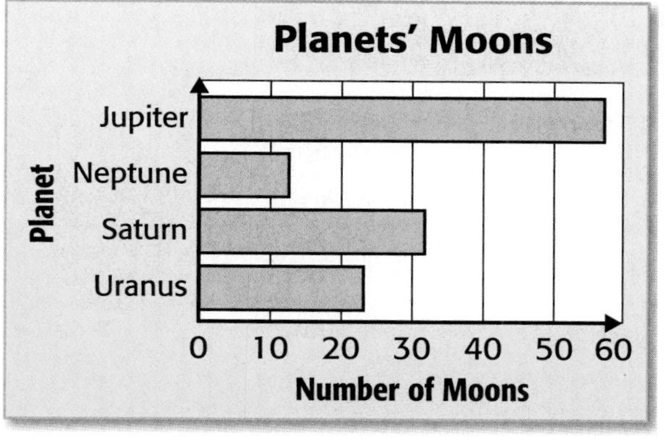

A 2

B 5

C 10

D 15

13. If Aric spins the arrow twice, which of these is **NOT** a possible combination? (Lesson 3-6)

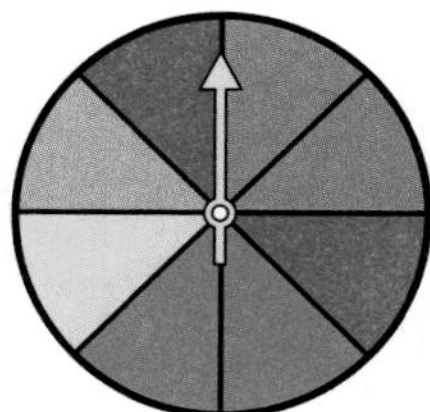

F Blue, blue

G Red, purple

H Yellow, red

J Green, blue

Spiral Review

For Exercises 14–16, use the graph showing average ages for cities in Texas. (Lesson 3-4)

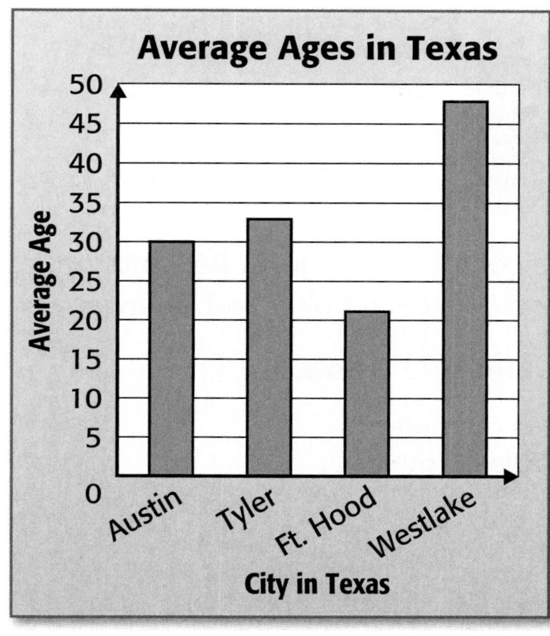

14. What city has the highest median age?

15. About what is the median age for people living in Tyler?

16. About how much younger is the population of Ft. Hood than the population of Westlake?

17. There were 2,367 students buying lunch on Monday. On Wednesday there were 2,745 buying lunch. If 45 more students bought lunch on Tuesday than Monday, how many lunches were sold on those three days in all?

3-7 Find Probability

GET READY to Learn

Two spinners are shown. What is the probability of the first spinner landing on red and the second spinner landing on yellow?

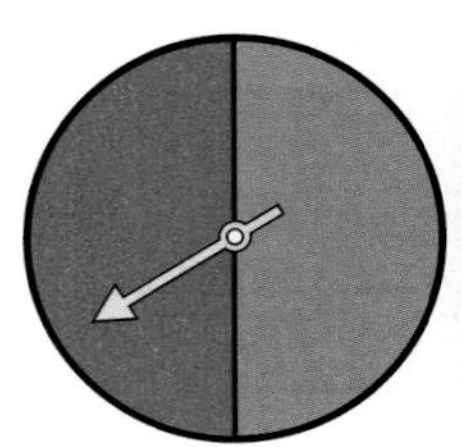

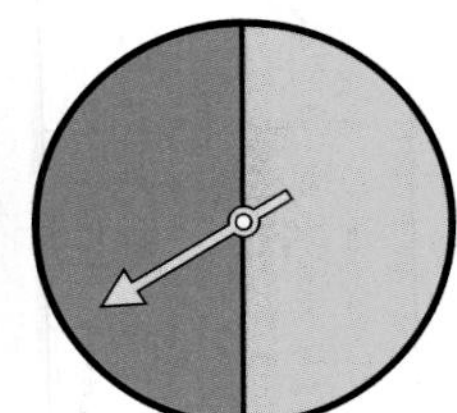

MAIN IDEA

I will find the probability of outcomes using a grid.

Targeted TEKS 4.13 The student solves problems by collecting, organizing, displaying, and interpreting sets of data. **(A) Use concrete objects or pictures to make generalizations about determining all possible combinations of a given set of data or of objects in a problem situation.** *Preparation for TEKS 5.12.*

New Vocabulary

probablility

grid

Probability describes the likelihood of an event taking place. A **grid** can be used to find the probability of a situation. On a grid, each outcome is shown where each row and column intersect.

EXAMPLE Use a Grid

1 The grid shows the results of spinning the spinners above. Find the probability of the first spinner landing on red and the second spinner landing on yellow.

Second Spinner

First Spinner		**Green**	**Yellow**
	Red	red, green	red, yellow
	Blue	blue, green	blue, yellow

There are four possible color combinations. Red and green, red and yellow, blue and green, and blue and yellow.

One of the outcomes is red and yellow.

$$\text{Probability} = \frac{\text{favorable outcome}}{\text{total possible outcomes}}$$

$$= \frac{1}{4}$$

So, the probability is 1 out of 4, or $\frac{1}{4}$.

Online **Personal Tutor at** tx.gr4math.com

EXAMPLE Make and Use a Grid

2 **Create a grid to show all the possible combinations of tossing two coins. Then find the probability of one coin landing on heads and one coin landing on tails.**

Step 1 Write the possible combinations for each coin on the side and top of the grid.

Step 2 Write the possible combinations for tossing two coins in the squares where each row and column intersect.

Second Coin

First Coin		heads	tails
	heads	heads, heads	heads, tails
	tails	tails, heads	tails, tails

There are four possible combinations. Two of the outcomes are heads, tails. So, the probability of heads, tails is 2 out of 4 or $\frac{2}{4}$.

CHECK What You Know

Two spinners are divided into four equal parts. The grid shows the possible outcomes when each spinner is spun once.

See Examples 1 and 2 (pp. 120–121)

Second Spinner

First Spinner	Red (R)	Blue (B)	Yellow (Y)	Green (G)
Red (R)	RR	RB	RY	RG
Blue (B)	BR	BB	BY	BG
Yellow (Y)	YR	YB	YY	YG
Green (G)	GR	GB	GY	GG

1. How many possible combinations are there?
2. What is the probability of spinning two different colors?
3. What is the probability of spinning green on the first spin?
4. Make a grid that shows the outcomes for two spinners that both have the colors green, blue, and orange. Find the probability of spinning at least one orange.
5. Talk About It Refer to Exercise 4. What generalization can you make about determining the total possible outcomes?

Practice and Problem Solving

See page R9.

One spinner is divided into four equal parts. A second spinner is divided into five equal parts. The grid shows the possible combinations when each spinner is spun once. See Examples 1 and 2 (pp. 120–121)

6. How many possible combinations are there?

7. What is the probability that an outcome contains numbers that are both greater than 3?

8. Find the probability of spinning the same two numbers.

Second Spinner

First Spinner	1	2	3	4
1	1, 1	1, 2	1, 3	1, 4
2	2, 1	2, 2	2, 3	2, 4
3	3, 1	3, 2	3, 3	3, 4
4	4, 1	4, 2	4, 3	4, 4
5	5, 1	5, 2	5, 3	5, 4

Make a grid to find each probability.

9. Two number cubes are numbered 1–6. Ravi needs to roll a sum of 8 or greater to win a game. Find the probability that Ravi will win.

10. There is one red shirt, one green shirt, and one blue shirt in a drawer. There are black and tan pants in another drawer. One shirt and pants are randomly chosen. Find the probability that a green shirt is chosen.

Real-World PROBLEM SOLVING

Nature A bush has flowers that can bloom in four different colors. Suppose it is equally likely for a bush to have any color flowers.

11. Two bushes are randomly chosen. What is the probability that at least one has blue flowers?

12. What is the probability that a bush will have the same color of flowers?

Bush 2

Bush 1	Blue (B)	Green (G)	Pink (P)	White (W)
Blue (B)	B, B	B, G	B, P	B, W
Green (G)	G, B	G, G	G, P	G, W
Pink (P)	P, B	P, G	P, P	P, W
White (W)	W, B	W, G	W, P	W, W

H.O.T. Problems

13. OPEN ENDED Draw and label a spinner so that the probability of spinning yellow is greater than the probability of spinning green.

14. WRITING IN MATH Create a real-world problem that involves probability and has an answer of one out of four.

Technology Activity for 3-7
Find Probability

You can use a spinner from the *Math Tool Chest* to solve problems.

MAIN IDEA

I will use technology to divide greater numbers.

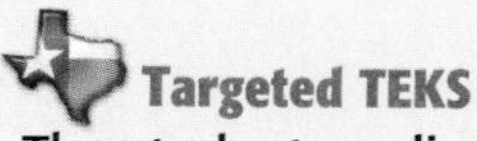

Targeted TEKS 4.14 The student applies Grade 4 mathematics to solve problems connected to everyday experiences and activities in and outside of school. (D) **Use tools such as** real objects, manipulatives, and **technology to solve problems.** *Also addresses TEKS 4.15(A).*

ACTIVITY

Angelo is using a spinner with four sections: one green, one red, one yellow, and one blue, to conduct an experiment. He spins the spinner 100 times and draws a bar graph of the results. Try the experiment for yourself.

- Click on the spinner button.
- Set the number of trials at 100.
- Click on the Spin Slow or Spin Fast.
- Click on the links at the bottom of the Data table.
- Choose Bar Graph. The program will create a bar graph to display the data.
- Which color did the spinner land on the most?

CHECK What You Know

Predict the outcome of the following spins. Use the computer spinner to test your prediction. Draw a bar graph for each, and state the color that the spinner landed on the most and the least. Compare the outcome to your prediction.

1. 15 times **2.** 25 times **3.** 30 times **4.** 50 times

Solve.

5. Spin a spinner with eight sections 25 times. Draw a bar graph to display the results. What color was spun the most?

6. **Analyze** How does using the spinner on the computer help you conduct these experiments?

CHAPTER 3

Study Guide and Review

FOLDABLES Study Organizer GET READY to Study

Be sure the following Key Vocabulary words and Key Concepts are written in your Foldable.

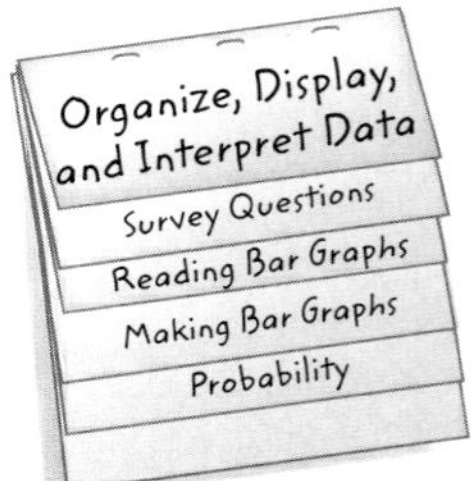

BIG Ideas

Displaying Data

- A **survey** is a way to collect data. **Data** can be organized in different ways, such as a tally chart and a frequency table. (p. 95)
- A **bar graph** is used to compare data by using bars of different heights to represent data. (p. 100)

Probability describes the likelihood of an event taking place. (p. 120)

The probability of two coins landing on heads after being tossed can be found by using the grid.

First Coin		Second Coin: Heads	Second Coin: Tails
	Heads	heads, heads	heads, tails
	Tails	tails, heads	tails tails

The probability of two coins landing on heads is 1 out of 4, or $\frac{1}{4}$.

Key Vocabulary

bar graph (p. 100)
data (p. 95)
probability (p. 120)
survey (p. 95)
tree diagram (p.117)

Vocabulary Check

Match each phrase with the correct vocabulary word above.

1. A survey is a way to collect ___?___ .
2. ___?___ describes the likelihood of an event taking place.
3. A ___?___ is used to compare data by using bars of different heights to represent values.
4. A ___?___ is a way to collect information that answers a question.
5. A ___?___ uses "branches" to show all possible combinations of a probability situation.
6. A grid can be used to find the ___?___ of a situation.

Math Online Vocabulary Review at tx.gr4math.com

Lesson-by-Lesson Review

3-1 Collect and Organize Data (pp. 95–97)

Example 1
Organize the data shown in a tally chart and frequency table.

Favorite Sports		
basketball	basketball	volleyball
basketball	basketball	volleyball
basketball	track	volleyball
basketball	track	volleyball

Favorite Sports	
Sport	**Tally**
Track	||
Basketball	~~||||~~ |
Volleyball	||||

Favorite Sports	
Sport	**Frequency**
Track	2
Basketball	6
Volleyball	4

Organize each set of data in a tally chart and frequency table.

7. Favorite after dinner activity.

After Dinner Activity		
nap	read	game
game	nap	read
game	game	read
read	game	game

8. Votes for president.

Votes for President		
Tom	Monica	Lamar
Monica	Tom	Tom
Tom	Monica	Monica
Lamar	Monica	Lamar

3-2 Problem-Solving Strategy: Make a Table (pp. 98–99)

Example 2
There are 144 students going on a class trip. If 36 students fit on each bus, how many buses are needed?

You know that there are 144 students and each bus holds 36. Make a table to find the number of buses needed.

Bus	Students
1	36
2	72
3	108
4	144

+36
+36
+36

So, 4 buses are needed.

Solve the problems using a table.

9. Jordan plans to read 30 out of 120 pages a night. Will he finish the book by Thursday? Explain.

Day	Pages Read
Sunday	30
Monday	60
Tuesday	■
Wednesday	■

10. There are 26 cars at a red light. The green light lets 2 cars go. How many lights will it take for all the cars to go through the light?

Study Guide and Review

3-3 Bar Graphs (pp. 100–102)

Example 3
How many children were at the park on Tuesday?

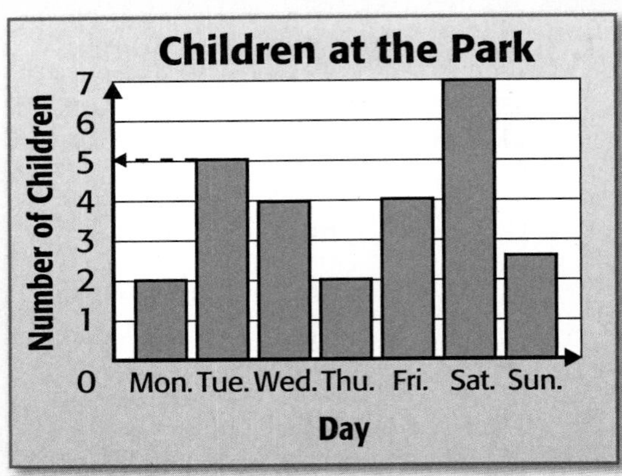

Compare the height of the bar that represents Tuesday to the scale on the left. So, five children were at the park on Tuesday.

For Exercises 11 and 12, use the graph.

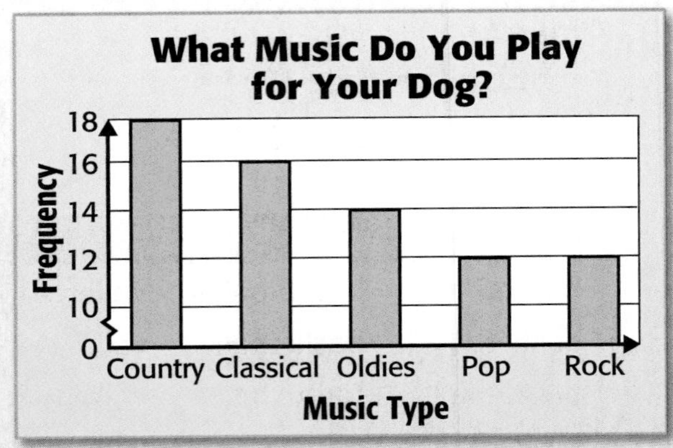

11. How many people played oldies for their dogs?

12. What is the total number of people who played pop and rock music for their dogs?

3-4 Bar and Double Bar Graphs (pp. 104–106)

Example 4
About how many rolls of wrapping paper did the third grade sell?

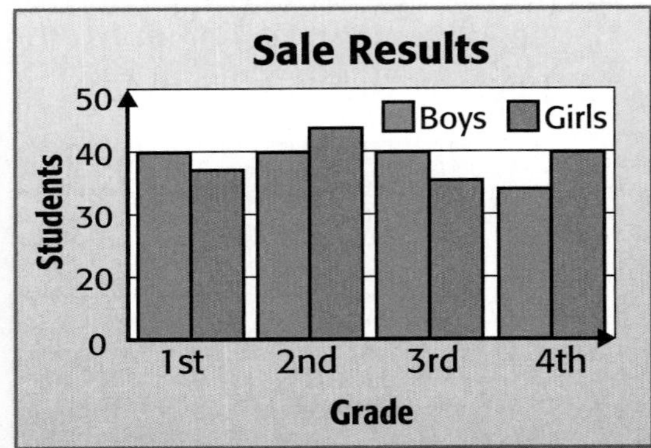

$35 + 40 = 75$. So, about 75 rolls of wrapping paper were sold.

For Exercises 13 and 14, use the graph.

13. What is the most popular spot?

14. What is the difference in number of students who liked the most popular and least popular vacation spots?

3-5 Problem-Solving Investigation: Choose a Strategy (pp. 110–111)

Example 5

Pia wants to earn \$75. If she earns \$15 each time she babysits, how many times will she have to babysit in order to earn \$75?

Understand

Pia earns \$15 each time she babysits. She wants to earn \$75. Find the number of days Pia needs to babysit to earn \$75.

Plan Organize the data in a table to solve the problem.

Solve

Day	Money Earned
1	\$15
2	\$30
3	\$45
4	\$60
5	\$75

Pia will have to babysit 5 times to earn \$75.

Check \$75 – \$15 = \$60
\$60 – \$15 = \$45
\$45 – \$15 = \$30
\$30 – \$15 = \$15
\$15 – \$15 = \$0

Subtracting \$15 from \$75 five times equals 0. So, the answer makes sense.

Use any strategy to solve.

15. Marcos has 19 baseball hats. Rashid has 5 more than Marcos. Shelly has 2 less than Rashid. How many baseball hats does Shelly have?

16. **Geometry** What 4 shapes come next in the pattern if it continues?

17. The sum of two numbers is 14. The difference between those same two numbers is 0. What are the two numbers?

18. **Geometry** What shape will be tenth in the pattern if it continues?

19. Grant's favorite video game takes him 132 minutes to win. Each level takes Grant about 22 minutes to clear. About how many levels does his video game have?

20. Doria works at a sandwich shop. There are 3 different kinds of bread and 5 different kinds of meat to choose from. How many different sandwiches can be made using one bread and one meat?

Chapter 3 Study Guide and Review

3-6 Determine Possible Combinations (pp. 116–119)

Example 6

Angie can use clay or paper for an art project. Her project can be blue or yellow. What are all the combinations of the art project?

Use a tree diagram.

Material	Color	Combination
clay	blue	clay, blue
	yellow	clay, yellow
paper	blue	paper, blue
	yellow	paper, yellow

There are four possible combinations.

Draw a tree diagram to find the number of possible combinations for each situation.

21. How many combinations are possible if the coin is tossed and the spinner is spun?

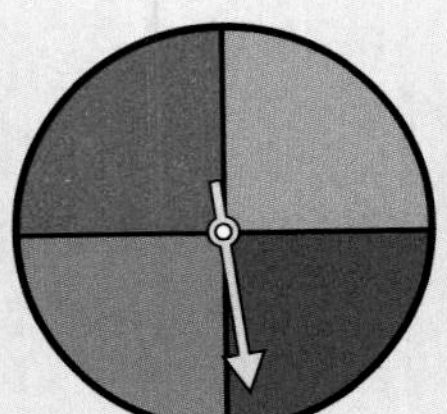

3-7 Find Probability (pp. 120–122)

Example 7

Each spinner is spun once. Find the probability of spinning blue and green.

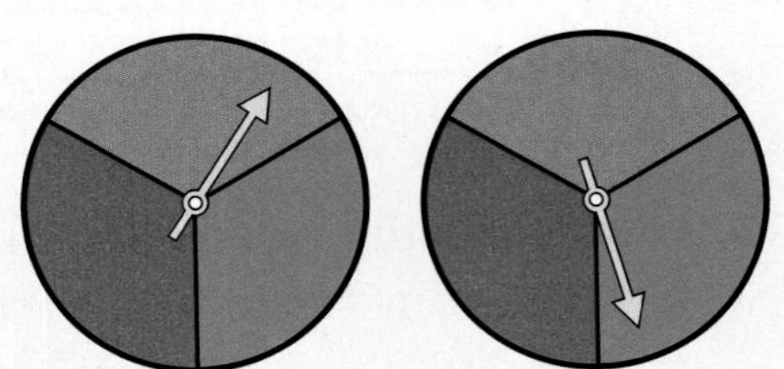

Spinner 1 (rows) / Spinner 2 (columns)

	Red (R)	Green (G)	Blue (B)
Red (R)	R, R	R, G	R, B
Green (G)	G, R	G, G	G, B
Blue(B)	B, R	B, G	B, B

Two of the outcomes are blue, green. So, the probability of blue, green is 2 out of 9 or $\frac{2}{9}$.

Two spinners are divided into three equal parts. The grid shows the possible combinations when each spinner is spun once.

Spinner 1 (rows) / Spinner 2 (columns)

	4	5	6
1	1, 4	1, 5	1, 6
2	2, 4	2, 5	2, 6
3	3, 4	3, 5	3, 6

22. How many combinations are possible?

23. What is the probability that both numbers are less than 5?

24. Find the probability that both numbers are odd.

Chapter 3 Chapter Test

For Exercises 1–2, tell whether each statement is *true* or *false*.

1. A double bar graph displays two sets of related data using bars of different colors and heights.

2. A tree diagram uses "branches" to show all possible combinations of a probability situation.

3. **TEST PRACTICE** Julio will spin the arrow on a spinner like the one shown below.

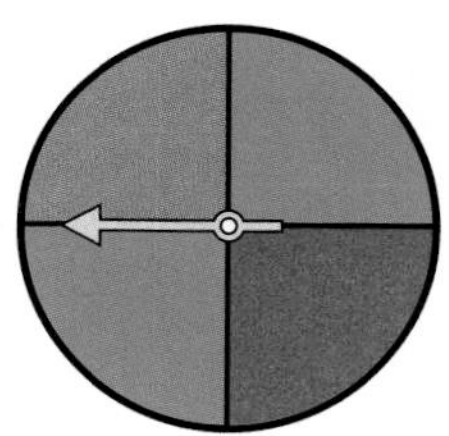

If Julio spins the arrow twice and it lands on two different spaces, which of the following is NOT a possible combination?

A Red, Blue

B Green, Green

C Red, Red

D Green, Red

Make a table to solve each problem.

4. A car needs an oil change every 3 months. Joe's car has had 4 oil changes so far. How many months have passed?

5. How much money will Kendall save if he saves $35 a month for a year?

6. Use the bar graph that shows the school choir membership. About how many members were added to the school choir in 2007?

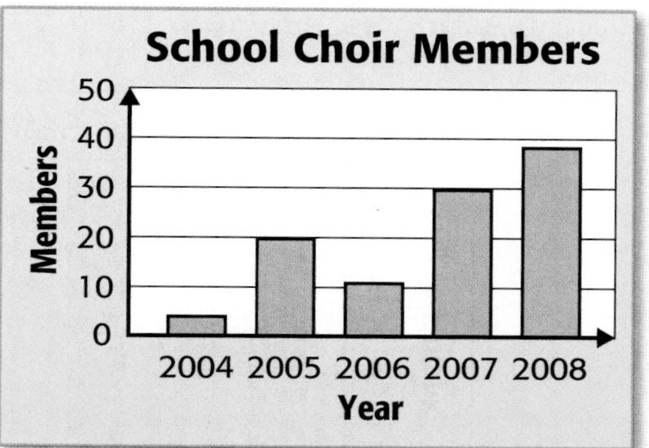

7. **TEST PRACTICE** The graph below shows the number of touchdowns made in four different games.

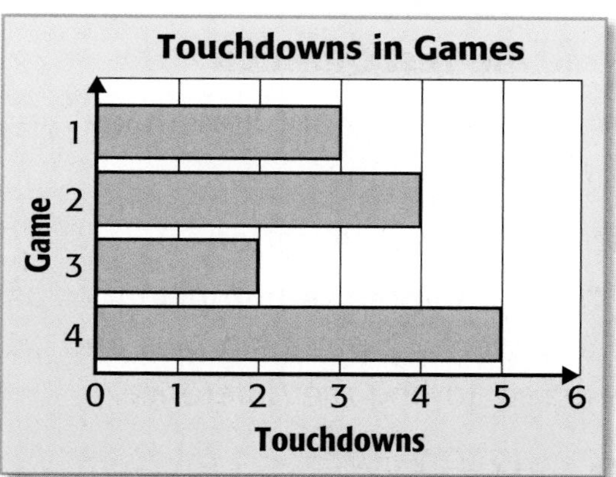

According to the graph, how many more touchdowns were made in game 4 than in game 1?

F 2 **H** 4

G 3 **J** 5

8. **WRITING IN MATH** Write two sentences to describe the graph in Exercise 7.

CHAPTER 3

Texas Test Practice

Cumulative, Chapters 1–3

TEST Example

Rey made a bar graph to show how many pies have been sold at a bake sale. How many more apple pies have been sold than pumpkin pies?

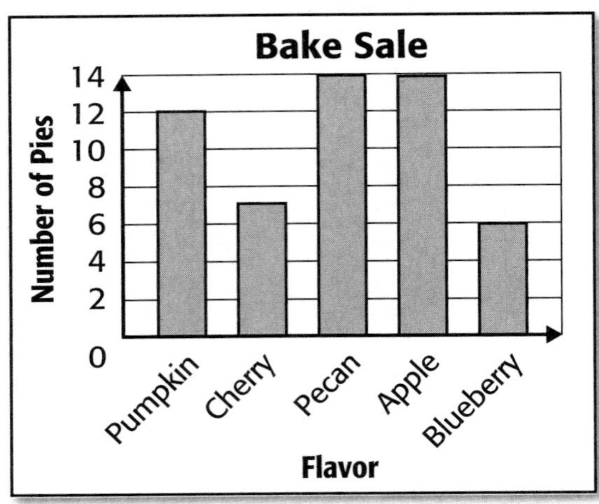

TEST-TAKING TIP

Get the information you need to answer each question correctly.

Read the Test Question

You need to find out how many more apple pies were sold than pumpkin pies.

Solve the Test Question

Find the number of pumpkin pies and apple pies sold. There were 12 pumpkin pies and 14 apple pies sold. Subtract to find the difference.

$14 - 12 = 2$

There have been 2 more apple pies sold than pumpkin pies.

Choose the best answer.

1. **Which number is 1,000 more than 82,753?**

   A 82,853 **C** 92,753

   B 83,753 **D** 92,735

2. **Which of the following has the greatest value?**

   F 804,703 **H** 810,609

   G 806,731 **J** 811,512

Get Ready for the Texas Test
For test-taking strategies and more practice, see pages TX1–TX21.

3. **A piggy bank has the coins shown below in it. If a coin is selected at random, what is the probability that the coin will be a penny?**

A 1 out of 5

B 2 out of 9

C 3 out of 11

D 3 out of 14

4. **The graph shows the cars sold by five salespeople this month.**

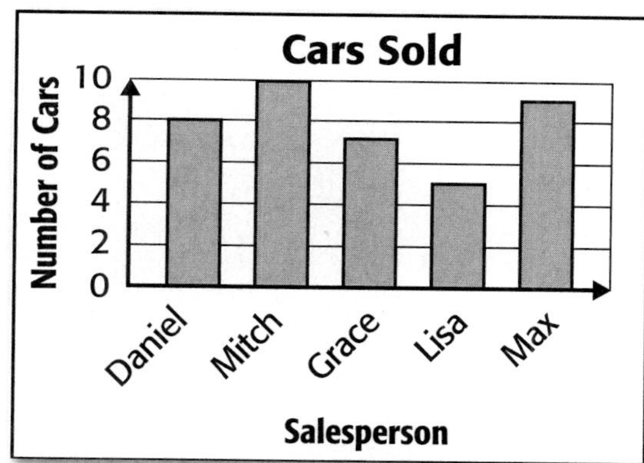

Which two salespeople have sold a total of 16 cars?

F Daniel and Lisa

G Mitch and Daniel

H Grace and Max

J Max and Lisa

5. **The table shows the number of baseball cards each of four friends has.**

Baseball Cards	
Jaden	41
Tala	68
Kenji	55
Sam	39

If Jaden gets 14 more baseball cards, which of the following will be true?

A Jaden will have the most cards.

B Sam will have more cards than Tala.

C Jaden will have 12 more cards than Sam.

D Kenji and Jaden will have the same number of cards.

6. **Last week there were 37 absent students at Victory Elementary School. This week there have been 5 more absent students. How many students have been absent this week?**

F 32

G 33

H 42

J 43

7. **What is $2,811,495 rounded to the nearest hundred thousand?**

A $2,000,000

B $2,800,000

C $2,900,000

D $3,000,000

Apply Multiplication and Division Facts

BIG Idea What are multiplication and division?

Multiplication means to find the total of equal groups.
Division means to separate an amount into equal groups.

Example Two years on Earth is about one year on Mars. Andrés is 10 years old. If he lived on Mars, he would be $10 \div 2$ or 5 years old.

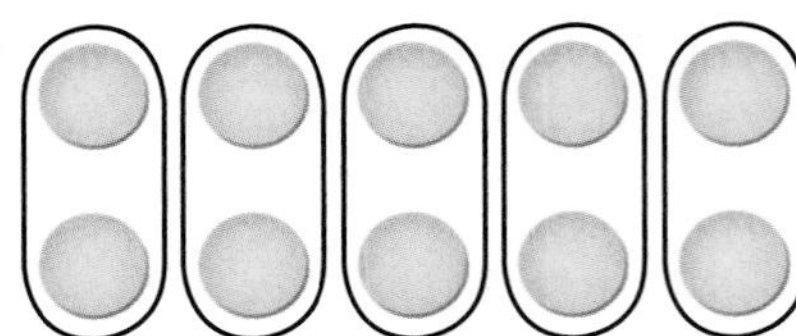

$10 \div 2$ means to separate 10 into equal groups of 2.
$10 \div 2 = 5$

What will I learn in this chapter?

- Use multiplication and division properties.
- Understand how multiplication and division are related.
- Multiply and divide facts through 12.
- Identify factors and multiples.
- Choose an operation to solve problems.

Key Vocabulary

Commutative Property of Multiplication
Associative Property of Multiplication
factor
multiple
Distributive Property of Multiplication

Student Study Tools at tx.gr4math.com

FOLDABLES™ Study Organizer

Make this Foldable to help you organize information about multiplication and division. Begin with four sheets of $8\frac{1}{2}'' \times 11''$ paper.

1. **Stack** 4 sheets of paper. Place each sheet $\frac{3}{4}$ inch apart.

2. **Roll** up the edges, so all tabs are the same size.

3. **Crease** and staple along the fold.

4. **Label** the tabs with the topics from the chapter.

ARE YOU READY for Chapter 4?

You have two ways to check prerequisite skills for this chapter.

Option 2

Math Online Take the Chapter Readiness Quiz at tx.gr4math.com.

Option 1

Complete the Quick Check below.

QUICK Check

Algebra Complete each number sentence. (Lesson 3-2)

1. $4 + 4 + 4 = \blacksquare$

2. $6 + 6 + \blacksquare + 6 = 24$

3. $9 + 9 + 9 = 3 \times \blacksquare$

4. $11 + 11 + 11 + 11 = \blacksquare \times 11$

5. Write the multiplication fact modeled by the array at the right.

Copy each array. Then circle equal groups of 3. (Prior grade)

6. ★★★★ ★★★★ ★★★★

7. ☾☾☾☾☾☾ ☾☾☾☾☾☾ ☾☾☾☾☾☾ ☾☾☾☾☾☾

8. Marcia has 15 action figures. If Marcia places the figures in 3 equal rows, how many figures will be in each row?

The number patterns below are formed by skip counting. Copy and complete each pattern. (Prior grade)

9. 2, 4, 6, ■, 10, ■, 14

10. 4, 8, 12, ■, 20, 24, ■

11. 5, ■, 15, 20, ■, 30, ■

12. ■, 18, 27, ■, 45, 54, ■

13. Write a number pattern that involves skip counting. Describe the pattern.

Math Activity for 4-1

Meaning of Multiplication and Division

You can use models to represent multiplication and division.

MAIN IDEA

I will use models to represent multiplication and division.

The student multiplies and divides to solve meaningful problems involving whole numbers. (B) **Represent multiplication and division situations in picture, word, and number form.**

You Will Need
counters
cups

1 Find 3 × 4.

Step 1 Model 3 × 4.

To model 3 × 4, arrange counters in an array with 3 rows and 4 columns.

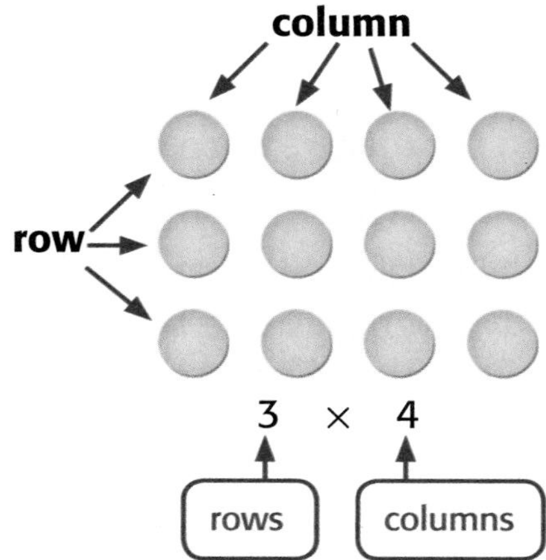

Step 2 Use repeated addition to find 3 × 4.

Add 3 rows of 4 counters.

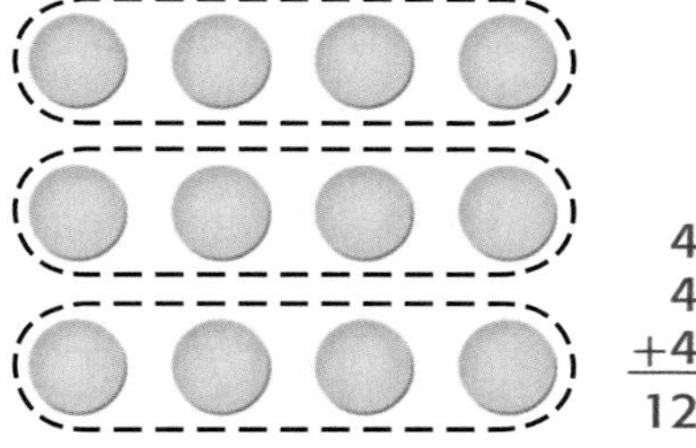

$$\begin{array}{r} 4 \\ 4 \\ +4 \\ \hline 12 \end{array}$$

Step 3 Make the connection.

Multiplication and repeated addition result in the same answer.

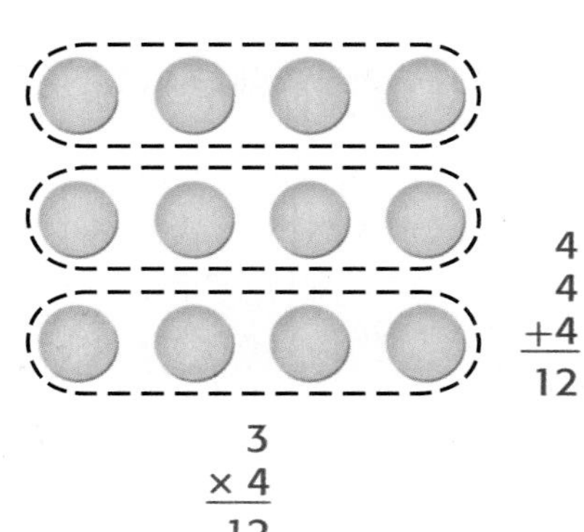

$$\begin{array}{r} 4 \\ 4 \\ +4 \\ \hline 12 \end{array} \qquad \begin{array}{r} 3 \\ \times 4 \\ \hline 12 \end{array}$$

So, 3 × 4 = 12.

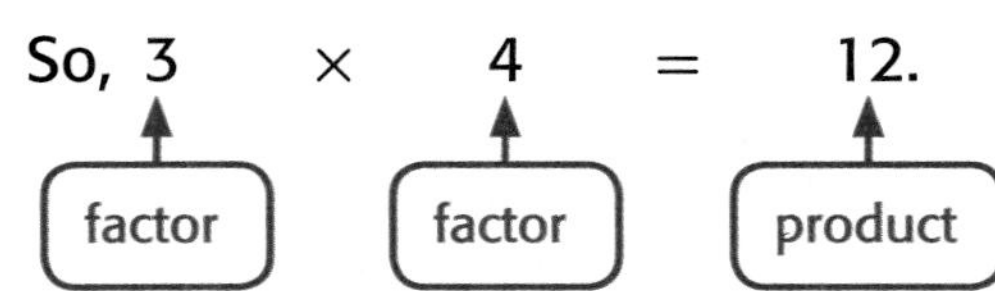

Animation
tx.gr4math.com

ACTIVITY

Hands-On Activity

2 **Find 15 ÷ 3.**

Step 1 **Model 15 ÷ 3.**

Use 15 counters. Put the counters in 3 rows since the divisor is 3.

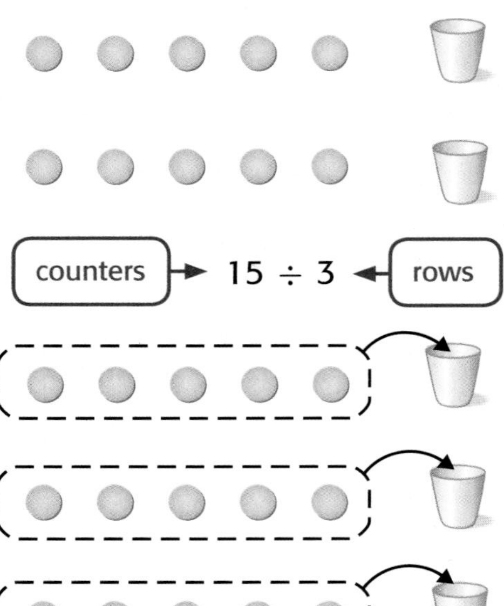

Step 2 **Place the counters in the cups.**

Divide the counters equally one by one into the cups until all 15 counters are gone.

Step 3 **Find 15 ÷ 3.**

There are 5 counters in each cup.

So, 15 ÷ 3 = 5.

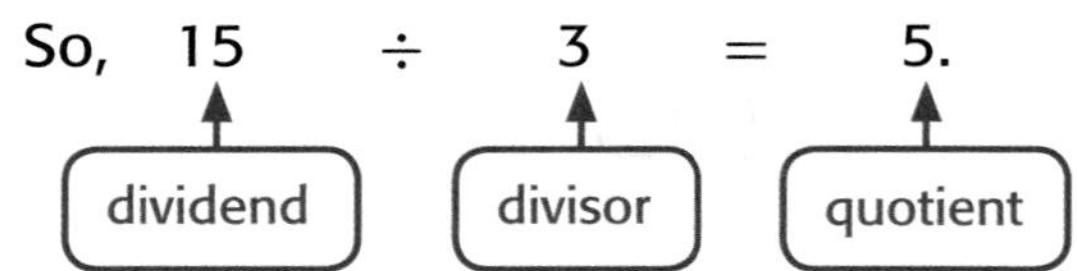

Think About It

1. How would you model 2 × 8?
2. How would you model 10 ÷ 5?

CHECK What You Know

Draw pictures to model. Then multiply or divide.

3. 3 × 7
4. 6 ÷ 3
5. 6 × 8
6. 24 ÷ 6

7. WRITING IN MATH Draw a picture explaining how to model 4 groups of 9. Write a number sentence to show the total amount in 4 groups of 9.

Relate Multiplication and Division

GET READY to Learn

Latanya and her father are baking. Her father asks her how many eggs they have. The eggs in the carton are arranged in an array.

MAIN IDEA

I will understand how multiplication and division are related.

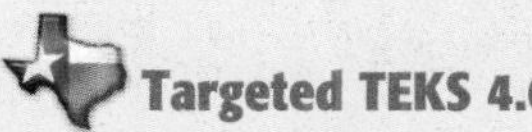

Targeted TEKS 4.6 The student uses patterns in multiplication and division. **(A)** **Use patterns and relationships to develop strategies to remember basic multiplication and division facts (such as the patterns in related multiplication and division number sentences (fact families) such as 9 × 9 = 81 and 81 ÷ 9 = 9.)** *Also addresses TEKS 4.4(A), (B).*

New Vocabulary

fact family

You can write related multiplication and division sentences to describe the array of eggs. You can think of this array as 2 rows and 3 columns or 3 rows and 2columns.

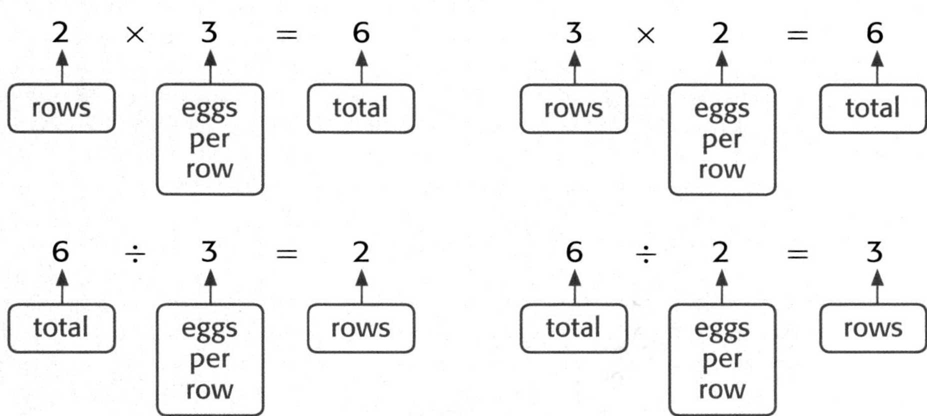

The number sentences above show a fact family. A **fact family** is a set of four related multiplication and division facts that use the same three numbers. The fact family follows a pattern.

EXAMPLE Write a Fact Family

1 Write a fact family for the array.

There are 3 rows, 4 columns, and a total of 12 objects.

3 × 4 = 12 **4 × 3 = 12**

12 ÷ 3 = 4 **12 ÷ 4 = 3**

You can use a related multiplication fact to help you divide.

Real-World EXAMPLE Use Related Facts

Remember

An array is a set of objects or symbols that are displayed in rows and columns.

2 BOOKS Vanesa has 36 books to put on 4 shelves. The same number of books will be placed on each shelf. How many books will be on each shelf?

Find 36 ÷ 4. You can use a related multiplication fact to help you divide.

36 ÷ 4 = ■

What number times 4 is 36?

36 ÷ 4 = 9

So, Vanesa will place 9 books on each shelf.

Online **Personal Tutor at** tx.gr4math.com

CHECK What You Know

Write a fact family for each array or set of numbers. See Example 1 (p. 137)

1. 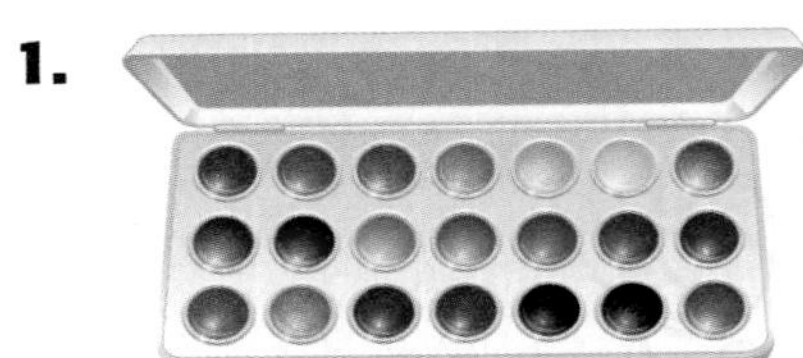

2.

3. 6, 8, 48

4. 3, 12, 4

Algebra Copy and complete each fact family. See Example 1 (p. 137)

5. 3 × 6 = ■ 6 × ■ = 18
   18 ÷ ■ = 3 18 ÷ 3 = ■

6. 5 × 7 = ■ ■ × 5 = 35
   35 ÷ ■ = 7 35 ÷ 7 = ■

Algebra Divide. Use a related multiplication fact. See Example 2 (p. 138)

7. 22 ÷ 2 = ■

8. 81 ÷ 9 = ■

9. Ed wants to share 18 grapes equally among himself and two friends. How many grapes will each get?

10. Talk About It How are multiplication and division related? Use examples to support your answer.

Practice and Problem Solving

EXTRA PRACTICE See page R9.

Write a fact family for each array or set of numbers. See Example 1 (p. 137)

11. 

12. 

13. 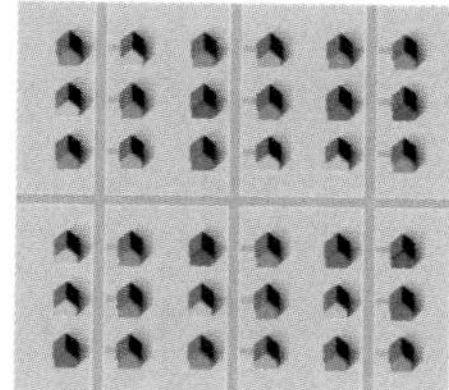

14. 

15. 6, 9, 54 **16.** 7, 8, 56 **17.** 9, 11, 99 **18.** 11, 12, 132

Algebra **Copy and complete each fact family.** See Example 1 (p. 137)

19. $4 \times 8 = ■$ $■ \times 4 = 32$
$32 \div ■ = 8$ $32 \div 8 = ■$

20. $■ \times 9 = 72$ $9 \times 8 = ■$
$72 \div ■ = 8$ $72 \div 8 = ■$

Algebra **Divide. Use a related multiplication fact.** See Example 2 (p. 138)

21. $18 \div 2 = ■$ **22.** $36 \div 6 = ■$ **23.** $63 \div 7 = ■$ **24.** $64 \div 8 = ■$

Real-World PROBLEM SOLVING

Data File The mockingbird became Texas' state bird in 1927.

Mockingbird

25. One mockingbird can sing up to 30 songs. Suppose a bird sings only 5 songs at one time. How many times would it have to sing before it completes all of its songs without repeating any?

26. The mockingbird lays 3 to 6 eggs in each clutch (a set of eggs laid at one time). Suppose 18 eggs were found in different nests throughout the park. There are 6 eggs in each nest. How many nests contained eggs?

H.O.T. Problem

27. **WRITING IN MATH** Explain how fact families and multiplication facts can help you solve division problems.

4-2 Properties of Multiplication and Division

GET READY to Learn

The table shows Jenny and Cliff's chores. Jenny earns \$3 for each chore and Cliff earns \$2 for each chore. How much does each person earn for completing chores?

Jenny	Cliff
Pack lunches	Set table
Take out trash	Clean room
Laundry	Walk dog
Clean room	Wash dishes
	Sweep floor

MAIN IDEA

I will use multiplication and division properties.

Targeted TEKS 4.6 The student uses patterns in multiplication and division. (A) **Use patterns and relationships to develop strategies to remember basic multiplication and division facts (such as the patterns in related multiplication and division number sentences (fact families) such as $9 \times 9 = 81$ and $81 \div 9 = 9$).**

New Vocabulary

Commutative Property of Multiplication

Associative Property of Multiplication

Identity Property of Multiplication

Zero Property of Multiplication

Multiplication also has properties similar to addition. You can use the patterns and relationships in these properties.

KEY CONCEPT — Multiplication Properties

Commutative Property of Multiplication
When multiplying, the order of the factors does not change the product.
$3 \times 2 = 6$
$2 \times 3 = 6$

Associative Property of Multiplication
The way in which the factors are grouped does not change the product.
$(5 \times 2) \times 3 = 30$
$5 \times (2 \times 3) = 30$

Identity Property of Multiplication
When any number is multiplied by 1, the product is that number.
$4 \times 1 = 4$

Zero Property of Multiplication
When any number is multiplied by 0, the product is 0.
$3 \times 0 = 0$

EXAMPLE Identify Properties

1 Identify the property shown by $8 \times 1 = 8$.

A number is multiplied by 1, and the product is that number. This is the Identity Property of Multiplication.

EXAMPLE Use Properties

2 **Complete (4 × 3) × 2 = 4 × (■ × 2). Identify the property used.**

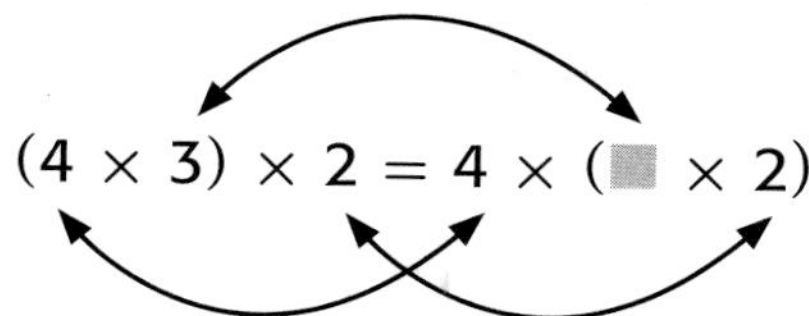

A 3 completes the number sentence. The way in which the factors are grouped does not change the product. This is the Associative Property of Multiplication.

 **Personal Tutor at** tx.gr4math.com

The following facts can help you with division.

Remember

Quotient is the name of the answer for division problems.

KEY CONCEPTS — Division Facts

Zeros in Division

When you divide 0 by any number other than 0, the quotient is 0. — $0 \div 5 = 0$

It is not possible to divide a number by 0. — 7 ÷ 0 (crossed out)

Ones in Division

When you divide any number by 1, the quotient is always the dividend. — $8 \div 1 = 8$

When you divide any number by itself, the quotient is always 1. This is true for all numbers except 0. — $9 \div 9 = 1$

Real-World EXAMPLE Use a Division Rule

3 **PARTIES There are 9 party favors and 9 guests. How many party favors will each guest get?**

$9 \div 9 = 1$

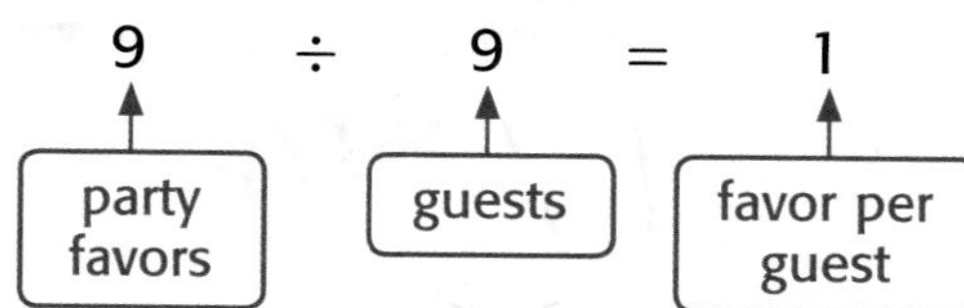

According to the rule, a non-zero number divided by the same number is 1. So, each guest will get 1 party favor.

CHECK What You Know

Identify the property shown by each number sentence.
See Examples 1–3 (pp. 140–141)

1. $12 \times 0 = 0$ **2.** $8 \times 5 = 5 \times 8$ **3.** $6 \div 1 = 6$

Algebra **Copy and complete each number sentence. Identify the property used.** See Example 2 (p. 141)

4. $7 \times \blacksquare = 7$ **5.** $(7 \times 2) \times 3 = 7 \times (\blacksquare \times 3)$ **6.** $5 \div \blacksquare = 1$

7. Brenda has 4 rows of 6 stickers. What is another way she can arrange the stickers? Write a number sentence.

8. Talk About It Explain why the Identity Property of Multiplication uses 1 while the Identity Property of Addition uses 0.

Practice and Problem Solving

Identify the property shown by each number sentence.
See Examples 1–3 (pp. 140–141)

9. $10 \div 10 = 1$ **10.** $6 \times (3 \times 4) = (6 \times 3) \times 4$ **11.** $8 \times 0 = 0$

12. $0 \div 12 = 0$ **13.** $(6 \times 3) \times 4 = (6 \times 4) \times 3$ **14.** $22 \times 1 = 22$

Algebra **Copy and complete each number sentence. Identify the property used.** See Example 2 (p. 141)

15. $3 \div \blacksquare = 1$ **16.** $\blacksquare \times 8 = 8 \times 4$ **17.** $\blacksquare \div 11 = 0$

18. $3 \times (\blacksquare \times 6) = (3 \times 3) \times 6$ **19.** $15 \times \blacksquare = 15$ **20.** $28 \times \blacksquare = 0$

Real-World PROBLEM SOLVING

Hiking Write a number sentence for each situation. Then solve.

21. On their first hiking trip, Tamika and Brian hiked 7 miles a day. They hiked for 5 days. Kurt and Suki hiked 5 miles a day. How many days did it take Kurt and Suki to hike the same distance as Tamika and Brian?

22. On their second trip, Tamika and Brian hiked twice as long as they did on their first trip. How many days will Kurt and Suki need to hike to go the same distance as Tamika and Brian?

Math Online Self-Check Quiz at tx.gr4math.com

H.O.T. Problems

23. **OPEN ENDED** Using the same three numbers, write two different multiplication expressions with a product of 60.

24. **NUMBER SENSE** When finding the value of the expression $(2 \times 9) \times 5$, is it easier to find 2×9 or 2×5 first? Explain.

25. **WRITING IN ▸MATH** Marcie thinks it is easier to find $(7 \times 6) \times 2$ than to find $7 \times (6 \times 2)$. What property tells her that the number sentences are equal? Why might Marcie think it is easier to find the answer to the first number sentence?

26. Luther's photo album has 6 pages with 8 photos on each page. Identify the number sentence that describes this situation. **(Lesson 4-2)**

A $8 \times 6 = 6 \times 8$

B $8 \times 6 > 6 \times 8$

C $8 \times 6 < 6 \times 8$

D $8 \times 8 > 6 \times 6$

27. Which number sentence is in the same fact family as $42 \div 7 = ■$? **(Lesson 4-1)**

F $7 + ■ = 42$

G $■ - 7 = 42$

H $7 \times ■ = 42$

J $42 \times 7 = 42$

Spiral Review

Algebra. Divide. Use a related multiplication fact. **(Lesson 4-1)**

28. $12 \div 3 = ■$

29. $16 \div 4 = ■$

30. $20 \div 5 = ■$

For Exercises 31 and 32, use the graph. **(Lesson 3-3)**

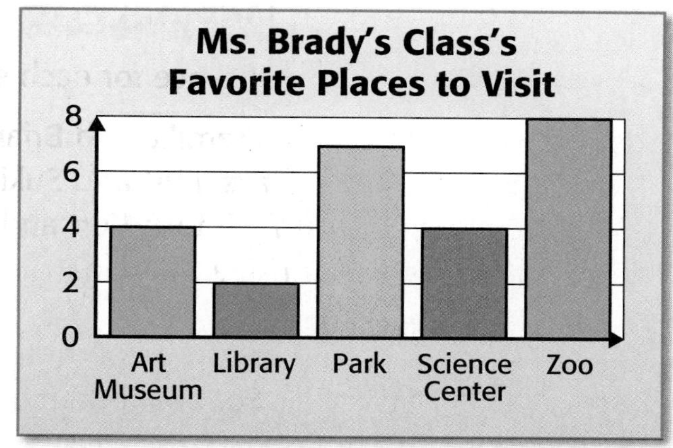

31. What is the most and least favorite place to visit?

32. Identify which two places to visit received a difference in votes of 5.

33. Fernando's two dogs eat 3 cups of food each day. How much food do his dogs eat in a week? Identify any extra or missing information. Then solve, if possible. **(Lesson 3-3)**

Multiply and Divide Facts Through 5

MAIN IDEA

I will recall multiplication and division facts 0 through 5.

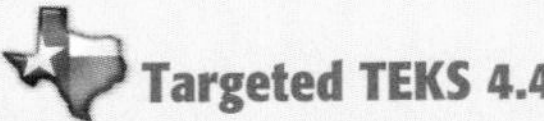

The student multiplies and divides to solve meaningful problems involving whole numbers. (A) **Model factors and products using arrays and area models.** (B) **Represent multiplication and division situations in picture, word, and number form.** *Also addresses TEKS 4.4(C), 4.6(A).*

GET READY to Learn

Charlotte is competing in a 3-mile race. Every 4 laps equals 1 mile. How many laps does she need to go in the race?

To find the number of laps that Charlotte needs to complete, multiply. There are different strategies that can be used to multiply.

Real-World EXAMPLE Multiply

1 RACING **How many laps does Charlotte need to go in the 3-mile race?**

You need to find 4 × 3.

One Way: **Skip Count**

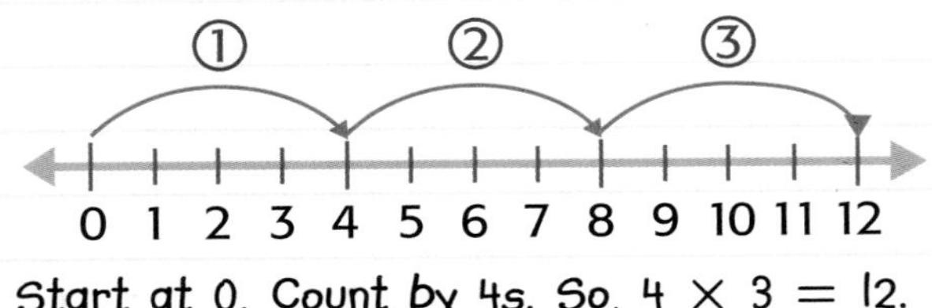

Start at 0. Count by 4s. So, 4 × 3 = 12.

Another Way: **Area Model**

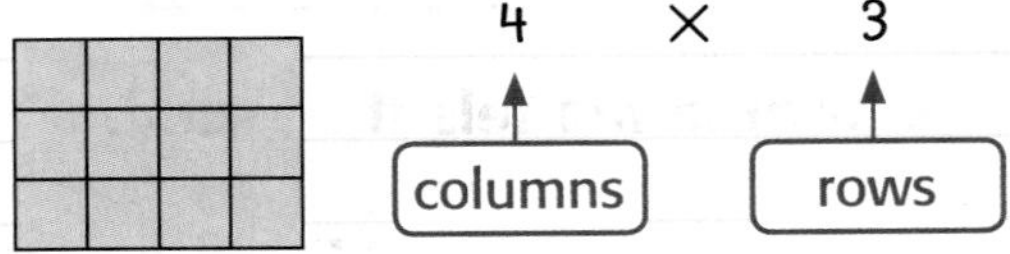

Count the squares. There is a total of 12 squares.

So, Charlotte must go 12 laps in the race.

Online Personal Tutor at tx.gr4math.com

There are different strategies to use when finding division facts.

Divide

2 **Omari has football practice 3 days a week. He drinks a sports drink during each practice. Suppose 12 sports drinks come in a package. How many weeks will a package of sports drinks last?**

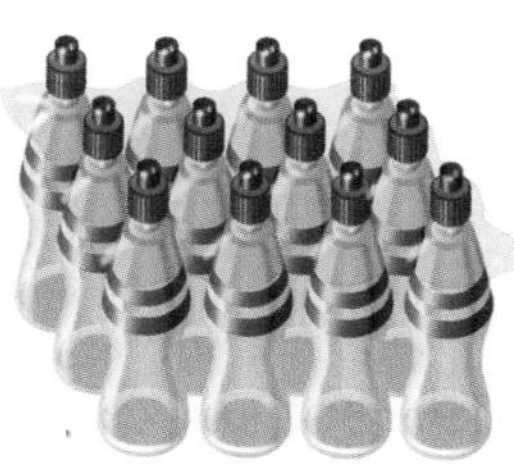

You need to find 12 ÷ 3.

Remember

You can also draw pictures, use a times table, or use models to help divide.

One Way: **Related Facts**

12 ÷ 3 = ■

THINK 3 × ■ = 12?

12 ÷ 3 = 4

Another Way: **Array**

Use an array to find 12 ÷ 3. Separate an array of 12 counters into 3 equal groups.

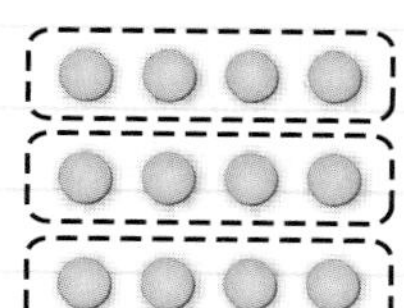

There are 4 counters in each group. So, 12 ÷ 3 = 4.

So, one package of sports drinks will last 4 weeks.

CHECK What You Know

Multiply or divide. Use arrays or area models if needed. See Examples 1 and 2 (pp. 144–145)

1. 5×3

2. 9×0

3. 1×5

4. 2×8

5. 6 ÷ 2

6. 24 ÷ 3

7. $5\overline{)10}$

8. $4\overline{)28}$

9. Nancy's dog gets 3 treats each day. There are 36 treats in a box. How many days will the treats last?

10. 

What multiplication fact can help you find 9 ÷ 3? Explain.

Practice and Problem Solving

EXTRA PRACTICE
See page R10.

Multiply or divide. Use arrays or area models if needed. See Examples 1 and 2 (pp. 144–145)

11. $\begin{array}{r} 5 \\ \times\ 6 \\ \hline \end{array}$ **12.** $\begin{array}{r} 2 \\ \times\ 3 \\ \hline \end{array}$ **13.** $\begin{array}{r} 9 \\ \times\ 2 \\ \hline \end{array}$ **14.** $\begin{array}{r} 8 \\ \times\ 4 \\ \hline \end{array}$

15. 7×1 **16.** 3×7 **17.** 9×5 **18.** 4×11

19. $8 \div 1$ **20.** $10 \div 2$ **21.** $12 \div 3$ **22.** $32 \div 4$

23. $2\overline{)24}$ **24.** $3\overline{)33}$ **25.** $4\overline{)40}$ **26.** $5\overline{)60}$

Algebra Complete each number sentence.

27. $2 \times ■ = 2$ **28.** $■ \times 5 = 35$ **29.** $33 \div ■ = 11$ **30.** $■ \div 5 = 10$

Algebra Solve.

31. If ☆ = 3, then what is ☆ + ☆ + ☆ + ☆ + ☆ + ☆ + ☆ ?

32. If ☺ + ☺ + ☺ + ☺ + ☺ + ☺ + ☺ + ☺ + ☺ = 45, then what is ☺ ?

33. There are 5 sets of paint in an art class. There are 25 students in the art class. How many students share each set of paint?

34. Fumiko has 6 packs of baseball cards. There are 5 cards in each pack. How many baseball cards does Fumiko have?

Real-World PROBLEM SOLVING

Technology The number of computers in classrooms is increasing. The results of a recent study are shown to the right.

http://
One computer for every 4 students in a classroom.

35. There are 5 computers in a fourth grade classroom. The number of students per computer matches the results of the study. How many students are in this classroom?

36. There are 24 students in Mr. Montoya's class. The number of computers per student matches the results of the study. How many computers are in Mr. Montoya's class?

Math Online Self-Check Quiz at tx.gr4math.com

H.O.T. Problems

37. OPEN ENDED Write three 2-digit numbers that are divisible by 2.

38. WHICH ONE DOESN'T BELONG? Identify the expression that does not belong with the other three. Explain.

2×4 $24 \div 3$ 3×4 $8 \div 1$

39. WRITING IN MATH Write a real-world problem that can be represented by $55 \div 5$.

TEST Practice

40. George scored 21 points during a basketball game. He scored three times as many points as Darien. Which number sentence shows a related fact that can be used to find how many points Darien scored? **(Lesson 4-2)**

A $7 + 3 = 10$

B $21 \div 7 = 3$

C $21 \div 3 = 7$

D $3 \times 7 = 21$

41. Which number is missing from the number sentence? **(Lesson 4-3)**

$$45 \div ■ = 9$$

F 2

G 3

H 4

J 5

Spiral Review

Algebra Copy and complete each number sentence. Identify the property used. **(Lesson 4-2)**

42. $8 \div ■ = 1$

43. $■ \times 5 = 5 \times 4$

44. $■ \div 12 = 0$

Algebra Copy and complete each fact family. **(Lesson 4-1)**

45. $4 \times 7 = ■$ $7 \times ■ = 28$

$28 \div ■ = 7$ $28 \div 7 = ■$

46. $8 \times 9 = ■$ $■ \times 8 = 72$

$72 \div ■ = 8$ $72 \div 9 = ■$

47. The number of children who visited a science museum is shown in the table. About how many children visited the museum during the weekend? **(Lesson 3-2)**

Museum Visitors							
Day	Mon.	Tues.	Wed.	Thur.	Fri.	Sat.	Sun.
Visitors	325	279	312	348	441	519	495

4-4 Problem-Solving Skill

MAIN IDEA I will choose an operation to solve a problem.

Targeted TEKS 4.14 The student applies Grade 4 mathematics to solve problems connected to everyday experiences and activities in and outside of school. **(C) Select or develop an appropriate problem-solving plan or strategy, . . . to solve a problem.** *Also addresses TEKS 4.14(B).*

There are 9 rows on the Twisted Zipper roller coaster. Each row has 4 seats. What operation do you need to use to find how many people can ride the roller coaster at a time?

Understand	**What facts do you know?** • There are 9 rows. • There are 4 seats per row. **What do you need to find?** • The operation you should use to find how many people can ride the roller coaster at a time.
Plan	There are groups with the same number in each group. So, multiply the number of rows by the number of seats per row.
Solve	Multiply to find the answer. $4 \times 9 = 36$ 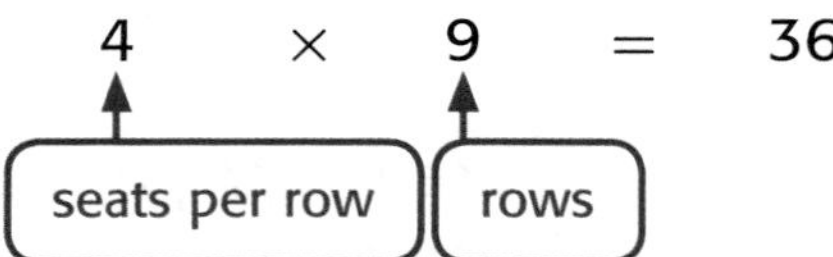 So, 36 people can ride the roller coaster at a time.
Check	Look back at the problem. Find 4×9 another way to see if you get the same answer. You can use an array. 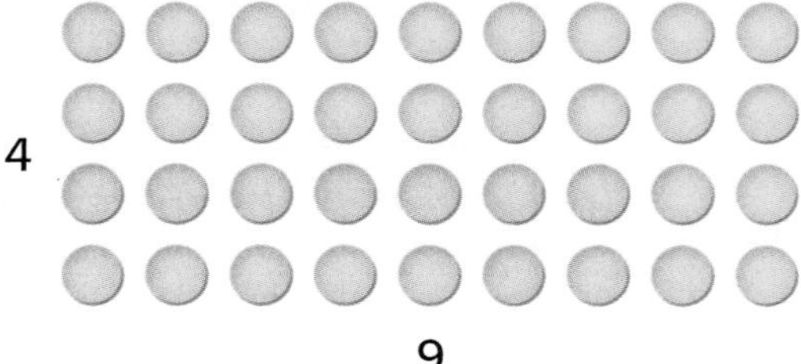 $4 \times 9 = 36$. So, the answer is correct.

ANALYZE the Skill

Refer to the problem on the previous page.

1. Explain why you multiplied 9 and 4 to find the answer.
2. What operation can be used to check the answer?
3. If 6 people can sit in each row, how many people could ride in all?
4. Refer to Exercise 3. How do you know the answer is correct?

PRACTICE the Skill

See page R10.

Tell which operation you would use to solve each problem. Then solve.

5. Fatima completed 28 problems for her math homework on Tuesday. She completed 17 more on Thursday than on Tuesday. How many problems did she complete on Thursday?
6. There are three jugglers in a circus. Each juggler can juggle 5 balls at a time. How many balls will they need for their act if they all perform at the same time?
7. A page from Dana's album is shown. Dana puts the same number of stickers on each page. She has 11 pages of stickers. How many stickers does she have in all?

8. Park Street School has 98 students who have perfect attendance. West Glenn School has 64 students. How many more students have perfect attendance at Park Street School?
9. The bar graph shows how long certain animals sleep. The koala sleeps 6 hours more than which animal?

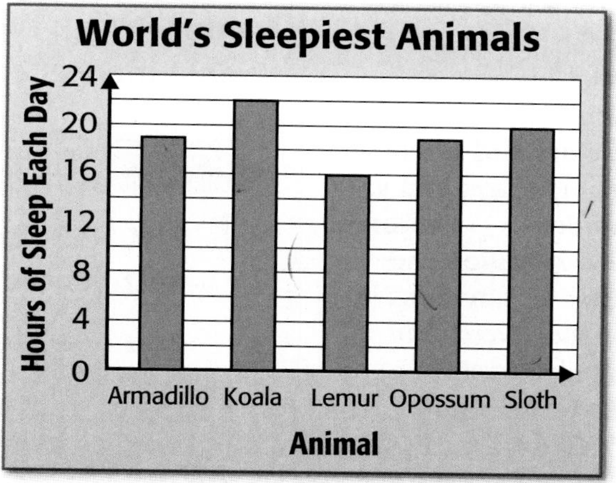

10. Use the graph above. How many more hours does a sloth sleep than a lemur?
11. Corey and his 2 friends earned $12 for doing yard work. How much money will each person get paid if they share the money evenly?
12. A lizard eats 6 crickets each day. How many crickets does it eat in one week?
13. **WRITING IN MATH** Explain how you chose an operation for Exercise 12.

4-5 Multiply and Divide Facts Through 10

MAIN IDEA

I will recall multiplication and division facts through 10.

Targeted TEKS 4.4 The student multiplies and divides to solve meaningful problems involving whole numbers. (A) **Model factors and products using arrays and area models.** (B) **Represent multiplication and division situations in picture, word, and number form.** *Also addresses TEKS 4.4(C), 4.6(A).*

Lorenzo is storing his friends' phone numbers in his cell phone. Each number has 7 digits. How many number buttons did Lorenzo press if he has 9 friends?

You can find how many number buttons Lorenzo pressed by multiplying. Two multiplication strategies that you can use are area models and related facts.

Real-World EXAMPLE Multiply

1 **PHONES Each number has 7 digits. How many number buttons did Lorenzo press if he has 9 friends?**

You need to find 7 × 9.

One Way: Area Model	Another Way: Related Fact
Make an area model.	Think of a related fact.
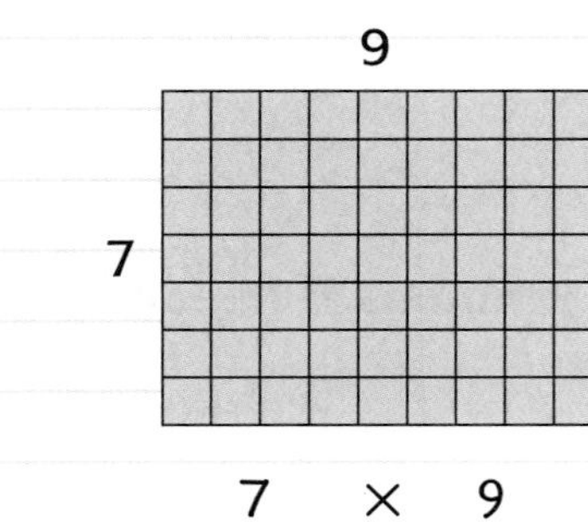	7 × 9 = ■ THINK ■ ÷ 7 = 9? 63 ÷ 7 = 9 7 × 9 = 63
There are 63 squares in all. So, 7 × 9 = 63.	

So, Lorenzo must press 63 number buttons.

Divide

2 **TELEVISION Carolyn noticed that 9 minutes of commercials play during a 30-minute television program. How many 30-minute shows did Carolyn watch during a weekend if she watched 54 minutes of commercials?**

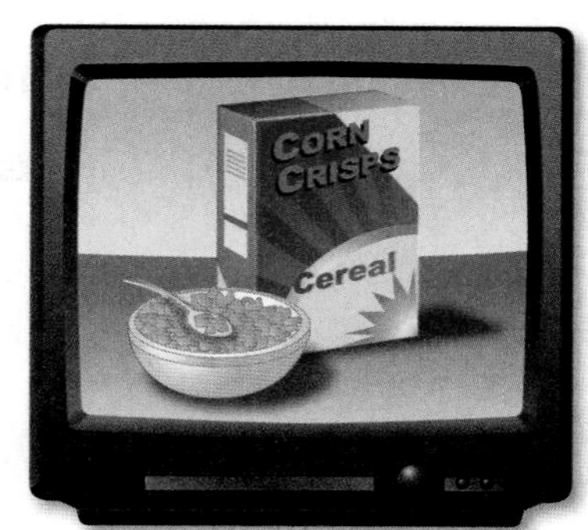

Remember

The factors in a multiplication problem become the divisor and quotient in the related division problem.

Each television program has 9 minutes of commercials. Divide 54 by 9 to find how many 30-minute shows Carolyn watched. You can use an array.

Separate an array of 54 counters into 9 equal groups.

There are 6 counters in each group.

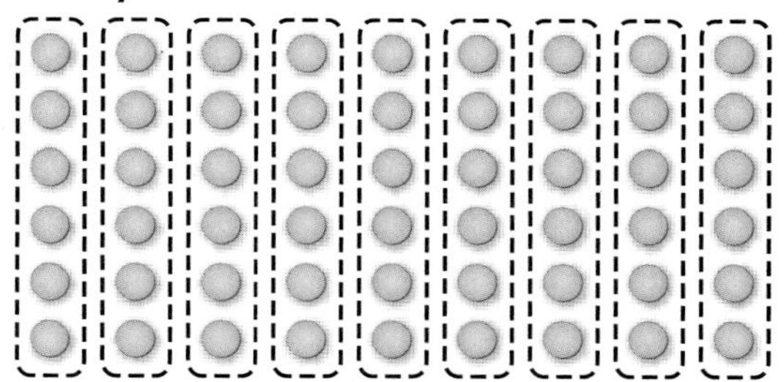

So, Carolyn watched 6 thirty-minute shows.

Check You can use a related fact to check your answer. Since $9 \times 6 = 54$, the answer is correct.

So, $54 \div 9 = 6$. ✓

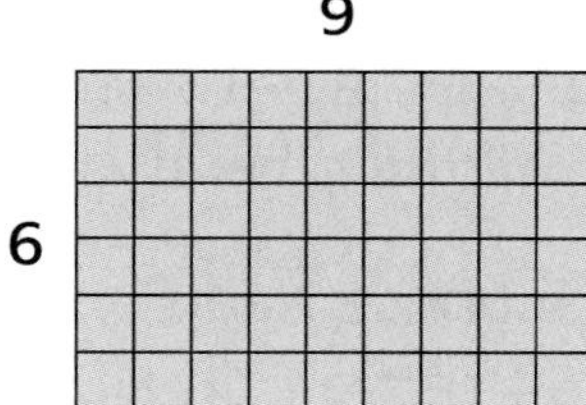

Online Personal Tutor at tx.gr4math.com

CHECK What You Know

Multiply or divide. Use arrays or area models if needed. See Examples 1 and 2 (pp. 150–151)

1. $\begin{array}{r} 9 \\ \times 8 \\ \hline \end{array}$

2. $\begin{array}{r} 10 \\ \times 7 \\ \hline \end{array}$

3. 6×4

4. 8×8

5. $49 \div 7$

6. $60 \div 6$

7. $8\overline{)48}$

8. $10\overline{)100}$

9. Linda sold 8 magazine subscriptions to make money for her school. Each magazine subscription costs $9. How much money did Linda collect?

10. Talk About It What do you notice when you multiply 10 and a number? Explain an easy method for finding a product when 10 is one of the factors.

Practice and Problem Solving

EXTRA PRACTICE See page R10.

Multiply or divide. Use arrays on area models if needed. See Examples 1 and 2 (pp. 150–151)

11. $\begin{array}{r} 6 \\ \times 6 \\ \hline \end{array}$

12. $\begin{array}{r} 10 \\ \times 8 \\ \hline \end{array}$

13. $\begin{array}{r} 7 \\ \times 7 \\ \hline \end{array}$

14. $\begin{array}{r} 6 \\ \times 7 \\ \hline \end{array}$

15. 9×4

16. 10×5

17. 6×8

18. 10×10

19. $30 \div 6$

20. $42 \div 7$

21. $72 \div 8$

22. $90 \div 10$

23. $7\overline{)70}$

24. $9\overline{)63}$

25. $8\overline{)56}$

26. $10\overline{)80}$

27. Juliana played 9 holes of miniature golf. Her total score was 54. Suppose she got the same score on each hole. What was Juliana's score per hole?

28. While on vacation, Felipe sent 42 postcards to his friends. How many friends did he send to if he sent 7 postcards to each person?

Real-World PROBLEM SOLVING

Fruit Oranges are the fruit of a citrus tree originally from southeast Asia. Oranges grow in different sizes and colors. Most oranges have 10 sections inside.

29. Nadia bought 2 oranges for each member of her family. Nadia has 4 family members. Each orange has 10 sections. How many sections will there be in all?

30. Suppose Nadia cuts 6 oranges in half. She finds that there are 54 sections in all. If there are the same number of sections in each orange, how many sections are in each orange?

H.O.T. Problems

31. OPEN ENDED Write three number sentences that each contain the number 6 and have a product greater than 40.

32. NUMBER SENSE Explain why the fact family of 7 and 49 only has two number sentences.

33. CHALLENGE The product of two numbers is 24. The sum of the numbers is 11. What are the two numbers?

34. WRITING IN MATH Is the quotient of $135 \div 9$ greater than or less than the quotient of $153 \div 9$? Explain how you know without finding the quotients.

Math Online Self-Check Quiz at tx.gr4math.com

CHAPTER 4

Mid-Chapter Check

Lessons 4-1 through 4-5

Write a fact family for each set of numbers. (Lesson 4-1)

1. 7, 28, 4

2. 3, 24, 8

Divide. Use a related multiplication fact. (Lesson 4-1)

3. 18 ÷ 2

4. 20 ÷ 5

5. 33 ÷ 3

6. 36 ÷ 4

7. TEST PRACTICE Which number sentence is in the same fact family as 63 ÷ 7 = ■? (Lesson 4-1)

A 7 + ■ = 63

B ■ − 7 = 63

C 7 × ■ = 63

D 63 × 7 = 63

Identify the property shown by each number sentence. (Lesson 4-2)

8. 15 × 0 = 0

9. 9 × 3 = 3 × 9

Algebra Copy and complete each number sentence. Identify the property used. (Lesson 4-2)

10. 5 ÷ ■ = 1

11. 7 × ■ = 0

Multiply or divide. (Lesson 4-3)

12. 20 ÷ 5

13. 4 × 3

14. Emmett brushes his teeth 3 times a day. How many times does Emmett brush his teeth in one week?

Algebra Complete each number sentence. (Lesson 4-3)

15. ■ × 5 = 45

16. 3 × ■ = 3

17. TEST PRACTICE Which number is missing from the number sentence? (Lesson 4-3)

27 ÷ ■ = 9

F 2

G 3

H 4

J 5

Tell which operation you would use to solve each problem. Then solve. (Lesson 4-4)

18. Lance walked 4 dogs on Monday. He walked twice that many on Tuesday. How many dogs did he walk on Tuesday?

19. Each row of the stadium can hold 9 people. Diana reserved 3 rows for her family. How many people in Diana's family will be at the stadium?

Multiply or divide. (Lesson 4-5)

20. 10 × 6

21. 56 ÷ 7

22. WRITING IN MATH Does the Associative Property work with division? Explain how you know.

Problem Solving in History

Did you know that pop was invented by doctors? Many people thought that the mineral water in natural springs had healing powers. In 1767, a doctor invented the first glass of carbonated water, which came to be known as "soda water."

About 80 years later, pharmacy owners and scientists began to add flavors to soda water. It was renamed "soda pop" in 1861. Soon, Americans could buy soda in bottles from grocery stores and vending machines. These drinks are still very popular.

1815
first soda fountain invented

1886
pharmacy owner sells 9 sodas per day at 5¢ each

1894
soda sells in cases of 24 bottles

Targeted TEKS 4.14 The student applies Grade 4 mathematics to solve problems connected to everyday experiences and activities in and outside of school. (A) Identify the mathematics in everyday situations.

Did You Know?

In 1929, there were more than 600 lemon-lime soda flavors to choose from!

Real-World Math

Use the information on pages 154 and 155 to solve each problem.

1. In 1886, how much money would a pharmacy owner make each day from selling soda?

2. How much money would the pharmacy owner make in a week?

3. Suppose the same pharmacy owner decreased the price of soda to 3¢ per bottle. How many sodas needed to be sold each day to make the same amount?

4. A 2-liter bottle of soda costs $3. How much will 16 liters of soda pop cost?

5. Soda was once sold in 8-ounce bottles. If you bought 96 ounces of soda, how many 8-ounce bottles did you buy? How many home-packs did you buy?

6. Suppose a customer buys $15 worth of 2-liter bottles, which cost $3 each. How many 2-liter bottles can the customer buy?

7. In 1894, a soda fountain owner sold 1 case of soda. How many different ways can you arrange the bottles in the case so that there are the same number of bottles in each row and column?

1923 soda is packaged in convenient six-bottle cartons, called "home-packs"

1977 soda is packaged in 2-liter bottles

4-6 Multiply with 11 and 12

MAIN IDEA

I will recall and apply multiplication facts for 11 and 12.

Targeted TEKS 4.4 The student multiplies and divides to solve meaningful problems involving whole numbers. (A) **Model factors and products using arrays and area models.** (B) **Represent multiplication and division situations in picture, word, and number form.** *Also addresses TEKS 4.4(C), 4.6(A).*

New Vocabulary

Distributive Property of Multiplication

GET READY to Learn

One day, a florist receives 7 orders for a dozen roses. How many roses does the florist need to make the 7 bouquets?

To multiply larger numbers, the Distributive Property of Multiplication is helpful. The **Distributive Property of Multiplication** says that you can multiply the addends of a number and then add the products.

Real-World EXAMPLE Multiply

1 How many roses does the florist need to make 7 bouquets?

There are 12 roses in one dozen. So, you need to find 7×12.

Think of 7×12 as $(7 \times 10) + (7 \times 2)$.

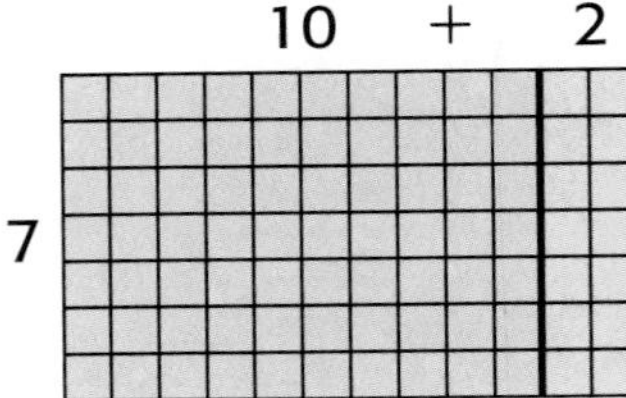

10 + 2

7 | 70 | 14

$$\begin{aligned} 7 \times 12 &= (7 \times 10) + (7 \times 2) \\ &= \quad 70 \quad + \quad 14 \\ &= \quad 84 \end{aligned}$$

So, 84 roses are needed to make 7 bouquets.

You can use a related multiplication fact to find the quotient in a division problem.

When solving a word problem, think about the facts you know and what you need to find.

Real-World EXAMPLE Divide

2 **MOVIES Shaun and 10 of his friends went to a movie. The total cost for the 11 movie tickets was \$66. How much did each ticket cost?**

You know that 11 tickets cost \$66.
Use a related multiplication fact to help you find \$66 ÷ 11.

Shaun + 10 friends

$\$66 \div 11 = \blacksquare$

THINK $11 \times \blacksquare = \$66?$
$11 \times \$6 = \$66$

$\$66 \div 11 = \$6$

So, each ticket cost \$6.

Check The area model shows that $\$6 \times 11 = \$66$.

So, $\$66 \div 11 = \$6$ is correct. ✓

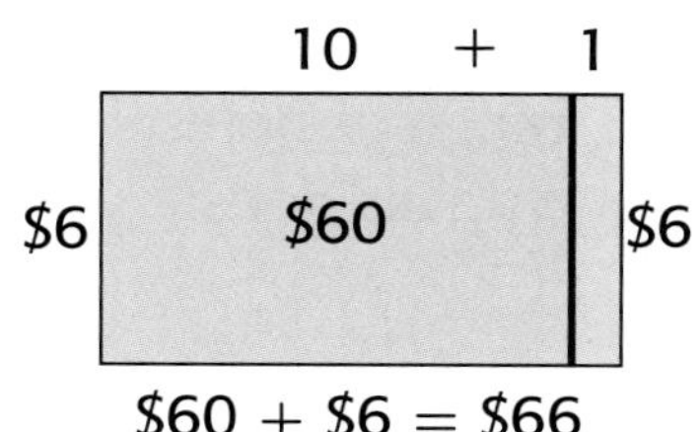

Personal Tutor at tx.gr4math.com

CHECK What You Know

Multiply or divide. Use arrays or area models if needed.

See Examples 1 and 2 (pp. 156–157)

1. $\begin{array}{r} 11 \\ \times 9 \\ \hline \end{array}$

2. $\begin{array}{r} 10 \\ \times 12 \\ \hline \end{array}$

3. 4×11

4. 6×12

5. $88 \div 11$

6. $108 \div 9$

7. $11\overline{)121}$

8. $12\overline{)132}$

9. There are 8 cartons of eggs on a grocery store shelf. Each carton contains one dozen eggs. How many eggs are on the shelf?

10. Talk About It How would you use two smaller area models to find 9×12? Draw the area models.

Practice and Problem Solving

EXTRA PRACTICE See page R11.

Multiply or divide. Use arrays or area models if needed. See Examples 1 and 2 (pp. 156–157)

11. 11×5 **12.** 12×5 **13.** 11×7 **14.** 12×8

15. 2×11 **16.** 12×7 **17.** 11×10 **18.** 12×12

19. $44 \div 11$ **20.** $72 \div 6$ **21.** $99 \div 11$ **22.** $120 \div 10$

23. $12\overline{)48}$ **24.** $11\overline{)66}$ **25.** $12\overline{)84}$ **26.** $11\overline{)110}$

Algebra Find the value of each number sentence if  **= 12 and** ☺ **= 11.**

27. ♡ × 6 **28.** 8 × ☺ **29.** 132 ÷ ☺ **30.** 144 ÷ 

Compare. Write >, <, or =.

31. 11×8 ■ 6×12 **32.** $132 \div 12$ ■ $99 \div 9$ **33.** 12×10 ■ 11×11

34. A piano has 88 keys. An octave, or range of notes, is 8 keys. How many octaves does a piano have?

35. Mrs. Hanson has 12 grandchildren. She gives each grandchild $10. How much money does she give in all?

Real-World PROBLEM SOLVING

Animals The table gives expected life spans for some animals when they live in the wild.

36. Identify the two animals that have life spans of 60 months.

37. What is the life span of a Tasmanian devil in months?

38. How many more months is a platypus expected to live than a koala?

39. A mongoose is 7 years old. How many months longer is it expected to live?

40. Find the difference between a mongoose's life span and a toucan's life span in months.

Animal Life Spans

Animal	Years
Bat	5 years
Gerbil	5 years
Koala	8 years
Mongoose	12 years
Platypus	10 years
Toucan	6 years
Tasmanian devil	8 years

H.O.T. Problems

41. OPEN ENDED Write three number sentences. Each should contain the number 12, a one-digit number as the other factor, and a product less than 60.

42. WHICH ONE DOESN'T BELONG? Identify the number sentence that does not belong with the other three. Explain.

9×11	$99 \div 9$	11×9	$88 \div 11$

43. WRITING IN MATH Write a problem about a real-world situation that involves finding the product of 6 and 12.

TEST Practice

44. In which number sentence does 8 make the number sentence true? (Lesson 4-5)

A $36 \div ■ = 4$

B $42 \div ■ = 6$

C $56 \div ■ = 7$

D $81 \div ■ = 9$

45. Look at the problem below.

$$\square = \triangle \times 12$$

If $\triangle = 10$, what is $\square$? (Lesson 4-6)

F 120

G 121

H 132

J 143

Spiral Review

Multiply or divide. Use an array or area model if needed. (Lesson 4-5)

46. 7×5

47. 8×9

48. $64 \div 8$

49. $10\overline{)90}$

Tell which operation you would use to solve each problem. Then solve. (Lesson 4-4)

50. There are 108 cotton balls in a bag. Each student needs 9 cotton balls for an art project. How many students will get the cotton balls?

51. There are 24 rocks in Hatsu's rock collection. She wants to display her rocks in an array. Identify 3 possible ways to display the rocks.

Algebra Complete each number sentence. (Lesson 4-3)

52. $3 \times ■ = 3$

53. $■ \times 4 = 28$

54. $22 \div ■ = 11$

55. $■ \div 4 = 10$

Problem-Solving Investigation

MAIN IDEA I will choose the best strategy to solve a problem.

Targeted TEKS 4.14 The student applies Grade 4 mathematics to solve problems connected to everyday experiences and activities in and outside of school. **(B) Solve problems that incorporate understanding the problem, making a plan, carrying out the plan, and evaluating the solution for reasonableness.** *Also addresses TEKS 4.14(C).*

P.S.I. TEAM +

KASA: I go to dance lessons every week. I dance for 2 hours at each lesson. I dance a total of 6 hours each week at lessons.

YOUR MISSION: Find how many dance lessons Kasa has in 4 weeks.

Understand Kasa dances for 2 hours at each lesson. She dances a total of 6 hours each week at lessons. Find how many lessons she has in 4 weeks.

Plan Divide the number of hours Kasa dances each week at lessons by the number of hours each lesson lasts. Then multiply by the number of weeks.

Solve

$$\underbrace{6}_{\text{hours per week}} \div \underbrace{2}_{\text{hours per lesson}} = \underbrace{3}_{\text{lessons per week}}$$

So, Kasa has 3 dance lessons each week.

$$\underbrace{3}_{\text{lessons per week}} \times \underbrace{4}_{\text{weeks}} = \underbrace{12}_{\text{lessons in 4 weeks}}$$

So, Kasa has 12 dance lessons in 4 weeks.

Check Look back at the problem. Check your answer by dividing the number of lessons in 4 weeks by the number of weeks. $12 \div 4 = 3$. Then, multiply the number of hours per lesson by the number of lessons each week. $2 \times 3 = 6$. So, the answer is correct.

Mixed Problem Solving

See page R11.

Use the *make a table* strategy or choose an operation to solve each problem.

PROBLEM-SOLVING STRATEGIES
- Make a table.
- Choose an operation

1. Mr. and Mrs. Lopez are putting square tiles on the floor in their bathroom. They can fit 6 rows of 4 tiles in the bathroom. How many tiles do they need to buy?

2. A teacher gives quizzes that are each worth 15 points. If the teacher gives 5 quizzes, how many points are all of the quizzes worth?

3. Marisol has 7 books from the library. She gets 5 new books and returns 3 books. How many library books does she have now?

4. Raheem is playing a game at a carnival. He needs to earn 400 points to win a large stuffed animal. The dartboard below shows 4 out of the 5 darts he has thrown. Is it possible for him to win the large stuffed animal? If so, how many points does he still need?

5. A scout troop went hiking on the trail shown below. They hiked 4 miles an hour. How long did they hike?

6. Wesley needs to finish reading a book before Monday. He started reading the 44-page book on Thursday. How many pages will he need to read each day if he reads an equal number of pages each day?

7. Twenty students want to raise money for new playground equipment. They need $2,200. Copy and complete the table to find out how much money each student needs to raise.

New Playground Equipment	
Money per Student	Total Raised
$90	$1,800
$95	$1,900
$100	$2,000
$105	■
■	■

8. **WRITING IN MATH** Tell which problem-solving strategy you used to solve Exercise 7. Explain how you used this strategy when solving Exercise 7.

4-8 Multiply Three Numbers

MAIN IDEA

I will multiply 3 factors.

Targeted TEKS 4.4 The student multiplies and divides to solve meaningful problems involving whole numbers.
(D) **Use multiplication to solve problems (no more than two digits times two digits without technology).**

GET READY to Learn

There are 2 baseball cards in each pack. There are 6 packs in each box. If Raul buys 3 boxes for his collection, how many cards will he have?

In Lesson 2-1, you learned to use the Associative Property of Addition to add more than two numbers. You can use the Associative Property of Multiplication to multiply more than two numbers.

Remember

To review the Associative Property of Multiplication, see Lesson 4-2 (p. 140).

Real-World EXAMPLE Associative Property

1 TRADING CARDS **How many baseball cards will Raul have?**

You need to find $2 \times 6 \times 3$. There are two ways to group the numbers.

One Way	Another Way
Multiply 2×6 first.	Multiply 6×3 first.
$2 \times 6 \times 3$	$2 \times 6 \times 3$
$(2 \times 6) \times 3$	$2 \times (6 \times 3)$
12×3	2×18
36	36

So, Raul will have 36 baseball cards.

Online Personal Tutor at tx.gr4math.com

CHECK What You Know

Multiply. See Example 1 (p. 162)

1. $3 \times 1 \times 5$ **2.** $2 \times 2 \times 3$ **3.** $3 \times 5 \times 3$

4. $6 \times 2 \times 3$ **5.** $4 \times 2 \times 7$ **6.** $3 \times 4 \times 8$

7. Art supply paint comes in a box that contains 3 sets of 8 bottles of paint. An art teacher ordered 2 boxes. How many bottles of paint were ordered?

8. Talk About It Identify the order that makes it easiest to multiply the factors in the expression $9 \times 6 \times 2$. Explain.

Practice and Problem Solving

EXTRA PRACTICE See page R11.

Multiply. See Example 1 (p. 162)

9. $6 \times 1 \times 5$ **10.** $2 \times 2 \times 7$ **11.** $5 \times 7 \times 2$

12. $10 \times 2 \times 5$ **13.** $3 \times 9 \times 3$ **14.** $2 \times 6 \times 7$

15. $4 \times 3 \times 7$ **16.** $2 \times 9 \times 4$ **17.** $5 \times 1 \times 12$

Algebra Copy and complete each number sentence.

18. $4 \times ■ \times 1 = 12$ **19.** $2 \times 6 \times ■ = 60$ **20.** $■ \times 3 \times 4 = 24$

Algebra Compare. Write >, <, or =.

21. $4 \times 2 \times 9$ ● $7 \times 4 \times 2$ **22.** $5 \times 2 \times 8$ ● $6 \times 2 \times 6$

Algebra Find the value of each number sentence if ☼ = 2, ☺ = 3, and ☆ = 4.

23. $5 \times 1 \times$ ☆ **24.** $6 \times$ ☼ $\times 9$ **25.** ☺ $\times 12 \times$ ☆ **26.** $10 \times$ ☼ $\times$ ☆

27. Gabriel is training for a race. He jogs 2 miles a day. He jogs this distance 4 days a week. How many miles will he jog in 6 weeks?

28. Measurement Blanca bikes 2 miles to her grandfather's house and 2 miles back to her house 5 times each month. How many miles does she bike?

29. Measurement For one week, 4 inches of snow fell every morning, and 3 inches fell every night. Was this enough snow to cover a bench that is 4 feet tall? Explain.

30. Helen borrowed 12 books from the library. The books are due in 4 weeks. If she reads 2 books 2 days a week, will she have enough time to read all of the books? Explain.

Real-World PROBLEM SOLVING

Animals Did you know that pigs are very smart animals? They are considered to be smarter than dogs. More information about farm animals is shown at the right.

DOWN ON THE FARM

Most pigs have an average of 8 piglets per litter.

Most chickens lay an average of 3 eggs per week.

31. There are 4 chickens on a farm. How many eggs will they lay in 4 weeks?

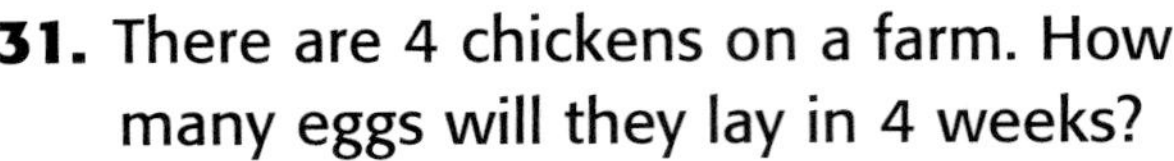

32. Use the number sentence $2 \times 3 \times$ ■ $= 30$ to find how many weeks it will take 2 chickens to lay 30 eggs.

33. On a farm there are 4 pigs that have had 2 litters of piglets. How many piglets have the sows had?

34. How many weeks would it take 2 chickens to have more eggs than the number of piglets that were mentioned in Exercise 33?

H.O.T. Problems

35. **OPEN ENDED** Copy and complete $2 \times 11 \times$ ■ $> 4 \times 9 \times 3$ to make a true sentence.

36. **FIND THE ERROR** Jamil and Denise are finding $4 \times$ ■ $\times 7 = 56$. Who is correct? Explain.

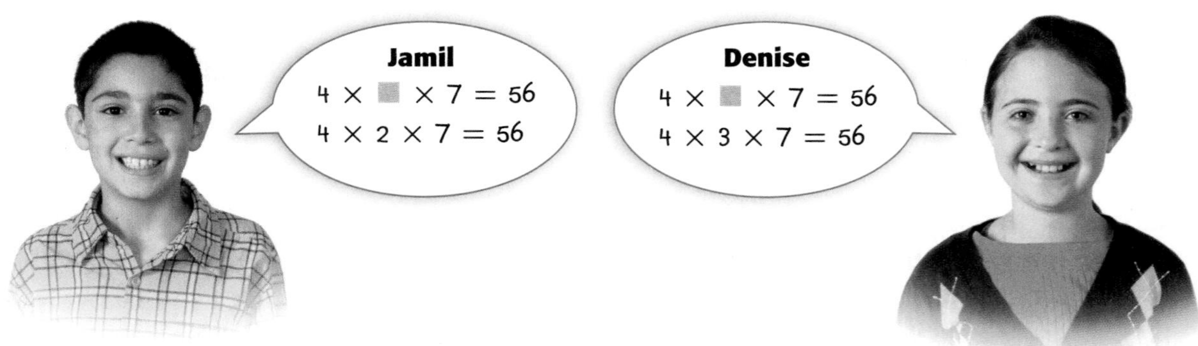

37. **CHALLENGE** Identify four factors that result in a product of 24.

38. **WRITING IN ► MATH** Manuel has 24 marbles in his collection. He wants to store his marbles in 2 cases. If the marbles are displayed in even rows and columns, what arrays could the marbles be displayed in?

Multiplication Bingo

Multiplication Facts

Get Ready!

Players: 3 or more players

You will need: 6 index cards

Get Set!

Make a game board like the one shown. Label each square with a number that can be found on a multiplication table. Cut each index card in half, and label each card with a number from 1 to 12.

6	27	12	9
36	18	10	45
8	54	32	15
72	144	16	81

Go!

- Shuffle the cards. Place them face-down in a stack on the table.
- Player 1 chooses a card.
- Players look at the game board to find a number that results from multiplying the number on the card times any other number. Color 1 square if it contains a product of the number.
- Player 2 chooses a card.
- Play continues the same way.
- The first player that colors 4 squares in a row, column, or diagonally wins.

4-9 Factors and Multiples

MAIN IDEA

I will find factors and multiples of whole numbers.

Targeted TEKS 4.4 The student multiplies and divides to solve meaningful problems involving whole numbers.
(B) **Represent multiplication and division situations in picture, word, and number form.**
(C) **Recall and apply multiplication facts 12×12.** *Also addresses TEKS 4.6(A).*

New Vocabulary

factor
multiple

GET READY to Learn

Mrs. Navarro is arranging desks in her classroom. There are 24 desks. How many ways can she arrange the desks so that the number of desks in each row is the same?

Two or more numbers that are multiplied together to form a product are called **factors**. To find the different arrangements of desks, break down or decompose 24 into its factors.

Real-World EXAMPLE Identify Factors

1. **SCHOOL How many ways can Mrs. Navarro arrange the desks in her classroom?**

Think of number pairs that result in a product of 24.

$1 \times 24 = 24$

$2 \times 12 = 24$

$3 \times 8 = 24$

THINK There are 4 more arrays:
24×1 8×3
12×2 6×4

$4 \times 6 = 24$

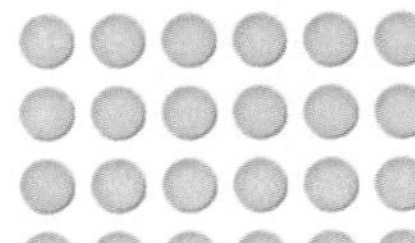

The factors of 24 are 1, 2, 3, 4, 6, 8, 12, and 24. So, the desks can be arranged in eight ways.

A **multiple** of a number is the product of that number and any whole number. For example, 15 is a multiple of 5 because it is composed or made up of 3 groups of 5.

EXAMPLE Identify Multiples

2 **Identify the first five multiples of 7.**

On a multiplication table, look across the row for 7, or down the column for 7. All of the numbers listed in the row or the column are multiples of 7.

> **Remember**
> The first multiple of a number is always zero.

×	0	1	2	3	4	5	6	7	8	9	10	11	12
0	0	0	0	0	0	0	0	0	0	0	0	0	0
1	0	1	2	3	4	5	6	7	8	9	10	11	12
2	0	2	4	6	8	10	12	14	16	18	20	22	24
3	0	3	6	9	12	15	18	21	24	27	30	33	36
4	0	4	8	12	16	20	24	28	32	36	40	44	48
5	0	5	10	15	20	25	30	35	40	45	50	55	60
6	0	6	12	18	24	30	36	42	48	54	60	66	72
7	0	7	14	21	28	35	42	49	56	63	70	77	84
8	0	8	16	24	32	40	48	56	64	72	80	88	96
9	0	9	18	27	36	45	54	63	72	81	90	99	108
10	0	10	20	30	40	50	60	70	80	90	100	110	120
11	0	11	22	33	44	55	66	77	88	99	110	121	132
12	0	12	24	36	48	60	72	84	96	108	120	132	144

So, the first five multiples of 7 are 0, 7, 14, 21, and 28.

Online **Personal Tutor at** tx.gr4math.com

CHECK What You Know

Find all of the factors of each number. See Example 1 (p. 166)

1. 6 **2.** 10 **3.** 12 **4.** 36

Identify the first five multiples for each number. See Example 2 (p. 167)

5. 2 **6.** 4 **7.** 9 **8.** 12

9. Elena is baking muffins in the pan shown at the right. How many muffins will Elena make if she uses 1, 2, 3, or 4 pans?

10. 

Explain the relationship between factors and multiples.

Practice and Problem Solving

EXTRA PRACTICE
See page R12.

Find all of the factors of each number. See Example 1 (p. 166)

11. 4
12. 7
13. 14
14. 20
15. 28
16. 30
17. 35
18. 42

Identify the first five multiples for each number. See Example 2 (p. 167)

19. 1
20. 3
21. 5
22. 6
23. 7
24. 8
25. 9
26. 11

Identify all of the factors that are related to each array.

27. 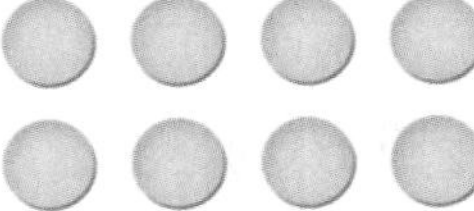

28. 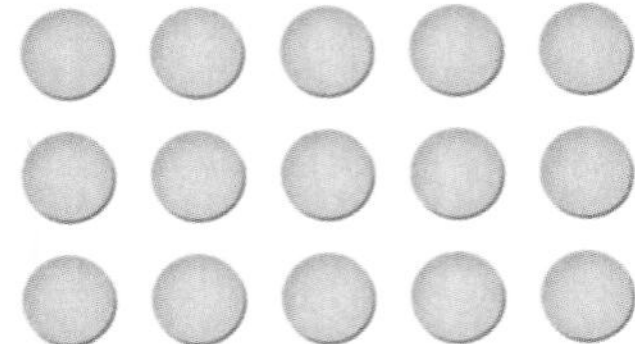

29. A chameleon eats 6 crickets a day. How many crickets does a chameleon eat in one week? in 8, 9, 10, and 11 days?

30. Pedro walks his dog 3 times a day. How many times does Pedro walk his dog in one week? in 10, 11, or 12 days?

31. There are 50 stars on the American flag. One way the stars can be arranged is a 5×10 array. Identify two more ways to arrange the stars.

32. There are 24 cans of soup on a shelf. One way the cans can be displayed is in a 4×6 array. Identify two more ways the cans can be displayed.

Real-World PROBLEM SOLVING

Science A certain comet can be seen every 6 years.

33. How old is a person who has seen the comet 4, 5, 6, or 7 times?

34. Warren is 10 years old. Warren's dad is 38 years old, and his mom is 36 years old. What is the total of the most number of times Warren and his parents could have seen the comet?

35. Suppose the comet can be seen every 4 years. Would your answer to Exercise 34 change? Explain.

H.O.T. Problems

36. **OPEN ENDED** List three numbers that have 2 and 3 as factors.

37. **CHALLENGE** Identify the number less than 144 with the most factors.

38. **WRITING IN ▸MATH** A fourth grade class is having a class picture taken for the yearbook. There are 24 students in the class. Explain why standing in 1 row of 24 is not the best way for the students to be arranged for the picture.

TEST Practice

39. In which number sentence does 9 make the equation true? (Lesson 4-8)

A $3 \times \blacksquare \times 4 = 108$

B $3 \times \blacksquare \times 7 = 108$

C $3 \times \blacksquare \times 9 = 108$

D $4 \times \blacksquare \times 7 = 108$

40. Which number has more than six factors? (Lesson 4-9)

F 6

G 12

H 15

J 36

Spiral Review

Multiply. (Lesson 4-8)

41. $2 \times 7 \times 3$

42. $3 \times 5 \times 4$

43. $11 \times 5 \times 2$

For Exercises 44 and 45, use the picture at the right. Identify the operation you used. (Lesson 4-7)

44. There are 5 people who want to play the game shown. How many marbles do they need in all?

45. There are 30 marbles on the game board at the start of a game. How many players are there?

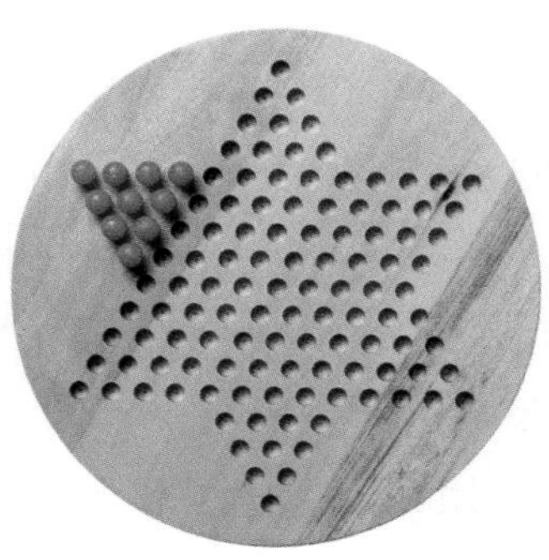

Algebra Find the value of each if ☆ = 11 and ☼ = 12. (Lesson 4-6)

46. ☆ × 6

47. 132 ÷ ☼

48. ☼ × ☆

CHAPTER 4

Study Guide and Review

Be sure the following Key Vocabulary words and Key Concepts are written in your Foldable.

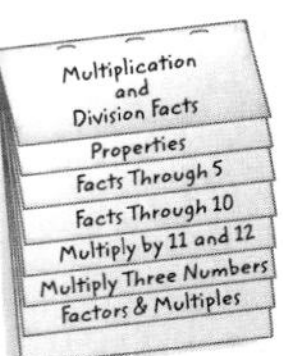

BIG Ideas

Relate Multiplication and Division (p. 137)

- A **fact family** is a set of four related multiplication and division facts.

$3 \times 4 = 12 \quad 4 \times 3 = 12$

$12 \div 4 = 3 \quad 12 \div 3 = 4$

Multiplication Properties (pp. 140–141)

$3 \times 4 = 4 \times 3$ Commutative Property

$3 \times 0 = 0$ Zero Property

$3 \times 1 = 3$ Identity Property

$3 \times (4 \times 2) = (3 \times 4) \times 2$ Associative Property

Factors and Multiples (pp. 166–167)

- Two or more numbers that are multiplied together to form a product are called **factors**.

factors of 6: 1, 2, 3, and 6

- A **multiple** of a number is the product of that number and any whole number.

multiples of 7: 0, 7, 14, 21, ...

Key Vocabulary

Associative Property of Multiplication (p. 140)
Commutative Property of Multiplication (p. 140)
Distributive Property of Multiplication (p. 156)
factor (p. 166)
multiple (p. 167)

Vocabulary Check

Complete each sentence with the correct vocabulary word.

1. Two or more numbers that are multiplied together to form a product are called ___?___ .

2. The ___?___ says that the order of the factors does not change the product when multiplying.

3. The ___?___ says that you can multiply the addends of a sum by a number and then add the products.

4. A(n) ___?___ of a number is the product of that number and any whole number.

Lesson-by-Lesson Review

4-1 Relate Multiplication and Division (pp. 137–139)

Example 1
Write a fact family for the array.

$2 \times 4 = 8$
$4 \times 2 = 8$
$8 \div 4 = 2$
$8 \div 2 = 4$

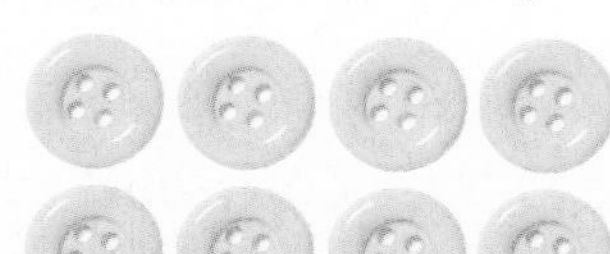

Example 2
Write a fact family for the numbers 3, 5, and 15.

$3 \times 5 = 15$ $\quad 5 \times 3 = 15$

$15 \div 3 = 5$ $\quad 15 \div 5 = 3$

Example 3
Stefanie and Eva want to share the shells that they collected on their trip to the beach. They have 18 shells in all. Use related facts and draw an array that will help them decide how they can divide their shells evenly.

$2 \times 9 = 18$

$9 \times 2 = 18$

$18 \div 2 = 9$

$18 \div 9 = 2$

So, each girl will have 9 shells.

Write a fact family for each array or set of numbers.

5. 3, 7, 21 **6.** 9, 5, 45

7.

8.

Solve. Use a related multiplication or division fact.

9. $4 \times 3 = ■$ **10.** $5 \times 6 = ■$

11. $36 \div 4 = ■$ **12.** $40 \div 8 = ■$

13. Lonzo bought four packs of trading cards. If there are eight cards in each pack, how many trading cards did Lonzo buy?

14. Andrea needs to read a book with 25 chapters. How many chapters will she need to read each day to finish the book in 5 days?

CHAPTER 4

Study Guide and Review

4-2 Properties of Multiplication and Division (pp. 140–143)

Example 4
Identify the property shown by $9 \times 1 = 9$.

A number is multiplied by 1, and the product is the number. This is the Identity Property of Multiplication.

Example 5
Complete $(5 \times 2) \times 3 = 5 \times (\blacksquare \times 3)$. Identify the property used.

$(5 \times 2) \times 3 = 5 \times (2 \times 3)$

The way in which the factors are grouped does not change the product.

This is the Associative Property of Multiplication.

Identify the property shown by each number sentence.

15. $12 \div 12 = 1$ **16.** $3 \times 6 = 6 \times 3$

Algebra Copy and complete each number sentence. Identify the property used.

17. $5 \div \blacksquare = 1$ **18.** $\blacksquare \div 14 = 0$

19. David has soccer practice for 3 hours each night. Sofia has softball practice for 2 hours each night. Will David and Sofia practice for the same amount of time in 5 nights? Use a multiplication property to justify your answer.

4-3 Multiply and Divide Facts Through 5 (pp. 144–147)

Example 6
Find 4×5.

You can use an area model to find 4×5.

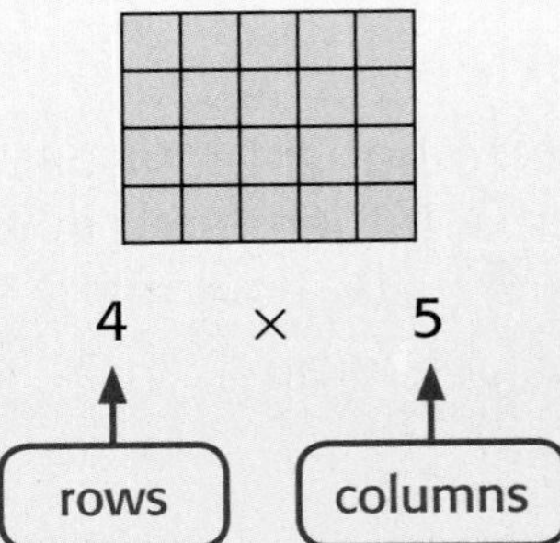

Count the squares. There is a total of 20 squares.

Multiply or divide.

20. 4×4 **21.** 5×3

22. $6 \div 3$ **23.** $9\overline{)18}$

Algebra Complete each number sentence.

24. $\blacksquare \times 3 = 6$ **25.** $4 \times \blacksquare = 32$

26. $56 \div \blacksquare = 8$ **27.** $44 \div \blacksquare = 11$

28. Algebra If ☆ = 2, then what is ☆ + ☆ + ☆ + ☆ + ☆?

4-4 Problem-Solving Skill: Choose an Operation (pp. 148–149)

Example 7
There are 9 rows on the bleachers. Each row holds 10 people. How many people can sit in the bleachers at once?

Understand

What facts do you know?

- There are 9 rows.
- There are 10 seats per row.

What do you need to find?

- The number of people that can sit in the bleachers at a time.

Plan There are groups with the same number in each group. So, multiply the number of rows by the number of seats per row.

Solve Multiply to find the answer.

$9 \times 10 = 90$

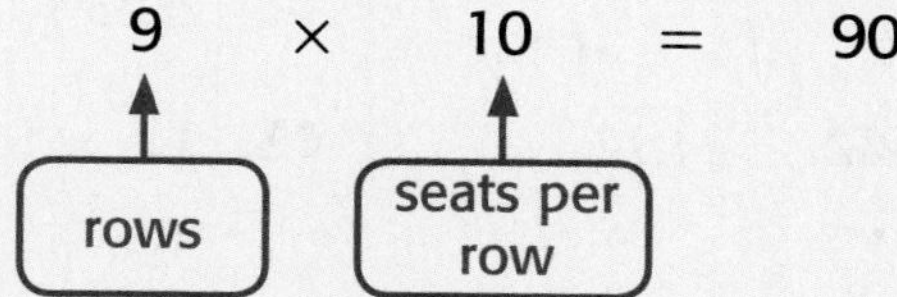

So, 90 people can sit on the bleachers at a time.

Check Look back at the problem. Use division to check the answer. Since $90 \div 10 = 9$, the answer is correct.

Tell which operation you would use to solve each problem. Then solve.

29. Loretta spent $80 on 10 tickets for a concert. Two tickets were for the front row. How many tickets did she buy for each of the other sections?

Smooth Jazz Concert	
Front row seats	$15
Center section	$10
Side sections	$5

30. Moses's vacation is 2 weeks long. Nina's vacation is 3 weeks longer than Moses's. How long is Nina's vacation?

31. Gavin purchased one bus ticket. He paid with a $10 bill. How much change did he get back?

Bus Tickets
1 for $4.50
2 for $10
3 for $15

32. There are 5 members in the band who play the drums. Three times as many members play the flute. How many band members play the flute?

33. West Elementary has 5 fourth grade classes. Each class made 12 posters. If 10 posters were destroyed before they could be put up on the wall, how many posters are there in all on the wall?

Study Guide and Review

4-5 Multiply and Divide Facts Through 10 (pp. 150–152)

Example 8
Find 4 × 7.

Make an area model to represent 4 × 7.

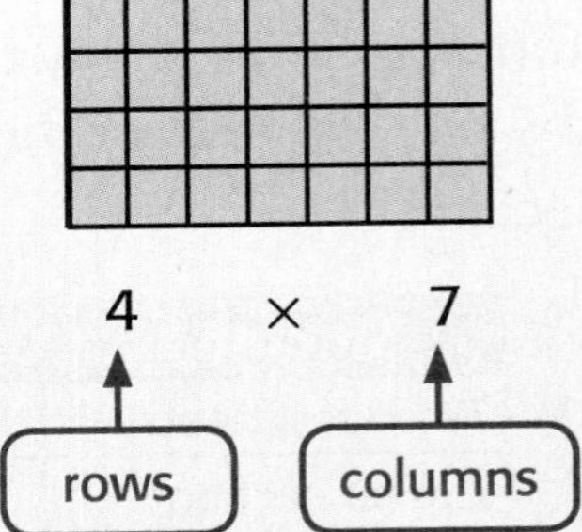

There are 28 squares in all.

So, 4 × 7 = 28.

Multiply or divide.

34. 4 × 8

35. 9 × 6

36. 10 ÷ 2

37. 90 ÷ 9

38. Spencer sold 9 magazine subscriptions to make money for his club. Each magazine subscription costs $7. How much money did Spencer collect?

39. Mr. Dunn has 6 rows of desks in his classroom. There are 5 desks in each row. How many desks are in Mr. Dunn's classroom?

4-6 Multiply with 11 and 12 (pp. 156–159)

Example 9
Marina has scored 9 points on each of 11 quizzes. How many points has she scored in all?

Think of 9 × 11 as (9 × 10) + (9 × 1).

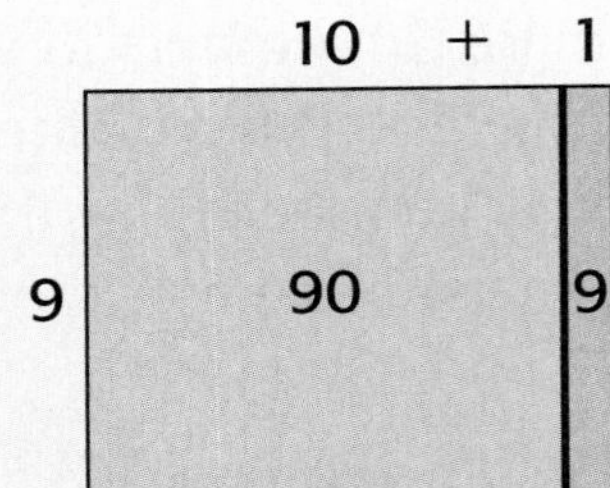

$$
\begin{aligned}
9 \times 11 &= (9 \times 10) + (9 \times 1) \\
&= 90 + 9 \\
&= 99
\end{aligned}
$$

So, Marina has scored 99 points.

Multiply or divide.

40. 72 ÷ 8

41. $\begin{array}{r} 12 \\ \times\ 6 \\ \hline \end{array}$

42. $12\overline{)84}$

43. 12 × 9

Compare. Write >, <, or =.

44. 108 ÷ 12 ■ 88 ÷ 8

45. 12 × 6 ■ 8 × 10

46. 36 ÷ 3 ■ 6 × 2

47. Kirsten's parents go to the grocery store once a week. How many times do they go to the grocery store in one year?

4-7 Problem-Solving Investigation: Choose a Strategy (pp. 160–161)

Example 10
Carlo wants to buy a frozen yogurt. The flavors of yogurt are vanilla, chocolate, or strawberry. The yogurt comes in a dish or on a cone. How many choices does he have?

Understand

What facts do you know?

- The yogurt flavors are vanilla, chocolate, and strawberry.
- Yogurt comes in a dish or on a cone.

What do you need to find?

- How many yogurt choices Carlo has.

Plan Make a table.

Solve

Flavor	Cone	Dish
Vanilla	X	X
Chocolate	X	X
Strawberry	X	X

Carlo has 6 choices for his yogurt.

Check There are 3 flavors and two choices for each flavor. So, Carlo has 6 choices. The answer is correct

Use the *make a table* strategy or choose an operation to solve each problem.

48. Amy wants to buy two dolls. Each doll costs $16. What is the total cost of the dolls?

49. Mr. Sullivan bought pizza for the reading club. Each pizza had 10 slices. How many pizzas did he buy if there were 120 slices?

50. Twyla worked five days in one week. She worked 40 hours during that week. She worked the same number of hours each day. How many hours did she work each day?

51. Conchita has 25 math problems for homework each day. Copy and complete the table to find how many problems she completes in five days.

Day	Problems Completed
1	25
2	50
3	75
4	■
5	■

52. Bradley has 3 tap dancing lessons each week. Each lesson is 2 hours long. How many hours of lessons will Bradley have completed in 4 weeks?

4-8 Multiply Three Numbers (pp. 162–165)

Example 11
Find 3 × 5 × 4.

There are two ways to group the numbers.

One Way	Another Way
Multiply 3 × 5 first.	Multiply 5 × 4 first.
3 × 5 × 4	3 × 5 × 4
(3 × 5) × 4	3 × (5 × 4)
15 × 4	3 × 20
60	60

So, 3 × 5 × 4 = 60.

Multiply.

53. 6 × 2 × 3
54. 2 × 4 × 9
55. 2 × 8 × 4
56. 5 × 1 × 11

Algebra Copy and complete each number sentence.

57. ■ × 7 × 3 = 42

58. 4 × ■ × 3 = 108

59. Jason goes to the park for 2 hours a day, 5 days a week. How many hours will he spend in the park in four weeks?

4-9 Factors and Multiples (pp. 166–169)

Example 12
Find all of the factors of 6.

Think of number pairs that result in a product of 6.

1 × 6

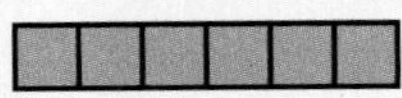

2 × 3

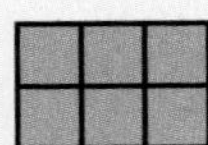

So, the factors of 6 are 1, 2, 3, and 6.

Example 13
Identify the first five multiples of 4.

Multiples of 4: 0, 4, 8, 12, 16, 20, 24, ...

The first five multiples of 4 are 0, 4, 8, 12, and 16.

Find all of the factors of each number.

60. 8
61. 12
62. 16
63. 28

Identify the first five multiples for each number.

64. 3
65. 5
66. 8
67. 10

68. Lora is arranging her 18 snow globes on a shelf. Write the different ways she can arrange the snow globes.

69. Glenn reads 11 pages in his book each day. How many pages will he read in one week? in 9, 10, or 11 days?

Chapter 4 Chapter Test

For Exercises 1–3, tell whether each statement is *true* or *false*.

1. Two or more numbers that are multiplied together to form a product are called factors.
2. Factors are numbers that do not divide into a whole number evenly.
3. A multiple of a number is the product of that number and any whole number.

Algebra Compare. Write >, <, or =.

4. $2 \times 7 \times 3$ ■ $8 \times 3 \times 4$
5. $5 \times 3 \times 9$ ■ $4 \times 2 \times 5$
6. There are 5 boxes of paints on an art store shelf. Each box contains one dozen colors. How many paint colors are on the shelf?

Find all of the factors of each number.

7.  2

8. 36

9. **TEST PRACTICE** Which number will make the number sentence true?

$$4 \times ■ \times 5 = 180$$

A 7
B 8
C 9
D 10

10. Write a fact family for the array.

Algebra Find the value of each number sentence if ♥ = 5 and ☺ = 10.

11. ♥ $\times 8$

12. ☺ $\div 5$

Copy and complete each number sentence. Identify each property shown.

13. ■ $\times 7 = 7 \times 4$

14. ■ $\div 12 = 0$

15. Identify all of the factors related to the array.

Identify the first five multiples for each number.

16. 7

17. 9

Multiply.

18. $6 \times 3 \times 12$

19. $4 \times 2 \times 7$

Divide.

20. $33 \div 11$

21. $36 \div 6$

22. **TEST PRACTICE** Which number has more than six factors?

F 6
G 12
H 15
J 64

23. **WRITING IN MATH** Explain how multiplication and division are related.

CHAPTER 4

Texas Test Practice

Cumulative, Chapters 1–4

Emily has 28 books. She wants to arrange an equal number on 4 shelves of a bookcase. How many books will she place on each shelf?

A 4 **C** 6

B 5 **D** 7

TEST-TAKING TIP

Be sure to read all the answer choices before choosing your answer.

Read the Test Question

You need to find an equal number of books that will fit on 4 shelves.

Solve the Test Question

Divide to solve the problem.
Think about a related multiplication fact.

$4 \times 7 = 28$ and $7 \times 4 = 28$

So, $28 \div 4 = 7$.

The answer is D.

Online **Personal Tutor at** tx.gr4math.com

Choose the best answer.

1. **Mr. Cook has 32 students in his homeroom. He makes groups with 8 students in each group. How many groups are there?**

   A 4 **C** 6

   B 5 **D** 7

2. **Kyra bought 72 eggs at the grocery store for the school breakfast. The eggs come in cartons of 12. How many cartons of eggs did Kyra buy?**

   F 4 **H** 6

   G 5 **J** 7

Get Ready for the Texas Test
For test-taking strategies and more practice, see pages TX1–TX21.

3. A drawer has 6 white, 2 blue, and 4 brown socks. If a sock is picked at random, what is the probability it will be white?

A 3 out of 4 **C** 6 out of 10

B 4 out of 8 **D** 6 out of 12

---

4. Which pair of numbers correctly completes this equation?

○ × 10 = □

F (5) and [50]

G (6) and [9]

H (2) and [200] 179

J (3) and [15]

---

5. Neil buys a sandwich for $3. He hands the cashier $20. How much change should he receive?

A $15 **C** $17

B $16 **D** $17.50

---

6. In which number sentence does 8 make the equation true?

F 28 ÷ ■ = 4 **H** 45 ÷ ■ = 5

G 32 ÷ ■ = 8 **J** 56 ÷ ■ = 7

---

7. GRIDDABLE Which number makes this equation true?

49 ÷ ■ = 7

---

8. Ajay wants to use one color pencil and one color crayon to make a drawing.

Pencil Colors	Crayon Colors
red	brown
blue	black
green	

Which of the following is possible if Ajay chooses one color pencil and one color crayon?

A red and green

B blue and purple

C green and brown

D blue and green

---

9. Which number is 10,000 less than 78,305?

F 68,305

G 77,305

H 78,205

J 88,305

Describe Algebraic Patterns

BIG Idea What are expressions and equations?

An **expression** is a statement with numbers and/or symbols, and at least one operation. An **equation** is a sentence that contains an equals sign, showing that two expressions are equal.

Example A tiger can live ■ years in the wild and 5 years longer than that in a zoo. The equation below can be used to find how long a tiger can live in the wild if it lives 20 years in a zoo.

■	+	5	=	20
years in wild				years in zoo

What will I learn in this chapter?

- Find patterns in sets of numbers.
- Write and find the value of expressions.
- Write and solve equations.
- Find and use a rule to write an equation.
- Identify extra and missing information.

Key Vocabulary

expression
parentheses
equation
pattern

Student Study Tools at tx.gr4math.com

FOLDABLES™
Study Organizer

Make this Foldable to help you organize information about using addition and subtraction in algebra. Begin with a piece of 11″ × 17″ paper.

1 **Fold** lengthwise 3″ from the bottom.

2 **Fold** the paper in half.

3 **Open** and staple on either side to form pockets.

4 **Label** as shown. Take notes on index cards.

ARE YOU READY for Chapter 5?

You have two ways to check prerequisite skills for this chapter.

Option 2

Math Online Take the Chapter Readiness Quiz at tx.gr4math.com.

Option 1

Complete the Quick Check below.

QUICK Check

Find the missing number. (Prior grade)

1. 8 + ■ = 11
2. ■ + 5 = 9
3. 6 + ■ = 15
4. 13 − ■ = 7
5. ■ − 4 = 8
6. 18 − ■ = 16
7. Use the number sentence 12 + 15 + ■ = 36 to find how many books Tony read in August.
8. What property is illustrated by 6 + 5 = 5 + 6?

Summer Reading Club	
Month	**Number of Books Read**
June	12
July	15
August	■

Find the value of each expression. (Prior grade)

9. 8 + 1 + 6
10. 7 + 2 − 3
11. 2 + 10 − 6
12. 11 + 6 − 6
13. 12 − 3 + 4
14. 16 + 4 − 10

Identify each pattern. Then find the next number in the pattern. (Prior grade)

15. 3, 6, 9, 12, 15
16. 7, 12, 17, 22, 27
17. 23, 19, 15, 11, 7
18. Each baseball uniform needs 3 buttons. Copy and complete the table to find how many buttons are needed for 12 uniforms.

Uniforms	3	6	9	12
Buttons	9	18	27	■

5-1 Addition and Subtraction Expressions

GET READY to Learn

Lia has 3 baseball cards. Her friend gave her some more. You can show the number of cards Lia now has by using the expression below.

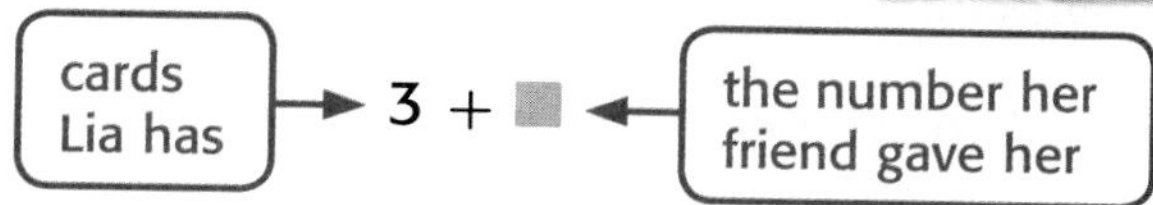

An **expression** like 3 + ■ is a statement with numbers and/or symbols, and at least one operation. A symbol can represent the unknown value. You can find the value of an expression if you know the value of the symbol.

MAIN IDEA

I will write and find the value of expressions.

Targeted TEKS 4.15 The student communicates about Grade 4 mathematics using informal language. (A) **Explain and record observations using objects, words, pictures, numbers, and technology.** *Preparation for TEKS 5.6.*

New Vocabulary

expression
parentheses

Real-World EXAMPLE Find Value of an Expression

1 **ALGEBRA If Lia's friend gives her 5 baseball cards, how many cards will she have?**

You need to find the value of 3 + ■ when ■ = 5.

3 + ■ Write the expression.

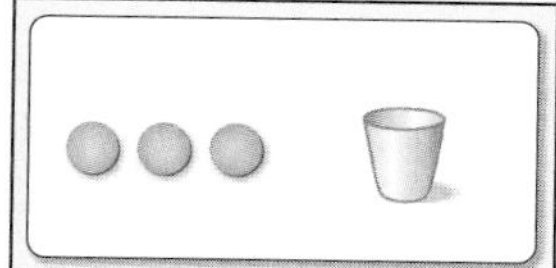

3 + **5** Replace ■ with 5.

8 Add 3 and 5.

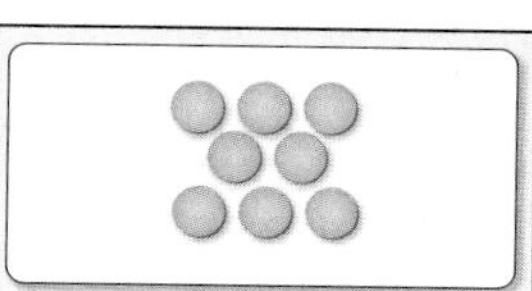

So, the value of 3 + ■ when ■ = 5 is 8.
Lia will have 8 baseball cards.

Animation
tx.gr4math.com

Some expressions contain parentheses, ( ). The **parentheses** tell you which operation to perform first.

EXAMPLE Find the Value of an Expression

2 **Find the value of 12 − (▲ + 2) if ▲ = 7.**

12 − (▲ + 2)	Write the expression.
12 − (7 + 2)	Replace ▲ with 7.
12 − 9	Find (7 + 2) first.
3	Next, find 12 − 9.

Real-World EXAMPLE Write an Expression

3 **ALGEBRA Latisha made 3 fewer baskets than Felisa. Write an expression for the number of baskets Latisha made.**

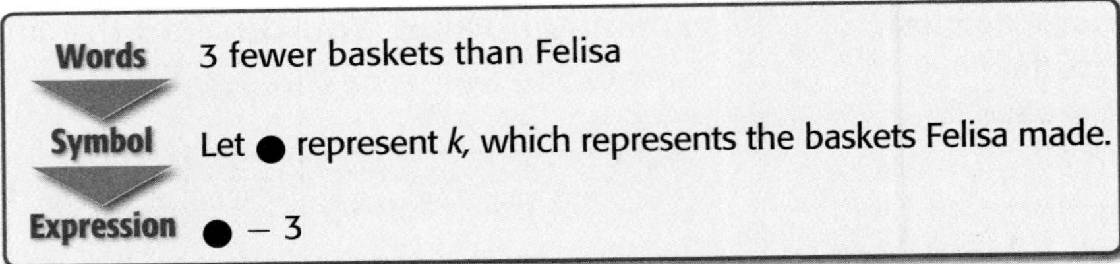

Words	3 fewer baskets than Felisa
Symbol	Let ● represent *k*, which represents the baskets Felisa made.
Expression	● − 3

So, Latisha made ● − 3 baskets.

Online Personal Tutor at tx.gr4math.com

CHECK What You Know

Find the value of each expression if ▲ = 4 and ■ = 8. See Examples 1 and 2 (pp. 183–184)

1. ▲ + 2 **2.** 19 − ■ **3.** 8 − (▲ + 1)

Write an expression for each situation. See Example 3 (p. 184)

4. two more than ● **5.** 44 minus ★ **6.** the sum of 17 and ◆

Measurement The length of a condor is 7 inches more than the length of a bald eagle.

7. If a bald eagle is 12 inches, what is the length of a condor?

8. Talk About It Describe a situation that could be represented by ● − 6.

Math Online Extra Examples at tx.gr4math.com

Practice and Problem Solving

EXTRA PRACTICE See page R12.

Find the value of each expression if ● = 9 and ■ = 5. See Examples 1 and 2 (pp. 183–184)

9. ● + 2 **10.** ■ + 9 **11.** ● − 4 **12.** 11 − ■

13. ● + 20 **14.** 14 + ■ **15.** 8 − ■ **16.** 12 − ●

17. (● − 3) + 7 **18.** 15 − (■ + 1) **19.** (● + 8) − 5 **20.** ■ + (17 − 9)

21. (● − 5) + 23 **22.** (■ − 2) + 8 **23.** 36 + (● − 1) **24.** (25 − 5) + ●

Write an expression for each situation. See Example 3 (p. 184)

25. three more than ■

26. the sum of ● and six

27. ten subtracted from ▲

28. the difference of ★ and fifty-six

29. the sum of ▲ and seven

30. thirteen more than ●

31. the sum of ■ and 5 subtracted from 16

32. the sum of ▼ and 23 subtracted from 100

Pablo had 3 cats. One of the cats had kittens. See Example 3 (p. 184)

33. Define a symbol. Then write an expression for the number of cats Pablo has now.

34. If the one cat has 4 kittens, how many cats will Pablo have?

Cole has 5 fewer soccer cards than his brother. See Example 3 (p. 184)

35. Define a symbol. Then write an expression for the number of cards Cole has.

36. If Cole's brother has 15 cards, how many cards does Cole have?

H.O.T. Problems

37. OPEN ENDED Describe a real-world situation for the expression ■ − 5.

38. WHICH ONE DOESN'T BELONG? Identify the expression that does not belong with the other three. Explain your reasoning.

3 − ●	2 + 5	4 − ▲	■ + 1

39. WRITING IN MATH Explain what a symbol means in an expression.

Algebra Activity for 5-2

Addition and Subtraction Equations

An **equation** is a sentence like 4 + 5 = 9 that contains an equals sign (=), showing that two expressions are equal. The equals sign shows that the expressions on each side of it are equal. Equations sometimes have a missing number.

4 + ▲ = 9   10 − ● = 6   ■ − 1 = 7

When you find the value of the missing number that makes the equation true, you **solve** the equation.

MAIN IDEA

I will explore addition and subtraction equations.

Targeted TEKS 4.15 The student communicates about Grade 4 mathematics using informal language. **(A) Explain and record observations using objects, words, pictures, numbers, and technology.** *Preparation for TEKS 5.6.*

You Will Need
counters
cups

1 Solve ■ + 3 = 5.

Step 1 Model the expression on the left side.

To model ■ + 3, use a cup to show ■ and 3 counters.

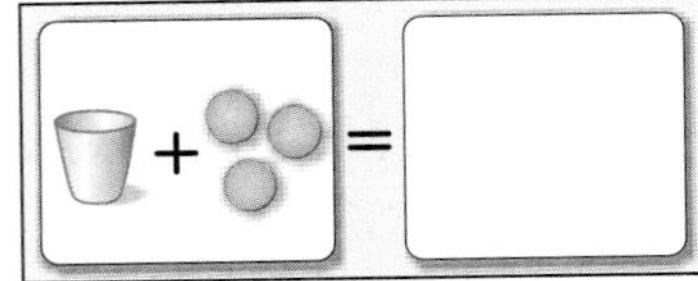

Step 2 Model the expression on the right side.

Place 5 counters on the right to show 5. An equals sign shows that both sides are the same.

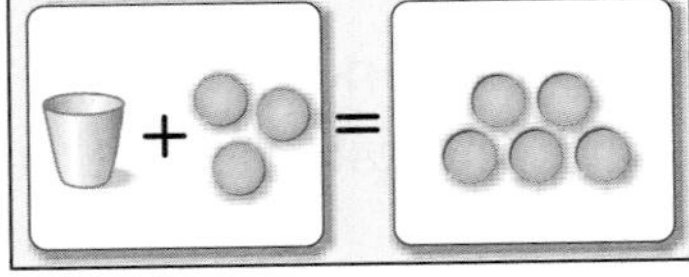

Step 3 Find the value of ■.

Put enough counters in the cup so that the number of counters on each side of the equals sign is the same.

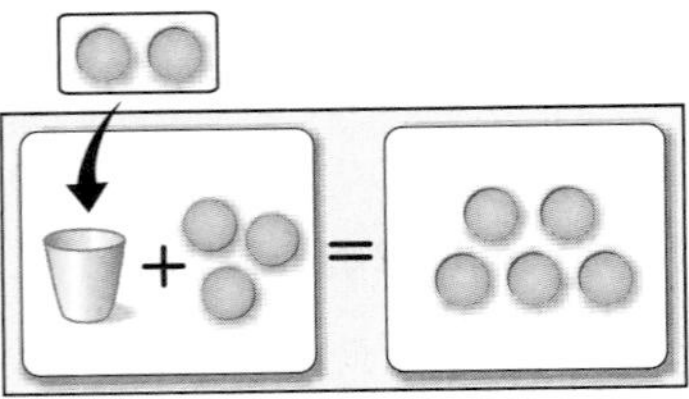

The value of ■ that makes ■ + 3 = 5 true is 2. So, ■ = 2.

You can also use counters to model equations involving subtraction.

ACTIVITY

2 **Solve ■ − 4 = 2.**

Step 1 **Model ■ − 4 = 2.**

Use a cup and counters to show ■ − 4 = 2

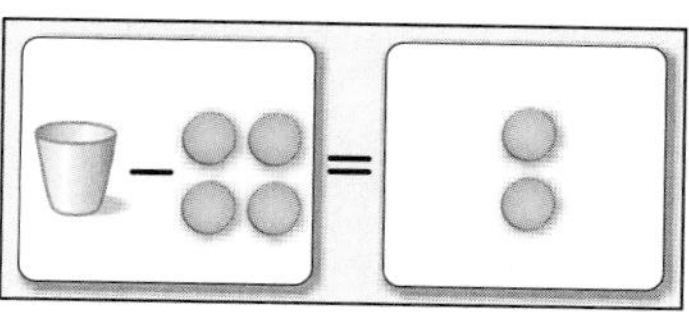

Step 2 **Find the value of ■.**

Think how many counters need to be placed in the cup so that when 4 are taken away 2 will be left.

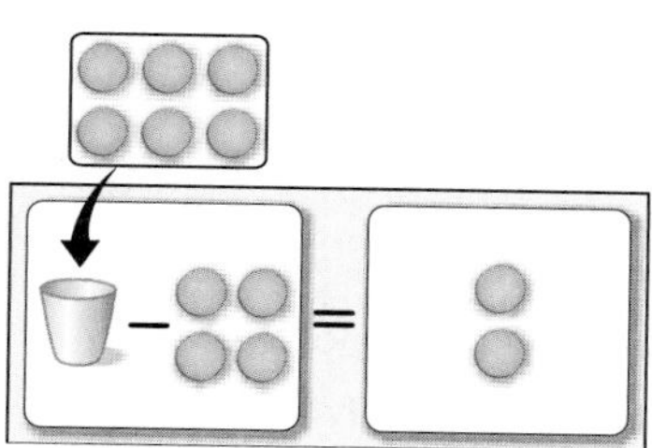

The number of counters in the cup is the missing number. So, the value of ■ that makes this equation true is 6. So, ■ = 6.

Think About It

1. How would you model ■ + 2 = 9?
2. What is the value of ■ in ■ + 2 = 9?
3. Explain how to check your answer.

CHECK What You Know

Write an equation for each model. Then find the value of ■.

4. 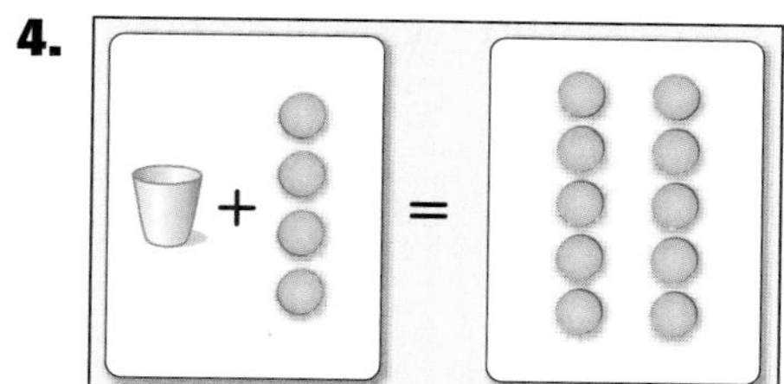

5. 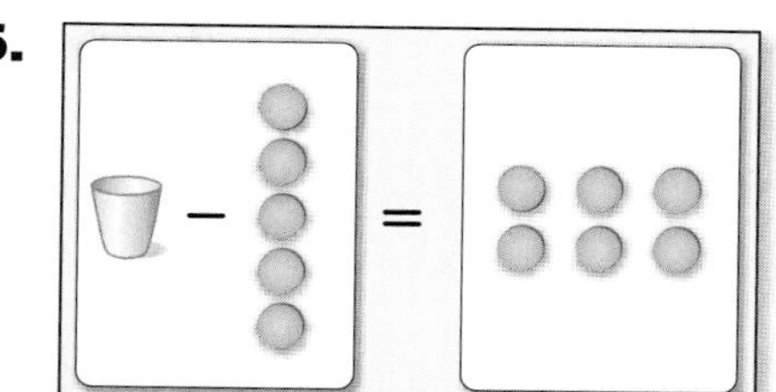

Use models to solve each equation.

6. ■ + 3 = 8
7. 14 − ■ = 8
8. 17 − ■ = 12
9. ■ + 9 = 19
10. **WRITING IN ▸MATH** Explain the difference between an expression and an equation. Give an example of each.

5-2 Solve Equations

MAIN IDEA

I will solve addition and subtraction equations.

Targeted TEKS 4.3 The student adds and subtracts to solve meaningful problems involving whole numbers and decimals. **(A) Use addition and subtraction to solve problems involving whole numbers.** *Also addresses TEKS 4.15(B).*

New Vocabulary

equation
solve

GET READY to Learn

Sashi downloaded 4 songs on Monday. After she downloaded some more songs on Tuesday, she had a total of 9 songs. How many songs did she download on Tuesday?

In the previous Explore Activity, you solved equations using models. Equations can also be solved mentally.

Real-World EXAMPLE — Solve Addition Equations

1 MUSIC How many songs did Sashi download on Tuesday?

One Way: Use Models

Step 1 Model the equation.

4 + ■ = 9

Step 2 Find the value of ■.

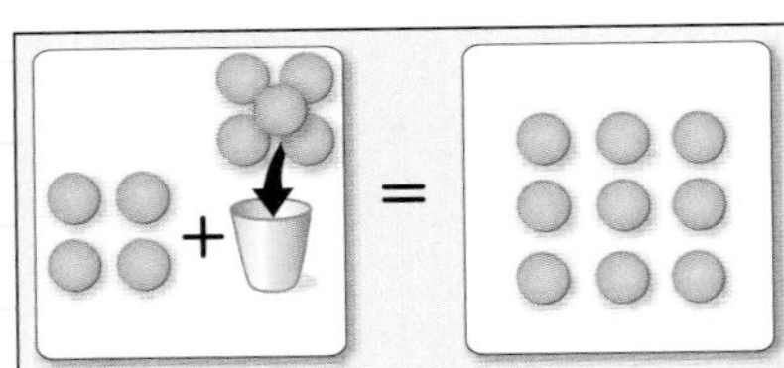

Another Way: Mental Math

4 + ■ = 9

THINK 4 plus what number equals 9?

4 + **5** = 9 You know that 4 + 5 = 9.

So, ■ = 5.

So, ■ = 5. Sashi downloaded 5 songs on Tuesday.

EXAMPLE Solve Subtraction Equations

2 **Solve 18 − ■ = 13.**

18 − ■ = 13 — 18 minus what number equals 13?

18 − 5 = 13 — You know that 18 − 5 = 13.

■ = 5

So, the value of ■ is 5.

Real-World EXAMPLE

3 ALGEBRA **Garcia had 9 video games. He bought some more video games and now has a total of 12. How many video games did he buy?**

Write and solve an equation.

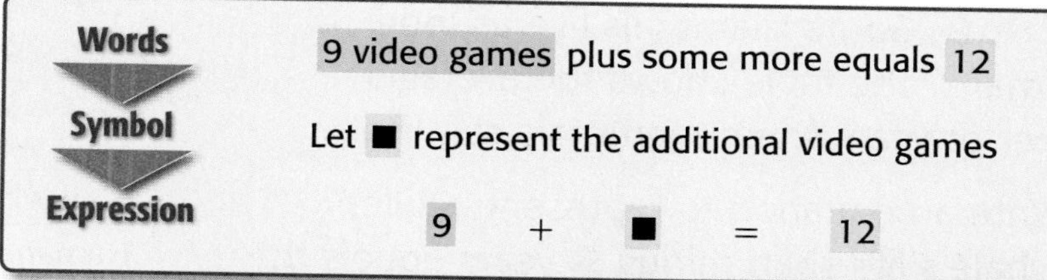

Words
9 video games plus some more equals 12
Symbol
Let ■ represent the additional video games
Expression
9 + ■ = 12

9 + ■ = 12 — 9 plus what number equals 12?

9 + 3 = 12 — You know that 9 + 3 = 12.

■ = 3

So, ■ = 3. Garcia bought 3 more video games.

Personal Tutor at tx.gr4math.com

CHECK What You Know

Solve each equation. See Examples 1 and 2 (pp. 188–189)

1. 5 + ■ = 11

2. ■ + 9 = 17

3. 13 + ■ = 20

4. 8 − ■ = 4

5. 14 − ■ = 9

6. ■ − 12 = 12

7. Keisha scored 14 points in the first half of a basketball game. At the end of the game, she had a total of 36 points. Write and solve an equation to find how many points she scored in the second half of the game. See Example 3 (p. 189)

8. Talk About It Explain how to solve ■ − 3 = 12.

Practice and Problem Solving

EXTRA PRACTICE
See page R12.

Solve each equation. See Examples 1 and 2 (pp. 188–189)

9. 1 + ■ = 4

10. ■ + 4 = 6

11. 6 + ■ = 10

12. ■ + 8 = 15

13. ■ + 10 = 17

14. 9 + ■ = 20

15. 4 − ■ = 2

16. ■ − 5 = 6

17. 7 − ■ = 2

18. ■ − 8 = 12

19. 9 = 15 − ■

20. 11 = ■ − 12

Write and solve an equation for each situation. See Example 3 (p. 189)

21. A number plus 8 equals 19.

22. The sum of 11 and a number is 35.

23. Nine subtracted from a number equals 12.

24. Fifteen less than a number is 15.

Real-World PROBLEM SOLVING

Science Some mammals live as long as humans. The table shows the average number of years some mammals can live.

Mammals that Live the Longest

Mammal	Years Lived
Killer whale	90
Blue whale	80
Human	76
African elephant	70
Gorilla	35

Source: *Scholastic Book of World Records*

25. Write an equation to represent a killer whale's life span minus ■ years equals the African elephant's life span. What is the value of ■?

26. Write an equation to represent the human's life span plus another mammal's life span (■) equals 111. What is the value of ■? Which animal does the ■ stand for?

H.O.T. Problems

27. **FIND THE ERROR** Caleb and Adriana say that the two equations have the same solution for ■. Are they correct? Explain.

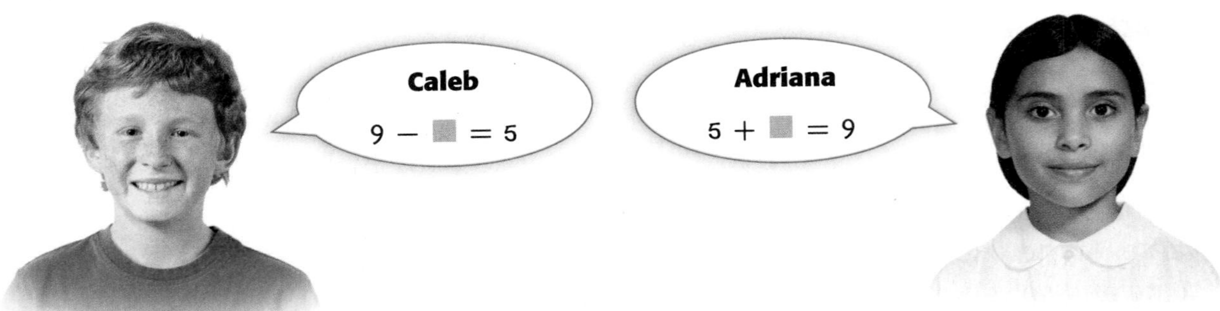

28. **WRITING IN ▸MATH** Write one or two sentences explaining how to solve an equation.

29. What is the value of the expression 16 − (8 + ■) if ■ = 2? (Lesson 5-1)

A 6

B 10

C 20

D 22

30. What is the value of ■ in the equation ■ + 18 = 48? (Lesson 5-2)

F 20

G 28

H 30

J 32

31. Ann sweeps the floor every third day. If she sweeps the floor on September 10, on which of the following days will she NOT have to sweep the floor? (Lesson 5-2)

September 2008

Sunday	Monday	Tuesday	Wednesday	Thursday	Friday	Saturday
	1	2	3	4	5	6
7	8	9	10	11	12	13
14	15	16	17	18	19	20
21	22	23	24	25	26	27
28	29	30				

A September 13

B September 19

C September 23

D September 28

Spiral Review

32. Write an expression for *three less than* ■. (Lesson 5-1)

Find all the factors of each number. (Lesson 4-9)

33. 36

34. 45

35. 100

36. The longest airport runway on Earth is 5,000 meters and is located in Russia. The shortest airport runway on Earth is 533 meters and located in the Netherlands Antilles. What is the difference in length of these two runways? (Lesson 2-5)

37. The local zoo has a giant panda bear. The bear eats 84 pounds of bamboo a day. Copy and complete the table to find out the total amount of bamboo the bear will eat in a week. (Lesson 3-2)

Day	1	2	■	4	5	■	7
Bamboo	84	■	252	336	■	504	■

Compare the numbers. Write >, <, or = for each ●. (Lesson 1-4)

38. 4,714 ● 4,741

39. 64,962 ● 64,926

5-3 Problem-Solving Skill

MAIN IDEA I will identify extra and missing information.

Targeted TEKS 4.14 The student applies Grade 4 mathematics to solve problems connected to everyday experiences and activities in and outside of school. (C) **Select or develop an appropriate problem-solving plan or strategy, . . . to solve a problem.** *Also addresses TEKS 4.14(B).*

Trina is making friendship bracelets to sell for $2 each. Last week, she sold 63 bracelets. Two weeks ago, she sold 21 bracelets. How many more bracelets did Trina sell last week than two weeks ago?

Understand

What facts do you know?

- Trina sells friendship bracelets for $2 each.
- She sold 63 bracelets last week.
- She sold 21 bracelets two weeks ago.

What do you need to find?

- Find how many more bracelets Trina sold last week than two weeks ago.

Plan

Once you identify the information needed to solve the problem you can write an equation. Look for any extra information.

Solve

Subtract 21 from 63. You do not need to know how much the bracelets cost. This is extra information.

$$\underbrace{63}_{\text{last week}} - \underbrace{21}_{\text{two weeks ago}} = \blacksquare$$

$$63 - 21 = 42$$

So, Trina sold 42 more bracelets last week than the week before.

Check

Look back at the problem. Check the subtraction with addition. Since $21 + 42 = 63$, the answer is correct.

ANALYZE the Skill

Refer to the problem on the previous page.

1. Explain why you do not need to know the cost of the bracelets.

2. Suppose the problem did not include how many bracelets were sold last week. Could you solve it? Explain.

3. If you need to find the difference in profit between the two weeks, is there enough information to solve the problem?

4. Find the difference in profit between the two weeks.

PRACTICE the Skill

EXTRA PRACTICE
See page R13.

Identify any missing or extra information. Then solve if possible.

5. Chango the monkey eats four apples and three bananas for lunch every day. He eats at 12:30 P.M. How much fruit does he eat for lunch in a week?

6. Nidia asked her classmates to name their favorite flavor of ice cream. Chocolate received 14 votes, which is 5 more votes than vanilla. How many students liked vanilla?

7. Sheri and two friends want to go to a movie. The movie starts at 2 P.M. How much will it cost for them to go to the movie?

MOVIE THEATER
Adult Ticket $6
Student Ticket $4
Movie Times 10A.M., 12P.M., 2P.M.

8. **Measurement** Each day, Zoe trains each of her horses for 30 minutes and then rides them for 20 minutes. How much time does Zoe spend with her horses in one day?

9. Julia wants to buy the fish aquarium supplies shown. How much change will she get back?

10. Three fourth-grade classes are going on a field trip. How many students are going on a field trip?

11. James and Donna have $18. Each pack of baseball cards costs $3. There are 8 cards in each pack. How many packs can they buy?

12. The Video Depot is having a sale on DVDs. The cost is $27 for 3. How many DVDS can Edgar buy?

13. **WRITING IN MATH** Explain how you identified any *extra or missing* information in Exercise 12.

5-4 Patterns

GET READY to Learn

Carla sold 3 picture frames for $15 and 4 for $20. If the price of the frames remains the same, how much will 6 frames cost?

MAIN IDEA

I will find patterns in sets of numbers.

Targeted TEKS 4.16 The student uses logical reasoning. **(A)** **Make generalizations from patterns or sets of examples and nonexamples.** *Also addresses TEKS 4.7.*

New Vocabulary

pattern

In this situation, there is a pattern in the cost of the frames. A **pattern** is a series of numbers or figures that follow a rule.

Real-World EXAMPLE Complete the Pattern

1 **MONEY** **How much will 6 frames cost?**

Find the cost of one frame by dividing the cost by the number of frames.

Since 3 frames cost $15, we can see that one frame will cost $5. $15 \div 3 = 5$

Also, we can check this by using the rest of the information.

Since 4 frames cost $20, then one frame will cost $5.
$20 \div 4 = 5$

Use a pattern to find how much money she will make.

1	2	3	4	5	6
$5	10	15	20	25	30

5 5 5 5 5

So, six frames will cost $30.

You can find and extend a pattern.

Online Personal Tutor at tx.gr4math.com

Real-World EXAMPLE Find the Rule

2 READING **Daniel is reading a book. There are 6 chapters in his book that follow a pattern. How many pages are in the sixth chapter? What is the page number for the last page of the chapter?**

Chapter	Ending Page	
1	16	+16
2	28	+12
3	44	+16
4	56	+12
5	72	+16
6		

The table shows that the odd numbered chapters have 16 pages. The even numbered chapters have 12 pages. Extend the pattern.

So, the sixth chapter will have 12 pages and the ending page will be 84.

Online Personal Tutor at tx.gr4math.com

Some patterns are not as easy to describe. So, look carefully at each example.

EXAMPLE Examples and Nonexamples

3 **Which figure will Alyssa color next?**

Alyssa is coloring these figures.

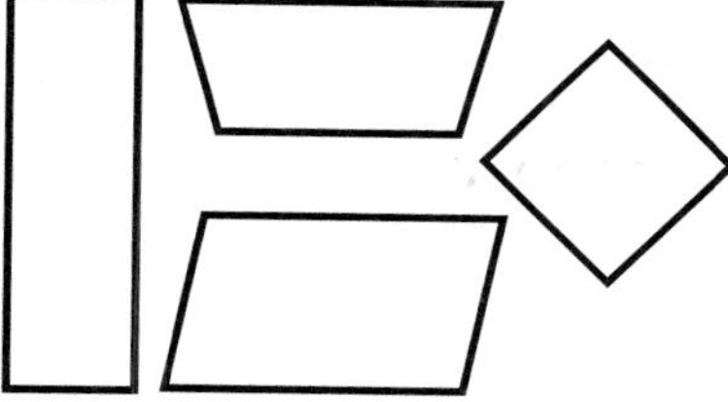

Barry is coloring these figures.

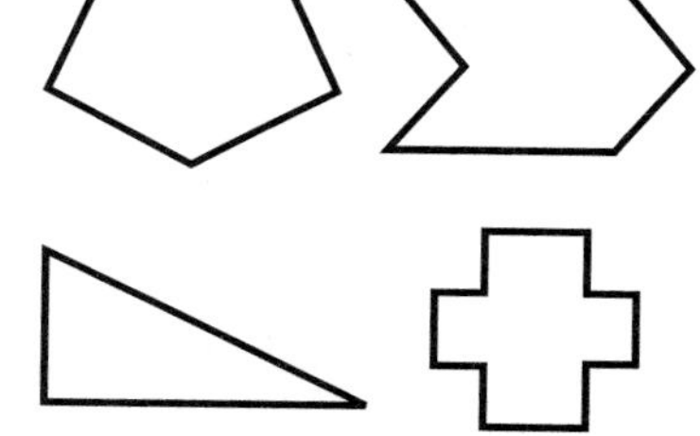

Alyssa's figures all have 4 sides.

Barry's figures do not have 4 sides.

These are the last figures. Which is a figure that Alyssa would color?

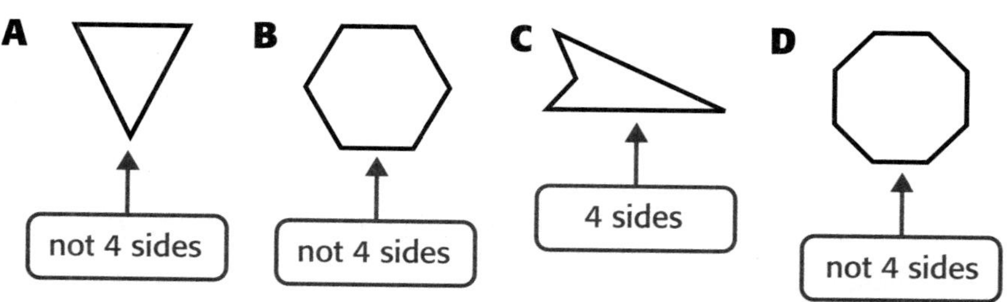

Alyssa would color figure C.

What You Know

Find the rule and find the next number in each pattern. See Examples 1 and 2 (pp. 194–195)

1. 9, 12, 15, 18, 21, ■ **2.** 5, 6, 4, 5, 3, ■ **3.** 3, 5, 7, 9, 11, ■

4. Marcos reads each day. What is the rule for the pattern shown in his reading log?

Reading Log					
Day	1	2	3	4	5
Min	30	60	90	120	150

5. Talk About It These are Inexes.

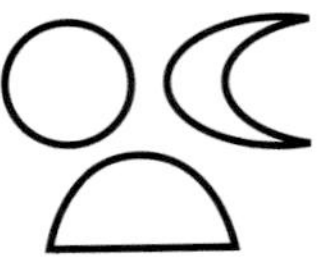

Explain why these are not Inexes.

Practice and Problem Solving

EXTRA PRACTICE See page R13.

Find the rule and find the next number in each pattern. See Examples 1 and 2 (pp. 194–195)

6. 26, 30, 34, 38, 42, ■ **7.** 13, 18, 23, 28, 33, ■ **8.** 8, 8, 6, 6, 4, ■

9. 10, 20, 30, 40, 50, ■ **10.** 28, 24, 28, 24, 28, ■ **11.** 3, 6, 12, 15, 21, ■

12. It is recommended to drink 64 fluid ounces of water each day. Below is a pattern to show how many days it would take to drink 448 fluid ounces.

64	128	192	256	320	384	448

+64 +64 +64 +64 +64 +64

Explain how another pattern could be used to find the same answer.

13. Bob goes swimming every afternoon. On even numbered dates he swims 10 laps, and on odd numbered dates he swims 15 laps. If it is the morning of the sixth, how many laps has he swum altogether for the month?

14. Explain why 75 is not an example of a number that would be in the number pattern in Exercise 9.

H.O.T. Problems

15. OPEN ENDED Create a number pattern involving two operations. Explain your pattern.

16. WRITING IN ►MATH Describe the pattern shown. What comes next?

△△▷▷△△△△▽▽△△△△△△◁◁

CHAPTER 5

Mid-Chapter Check

Lessons 5-1 through 5-4

Find the value of each expression if ▲ = 2 and ■ = 8. (Lesson 5-1)

1. ▲ + 3
2. 18 − ■
3. ■ − (1 + 4)
4. (■ − 2) + ▲

Write an expression for each situation. (Lesson 5-1)

5. three more than ■
6. the sum of 27 and ■

Amado has 13 more books than Sara. (Lesson 5-1)

7. Define a symbol. Then write an expression for the number of books Amado has.
8. If Sara has 8 books, how many does Amado have?

Solve each equation. (Lesson 5-2)

9. 7 + ■ = 11
10. ■ − 4 = 12

11. **TEST PRACTICE** Which number will make the equation true? (Lesson 5-2)

67 + ■ = 121

A 54
B 56
C 64
D 68

Write and solve the equation for the situation. (Lesson 5-2)

12. A number plus 7 equals 19. What is the number?

Identify any missing or extra information. Then solve. (Lesson 5-3)

13. Raekwon bought his lunch every day this week. How much did he spend on lunches this week?

14. Dakota is buying a basketball for $12 and an air pump for $5. She wants to buy a baseball for $6. After purchasing the basketball and pump the cashier gives Dakota $3. How much money did Dakota give the cashier?

15. **TEST PRACTICE** Identify the equation that describes the pattern. (Lesson 5-4)

Input (▲)	16	19	22	25	28	31
Output (■)	9	12	15	■	■	■

F 16 − 7 = ■
G ▲ + 6 = ■
H ▲ − 7 = ■
J ■ + 6 = ▲

16. Write an equation to describe the pattern. Then use the equation to find the next three numbers in the pattern. (Lesson 5-4)

Input (▲)	3	6	9	12	15	18
Output (■)	7	10	13	■	■	■

17. **WRITING IN MATH** Explain how the pattern of the input numbers is related to the pattern of the output numbers. (Lesson 5-4)

Addition and Subtraction Relationships

GET READY to Learn

Mr. Mathis put the following input number into his number machine and got the output number shown.

MAIN IDEA

I will find a rule to describe the relationship of sets of data and use the rule to write an equation.

Targeted TEKS 4.7 The student uses organizational structures to analyze and describe patterns and relationships. **Describe the relationship between two sets of related data such as ordered pairs in a table.**

The numbers from the number machine above form a pattern. You can write an equation to describe and extend a pattern.

EXAMPLES Find an Addition Rule

1 Write an equation that describes the pattern in the table.

Input (▲)	Output (■)
2	9
4	11
6	13
8	■
10	■
12	■

Pattern: 2 + 7 = 9
4 + 7 = 11
6 + 7 = 13

Rule: Add 7.

Equation: ▲ + 7 = ■

input (▲) output (■)

2 Use the equation to find the next three numbers.

Find the next three numbers when the input (▲) is 8, 10, and 12.

▲ + 7 = ■	▲ + 7 = ■	▲ + 7 = ■
8 + 7 = 15	10 + 7 = 17	12 + 7 = 19

So, the next three numbers in the pattern are 15, 17, and 19.

Real-World EXAMPLE Find a Subtraction Rule

Remember

Always check to make sure the equation works for each pair of numbers in the table.

3 **ALGEBRA A pizza shop offers $3 off any order over $10. Write an equation that describes the pattern. Then use the equation to find the next three costs.**

Input (▲)	Output (■)
$11	$8
$12	$9
$14	$11
$16	■
$18	■
$20	■

Identify the rule and write it as an equation.

Rule: Subtract 3.

Equation: ▲ − $3 = ■

(▲ = input, ■ = output)

Find the next three numbers when the input (▲) is $16, $18, and $20.

▲ − $3 = ■	▲ − $3 = ■	▲ − $3 = ■
$16 − $3 = $13	**$18** − $3 = $15	**$20** − $3 = $17

So, the next three amounts are $13, $15, and $17.

Online **Personal Tutor at** tx.gr4math.com

CHECK What You Know

Write an equation that describes the pattern. Then use the equation to find the next three numbers.

See Examples 1–3 (pp. 198–199)

1.

Input (▲)	5	9	13	17	21	25
Output (■)	9	13	17	■	■	■

2.

Input (▲)	11	16	21	26	31	36
Output (■)	2	7	12	■	■	■

3. The amounts a bus company charges to take students on a field trip are shown at the right. How much would it cost for 30, 40, and 50 students to go on a field trip?

Students	Cost ($)
10	$60
20	$70
30	■
40	■
50	■

4. **Talk About It** Explain what you should do if you test a number in an equation and it does not work.

Practice and Problem Solving

EXTRA PRACTICE See page R13.

Write an equation that describes the pattern. Then use the equation to find the next three numbers. See Examples 1–3 (pp. 198–199)

5.

Input (▲)	3	6	9	12	15	18
Output (■)	6	9	12	■	■	■

6.

Input (▲)	2	6	10	14	18	22
Output (■)	15	19	23	■	■	■

7.

Input (▲)	16	22	28	34	40	46
Output (■)	5	11	17	■	■	■

8.

Input (▲)	14	19	24	29	34	39
Output (■)	9	14	19	■	■	■

Create an input/output table for each equation.

9. ▲ + 4 = ■
10. ▲ + 11 = ■
11. ▲ − 7 = ■
12. ▲ − 10 = ■

Real-World PROBLEM SOLVING

Money The table shows what a taxi company charges (■) for every ▲ miles traveled.

Input (▲)	Output (■)
10	$12
15	$17
20	■
25	■
30	■

13. Use the table to write an equation for this situation.

14. Find the costs of a 20-mile, 25-mile, and 30-mile trip.

15. Use the equation you wrote for Exercise 13 to find the cost of a 60-mile trip.

16. Write an equation for the number of miles traveled and $4 charged for each trip.

17. Create a table for the equation in Exercise 16. How much would a 40-mile trip cost?

H.O.T. Problems

18. **OPEN ENDED** Write a real-world situation that can be represented by the table.

Input (▲)	1	2	3	4	5
Output (■)	$10	$20	■	■	■

19. **WRITING IN MATH** Explain how the pattern of the input numbers is related to the pattern of the output numbers.

20. Which of the following describes the rule for this pattern? **(Lesson 5-4)**

16, 12, 15, 11, 14, 10, 13

A Add 4, subtract 3.

B Subtract 4, add 3.

C Subtract 3, add 4.

D Add 3, subtract 4.

21. Each number in Set R is paired with a number in Set S. **(Lesson 5-5)**

Set R	Set S
2	10
5	13
6	14

The relationship for each pair of numbers is the same. If the number in Set R is 12, how will you find its paired number in Set S?

F Add 8 to 8.

G Subtract 8 from 12.

H Add 8 to 12.

J Subtract 12 from 12.

Spiral Review

Find the rule for each pattern. (Lesson 5-4)

22. 28, 25, 22, 19, 16, 13

23. 9, 12, 15, 18, 21, 24

Identify any missing or extra information. Then solve if possible. (Lesson 5-3)

24. A cat named Socks is two years old. Socks eats treats twice a day. If there are 365 days in a year, how many days old is Socks?

25. Camille scored 12 points in the first half of a basketball game. She scored a total of 26 points at the end of the game. How many points did she score during the second half of the game?

Solve each equation. (Lesson 5-2)

26. $\blacksquare + 15 = 25$

27. $\blacksquare - 36 = 4$

28. $12 + \blacksquare = 26$

Round each number to the given place value. (Lesson 1-6)

29. 16,543; hundreds

30. 2,345; tens

31. 67,343; thousands

Do Flying Squirrels Really Fly?

There are 36 types of flying squirrels. Southern flying squirrels and Northern flying squirrels are found in the United States. These squirrels do not actually fly. They glide from tree to tree. These animals climb as high as 30 feet into trees. Then they use their hind legs to push off from branches.

Flying squirrels build their nests in trees, where they collect nuts and berries. They store up to 15,000 nuts in a season. What an appetite.

Southern Flying Squirrel Facts

Length of Body, including Tail . . . . 14 inches
Length of Tail . . . . 6 inches
Weight of Adult . . . . 3 ounces
Life Span . . . . 5 years

How Far Flying Squirrels Glide

Height of Squirrel in Tree (ft)	5	10	15	20
Distance of Glide (ft)	11	16	21	26

Targeted TEKS 4.14 The student applies Grade 4 mathematics to solve problems connected to everyday experiences and activities in and outside of school. **(A) Identify the mathematics in everyday situations.**

Did You Know?

Some flying squirrels can glide as far as 1,500 feet!

Real-World Math

Use the information on pages 202 and 203 to solve each problem.

1. What is the length of a Southern flying squirrel's body? Write and find the value of an expression.

2. The length of a Northern squirrel's body, including the tail, is 16 inches. Its tail is the same length as a Southern squirrel's tail. Write and find the value of an expression to find the length of the Northern squirrel's body.

3. A Southern flying squirrel lives to be 8 years old. How many years did this squirrel live beyond its average life span? Write and find the value of an expression.

4. Write a rule that describes how far a flying squirrel will glide when it jumps from a given height.

5. Suppose a squirrel jumps from a tree that is 25 feet tall. How far will the squirrel glide?

6. A squirrel jumps from a tree that is 30 feet tall. Will it glide farther than 40 feet? Explain.

7. What is the difference in gliding distances of a squirrel that jumps from a 40-foot tree than a squirrel that jumps from a 50-foot tree?

Multiplication and Division Expressions

MAIN IDEA

I will write and find the value of multiplication and division expressions.

Targeted TEKS 4.15 The student communicates Grade 4 mathematics using informal language. (A) **Explain and record observations using objects, words, pictures,** and technology. *Preparation for TEKS 5.6.*

Liza has 4 cans of tennis balls. The total number of balls can be represented by the expression below.

cans → 4 × ■ ← balls per can

Finding the value of multiplication and division expressions is similar to finding the value of addition and subtraction expressions.

Real-World EXAMPLE Find Value of an Expression

1 **ALGEBRA If there are 3 balls in each can, what is the total number of tennis balls? Find the value of 4 × ■ if ■ = 3.**

4 × ■	Write the expression.	
4 × 3	Replace ■ with 3.	
12	Multiply 4 and 3.	

So, the value of ■ is 12. Liza has a total of 12 tennis balls.

Review Vocabulary

expression a statement with numbers and/or symbols, and at least one operation; *Example:* ■ + 3; 4 × ■

Recall that you perform the operations inside parentheses first.

EXAMPLE Find the Value of an Expression

2 **Find the value of 2 × (15 ÷ ■) if ■ = 5.**

2 × (15 ÷ ■)	Write the expression.
2 × (15 ÷ 5)	Replace ■ with 5.
2 × 3	Find (15 ÷ 5) first.
6	Next, find 2 × 3.

You can write expressions for real-world situations.

Real-World EXAMPLE Write an Expression

3 Jorge has ■ dollars to buy airplane models. Write an expression for the number of models Jorge can buy with his money.

Write an expression.

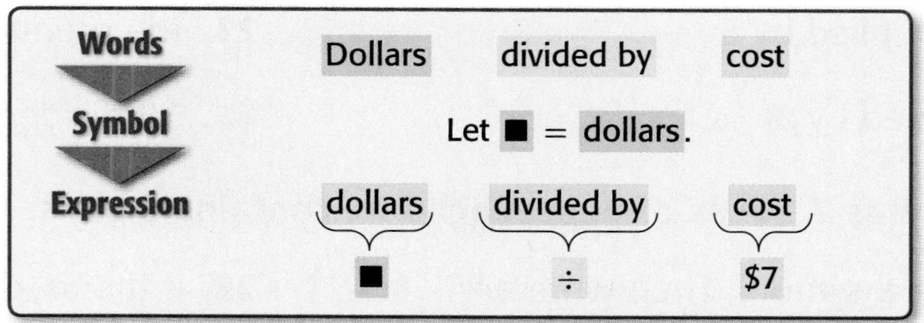

So, the number of airplane models Jorge can buy is ■ ÷ $7.

Online Personal Tutor at tx.gr4math.com

CHECK What You Know

Find the value of each expression if ● = 3 and ▲ = 6. See Examples 1 and 2 (p. 204)

1. 2 × ●
2. ▲ ÷ ●
3. (15 ÷ ●) × 6

Write an expression for each situation. See Example 3 (p. 205)

4. 9 times ▲
5. ▲ multiplied by 12
6. a number divided by 8
7. 24 divided by a number

For Exercises 8 and 9, use the following information. See Example 3 (p. 205)
Luis has four times as much money as Kyle.

8. Define a symbol. Then write an expression for the amount of money Luis has.
9. If Kyle has $8, how much money does Luis have?
10. Talk About It How do you find the value of 9 × (▲ ÷ 4) when ▲ = 20?

Practice and Problem Solving

EXTRA PRACTICE See page R14.

Find the value of each expression if ▼ = 10 and ● = 5.
See Examples 1 and 2 (p. 204)

11. 6 × ●

12. ▼ × 7

13. ▼ ÷ 5

14. ● ÷ 5

15. ● × ▼

16. ▼ ÷ ●

17. 4 × (▼ ÷ 2)

18. (▼ ÷ ●) × 9

19. (▼ × ●) ÷ 5

Write an expression for each situation. See Example 3 (p. 205)

20. ■ multiplied by 5

21. the product of 2 and a number

22. 8 divided by ■

23. 18 divided by a number

A teacher has 7 boxes of pens. Each box contains 8 pens. See Example 3 (p. 205)

24. Define a symbol. Then write an expression for the number of pens the teacher has.

25. If the teacher bought 2 more boxes of pens, how many pens will the teacher have?

Eduardo has 5 CDs with 9 songs on each of them. See Example 3 (p. 205)

26. Define a symbol. Then write an expression for the number of songs that are on the CDs.

27. If Eduardo lets a friend borrow 2 of his CDs, how many songs will be on the CDs he has left?

Real-World PROBLEM SOLVING

Data File The largest freshwater turtle in the world is the alligator snapping turtle. It can be found in the western and central areas of Texas.

28. Write an expression for the total weight of ■ turtles.

29. **Measurement** Find the total length of four turtles that are laid head to tail.

Turtles

Alligator Snapping Turtle	
Length	30 inches
Weight	175 pounds

H.O.T. Problems

30. **OPEN ENDED** Write a division expression that has a value of 3 if ■ = 7.

31. **WRITING IN MATH** Write a problem that uses the expression (4 × ■) ÷ 7.

Equation Race

Solve Equations

Get Ready!

Players: 2 players

Get Set!

Label 16 index cards as shown.

Go!

- Shuffle the cards. Then spread out the cards face down.
- Player 1 turns over one equation card.
- Both players use mental math to solve the equation.
- The first player to correctly solve the equation gets 1 point.
- Player 2 turns over another equation card. Repeat steps until all of the cards have been used.
- The player with the most points wins.

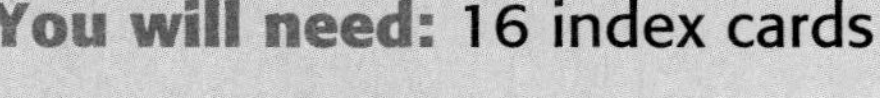
You will need: 16 index cards

$\blacksquare - 9 = 7$	$\blacksquare \div 11 = 10$	
$15 - \blacksquare = 3$	$\blacksquare - 8 = 6$	$35 - \blacksquare = 5$
$24 \div \blacksquare = 12$	$\blacksquare \div 4 = 9$	$144 \div \blacksquare = 12$
$12 + \blacksquare = 108$	$\blacksquare + 9 = 18$	$8 + \blacksquare = 64$
$5 \times \blacksquare = 45$	$\blacksquare \times 4 = 40$	$3 \times \blacksquare = 36$
$\blacksquare + 7 = 42$	$\blacksquare \times 11 = 22$	

Problem-Solving Investigation

MAIN IDEA I will choose the best strategy to solve a problem.

Targeted TEKS 4.14 The student applies Grade 4 Mathematics to solve problems connected to everyday experiences and activities in and outside of school. (B) **Solve problems that incorporate understanding the problem, making a plan, carrying out the plan, and evaluating the solution for reasonableness.** *Also addresses TEKS 4.14(C).*

P.S.I. TEAM +

TASHA: My soccer team is raising money by having a car wash. We earn $36 each hour of washing cars.

YOUR MISSION: Find how much money Tasha's soccer team will make in 5 hours.

Understand The soccer team earns $36 each hour. You need to find how much money the team will make in 5 hours.

Plan You can make a table that shows how much the team will earn in 1, 2, 3, 4, and 5 hours.

Solve The table shows how much money the team earns in 1, 2, 3, 4, and 5 hours.

Hours	1	2	3	4	5
Money	$36	$72	$108	$144	$180

+36 +36 +36 +36

So, Tasha's soccer team will make $180 in 5 hours.

Check Look back at the problem. Start with $180. Subtract $36 five times.

$180 − **$36** = $144
$144 − **$36** = $108
$108 − **$36** = $72
$72 − **$36** = $36
$36 − **$36** = $0

So, you know the answer is correct.

Mixed Problem Solving

See page R14.

Use any strategy shown below to solve. Tell what strategy you used.

PROBLEM-SOLVING STRATEGIES
- Draw a picture.
- Look for a pattern.
- Make a table.

1. Gigi is planting flowers in her garden in the pattern shown. How many daisies will she have if she plants 24 flowers?

2. Julio is setting up square tables for a party. One person can sit at each side of a table. He connects the tables together to form one long table. He invited 9 friends. How many tables does he need for everyone, including himself?

3. Copy and complete the number pattern.

   15, 20, 18, 23, 21, ■, ■, ■

4. Misu wants to buy juice, a fruit cup, and a salad for lunch. She has $5. How much change will she get back?

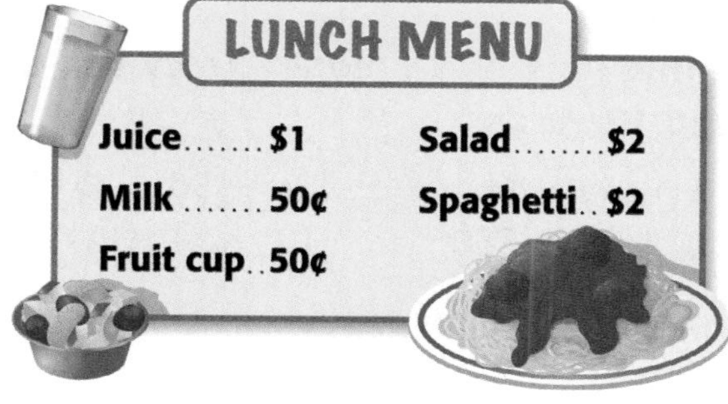

LUNCH MENU
Juice....... $1
Milk....... 50¢
Fruit cup.. 50¢
Salad........ $2
Spaghetti.. $2

5. **Measurement** Kirk rode his bike to school, which is 2 miles away. After school, he rode to his friend's house, which is 1 mile from school. Then he rode home. If he rode a total of 4 miles, how far does he live from his friend?

6. Miko made 2 bowls of fruit punch for a family reunion. Each bowl fills 24 glasses. There are 12 family members at the reunion. How many glasses of punch can each person get?

7. Victor wants to buy CDs that cost $12 each. He has $40. How many CDs can he buy?

8. Polly is making a scrapbook. She is making the pattern shown as a border for one of the pages. How many bones will she need to glue to the page if she uses 36 shapes in all?

   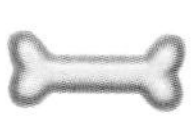  

9. Darnell has baseball practice four days a week. Practice lasts for two hours each day. How many hours does he practice in four weeks?

10. **WRITING IN MATH** Niles's bedtime was 8:00 P.M. in first grade. It was 8:30 P.M. in second grade and 9:00 P.M. in third grade. The answer is 10:00 P.M. What is the question?

5-8 Multiplication and Division Relationships

GET READY to Learn

Tracy rakes yards to earn money. If she rakes 2 yards a day, she earns \$12. If she rakes 4 yards, she earns \$24. If she rakes 6 yards, she earns \$36. How much money will she earn if she rakes 10 yards?

MAIN IDEA

I will find and use a rule to write an equation.

Targeted TEKS 4.7 The student uses organizational structures to analyze and describe patterns and relationships. **Describe the relationship between two sets of related data such as ordered pairs in a table.**

You can write an equation to describe and extend a pattern.

Real-World EXAMPLES Find a Multiplication Rule

1 MONEY Write an equation that describes the amount of money Tracy earns.

Show the information in a table. Then look for the pattern that describes the rule.

Yards Raked	Amount Earned (\$)
Input (▲)	Output (■)
2	12
4	24
6	36
8	■
10	■
12	■

Pattern: $2 \times \mathbf{6} = 12$
$4 \times \mathbf{6} = 24$
$6 \times \mathbf{6} = 36$

Rule: Multiply by 6.

Equation: ▲ × 6 = ■

(▲ = input, ■ = output)

2 Use the equation to find how much money Tracy will earn if she rakes 8, 10, and 12 yards.

▲ × **\$6** = ■
8 × **\$6** = \$48

▲ × **\$6** = ■
10 × **\$6** = \$60

▲ × **\$6** = ■
12 × **\$6** = \$72

So, Tracy will earn \$48, \$60, and \$72.

Always check to make sure the rule works for each number in the table.

Real-World EXAMPLES Find a Division Rule

3 **MONEY The cost of crackers is shown. Write an equation that describes the pattern.**

Total Cost ($)	Boxes of Crackers
Input (▲)	Output (■)
4	1
8	2
12	3
16	■
20	■
24	■

Look for the pattern that describes the rule.

Pattern: $4 \div 4 = 1$
$8 \div 4 = 2$
$12 \div 4 = 3$

Rule: Divide by 4.

Equation: ▲ ÷ 4 = ■

input output

4 **Use the equation to find how many boxes you get for $16, $20, or $24.**

▲ ÷ 4 = ■	▲ ÷ 4 = ■	▲ ÷ 4 = ■
$16 ÷ 4 = 4	$20 ÷ 4 = 5	$24 ÷ 4 = 6

So, $16, $20, or $24 will buy 4, 5, or 6 boxes of crackers.

CHECK What You Know

Write an equation that describes the pattern. Then use the equation to find the next three numbers. See Examples 1–4 (pp. 210–211)

1.

Input (▲)	2	4	6	8	10	12
Output (■)	12	24	36	■	■	■

2.

Input (▲)	16	24	32	40	48	56
Output (■)	2	3	4	■	■	■

3. The table shows the cost of movie tickets. How many tickets will you get for $72? See Examples 1–4 (pp. 210–211)

Total Cost	Input (▲)	$12	$24	$36	$48	$60	$72
Tickets	Output (■)	2	4	6	■	■	■

4. Talk About It How are a rule and an equation alike? How are they different?

Practice and Problem Solving

EXTRA PRACTICE See page R15.

Write an equation that describes each pattern. Then use the equation to find the next three numbers. See Examples 1–4 (pp. 210–211)

5.

Input (▲)	1	3	5	7	9	11
Output (■)	5	15	25	■	■	■

6.

Input (▲)	2	4	6	8	10	12
Output (■)	14	28	42	■	■	■

7.

Input (▲)	3	9	15	21	27	33
Output (■)	1	3	5	■	■	■

8.

Input (▲)	10	20	30	40	50	60
Output (■)	2	4	6	■	■	■

9. A local sports team sells $6 tickets for $3, $8 tickets for $4, and $10 tickets for $5. Write a rule and equation to find the cost of a $20 ticket.

10. The admission for an art museum costs $5 per person. Make a table to find how much it would cost for 2, 3, 4, 5, and 6 people to attend the exhibit.

Real-World PROBLEM SOLVING

Art Sari makes bead necklaces. The table shows the relationship between the number of blue beads and green beads Sari uses.

Blue Beads	Green Beads
Input (▲)	Output (■)
3	1
9	3
15	5
21	■
27	■
33	■

11. Write an equation that describes the relationship between green beads and blue beads.

12. How many green beads does Sari need if she is using 36 blue beads?

13. How many beads does Sari have in all if she has 9 green beads?

H.O.T. Problems

14. **OPEN ENDED** Create a table that shows inputs and outputs. Choose a multiplication or division rule for the table. Then choose six input numbers and find the output numbers.

15. **CHALLENGE** Can both an addition equation and a multiplication equation be written for the number pattern in the table to the right? Explain.

Input (▲)	Output (■)
1	2
2	4
3	6

16. **WRITING IN MATH** Write a problem about a real-world situation that involves a pattern. What equation describes the pattern?

Math Online Self-Check Quiz at tx.gr4math.com

17. What is the value of the expression below if ● = 6? (Lesson 5-6)

9 × ● + 3

A 18

B 27

C 57

D 81

18. What is the value of the expression below? (Lesson 5-6)

8 × (9 − 6)

F 11

G 24

H 48

J 66

19. Which equation can be used to describe the pattern in the table? (Lesson 5-8)

Input (▲)	Output (■)
1	■
3	9
5	15
7	21
9	27

A ▲ + 3 = ■

B ▲ + 6 = ■

C ▲ × 3 = ■

D ■ × 3 = ▲

Spiral Review

Find a rule and equation that describes each pattern. Then use the equation to find the next two numbers. (Lesson 5-5)

20.

Input (?)	Output (?)
30	20
24	14
18	8
15	■
16	■

21.

Input (▲)	Output (■)
3	15
5	17
7	19
9	■
11	■

Find the value of each expression if ▲ = 12 and ■ = 3. (Lesson 5-5)

22. ■ × 6

23. ▲ ÷ 4

24. ▲ ÷ ■

Write an equation for each situation. Then solve. (Lesson 5-5)

25. The product of a number and 7 equals 49. What is the number?

26. 132 divided by a number equals 11. What is the number?

CHAPTER 5

Study Guide and Review

FOLDABLES™ Study Organizer — GET READY to Study

Be sure the following Key Vocabulary words and Key Concepts are written in your Foldable.

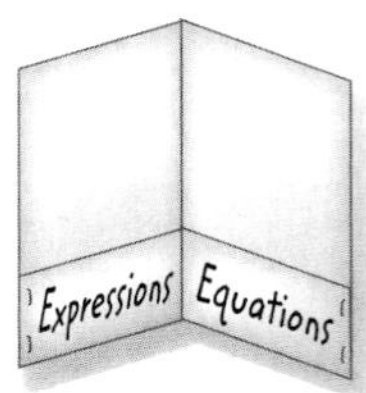

BIG Ideas

Expressions

- An **expression** is a statement with numbers and/or symbols, and at least one operation. (p. 183)

■ − 3

Equations

- An **equation** is a statement with an equals (=) sign, showing that two expressions are equal. (p. 188)

▲ + 8 = 17

- An equation can be used to describe the pattern in a table. (p. 194)

Input (▲)	8	10	15	26	28
Output (■)	12	14	19	■	■

Rule: Add 4.

Equation: ▲ + 4 = ■

Key Vocabulary

equation (p. 188)
expression (p. 183)
parentheses (p. 184)
pattern (p. 194)

Vocabulary Check

Choose the vocabulary word that completes each sentence.

1. 6 + ■ is a(n) ___?___.
2. 9 + ■ = 19 is a(n) ___?___.
3. An ___?___ shows that two expressions are equal.
4. 6 − 2 = 4 is a(*n*) ___?___.
5. In the expression 2 + (7 − 3) you should do what is in the ___?___ first.
6. ■ + 18 is a(*n*) ___?___.

Lesson-by-Lesson Review

5-1 Addition and Subtraction Expressions (pp. 183–185)

Example 1
What is the value of 5 + ▲ if ▲ = 2?

5 + ▲ Write the expression.

5 + 2 Replace ▲ with 2.

7 Add 5 and 2.

Example 2
Find the value of 13 − (■ + 3) if ■ = 8.

13 − (■ + 3) Write the expression.

13 − (8 + 3) Replace ■ with 8.

13 − 11 Add (8 + 3) first.

2 Subtract 13 − 11.

Find the value of each expression if ▲ = 9 and ■ = 5.

7. ▲ + 3 **8.** 12 + ■

9. (▲ − 2) + 6 **10.** 14 − (■ + 2)

Write an expression for each situation.

11. five more than ■

12. the sum of ▲ and four

13. seven subtracted from ■

Hayden's score was 15 more than Mario's.

14. Define a symbol. Then write an expression for Hayden's score.

15. If Mario's score was 60, what was Hayden's score?

5-2 Solve Equations (pp. 188–191)

Example 3
Solve 4 + ■ = 10.

4 + ■ = 10 4 plus what equals 10?

4 + 6 = 10 4 + 6 = 10

■ = 6

Example 4
Solve 18 − ■ = 12.

18 − ■ = 12 18 minus what equals 12?

18 − 6 = 12 18 − 6 = 12

■ = 6

Solve each equation.

16. ■ + 10 = 18 **17.** ■ − 8 = 11

18. 7 − ■ = 3 **19.** ■ + 9 = 15

Write and solve an equation for each situation.

20. A number plus 7 equals 19. What is the number?

21. Five subtracted from a number equals 12. What is the number?

5-3 Problem-Solving Skill: Missing and Extra Information

(pp. 192–193)

Example 5
Troy's family went to the zoo. Admission to the local zoo is $12 for adults and $5 for children. How much did it cost for Troy's family to go to the zoo?

Understand

What facts do you know?

Troy's family went to the zoo.

Zoo admission is $12 for adults and $5 for children.

What do you need to find?

Find the cost for Troy's family to go to the zoo.

Plan Identify the information needed to solve the problem. Look for any extra or missing information.

Solve To find the cost of admission, add the cost of each family member.

This information is missing, so the problem can not be solved.

Check Since no answer was found, there is no answer to check.

Identify any missing or extra information. Then solve if possible.

22. The table shows the points Yoshi scored in a basketball game. How many points did she score in the second half of the game?

first half	second half	total
12 points	■	26 points

23. The Cougars scored 36 points and defeated the Falcons by 12 points. How many points did the Falcons score?

24. A pet frog is two years old. It eats four times a week. If there are 365 days in a year, how many days old is the frog?

25. Kendra's parents drove 269 miles to Seattle. Kendra's aunt flew 457 miles to Seattle. What is the total round-trip distance Kendra's parents will drive to Seattle and back?

5-4 Patterns (pp. 194–196)

Example 6

Look at the series of numbers. Find the rule and extend the pattern.

12, 16, 20, 24, ■, ■

+ 4 + 4 + 4 + 4 + 4

$24 + 4 = 28$

$28 + 4 = 32$

So, the rule is +4 and the next two numbers in the series are 28 and 32.

Example 7

Harry plays ball with his friends. The table shows how long he spends each day playing. If this pattern continues, how long will he play ball on Friday?

Day	Time
Monday	15 minutes
Tuesday	30 minutes
Wednesday	45 minutes
Thursday	60 minutes
Friday	75 minutes

+15 +15 +15 +15

Since each day he played 15 minutes longer, by Friday he will play 75 minutes or 1 hour and 15 minutes.

Example 8

Genni drew these figures.

Which of the following is like the figures she drew? Explain.

Since she has drawn triangles, the triangles will be most like the others.

Look at the series of numbers. Find the rule and extend the pattern.

26. 26, 23, 20, 17, ■, ■

27. 200, 175, 150, ■, ■

28. Tomás is making a pattern with shells from his family vacation. In the first row there are 4 shells. In the second row there are 12 shells and in the third row there are 16 shells. How many shells will be in the fourth and fifth rows?

29. Cynthia made oatmeal bars for the bake sale. She sold them at 4 for \$1. How much would 10 oatmeal bars cost?

30. The table shows the cost of admission to the outdoor theater. How much will it cost for 5 people to go to the theater?

# of People	Cost (\$)
1	8
2	16
3	24
4	32
5	■

31. 

Which of the following would not belong in this group of figures? Explain.

A ◇ **B** ○ **C** ◺ **D** ⬠

5-5 Addition and Subtraction Relationships (pp. 198–201)

Example 9
Write an equation that describes the pattern in the table. Then use the equation to find the next two numbers in the pattern.

Input (▲)	Output (■)
12	2
17	7
22	12
27	■
32	■
37	■

First, write an equation.

Pattern: 12 − **10** = 2
17 − **10** = 7
22 − **10** = 12

Rule: Subtract 10.

Equation: ▲ − 10 = ■

Then use the equation to find the next three numbers.

Find the next three numbers when the input (▲) is 27, 32, and 37.

▲ − 10 = ■

27 − 10 = 17

32 − 10 = 22

37 − 10 = 27

So, the next three numbers in the pattern are 17, 22, and 27.

Write an equation to describe the pattern. Then use the equation to find the next two numbers.

32.

Input (▲)	Output (■)
14	5
21	12
27	18
33	■
39	■
45	■

33.

Input (▲)	Output (■)
15	21
20	26
25	31
30	■
35	■
40	■

34.

Input (▲)	Output (■)
11	7
13	9
15	11
17	■
19	■
21	■

5-6 Multiplication and Division Expressions (pp. 204–207)

Example 10
Find the value of 5 × ■ if ■ = 3.

5 × ■ Write the expression.

5 × 3 Replace ■ with 3.

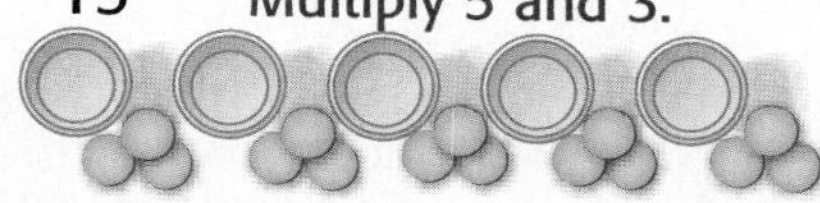

15 Multiply 5 and 3.

Example 11
Find the value of 3 × (12 ÷ ■) if ■ = 6.

3 × (12 ÷ ■) Write the expression.

3 × (12 ÷ 6) Replace ■ with 6.

3 × 2 Find (12 ÷ 6) first.

6 Multiply 3 × 2.

Example 12

Maggie has some money to buy kites for her club. Write an expression for the number of kites Maggie can buy with her money.

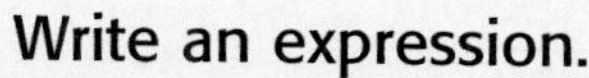

Write an expression.

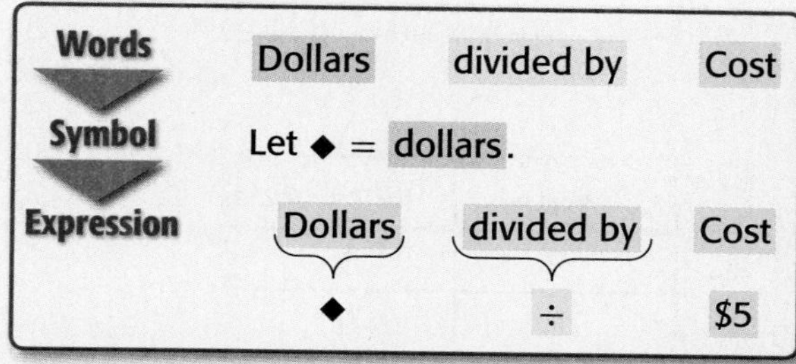

Words	Dollars	divided by	Cost
Symbol	Let ◆ = dollars.		
Expression	Dollars	divided by	Cost
	◆	÷	$5

So, the number of kites Maggie can buy is ◆ ÷ $5.

Find the value of each expression if ■ = 4 and ▲ = 6.

35. ■ × 3

36. ▲ ÷ 2

37. 24 ÷ (▲ × 2)

38. (16 ÷ ■) × ▲

Write an expression for each situation.

39. a number divided by 7

40. 32 divided by a number

41. Terri has 4 times as many coins as Kuni. If Kuni has 7 coins, how many do they have in all? Write an expression. Then solve.

42. Jason wants to buy five toy cars.

Write an expression to show how much he will pay for the cars.

43. Joni has 3 times as much paper as Korra. If Korra has 10 sheets of paper, how many sheets does Joni have? Write an expression. Then solve.

5-7 Problem-Solving Investigation: Choose a Strategy (pp. 208–209)

Example 13

Sonia's bank account increases with each paycheck. Use the table to find how much her account increased after her fourth and fifth paychecks.

Number of Paychecks	Account Total
1	$25
2	$75
3	$125
4	■
5	■

Use the table to find a pattern. Each paycheck shows a rule of +$50. So, the missing outputs are $175 and $225.

Use any strategy to solve.

44. Lucas is collecting coupons to raise funds for his school. The first week he collects 525. The second week he collects 600. He collects 675 the third week. If this pattern continues, how many should he collect the 7th week?

45. Karina has $27 and Jessica has $48. Do they have enough money to buy the $82 concert tickets they want? Explain.

5-8 Multiplication and Division Relationships (pp. 210–213)

Example 14
Write an equation that describes the pattern in the table.

Input (▲)	Output (■)
5	1
10	2
15	3

Divide by 5.

So, ▲ ÷ 5 = ■ will be the equations.

input output

Write an equation that describes the pattern. Then use the equation to find the next number.

46.

Input (▲)	Output (■)
1	7
3	21
5	35
7	■

47.

Input (▲)	Output (■)
9	3
18	6
27	9
36	■

Chapter 5 Chapter Test

For Exercises 1–3, tell whether each statement is *true* or *false*.

1. The parentheses tell you which operation to perform first.

2. An expression is a math statement without numbers and symbols.

3. A pattern is a series of numbers or figures that follow a rule.

Write an expression for each situation.

4. thirty subtracted from ▲

5. the difference of ■ and twenty-six

6. the sum of ■ and 13

7. eight more than ■

Solve each equation.

8. 13 + ■ = 25 9. ■ − 12 = 22

10. Justice rode his bike for 35 minutes on Monday, 20 minutes on Tuesday, and 44 minutes on Saturday. Did he spend more than an hour riding his bike on Monday and Tuesday? Identify any missing or extra information.

11. **TEST PRACTICE** Which number would make the equation true?

17 + ▲ = 20

A 2 **C** 37

B 3 **D** 33

Solve each equation.

12. ■ ÷ 10 = 12 13. 6 × ■ = 54

14. The product of a number and 12 is 84. Write an equation to find the number.

15. **TEST PRACTICE** Which equation describes the pattern?

Input (▲)	Output (■)
8	1
24	3
40	5
56	7
72	9

F ▲ − 7 = ■ **H** ▲ ÷ 8 = ■

G ▲ ÷ 7 = ■ **J** ■ + 7 = ■

16. The ski club is having a car wash. They make $5 for each car they wash. Write a rule and an equation to find how much money they will make if they wash 4 cars.

Show the equality is not changed.

17. ■ ÷ 8 = 12
■ ÷ 8 × 8 = 12 × 8

18. **WRITING IN MATH** Explain how to find the missing number in the equation (9 × 4) ÷ ■ = 60 ÷ 10.

CHAPTER 5

Texas Test Practice

Cumulative, Chapters 1–5

TEST Example

Sonia wrote the following numbers on the chalkboard.

4, 7, 10, 13, 16, 19, ________

What number should come next in the pattern?

A 20

B 21

C 22

D 23

Read the Test Question

You need to find the next number in the pattern of numbers.

Solve the Test Question

Look for a pattern in the numbers.

$4 + 3 = 7$
$7 + 3 = 10$
$10 + 3 = 13$
$13 + 3 = 16$
$16 + 3 = 19$

Each number is 3 more than the previous number. So the next number in the pattern will be $19 + 3 = 22$.

The answer is C.

TEST-TAKING TIP

Look for a pattern in the numbers to solve the problem.

online **Personal Tutor at** tx.gr4math.com

Choose the best answer.

1. What number comes next in the pattern below?

5, 10, 15, 20, 25, ________

A 27

B 28

C 29

D 30

2. What number comes next in the pattern below?

7, 13, 19, 25, 31, ________

F 37

G 38

H 39

J 41

Get Ready for the Texas Test
For test-taking strategies and more practice, see pages TX1–TX21.

3. What multiplication expression does this model represent?

A 2×9　　**C** 3×10

B 3×8　　**D** 3×9

---

4. The graph shows the number of points scored by Mark and Kim during the first 4 games of the basketball season.

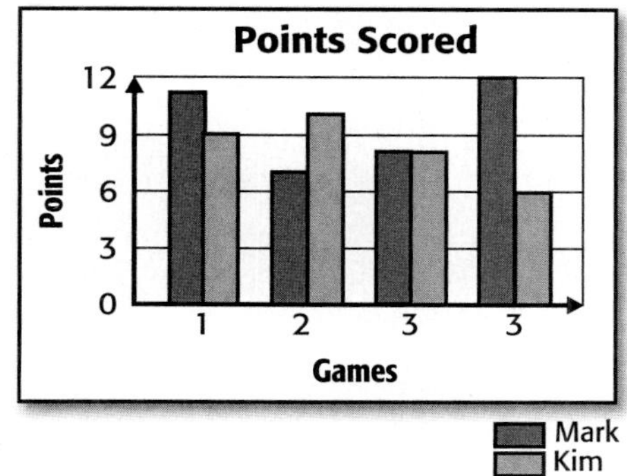

How many more points did Kim score than Mark in Game 2?

F 2 points　　**H** 4 points

G 3 points　　**J** 5 points

---

5. Refer to the double bar graph of points scored in Exercise 4. During which game did both players score the same number of points?

A Game 1　　**C** Game 3

B Game 2　　**D** Game 4

---

6. There are 48 students traveling on a field trip. Each van holds 8 students. How many vans are needed in all?

F 6　　**H** 8

G 7　　**J** 9

---

7. GRIDDABLE Which number makes this equation true?

$$7 \times \square = 63$$

---

8. Which of the following statements best describes the relationship between ▲ and ■ in the table?

▲	■
1	3
2	6
3	9
4	12
5	15

A ■ is 3 more than ▲

B ■ is 3 times ▲

C ■ is 3 less than ▲

D ■ is 2 times ▲

CHAPTER 6

Multiply Whole Numbers

BIG Idea How do you multiply by one-digit numbers?

Multiply each digit by the one-digit number, starting with the ones place. Regroup when necessary.

Example A great white shark has 50 teeth. If it has 3 sets of these in a lifetime, how many teeth would it have had?

Multiply using multiples of 10.

$$5 \times 3 = 15$$
$$5\mathbf{0} \times 3 = 15\mathbf{0}$$

The shark would have had 150 teeth in its lifetime.

What will I learn in this chapter?

- Multiply by multiples of 10 and 100.
- Estimate products.
- Multiply multi-digit numbers.
- Determine reasonable answers.

Key Vocabulary

multiply

estimate

product

Distributive Property of Multiplication

Student Study Tools at tx.gr4math.com

FOLDABLES™ Study Organizer

Make this Foldable to help you organize information about multiplying by one-digit numbers. Begin with one sheet of 11″ × 17″ paper.

1. **Fold** the short sides so they meet in the middle.

2. **Fold** the top to the bottom.

3. **Unfold** and cut to make four tabs.

4. **Label** each tab as shown.

ARE YOU READY for Chapter 6?

You have two ways to check prerequisite skills for this chapter.

Option 2

Math Online Take the Chapter Readiness Quiz at tx.gr4math.com.

Option 1

Complete the Quick Check below.

QUICK Check

Multiply. Use models if needed. (Lessons 4-3 and 4-5)

1. 2×3 **2.** $4 \times \$4$ **3.** 5×6 **4.** $7 \times \$8$

5. 9×4 **6.** 8×3 **7.** $\$7 \times 5$ **8.** 9×9

9. Evan's photo album has 8 pages of pictures. How many photos are in Evan's album if the same number of photos are on each page?

Identify the place value of the underlined digit. (Lesson 1-1)

10. 1,<u>6</u>30 **11.** $<u>5</u>,367 **12.** 20,4<u>9</u>5 **13.** $<u>8</u>9,196

14. Measurement Mount Everest's tallest peak is 29,035 feet tall. It is the highest point on Earth. Identify the place value of each digit in 29,035.

Round each number to its greatest place value. (Lesson 1-6)

15. 26 **16.** $251 **17.** 4,499 **18.** $33,103

19. There are 1,366 students at Sunrise Elementary School. Approximately how many students attend the school rounded to the greatest place value?

6-1 Multiples of 10 and 100

GET READY to Learn

Houston is known as the Lightning Capital of Texas. Suppose 60 bolts of lightning strike Houston in one storm. How many will strike in 4 storms?

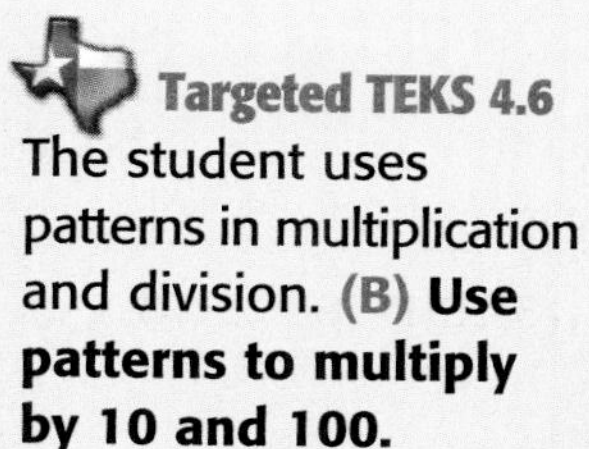

MAIN IDEA

I will multiply multiples of 10 and 100 using basic facts and patterns.

Targeted TEKS 4.6 The student uses patterns in multiplication and division. **(B) Use patterns to multiply by 10 and 100.**

You can use basic facts and number patterns to multiply.

Real-World EXAMPLE Multiples of 10

1 WEATHER **How many strikes will there be in 4 storms?**

You need to find 4×60. Use basic facts and patterns.

$4 \times 6 = 24$ $\quad$ 4 × 6 ones = 24 ones = 24

$4 \times 60 = 240$ $\quad$ 4 × 6 tens = 24 tens = 240

So, there would be 240 strikes in 4 storms. Notice that the pattern is 4×6 with one zero at the end.

Real-World EXAMPLE Multiples of 100

2 ANIMALS **The whale shark's mouth is 5 feet long, and each foot contains 600 teeth. How many teeth does a whale shark have?**

You need to find 5×600. Use basic facts and patterns.

$5 \times 6 = 30$ $\quad$ 5 × 6 ones = 30 ones = 30

$5 \times 60 = 300$ $\quad$ 5 × 6 tens = 30 tens = 300

$5 \times 600 = 3{,}000$ $\quad$ 5 × 6 hundreds = 30 hundreds = 3,000

So, a whale shark has 3,000 teeth. Notice that this pattern is 5×6 with two zeros at the end.

When you know basic facts and number patterns, you can multiply mentally.

Real-World EXAMPLE Multiples of 1,000

> **Remember**
>
> As the number of zeros in a factor increases, the number of zeros in the product increases.

3 ANIMALS **Female elephants' average weight is about 8,000 pounds. How much would 3 female elephants weigh?**

Find $3 \times 8{,}000$.

$3 \times 8 = 24$	3 × 8 ones = 24 ones = 24
$3 \times 80 = 240$	3 × 8 tens = 24 tens = 240
$3 \times 800 = 2{,}400$	3 × 8 hundreds = 24 hundreds = 2,400
$3 \times 8{,}000 = 24{,}000$	3 × 8 thousands = 24 thousands = 24,000

So, $3 \times 8{,}000$ is 24,000. Notice that this pattern is 3×8 with three zeros at the end.

Personal Tutor at tx.gr4math.com

CHECK What You Know

Multiply. Use basic facts and patterns. See Examples 1–3 (pp. 227–228)

1. 2×1
2×10
2×100
$2 \times 1{,}000$

2. 6×8
6×80
6×800
$6 \times 8{,}000$

3. 7×9
7×90
7×900
$7 \times 9{,}000$

Multiply. See Examples 1–3 (pp. 227–228)

4. 3×20

5. 8×600

6. $9 \times 9{,}000$

7. A zookeeper is in charge of feeding 70 monkeys. Each day the monkeys eat 3 meals. How many meals does the zookeeper prepare each day?

8. Talk About It What is the product of 4 and 500? Explain why there are more zeros in the product than in the factors in the problem.

Practice and Problem Solving

EXTRA PRACTICE
See page R16.

Multiply. Use basic facts and patterns. See Examples 1–3 (pp. 227–228)

9. 5 × 3
5 × 30
5 × 300
5 × 3,000

10. 3 × 4
3 × 40
3 × 400
3 × 4,000

11. 2 × 9
2 × 90
2 × 900
2 × 9,000

12. 6 × 7
6 × 70
6 × 700
6 × 7,000

13. 9 × 1
9 × 10
9 × 100
9 × 1,000

14. 8 × 5
8 × 50
8 × 500
8 × 5,000

Multiply. See Examples 1–3 (pp. 227–228)

15. 4 × 30

16. 6 × 40

17. 7 × 200

18. 4 × 500

19. 3 × 9,000

20. 9 × 6,000

Algebra Copy and complete.

21. If 6 × ■ = 42,
then 60 × ■ = 4,200.

22. If 5 × 7 = ■,
then 50 × ■ = 3,500.

23. Mr. Singh's car payments are $300 a month. How much money will he pay in 6 months?

24. Mia's cell phone plan includes 2,000 monthly minutes. How many minutes does she get over 6 months?

Real-World PROBLEM SOLVING

Travel The Williams family is going to a theme park.

25. Admission tickets cost $30 for each person. What is the total cost for the 5 family members for one day?

26. The cost for each person to eat for one week is $100. Find the total cost for the family to eat for one week.

27. Suppose each family member goes on 70 rides during the week. How many rides will they go on altogether?

H.O.T. Problems

28. OPEN ENDED Write two multiplication expressions that have a product of 20,000.

29. WRITING IN MATH Which basic fact would you use to find 1 × 10,000? Explain. What is 1 × 10,000?

6-2 Problem-Solving Skill

MAIN IDEA I will decide whether an answer to a problem is reasonable.

Targeted TEKS 4.14 The student applies Grade 4 mathematics to solve problems connected to everyday experiences and activities in and outside of school. **(C) Select or develop an appropriate problem-solving plan or strategy, . . . to solve a problem.** *Also addresses TEKS 4.14(B).*

Odell donated 3 cases of dog treats to a dog shelter. Each case has 900 treats. The dogs eat 2,500 treats each month. Odell says he has donated enough treats for more than one month. Is his claim reasonable?

Understand	**What facts do you know?** • 3 cases of treats were donated. • Each case has 900 treats. • The animals eat 2,500 treats each month. **What do you need to find?** • Is it reasonable to say that the 3 cases of treats will last longer than one month?
Plan	Find 3×900. Then determine if the amount is reasonable.
Solve	3×900 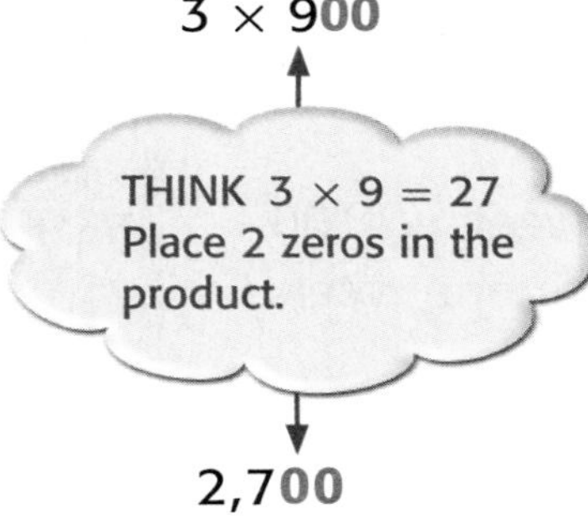 THINK $3 \times 9 = 27$ Place 2 zeros in the product. 2,700 Since $2{,}700 > 2{,}500$, it is reasonable to say that the three cases will last longer than one month.
Check	You can add to check the multiplication. $900 + 900 + 900 = 2{,}700$ So, the answer is correct.

ANALYZE the Skill

Refer to the problem on the previous page.

1. Explain why 3 is multiplied by 900 to decide if Odell's claim was reasonable.
2. Explain why there are 2 zeros at the end of the product of 3 and 900.
3. Look back at the example. What would make Odell's claim *not* reasonable?
4. Suppose Odell donates 5 cases of treats. Is it reasonable to believe the treats will last 2 months? Explain.

PRACTICE the Skill

EXTRA PRACTICE
See page R16.

Decide whether each answer is reasonable. Explain your reasoning.

5. Ben delivers 40 newspapers each day. Is 400 a reasonable estimate for the number of newspapers Ben delivers each week?
6. The calendar shows the number of days each month Olivia rides her bike.

September

Sun	Mon	Tues	Wed	Thurs	Fri	Sat
					1	2 (B)
3 (B)	4	5	6	7	8 (B)	9
10 (B)	11	12	13 (B)	14	15	16 (B)
17	18	19	20	21	22 (B)	23
24 (B)	25	26	27	28 (B)	29	30 (B)

Each time she rides her bike, she travels 10 miles. Is it reasonable to say that Olivia will bike more than 500 miles in 6 months?

7. Jay makes $40 a week doing yard work. He is saving his money to buy a laptop computer that costs $400. He has already saved $120. Is it reasonable to say that Jay will save enough money to buy the laptop in 6 weeks?
8. **Measurement** The distance from Ian's home to the museum is 640 yards. Is it reasonable to say that Ian's home is more than 800 feet away from the museum?
9. Kiri spends 60 minutes a week walking to school. Is it reasonable to say that she spends 240 minutes walking to school in four weeks?
10. The table below shows the number of pennies collected by four children.

Pennies Collected

Child	Number of Pennies
Myron	48
Teresa	52
Veronica	47
Warren	53

Is it reasonable to say that the children collected about 200 pennies in all?

11. **WRITING IN MATH** Write a problem where $180 would be a reasonable answer.

6-3 Estimate Products

MAIN IDEA

I will estimate products by rounding.

 **Targeted TEKS 4.5** The student estimates to determine reasonable results. (B) **Use strategies including rounding and compatible numbers to estimate solutions to multiplication** and division problems.

GET READY to Learn

The fastest passenger train in the world actually floats above its track. This train in China can travel up to 267 miles per hour. About how far can the train travel in 3 hours?

To estimate products, round factors to their greatest place or use compatible numbers.

Real-World EXAMPLE Estimate Products

1 TRAVEL **About how far can the train travel in 3 hours?**

Estimate 3×267. Round the greater factor to its greatest place. Then use basic facts and patterns to multiply.

3×267

↓ THINK 267 rounds to 300.

3×300

So, the train can travel about 900 miles in 3 hours. Since 267 was rounded up, the estimated product is greater than the actual product.

EXAMPLE Use Compatible Numbers

2 **Estimate 8×249.**

8×249

↓ THINK Change 249 to 200 since we know $8 \times 2 = 16$.

8×200 $\quad$ $8 \times 20 = 160$

$8 \times 2 = 16$ $\quad$ $8 \times 200 = 1{,}600$

So, 8×249 is about 1,600. Since 249 was rounded down, the estimated product is less than the actual product.

You can also estimate products involving money.

Real-World EXAMPLE Estimate Money

3 MONEY Ava is going to a four-year college. The tuition is $8,562 each year. About how much will 4 years of college tuition cost?

You need to estimate $4 \times \$8,562$.

First round, then multiply using patterns.

$4 \times \$8,562$

THINK 8,562 rounds to 9,000.

$$4 \times 9 = 36$$
$$4 \times 90 = 360$$
$$4 \times 900 = 3,600$$
$$4 \times \$9,000 = \$36,000$$

So, tuition will cost about $36,000.

Online Personal Tutor at tx.gr4math.com

CHECK What You Know

Estimate each product by rounding or using compatible numbers. Then tell if the estimate is *greater than* or *less than* the actual product. See Examples 1–3 (pp. 232–233)

1. 49×5

2. $\$87 \times 9$

3. 293×3

For Exercises 4 and 5, use the data at the right.

4. Mr. and Mrs. Rivera are going on an African safari. They have saved $1,125 a year for 8 years. Estimate the amount they saved. Do they have enough money? Explain.

5. Talk About It Suppose Mr. and Mrs. Rivera saved $1,499 a year for 8 years. Why would an estimated answer be misleading for the amount saved?

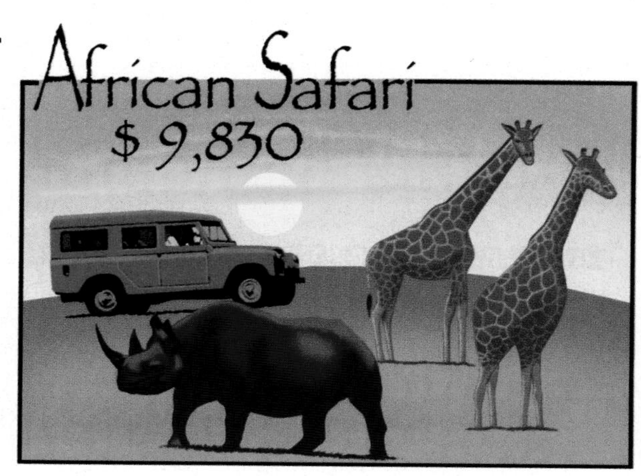

Practice and Problem Solving

EXTRA PRACTICE See page R17.

Estimate each product by rounding or using compatible numbers. Then tell if the estimate is *greater than* or *less than* the actual product. See Examples 1–3 (pp. 232–233)

6. 56×6

7. 89×2

8. 72×8

9. 94×4

10. 2 × $43

11. 8 × $64

12. 5 × $35

13. 7 × $45

14. 7 × 112

15. 3 × 548

16. 9 × 350

17. 6 × 881

18. 4 × $650

19. 7 × $885

20. 9 × $949

21. 7 × $931

22. There are 24 students in each class at Watson Elementary School. About how many students are there if there are 8 classes?

23. The round-trip distance from Austin to Dallas is 196 miles. Mr. Chen travels this distance 6 days a week. About how many miles does he travel each week?

Real-World PROBLEM SOLVING

Entertainment Toby and Lena like to go to the arcade. They earn points toward prizes.

24. Toby went to the arcade 9 times. He earned 275 points each time. What is the biggest prize Toby can get?

25. Lena went to the arcade 7 times. She earned 375 points each time. How many balls could Lena get with her points?

H.O.T. Problems

26. NUMBER SENSE Explain how you can tell if your estimated answer is more or less than the exact answer to a multiplication problem.

27. WRITING IN ▶MATH Suppose you need to find the exact answer to 4 × $189. How can you use estimation to check the reasonableness of your answer?

Estimation Station

Estimate Products

Get Ready!

Players: 2 players
You will need: spinner, 1 number cube, 2 whiteboards

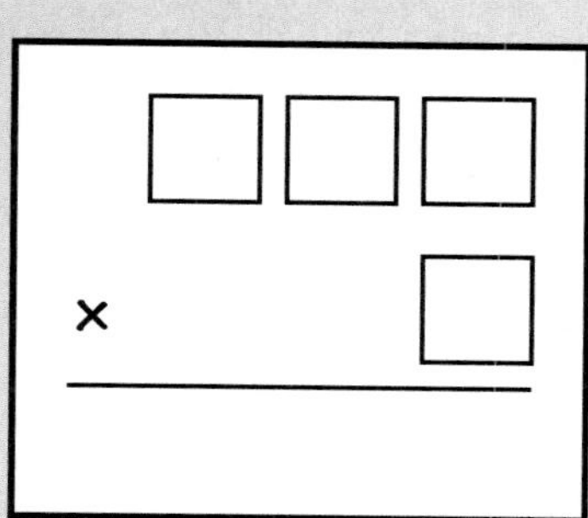

Get Set!

Each player makes a spinner and a game board as shown.

Go!

- Player 1 rolls the number cube to find a one-digit factor. Record the number in the second row on the game board.
- Player 1 then spins to find out how many digits will be in the second factor.
- Player 1 rolls the number cube to find the digits in the second factor. Record each digit.
- Player 1 estimates the product and gets 1 point if the estimate is correct.
- Player 2 takes a turn.
- Continue playing. The player who earns 10 points first wins.

Multiply One-Digit by Two-Digit Numbers

GET READY to Learn

Hands-On Mini Activity

Materials: base-ten blocks

Base-ten blocks can be used to explore multiplying two-digit numbers. In this activity, you will find 4 × 13.

Step 1 Model 4 groups of 13.

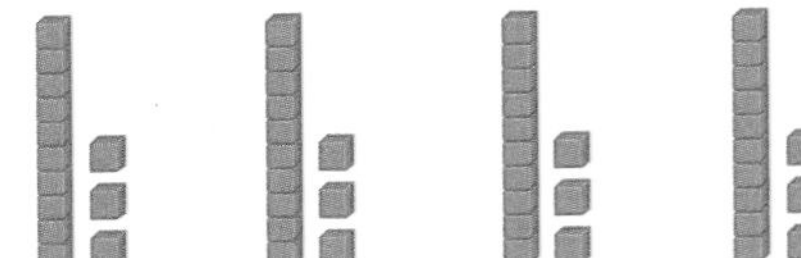

Step 2 Combine the tens and ones. Regroup 12 ones as 1 ten and 2 ones.

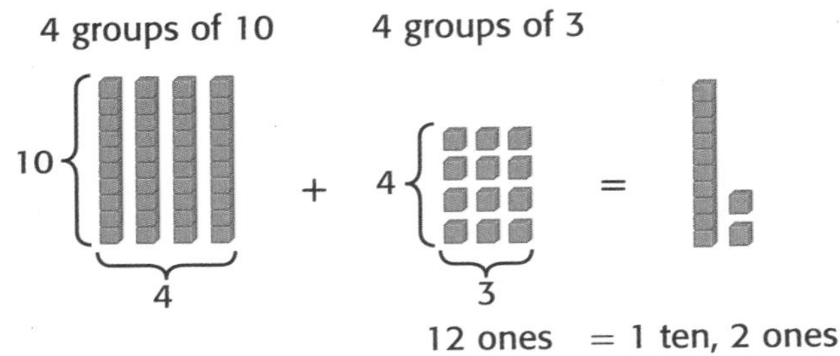

Step 3 Add the partial products.

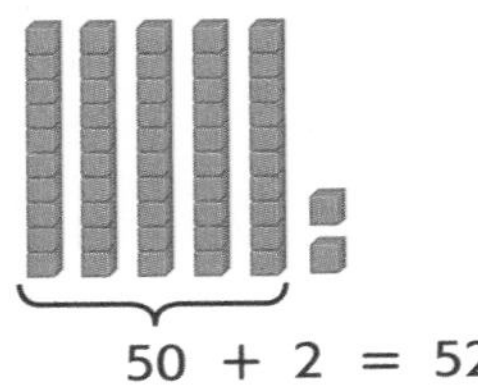

So, 4 × 13 = 52.

Find each product. Use base-ten blocks.

1. 3 × 18 **2.** 4 × 19 **3.** 3 × 21

4. Multiplication is a shortcut for which operation?

5. When is it necessary to regroup in a multiplication problem? When is regrouping not needed?

MAIN IDEA

I will multiply a two-digit number by a one-digit number.

Targeted TEKS 4.4 The student multiplies and divides to solve meaningful problems involving whole numbers. **(D) Use multiplication to solve problems (no more than two digits times two digits without technology).** *Also addresses TEKS 4.14(D).*

Using place-value models is not the only way to multiply a two-digit number by a one-digit number.

EXAMPLE Multiply with Regrouping

Remember

To review the Distributive Property of Multiplication, see Lesson 4-6 (p. 156).

1 **Find 6 × 38.** **Estimate** $6 \times 38 \longrightarrow 6 \times 40 = 240$

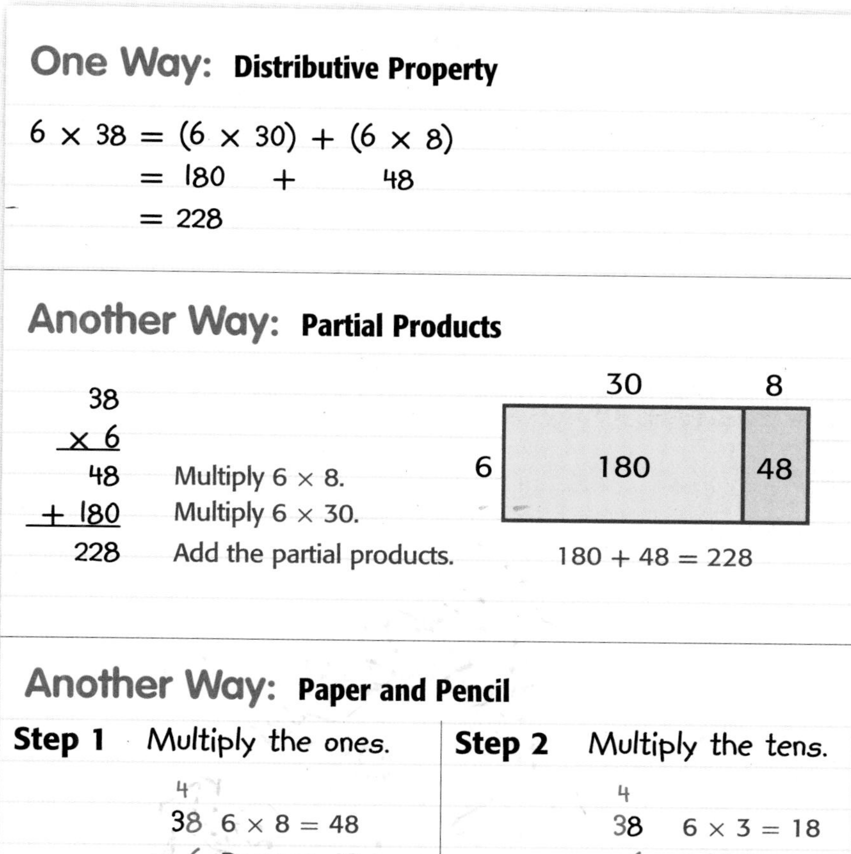

One Way: Distributive Property

$$6 \times 38 = (6 \times 30) + (6 \times 8)$$
$$= 180 + 48$$
$$= 228$$

Another Way: Partial Products

$$\begin{array}{r} 38 \\ \times\ 6 \\ \hline 48 \\ +\ 180 \\ \hline 228 \end{array}$$

Multiply 6 × 8.
Multiply 6 × 30.
Add the partial products.

180 + 48 = 228

Another Way: Paper and Pencil

Step 1 Multiply the ones.

$$\begin{array}{r} ^{4}\ \ \\ 38 \\ \times\ 6 \\ \hline 8 \end{array}$$

6 × 8 = 48
Regroup 48 ones as 4 tens and 8 ones.

Step 2 Multiply the tens.

$$\begin{array}{r} ^{4}\ \ \\ 38 \\ \times\ 6 \\ \hline 228 \end{array}$$

6 × 3 = 18
Add the regrouped tens, 4.

Check for reasonableness

The product, 228, is close to the estimate, 240. ✓

Online Personal Tutor at tx.gr4math.com

CHECK What You Know

Multiply. Check for reasonableness. See Example 1 (p. 237)

1. $\begin{array}{r} 23 \\ \times\ 2 \\ \hline \end{array}$

2. $\begin{array}{r} 42 \\ \times\ 2 \\ \hline \end{array}$

3. 8 × $98

4. Haley can fit 25 books on each of 5 shelves. How many books will fit in all?

5. Talk About It Explain how to find 6 × 37.

Practice and Problem Solving

EXTRA PRACTICE See page R17.

Multiply. Check for reasonableness. See Example 1 (p. 237)

6. $\begin{array}{r} 33 \\ \times\ 2 \\ \hline \end{array}$

7. $\begin{array}{r} \$24 \\ \times\ 2 \\ \hline \end{array}$

8. $\begin{array}{r} 11 \\ \times\ 7 \\ \hline \end{array}$

9. $\begin{array}{r} 13 \\ \times\ 3 \\ \hline \end{array}$

10. 2 × $27

11. 4 × 29

12. 5 × 18

13. 7 × $36

14. 6 × 52

15. 8 × 75

16. 4 × $83

17. 9 × 99

18. Will makes $4 an hour shampooing dogs at a pet shop. Last month he worked 26 hours. How much money did Will earn?

19. If a sales tax is 7 cents for each dollar that is spent on any item, how much sales tax in cents is charged for a badminton set that costs $35?

Real-World PROBLEM SOLVING

Data File The Natural Bridge Caverns are located near San Antonio, Texas.

20. The Diaz family has 5 members. How much would it cost for the family to go on a North Cavern Tour?

21. The Diaz family has $475. Is this enough to go on the Adventure Tour? Explain.

22. Find the total cost of 5 North Cavern Tours and 3 Jaremy Room Flashlight Tours.

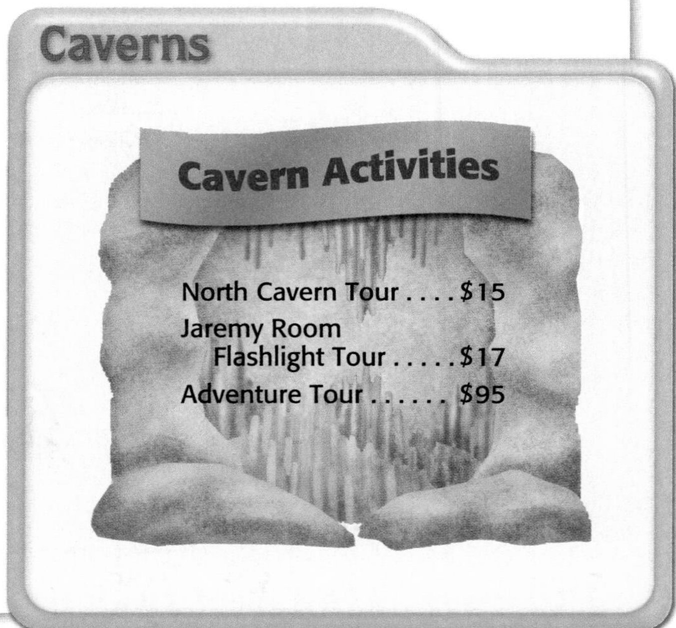

Caverns
Cavern Activities
North Cavern Tour $15
Jaremy Room Flashlight Tour $17
Adventure Tour $95

H.O.T. Problems

23. OPEN ENDED Write two problems that result in a product of 120.

24. WHICH ONE DOESN'T BELONG? Which multiplication problem does not belong with the other three? Explain.

$\begin{array}{r} 12 \\ \times 8 \\ \hline \end{array}$ $\begin{array}{r} 22 \\ \times 4 \\ \hline \end{array}$ $\begin{array}{r} 52 \\ \times 2 \\ \hline \end{array}$ $\begin{array}{r} 33 \\ \times 3 \\ \hline \end{array}$

25. WRITING IN MATH How do you use partial products to find 6 × 42?

Math Online **Self-Check Quiz at** tx.gr4math.com

CHAPTER 6

Mid-Chapter Check

Lessons 6-1 through 6-4

Multiply. Use basic facts and patterns. (Lesson 6-1)

1. 3 × 4
3 × 40
3 × 400
3 × 4,000

2. 12 × 5
12 × 50
12 × 500
12 × 5,000

3. Toshi needs 292 toothpicks for a project. A box holds 150 toothpicks. Is it reasonable to buy 2 boxes? Explain. (Lesson 6-2)

4. Mara and Billy bought 6 bags of balloons for a party. Is it reasonable to say they will have more than 75 balloons? (Lesson 6-2)

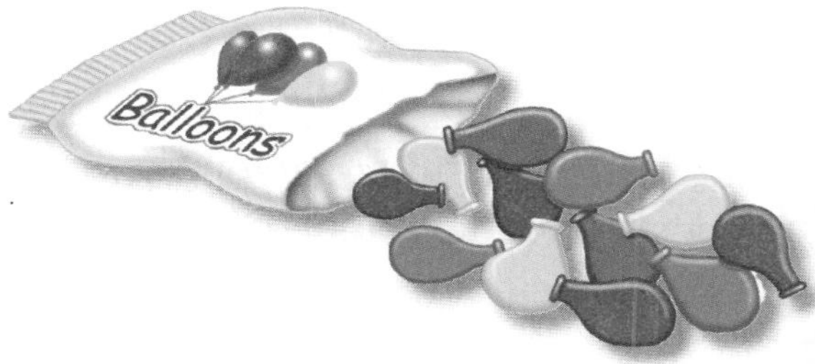

Estimate each product. (Lesson 6-3)

5. 3 × 252

6. 5 × 7,49

7. **TEST PRACTICE** Jada pays $1,875 a year in car payments. About how much money will she pay in 5 years? (Lesson 6-3)

A $5,000 **B** $7,500

C $9,375 **D** $10,000

8. Juan plans to read 264 pages a month to complete his book in 6 months. About how many pages are in his book? (Lesson 6-3)

9. **Measurement** Each gallon of paint covers about 350 square feet. Ann estimated that 3 gallons of paint would be enough to cover 1,400 square feet. Will Ann have enough paint? Explain.

Multiply. Check for reasonableness. (Lesson 6-3)

10.
$$\begin{array}{r} 43 \\ \times\ 2 \\ \hline \end{array}$$

11.
$$\begin{array}{r} \$51 \\ \times\ 3 \\ \hline \end{array}$$

12. 9 × 62

13. 8 × 47

14. There are 24 pencils in a package. How many pencils will you have if you buy 6 packages? (Lesson 6-4)

15. **TEST PRACTICE** There are 27 boxes of markers in the art room. If each box holds 8 markers, how many markers are in the art room? (Lesson 6-4)

F 106 **H** 216

G 166 **J** 226

16. **WRITING IN MATH** Cassie got the following problem wrong on her math test. Explain what she did wrong. (Lesson 6-4)

$$\begin{array}{r} {}^{5}\ \ \\ 47 \\ \times\ 8 \\ \hline 326 \end{array}$$

Problem-Solving Investigation

MAIN IDEA I will choose the best strategy to solve a problem.

Targeted TEKS 4.14 The student applies Grade 4 mathematics to solve problems . . . (B) **Solve problems that incorporate understanding the problem, making a plan, carrying out the plan, and evaluating the solution for reasonableness.** *Also addresses TEKS 4.14(C).*

P.S.I. TEAM +

ISABEL: **I am making punch for a party. One bowl of punch serves 35 guests. I am going to make four bowls of punch.**

YOUR MISSION: **Find how many guests will be served by four bowls.**

Understand	One bowl of punch serves 35 guests. Isabel is making four bowls of punch. Find how many guests will be served by four bowls of punch.
Plan	Use the *four-step plan* and write a number sentence. Multiply the number of guests served by one bowl of punch by the number of bowls being made.
Solve	You need to find $35 \times 4 = \blacksquare$. $\begin{array}{r} 35 \\ \times\ 4 \\ \hline 120 \\ +\ 20 \\ \hline 140 \end{array}$ Multiply 4×30. Multiply 4×5. Add. 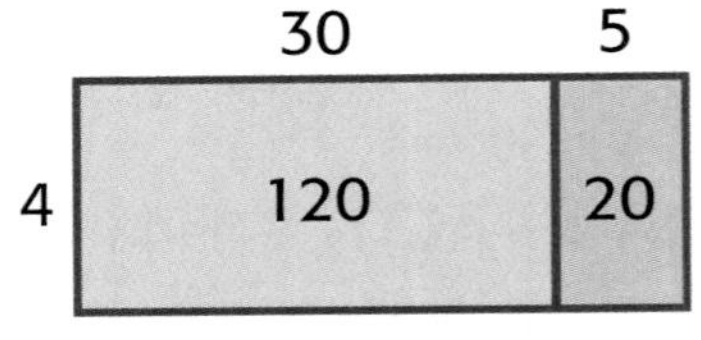 $120 + 20 = 140$ So, four bowls of punch will serve 140 guests.
Check	Look back at the problem. You can use repeated addition to check your answer. $35 + 35 + 35 + 35 = 140$. So, the answer is correct.

Mixed Problem Solving

EXTRA PRACTICE
See page R18.

Use any strategy shown below to solve. Tell what strategy you used.

PROBLEM-SOLVING STRATEGIES

- Draw a picture.
- Look for a pattern.
- Make a table.
- Work backward.

1. There are 12 members in each scout troop. Make a table to find out how many members are in 10, 11, 12, or 13 scout troops.

2. Nate is choosing 1 dinner, 1 side, and 1 beverage from the menu below. What are 3 possible combinations?

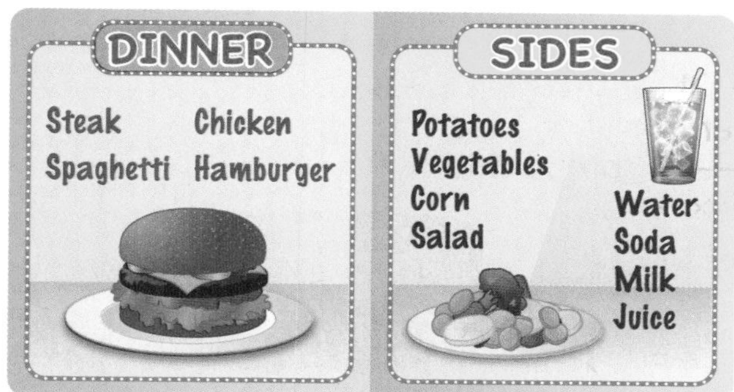

3. Kishi is choosing an outfit to wear to school. She has 3 shirts, 2 pants, and 3 shoes to choose from. How many different outfits does she have to choose from?

4. Four bears eat 2,000 ants per day. How many ants will 2 bears eat in one day?

5. There are 18 stickers on each sheet. There are five sheets in one pack. How many stickers are in one pack?

6. **Algebra** Copy and complete the pattern below. Describe the pattern.

   100, 200, 400, ■, 1,600, ■, 6,400

7. **Geometry** If this pattern continues, identify the 18th shape in the pattern.

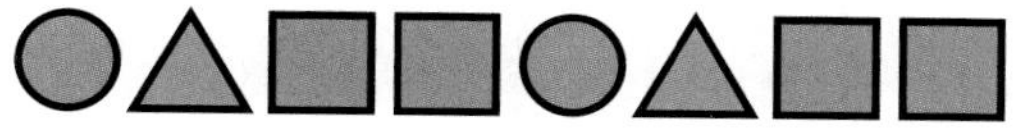

8. Reginald is decorating his room with 4 posters. One wall has an animal poster to the right of a car poster. A space poster is last. A music poster is to the left of the space poster. What is the order of the posters?

9. Emma now has $32. She earned $12 babysitting, and she received $5 for her allowance. How much money did she have originally?

10. The Turner family played miniature golf. What is the total cost if 2 adults and 3 children played 18 holes of golf?

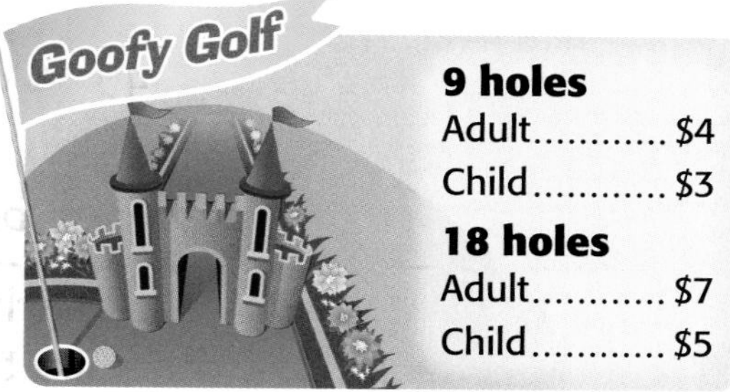

11. **WRITING IN MATH** Look at Exercise 9. Identify the strategy you used. Explain how you used this strategy to solve the problem.

Multiply One-Digit by Three-Digit Numbers

GET READY to Learn

Today is Laura's birthday, and she is nine years old. There are 365 days in one year. How many days old is Laura?

MAIN IDEA

I will multiply a three-digit number by a one-digit number.

The student multiplies and divides to solve meaningful problems involving whole numbers. (D) **Use multiplication to solve problems (no more than two digits times two digits without technology).** *Also addresses TEKS 4.14(D). Preparation for TEKS 5.3(B).*

You multiply multi-digit numbers the same way you multiply a two-digit number by a one-digit number.

Partial Products

1 TIME How many days old is Laura?

To find how many days old Laura is, multiply the number of days in a year by the number of years.

First estimate: $365 \times 9 \rightarrow 400 \times 9 = 3{,}600$.

You can use a calculator to find 365×9.

Press 3 6 5

Press ×

Press 9

Press =

Results 3,285

So, Laura is 3,285 days old. This is reasonable since 3,285 is close to 3,600.

You can also use paper and pencil to multiply.

EXAMPLE **Multiply Money**

> **Remember**
>
> Always check for reasonableness.
>
> 3 × $175
> ↓
> 3 × $200 = $600
>
> Since $525 is close to $600, the answer is reasonable.

2 **Find 3 × $175.**
Estimate: 3 × $175 → 3 × $200 = $600

One Way: Use Technology	**Another Way: Pencil and Paper**
Multiply using a calculator.	**Step 1** Multiply the ones.
	$\begin{array}{r} \overset{1}{} \\ \$\ 175 \\ \times\ \ 3 \\ \hline 5 \end{array}$ 3 × 5 ones = 15. Regroup 15 ones as 1 ten and 5 ones.
Press: 1 7 5	**Step 2** Multiply the tens.
Press: ×	$\begin{array}{r} \overset{2\,1}{} \\ \$\ 175 \\ \times\ \ 3 \\ \hline 25 \end{array}$ 3 × 7 tens = 21 tens. Add the regrouped tens. 21 tens + 1 ten = 22 tens. Regroup 22 tens as 2 hundreds and 2 tens.
Press 3	**Step 3** Multiply the hundreds.
Press =	$\begin{array}{r} \overset{2\,1}{} \\ \$\ 175 \\ \times\ \ 3 \\ \hline 525 \end{array}$ 3 × 1 hundred = 3 hundreds. Add the regrouped hundreds. 3 hundreds + 2 hundreds = 5 hundreds
Results 525	

So, 3 × 175 = 525.

Personal Tutor at tx.gr4math.com

CHECK What You Know

Use technology to multiply. See Examples 1 and 2 (pp. 242–243)

1. $\begin{array}{r} 135 \\ \times\ 2 \\ \hline \end{array}$

2. $\begin{array}{r} 532 \\ \times\ 6 \\ \hline \end{array}$

3. 2 × $957

4. 7 × 832

5. A vacation costs $389 for one person. What is the total cost of this vacation for a family of four?

6. Talk About It Explain why it is a good idea to estimate answers to multiplication problems.

Practice and Problem Solving

EXTRA PRACTICE
See page R18.

Use technology to multiply. See Examples 1 and 2 (pp. 242–243)

7. $168 × 2

8. 313 × 3

9. 252 × 2

10. $338 × 3

11. 238 × 4

12. 819 × 5

13. $781 × 5

14. 340 × 6

Algebra Find the value of each expression if ■ = 8.

15. ■ × 295

16. 737 × ■

17. ■ × $273

18. 737 × ■

Compare. Use >, <, or =.

19. 4 × 198 ● 3 × 248

20. 7 × 385 ● 6 × 457

21. Ms. Gomez buys 8 cases of seeds at the school plant sale. If there are 144 packages of seeds in each case, how many packages of seeds has she bought?

22. **Measurement** On average 1,668 gallons of water are used by each person in the United States daily. How much water is used by one person in a week?

Real-World PROBLEM SOLVING

Science The rainforests are the richest, oldest, and most productive ecosystems on Earth. Animals such as anacondas, iguanas, monkeys, and parrots live in rainforests. Use technology to solve.

23. A four-square-mile section of rainforest has 125 mammals. How many mammals would live in an area 3 times that size?

24. Rainforest land that is used to raise cattle is worth $60 an acre. Rainforest land that is used for its plants is worth $2,400 an acre. Find the difference in worth of 5 acres of land used to raise cattle compared to the same amount of land used for its plants.

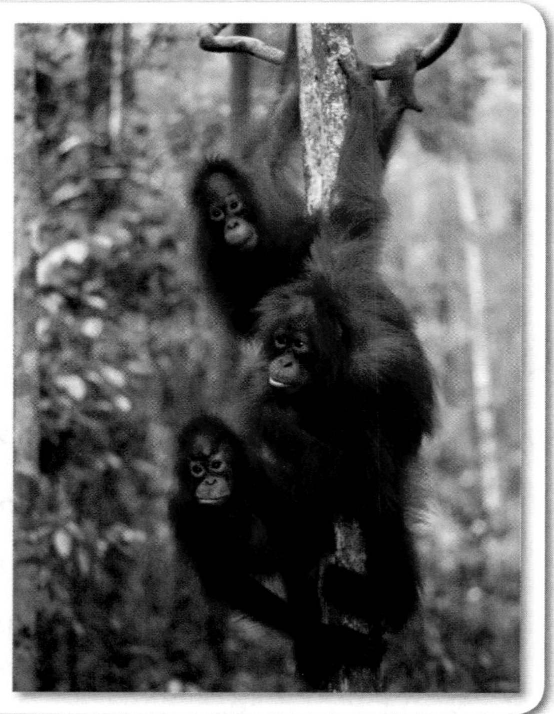

H.O.T. Problems

25. **OPEN ENDED** Write a four-digit number and a one-digit number whose product is greater than 6,000 and less than 6,200.

26. **FIND THE ERROR** Roberta and Camden are finding 362 × 2. Who is correct? Explain.

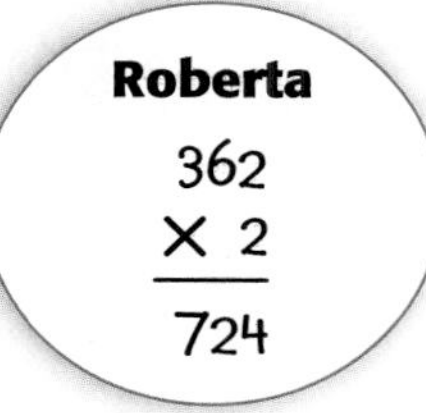

27. **WRITING IN MATH** Write a real-world problem that involves multiplying a three-digit by a one-digit number, and regrouping.

28. Approximately how long would 6 train cars be? (Lesson 6-4)

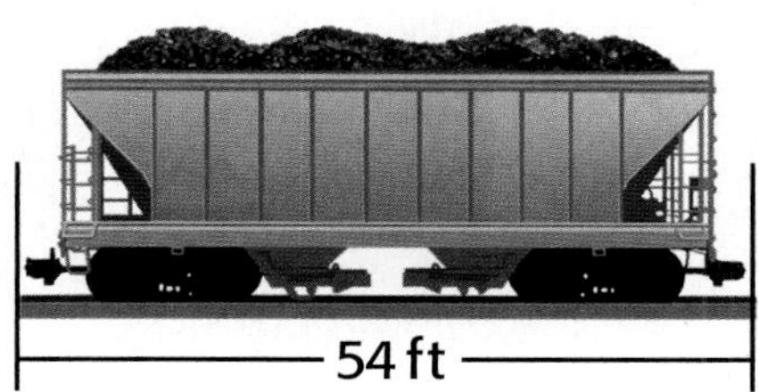

A 300 ft
B 324 ft
C 330 ft
D 360 ft

29. There are 1,440 minutes in a day. How many minutes are in 7 days? (Lesson 6-6)

F 7,880
G 9,880
H 10,080
J 11,080

Multiply. Check for reasonableness. (Lesson 6-4)

30. 3 × 21 **31.** 5 × 34 **32.** 8 × $72

Estimate each product by rounding or using compatible numbers. (Lesson 6-3)

33. 2 × 265 **34.** 3 × 849 **35.** 7 × 5,513

36. There are 26 students, 1 teacher, and 4 parents going on a field trip. Each car can hold 4 people. Is it reasonable to say that 7 cars will allow every person to go on the field trip? Explain. (Lesson 6-2)

Problem Solving in Science

Emperors of the ICE

There are 17 different types of penguins. Emperor penguins are the tallest and heaviest penguins. An Emperor penguin is over 3 feet tall and can weigh from 42 to 101 pounds. The average Emperor penguin weighs 66 pounds and can swim 15 miles per hour.

About 200,000 pairs of Emperor penguins live in 40 different groups in Antarctica. Penguins huddle together to share their body heat during the cold winter temperatures and bitter winds.

Did You Know?

Emperor penguins usually dive 60 to 70 feet. An average dive lasts 3 to 6 minutes.

Targeted TEKS 4.14 The student applies Grade 4 mathematics to solve problems connected to everyday experiences and activities in and outside school. **(A) Identify the mathematics in everyday situations.**

Real-World Math

Use the information on pages 246 and 247 to solve each problem. Use a calculator when needed.

1. Suppose that eight average-sized Emperor penguins are standing together. What is their total weight?
2. Six penguins of varying weights are standing together. What is the least they can weigh? the most?
3. Suppose a penguin's dive lasts 4 minutes. How many times did its heart beat during the dive?
4. How many miles can a penguin swim in 3 hours?
5. Suppose it takes a penguin 3 minutes to walk from its resting place to the place where it dives. What is a reasonable number of times its heart beats in these three minutes before it dives?
6. Based on the following table, estimate how many times a penguin's heart beats after completing all of the activities listed for two minutes each.

PENGUIN HEARTBEAT

Activity	Heartbeat (beats per minute)
Resting	65
Before a dive	180–200
Hitting the water	100
Diving	20
Returning to surface	200

6-7 Multiply by Tens

GET READY to Learn

Rita took 20 pictures at her family reunion. She printed the pictures so that each of her 25 family members could have them. How many pictures did Rita print?

MAIN IDEA

I will multiply a whole number by a multiple of ten.

Targeted TEKS 4.4 The student multiplies and divides to solve meaningful problems involving whole numbers. **(D) Use multiplication to solve problems (no more than two digits times two digits without technology).**

When you multiply a two-digit number by a multiple of ten such as 20, 30, 40, ..., the digit in the ones place is always a zero.

Real-World EXAMPLE Multiply by Tens

1 PHOTOGRAPHS How many pictures did Rita have printed?

You need to find 20×25.

25×20	Write the problem.
$25 \times (10 \times 2)$	Think of 20 as 10×2.
$25 \times (2 \times 10)$	Commutative Property
$(25 \times 2) \times 10$	Associative Property
50×10	Multiply. $25 \times 2 = 50$
500	Use mental math.

So, Rita printed 500 pictures.

CHECK What You Know

Multiply. See Example 1 (p. 248)

1. $\begin{array}{r} 36 \\ \times\ 10 \\ \hline \end{array}$

2. $\begin{array}{r} 53 \\ \times\ 30 \\ \hline \end{array}$

3. $\begin{array}{r} 79 \\ \times\ 80 \\ \hline \end{array}$

4. $25 $\times$ 20

5. $89 $\times$ 40

6. $58 $\times$ 70

7. Latasha bikes 20 miles every week. There are 52 weeks in a year. How many miles does she bike in a year?

8. **Talk About It** Joey is finding 40×67. Explain why he can think of 40×67 as $4 \times 10 \times 67$.

Practice and Problem Solving

EXTRA PRACTICE See page R19.

Multiply. See Example 1 (p. 248)

9. 15×20

10. 27×30

11. 46×40

12. 53×60

13. 80×80

14. 94×90

15. $\$275 \times 10$

16. $\$312 \times 30$

17. $\$38 \times 50$

18. $\$47 \times 50$

19. $\$56 \times 70$

20. $\$69 \times 80$

21. If $7 \times 29 = 203$, then what is 70×29?

22. If $3 \times 52 = 156$, then what is 30×52?

23. Baby robins eat 14 feet of earthworms each day. How many feet of worms does a baby robin eat in 20 days?

24. Mozart could learn a piece of music in 30 minutes. How long would it take him to learn 15 pieces of music?

Real-World PROBLEM SOLVING

Birds Hummingbirds feed every 10 minutes. They fly about 25 miles per hour and flap their wings 60 to 80 times each second.

25. What is the least number of times a hummingbird will flap its wings in 15 seconds?

26. What is the greatest number of times it will flap its wing in 15 seconds?

27. How many minutes have passed if a hummingbird has eaten 45 times?

28. If a hummingbird flies a total of 20 hours, how far did it fly?

H.O.T. Problems

29. OPEN ENDED Create a number sentence with two 2-digit factors whose product has three zeros.

30. WHICH ONE DOESN'T BELONG? Identify the multiplication problem that does not belong with the other three. Explain.

15 × 30	28 × 20	41 × 21	67 × 40

31. WRITING IN ▶MATH How many zeros would be in the product of 50 and 60? Explain.

Math Activity for 6-8

Multiply Two-Digit by Two-Digit Numbers

In Lesson 4-6, you learned that the **Distributive Property of Multiplication** allows you to break apart factors to find a product. You can use the Distributive Property to multiply two-digit numbers.

MAIN IDEA

I will explore multiplying by two-digit numbers.

The student multiplies and divides to solve meaningful problems involving whole numbers. (D) **Use multiplication to solve problems (no more than two digits times two digits without technology).** *Also addresses TEKS 4.4(A), 4.4(B).*

You Will Need
colored pencils
graph paper

KEY CONCEPT — Distributive Property

To multiply a sum by a number, multiply each addend by the number and add the products.

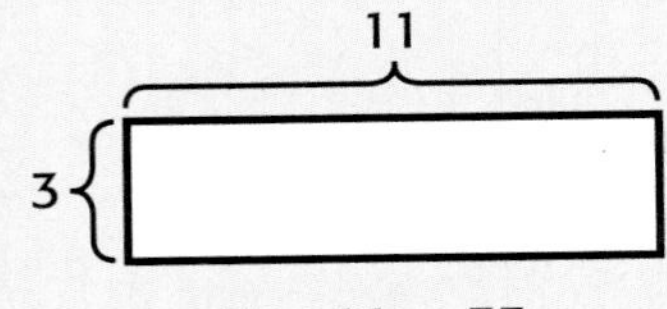

$3 \times 11 = 33$

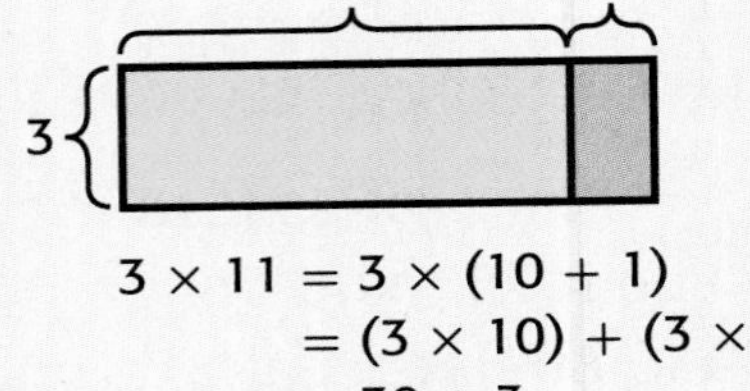

$$\begin{aligned} 3 \times 11 &= 3 \times (10 + 1) \\ &= (3 \times 10) + (3 \times 1) \\ &= 30 + 3 \\ &= 33 \end{aligned}$$

ACTIVITY **Find 12×15.**

Step 1 **Draw a rectangle.**

Draw a rectangle on graph paper. Use 12 and 15 as the dimensions.

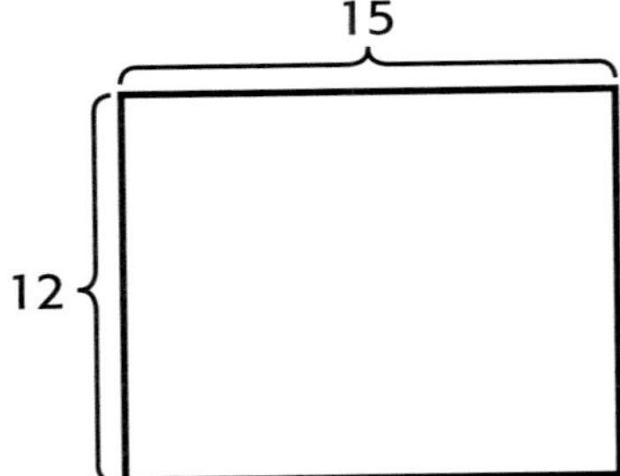

Step 2 **Separate the tens and ones.**

First, break up the 15 to 10 and 5. Next, break up the 12 to 10 and 2.

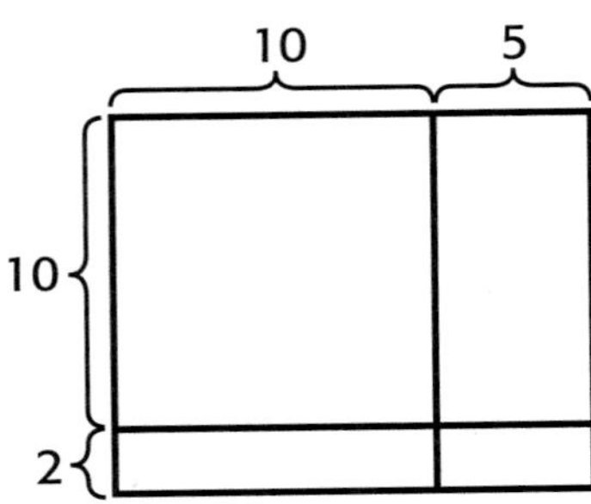

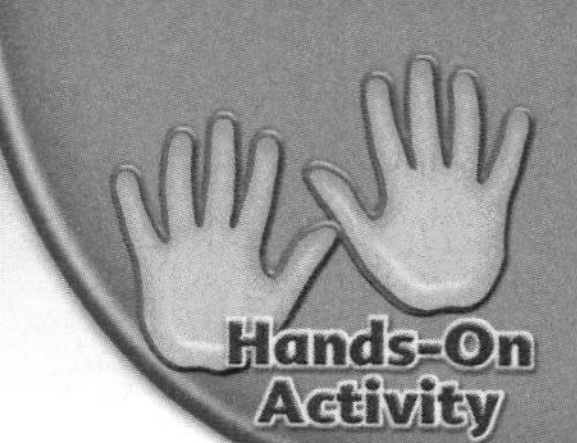

Step 3 **Find each product. Then add.**

10 × 10	=	**100**
10 × 5	=	**50**
2 × 10	=	**20**
2 × 5	=	**+ 10**
		180

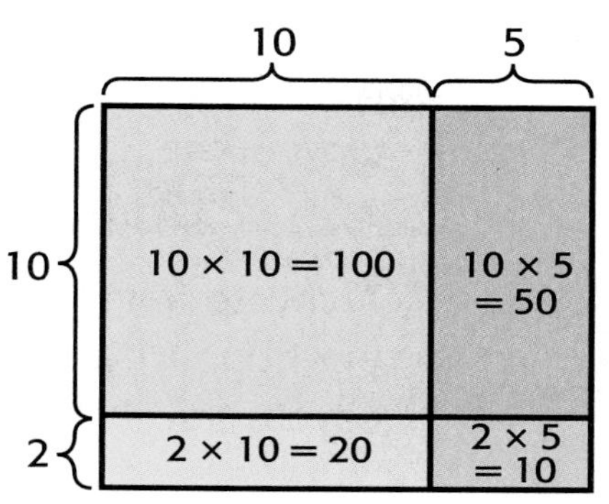

Step 4 **Make the connection.**
Distributive Property

$12 \times 15 = (10 \times 15) + (2 \times 15)$
$= (10 \times 10) + (10 \times 5) + (2 \times 10) + (2 \times 5)$
$= 100 + 50 + 20 + 10$
$= 180$

Partial Products

1	
× 12	
10	2 × 5
20	2 × 10
50	10 × 5
+ 100	10 × 10
180	Add partial products.

Think About It

1. How would you use the Distributive Property to find 12 × 18?

CHECK What You Know

Write the multiplication sentence for each area model. Multiply.

2.

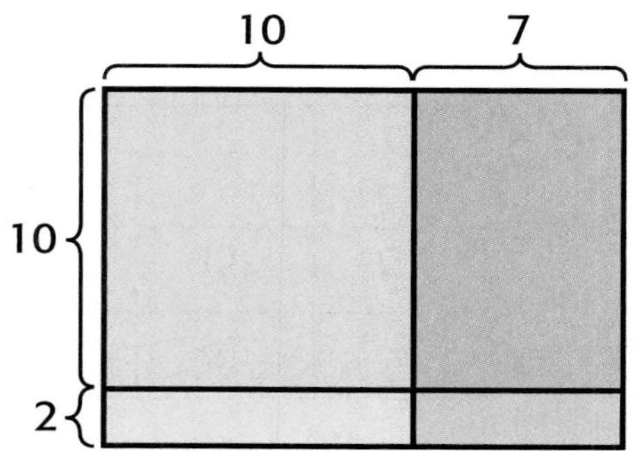

3.

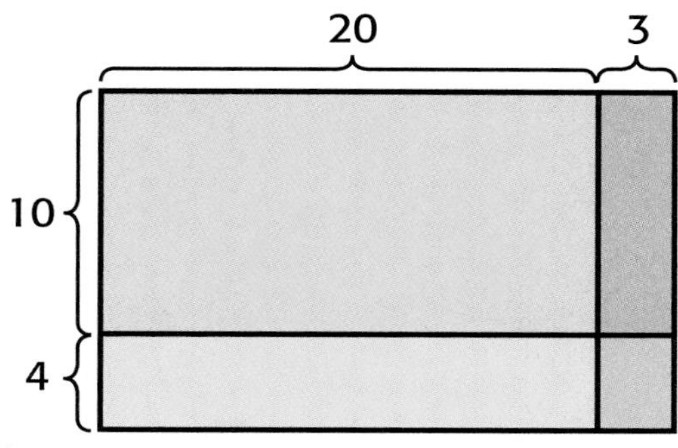

Multiply. Use an area model and the Distributive Property.

4. 12 × 10 **5.** 14 × 18 **6.** 25 × 28

7. WRITING IN ▶MATH Explain how to find 16 × 19.

6-8 Multiply Two-Digit by Two-Digit Numbers

GET READY to Learn

A coyote travels 27 miles per hour. How far would a coyote travel in 12 hours?

MAIN IDEA

I will multiply two-digit numbers.

Targeted TEKS 4.4 The student multiplies and divides to solve meaningful problems involving whole numbers. (D) **Use multiplication to solve problems (no more than two digits times two digits without technology).**

There is more than one way to multiply two-digit numbers.

Real-World EXAMPLE

1 MEASUREMENT A coyote travels 27 miles each hour. Multiply 27 × 12 to find how far a coyote can travel in 12 hours.

One Way: Partial Products

27	
× 12	
14	Multiply 2 × 7.
40	Multiply 2 × 20.
70	Multiply 10 × 7.
+ 200	Multiply 10 × 20.
324	Add partial products.

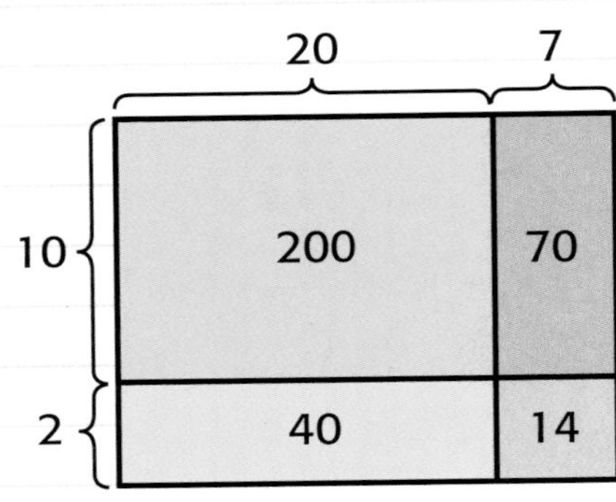

Another Way: Partial Products

To find 27 × 12, think of 27 as 20 + 7 and 12 as 10 + 2. Then multiply each part of one sum by each part of the other, and add the results.

27 ×12	20	7
10	200	70
2	40	14

200 + 70 + 40 + 14 = 324

So, a coyote can travel 324 miles in 12 hours.

Real-World EXAMPLE Multiply Money

2 EXPENSES Heidi's monthly bills are shown. How much does she spend on her cell phone service in 2 years?

Monthly Bills	
Cable	$55
Cell phone	$38
Movie club	$21
Water	$93

Heidi's cell phone bill is $38. There are 24 months in 2 years. So multiply $38 by 24 to find how much she spends in 2 years.

> **Remember**
> Make an estimate to check the reasonableness of the answer.

Estimate $40 \times 20 = 800$

Step 1 Multiply the ones.

$$\begin{array}{r} \$\ 38 \\ \times\ 24 \\ \hline 152 \end{array} \leftarrow 4 \times 38$$

Step 2 Multiply the tens.

$$\begin{array}{r} \$38 \\ \times\ 24 \\ \hline 152 \\ +\ 760 \\ \hline \end{array} \leftarrow 20 \times 38$$

Step 3 Add the products.

$$\begin{array}{r} \$38 \\ \times\ 24 \\ \hline 152 \\ +760 \\ \hline 912 \end{array} \leftarrow \text{Add.}$$

Check $600 + 160 + 120 + 32 = 912$

So, the cost of cell phone service for 2 years is $912.

Check for reasonableness

912 is close to the estimate of 800. The answer is reasonable. ✓

Online **Personal Tutor at** tx.gr4math.com

CHECK What You Know

Multiply. See Examples 1 and 2 (pp. 252–253)

1. $\begin{array}{r} 35 \\ \times\ 24 \\ \hline \end{array}$

2. $\begin{array}{r} \$57 \\ \times\ 42 \\ \hline \end{array}$

3. 92×81

4. A farmer plants 35 rows of tomatoes. There are 25 plants in each row. How many plants are there altogether?

5. Talk About It Explain the steps needed to find the product of 23 and 56.

Practice and Problem Solving

EXTRA PRACTICE See page R19.

Multiply. See Examples 1 and 2 (pp. 252–253)

6. 19×15

7. 36×24

8. 42×38

9. 52×47

10. $\$54 \times 51$

11. $\$68 \times 46$

12. $\$74 \times 63$

13. $\$82 \times 49$

14. 47×24

15. 64×46

16. 83×67

17. 91×78

18. Bamboo plants can grow up to 36 inches in a day. How many inches could they grow in 3 weeks?

19. Josie earns about 28 points on each quiz she takes. How many points will Josie earn on 12 quizzes?

20. A greyhound dog can jump a distance of 27 feet. How many feet will a greyhound travel if it jumps 12 times?

21. Each day, enough paper is recycled in the U.S. to fill 15 miles of train boxcars. How many miles of boxcars could be filled over 25 days?

Real-World PROBLEM SOLVING

Food The table shows the average amount of hot dogs and pizza slices each person eats per year.

Amount of Food Eaten Each Year

Food	Number
Hot dog	60
Slice of pizza	46

22. How many hot dogs will a person eat in 11 years?

23. How many slices of pizza will a person eat in 12 years?

24. How many more hot dogs than pizza slices will a person eat in 15 years?

H.O.T. Problems

25. OPEN ENDED Copy and complete the multiplication problem to make a true sentence.

$$\begin{array}{r} 20 \\ \times\ \blacksquare\blacksquare \\ \hline \blacksquare 00 \end{array}$$

26. WHICH ONE DOESN'T BELONG? Identify the multiplication problem that does not belong with the other three. Explain.

22×15	$\$45 \times 28$	37×18	$\$65 \times 25$

27. WRITING IN ▸MATH Explain why the product of two 2-digit whole numbers can never be two digits.

TEST Practice

28. While riding in a car, Dexter counted 17 blue cars on a highway in 1 minute. At this rate, how many blue cars will Dexter see in 45 minutes? (Lesson 6-7)

A 360

B 400

C 765

D 775

29. There are 24 hours in a day and 365 days in a year. About how many hours are in a year? (Lesson 6-8)

F 2,100

G 7,400

H 8,000

J 8,700

Spiral Review

Multiply. (Lesson 6-7)

30. 28×10

31. 44×50

32. 79×80

Estimate. Tell whether the estimate is greater or less than the actual product. (Lesson 6-6)

33. 26×17

34. 61×33

35. $\$87 \times 75$

36. For every 4 magazines Silvia sells, she receives $2. Use the table to find how much money she will raise if she sells 18 magazines. (Lesson 6-5)

Magazines Sold	4	8	12	16	20
Money	$2	$4	$6	■	■

Multiply. (Lesson 6-4)

37. 34×5

38. 55×9

39. $\$272 \times 6$

Find the value of each expression. (Lesson 5-6)

40. $24 \div (3 + 5) - 2$

41. $4 \times (11 - 4) + 6$

42. $(9 + 6) \div (10 - 7)$

Find all of the factors of each number. (Lesson 4-9)

43. 8

44. 11

45. 24

46. 36

CHAPTER 6

Study Guide and Review

FOLDABLES Study Organizer — GET READY to Study

Be sure the following Key Vocabulary words and Key Concepts are written in your Foldable.

Estimate Products	Multiply One-Digit by Two-Digit Numbers
Multiply One-Digit by Three-Digit Numbers	Multiply Two-Digit by Two-Digit Numbers

BIG Ideas

Multiply Multiples of 10 and 100

Use basic facts and patterns. (p. 227)

$3 \times 7 = 21$	3×7 ones
$3 \times 70 = 210$	3×7 tens
$3 \times 700 = 2{,}100$	3×7 hundreds
$3 \times 7{,}000 = 21{,}000$	3×7 thousands

Estimate Products (p. 232)

$4 \times 192 \rightarrow 4 \times 200 = 800$

Multiply by One-Digit Numbers (p. 236)

There are many ways you can multiply.

500 + 0 + 2

6	3,000	0	12

$$\begin{array}{r} 3{,}000 \\ 0 \\ +\ 12 \\ \hline 3{,}012 \end{array}$$

$$\begin{array}{r} \scriptstyle 1 \\ 502 \\ \times\ 6 \\ \hline 3{,}012 \end{array}$$

Multiply the ones, tens, hundreds, and thousands. Regroup as needed.

Key Vocabulary

Distributive Property of Multiplication (pp. 156, 237)

estimate (pp. 58, 232)

multiply (pp. 137, 227)

product (p. 232)

Vocabulary Check

Choose the vocabulary word that completes the sentence.

1. When you do not need an exact answer you can ___?___.

2. Finding the product means you need to ___?___.

3. The ___?___ says that you can multiply the addends of a number and then add the products.

4. To ___?___ products, round factors to their greatest place.

5. When two factors are multiplied together, the result is a(n) ___?___.

6. You need to ___?___ to find the total of equal groups.

Lesson-by-Lesson Review

6-1 Multiples of 10 and 100 (pp. 227–229)

Example 1
Find 7 × 600.

Use basic facts and patterns to find 7 × 600.

7 × 6 = 42	7 × 6 ones
7 × 60 = 420	7 × 6 tens
7 × 600 = 4,200	7 × 6 hundreds

So, 7 × 600 = 4200.
Notice that the pattern is 7 × 6 with two zeros added to the end.

Multiply. Use basic facts and patterns.

7. 2 × 50
8. 4 × 90
9. 5 × 400
10. 8 × 600
11. 6 × 3,000
12. 9 × 7,000

13. Measurement One ton is equal to 2,000 pounds. How many pounds are equal to 7 tons?

6-2 Problem-Solving Skill: Reasonable Answers (pp. 230–231)

Example 2
Andrés walks 40 miles each month. Is it reasonable to say that he will walk more than 300 miles in 6 months? Explain.

Andrés walks 40 miles each month. Find if it is reasonable to say he will walk more than 300 miles in 6 months. Find 6 × 40 and then compare.

6 × 4 = 24

6 × 40 = 240

240 < 300. So, it is not reasonable to say Andrés will walk more than 300 miles in 6 months.

14. Jaime's family eats 12 cups of fruit each week. Is 200 a reasonable estimate for the number of cups of fruit they will eat each month? Explain.

15. There are 8 party bags. Each bag contains the items shown. Is it reasonable to say that the bags will have 75 items in all? Explain.

16. Ahmik donates $200 each month to the local homeless shelter. Is it reasonable to say that he will give more than $3,000 a year? Explain.

Study Guide and Review

6-3 Estimate Products (pp. 232–235)

Example 3
Estimate 4 × 859.

First round. Then use basic facts and patterns to multiply.

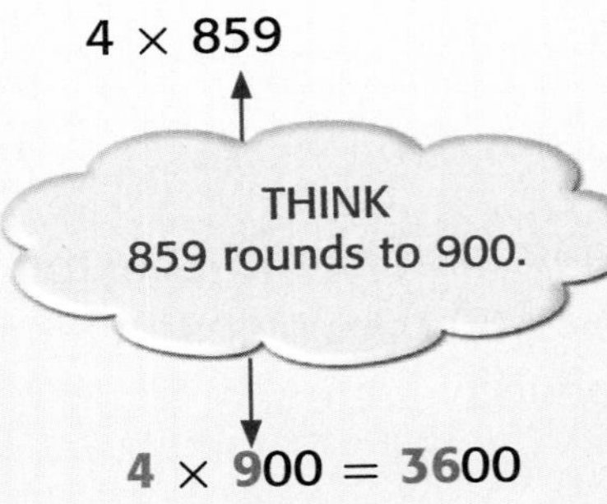

So, 4 × 859 is about 3,600.

Estimate each product by rounding or using compatible numbers. Then tell if the estimate is *greater than* or *less than* the actual product.

17. 5 × 248

18. 7 × 584

19. $\begin{array}{r} 147 \\ \times\ 4 \\ \hline \end{array}$

20. $\begin{array}{r} 938 \\ \times\ 8 \\ \hline \end{array}$

21. About how many children play football if there are 9 teams of 18 children?

22. Rob can read a 240-page book in a week. About how many pages can he read in 6 weeks?

6-4 Multiply One-Digit by Two-Digit Numbers (pp. 236–238)

Example 4
Tania has four decks of 52 cards. How many cards does Tania have?

Find 4 × 52.

Step 1 Multiply the ones.

$\begin{array}{r} 52 \\ \times\ 4 \\ \hline 8 \end{array}$ $4 \times 2 = 8$

Step 2 Multiply the tens.

$\begin{array}{r} 52 \\ \times\ 4 \\ \hline 208 \end{array}$ $4 \times 5 = 20$

So, Tania has 208 cards.

Multiply. Check for resonableness.

23. $\begin{array}{r} 62 \\ \times\ 7 \\ \hline \end{array}$

24. $\begin{array}{r} 77 \\ \times\ 9 \\ \hline \end{array}$

25. 3 × 35

26. 5 × 88

27. **Measurement** A kangaroo can jump as far as 44 feet in a single jump. What distance would three jumps of this size cover?

28. Paulo watched 7 movies in one month. Each movie was 120 minutes long. How many minutes did Paulo watch movies?

6-5 Problem-Solving Investigation: Choose a Strategy (pp. 240–241)

Example 5

Iván is making dinner. Setting the table and preparing a salad will take 15 minutes each. Making the entree will take 1 hour. If dinner is to be served at 6:00 P.M., what time does he need to start preparing dinner?

Use the *work backward* strategy.

6 P.M.	end
− 1 hour	entree
5 P.M.	
−15 minutes	salad
4:45 P.M.	
−15 minutes	set table
4:30 P.M.	

So, Iván needs to start at 4:30 P.M.

Use any strategy to solve.

29. There are 11 fish in an aquarium. Three of the fish are yellow. There are twice as many blue fish as yellow fish. The rest of the fish are red. How many red fish are there?

30. Adelina earns $35 a day for baby-sitting. She earns a total of $315. How many days did she baby-sit?

31. Katelyn is going to rent a movie last. She is going to the post office second. She is going to the pet store before the post office. She is going to the library before she rents a movie. In what order is she completing her errands ?

6-6 Multiply One-Digit by Three-Digit Numbers (pp. 242–245)

Example 6

Use a calculator to find 276 × 4.

Press  

Press 

Press 

Press 

Results 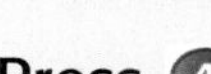 1,104

So, 276 × 4 is 1,104.

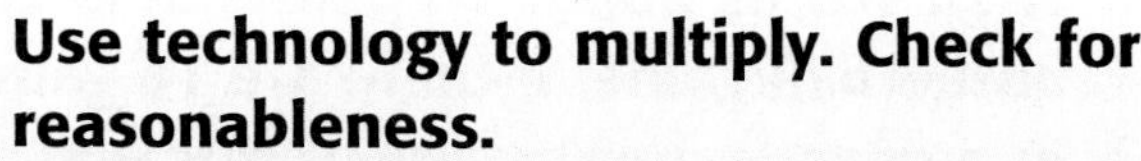

Use technology to multiply. Check for reasonableness.

32. 6 × 109

33. 8 × 854

34. 4,355 × 3

35. 5,820 × 7

36. An average hen lays 228 eggs in one year. How many eggs does a hen lay in four years?

37. There are 365 days in one year. Kevin is 9 years old. How many days old is Kevin?

Study Guide and Review

6-7 Multiply by Tens (pp. 248–249)

Example 7

A football coach is ordering 30 jerseys for his football team. The jerseys cost $29 each. What will the total cost of the jerseys be?

Step 1 Multiply the ones.

$$\begin{array}{r} 29 \\ \times\ 30 \\ \hline 0 \end{array}$$

0 ones × 29 = 0

Step 2 Multiply the tens.

$$\begin{array}{r} 29 \\ \times\ 30 \\ \hline 870 \end{array}$$

3 tens × 29 = 87 tens

So, the total cost will be $870.

Multiply.

38. $\begin{array}{r} 90 \\ \times\ 90 \\ \hline \end{array}$

39. $\begin{array}{r} 34 \\ \times\ 80 \\ \hline \end{array}$

40. $28 × 40

41. $45 × 30

42. Jeremy reads the number of books shown in a month. How many books will he read in 2 years?

43. A school has 27 classrooms. There are 30 students in each classroom. How many students are there?

6-8 Multiply Two-Digit by Two-Digit Numbers (pp. 252–255)

Example 8

Trish scores about 18 points in each basketball game. If there are 14 games in a season, how many points will Trish score?

Multiply the number of games by the number of points scored in each game.

$$\begin{array}{r} {}^{3} \\ 18 \\ \times 14 \\ \hline 72 \\ +180 \\ \hline 252 \end{array}$$

Multiply the ones.
Multiply the tens.
Add the products.

So, Trish will score 252 points.

Multiply.

44. $\begin{array}{r} 63 \\ \times\ 46 \\ \hline \end{array}$

45. $\begin{array}{r} 26 \\ \times 34 \\ \hline \end{array}$

46. $\begin{array}{r} \$72 \\ \times\ 49 \\ \hline \end{array}$

47. $\begin{array}{r} \$55 \\ \times\ 41 \\ \hline \end{array}$

48. 37 × 68

49. 89 × 53

50. $19 × 72

51. 95 × 84

52. **Measurement** Kittens can run up to 31 miles per hour. At this rate, how far could a kitten run in a day?

CHAPTER 6

Chapter Test

Multiply. Use basic facts and patterns.

1. 5 × 4
5 × 40
5 × 400
5 × 4,000

2. 9 × 6
9 × 60
9 × 600
9 × 6,000

3. School supplies cost $30. Is it reasonable for 9 students to purchase supplies with $300? Explain.

4. **TEST PRACTICE**
Which pair of numbers best completes the equation?

□ × 100 = ◯

A 65 and 650

B 65 and 6,500

C 605 and 6,500

D 650 and 6,500

5. Fiona makes $25 a day babysitting. Is it reasonable to say she will have more than $200 at the end of a week? Explain.

Estimate each product.

6. 4 × 657

7. 7 × 9,431

Multiply.

8. 5 × 64

9. 9 × 75

10. Nia takes 60-minute tennis lessons twice a week. How many minutes of tennis lessons does Nia take in four weeks?

Multiply.

11. 26 × 10

12. 43 × 30

13. 89 × 33

14. 82 × 91

15. **Measurement** The table shows how many miles Ari biked each week of a month. At this rate, how many miles will Ari bike in a year?

Distance Biked	
Week	Miles
1	12
2	14
3	8
4	10

Algebra **Copy and complete.**

16. If 3 × ■ = 21,
then 30 × ■ = 2,100.

17. If 8 × ■ = 48,
then 80 × ■ = 4,800.

18. **TEST PRACTICE**
A plane carries 234 passengers. If the plane makes 4 trips a day, how many passengers is the plane transporting a day?

F 826

G 926

H 936

J 981

19. **WRITING IN ▸MATH** Joshua does not understand why 4,200 is not the best estimate for 681 × 7. Explain.

Texas Test Practice

Cumulative, Chapters 1–6

GRIDDABLE How many CDs are there in 8 packages?

TEST-TAKING TIP

You can use basic facts and mental math to help you find the correct answer.

Read the Test Question

You need to find the number of CDs in 8 packages.

Solve the Test Question

Look for a basic fact in the problem.

$8 \times 5 = 40$

$8 \times 50 = 400$

So, $50 \times 8 = 400$.

There are 400 CDs in 8 packages.

4	0	0	.
⓪	●	●	
①	①	①	
②	②	②	
③	③	③	
●	④	④	
⑤	⑤	⑤	
⑥	⑥	⑥	
⑦	⑦	⑦	
⑧	⑧	⑧	
⑨	⑨	⑨	

Personal Tutor at tx.gr4math.com

Choose the best answer.

1. **There are 1,400 sheets of paper in all in 7 packages. The same number of sheets are in each package. How many sheets are in each package?**

   A 100 **C** 175

   B 150 **D** 200

2. **Fran baked 15 trays of cookies for a bake sale. Each tray has 14 cookies. How many cookies did Fran bake in all?**

   F 200 **H** 225

   G 210 **J** 240

Get Ready for the Texas Test
For test-taking strategies and more practice, see pages TX1–TX21.

3. **A roller coaster at an amusement park runs 21 times every half hour. About how many times does the ride run each hour?**

   A 20 **C** 40
   B 30 **D** 50

4. **The manager of a new clothing store mailed out 500 flyers during the first week. During the second week, the store manager mailed out 10 times as many flyers. How many flyers were mailed in the second week?**

   F 750 **H** 2,500
   G 1,000 **J** 5,000

5. **Hugh practices the piano 30 minutes per day 6 days per week. Which expression shows how many minutes he practices in 10 weeks?**

   A $6 \times 10 + 30$ **C** $6 \times 10 \times 30$
   B $6 + 10 + 30$ **D** $30 \div 10 \times 6$

6. **Carlos has 3 red crayons, 2 blue crayons, and 4 green crayons. If a crayon is selected at random, what is the probability that it will be blue?**

   F 3 out of 9
   G 2 out of 5
   H 2 out of 7
   J 2 out of 9

7. **GRIDDABLE How many cans of green beans are there in 5 boxes?**

8. **How many sheets of paper are there in 6 packages?**

   A 3,000
   B 3,200
   C 3,500
   D 4,000

9. **Which is the value of the digit 3 in 564,327?**

   F 30
   G 300
   H 3,000
   J 30,000

Chapter 7 Divide by One-Digit Numbers

BIG Idea How do you divide by a one-digit number?

Divide each digit of the dividend by the divisor.

Example A toll worker for the METRORail collected $99 for 7-day passes. The 7-day pass sells for $9. How many passes did the worker sell?

```
   11
9)99    Divide $99 by $9.
 -9↓    For each place, divide, multiply, subtract, and compare.
  09    Then bring down the next digit in the dividend.
 - 9
   0
```

So, the worker sold 11 7-day passes.

What will I learn in this chapter?

- Divide a two- or three-digit number by a one-digit number.
- Divide a multi-digit number by a one-digit number.
- Estimate quotients.
- Solve problems by using the *guess and check* strategy.

Key Vocabulary

dividend **remainder**
divisor **compatible numbers**
quotient

Student Study Tools
at tx.gr4math.com

FOLDABLES™ Study Organizer

Make this Foldable to help you organize information about dividing by one-digit numbers. Begin with 5 sheets of 11″ × 17″ paper.

1. **Fold** one sheet in half widthwise.
2. **Open** and fold the bottom to form a pocket. Glue.
3. **Repeat** Steps 1 and 2 four times. Glue the back of one folder to the front of another.
4. **Label** the pockets as shown. Place an index card in each pocket.

ARE YOU READY for Chapter 7?

You have two ways to check prerequisite skills for this chapter.

Option 2

Math Online Take the Chapter Readiness Quiz at tx.gr4math.com.

Option 1

Complete the Quick Check below.

QUICK Check

Subtract. **(Prior grade)**

1. $\begin{array}{r} 25 \\ -\ 6 \\ \hline \end{array}$ **2.** $\begin{array}{r} 42 \\ -\ 8 \\ \hline \end{array}$ **3.** $\begin{array}{r} 67 \\ -\ 29 \\ \hline \end{array}$ **4.** $\begin{array}{r} 93 \\ -\ 54 \\ \hline \end{array}$

5. 24 − 15 **6.** 31 − 17 **7.** 50 − 23 **8.** 86 − 49

9. There are 81 pages in Gerardo's book. He has read 38 pages. How many pages are left?

Divide. **(Lesson 5-5)**

10. $2\overline{)3}$ **11.** $4\overline{)5}$ **12.** $6\overline{)7}$ **13.** $8\overline{)9}$

14. 4 ÷ 3 **15.** 7 ÷ 5 **16.** 9 ÷ 6 **17.** 9 ÷ 7

18. Sharon has $32. She wants to buy CDs that cost $8 each. How many can she buy?

Round each number to its greatest place value. **(Lesson 1-6)**

19. 269 **20.** $2,513 **21.** 14,895 **22.** 56,071

23. There are 2,515 mammals at a zoo and 3,496 animals that are not mammals at the zoo. About how many animals are there in all?

Math Activity for 7-1
Model Division

In division, the **dividend** is the number that is being divided. The **divisor** is the number that divides the dividend. The **quotient** is the result.

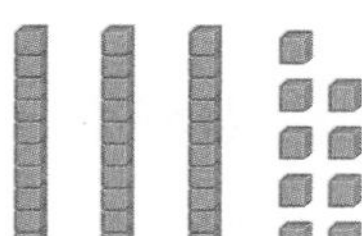

MAIN IDEA

I will explore dividing by one-digit numbers.

Targeted TEKS 4.4 The student multiplies and **divides to solve meaningful problems involving whole numbers.** (B) **Represent** multiplication and **division situations in picture, word, and number form.** (E) **Use division to solve problems** (no more than one-digit divisors and three-digit dividends without technology). *Also addresses TEKS 4.15(A).*

You Will Need
base-ten blocks

New Vocabulary
- dividend
- divisor
- quotient
- remainder

ACTIVITY

1 Find 39 ÷ 3.

Step 1 Model the dividend, 39.

Use 3 tens and 9 ones to show 39.

Step 2 Divide the tens.

The divisor is 3. So, divide the tens into 3 equal groups. There is a ten in each group.

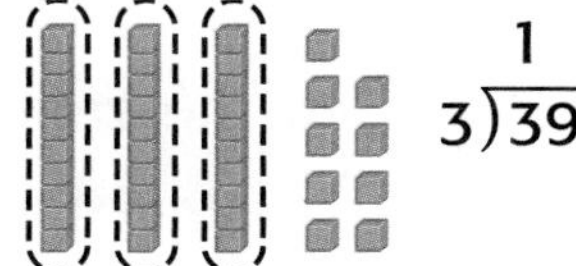

Step 3 Divide the ones.

Divide the ones into 3 equal groups. There is 1 ten and 3 ones in each group.
So, 39 ÷ 3 = 13.

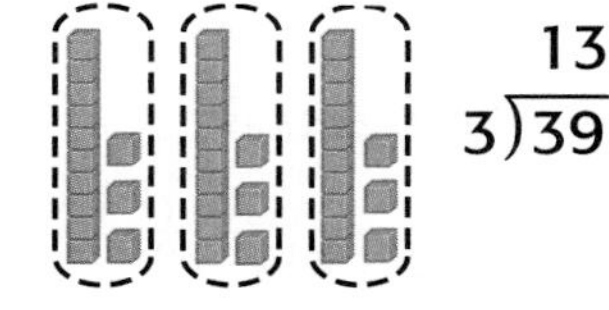

ACTIVITY

Hands-On Activity

2 **Find 68 ÷ 5.**

Step 1 **Model the dividend 68.**

Use 6 tens and 8 ones to show 68.

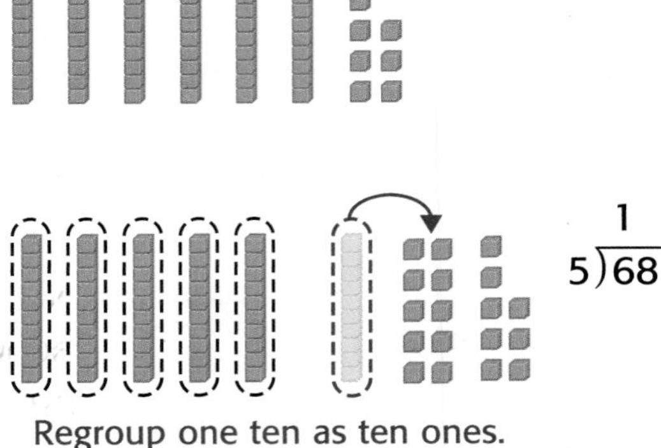

Step 2 **Divide the tens.**

The divisor is 5. So, divide the tens into 5 equal groups. There is a ten in each group.

$5\overline{)68}$ with quotient 1

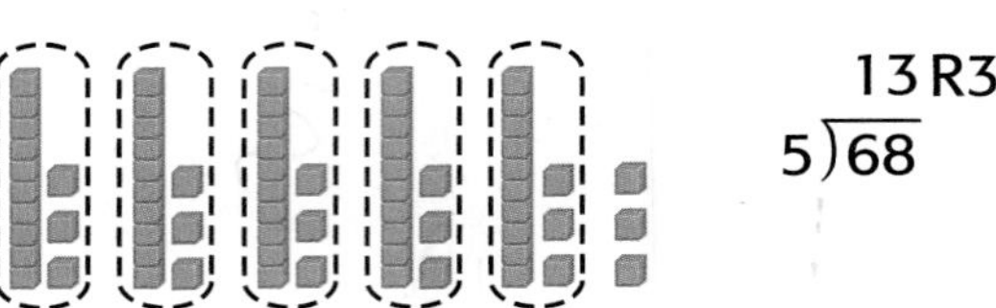

Regroup one ten as ten ones.

Step 3 **Divide the ones.**

Divide the ones into 5 equal groups. There is 1 ten and 3 ones in each group. There are 3 ones left over. The 3 is the **remainder**.

So, 68 ÷ 5 = 13 R3.

$5\overline{)68}$ with quotient 13 R3

Think About It

1. How would you use base-ten blocks to find 58 ÷ 4?
2. Explain what it means to have a remainder when dividing.

CHECK What You Know

Write the division expression shown by each model. Then divide.

3. 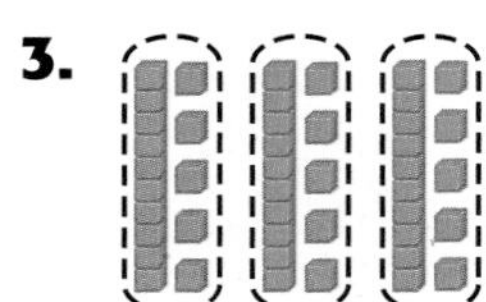

4. 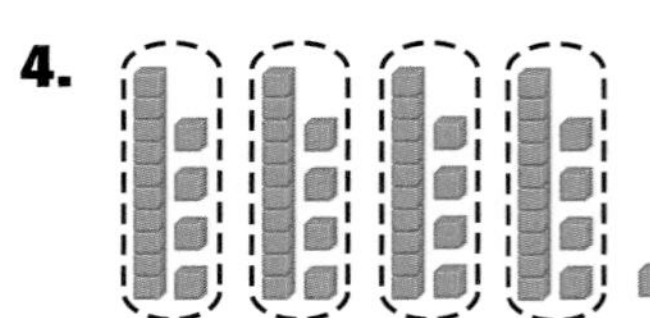

Use models or pictures to find each quotient.

5. 36 ÷ 2 **6.** 48 ÷ 3 **7.** 57 ÷ 4 **8.** 77 ÷ 5

9. WRITING IN ►MATH Explain how to use models or pictures to find 79 ÷ 6.

7-1 Division with Remainders

MAIN IDEA

I will carry out division with and without remainders.

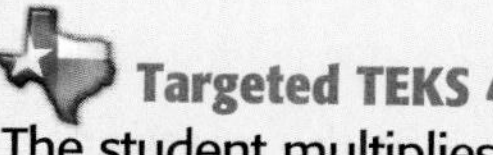

Targeted TEKS 4.4 The student multiplies and **divides to solve meaningful problems involving whole numbers. (B) Represent** multiplication and **division situations in picture, word, and number form. (E) Use division to solve problems** (no more than one-digit divisors and three-digit dividends without technology).

GET READY to Learn

Mr. Hein's class is going to a natural history museum. Each seat on the bus can hold 2 people. There are 28 students and 8 adults. How many bus seats are needed?

You have used models to divide. You can also use paper and pencil.

Real-World EXAMPLE

1 SCHOOL **How many bus seats are needed for the field trip?**

There are 36 people. Each seat holds 2 people. Find $36 \div 2$.

Step 1 Divide the tens.

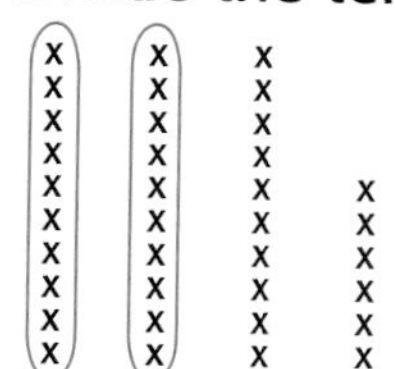

$2\overline{)36}$ → $\begin{array}{r} 1 \\ 2\overline{)36} \end{array}$

Can 3 tens be divided equally into groups of 2?

Yes, there is one ten in each group.

Step 2 Multiply, subtract, and compare.

$$\begin{array}{r} 1 \\ 2\overline{)36} \\ -2 \\ \hline 1 \end{array}$$

Multiply. $2 \times 1 = 2$
Subtract. $3 - 2 = 1$
Compare. $1 < 2$

Step 3 Bring down the ones.

$$\begin{array}{r} 1 \\ 2\overline{)36} \\ -2\downarrow \\ \hline 16 \end{array}$$

Bring down 6 ones
16 ones in all.

Step 4 Divide the ones.

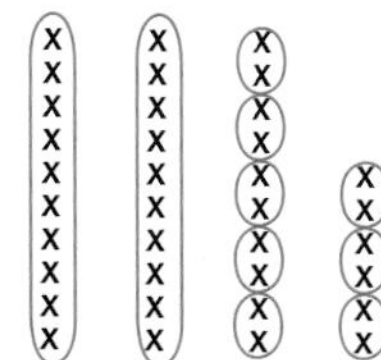

$$\begin{array}{r} 18 \\ 2\overline{)36} \\ -2\downarrow \\ \hline 16 \\ -16 \\ \hline 0 \end{array}$$

Divide. $16 \div 2 = 8$
Put 8 in the quotient.

Multiply. $2 \times 8 = 16$
Subtract. $16 - 16 = 0$
Compare. $0 < 2$

So, 18 bus seats are needed.

You can interpret the remainder in division problems.

Remember

To check a division answer, multiply the quotient by the divisor.

$$\begin{array}{r} 18 \\ \times\ 4 \\ \hline 72 \\ +\ 2 \\ \hline 74 \end{array}$$

← Add the remainder.

Real-World EXAMPLE — Division with Remainders

2 MONEY Manuel's comic books are worth \$74. He has 4 comic books. They are each worth the same amount. How much is each book worth?

Manuel has 4 comic books that are worth \$74. Each comic book is worth the same amount. So, divide \$74 by 4 to find how much each book is worth.

Step 1 Divide the tens.

$$\begin{array}{r} 1 \\ 4\overline{)\$74} \\ -4 \\ \hline 3 \end{array}$$

Divide. $7 \div 4 = 1$ so one ten is in each group.
Multiply. $4 \times 1 = 4$
Subtract. $7 - 4 = 3$
Compare. $3 < 4$

Step 2 Divide the ones.

$$\begin{array}{r} 18 \text{ R2} \\ 4\overline{)\$74} \\ -4\downarrow \\ \hline 34 \\ -32 \\ \hline 2 \end{array}$$

Bring down the ones.
Divide. $34 \div 4 = 8$
Put 8 in the quotient.
Multiply. $4 \times 8 = 32$
Subtract. $34 - 32 = 2$
Compare. $2 < 4$
Remainder $= 2$

So, each comic book is worth a little more than \$18.

Check The picture shows that $\$74 \div 4 = 18$ R2.

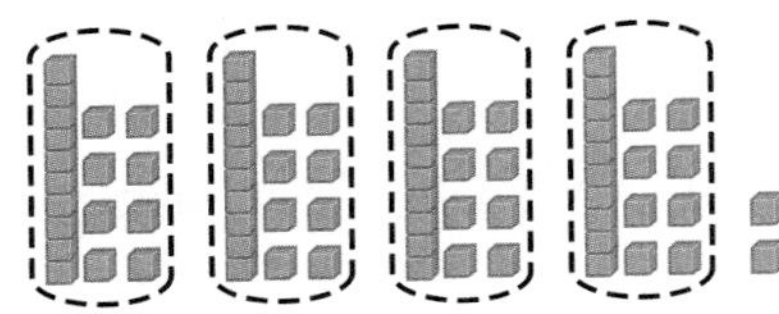

Online **Personal Tutor at** tx.gr4math.com

CHECK What You Know

Divide. Draw a picture to help. Check each answer. See Examples 1 and 2 (pp. 269–270)

1. $2\overline{)26}$
2. $3\overline{)36}$
3. $5\overline{)59}$
4. $8\overline{)84}$
5. $93 \div 3$
6. $84 \div 4$
7. $61 \div 2$
8. $86 \div 3$

9. Four zookeepers each feed the same number of animals. If there are 84 animals, how many will each zookeeper feed?

10. Talk About It Why is the remainder always less than the divisor?

Practice and Problem Solving

EXTRA PRACTICE
See page R20.

Divide. Draw a picture to help. Check each answer. See Examples 1 and 2 (pp. 269–270)

11. $2\overline{)28}$ **12.** $4\overline{)48}$ **13.** $3\overline{)33}$ **14.** $2\overline{)26}$

15. $5\overline{)53}$ **16.** $6\overline{)67}$ **17.** $7\overline{)73}$ **18.** $9\overline{)96}$

19. $93 \div 3$ **20.** $84 \div 4$ **21.** $64 \div 2$ **22.** $69 \div 3$

23. $79 \div 2$ **24.** $91 \div 4$ **25.** $77 \div 3$ **26.** $99 \div 4$

27. Marlene makes $4 an hour babysitting. If she earned $48, how many hours did she babysit?

28. Seven scouts need to sell 75 boxes of cookies. Each scout gets the same number of boxes. How many boxes does each scout need to sell?

Real-World PROBLEM SOLVING

Science There are many different insects and worms on Earth.

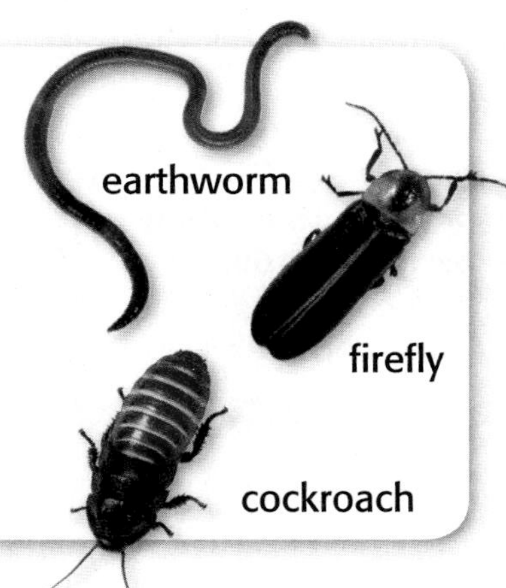

29. The lifespan of a firefly is 7 days. How many generations of fireflies have lived in 77 days?

30. A cockroach can travel 3 miles per hour. How long would it take the cockroach to travel 32 miles?

H.O.T. Problems

31. OPEN ENDED Identify a two-digit dividend that will result in a quotient with a remainder of 1 when the divisor is 4.

32. FIND THE ERROR Kate and Yutaka found 46 ÷ 4. Who is correct? Explain.

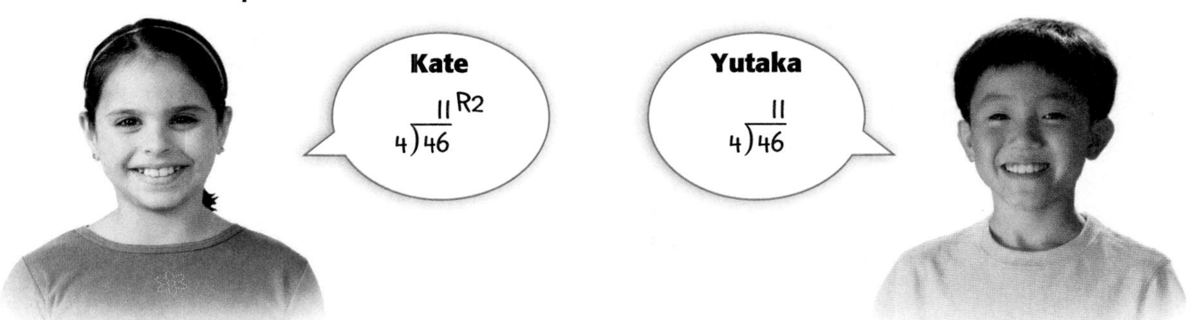

33. WRITING IN MATH When you divide a number by 6, can the remainder be 6? Explain.

7-2 Divide Multiples of 10 and 100

GET READY to Learn

A certain amusement park has 5 entrances. If 1,500 people entered the amusement park and separated into equal lines, how many people are in each line?

MAIN IDEA

I will use basic facts and patterns to divide mentally.

Targeted TEKS 4.6 The student uses patterns in multiplication and division. (B) **Use patterns to multiply by 10 and 100.** *Also addresses TEKS 4.6(A).*

You can find patterns when dividing multiples of 10. Using patterns makes it easy to divide multiples of 10.

Real-World EXAMPLE — Divide Multiples of 10

1 **AMUSEMENT PARKS How many people are in each line at the amusement park?**

You need to divide 1,500 people into 5 equal groups. Find 1,500 ÷ 5.

One Way: Use a Multiplication Pattern

$5 \times 3 = 15 \longrightarrow 15 \div 5 = 3$

$5 \times 30 = 150 \longrightarrow 150 \div 5 = 30$

$5 \times 300 = 1{,}500 \longrightarrow 1{,}500 \div 5 = 300$

Another Way: Use a Basic Fact

The basic fact for 1,500 ÷ 5 is 15 ÷ 5.

$15 \div 5 = 3$ ← basic fact

$150 \div 5 = 30$

$1{,}500 \div 5 = 300$

So, there are 300 people in each line.

EXAMPLE Divide Multiples of 10

Remember

Multiplication can be used to check division.

2 **Find the quotient of 2,400 and 40.**

One Way: Use a Multiplication Pattern

$4 \times 6 = 24 \rightarrow 24 \div 4 = 6$

$40 \times 6 = 240 \rightarrow 240 \div 40 = 6$

$40 \times 60 = 2{,}400 \rightarrow 2{,}400 \div 40 = 60$

Another Way: Use a Basic Fact

The basic fact for $2{,}400 \div 40$ is $24 \div 4$.

$24 \div 4 = 6$ ← basic fact

$240 \div 4 = 60$

$2{,}400 \div 40 = 60$

So, $2{,}400 \div 40$ is 60.

Online Personal Tutor at tx.gr4math.com

CHECK What You Know

Copy and complete each set of patterns. See Examples 1 and 2 (pp. 272–373)

1. $12 \div 4 = \blacksquare$
$120 \div 4 = \blacksquare$
$1{,}200 \div 4 = \blacksquare$

2. $\$36 \div 6 = \blacksquare$
$\$360 \div 60 = \blacksquare$
$\$3{,}600 \div 60 = \blacksquare$

3. $45 \div 9 = \blacksquare$
$450 \div 90 = \blacksquare$
$4{,}500 \div 90 = \blacksquare$

Divide. Use patterns. See Examples 1 and 2 (pp. 272–273)

4. $\$400 \div 20$

5. $1{,}600 \div 40$

6. $\$3{,}200 \div 80$

For Exercise 7, use the information to the right.

7. There are 4 members of a family planning a weekend camping trip. How much will the trip cost cost for each person?

Family Vacation

Item	Total Cost
Campsite rental cost	$50
Camping supplies	$75
Food	$75

8. Talk About It What basic fact will help you find the quotient of 4,200 and 70?

Practice and Problem Solving

EXTRA PRACTICE See page R20.

Copy and complete each set of patterns. See Examples 1 and 2 (pp. 272–273)

9. 12 ÷ 4 = ■
120 ÷ 4 = ■
1,200 ÷ 4 = ■

10. \$28 ÷ 7 = ■
\$280 ÷ 7 = ■
\$2,800 ÷ 7 = ■

11. 54 ÷ 9 = ■
540 ÷ 9 = ■
5,400 ÷ 9 = ■

12. \$36 ÷ 4 = ■
\$360 ÷ 40 = ■
\$3,600 ÷ 40 = ■

13. 42 ÷ 6 = ■
420 ÷ 60 = ■
4,200 ÷ 60 = ■

14. \$72 ÷ 8 = ■
\$720 ÷ 80 = ■
\$7,200 ÷ 80 = ■

Divide. Use patterns. See Examples 1 and 2 (pp. 272–273)

15. 200 ÷ 50
16. \$600 ÷ 30
17. 800 ÷ 20
18. 900 ÷ 30
19. \$1,400 ÷ 70
20. 4,500 ÷ 50
21. 6,300 ÷ 90
22. \$6,400 ÷ 80
23. \$3,500 ÷ 50
24. 1,600 ÷ 80
25. 5,400 ÷ 60
26. \$8,100 ÷ 90

27. The cost of a car is \$5,400. If the payments are spread over 60 months, what is the payment each month?

28. The Nair family collected 2,400 pennies. The pennies will be divided evenly among the 4 children. How many dollars will each child get?

Real-World PROBLEM SOLVING

Measurement Animals migrate due to factors such as climate and food availability. The table shows a few migration distances.

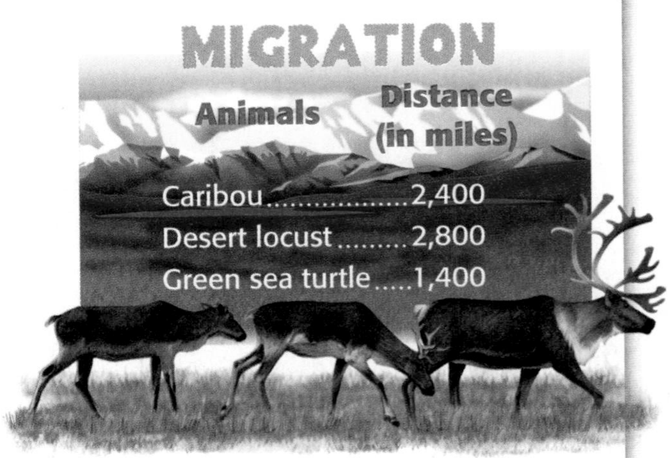

MIGRATION

Animals	Distance (in miles)
Caribou	2,400
Desert locust	2,800
Green sea turtle	1,400

29. If a group of green sea turtles travel 20 miles a day, how many days will the migration take?

30. A swarm of desert locusts is traveling about 70 miles a day. How many days will the migration take?

31. A herd of caribou migrated the distance shown in 8 months. If they traveled the same distance each month, how many miles did the herd travel each month?

H.O.T. Problems

32. **NUMBER SENSE** Without actually dividing, tell which has the greater quotient, 1,500 ÷ 30 or 2,400 ÷ 60. Explain.

33. **WRITING IN ▶MATH** Explain how you would know that the quotient of 600 ÷ 2 is a three-digit number.

TEST Practice

34. Rosita read a 75-page book in 5 days. She read the same number of pages each day. How many pages did she read each day? (Lesson 7-1)

A 5

B 10

C 15

D 150

35. Antoine went to his sister's college graduation. There were 1200 students graduating. They were separated equally into 4 sections of the auditorium. How many students were seated in each section? (Lesson 7-2)

F 3

G 30

H 300

J 3,000

Spiral Review

Divide. Check each answer. (Lesson 7-1)

36. $2\overline{)37}$

37. $5\overline{)49}$

38. $7\overline{)81}$

Multiply. (Lesson 6-8)

39. 72×18

40. 61×39

41. 44×65

For Exercises 42–44, use the table. It shows the life spans of reptiles. Choose the best operation. Then solve. (Lesson 5-4)

42. How many years will three generations of Galapagos turtles live?

43. How much longer can an American alligator live than a komodo dragon?

44. Which animal lives 90 years longer than the boa constrictor?

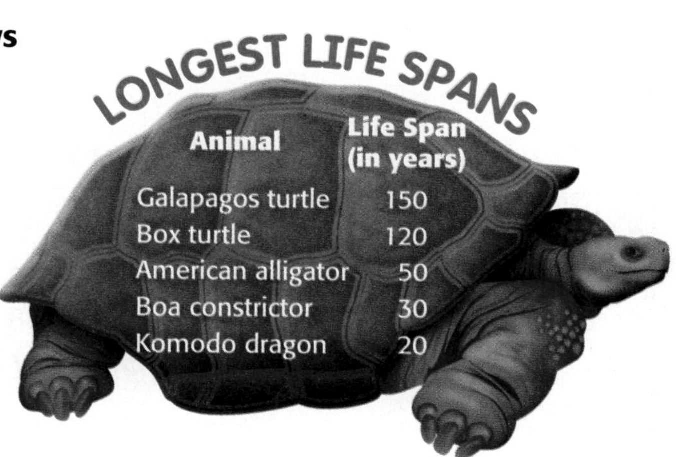

Animal	Life Span (in years)
Galapagos turtle	150
Box turtle	120
American alligator	50
Boa constrictor	30
Komodo dragon	20

7-3 Problem-Solving Strategy

MAIN IDEA I will solve problems by using the *guess and check* strategy.

Targeted TEKS 4.14 The student applies Grade 4 mathematics to solve problems connected to everyday experiences and activities in and outside of school. **(C) Select or develop an appropriate problem-solving plan or strategy, including . . . systematic guessing and checking, . . .** to solve a problem. *Also addresses TEKS 4.14(B).*

Ruben bought 3 gifts for his sisters. Two of the gifts cost the same. The other gift costs \$3 more than the other two. If the total amount of money spent was \$27, how much did each gift cost?

Understand

What facts do you know?

- There are three gifts, and two gifts cost the same.
- One gift is \$3 more than the other two.
- Ruben spent \$27 on all three gifts.

What do you need to find?

- The cost of each gift.

Plan

You can guess and check to solve the problem.

Solve

Use gift + gift + (gift + \$3) = \$27 and make logical guesses.

Start with numbers less than \$10 because \$10 × 3 = \$30 and the total is less than \$30.

Try \$9.
\$9 + \$9 + (\$9 + \$3) = \$30   No, too large.

Try \$8.
\$8 + \$8 + (\$8 + \$3) = \$27   Yes

So, two gifts cost \$8 each, and the third gift costs \$8 + \$3, or \$11.

Check

Subtract the cost of each gift from the total cost.

First gift: \$27 − \$8 = \$19
Second gift: \$19 − \$8 = \$11
Third gift: \$11 − \$11 = \$0

So, the answer is correct.

ANALYZE the Strategy

Refer to the problem on the previous page.

1. Explain why gift + gift + (gift + $3) is used to solve the equation.

2. Explain why the first guess was $9 instead of a smaller number.

3. Suppose Ruben spent $39 on the gifts. How much does each gift cost?

4. Explain how you found the answer to Exercise 3.

PRACTICE the Strategy

EXTRA PRACTICE
See page R21.

Solve. Use the *guess and check* strategy.

5. Kendra photographed the Dogs-n-Suds annual car wash. She photographed 20 dogs and owners in all. If there was a total of 64 legs, how many dogs and owners were there?

6. Corrine is making twice as much fruit punch as lemonade. She is making 12 gallons total. How many gallons will be fruit punch and how many will be lemonade?

7. **Measurement** Theo lives twice as far from Cassidy as Jarvis. How far do Theo and Jarvis live from Cassidy?

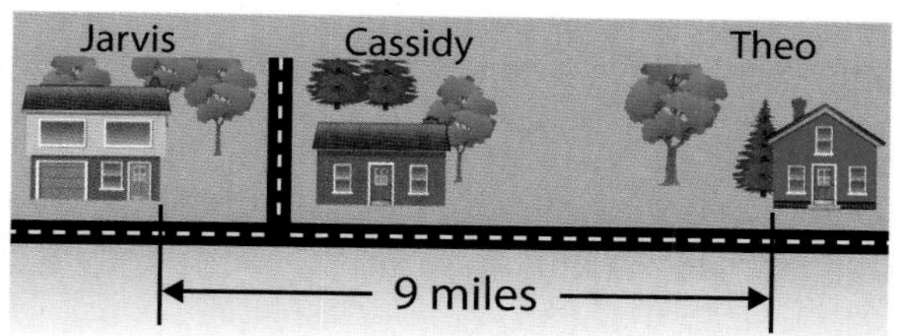

8. The total number of tickets sold for a play was 450. On Friday, 150 tickets were sold. Fifty more tickets sold on Saturday than on Sunday. How many tickets sold on Saturday and Sunday?

9. At a zoo gift shop, Jeffrey bought two of the items shown. He paid the cashier $20, and received $4 in change. Which two items did he buy?

10. Ahmed and Marco collect miniature cars. Marco has 37 fewer cars than Ahmed. They have 249 cars altogether. How many cars does each boy have?

11. Mirna's basketball team has played 14 games. They have lost and tied an equal number of times. They have won 5 times as many games as they have lost. How many games have they won, lost, and tied?

12. **WRITING IN MATH** Explain what it means to solve a problem by *guess and check.*

7-4 Estimate Quotients

GET READY to Learn

Circuses have been around for more than 200 years. They sometimes travel by train. Suppose a circus train travels 642 miles in 8 hours. *About* how fast did the train travel?

MAIN IDEA

I will estimate quotients using compatible numbers.

Targeted TEKS 4.5 The student estimates to determine reasonable results. (B) **Use strategies including rounding and compatible numbers to estimate solutions to** multiplication and **division problems.** *Also addresses TEKS 4.4(C), 4.6(B).*

New Vocabulary

compatible numbers

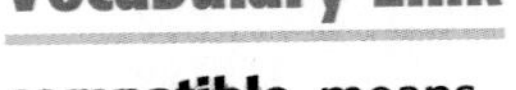

Vocabulary Link

compatible means well matched

There are different ways to estimate quotients. One way is to use compatible numbers. **Compatible numbers** are numbers that are easy to divide mentally.

Real-World EXAMPLE — Estimate Quotients

1 TRAVEL **Estimate the quotient of 642 and 8 to find how fast the train is traveling.**

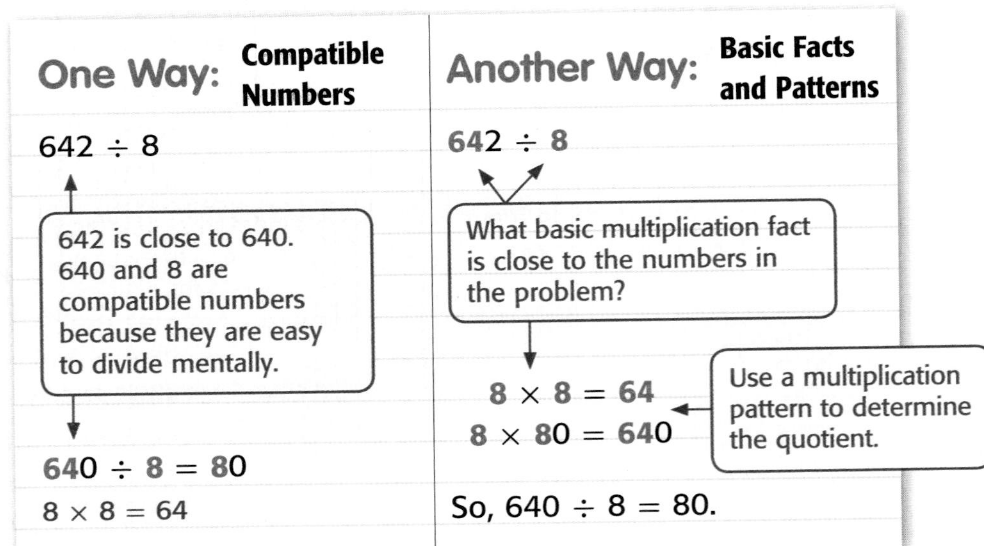

One Way: **Compatible Numbers**	Another Way: **Basic Facts and Patterns**
$642 \div 8$	$642 \div 8$
642 is close to 640. 640 and 8 are compatible numbers because they are easy to divide mentally.	What basic multiplication fact is close to the numbers in the problem?
$640 \div 8 = 80$	$8 \times 8 = 64$ $8 \times 80 = 640$ — Use a multiplication pattern to determine the quotient.
$8 \times 8 = 64$	So, $640 \div 8 = 80$.

So, the circus train is traveling about 80 miles per hour.

Check

You know that $640 \div 8 = 80$ because $8 \times 80 = 640$. ✓

Online Personal Tutor at tx.gr4math.com

Real-World EXAMPLE Estimate Quotients

2 **DOLLS Isabella has 6 dolls in her doll collection. The collection is worth $1,168. Each doll is worth the same amount of money. About how much is each doll worth?**

You need to estimate $1,168 ÷ 6.

One Way: Compatible Numbers	**Another Way:** Use Rounding
$1,168 ÷ 6	$1,168 ÷ 6
$1,168 is close to $1,200. $1,200 and 6 are compatible numbers because they are easy to divide mentally.	Round 1,168 to the nearest hundred.
	1,200 ÷ 6
	Use a multiplication pattern to solve.
$1,200 ÷ 6 = 200 6 × 2 = 12	6 × 2 = 12
	6 × 20 = 120
	6 × 200 = 1,200
	So, $1,200 ÷ 6 = 200.

So, each doll is worth about $200.

Check

You know that $1,200 ÷ 6 = $200 because
6 × $200 = $1,200. ✓

CHECK What You Know

Estimate. Use compatible numbers. See Examples 1 and 2 (pp. 278–279)

1. 161 ÷ 4   **2.** $424 ÷ 6   **3.** 715 ÷ 8

Estimate. Round to the nearest hundred. See Examples 1 and 2 (pp. 278–279)

4. 2,660 ÷ 9   **5.** $5,643 ÷ 8   **6.** 8,099 ÷ 9

7. On Saturday, 1,163 people saw a movie at Upcity Theater. There were a total of 4 movie screens with the same number of people in each audience. About how many people watched each screen?

8. Talk About It Explain how to estimate $4,782 ÷ 6 using compatible numbers.

Practice and Problem Solving

EXTRA PRACTICE See page R21.

Estimate. Use compatible numbers. See Examples 1 and 2 (pp. 278–279)

9. 123 ÷ 3 **10.** $244 ÷ 6 **11.** 162 ÷ 2 **12.** 345 ÷ 7

13. $538 ÷ 6 **14.** 415 ÷ 6 **15.** $1,406 ÷ 7 **16.** 2,431 ÷ 8

Estimate. Round to the nearest hundred. See Examples 1 and 2 (pp. 278–279)

17. $2,719 ÷ 9 **18.** 4,187 ÷ 7 **19.** $7,160 ÷ 9 **20.** 8,052 ÷ 9

21. Tran earned 806 points on 9 tests. If he earned about the same number of points on each test, about how many points did he earn on each test?

22. **Measurement** Gloria ran 1,575 miles in 8 months. She ran the same number of miles each month. About how many miles did she run each month?

Real-World PROBLEM SOLVING

Data File You can go hut hiking in Big Bend National Park. Hut hiking involves hiking and spending the night in huts instead of tents.

Parks

BIG BEND
NATIONAL PARK
UNITED STATES DEPARTMENT OF THE INTERIOR
NATIONAL PARK SERVICE

23. The total cost for the 5 members in the Valdez family to hut hike for 6 days is $2,475. About how much does it cost for each family member?

24. Harold needs to climb a 361-foot hill to get to the next hut. About how many yards away is he from the next hut? (*Remember:* 3 feet = 1 yard)

H.O.T. Problems

25. **OPEN ENDED** The estimated quotient of a division sentence is 200. What could the division sentence be?

26. **WRITING IN MATH** Estimate 5,425 ÷ 6 using 5,400 ÷ 6. Is the estimate greater than or less than the actual quotient? Explain.

CHAPTER 7

Mid-Chapter Check

Lessons 7-1 through 7-4

Divide. Check each answer. (Lesson 7-1)

1. 92 ÷ 3

2. 37 ÷ 2

3. Gwen earns $5 an hour delivering newspapers. If she earned $35 this week, how many hours did she spend delivering newspapers? (Lesson 7-1)

4. **TEST PRACTICE** Gabriel solved the problem below. Which expression could be used to check his answer? (Lesson 7-1)

136 ÷ 5 = 27 R1

A (27 × 1) + 5

B (27 × 5) + 1

C (27 + 5) × 1

D (27 + 1) × 5

Copy and complete each set of patterns. (Lesson 7-2)

5. 42 ÷ 7 = ■
420 ÷ 7 = ■
4,200 ÷ 7 = ■

6. 25 ÷ 5 = ■
250 ÷ 5 = ■
2,500 ÷ 5 = ■

Divide. Use patterns. (Lesson 7-2)

7. 150 ÷ 50

8. 600 ÷ 20

9. Jairo has 200 minutes left on his cell phone plan for the last five days of the month. If Jairo uses the same number of minutes each day, how many minutes can Jairo use his cell phone per day?

Solve. Use the *guess and check* strategy. (Lesson 7-3)

10. Patricia and Ashley collect stamps. Patricia has 13 more stamps than Ashley. Together they have 229 stamps. How many stamps does each girl have?

11. Dion bought three of the items shown below. He paid the cashier $10 and received $4 in change. Which three items did he buy?

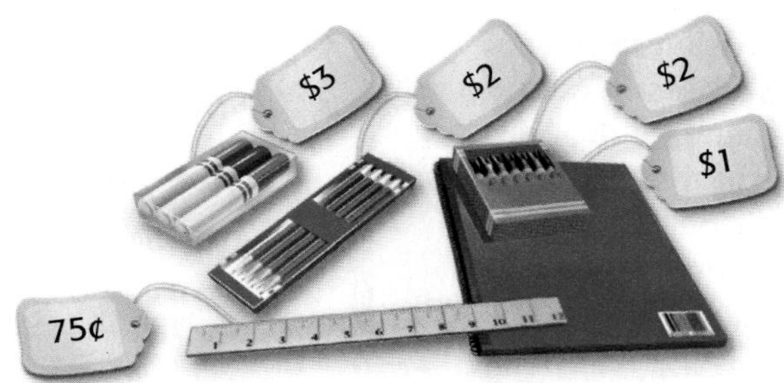

Estimate. Check your estimate. (Lesson 7-4)

12. 156 ÷ 3

13. 182 ÷ 9

14. **TEST PRACTICE** Vikas drove 325 miles in five hours. Approximately how many miles did Vikas drive each hour? (Lesson 7-4)

F 60

G 65

H 68

J 70

15. **WRITING IN MATH** (Lesson 7-4)
If you estimate 4,225 ÷ 6 using 4,200 ÷ 6, is the estimate greater or less than the actual quotient? Explain.

7-5 Two-Digit Quotients

MAIN IDEA

I will divide a two-digit dividend by a one-digit number.

Targeted TEKS 4.4 The student multiplies and divides to solve meaningful problems involving whole numbers. (E) **Use division to solve problems** (no more than one-digit divisors and three-digit dividends without technology). *Also addresses TEKS 4.5(B).*

GET READY to Learn

Most of the world's geysers are found in Yellowstone National Park. Suppose one of Yellowstone's geysers erupts every 7 minutes. How many times does it erupt in 95 minutes?

Recall that to divide a two-digit number by a one-digit number, you need to divide the tens. Then divide the ones.

Real-World EXAMPLE Two-Digit Quotients

1 How many times does the geyser erupt in 95 minutes?

The geyser erupts every 7 minutes. You need to find the number of times it erupts in 95 minutes. So, find $95 \div 7$.

Estimate $95 \div 7 \longrightarrow 100 \div 10 = 10$

Step 1 Divide the tens.

$$\begin{array}{r} 1 \\ 7\overline{)95} \\ -7 \\ \hline 2 \end{array}$$

Divide. $9 \div 7 = 1$
Put 1 in the quotient.
Multiply. $7 \times 1 = 7$
Subtract. $9 - 7 = 2$
Compare. $2 < 7$

Step 2 Divide the ones.

$$\begin{array}{r} 13 \text{ R4} \\ 7\overline{)95} \\ -7\downarrow \\ \hline 25 \\ -21 \\ \hline 4 \end{array}$$

Bring down the ones.
Divide. $25 \div 7 = 3$
Put 3 in the quotient.
Multiply. $7 \times 3 = 21$
Subtract. $25 - 21 = 4$
Remainder = 4
Compare. $4 < 7$

So, the geyser will erupt about 13 times in 95 minutes.

Check for Reasonableness

13 is close to the estimate. The answer is reasonable. ✓

Sometimes it is not possible to divide the first digit of the dividend by the divisor.

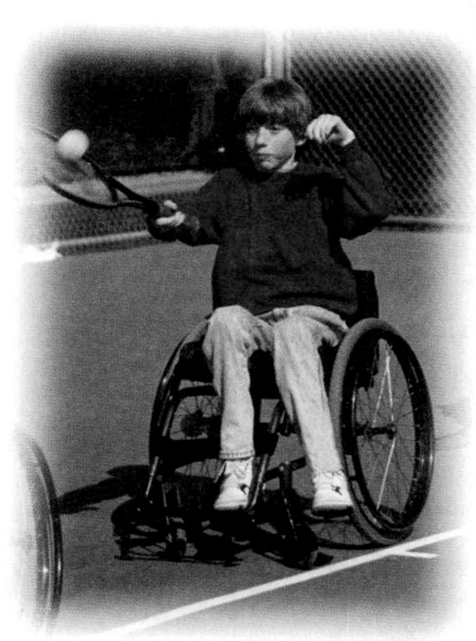

Real-World EXAMPLE Divide with Remainders

2 SPORTS A tennis coach has 123 tennis balls. There are 4 members on the team. If the tennis balls are divided as evenly as possible, how many balls does each member get for practice?

There are 123 tennis balls and 4 team members. Divide 123 by 4 to find how many balls each player gets.

Estimate $123 \div 4 \longrightarrow 120 \div 4 = 30$

Step 1 Estimate to place the first digit.

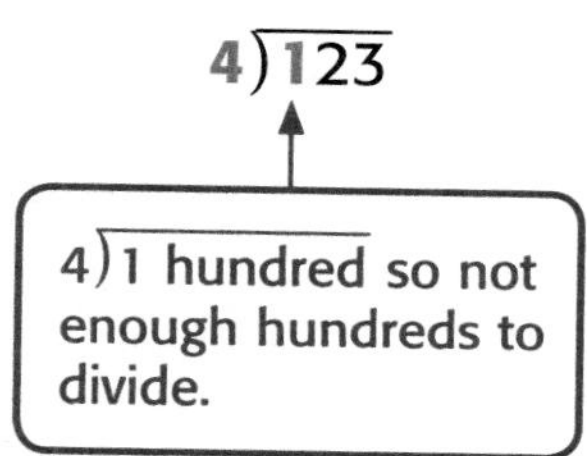

x
4)123

4)12 tens so enough tens to divide. So, the first digit is in the tens digit.

Step 2 Divide the tens.

```
   3
4)123
 -12
   0
```

Divide. $12 \div 4 = 3$
Put 3 in the quotient.
Multiply. $4 \times 3 = 12$
Subtract. $122 - 12 = 0$
Compare. $0 < 4$

Step 3 Divide the ones.

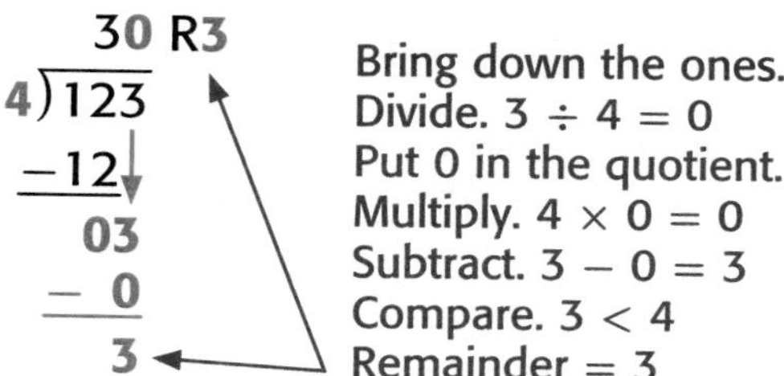

Bring down the ones.
Divide. $3 \div 4 = 0$
Put 0 in the quotient.
Multiply. $4 \times 0 = 0$
Subtract. $3 - 0 = 3$
Compare. $3 < 4$
Remainder = 3

So, each member gets 30 balls for practice, with 3 balls leftover.

Check for Reasonableness
The answer is close to the estimate. So, it is reasonable. ✓

Remember

When a real world problem has a remainder, you have to interpret the remainder.

Online **Personal Tutor at** tx.gr4math.com

CHECK What You Know

Divide. Use estimation to check. See Examples 1 and 2 (pp. 282–283)

1. $2\overline{)33}$ **2.** $4\overline{)56}$ **3.** $5\overline{)71}$

4. 179 ÷ 3 **5.** 387 ÷ 4 **6.** 697 ÷ 7

7. Holden and Alma earned $32 by doing yard work in their neighborhood. They will share their money. How much money will each person get?

8. Talk About It Estimation is one method that can be used to check division answers. Identify another method.

Practice and Problem Solving

EXTRA PRACTICE See page R22.

Divide. Use estimation to check. See Examples 1 and 2 (pp. 282–283)

9. $2\overline{)37}$ **10.** $3\overline{)64}$ **11.** $4\overline{)79}$ **12.** $5\overline{)82}$

13. $7\overline{)74}$ **14.** $6\overline{)91}$ **15.** $2\overline{)151}$ **16.** $3\overline{)286}$

17. 387 ÷ 5 **18.** 493 ÷ 5 **19.** 567 ÷ 6 **20.** 682 ÷ 7

21. 694 ÷ 7 **22.** 783 ÷ 8 **23.** 795 ÷ 8 **24.** 883 ÷ 9

25. There are 78 campers at a summer camp. There are 6 campers per cabin. How many cabins are there?

26. Carlo has $46 to spend on trading cards. If each pack of cards costs $3, how many packages can he buy?

Real-World PROBLEM SOLVING

Recycling Every month, Americans throw out enough bottles and jars to fill up a giant skyscraper. All of these jars are recyclable.

27. When one aluminum can is recycled, enough energy is saved to run a television for 3 hours. How many cans need to be recycled to run a television for 75 hours?

28. Most Americans use 7 trees a year in products that are made from trees. How old is a person who has used 85 trees?

Math Online Self-Check Quiz at tx.gr4math.com

H.O.T. Problems

29. OPEN-ENDED When Kira's father's age is divided by Kira's age, you get a quotient of 13 R1. Identify one possibility for their ages.

30. FIND THE ERROR Amber and Paul are finding 53 ÷ 3. Who is correct? Explain.

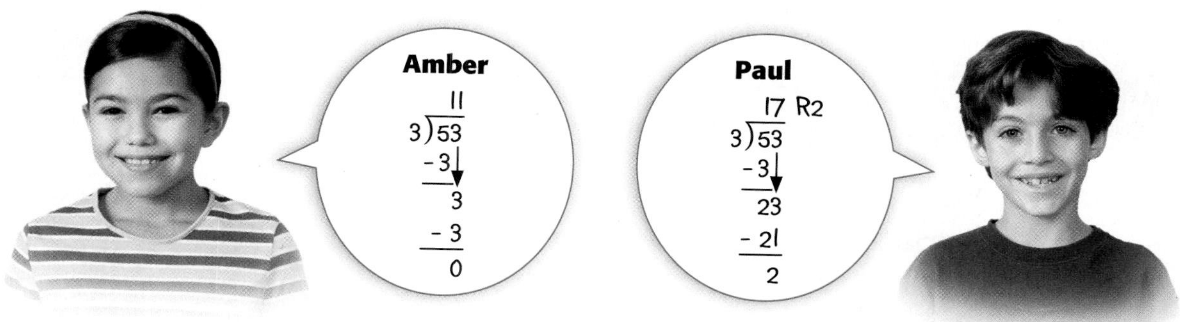

31. WRITING IN MATH Write a division problem that requires regrouping and a remainder in the quotient. Give to a classmate to solve.

TEST Practice

32. Martín biked 78 miles in 5 days. About how many miles did he bike each day? (Lesson 7-4)

A 14 **C** 16

B 15 **D** 17

33. Raj ran 56 feet during a football game. If there are 3 feet in one yard, how many yards did he run? (Lesson 7-5)

F 17 R2 **H** 18 R2

G 18 **J** 19 R1

Spiral Review

Estimate. Check your estimate. (Lesson 7-4)

34. 139 ÷ 2 **35.** \$449 ÷ 5 **36.** 562 ÷ 7 **37.** \$805 ÷ 9

38. Pablo works at an animal hospital. Last week he took care of 49 birds and snakes. He took care of four birds for every three snakes. How many of each animal did he take care of? (Lesson 7-3)

Divide. Use patterns. (Lesson 7-2)

39. \$600 ÷ 30 **40.** 2,400 ÷ 40 **41.** 4,900 ÷ 70 **42.** 4,800 ÷ 80

43. Jerry was given 3 CDs from his friends, 4 from his parents, and 1 from his sister. He now has 38. How many did he have originally? (Lesson 7-3)

Problem-Solving Investigation

MAIN IDEA I will choose the best strategy to solve a problem.

Targeted TEKS 4.14 The student applies Grade 4 mathematics to solve problems . . . in and outside of school. (B) **Solve problems that incorporate understanding the problem, making a plan, and evaluating the solution for reasonableness.** *Also addresses TEKS 4.14(C).*

P.S.I. TEAM +

CINDY: I had some stamps. I bought 6 more stamps. I traded 4 of my stamps for 8 of my friend's stamps. I now have 32 stamps.

YOUR MISSION: Find how many stamps Cindy started with.

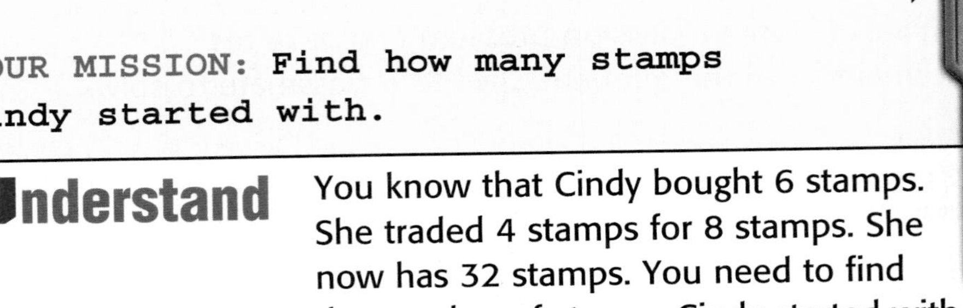

Understand

You know that Cindy bought 6 stamps. She traded 4 stamps for 8 stamps. She now has 32 stamps. You need to find the number of stamps Cindy started with.

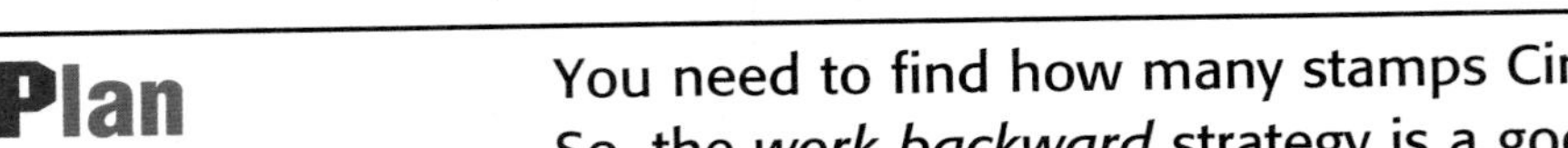

Plan

You need to find how many stamps Cindy started with. So, the *work backward* strategy is a good choice.

Solve

Start with the end result, then work backward.

End result ⟶ 32 stamps Cindy has now
-8 stamps Cindy received from a friend
24

24
$+4$ stamps Cindy gave to a friend
28

28
-6 stamps Cindy bought
22

Check

Look back at the problem. Cindy gained 14 stamps and lost 4. This means she has 10 more stamps then she started with. If she now has 32 stamps, then she started with 22 stamps. The answer is correct.

Mixed Problem Solving

See page R22.

Use any strategy shown below to solve. Tell what strategy you used.

PROBLEM-SOLVING STRATEGIES
- Look for a pattern.
- Make a table.
- Work backward.
- Act it out.
- Guess and check.

1. Ellis rode his bike to and from his cousin's home over the weekend. His cousin lives 5 miles away. If Ellis rode a total of 20 miles, how many times did he visit his cousin?

2. What is the next number in the pattern 2, 5, 11, 23, ■?

3. Judie and her dad caught 63 fish over the summer. The license allowed them to keep fish longer than 8 inches. Only 2 out of every 5 fish were long enough to keep. About how many did they keep?

4. Alvin buys 2 pairs of jeans, 2 pairs of shoes, 3 T-shirts, and 2 dress shirts for school. How much did he spend?

5. There are 24 cars in a parking lot. There are twice as many 4-door cars as 2-door. How many of each are there?

6. **Measurement** Lucy the Great Dane eats the amount of dog food shown each day. Roscoe the Pug eats 1 cup for every 2 that Lucy eats each day. How much food does Roscoe eat in a week?

7. A worker at an arcade is handing out 30 tokens for a party. There are more than 6 people at the party. The tokens are shared equally among the people. After the tokens are handed out, 6 are left. How many people are at the party? How many tokens does each person get?

8. Anoki has 5 coins that total 62¢. What are the coins?

9. Selena is going to a birthday party at 12 P.M. She needs to complete the activities shown before the party starts. What time should Selena start to get ready?

Activity	Time
Shower/get ready	30 minutes
Eat breakfast	30 minutes
Chores	2 hours
Pick up Felix and go	30 minutes

10. **WRITING IN ▶MATH** Identify the problem-solving strategy you used to solve Exercise 9. Explain how you used the strategy to solve the problem.

7-7 Three-Digit Quotients

GET READY to Learn

There are 636 people in line to ride a roller coaster. Each coaster car holds 6 people. How many coaster cars are needed so that everyone in line rides the coaster once?

MAIN IDEA

I will divide a three-digit dividend by a one-digit number.

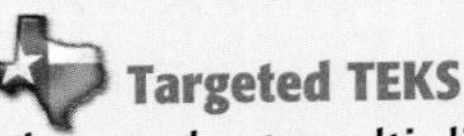

Targeted TEKS 4.4 The student multiplies and divides to solve meaningful problems involving whole numbers. **(E) Use division to solve problems** (no more than one-digit divisors and three-digit dividends without technology). *Also addresses TEKS 4.5(B).*

Finding a quotient like $636 \div 6$ is similar to dividing a two-digit number by a one-digit number.

Real-World EXAMPLE Three-Digit Quotients

1 **ROLLER COASTERS How many coaster cars are needed?**

Divide 636 by 6 to find the number of coaster cars needed.

Estimate $636 \div 6 \longrightarrow 600 \div 6 = 100$

Step 1 Divide the hundreds.

```
   1
6)636
 -6
  0
```

Divide. $6 \div 6 = 1$
Put 1 in the quotient.
Multiply. $6 \times 1 = 6$
Subtract. $6 - 6 = 0$
Compare. $0 < 6$

Step 2 Divide the tens.

```
   10
6)636
 -6↓
  03
  -0
   3
```

Bring down the tens.
Divide. $3 \div 6 = 0$
Put 0 in the quotient.
Multiply. $6 \times 0 = 0$
Subtract. $3 - 0 = 3$
Compare. $3 < 6$

Step 3 Divide the ones.

```
   106
6)636
 -6↓
  03
  -0↓
   36
  -36
    0
```

Bring down the ones.
Divide.
Divide. $36 \div 6 = 6$
Multiply. $6 \times 6 = 36$
Subtract. $36 - 36 = 0$
Compare. $0 < 6$

So, 106 coaster cars are needed.

When dividing three-digit numbers, you can have a remainder like you sometimes have when dividing two-digit numbers.

Remember

Always start a division problem by dividing the greatest place value.

Real-World EXAMPLE — Three-Digit Quotients with Remainders

2 MEASUREMENT **A roller coaster whose track is 985 feet long takes about 2 minutes to travel the track. How many feet does the coaster travel in one minute?**

The coaster travels 985 feet in 2 minutes. To find how far it travels in 1 minute, divide 985 by 2.

Estimate 985 ÷ 2 ⟶ 1,000 ÷ 2 = 500

$$\begin{array}{r} 492 \text{ R1} \\ 2\overline{)985} \\ -8\downarrow \\ \hline 18 \\ -18\downarrow \\ \hline 05 \\ -4 \\ \hline 1 \end{array}$$

THINK A remainder of 1 tells you that the quotient is just over 492.

So, the roller coaster travels a little more than 492 feet each minute.

Check for Reasonableness

The answer, a little more than 492, is close to the estimate. So, it is reasonable. ✓

Online **Personal Tutor at** tx.gr4math.com

CHECK What You Know

Divide. Use estimation to check. See Examples 1 and 2 (pp. 288–289)

1. $2\overline{)286}$ **2.** $3\overline{)345}$ **3.** $4\overline{)492}$

4. 745 ÷ 2 **5.** 679 ÷ 3 **6.** 917 ÷ 4

7. **Measurement** A tug-of-war team weighs a total of 774 pounds. The 6 members on the team weigh the same amount. How much does each person weigh?

8. Talk About It How would you mentally figure out how many digits the quotient of 795 ÷ 5 will have? Explain your reasoning.

Practice and Problem Solving

EXTRA PRACTICE See page R23.

Divide. Use estimation to check. See Examples 1 and 2 (pp. 288–289)

9. $2\overline{)324}$ **10.** $3\overline{)585}$ **11.** $5\overline{)775}$ **12.** $6\overline{)696}$

13. $7\overline{)847}$ **14.** $7\overline{)973}$ **15.** $2\overline{)573}$ **16.** $3\overline{)787}$

17. $849 \div 2$ **18.** $994 \div 4$ **19.** $963 \div 3$ **20.** $976 \div 4$

21. A coach ordered 6 lacrosse sticks for $678. How much did each stick cost?

22. Britney needs to finish reading a book in 3 days. If the book is 348 pages long, how many pages does she need to read each day?

23. Maria is making friendship necklaces. She needs 2 feet of ribbon for each necklace. How many necklaces can she make if she has 439 feet of ribbon?

24. The students at Kennedy Elementary School have collected 926 cans of food. The cans will be divided equally among 4 shelters. About how many cans will be given to each shelter?

H.O.T. Problems

25. OPEN ENDED Write a division problem that results in a quotient that is greater than 200 and less than 250.

26. WHICH ONE DOESN'T BELONG? Identify the problem that will have a quotient whose number of digits is different from the rest.

$2\overline{)478}$ $3\overline{)264}$ $4\overline{)652}$ $5\overline{)815}$

27. WRITING IN MATH Write a real-world division problem that involves dividing a 3-digit number by a 1-digit number that results in a 2-digit quotient with a remainder.

Technology Activity for 7-7
Division

MAIN IDEA

I will use technology to divide greater numbers.

Targeted TEKS 4.14 The student applies Grade 4 mathematics to solve problems connected to everyday experiences and activities in and outside of school. **(D)** **Use tools such as** real objects, manipulatives, and **technology to solve problems.** *Also addresses TEKS 4.15(A).*

Rigo downloads many CDs throughout the year. His total cost for last year was \$324. If he paid this in 6 payments, how much would each payment be?

You can use the division mat on the base-ten models from the *Math Tool Chest* to show \$324 divided by 6.

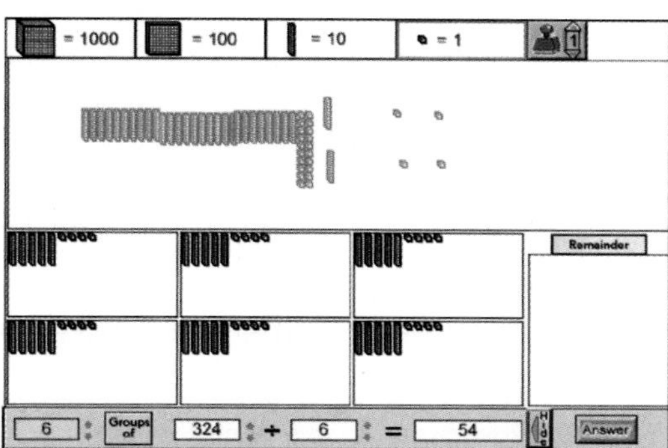

- Choose division as the type of mat.
- Stamp out 3 hundreds, 2 tens, and 4 ones.
- Then divide by 6.
- Press answer to find out the amount each payment will be.

$\$324 \div 6 = 54$

Rigo pays \$54 each time.

CHECK What You Know

Use the computer to model each problem. Then write the quotient.

1. $155 \div 7$ **2.** $225 \div 8$ **3.** $352 \div 4$

Use technology to solve.

4. A group of friends bought tickets to a professional baseball game for a total cost of \$153. A group of 9 people is going to the game. What was the cost of each ticket to the baseball game?

5. A case of trading cards has 5 boxes. The total cost of the case is \$130. What is the value of a each box of trading cards?

6. **Analyze** How can modeling the problem help you divide?

7-8 Quotients with Zeros

MAIN IDEA

I will divide with zeros in the quotients.

Targeted TEKS 4.4 The student multiplies and **divides to solve meaningful problems involving whole numbers. (E) Use division to solve problems** (no more than one-digit divisors and three-digit dividends without technology). *Also addresses TEKS 4.5(B).*

GET READY to Learn

The Ramos family is going on a behind the scenes tour of a wildlife reserve in a park. How much will it cost for each person?

Cost of Tour	
Number of People	Cost ($)
3	$327

In division, a quotient will sometimes contain zeros.

Real-World EXAMPLE Divide Greater Numbers

1 ANIMALS How much it will cost for each person to go on the tour?

You need to find $327 ÷ 3.

Step 1 Divide the hundreds.

$$\begin{array}{r} \$1 \\ 3\overline{)\$327} \\ -3 \\ \hline 0 \end{array}$$

Divide. 3 ÷ 3 = 1
Put 1 in the quotient.
Multiply. 3 × 1 = 3
Subtract. 3 − 3 = 0
Compare. 0 < 3

Step 2 Divide the tens.

$$\begin{array}{r} \$10 \\ 3\overline{)\$327} \\ -3\downarrow \\ \hline 02 \\ -0 \\ \hline 0 \end{array}$$

Bring down the tens.
Divide. Since 2 < 3, there is not enough to divide. So, put 0 in the quotient.
Multiply. 3 × 0 = 0
Subtract. 2 − 0 = 2
Compare. 2 < 3

Step 3 Divide the ones.

$$\begin{array}{r} \$109 \\ 3\overline{)\$327} \\ -3\downarrow \\ \hline 02 \\ -0\downarrow \\ \hline 27 \\ -27 \\ \hline 0 \end{array}$$

Bring down the ones.
Divide. 27 ÷ 3 = 9
Put 9 in the quotient.
Multiply. 3 × 9 = 27
Subtract. 27 − 27 = 0
Compare. 0 < 3

So, it will cost each person $109.

Divide with Remainders

2 **VACATIONS** **The Kincaids have to drive a total of 415 miles to get to and from Dolphin Cove. How far is it to Dolphin Cove?**

415 miles

The total distance the Kincaids will travel is 415 miles. To find the distance to Dolphin Cove, divide 415 by 2.

Estimate 415 ÷ 2 ⟶ 400 ÷ 2 = 200

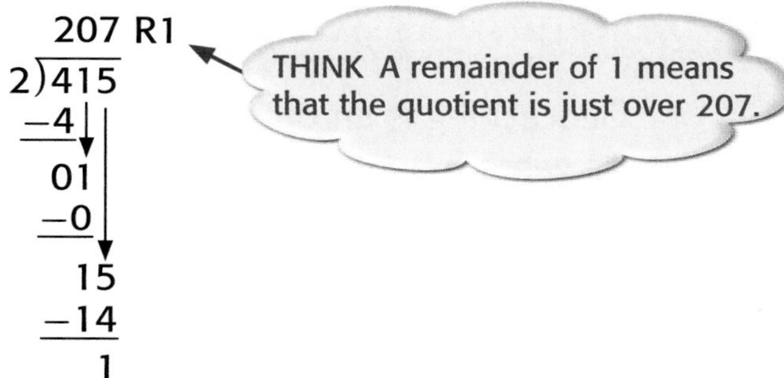

Remember

Remember to divide, multiply, subtract, and compare. Then bring down the next number in the dividend.

So, the distance to Dolphin Cove is a little more than 207 miles.

Check for Reasonableness

The quotient, 207 R1, is close to the estimate. So, the answer is reasonable. ✓

CHECK What You Know

Divide. Use estimation to check. See Examples 1 and 2 (pp. 292–293)

1. 2)212 **2.** 3)$627 **3.** 4)416

4. 617 ÷ 2 **5.** $913 ÷ 3 **6.** 825 ÷ 4

7. Clara's total score for 3 games of bowling is 312. If Clara earned the same score for each game, what was her score for each game?

8. Talk About It Explain how to find 624 ÷ 3.

Practice and Problem Solving

EXTRA PRACTICE See page R23.

Divide. Use estimation to check. See Examples 1 and 2 (pp. 292–293)

9. $2\overline{)214}$ **10.** $3\overline{)327}$ **11.** $5\overline{)\$545}$ **12.** $6\overline{)648}$

13. $7\overline{)742}$ **14.** $8\overline{)\$824}$ **15.** $2\overline{)417}$ **16.** $3\overline{)622}$

17. $613 ÷ 3 **18.** 837 ÷ 4 **19.** 819 ÷ 2 **20.** $929 ÷ 3

21. There are 412 toys to be put on 4 shelves at a toy store. If the same number of toys fit on each shelf, how many toys fit on each shelf?

22. There are 408 students at a school. There are 4 lunch periods. If there are the same number of students in each lunch period, how many students are in each period?

Real-World PROBLEM SOLVING

Treasure Geocaching is an outdoor treasure hunting game in which participants use a Global Positioning System to hide and seek "treasures" all over the world. The "treasures" are usually toys or trinkets.

23. Chad is saving his money to buy a Global Positioning System receiver so that he can go geocaching. He has 2 months to save $216. How much money does he need to save each month?

24. Some of the treasures have been hidden on mountains. If the treasure is 325 feet away, how many yards away is it? (*Remember:* 3 feet = 1 yard.)

H.O.T. Problems

25. OPEN ENDED Identify a three-digit dividend that will result in a three-digit quotient that has a zero in the tens place when the divisor is 6.

26. WRITING IN MATH Explain how an estimate could help you remember to write a zero in a quotient that results in a two-digit quotient with a remainder.

Math Online **Self-Check Quiz at** tx.gr4math.com

Division Shuffle

Division of Multi-Digit Numbers

Get Ready!

Players: 2 players

You will need: 5 index cards, 2 white boards, 2 dry erase markers

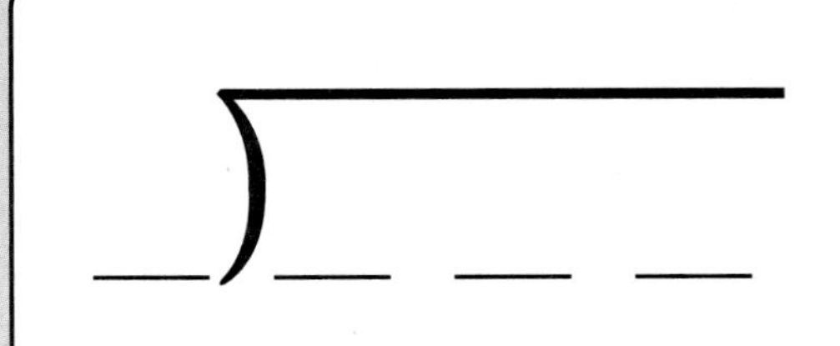

Get Set!

- Cut each index card in half. Label each card with one number so that the cards are labeled 0 through 9.

Go!

- Shuffle and then place the cards face down on the table.
- Both players draw a division house on their dry erase boards.
- Player 1 draws four cards, and then turns them over one at a time. After each card is turned over, players 1 and 2 write each number in any blank on their dry erase boards.
- After all the numbers are recorded, Players 1 and 2 find the quotients.
- The player that has the greatest quotient gets 1 point.
- Continue playing until a player earns 5 points. Reshuffle the cards if needed.

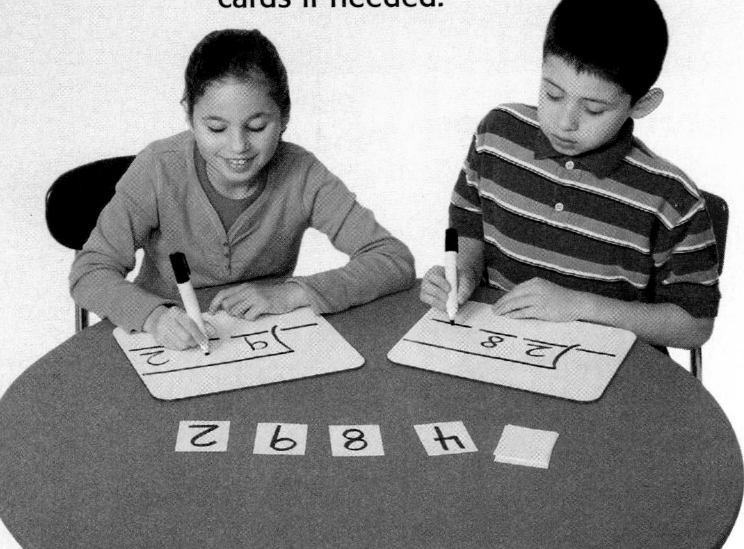

Problem Solving in Science

A DESERT SAFARI

The Sahara desert in Africa is 800–1,200 miles wide and 3,000 miles long. Animals like elephants, giraffes, lions, and chimpanzees live in or near this desert. Many African desert animals can also be found in zoos, where they are protected and fed. Some animals, such as the elephant, are very large. An average elephant weighs 12,250 pounds, and its trunk weighs 400 pounds!

Food Eaten by Zoo Animals

Animal	Number	Daily Food (lb)
Hippo	6	900
Elephant	10	1,600
Giraffe	6	360
Lion	7	218
Camel	5	94
Hyena	8	144
Chimpanzee	9	117
Flamingo	8	1

Targeted TEKS 4.14 The student applies Grade 4 mathematics to solve problems connected to everyday experiences and activities in and outside of school. **(A) Identify the mathematics in everyday situations.**

Real-World Math

Use the information on page 296 to solve each problem.

1. Suppose each camel eats the same amount of food. About how much food would one camel eat in one week?

2. A visitor travels the Sahara desert from east to west in 10 days and travels the same amount each day. How many miles does the visitor travel each day?

3. Suppose each elephant eats the same amount of food. How much food do four elephants eat in a day?

4. How many ounces of food does each flamingo eat per day? (Hint: 1 pound = 16 ounces)

5. Does a hyena or a chimpanzee eat more each day? Explain.

6. How much more do three elephants eat than three hippos?

7. How much food is eaten each day by one giraffe, one hyena, and one lion? Order these animals in order from greatest to least with respect to the amount of food each eats.

Did You Know?

The African elephant is the largest land mammal.

7-9 Divide Greater Numbers

MAIN IDEA

I will divide four- and five-digit dividends by a one-digit number.

Targeted TEKS 4.4 The student multiplies and divides to solve meaningful problems involving whole numbers. (E) **Use division to solve problems (no more than one-digit divisors and three-digit dividends without technology).** *Also addresses TEKS 4.5(B), 4.15(A).*

Pennies are made from copper. One of the largest holes in the world is a copper mine. It is 5,808 feet wide. How many yards wide is the hole?

You can use the same process to divide greater numbers that you use with lesser numbers.

Real-World EXAMPLE Use Technology

1 MEASUREMENT How many yards wide is the copper mine?

The mine is 5,808 feet wide. There are 3 feet in 1 yard. So, to find the width in yards, divide 5,808 by 3.

Use a Calculator

Enter:    

Press: 

Enter: 3

Press: 

Solution: 1936

So, the copper mine is 1,936 yards wide.

Real-World EXAMPLE Divide Greater Numbers

2 **MONEY The largest gold nugget ever found was in California. It weighed 195 pounds and was worth $43,536 at the time it was found. Suppose that 4 people found it, sold it, and divided the money evenly. How much money would each person get?**

Divide $43,536 by 4 to find out how much money each person will get.

Remember

When using a calculator to divide, the dividend should be the first number entered into the calculator.

Enter: 4 3 5 3 6

Press: ÷

Enter: 4

Press: =

Solution: 10884

So, each person would get $10,884.

Online Personal Tutor at tx.gr4math.com

CHECK What You Know

Use a calculator to divide. See Examples 1 and 2 (pp. 298–299)

1. $2\overline{)2{,}764}$

2. $3\overline{)\$6{,}163}$

3. $5\overline{)8{,}045}$

4. 60,436 ÷ 4

5. $81,486 ÷ 6

6. 98,194 ÷ 8

7. An art museum hosted an exhibit. One day, 6,414 people attended the exhibit in 6 hours. If the same number of people attended each hour, how many people attended each hour?

8. Talk About It Explain how dividing a 5-digit dividend by a 1-digit divisor is similar to dividing a 3-digit dividend by a 1-digit divisor. How is it different?

Practice and Problem Solving

EXTRA PRACTICE See page R24.

Use a calculator to divide. See Examples 1 and 2 (pp. 298–299)

9. $2\overline{)2{,}418}$

10. $3\overline{)3{,}428}$

11. $4\overline{)\$4{,}228}$

12. $5\overline{)7{,}465}$

13. $6\overline{)8{,}802}$

14. $8\overline{)\$9{,}597}$

15. $7\overline{)70{,}245}$

16. $8\overline{)92{,}072}$

17. $58,412 ÷ 4

18. 59,562 ÷ 6

19. 184,932 ÷ 2

20. $291,387 ÷ 3

21. Kirby bought a used car for $3,624. He plans on paying for it in two years. How much will he pay each year?

22. **Measurement** The farthest distance a pumpkin has ever been thrown is 4,434 feet. How many yards is this?

Real-World PROBLEM SOLVING

Measurement The map shows distances between cities in the United States.

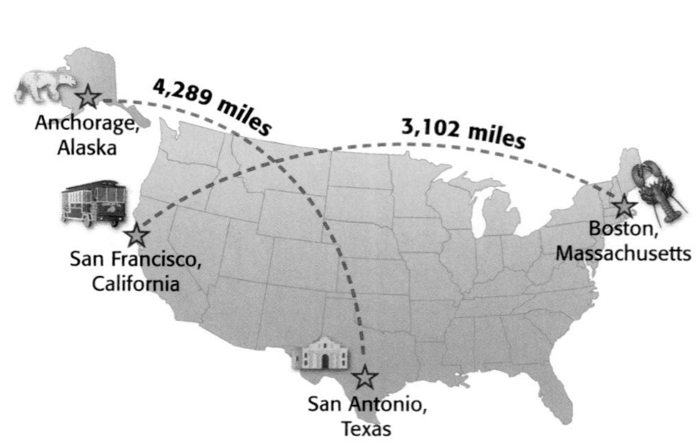

23. The Regan family drove from San Francisco, California, to Boston, Massachusetts. They drove an equal distance each day. How many miles did they drive each day if they made the trip in 6 days?

24. The Collins family moved to San Antonio, Texas, from Anchorage, Alaska. They drove an equal distance each day. How many miles did they drive each day if they made the trip in 8 days?

H.O.T. Problems

25. OPEN ENDED Write a division problem that involves dividing a three-digit number by a one-digit number. The quotient must be between 100 and 1,000.

26. WHICH ONE DOESN'T BELONG? Identify the expression that does not belong. Explain.

$3\overline{)693}$ $5\overline{)673}$ $8\overline{)168}$ $9\overline{)918}$

27. WRITING IN MATH How many digits would be in the quotient of 12,495 ÷ 5? Use a calculator to help explain.

TEST Practice

28. The map shows the distance in feet to the treasure.

Find 318 ÷ 3 to find how many yards it is from X to the treasure. (Lesson 7-8)

A 104 **C** 106

B 105 **D** 107

29. Rodrigo's horse ate 351 pounds of food in 3 weeks. How many pounds of food did it eat each week? (Lesson 7-9)

F 100 pounds

G 117 pounds

H 120 pounds

J 121 pounds

Spiral Review

Divide. Use estimation to check. (Lesson 7-8)

30. $3\overline{)624}$ **31.** $4\overline{)\$824}$ **32.** $5\overline{)537}$

Divide. Use estimation to check. (Lesson 7-7)

33. $2\overline{)468}$ **34.** $3\overline{)\$645}$ **35.** $4\overline{)872}$

36. Janise bought the items shown to the right. If the shirts are equal in price and the total cost was $80, how much did each item cost? (Lesson 7-6)

CHAPTER 7

Study Guide and Review

FOLDABLES Study Organizer GET READY to Study

Be sure the following Key Vocabulary words and Key Concepts are written in your Foldable.

BIG Ideas

Division of Multi-Digit Numbers (p. 288)

- Divide a multi-digit number by a one-digit number.

```
     $234
  2)$468
    -4
     06
    - 6
      08
    - 8
       0
```

For each place, divide, multiply, subtract, and compare. Then bring down the next digit in the dividend.

Estimate Quotients (p. 278)

- You can use compatible numbers to estimate quotents.

$722 \div 9$

THINK 722 is close to 720. 720 and 9 are compatible numbers because they are easy to divide mentally.

$720 \div 9 = 80 \quad 9 \times 8 = 72$

Key Vocabulary

compatible numbers (p. 278)
dividend (p. 267)
divisor (p. 267)
quotient (p. 267)
remainder (p. 268)

Vocabulary Check

Complete each sentence with the correct vocabulary word.

1. The number that is left over in a division problem is the ___?___.
2. The number that divides the dividend is the ___?___.
3. The number you are dividing is the ___?___.
4. ___?___ are numbers that are easy to divide mentally.
5. The result of a division problem is the ___?___.
6. In division, the ___?___ is the number that is being divided.

Math Online **Vocabulary Review at** tx.gr4math.com

Lesson-by-Lesson Review

7-1 Division with Remainders (pp. 269–271)

Example 1
Find 59 ÷ 3.

$$\begin{array}{r} 19 \text{ R2} \\ 3\overline{)59} \\ -3\downarrow \\ \hline 29 \\ -27 \\ \hline 2 \end{array}$$

For each place, divide, multiply, subtract, and compare.

Then bring down the next digit in the dividend.

Check

$$\begin{array}{r} 19 \\ \times\ 3 \\ \hline 57 \\ +\ 2 \\ \hline 59 \end{array}$$

So, the answer is correct. ✓

Divide.

7. $5\overline{)53}$ **8.** $6\overline{)67}$

9. 91 ÷ 4 **10.** 77 ÷ 3

11. Christy has 37 books. She wants to put them evenly on her 4 shelves. How many books will she not be able to fit?

12. Rafael wants to earn $40 for a new pair of skates. He earns $6 an hour for yard work. How many hours will he have to work to have the money for the skates?

7-2 Divide Multiples of 10 and 100 (pp. 272–275)

Example 2
Find 1,600 ÷ 4.

Use patterns to divide.

16 ÷ 4 = 4
160 ÷ 4 = 40
1,600 ÷ 4 = 400

So, 1,600 ÷ 4 = 400.

Check

Use addition to check.

$$\begin{array}{r} 400 \\ 400 \\ 400 \\ +\ 400 \\ \hline 1{,}600 \end{array}$$

So, the answer is correct. ✓

Divide.

13. 27 ÷ 9 = ■
270 ÷ 9 = ■
2,700 ÷ 9 = ■

14. 49 ÷ 7 = ■
490 ÷ 7 = ■
4,900 ÷ 7 = ■

15. 900 ÷ 3 **16.** 1,800 ÷ 9

17. 3,600 ÷ 40 **18.** 4,900 ÷ 70

19. 6,400 ÷ 80 **20.** 7,200 ÷ 90

21. Chuck collected 150 shells during his five days of vacation. Chuck collected the same number of shells each day. How many shells did he collect each day?

7-3 Problem-Solving Strategy: Guess and Check (pp. 276–277)

Example 3
Opal and Steve collect coins. Opal has 32 more coins than Steve. They have 146 coins altogether. How many coins does each person have?

Understand

What facts do you know?

- Opal has 32 more coins than Steve.
- They have 146 coins altogether.

What do you need to find?

- The number of coins each person has.

Plan You can guess and check to solve the problem.

Solve Make logical guesses.

$146 \div 2 = 73$, so Opal will have more than 73, and Steve will have less than 73.

Check Think of two addends that have a difference of about 30, and a sum of about 150.

Try $90 + 60$. $90 + 60 = 150$

The sum is too high. Try smaller numbers until you find the correct answer.

The correct answer is 89 and 57 because $89 + 57 = 146$.

Solve. Use the *guess and check* Strategy.

22. Juanita made a vegetable tray with 3 different vegetables. There are 2 times more cucumbers than tomatoes and 4 times more carrots than cucumbers. If there are 5 tomatoes, how many carrots and cucumbers are there?

23. Toru bought a CD and a DVD. The CD cost $5 less than the DVD and the total was $29. How much was each item?

24. There are rabbits, ponies, and goats at a petting zoo. There are eight times as many goats as ponies. There are six more rabbits than ponies. The number of ponies is shown. Find how many rabbits and goats.

25. Etta is buying a sweater and a pair of pants. The sweater costs $12 more than the pants. The total cost is $84. What is the cost of each clothing item?

7-4 Estimate Quotients (pp. 278–280)

Example 4
Find 273 ÷ 9.

273 ÷ 9

THINK 273 is close to 270. 270 and 9 are compatible numbers because they are easy to divide mentally.

270 ÷ 9 = 30

So, 273 ÷ 9 is about 30.

Estimate.

26. $254 ÷ 5

27. 634 ÷ 7

28. 5,571 ÷ 8

29. 7,218 ÷ 9

30. **Measurement** A roller coaster car made it to the bottom of a 318-foot hill in 5 seconds. About how many feet did the car travel each second?

31. A skate park has $3,225 to spend on 8 new ramps. About how much can be spent on each ramp?

7-5 Two-Digit Quotients (pp. 282–285)

Example 5
Find 95 ÷ 4.

Step 1 Divide the tens.

$$\begin{array}{r} 2 \\ 4\overline{)95} \\ -8 \\ \hline 1 \end{array}$$

Divide. 9 ÷ 4 = 2
Put 2 in the quotient.
Multiply. 4 × 2 = 8
Subtract. 9 − 8 = 1
Compare. 1 < 4

Step 2 Divide the ones.

$$\begin{array}{r} 23 \text{ R3} \\ 4\overline{)95} \\ -8\downarrow \\ \hline 15 \\ -12 \\ \hline 3 \end{array}$$

Bring down the ones.
Divide. 15 ÷ 4 = 3
Put 3 in the quotient.
Multiply. 4 × 3 = 12
Subtract. 15 − 12 = 3
Compare. 3 < 4
Remainder = 3

So, 95 ÷ 4 = 23 R3.

Divide.

32. $3\overline{)86}$

33. $6\overline{)96}$

34. 87 ÷ 4

35. 95 ÷ 3

36. There are 85 crayons in Miranda's crayon box. She wants to share them equally with two of her friends. How many crayons will Miranda and her friends each get? How many will be left over?

37. Garcia placed his baseball cards into 3 envelopes. He ended up with 17 cards in each envelope and 2 left over. How many cards did Garcia have to begin with?

Problem-Solving Investigation: Choose a Strategy (pp. 286–287)

Example 6

There are 333 students trying out for basketball teams. Is it reasonable to say that more than 40 teams will be formed if there are nine players on each team?

Understand

There are 333 students trying out for basketball teams. Nine players will be on each team.

Will there be more than 40 teams formed?

Plan Divide the number of students trying out by the number of players per team.

Solve Divide 333 by 9.

$$\begin{array}{r} 37 \\ 9\overline{)333} \\ -27\downarrow \\ 63 \\ -63 \\ 0 \end{array}$$

There will be 37 teams. So, it is not reasonable to say there will be more than 40 teams.

Check Use multiplication to check.

$9 \times 37 = 333$

So, the answer is correct.

Use any strategy to solve.

38. Frida had 3 pencils. Then her teacher gave her some new packs of pencils. Now Frida has 11 pencils. How many packs of pencils did the teacher give Frida?

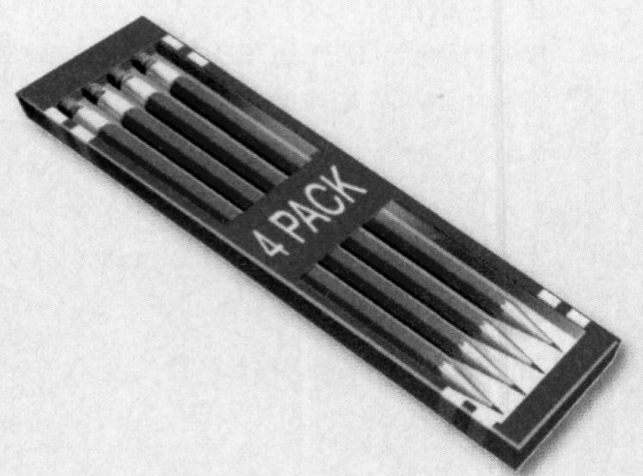

39. Each hand in the human body has 27 bones. There are 6 more bones in the fingers than in the wrist. There are 3 fewer bones in the palm than in the wrist. How many bones are in the fingers and wrist?

40. How many different posters can be made using red, yellow, and black paper one time each if the paper is placed in a row?

41. What number is missing from the pattern below?

2, 7, 12, 17, ■

42. A number is divided by 5. Next, 4 is subtracted from the quotient. Then, 6 is added to the difference. The result is 10. What is the number?

7-7 Three-Digit Quotients (pp. 288–290)

Example 7
Find 426 ÷ 4.

Estimate 426 ÷ 4 → 400 ÷ 4 = 100

$$
\begin{array}{r}
106 \text{ R2} \\
4\overline{)426} \\
-4\downarrow \\
02 \\
-\ 0\downarrow \\
26 \\
-24 \\
2
\end{array}
$$

For each place, divide, multiply, subtract, and compare.

Then bring down the next digit in the dividend.

So, 426 ÷ 4 = 106 R2.

Check for reasonableness
The quotient, 106 R2, is close to the estimate. So, the answer is reasonable. ✓

Divide.

43. $3\overline{)787}$

44. 994 ÷ 4

45. There are 7 classes and 147 students in the 4th grade. If the same number of students are in each class, how many students will be in each class?

46. There are 1,035 cars in the airport parking lot. The lot has 9 rows of parked cars. How many cars are in each row if the same number of cars are in each row?

47. Explain how to check Exercise 46 to be sure your answer is correct.

7-8 Quotients with Zeros (pp. 292–294)

Example 8
Find \$416 ÷ 2.

$$
\begin{array}{r}
\$208 \\
2\overline{)\$416} \\
-4\downarrow \\
01 \\
-0\downarrow \\
16 \\
-16 \\
0
\end{array}
$$

For each place, divide, multiply, subtract, and compare.

Then bring down the next digit in the dividend.

So, \$416 ÷ 2 = \$208.

Divide.

48. $2\overline{)217}$

49. $3\overline{)621}$

50. 817 ÷ 4

51. 925 ÷ 3

52. 432 students ride the bus home each day. The school has 8 buses. How many students fit on each bus?

53. Tamera wants to fit all of her 749 marbles into 7 jars. How many should she put in each jar?

7-9 Divide Greater Numbers (pp. 298–301)

Example 9
Find 6,213 ÷ 3.

Use a calculator.

Enter: 6 2 1 3

Press:    

Enter: 3

Press: =

Solution: 

So, 6,213 ÷ 3 = 2,071.

Use a calculator to divide.

54. $3\overline{)\$6{,}597}$

55. $5\overline{)8{,}804}$

56. 79,562 ÷ 6

57. $91,384 ÷ 8

58. Candice is making hair bows. She uses a 9-inch piece of ribbon for each bow. How many bows can she make with 1,827 inches of ribbon?

59. A total of 33,915 people are attending three shows of an orchestra concert. How many people are attending each show if the same number of people attend each show?

60. There are 1,440 students who attend a school. There are four lunch periods. If the same number of students eat during each lunch period, how many students eat during each lunch period?

61. **Measurement** A 5-kilometer race is about 16,404 feet long. How many yards long is the race? (*Remember:* 3 feet = 1 yard.)

CHAPTER 7

Chapter Test

For Exercises 1 and 2, decide whether each statement is *true* or *false*.

1. A quotient is the number being divided.

2. In the problem 62 ÷ 2, the number 2 is the divisor.

Divide. Check each answer.

3. $2\overline{)45}$

4. 73 ÷ 4

5. **TEST PRACTICE** There are 5,280 feet in a mile. Since 1 yard equals 3 feet, about how many yards are in one mile?

A 1,700 yd **C** 1,900 yd
B 1,800 yd **D** 2,000 yd

Copy and complete each set of patterns.

6. 24 ÷ 4 = ■
240 ÷ 4 = ■
2,400 ÷ 4 = ■

7. 18 ÷ 2 = ■
180 ÷ 2 = ■
1,800 ÷ 2 = ■

Divide. Use patterns.

8. $3,200 ÷ 40

9. 5,400 ÷ 60

10. Three members of the Cotter family are flying to Washington, D.C., for vacation. The total cost of the tickets is $950. About how much was each person's ticket?

Divide. Use estimation to check.

11. $5\overline{)410}$

12. 863 ÷ 3

13. Sara earned the same score on her last 2 tests. Her total score was 184. What was her score on each of the 2 tests?

Divide. Use estimation to check.

14. $2\overline{)417}$

15. $929 ÷ 3

16. **Measurement** The Toshiro family is moving. They will drive a total of 830 miles over 2 days. If they drive the same distance each day, how far will they drive each day?

17. A family is buying a boat for $999. They hope to have it paid off in 3 years. How much do they have to pay each year to reach their goal?

18. **TEST PRACTICE** There were 436 people at 4 different movies. The same number of people went to each movie. Which shows the number of people that went to each movie?

F 109 **H** 110
G 108 **J** 111

19. **WRITING IN MATH** How many digits would be in the quotient of 12,795 ÷ 5? Use a calculator to help explain.

Math Online Chapter Test at tx.gr4math.com

CHAPTER 7

Texas Test Practice

Cumulative, Chapters 1–7

Penny has 125 photos. Her photo album has slots for 6 photos on a page. About how many pages will she need for her photo album?

A 19 **C** 21

B 20 **D** 22

TEST-TAKING TIP

You can estimate to see whether your answer is reasonable.

Read the Test Question

You need to find a close estimate for the number of pages Penny will need.

Solve the Test Question

Think about a related multiplication fact to estimate the quotient.

$6 \times 2 = 12$ and $6 \times 20 = 120$

So, a quotient of $125 \div 6$ is greater than 20.

Divide.

$125 \div 6 = 20$ R5

Round up since Penny will need a page for the 5 remaining photos. The answer is C.

 **Personal Tutor at** tx.gr4math.com

Choose the best answer.

1. **There are 256 students going on a field trip. There are 6 buses. About how many students will there be on each bus?**

   A 70 **C** 50

   B 60 **D** 40

2. **Rosa has 150 goldfish. She wants to put about the same number of fish into each of 8 ponds. About how many fish will be in each pond?**

   F 18 **H** 20

   G 19 **J** 21

Get Ready for the Texas Test
For test-taking strategies and more practice, see pages TX1–TX21.

3. **Valerie has 84 beads. She wants to arrange them into 12 equal groups. How many beads will be in each group?**

   A 5 **C** 7
   B 6 **D** 8

4. **Which number makes this equation true?**

   $$88 \div \blacksquare = 11$$

   F 8
   G 9
   H 10
   J 11

5. **Booker packed 720 cans evenly into 9 crates. How many cans were in each crate?**

   A 60 **C** 80
   B 70 **D** 90

6. **GRIDDABLE Jason bought 7 packages of baseball cards. Each package contains 6 cards. How many cards did Jason buy in all?**

7. **There are 8,000 fans at a sold out baseball game. Each section of the stadium holds 100 people. How many sections are there in the stadium?**

   F 8 **H** 80
   G 40 **J** 800

8. **Which number is 100,000 more than 7,186,335?**

   A 7,086,335
   B 7,196,335
   C 7,286,335
   D 8,186,335

9. **Carlos rode his bike 115 miles in 5 days. How many miles did he ride each day?**

   F 13 **H** 25
   G 23 **J** 33

10. **A radio survey company called 600 homeowners last month. This month the company will call 10 times as many homeowners. How many homeowners will be called this month?**

   A 60 **C** 6,000
   B 600 **D** 60,000

Identify and Describe Geometric Figures

What are solid and plane figures?

A **solid figure**, or three-dimensional figure, is a figure with length, width, and height. A **plane figure**, or two-dimensional figure, is a figure with length and width.

Example Plane and solid figures are often found in traffic signs.

What will I learn in this chapter?

- Identify, describe, and classify solid and plane figures.
- Identify angles.
- Identify and make nets.
- Solve problems by looking for a pattern.

Key Vocabulary

solid figure
plane figure
angle
right angle

Student Study Tools at tx.gr4math.com

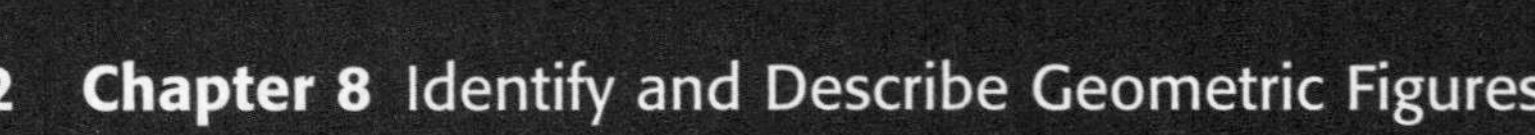

FOLDABLES™ Study Organizer

Make this Foldable to help you organize information about geometry. Begin with 10 sheets of notebook paper.

1. **Staple** the sheets of notebook paper together to form a booklet.

2. **Cut** a tab as shown. On the third page, make the tab longer, and so on.

3. **Write** the chapter title on the cover. Label each tab with a lesson number.

ARE YOU READY for Chapter 8?

You have two ways to check prerequisite skills for this chapter.

Option 2

Math Online Take the Chapter Readiness Quiz at tx.gr4math.com.

Option 1

Complete the Quick Check below.

QUICK Check

Identify each figure. (Prior grade)

1. 

2. 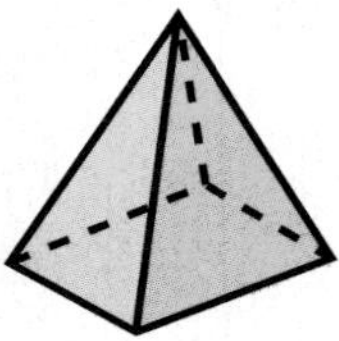

3. 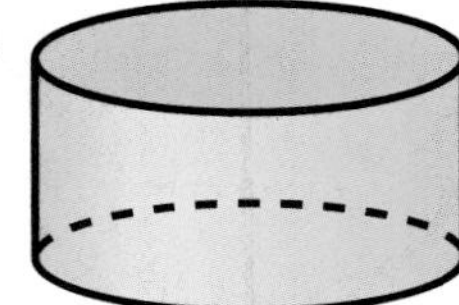

4. Identify the solid figure the objects at the right represent.

How many sides does each figure have? (Prior grade)

5. 

6. 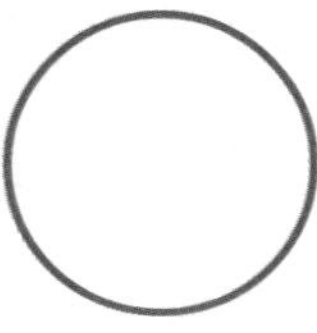

7. 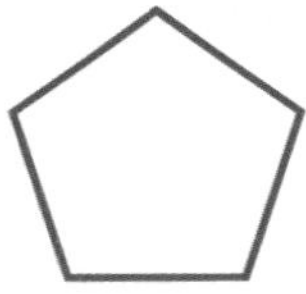

8. The musical instrument at right resembles a triangle. How many sides does the instrument have?

Identify each figure. (Prior grade)

9. 

10. 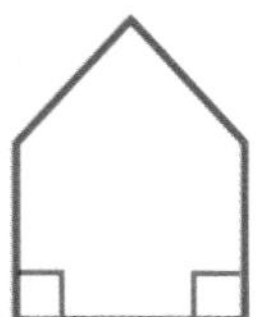

11. 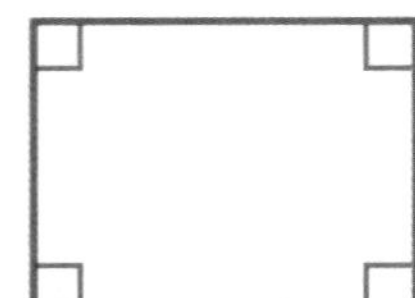

12. Explain how you know what the two-dimensional figure is.

8-1 Three-Dimensional Figures

MAIN IDEA

I will identify and describe solid figures, and identify and draw nets.

Targeted TEKS 4.8 The student identifies and describes attributes of geometric figures using formal geometric language. (C) **Use essential attributes to define** two- and **three-dimensional geometric figures.** *Also addresses TEKS 4.16(A).*

New Vocabulary

solid figure
face
edge
vertex
net

GET READY to Learn

A dog crate is shown. It resembles a solid figure. A **solid figure** is a three-dimensional figure with length, width, and height.

- A **face** is a flat side.
- Two faces meet at an **edge**.
- A **vertex** is where three or more faces meet.

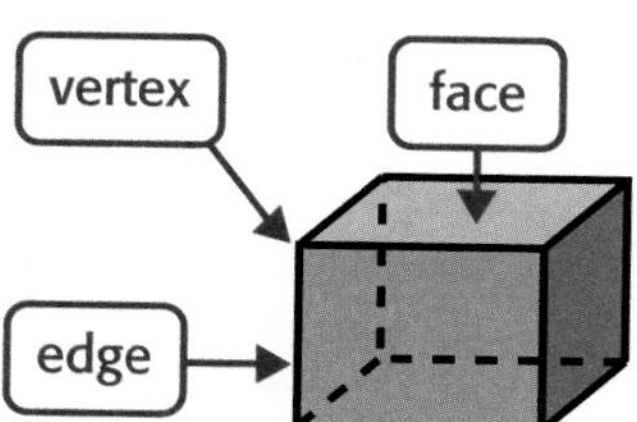

KEY CONCEPT Solid Figures

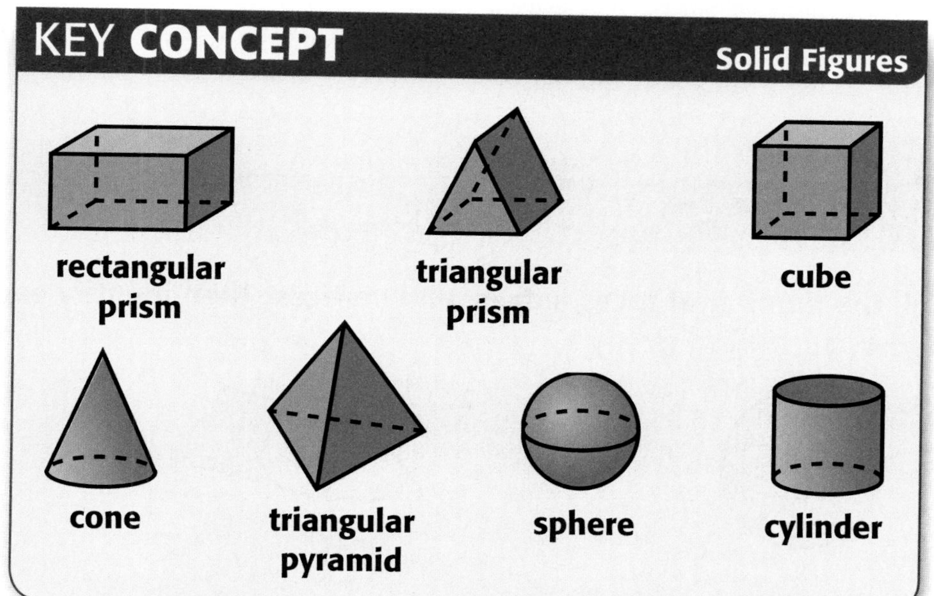

Real-World EXAMPLE Identify Solid Objects

1 **Tell the number of faces, edges, and vertices. Then identify the shape of the gift box.**

It has 6 faces, 12 edges, and 8 vertices. The gift box is a rectangular prism.

Online Personal Tutor at tx.gr4math.com

A **net** is a two-dimensional figure that can be folded to make a solid figure.

Hands-On Mini Activity

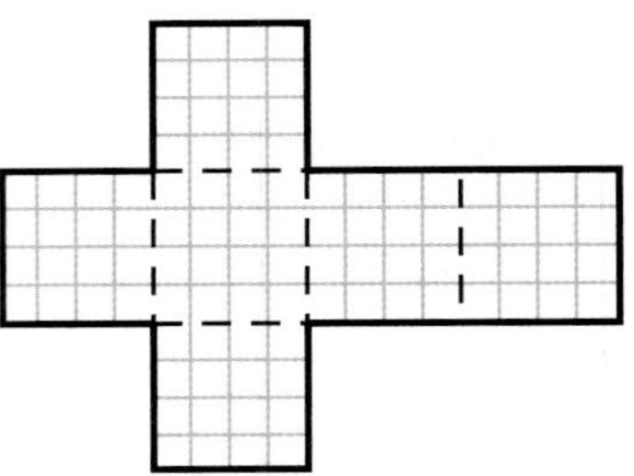

Step 1 Using grid paper, draw and cut out the net shown.

Step 2 Fold along the dotted lines. Tape the edges.

Step 3 Identify the solid.

1. Draw another net that could be used to form a cube.
2. Identify the solid figure the net shown at the right makes.
3. Explain how you can identify a shape from its net without folding the paper.

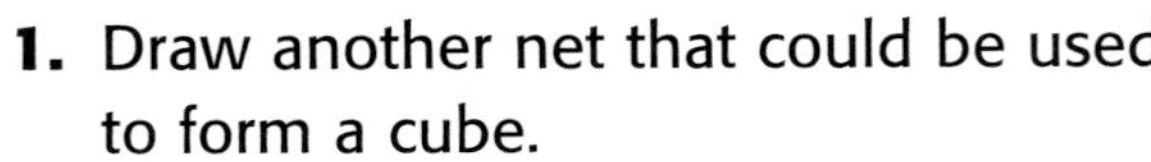

Remember

A prism has rectangular sides. A pyramid has triangular sides.

CHECK What You Know

Tell the number of faces, edges, and vertices. Then identify each figure. See Example 1 (p. 315)

1. 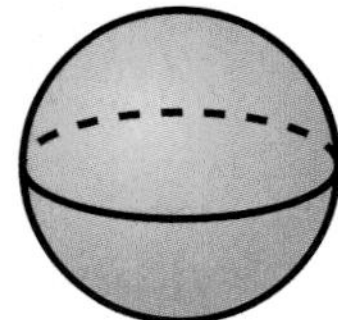

2. 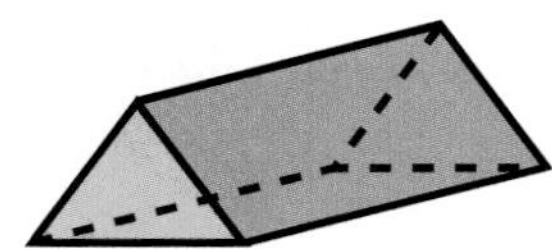

3. 

Identify the solid figure each net makes.

4. 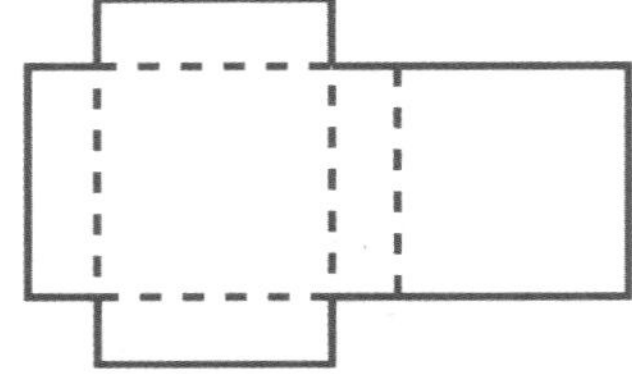

5. 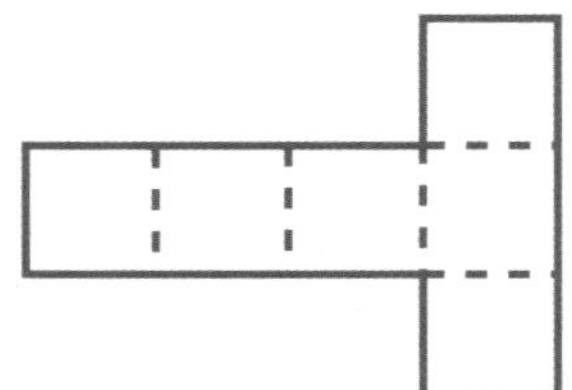

6. 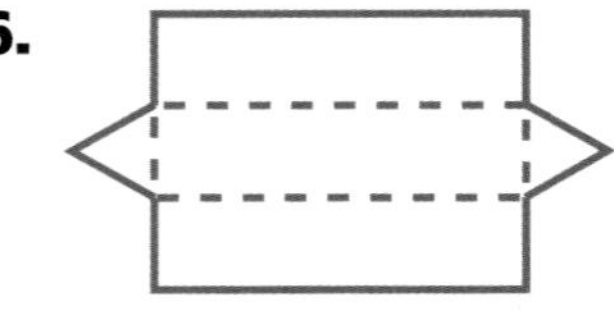

7. Name two solid figures that have 6 faces.

8. 

Compare a triangular prism and a triangular pyramid.

Practice and Problem Solving

EXTRA PRACTICE See page R24.

Tell the number of faces, edges, and vertices. Then identify each figure.
See Example 1 (p. 315)

9. 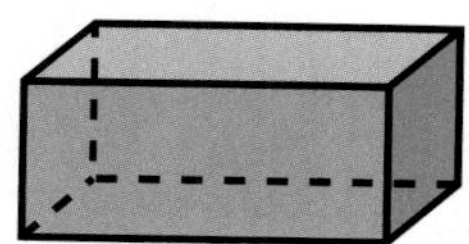

10. 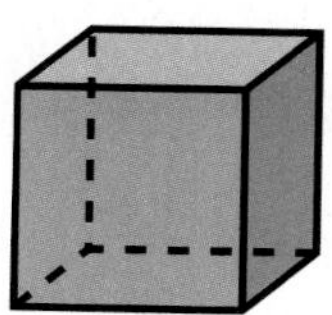

11. 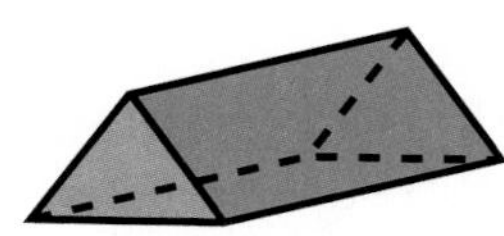

12. 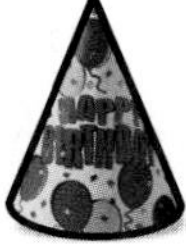

13. 

14. 

Identify the solid figure each net makes.

15. 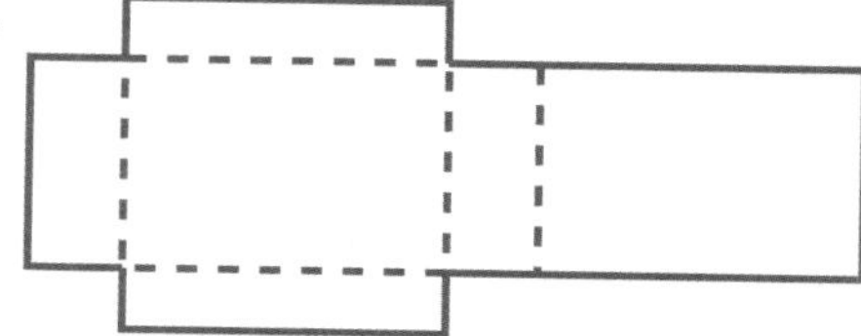

16. 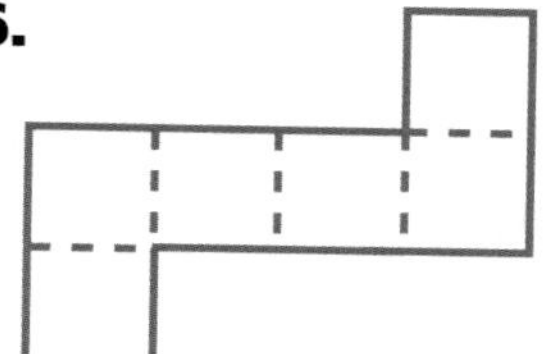

17. 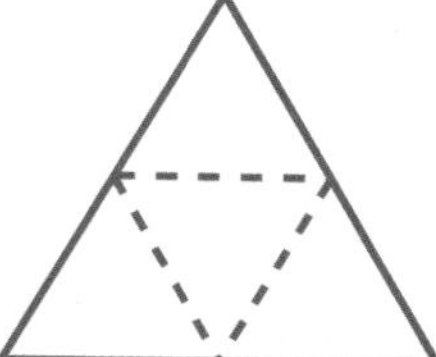

18. 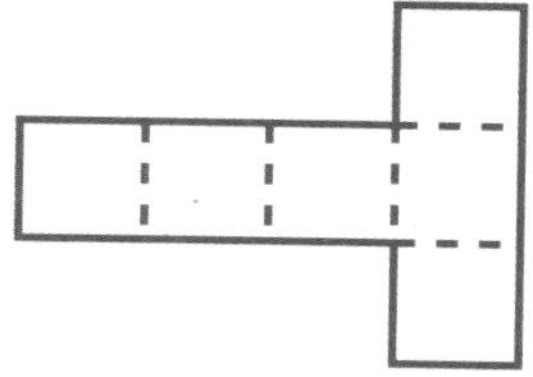

19. 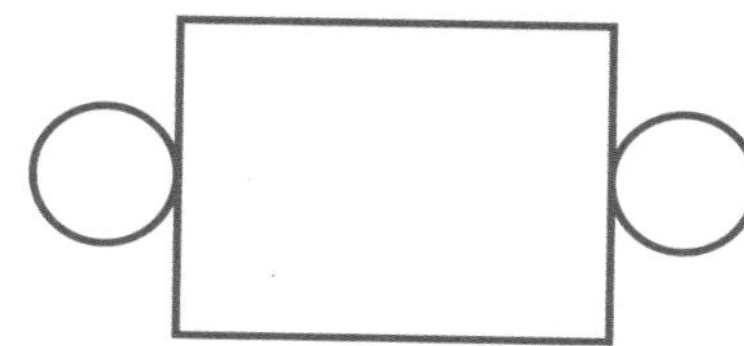

20. 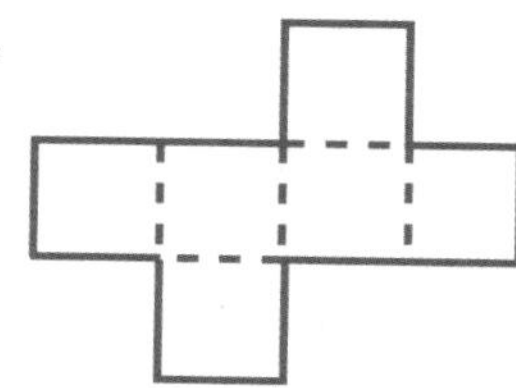

21. This solid has 4 faces, 6 edges, and 4 vertices. What solid is it?

22. This solid can be made using 2 circles and 1 large rectangle. What solid is it?

H.O.T. Problems

23. **OPEN ENDED** Draw any solid. Then describe its faces, edges, and vertices.

24. **WHICH ONE DOESN'T BELONG?** Identify the figure that does not belong with the other three. Explain.

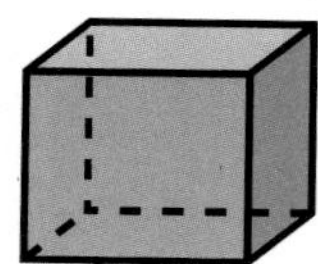

25. **WRITING IN ▶MATH** How are a cone and cylinder alike? How are they different?

8-2 Two-Dimensional Figures

GET READY to Learn

These are traffic signs that you may see every day. What shapes are the signs?

MAIN IDEA

I will identify, describe, and classify plane figures.

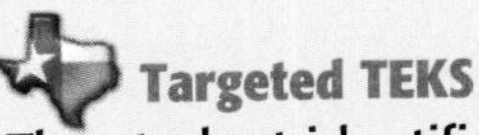

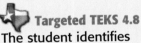

Targeted TEKS 4.8 The student identifies and describes attributes of geometric figures using formal geometric language. (C) **Use essential attributes to define two-** and three-**dimensional geometric figures.**

New Vocabulary

- plane figure
- polygon
- sides
- triangle
- quadrilateral
- pentagon
- hexagon
- octagon

The shapes of the signs are plane figures. A **plane figure** is a two-dimensional figure with length and width. **Polygons** are closed plane figures that have three or more line segments called **sides**.

KEY CONCEPT — Polygons

A **triangle** has 3 sides.

A **quadrilateral** has 4 sides.

A **pentagon** has 5 sides.

A **hexagon** has 6 sides.

An **octagon** has 8 sides.

Real-World EXAMPLE — Identify a Polygon

1 **SPORTS Identify the shape of home plate.**

Look at the shape of the home plate. It has 5 sides.

So, this figure is a pentagon.

A circle is not a polygon because it does not have straight sides. Other shapes are not polygons as well.

Polygons have straight sides only, not curved sides.

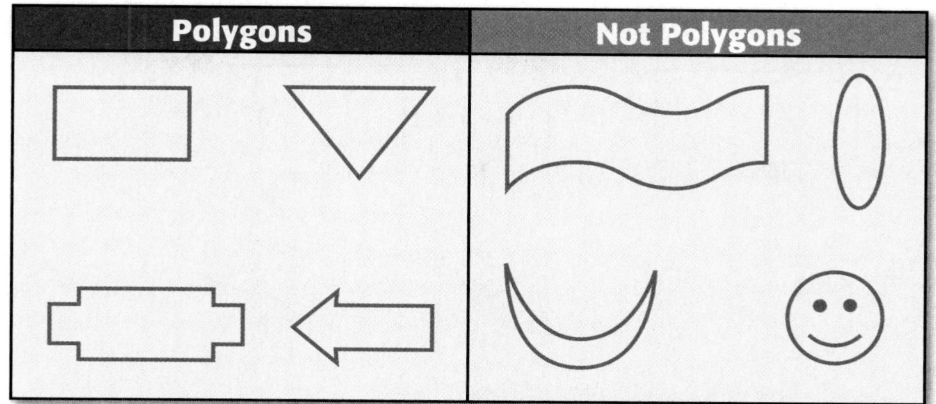

EXAMPLES Identify a Polygon

Tell whether each shape is a polygon.

2

The figure has curved sides. It is not a polygon.

3

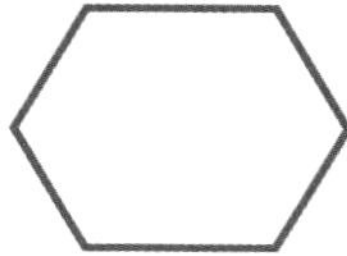

The figure has 6 sides. The sides are straight. So, it is a polygon.

Online Personal Tutor at tx.gr4math.com

CHECK What You Know

Identify each polygon. See Example 1 (p. 318)

1. 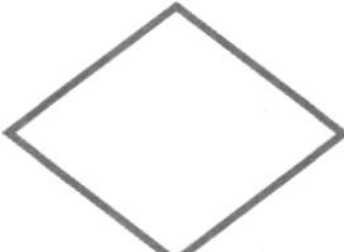

2. 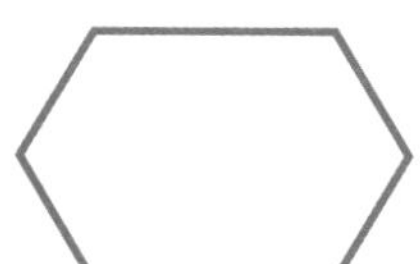

3. 

Tell whether each shape is a polygon. See Examples 2 and 3 (p. 319)

4. 

5. 

6. 

7. Identify two polygons on the soccer ball.

8. 

If we take a quadrilateral and cut it into two pieces, what shapes could the pieces be?

Practice and Problem Solving

EXTRA PRACTICE
See page R25.

Identify each polygon. See Example 1 (p. 318)

9. 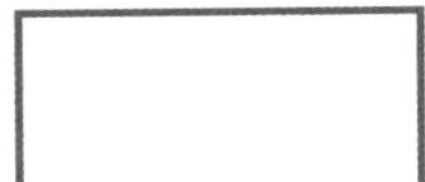

10. 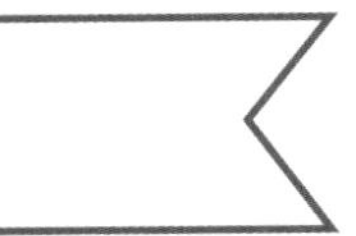

11. 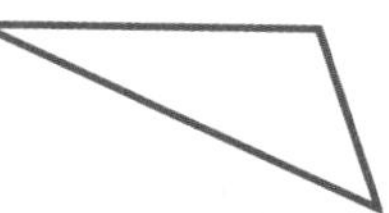

12. 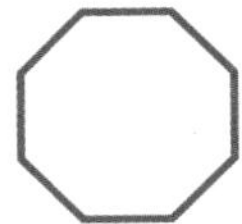

13. 

14. 

Tell whether each shape is a polygon. See Examples 2 and 3 (p. 319)

15. 

16. 

17. 

18. 

19. 

20. 

Identify two polygons in each real-world object.

21. 

22. 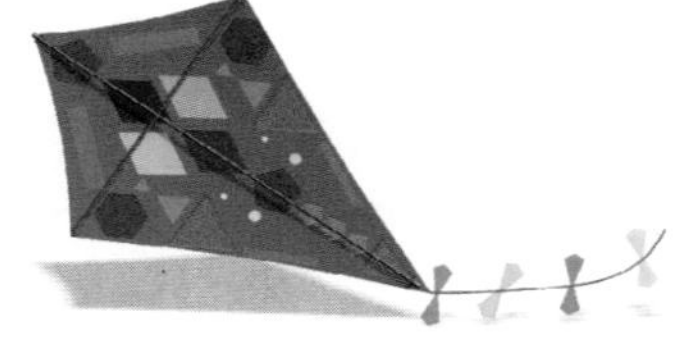

Real-World PROBLEM SOLVING

Art Polygons and other shapes are used in the painting *Castle and Sun*.

23. Name three polygons in the painting.

24. Is the sun a polygon? Explain.

25. What polygon is in the painting most often?

26. What polygon in the painting has the most sides?

H.O.T. Problems

27. **OPEN ENDED** Draw and identify a polygon.

28. **FIND THE ERROR** Carlota and Gabe are drawing a polygon. Who is correct? Explain.

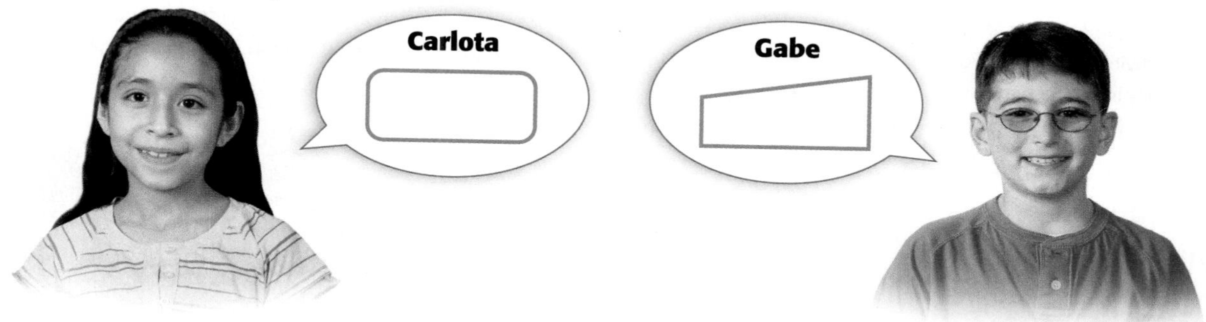

29. **WRITING IN ▸MATH** Write about a real-world object that is made up of polygons.

TEST Practice

30. Which figure can form a cube when folded on the dotted lines without overlapping? (Lesson 8-1)

A

C

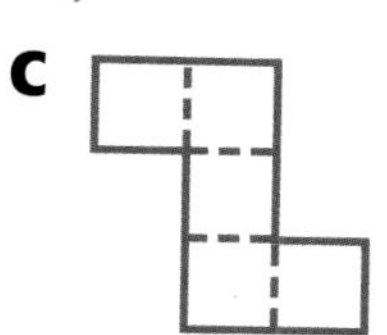

B

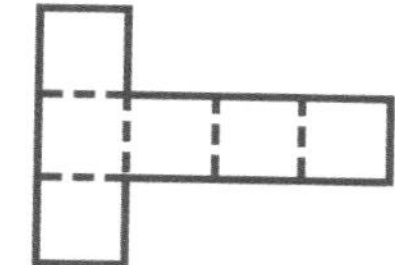

D

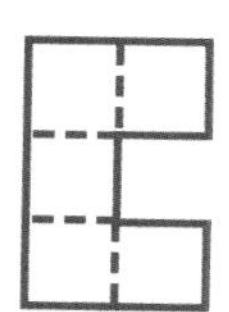

31. Which statement about these figures is true? (Lesson 8-2)

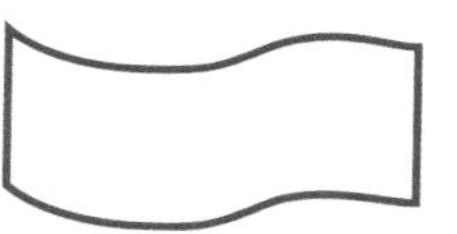

F There is one polygon.

G These are all polygons.

H There are two polygons.

J None of these are polygons.

Spiral Review

Identify each figure. Then tell the number of faces, edges, and vertices. (Lesson 8-1)

32. 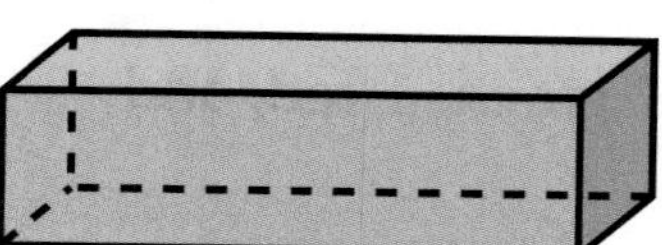

33. 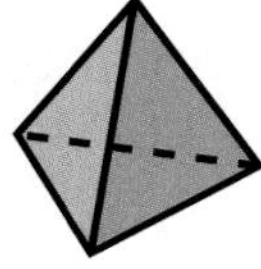

Divide. Use technology if needed. (Lesson 7-9)

34. 549 ÷ 3

35. \$485 ÷ 5

36. $7\overline{)504}$

37. $9\overline{)\$423}$

Problem-Solving Strategy

MAIN IDEA I will solve problems by looking for a pattern.

Targeted TEKS 4.14 The student applies Grade 4 mathematics to solve problems connected to everyday experiences and activities in and outside of school. **(C) Select or develop an appropriate problem-solving plan or strategy,** including . . . **looking for a pattern, . . . to solve a problem.** *Also addresses TEKS 4.14(B).*

Amado is helping his dad put tile on a table top. They are laying the tiles in a pattern. They have run out of tiles and need to buy more. What color of tiles need to be purchased to complete the table?

Understand	**What facts do you know?** • You know the tiles form a pattern. • You know they need to buy more tiles. **What do you need to find?** • Find the tile colors that need to be purchased.
Plan	Look for a pattern. Then continue the pattern to find the missing tiles.
Solve	There are two rows of tile, and the tiles repeat red, green, blue, and yellow.  In the first row, the missing tiles are blue and green. In the second row, the missing tiles are red, blue, and yellow. So, Amado and his father need 2 blue, 1 green, 1 red, and 1 yellow tile.
Check	Look back at the problem. The answer makes sense for the facts given. So, the answer is correct.

ANALYZE the Strategy

Refer to the problem on the previous page.

1. How do you identify a pattern in a problem-solving situation?

2. If Amado and his dad used 36 tiles, how many tiles would they use of each color?

3. Suppose Amado and his dad laid 3 more rows of tiles. How many green tiles would they need in all?

4. Look back at Exercise 3. Check your answer. Explain how you know the answer is correct.

PRACTICE the Strategy

See page R25.

Solve. Use the *look for a pattern* strategy.

5. Draw the next three shapes in the pattern below.

6. **Algebra** Copy and complete the table. What is the pattern?

Input (*g*)	Output (*h*)
6	24
8	32
5	20
3	■
■	36

7. Claudia will arrive at the airport on the first plane after 9 A.M. Planes arrive every 45 minutes after 6 A.M. When will Claudia's plane arrive?

8. Ming gathered 8 seashells on the first day, 20 on the second day, and 32 on the third day. If the pattern continues, how many shells will she gather on the fifth day?

9. Describe the pattern below. Then find the missing number.

   2, 4, 8, ■, 32

10. Two hikers take turns carrying a backpack during a hike. The first hiker carries the pack. They change every 3 miles. They have hiked 14 miles so far. How many times have they changed? Who has the pack now?

11. A pattern of figures is shown below. Draw the next two figures in the pattern.

12. A border on a scrapbook page has a repeating design that shows a triangle, a pentagon, and a hexagon. Draw the first eight figures in the pattern.

13. **WRITING IN MATH** Create a pattern with geometric shapes. Give it to a classmate and see if he or she can continue it.

8-4 Angles

GET READY to Learn

Brent's teacher assigned ten problems for homework. Brent started his homework at 4:00 P.M. He completed it at the time shown. How far has the minute hand turned?

MAIN IDEA

I will identify, describe and classify angles.

Targeted TEKS 4.8 The student identifies and describes attributes of geometric figures using formal geometric language. (A) **Identify and describe right, acute, and obtuse angles.**

New Vocabulary

- angle
- right angle
- acute angle
- obtuse angle

An **angle** is a figure made from two rays that have the same endpoint. Angles are measured in degrees (°).

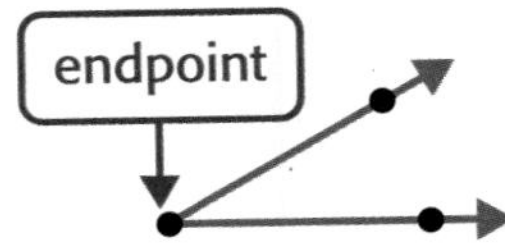

KEY CONCEPT Turns and Angles

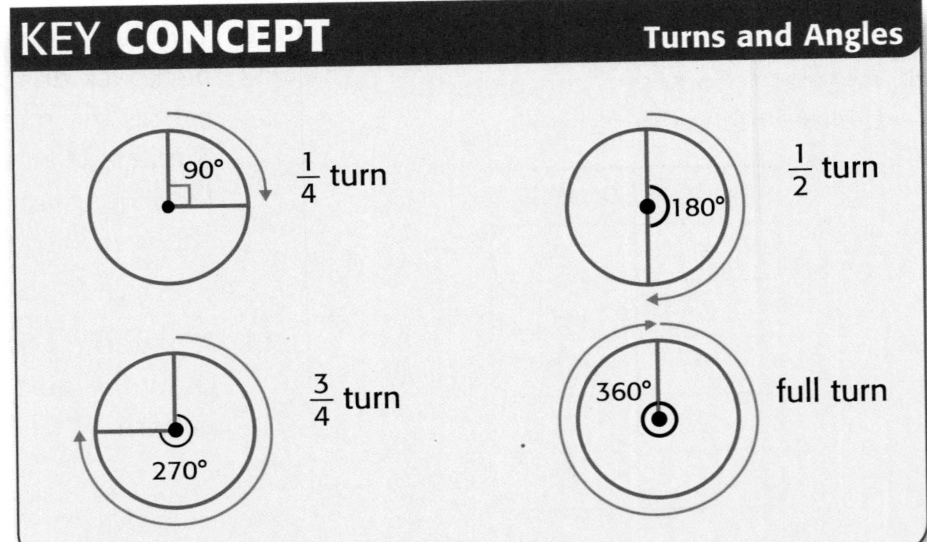

Real-World EXAMPLE Turns and Angles

1 **MEASUREMENT Refer to the clock above. Write how far the minute hand has turned in degrees and as a fraction.**

Compare the angle shown on the clock to the angles shown in the Key Concept box.

So, the angle shown on the clock is 90° or a $\frac{1}{4}$ turn.

Remember

A corner, like the corners on a desk, is a right angle.

KEY CONCEPT — Types of Angles

A **right angle** measures 90°. A right angle is formed by perpendicular lines.

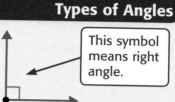

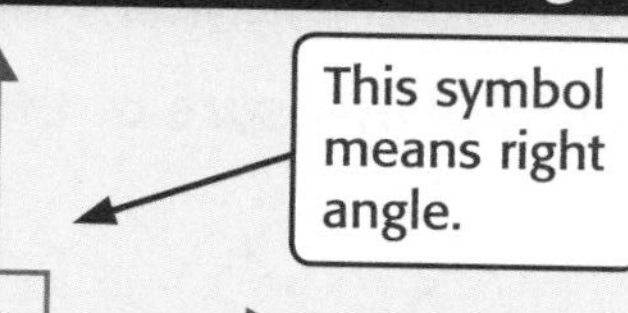
This symbol means right angle.

An **acute angle** measures greater than 0° and less than 90°.

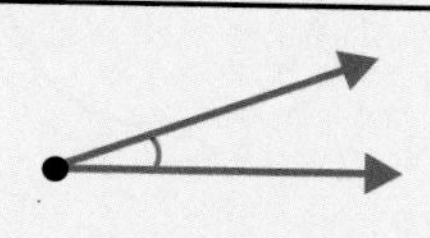

An **obtuse angle** measures greater than 90°, but less than 180°.

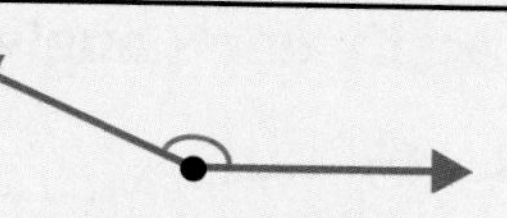

EXAMPLES Classify an Angle

Classify each angle as *right, acute,* or *obtuse*.

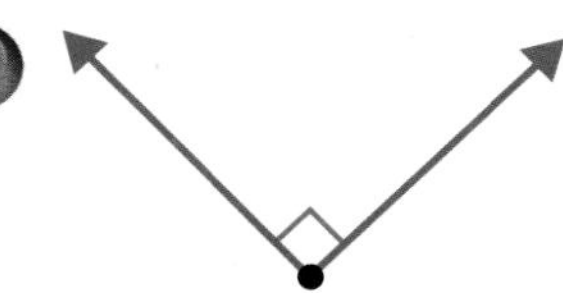

The angle is 90°.
So, it is a right angle.

3

The angle is greater than 90° and less than than 180°.
It is an obtuse angle.

Online Personal Tutor at tx.gr4math.com

CHECK What You Know

Write the measure of each angle in degrees and as a fraction of a full turn. See Example 1 (p. 324)

1. 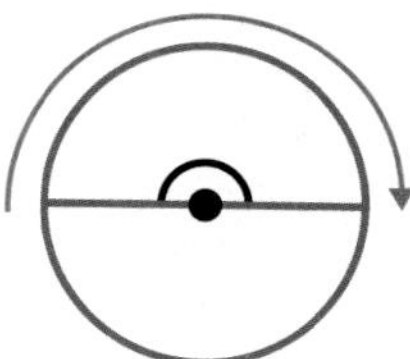

2. 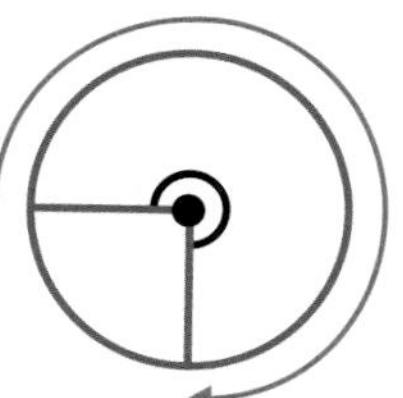

3. 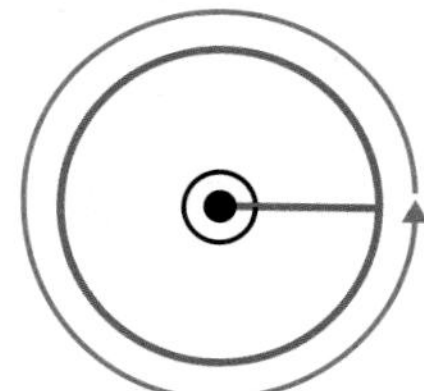

Classify each angle as *right, acute,* or *obtuse*. See Examples 2 and 3 (p. 325)

4. 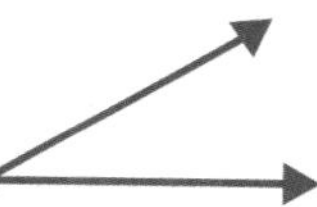

5. 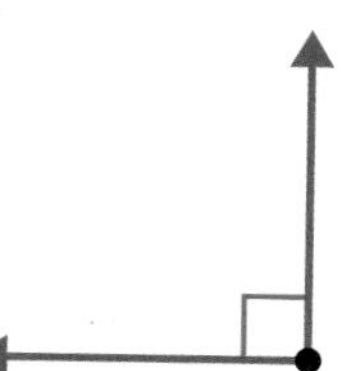

6. 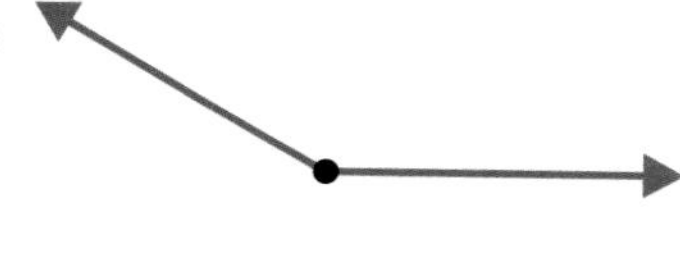

7. **Talk About It** Describe what makes each type of angle an *acute*, *obtuse*, or *right* angle.

Practice and Problem Solving

EXTRA PRACTICE See page R26.

Write the measure of the angle in degrees and as a fraction of a full turn. See Example 1 (p. 324)

8. 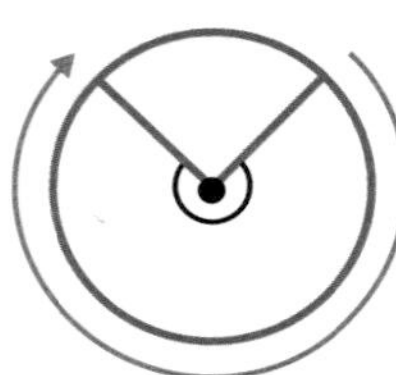

9. 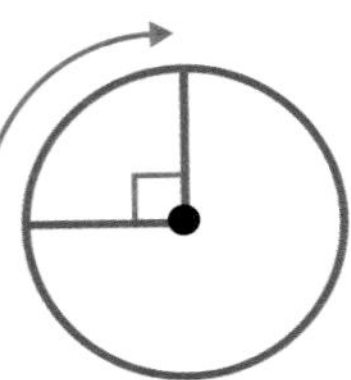

10. 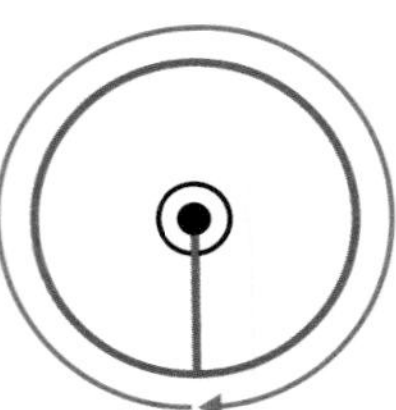

Classify each angle as *right*, *acute*, or *obtuse*. See Examples 2 and 3 (p. 325)

11.

12. 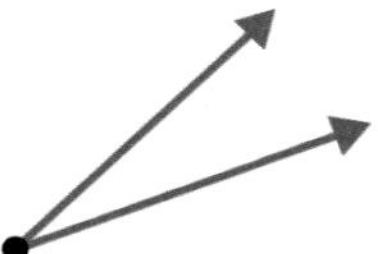

13. 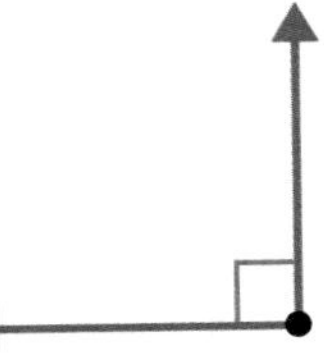

14. 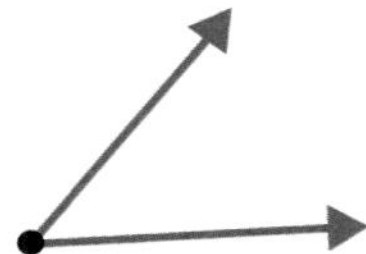

15. 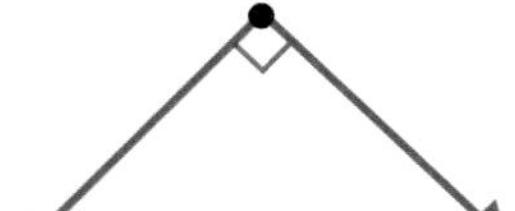

16. 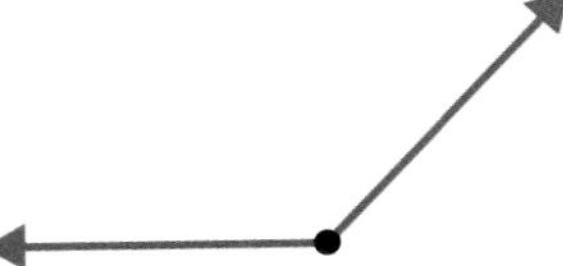

17. The timer is set to 30 minutes. How many degrees will the dial have turned when the timer goes off?

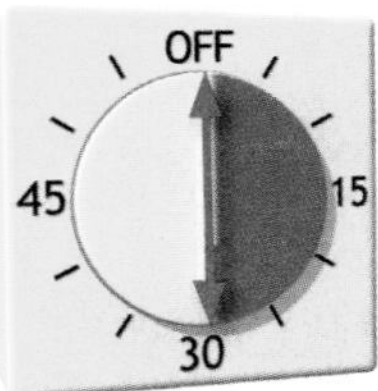

18. Classify the angle shown on the gas gauge below.

Real-World PROBLEM SOLVING

Geography A compass can be used to find direction. The arrow on a compass always faces north.

19. If you are facing north and turn west, what angle could be drawn to represent your movement?

20. You are facing east and are told to turn 180°. What direction will you be facing? Write the angle your body has turned as a fraction of a full turn.

H.O.T. Problems

21. **OPEN ENDED** Draw three different acute angles.

22. **WRITING IN MATH** Choose three objects in your classroom that have angles. Describe how to classify each angle as *acute*, *obtuse*, or *right*.

Math Online Self-Check Quiz at tx.gr4math.com

CHAPTER 8 Mid-Chapter Check

Lessons 8-1 through 8-4

Tell the number of faces, edges, and vertices. Then identify each figure. (Lesson 8-1)

1. 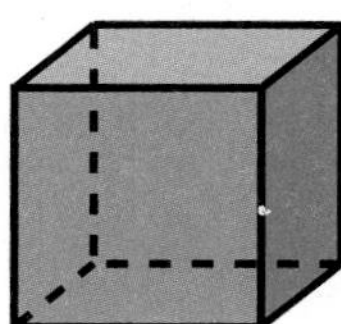

2. 

3. Identify the solid figure the net would make. (Lesson 8-1)

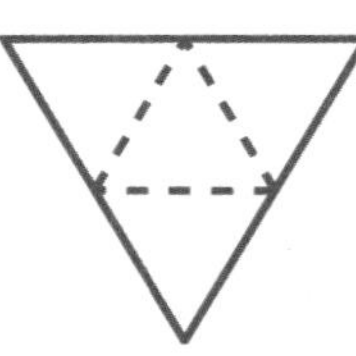

Identify each polygon. (Lesson 8-2)

4. 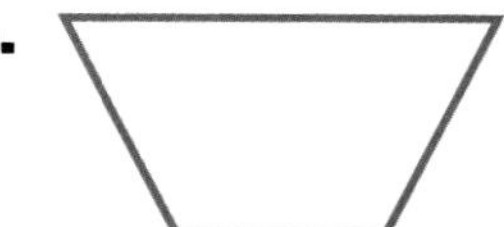

5. 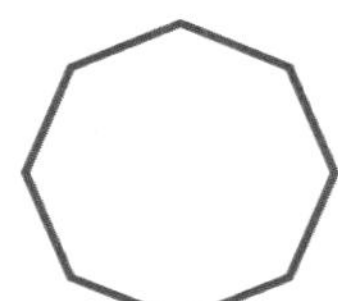

6. **TEST PRACTICE** Look at the figures below. (Lesson 8-2)

Which statement is true?

A There is one polygon.

B These are all polygons.

C There are two polygons.

D None of these are polygons.

7. Identify two polygons on the bird house. (Lesson 8-2)

8. **TEST PRACTICE** What is the figure called? (Lesson 8-2)

F hexagon

G triangle

H octagon

J pentagon

For Exercises 9 and 10, solve. Use the *look for a pattern* strategy. (Lesson 8-3)

9. Describe the pattern in 3, 9, 27, ■, 243. Then find the missing number.

10. A ferry leaves the harbor every 35 minutes. The first ferry leaves at 6:30 A.M. Davion plans on taking the first ferry after 8 A.M. When will his ferry leave?

Write the measure of each angle in degrees and as a fraction. (Lesson 8-4)

11. 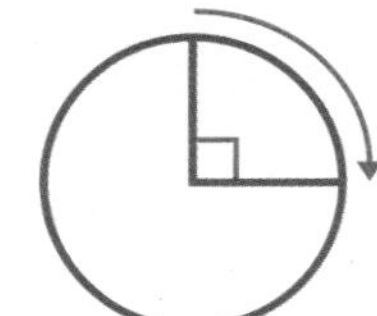

12. 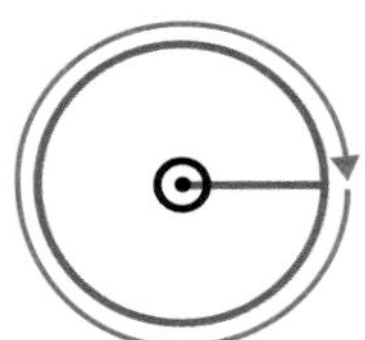

13. WRITING IN ▶MATH Can a figure be a polygon and a solid? Explain.

8-5 Triangles

GET READY to Learn

This sandwich is cut in half. What figure does each half resemble?

MAIN IDEA

I will identify, describe, and classify triangles.

Targeted TEKS 4.8 The student identifies and describes attributes of geometric figures using formal geometric language. **(C) Use essential attributes to define two-** and three-**dimensional geometric figures.** *Also addresses TEKS 4.8(A).*

New Vocabulary

- **isosceles triangle**
- **equilateral triangle**
- **scalene triangle**
- **right triangle**
- **acute triangle**
- **obtuse triangle**

There are many different types of triangles. You can classify triangles by the lengths of their sides.

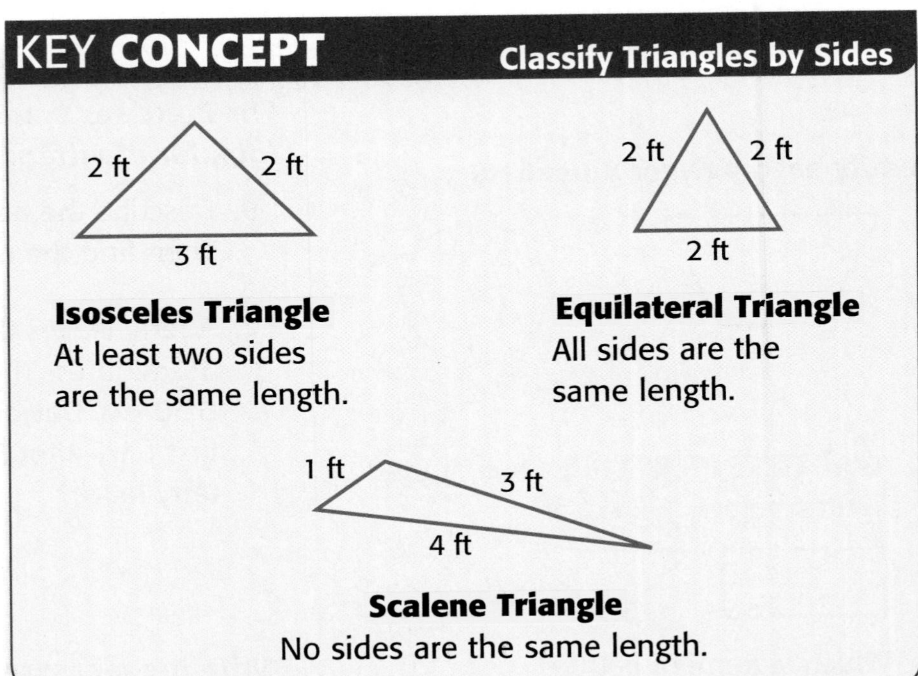

KEY CONCEPT Classify Triangles by Sides

Isosceles Triangle
At least two sides are the same length.

Equilateral Triangle
All sides are the same length.

Scalene Triangle
No sides are the same length.

EXAMPLE Classify by Sides

1 Classify the triangle. Use *isosceles, equilateral,* or *scalene*.

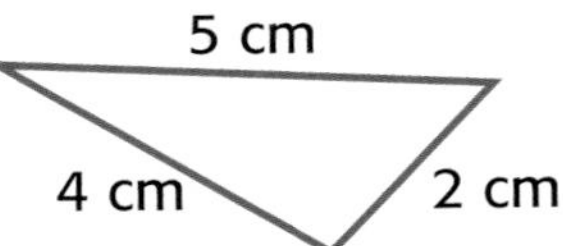

Since no sides are the same length, the triangle is scalene.

Triangles can also be classified by the measure of their angles.

KEY CONCEPTS — Classify Triangles by Angles

A **right triangle** has one right angle.

An **acute triangle** has three angles that are less than 90°.

An **obtuse triangle** has one obtuse angle.

EXAMPLE — Classify by Sides and Angles

2 **Classify the triangle. Use *isosceles, equilateral,* or *scalene* and *acute, right,* or *obtuse*.**

All of the sides are the same length. The triangle is equilateral. The triangle has three angles that are less than 90°, so it is also acute.

Online Personal Tutor at tx.gr4math.com

CHECK What You Know

Classify each triangle. Use *isosceles, equilateral,* or *scalene* and *acute, right,* or *obtuse*. See Examples 1 and 2 (pp. 328–329)

1.

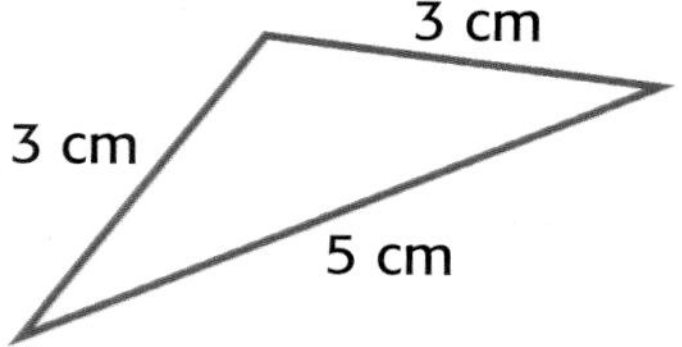

2.

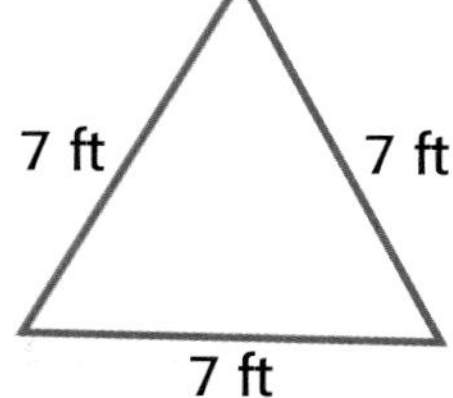

3.

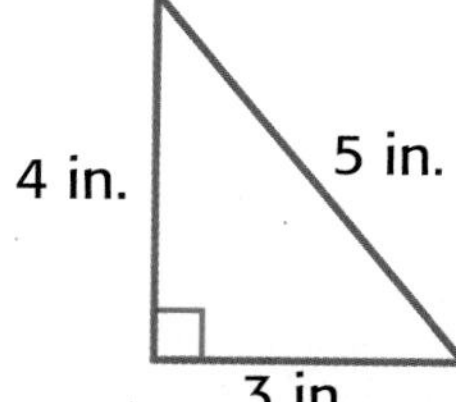

4. Rex has a pennant hanging in his room. What type of triangle is the pennant?

5. Talk About It Two sides of an equilateral triangle measure 3 feet. What is the measure of the third side? Explain.

Practice and Problem Solving

EXTRA PRACTICE
See page R26.

Classify each triangle. Use *isosceles, equilateral,* or *scalene* and *acute, right,* or *obtuse*. See Examples 1 and 2 (pp. 328–329)

6. 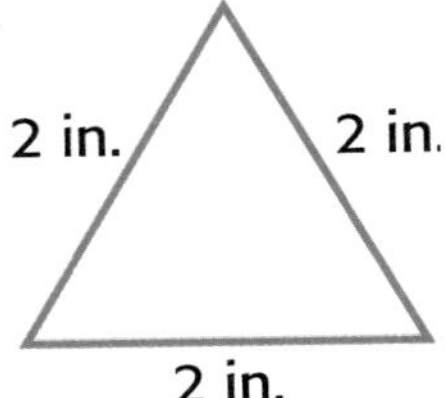

7. 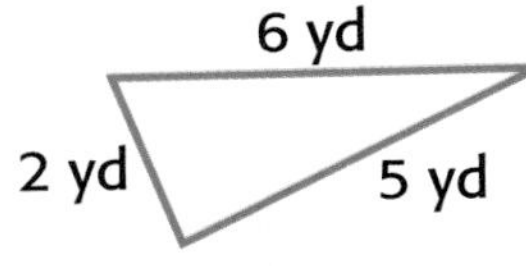

8. 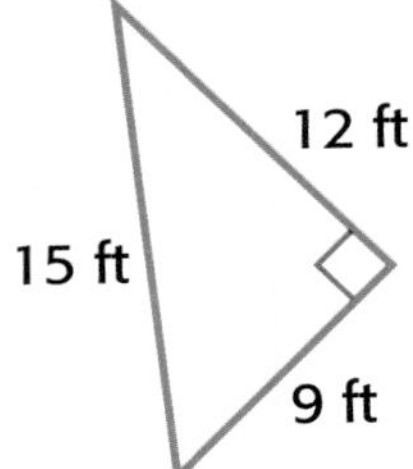

9. 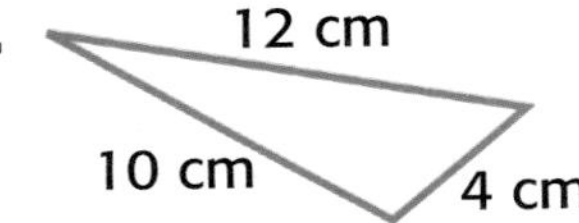

10. 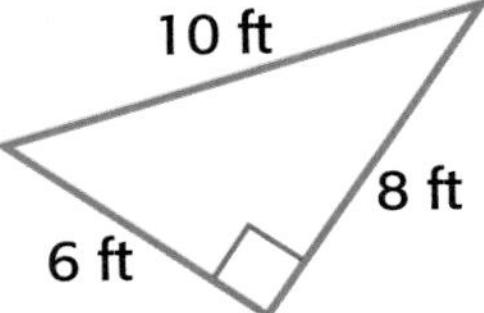

11. 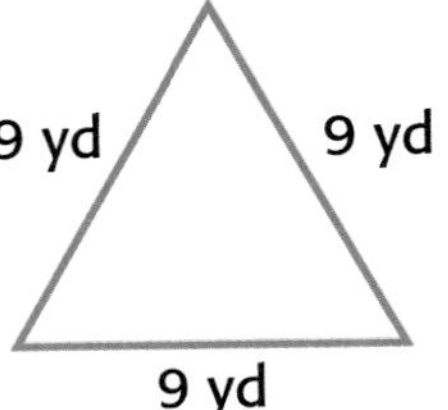

Draw an example of each triangle.

12. scalene right triangle

13. isosceles obtuse triangle

14. Describe the triangle formed by the ladder and the wall.

15. Classify the triangle on the wedge of cheese.

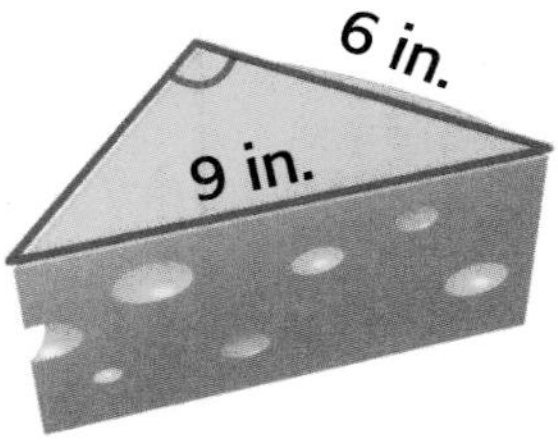

16. Shonda draws an equilateral triangle with 2 sides that equal 12 inches in length when added together. What is the length of the third side?

17. **Measurement** Ross draws an isosceles triangle with sides 5 centimeters and 3 centimeters. What could the measure of the third side be?

18. **Algebra** Copy and complete the table.

Polygon	Triangle	Square	Pentagon	Hexagon	Octagon
Number of Triangles in Polygon	1	2	3	■	■
Number of Sides in Polygon	3	4	■	6	8

H.O.T. Problems

19. OPEN ENDED Draw a triangle. Describe it in as many ways as you can.

20. WHICH ONE DOESN'T BELONG? Identify the term that does not belong with the other three. Explain.

right | obtuse | scalene | acute

21. WRITING IN ▸MATH Can an equilateral triangle be obtuse? Explain your answer.

TEST Practice

22. In the figure, which two angles appear to be obtuse? **(Lesson 8-5)**

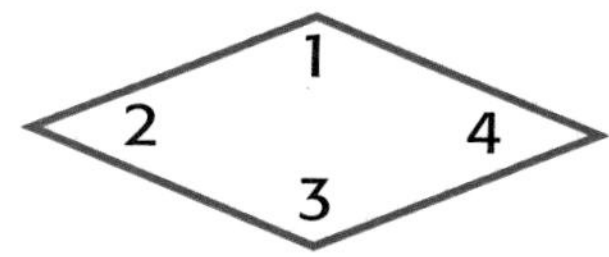

A Angles 1 and 2

B Angles 1 and 3

C Angles 1 and 4

D Angles 2 and 4

23. What kind of triangle always has 3 acute angles and 3 sides the same length? **(Lesson 8-5)**

F isosceles

G right

H equilateral

J scalene

Spiral Review

24. Suppose the pattern at the right was extended to 30 shapes in all. How many pentagons and octagons would there be? **(Lesson 8-3)**

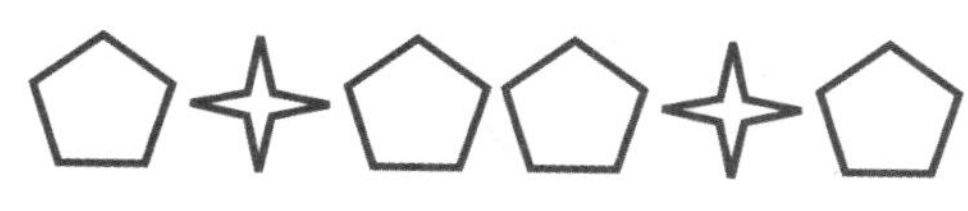

Classify each angle as *right, acute,* or *obtuse.* **(Lesson 8-4)**

25.

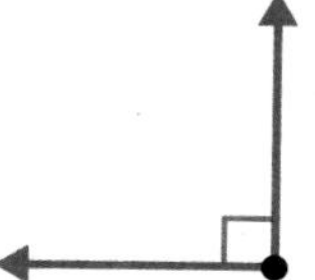

26.

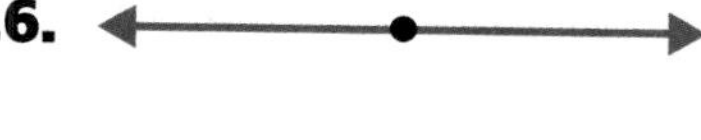

27.

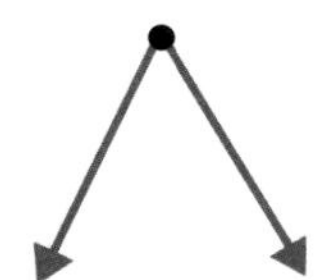

Identify the first five multiples for each number. **(Lesson 4-9)**

28. 3

29. 5

30. 8

31. 11

8-6 Quadrilaterals

GET READY to Learn

There are many quadrilaterals in these fields. How can you describe some of the different figures?

MAIN IDEA

I will identify, describe, and classify quadrilaterals.

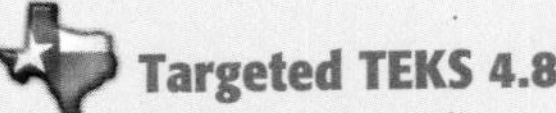

Targeted TEKS 4.8 The student identifies and describes attributes of geometric figures using formal geometric language. (C) **Use essential attributes to define two-** and three- **dimensional geometric figures.**

New Vocabulary

rectangle
square
rhombus
parallelogram
trapezoid

All quadrilaterals have 4 sides and 4 angles.

KEY CONCEPT — Quadrilaterals

A **rectangle** has 4 right angles, with opposite sides equal and parallel.

A **square** has 4 right angles, with opposite sides parallel. All sides are equal in length.

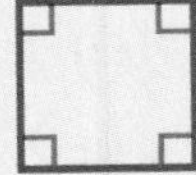

A **rhombus** has 4 equal sides and opposite sides are parallel.

These marks show equal sides.

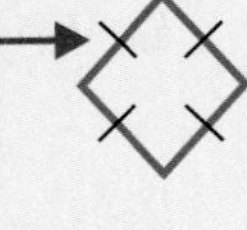

A **parallelogram** has opposite sides equal in length and parallel.

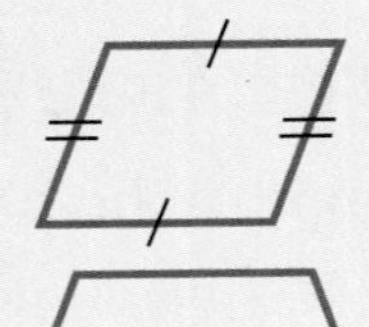

A **trapezoid** has exactly 1 pair of parallel sides.

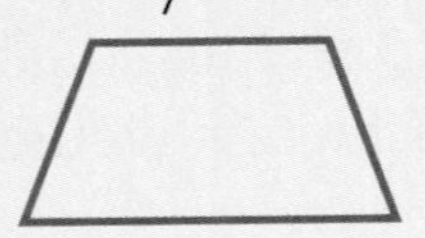

EXAMPLE Classify a Quadrilateral

1 Classify the quadrilateral in as many ways as possible.

It can be classified as a parallelogram, rectangle, square, and rhombus.

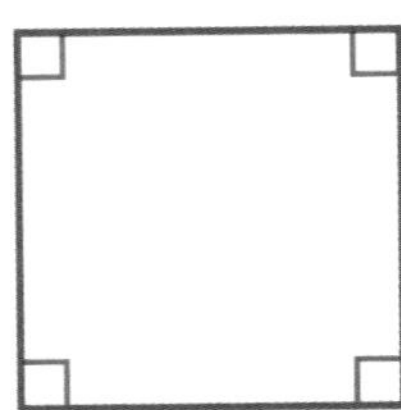

Many real-world objects have the shapes of quadrilaterals.

Real-World EXAMPLES Real-World Shapes

2 **VIDEO GAMES** **Write the type of quadrilateral that best describes the shape around the game controller.**

The shape has one pair of parallel sides. So, it is a trapezoid.

3 **Identify the shape outlined in the sculpture.**

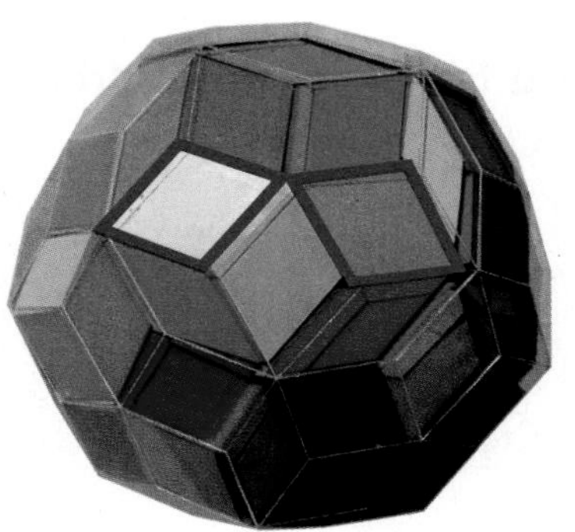

The opposite sides of the shape are equal and parallel. So, the shape is a parallelogram.

Online **Personal Tutor at** tx.gr4math.com

CHECK What You Know

Classify each quadrilateral in as many ways as possible.

See Example 1 (p. 332)

1. 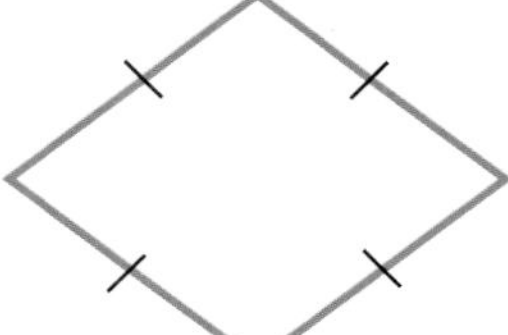

2. 

3. 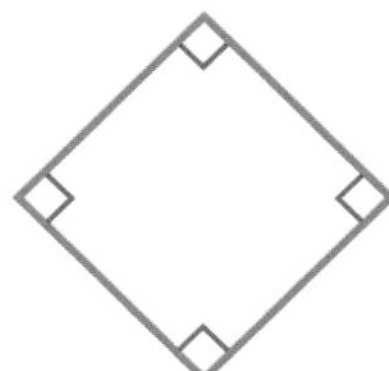

Write the type of quadrilateral that best describes the shape.

See Examples 2–3 (p. 333)

4. 

5. 

6. 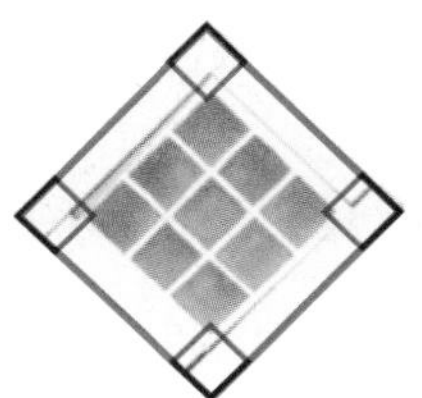

7. Talk About It How are a square and a rhombus alike? How are they different?

Practice and Problem Solving

EXTRA PRACTICE See page R27.

Classify each quadrilateral in as many ways as possible.

See Example 1 (p. 332)

8. 

9. 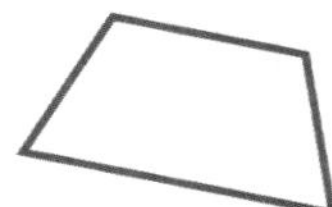

10. 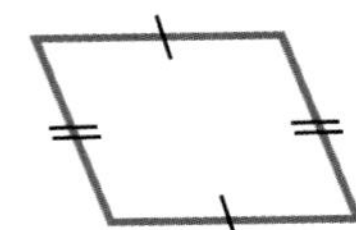

11. 

12. 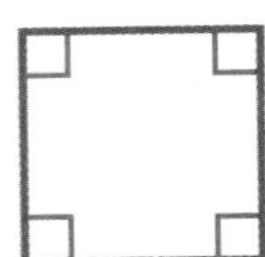

13. 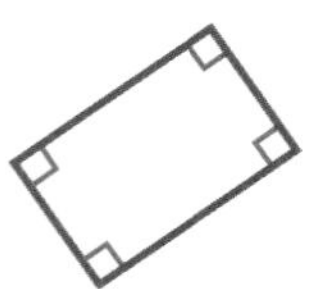

Write the type of quadrilateral that best describes the shape.

See Examples 2 and 3 (p. 333)

14. 

15. 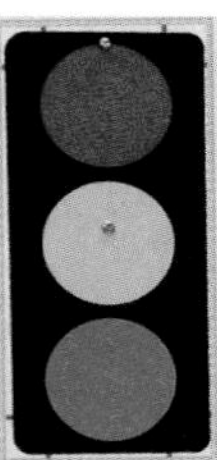

16. 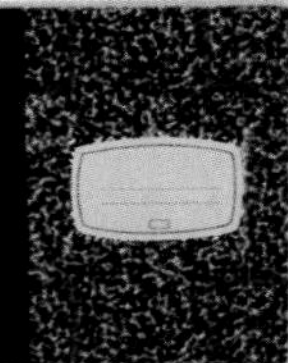

17. 

18. 

19. 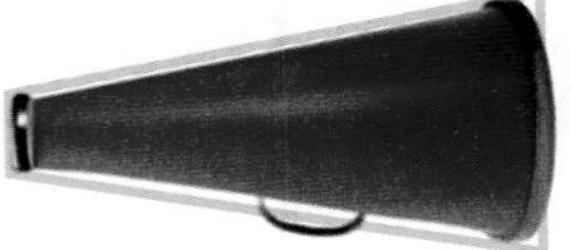

20. A quadrilateral has 4 sides with opposite sides parallel and 4 right angles. Two sides are longer than the others. What is the quadrilateral?

21. Phillip draws a quadrilateral. It has all 4 sides the same length. Its opposite sides are parallel. What quadrilateral did he draw?

H.O.T. Problems

22. **OPEN ENDED** Draw two quadrilaterals that can be classified as parallelograms.

REASONING Tell whether each statement is *true* or *false*.

23. A rhombus is a square.

24. A rectangle is a parallelogram.

25. **WRITING IN MATH** True or false: All squares are rectangles, but not all rectangles are squares. Explain.

Shape Up

Draw Polygons

Get Ready!

Players: 2

You will need: 10 index cards

Get Set!

Cut the cards in half. Then label the cards with the terms shown.

polygon	right angle
quadrilateral	acute angle
triangle	obtuse angle
pentagon	straight angle
hexagon	rectangle
parallelogram	square
trapezoid	rhombus

Go!

- Shuffle the cards. Then spread the cards face down on the table.
- Player 1 turns over a card and draws an example of the polygon.
- If Player 1 cannot draw the polygon, Player 2 is given a chance to draw the polygon.
- Player 2 keeps the card if he or she can draw the polygon. If he or she cannot, the card is put back.
- Player 2 selects a card.
- Continue playing until all cards are gone. The player who collects the most cards wins.

Problem-Solving Investigation

MAIN IDEA I will choose the best strategy to solve a problem.

Targeted TEKS 4.14 The student applies Grade 4 mathematics to solve problems connected to everyday experiences and activities in and outside of school. (B) **Solve problems that incorporate understanding the problem, making a plan, carrying out the plan, and evaluating the solution for reasonableness.** *Also addresses TEKS 4.14(C).*

P.S.I. TEAM +

ARTURO: I have the five puzzle pieces shown. I need to form a square using all of the pieces.

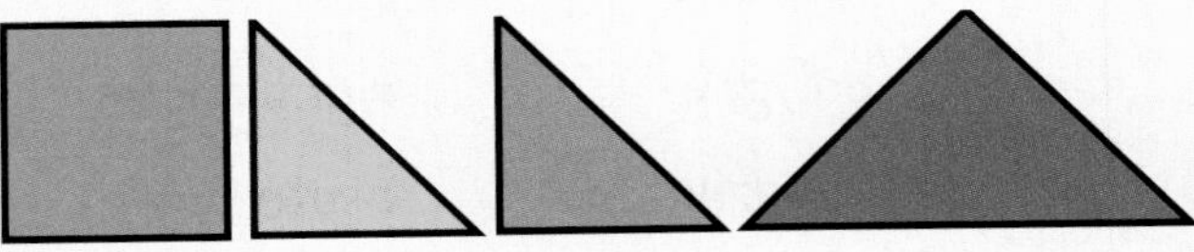

YOUR MISSION: Arrange the five puzzle pieces to form a square.

Understand	You know there are five puzzle pieces. Find how to arrange the pieces to form a square.
Plan	Use the *act it out* strategy. Trace the pieces and cut them out of paper. Then arrange the polygons in different ways to figure out how they will form a square.
Solve	Arrange the pieces in different ways until you form a square. 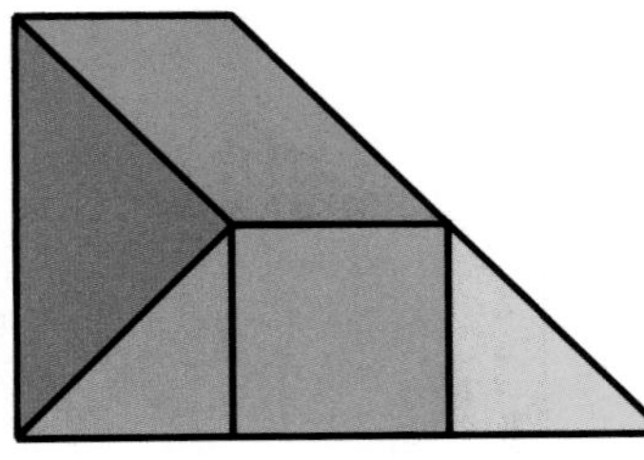 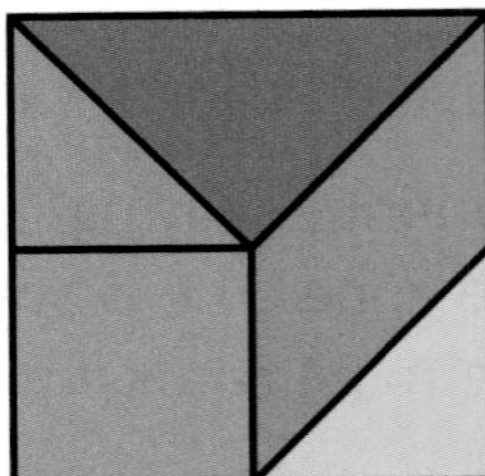
Check	Look back at the problem. The figure formed by the pieces is a square because it is a rectangle that has four equal sides. So, the answer is correct.

Mixed Problem Solving

Use any strategy shown below to solve. Tell what strategy you used.

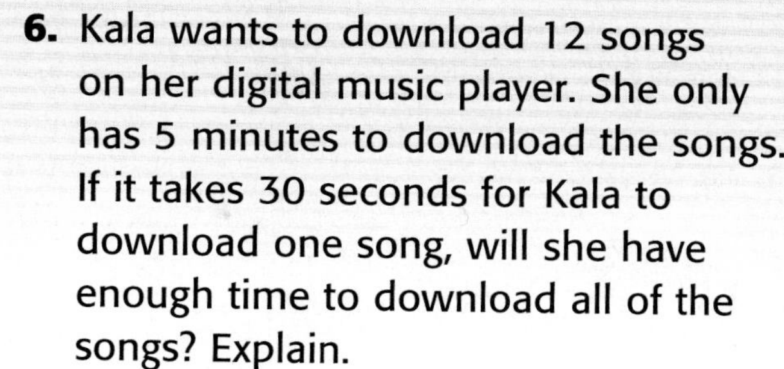

PROBLEM-SOLVING STRATEGIES

- Make a table.
- Act it out.
- Guess and check.

1. Keli can run 3 miles in 36 minutes. She plans to improve her time by running 1 mile one minute faster every 2 weeks. Is it reasonable to say that Keli will be able to run 3 miles in 25 minutes in 3 weeks? Explain.

2. Identify four bills worth $50 using $1, $5, $10, and $20 bills.

3. Draw the next three figures in the pattern below.

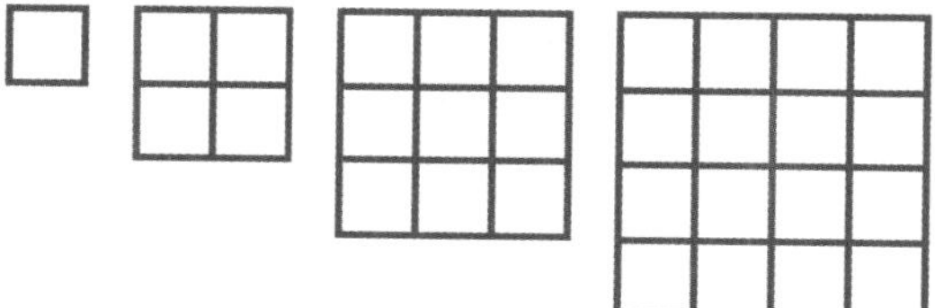

4. Pilar had 8 trading cards. She then bought some packs with 6 cards in each pack. Pilar now has 44 cards. How many packs did she buy?

5. Kareem has $20. He wants to buy the items shown. Will he have enough money? Explain. **(Lesson 1-3)**

$9 $8 $4

6. Kala wants to download 12 songs on her digital music player. She only has 5 minutes to download the songs. If it takes 30 seconds for Kala to download one song, will she have enough time to download all of the songs? Explain.

7. The polygons below form a pattern. How many sides will the ninth polygon have?

8. Mason has $12. He earns $5 every week for doing chores. Is it reasonable to say that Mason will be able to buy a skateboard that costs $60 in 10 weeks? Explain.

9. A number is multiplied by 2. Then 4 is subtracted from the product. The result is 8. What was the original number?

10. During football practice, Emilio is running drills. He runs 20 yards forward and then 10 yards backward starting at the goal line. How many sets will it take him to reach the other goal line?

11. **WRITING IN MATH** Look at Exercise 7. Which problem-solving strategy did you use to find the answer? Explain how you used this strategy to solve the problem.

Problem Solving in Art

Garden Art

Four-Sided Pyramid

The Sculpture Garden in Washington, D.C., is filled with many shapes. It has 17 large sculptures. Many of these sculptures are made of different solid figures. For example, the *Four-Sided Pyramid* is made of concrete cubes. It is about 32 feet tall and 33 feet wide.

Another sculpture in this garden, *Cluster of Four Cubes,* is made of four metal cubes that spin in the breeze. These cubes are about 9 feet high in the air. *Moondog* is a metal sculpture that has triangles, hexagons, and pentagons in its shape. It is so large you can walk under it!

Did You Know?

There are 624 cubes in *Four-Sided Pyramid.*

Targeted TEKS 4.14 The student applies Grade 4 mathematics to solve problems connected to everyday experiences and activities in and outside of school. **(A) Identify the mathematics in everyday situations.**

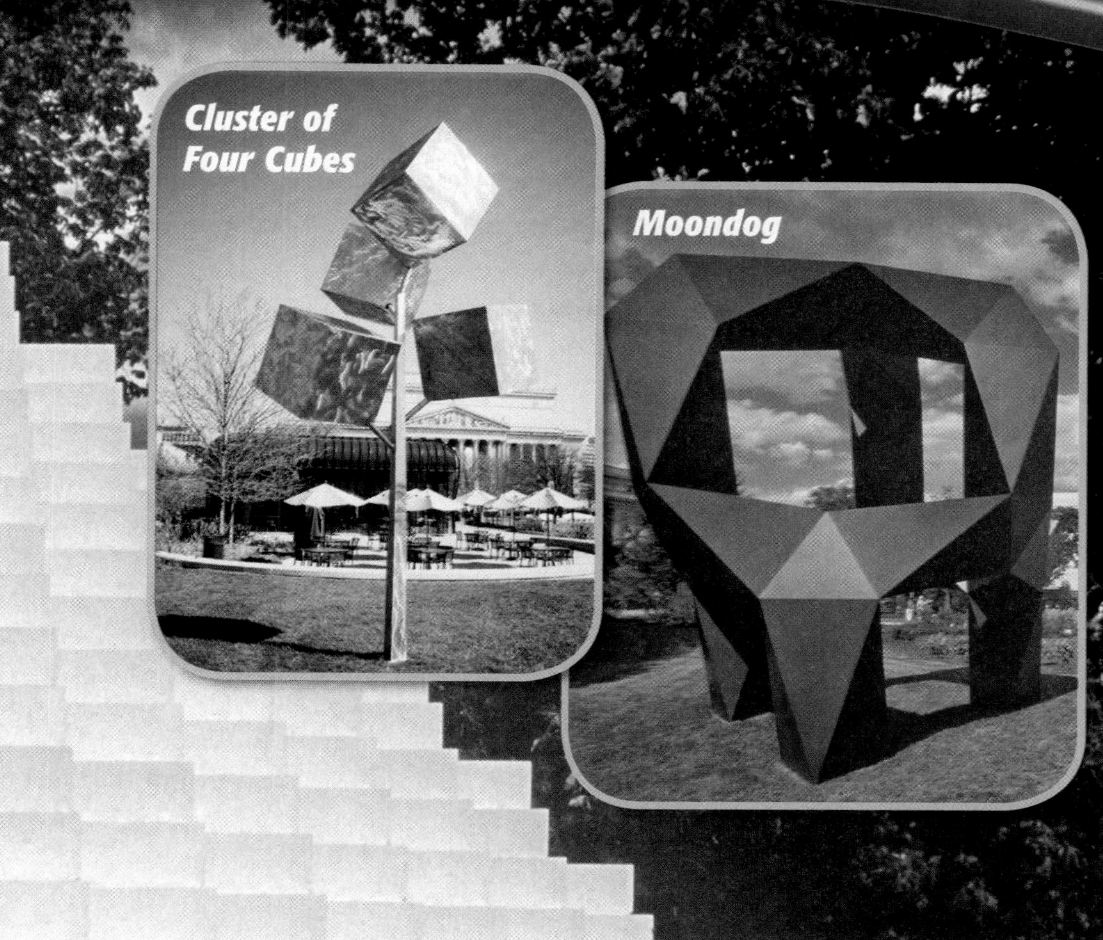

Real-World Math

Use the sculptures *Moondog, Four-Sided Pyramid,* and *Cluster of Four Cubes* to solve each problem.

1. What geometric shape does *Four-Sided Pyramid* resemble?

2. How many faces, edges, and vertices does *Four-Sided Pyramid* have?

3. How many edges does one cube in *Cluster of Four Cubes* have?

4. Can you see a rectangle in the picture of *Moondog*? Explain.

5. How many equilateral triangles do you see in the picture of the *Moondog*?

6. All the edges of the *Four-Sided Pyramid* are equal. What kind of triangles make up the faces? How many triangles are there?

7. Suppose one face of a cube on *Cluster of Four Cubes* is cut diagonally. What kind of triangle will it make?

CHAPTER 8

Study Guide and Review

FOLDABLES Study Organizer GET READY to Study

Be sure the following Key Vocabulary words and Key Concepts are written in your Foldable.

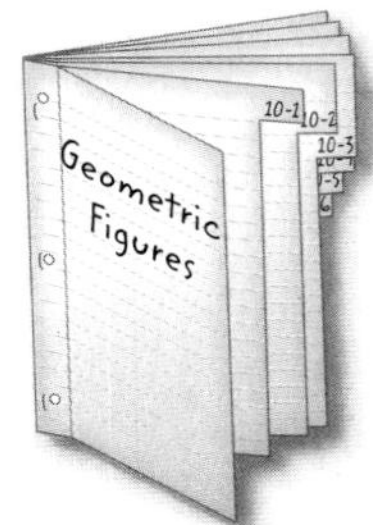

BIG Ideas

- A **solid figure** is a three-dimensional figure with length, width, and height. (p. 315)

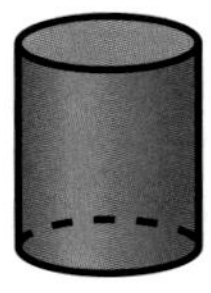 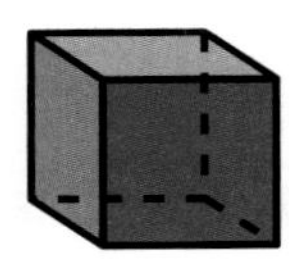 

- A **plane figure** is a two-dimensional figure with length and width. (p. 318)

- Angles are made from two rays that have the same endpoint.

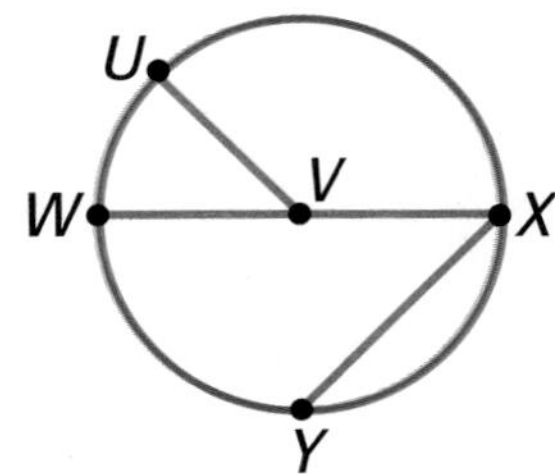

Key Vocabulary

angle (p. 324)
plane figure (p. 318)
solid figure (p. 315)
right angle (p. 325)

Vocabulary Check

Decide which vocabulary word best completes each sentence.

1. A(n) ___?___ is a figure where all the points are the same distance from the center.
2. A(n) ___?___ is a three-dimensional figure with length, width, and height.
3. A(n) ___?___ is a figure made from two rays that have the same endpoint.
4. A(n) ___?___ is a two-dimensional figure with length and width.
5. A(n) ___?___ is formed by perpendicular lines.

Math Online Vocabulary Review at tx.gr4math.com

Lesson-by-Lesson Review

8-1 Three-Dimensional Figures (pp. 315–317)

Example 1
Identify the shape of the paint can. Then tell the number of faces, edges, and vertices.

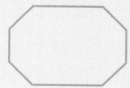

The paint can is a cylinder.

It has 2 faces, 0 edges, and 0 vertices.

Identify each figure. Then tell how many faces, edges, and vertices it has.

6. 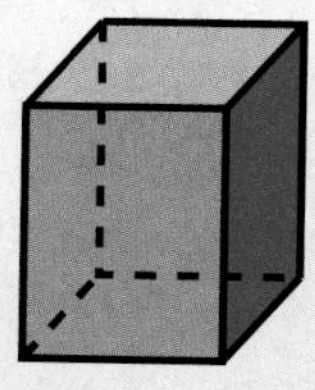

7. 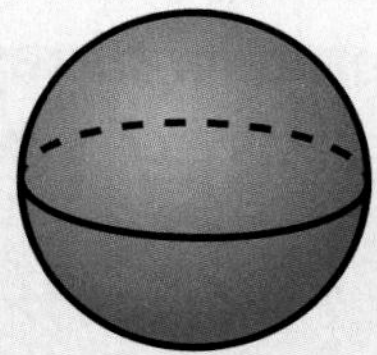

8. Identify the solid figure the net would make.

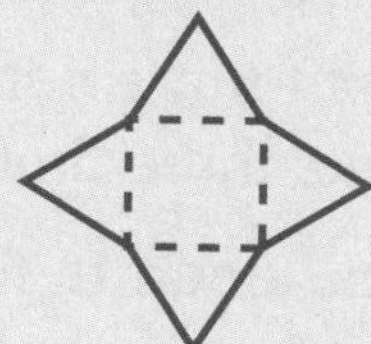

8-2 Two-Dimensional Figures (pp. 318–321)

Tell whether each shape is a polygon.

Example 2

The moon has curved sides. So, it is not a polygon.

Example 3

This figure has 8 sides. The sides are straight. So, it is a polygon.

Identify each polygon.

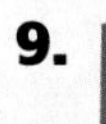

9. 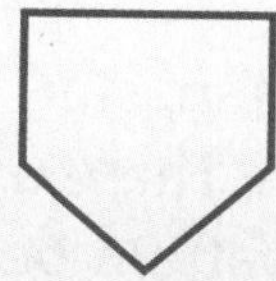

10. 

11. 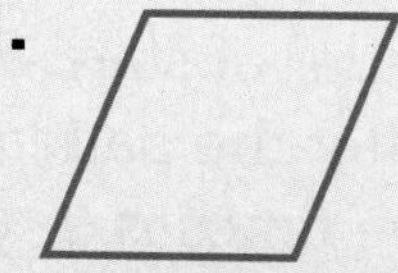

12. 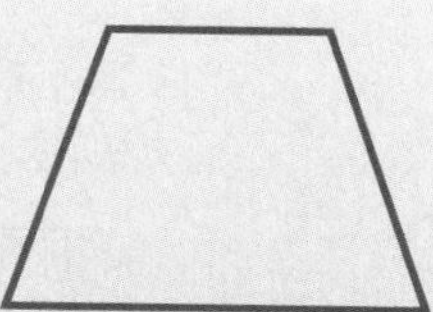

Tell whether the shape is a polygon.

13. 

14. 

8-3 Problem-Solving Strategy: Look for a Pattern (pp. 322–323)

Example 4
Bruce is creating the pattern below on a bowl in art class. There is enough space on the bowl for the pattern to repeat three times. How many stars will he make?

Understand

What facts do you know?

- The figures form a pattern that repeats three times.

What do you need to find?

- The number of stars Bruce will make.

Plan Look for a pattern to solve.

Solve The pattern is sun, star, moon, sun, star, moon. There are 2 stars in the pattern before it repeats.

So, the number of stars Bruce will make after the pattern repeats three times is 2×3 or 6.

Check The answer makes sense for the facts given. The answer is correct.

15. Describe the pattern below. Then find the missing number.

45, 36, 27, ■, 9

16. Copy and complete the pattern. What are the next two figures in this pattern?

17. Algebra Copy and complete the table. What is the pattern?

Input ( )	Output ( )
8	40
4	20
9	45
7	■
■	15

18. Nell jogged for 8 minutes on Monday. Then she jogged for 13 minutes on Tuesday. She jogged for 18 minutes on Wednesday. How many minutes will Nell jog on Sunday?

19. The pattern below can also be shown as 1, 4, 7, 10. Draw the next two figures. What are the next two numbers?

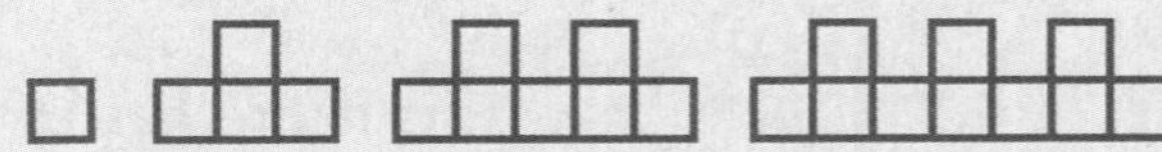

20. Describe the pattern below. Then find the missing number.

1, 3, 7, 15, ■

8-4 Angles (pp. 324–326)

Example 5

Write the measure of the angle shown below in degrees and as a fraction of a full turn.

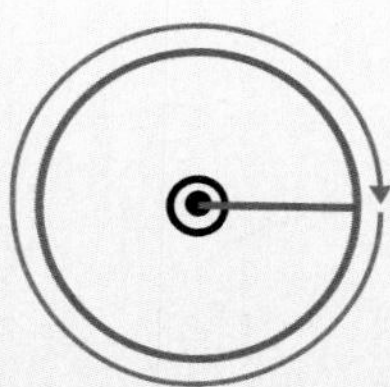

The angle shown is 360° or a full turn.

Write the measure of each angle in degrees and as a fraction of a full turn.

21. 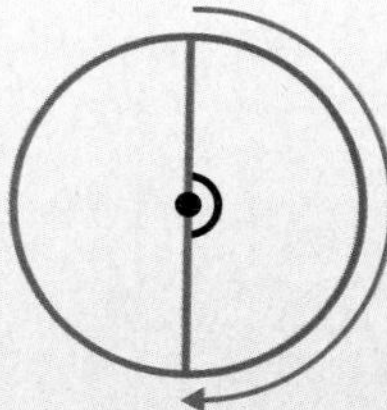

22. 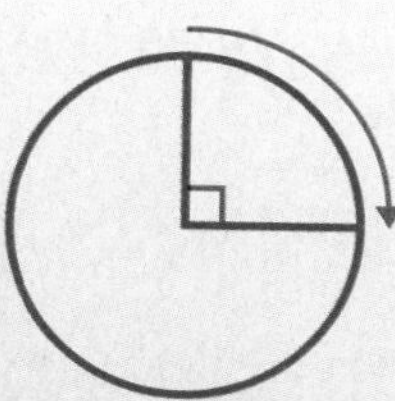

Classify each angle as *right, acute,* or *obtuse*.

23. 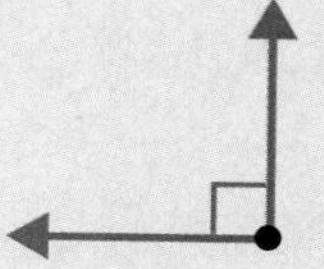

24.

8-5 Triangles (pp. 328–331)

Example 6

Classify the triangle. Use *isosceles, equilateral,* or *scalene* and *acute, right* or *obtuse*.

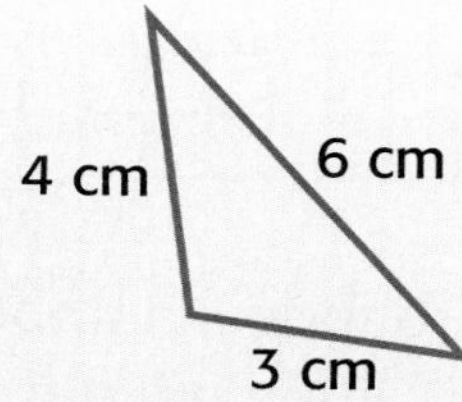

Since no sides are the same length, the triangle is scalene.

The triangle has one obtuse angle, so it is obtuse.

Classify each triangle. Use *isosceles, equilateral,* or *scalene* and *acute, right,* and *obtuse*.

25. 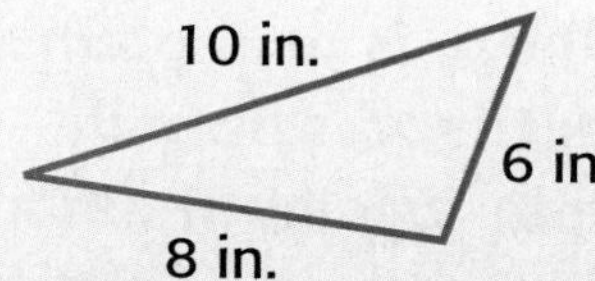

26. 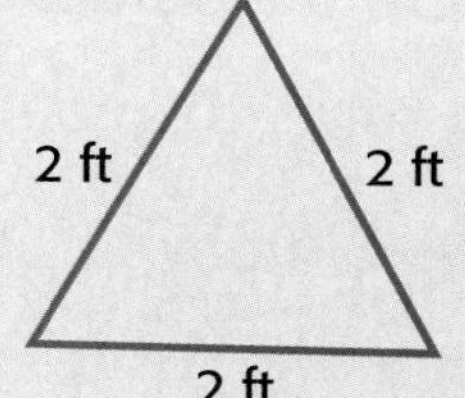

27. 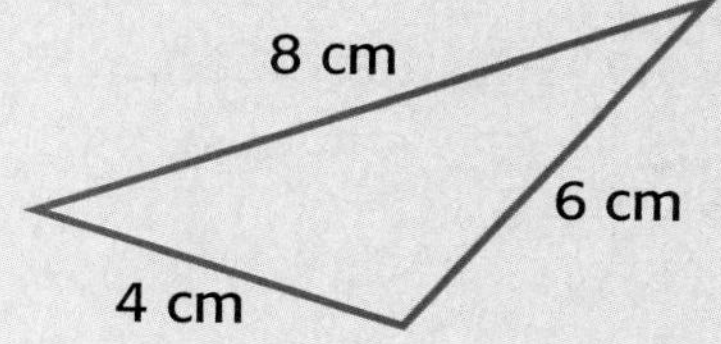

Study Guide and Review

8-6 Quadrilaterals (pp. 332–334)

Example 7
Classify the quadrilateral in as many ways as possible.

The figure has parallel sides. So, it is a parallelogram.

It has 4 right angles. So, is a rectangle.

So, the quadrilateral can be classified as a parallelogram and rectangle.

Classify each quadrilateral in as many ways as possible.

28. 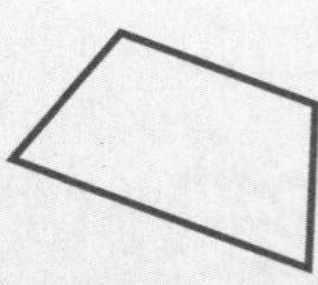

29. 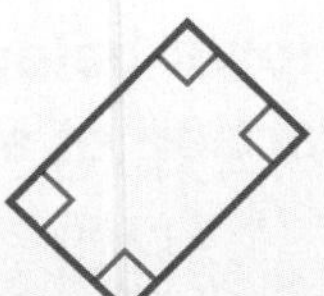

30. 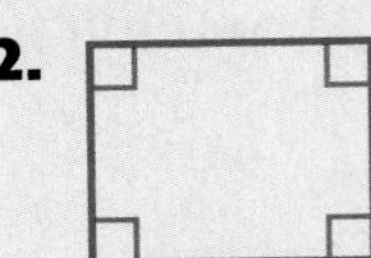

31. 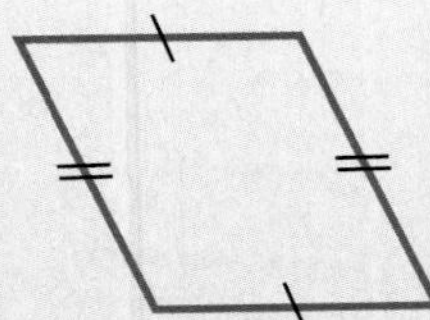

32. 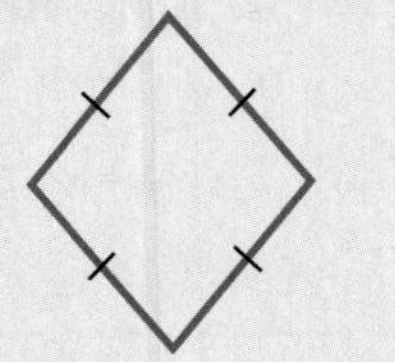

33.

8-7 Problem-Solving Investigation: Choose a Strategy (pp. 336–337)

Example 8
Students are lining up by birthdays. Nathan's birthday is in September, so he is first. Beatriz was born in December. Ruby was born before Beatriz. Carlie was born in October. What is the order of the students?

Work backward to solve the problem.

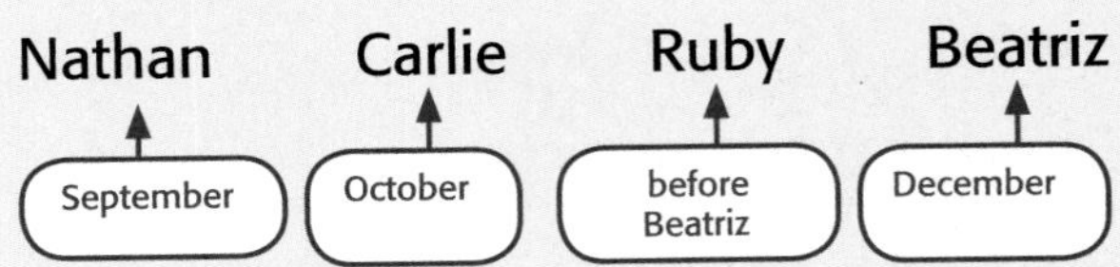

So, the order is Nathan, Carlie, Ruby, and Beatriz.

Use any strategy to solve.

34. Draw the next two figures in the pattern.

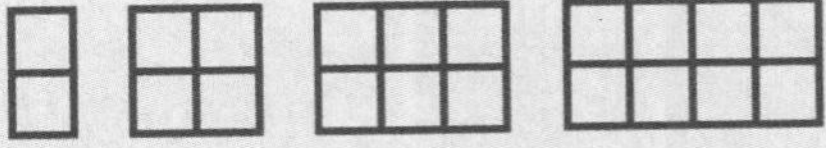

35. Liana rounds a number to the nearest hundred and gets 200. What is the least number it could be? the greatest number?

36. **Algebra** Logan has 7 jars of coins. Each jar has 35 coins. How many coins does he have?

CHAPTER 8

Chapter Test

For exercises 1–3, decide whether each statement is *true* or *false*.

1. A square is a plane figure in which all the sides are the same length.

2. A trapezoid has 2 pairs of parallel sides.

3. An obtuse triangle has two obtuse angles.

Classify each quadrilateral in as many ways as possible.

4. 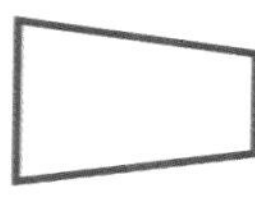

5. 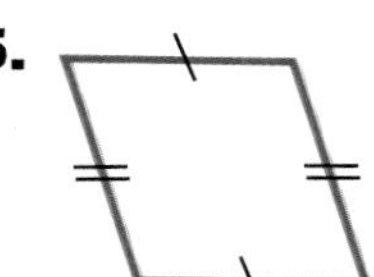

6. **TEST PRACTICE** How many faces does this shape have?

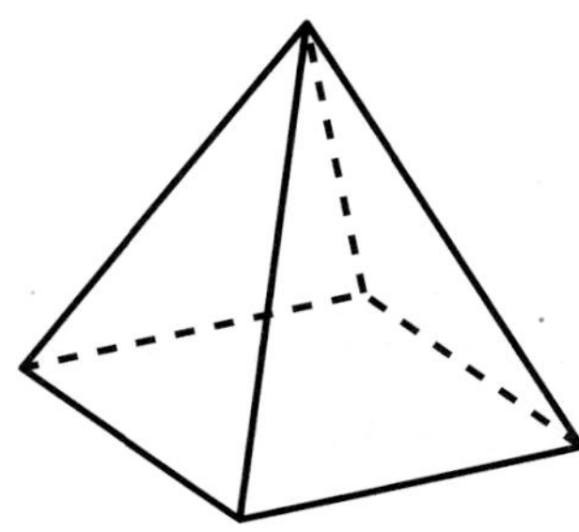

A 3

B 4

C 5

D 6

Classify each triangle. Use *isosceles, equilateral,* or *scalene* and *acute, right,* or *obtuse*.

7. 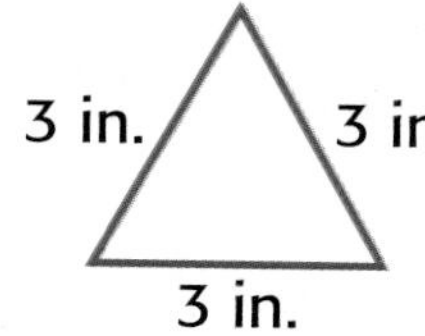

8. 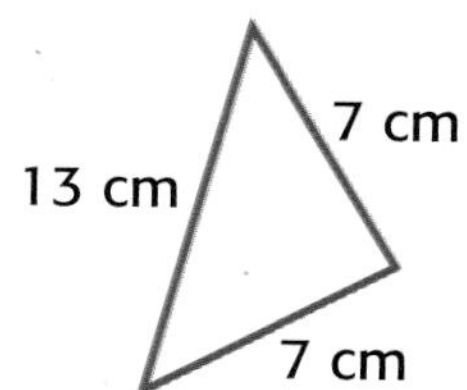

Classify each angle as *right, acute,* or *obtuse*.

9. 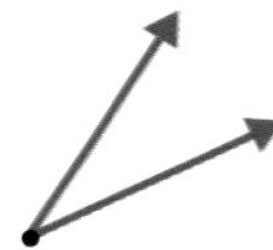

10. 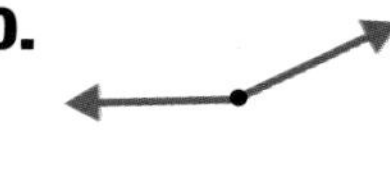

11. Draw the next 2 shapes in the pattern below.

12. **TEST PRACTICE** In the figure below, which two angles appear to be acute?

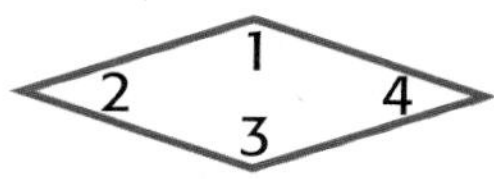

F Angles 1 and 2 **H** Angles 1 and 4

G Angles 1 and 3 **J** Angles 2 and 4

13. **WRITING IN MATH** Is it possible to draw an isosceles triangle that is acute? Explain. Draw a picture to support your answer.

CHAPTER 8

Texas Test Practice

Cumulative, Chapters 1–8

Nara is wrapping a gift in a box shaped like a rectangular prism. How many faces does a rectangular prism have?

A 4　　**C** 8

B 6　　**D** 12

TEST-TAKING TIP

A face of a solid figure is a flat surface of the figure.

Read the Test Question

You need to find the number of faces of a rectangular prism.

Solve the Test Question

Draw a net to show the faces of a rectangular prism. Then count the faces.

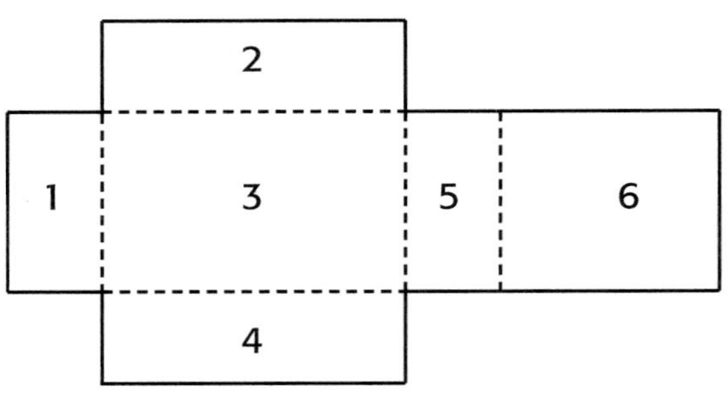

A rectangular prism has 6 faces. The answer is B.

Personal Tutor at tx.gr4math.com

Choose the best answer.

1. **How many vertices does a cube have?**

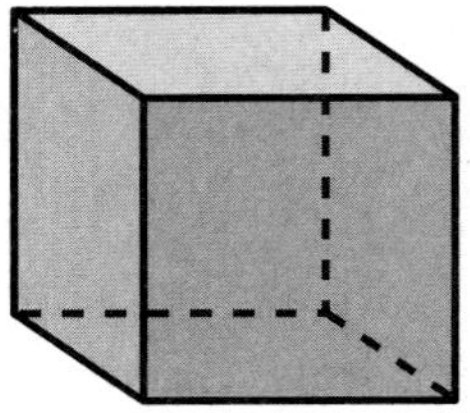

A 4

B 6

C 8

D 10

2. **What solid figure has one circular face and one vertex?**

F cone

G cylinder

H prism

J sphere

Get Ready for the Texas Test
For test-taking strategies and more practice, see pages TX1-TX21.

3. What number comes next in the pattern below?

20, 17, 14, 11, 8, __

A 3
B 4
C 5
D 6

4. Which of the following best describes the lines below?

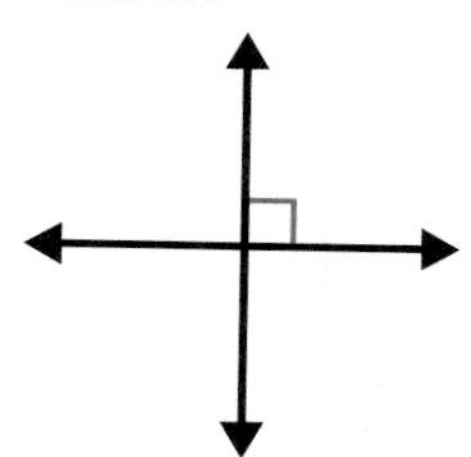

F The lines are parallel.
G The lines are perpendicular.
H The lines form an acute angle.
J The lines do not intersect.

5. Which number makes this equation true?

126 ÷ ■ = 9

A 10
B 11
C 12
D 14

6. Nicolas has 182 pennies. He wants to put about the same number of pennies into each of 8 jars. About how many pennies will be in each jar?

F 21
G 22
H 23
J 24

7. How many lines of symmetry does the figure below have?

A 0
B 1
C 2
D 4

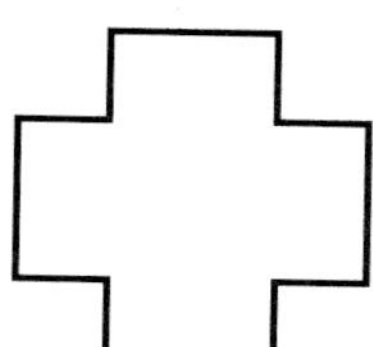

8. Which of the following angles appears to be acute?

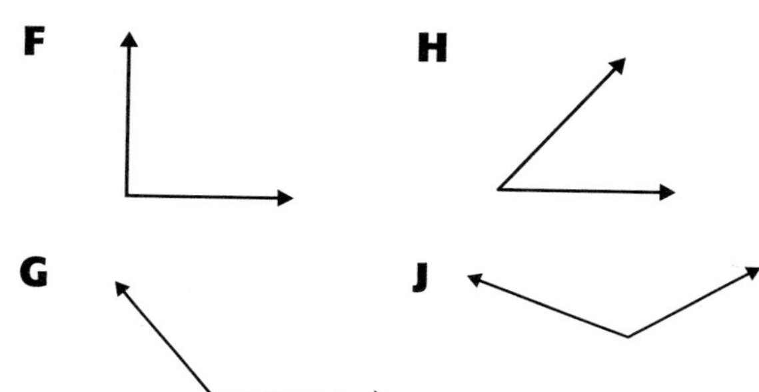

9. GRIDDABLE Coach Sanchez wants to organize 132 players into teams of 11. How many teams will there be?

10. What is the quotient when 806 is divided by 31?

A 26
B 29
C 34
D 37

Understand and Develop Spatial Reasoning

BIG Idea What is spatial reasoning?

Spatial reasoning is the ability to visualize changes in the world around you, such as changes in location and shapes.

Example When you look at a map, you use spatial reasoning to find the best way of getting somewhere. Look at this map. Would it be better to take Park Avenue or South View Boulevard to get from Lane Street to Jefferson Way?

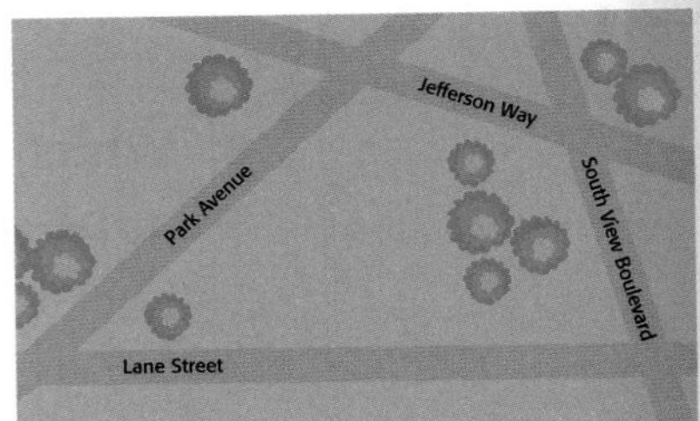

What will I learn in this chapter?

- Find points on number lines and coordinate planes.
- Identify, describe, and classify lines, line segments, and rays.
- Demonstrate rotations, reflections, and translations and use them to identify congruent figures and symmetry in figures.
- Solve problems by making an organized list.

Key Vocabulary

number line **transform**
point **congruent**
coordinate plane

Student Study Tools at tx.gr4math.com

FOLDABLES™ Study Organizer

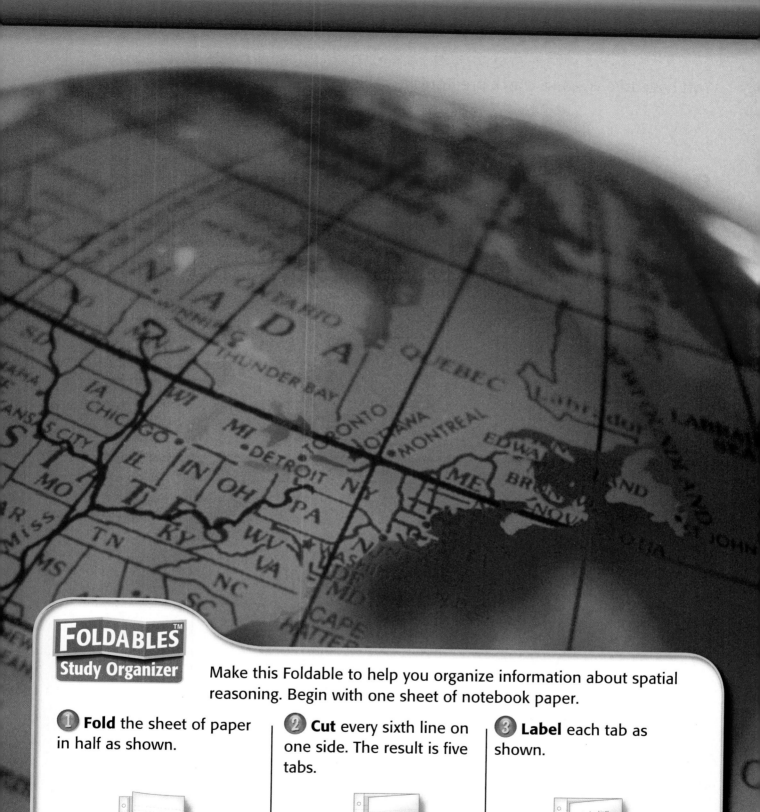

Make this Foldable to help you organize information about spatial reasoning. Begin with one sheet of notebook paper.

1. **Fold** the sheet of paper in half as shown.

2. **Cut** every sixth line on one side. The result is five tabs.

3. **Label** each tab as shown.

ARE YOU READY for Chapter 9?

You have two ways to check prerequisite skills for this chapter.

Option 2

Math Online Take the Chapter Readiness Quiz at tx.gr4math.com.

Option 1

Complete the Quick Check below.

QUICK Check

Tell whether each figure could be divided in half by the dashed line. Write *yes* or *no*. (Prior grade)

1.

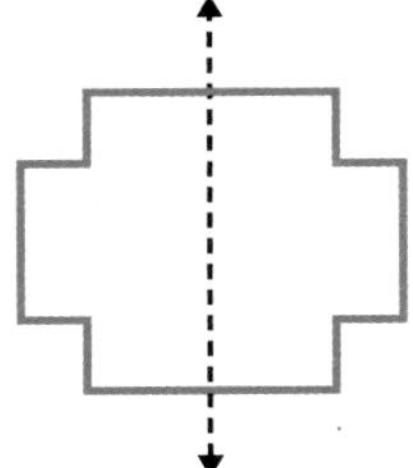

2.

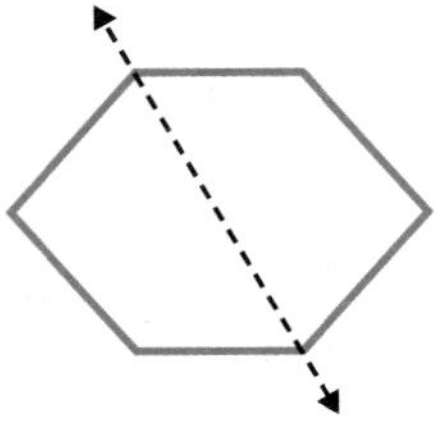

3.

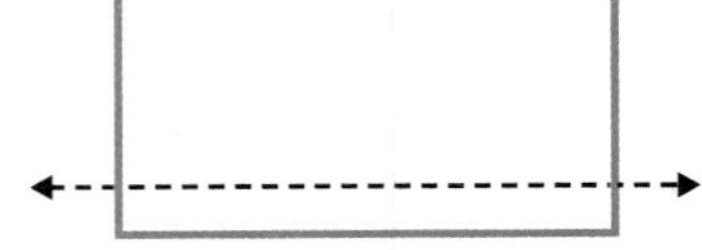

4. Jon is sharing his sandwich with his brother. Is the sandwich divided in half?

Identify the figure that is different.

5.

6.

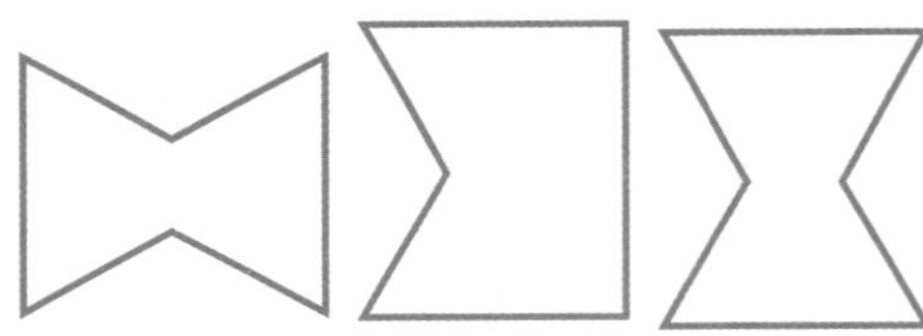

Identify each polygon. (Lesson 8-2)

7.

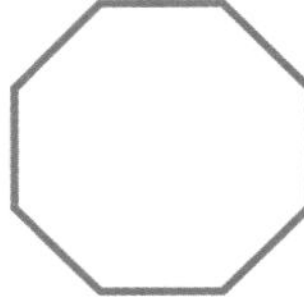

8.

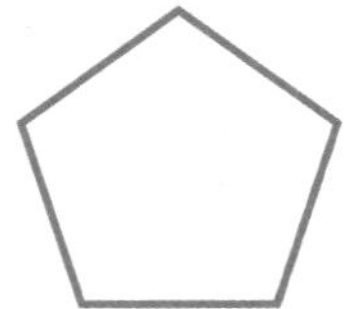

9.

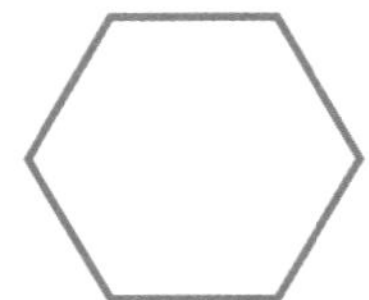

10. Peyton is looking in a kaleidoscope. Identify two of the polygons that can be seen.

9-1 Locate Points on a Number Line

GET READY to Learn

Andrés is trying to find what whole number is represented by the point *T* on the number line shown. Name each point represented by a letter.

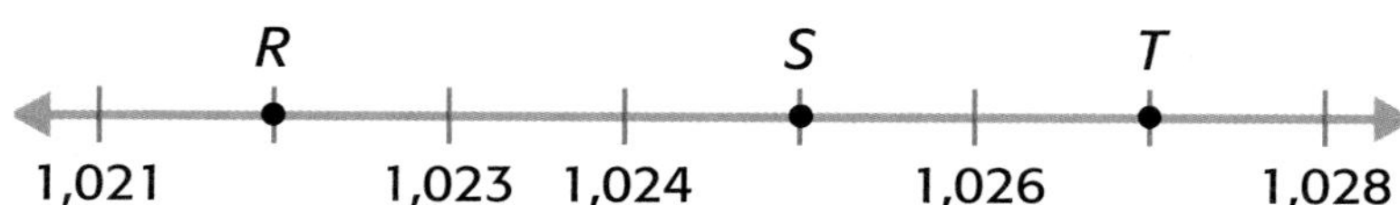

MAIN IDEA

I will find points on a number line.

Targeted TEKS 4.10 The student recognizes the connection between numbers and their properties and points on a line. **Locate and name points on a number line using whole numbers,** fractions such as halves and fourths, and decimals such as tenths.

New Vocabulary

number line
point

A **number line** is a line that represents numbers as points. A **point** is an exact location in space. Number lines can be used to compare and order numbers.

EXAMPLE .Name Points on a Number Line

1 Name each point represented by a letter.

To find out what number each letter represents, use the information given.

The scale for the number line is in one-unit intervals. Count to find out what each letter is.

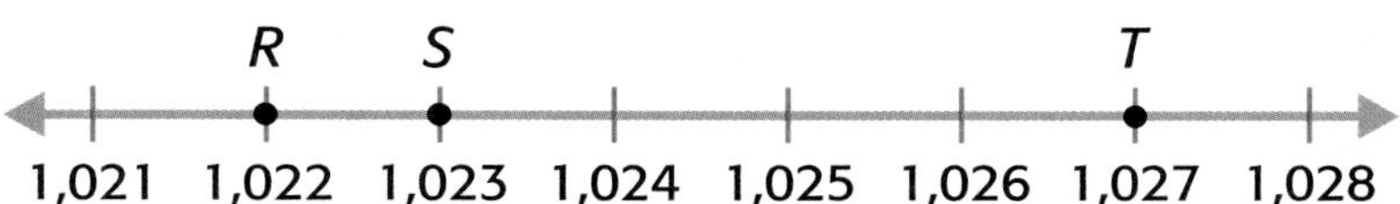

$T = 1{,}027$ So, *T* is 1,027.

EXAMPLE Name Points on a Number Line

2 Name the point *Z* represents on the number line.

Locate *Z* on the number line.

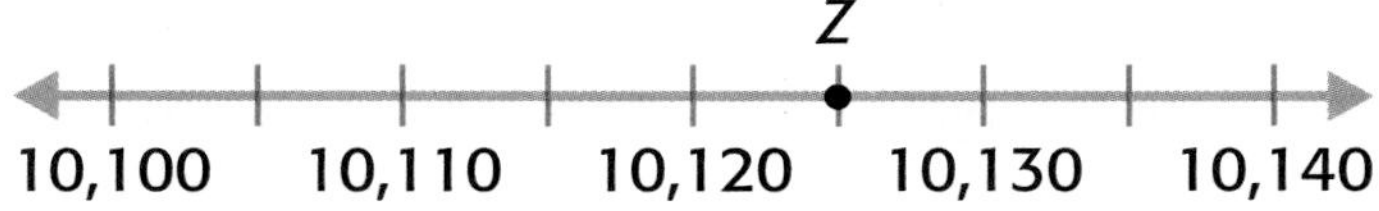

The scale is in intervals of 5. Count by fives to find out what point *Z* represents. So, *Z* is 10,125. $Z = 10{,}125$

EXAMPLE Name Points on a Number Line

3 Write the number *Z* represents on the number line.

Locate *Z* on the number line.

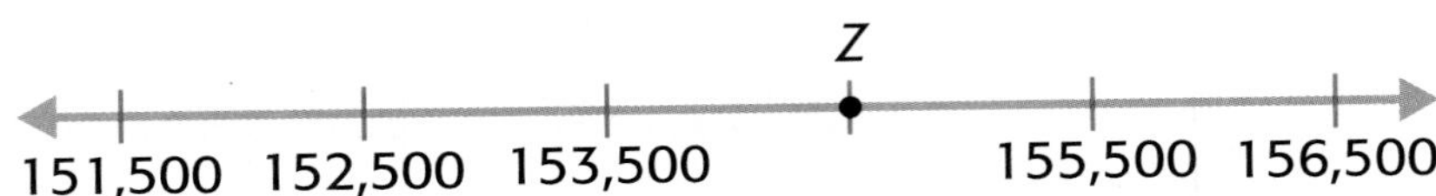

The scale is in intervals of 1,000. Count by thousands to find out what point *Z* represents.

So, *Z* is 154,500. *Z* = 154,500

Online Personal Tutor at tx.gr4math.com

CHECK What You Know

Write the number represented by a letter. See Example 1 (p. 351)

1.

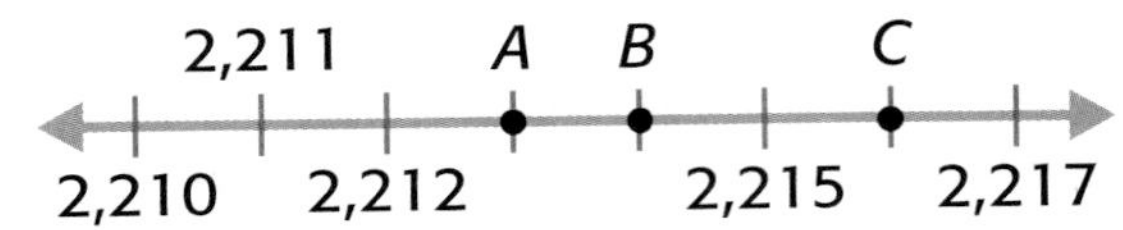

A = *B* =

2.

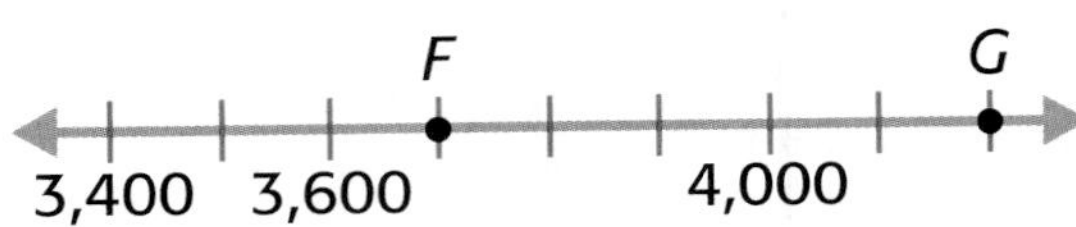

F = *G* =

Write the number *Z* represents on each number line. See Examples 1 and 2 (pp. 351–352)

3.

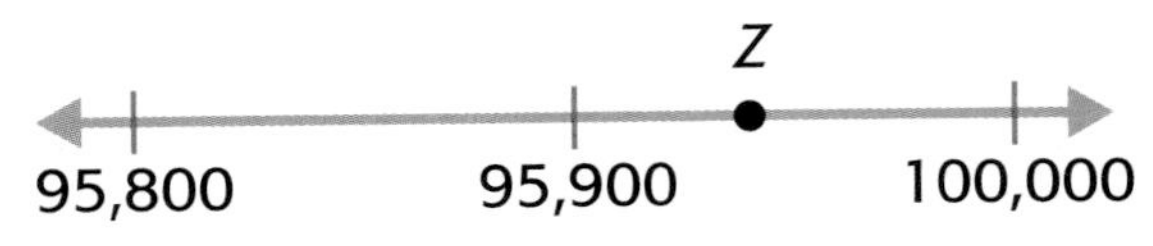

Z =

4.

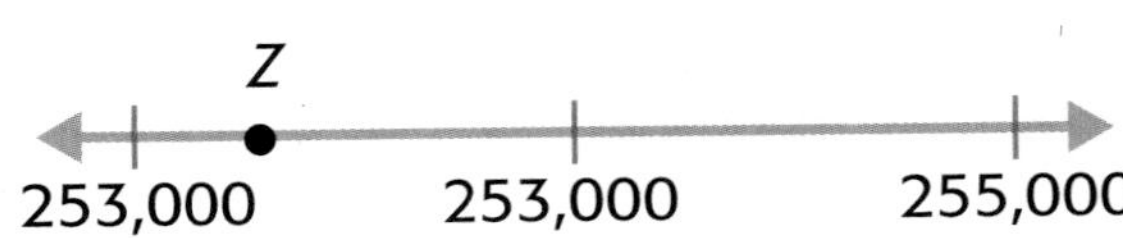

Z =

5. Dani is looking at a timeline. The timeline reads that in 1787 Delaware became the first state in the United States. In 1803, Ohio became the seventeenth state. Forty-two years later, Texas became the twenty-eighth state. Create a number line of what Dani saw. Use intervals of 20 years on your number line.

6. Talk About It Why do most number lines have intervals greater than one?

Practice and Problem Solving

EXTRA PRACTICE See page R28.

Name each point represented by a letter. See Example 1 (p. 351)

7.

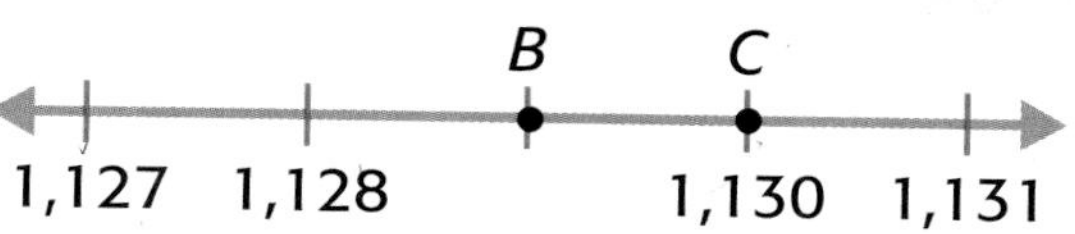

$B =$ $C =$

8.

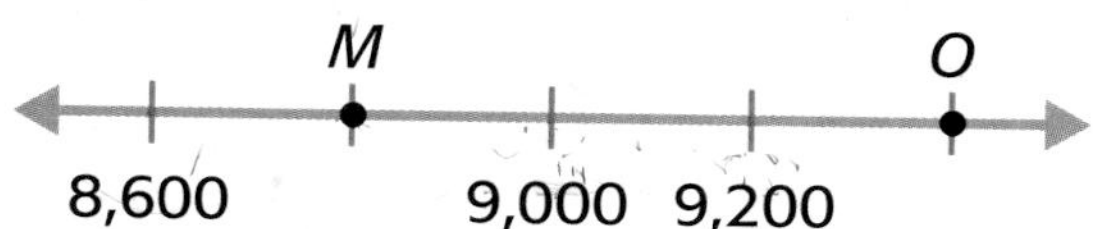

$M =$ $O =$

9.

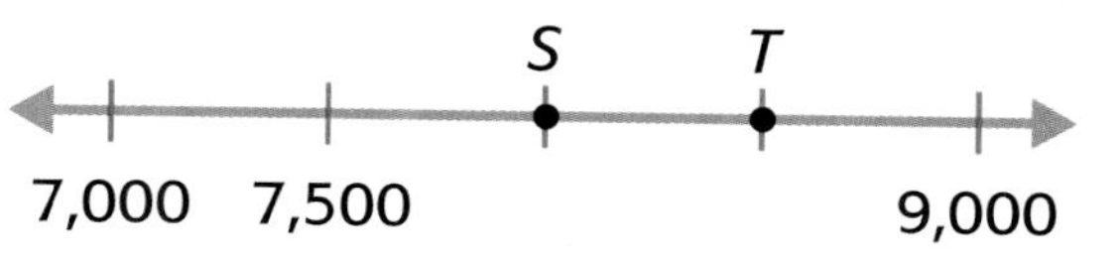

$S =$ $T =$

10.

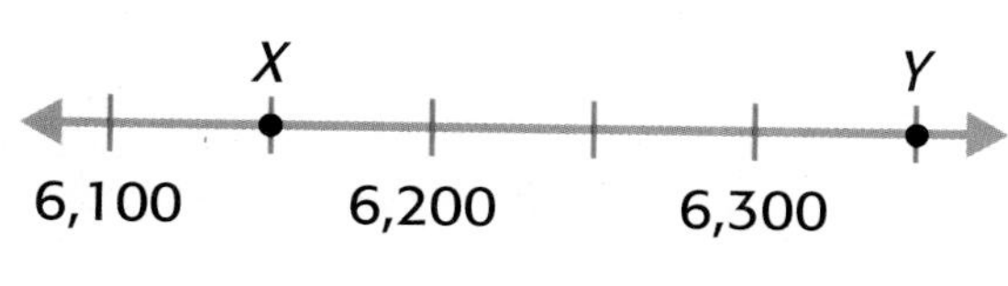

$X =$ $Y =$

Write the point *Z* represents on each number line. See Examples 1 and 2 (p. 351–352)

11.

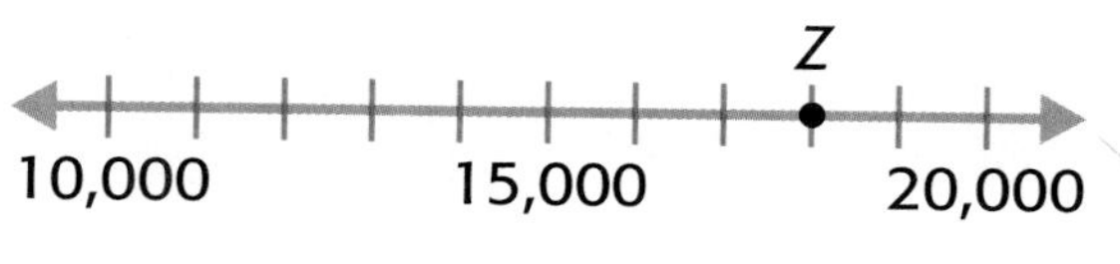

$Z =$

12.

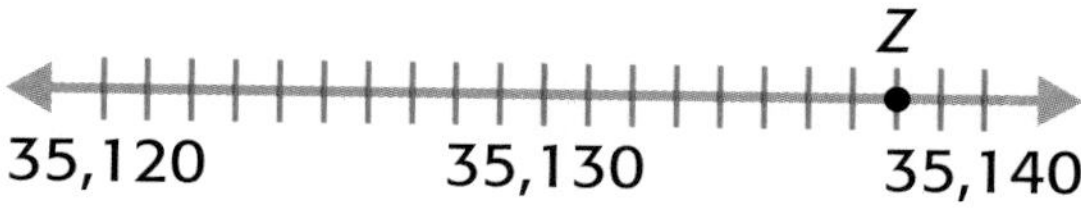

$Z =$

13.

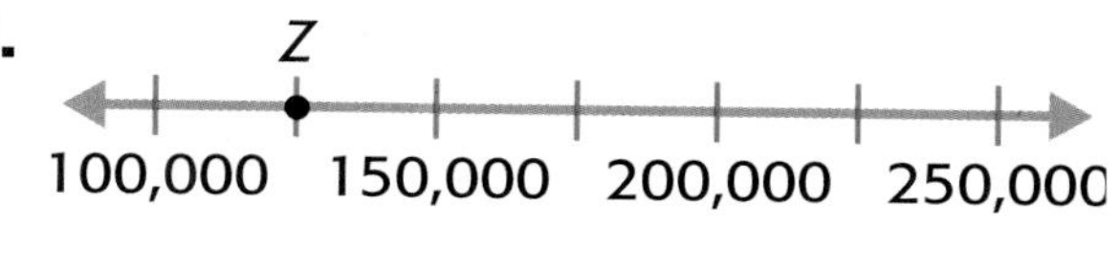

$Z =$

14.

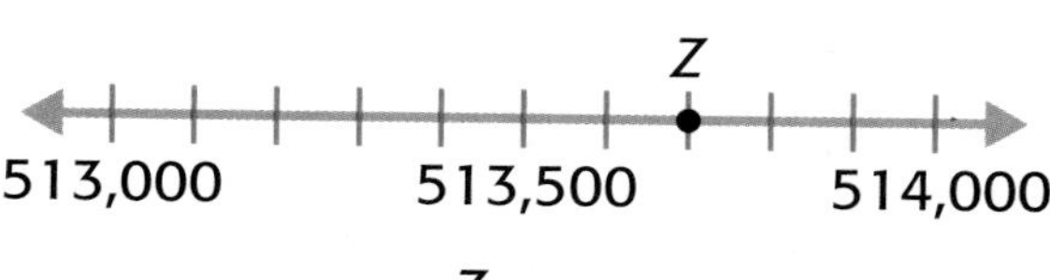

$Z =$

15. A timeline shows that in 1856 Booker T. Washington was born. Then, in 1881 he helped to open the first African-American university. How old was Booker T. Washington when he founded the first African-American university?

16. A number line starts with 30,405 and ends on 30,415. It is marked with intervals of 1. The letter *N* is halfway between 30,405 and 30,415. What is the value for *N*?

H.O.T. Problems

17. OPEN ENDED Create a number line that starts on an even number and has a scale of 5.

18. CHALLENGE Estimate the value of each letter.

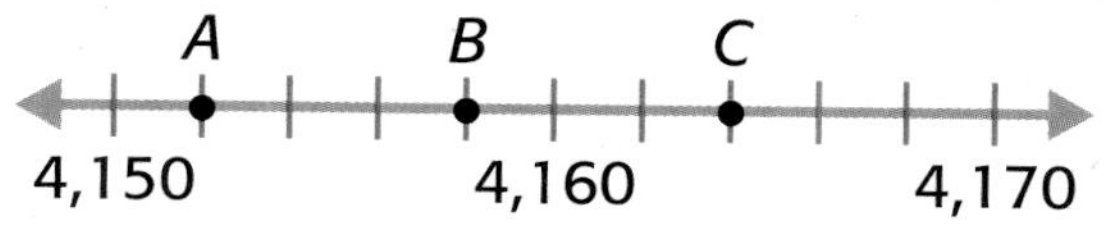

$A =$ $B =$ $C =$

19. WRITING IN ▶MATH Explain how to find points on a number line.

Explore

Math Activity for 9-2

Identify and Describe Parallel and Intersecting Lines

In this activity, you will use pattern blocks to discover parallel and intersecting lines. You will also decide if the intersecting lines are perpendicular.

MAIN IDEA
I will identify and describe parallel and intersecting lines.

 **Targeted TEKS 4.8** The student identifies and describes attributes of geometric figures using formal geometric language. (B) **Identify and describe parallel and intersecting (including perpendicular) lines using concrete and pictorial models.**

You Will Need
pattern blocks
paper and pencil
ruler
index cards

ACTIVITY

1 Discover parallel and intersecting lines.

Step 1 **Observe.**
Take your trapezoid pattern block. Notice that there are four corners. At each corner there is a point of intersection, where two lines cross.

Step 2 **Trace the shape.**
Now take the trapezoid and place it on a piece of paper. Trace around it.

Step 3 **Extend the lines.**
Now take a ruler and carefully extend the lines. Notice how the sides intersect above the trapezoid. The top and bottom lines appear to be parallel. They do not intersect. To make sure they are parallel, take the ruler and measure the distance between the lines in several places. If the distance is the same, they are parallel. In this case, they are.

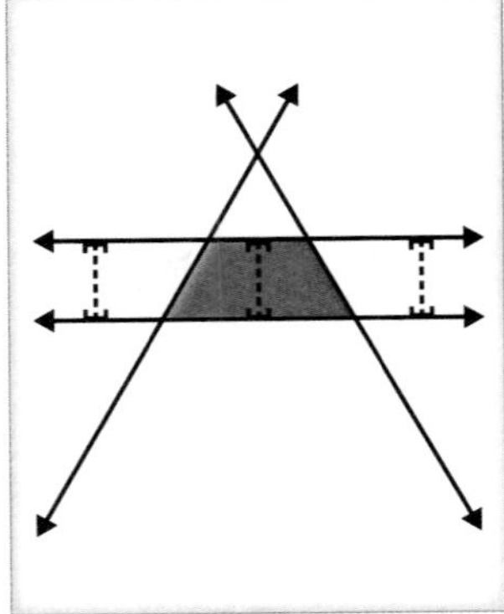

ACTIVITY

2 Model Intersecting Lines

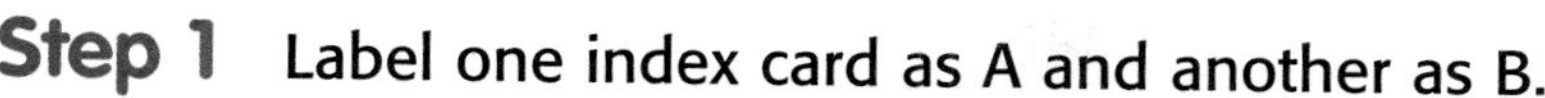

Step 1 Label one index card as A and another as B.

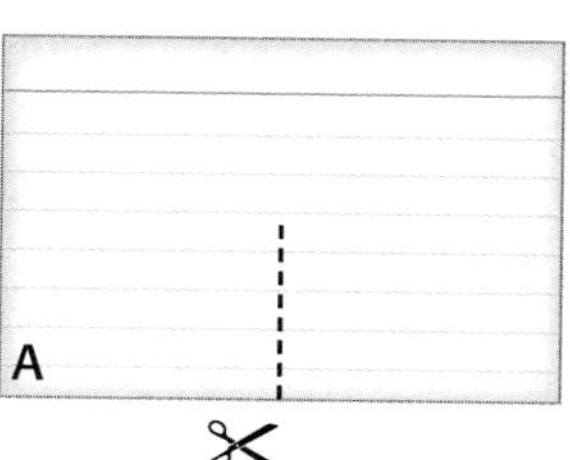

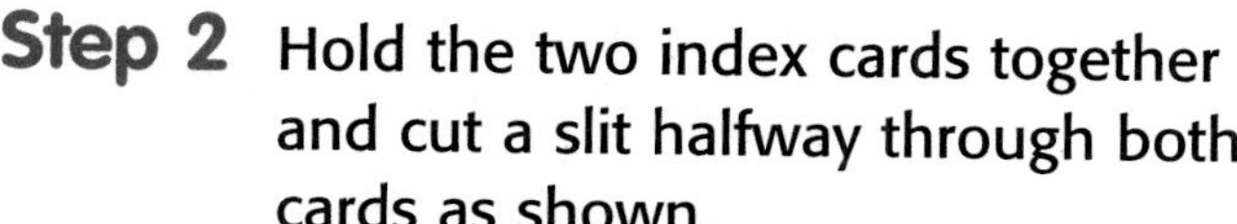

Step 2 Hold the two index cards together and cut a slit halfway through both cards as shown.

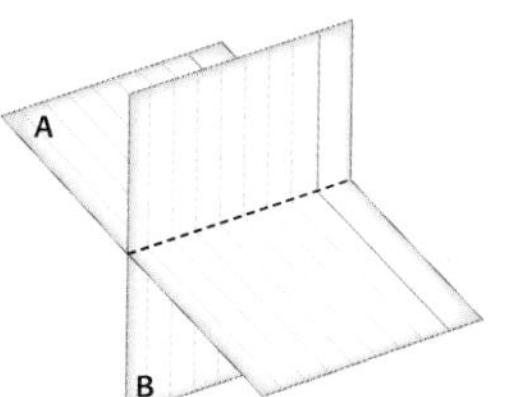

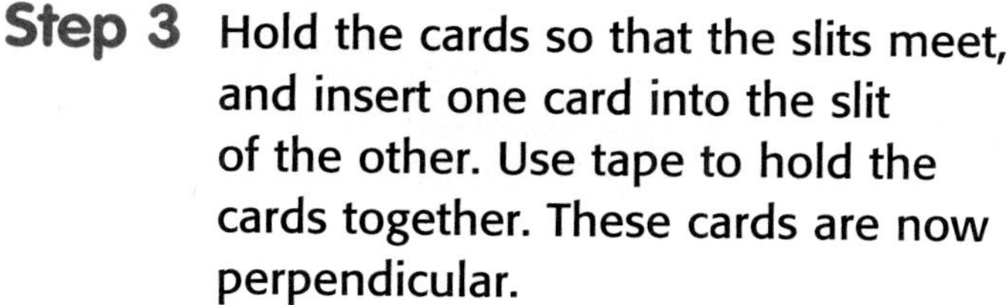

Step 3 Hold the cards so that the slits meet, and insert one card into the slit of the other. Use tape to hold the cards together. These cards are now perpendicular.

Step 4 Use the cards to check objects around the room for perpendicular corners.

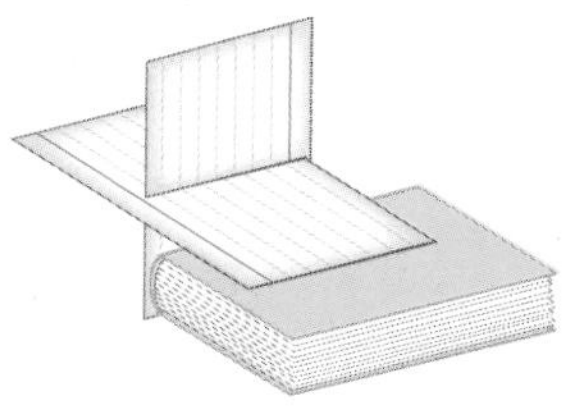

Hands-On Activity

Think About It

1. Are any of the intersecting lines perpendicular on the trapezoid?
2. Name two other shapes that have parallel lines.
3. Name two other shapes that have perpendicular lines of intersection.

CHECK What You Know

Identify and describe lines as *parallel, intersecting,* or *perpendicular.*

4. 

5. 

6. WRITING IN ➤MATH How would you find out if two lines are parallel if you can not tell by extending the lines?

Lines, Line Segments, and Rays

MAIN IDEA

I will identify, describe, and classify lines, line segments, and rays.

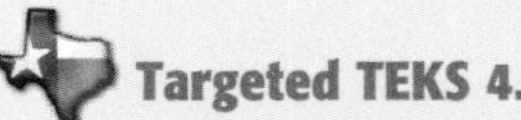

The student identifies and describes attributes of geometric figures using formal geometric language. (B) **Identify and describe parallel and intersecting (including perpendicular) lines using concrete and pictorial models.**

New Vocabulary

line
ray
endpoint
line segment
parallel
intersecting
perpendicular

GET READY to Learn

Farmers often plant crops like corn in rows. The rows resemble line segments.

KEY CONCEPT — Lines, Rays, Segments

Words	Model
A **line** is a straight set of points that extend in opposite directions without ending.	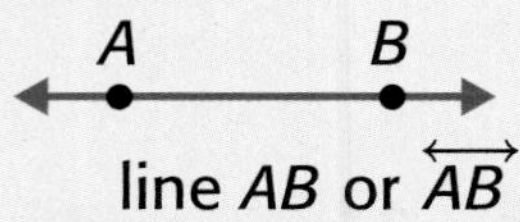 line AB or $\overleftrightarrow{AB}$
A **ray** is a part of a line that has one **endpoint** and extends in one direction without ending.	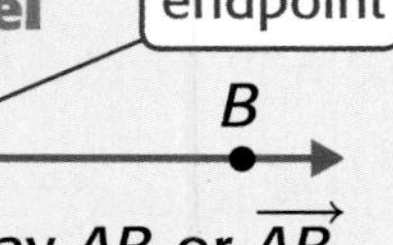 ray AB or $\overrightarrow{AB}$
A **line segment** is a part of a line between two endpoints.	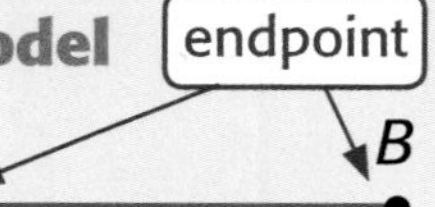

EXAMPLES Identify Lines, Rays, or Line Segments

Identify each figure.

1. 

The figure extends in opposite directions without ending. Line XY or $\overleftrightarrow{XY}$.

2.  

This figure has one endpoint and extends in one direction without ending. Ray AB or $\overrightarrow{AB}$.

Math Online Extra Examples at tx.gr4math.com

You can describe lines, rays, and line segments by the way they meet or cross each other. In the previous Explore Activity, you learned how to identify parallel and intersecting lines.

> **Remember**
>
> The symbol || means parallel. The symbol ⊥ means perpendicular. The symbol ˥ means right angle.

KEY **CONCEPTS** — Types of Lines

Words **Parallel** lines are always the same distance apart. They do not meet.

Model

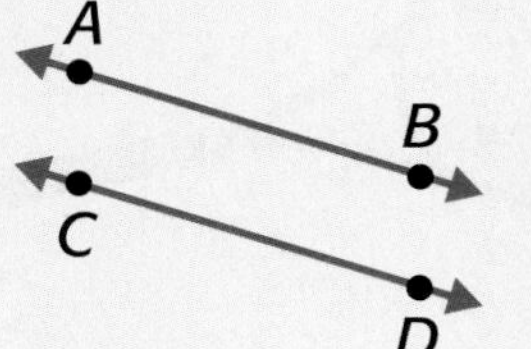

line *AB* is parallel to line *CD*

$\overleftrightarrow{AB} \parallel \overleftrightarrow{CD}$

Words Lines that meet or cross each other are called **intersecting** lines.

Model

line *AB* intersects line *CD*

$\overleftrightarrow{AB}$ intersects $\overleftrightarrow{CD}$

Words Lines that meet or cross each other to form right angles are called **perpendicular** lines.

Model

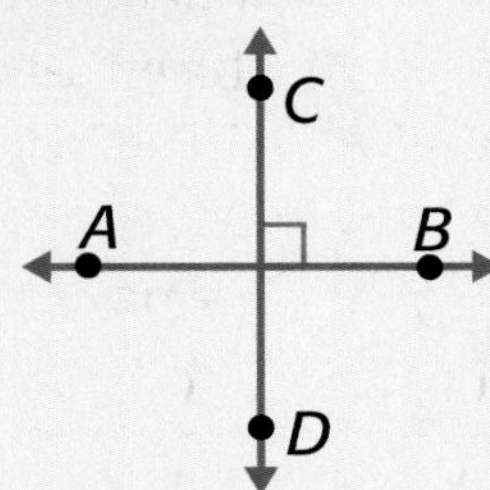

line *AB* is perpendicular to line *CD*

$\overleftrightarrow{AB} \perp \overleftrightarrow{CD}$

EXAMPLE — Describe Lines

3 Describe the figure.

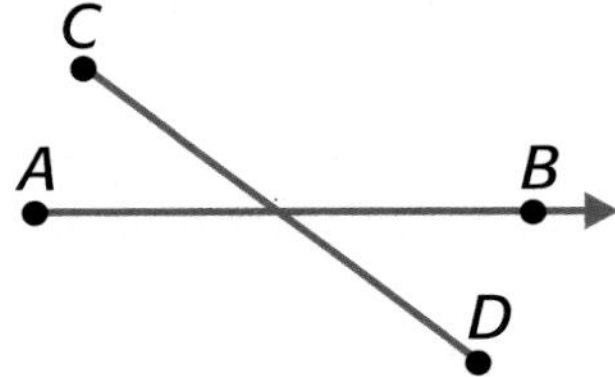

The figure shows ray *AB* and line segment *CD*. Notice that ray *AB* intersects line segment *CD*.

$\overrightarrow{AB}$ intersects $\overline{CD}$.

Online Personal Tutor at tx.gr4math.com

CHECK What You Know

Identify each figure. See Examples 1 and 2 (p. 356)

1. Q R

2.

3. A C

4. Describe the line segments formed on a tennis racquet. See Example 3 (p. 397)

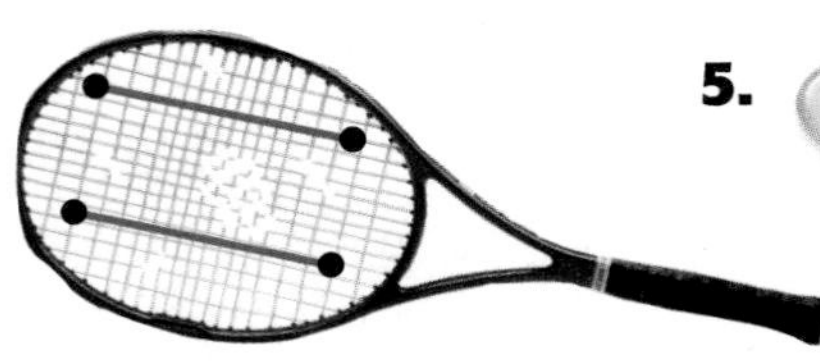

5. Talk About It List a real-world example for a line segment, parallel lines, and intersecting lines.

Practice and Problem Solving

EXTRA PRACTICE See page R28.

Identify each figure. See Examples 1 and 2 (p. 356)

6.

7.

8.

Describe the line segments. See Example 3 (p. 357)

9.

10.

11.

Real-World PROBLEM SOLVING

Geography On a map, streets resemble lines. Use the map to answer Exercises 12–15.

12. Identify two streets that are parallel to Oak Street.

13. Tell whether Center Street and Johnston Street are parallel, intersecting, or perpendicular lines. Explain.

14. Identify two streets that are parallel.

15. Are there any streets that are intersecting? Explain.

Pine St
Stephenson St
School St
Queen St
Johnston St
Oak St
Oak St
Church St
Center St
Main St

H.O.T. Problems

OPEN ENDED Draw an example of each figure described.

16. ray CD

17. $\overleftrightarrow{DE} \parallel \overleftrightarrow{FG}$

18. $\overline{RS}$ intersecting $\overline{TU}$

REASONING Tell whether each statement is *true* or *false*.

19. If two lines are parallel, they are the same distance apart.

20. If two lines are parallel, they are also perpendicular.

21. **WRITING IN MATH** Can you draw two lines on a sheet of paper that are both parallel and perpendicular? Explain.

TEST Practice

22. What number on the number line does point B best represent? (Lesson 9-2)

A 900

B 950

C 970

D 1,000

23. Which figure shows parallel lines? (Lesson 9-4)

F

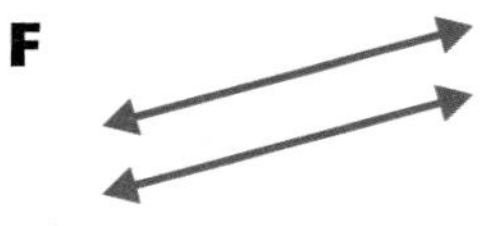

H

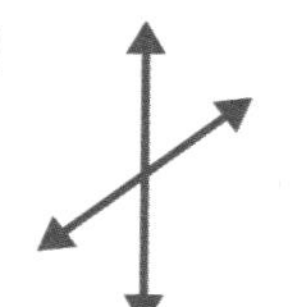

G

J

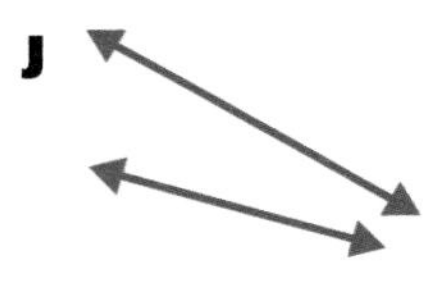

Spiral Review

For Exercises 24 and 25, use the table. (Lesson 8-3)

24. Mr. Ito's class is playing a game. The table shows how many playing pieces are needed. Copy and complete the table.

25. Explain how to find the number of pieces needed if you know the number of students playing.

Game Pieces Needed

Students	Number of Pieces
4	36
7	63
■	72
9	■
10	90

Identify each polygon. (Lesson 8-2)

26.

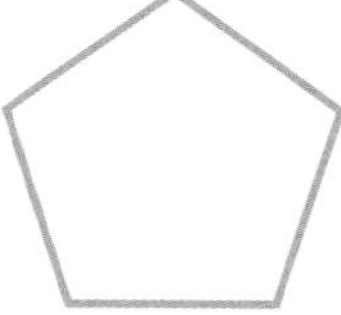

27.

28.

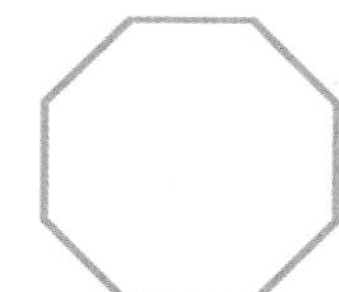

9-3 Problem-Solving Strategy

MAIN IDEA I will make an organized list to solve problems.

Targeted TEKS 4.14 The student applies Grade 4 mathematics to solve problems connected to everyday experiences and activities in and outside of school. **(C)** **Select or develop appropriate problem-solving plan or stategy, . . . to solve a problem.** *Also addresses TEKS 4.14(B).*

The Burke family is going camping for the weekend. There are four children in the Burke family, Devon, Nikki, Jade, and Terrell. They will sleep in two tents, with two children in each tent. How many different combinations are possible?

Understand	**What facts do you know?** • There are 4 children going camping. • Two children will sleep in each tent. **What do you need to find?** • Find how many combinations are possible.
Plan	You can make a list of all the possible combinations. Then count the total number of different combinations.
Solve	First, write the name of one of the children. Then, write the name of another child by the first child's name. Continue to do this with each child. Do not repeat pairs. **Nikki—Jade** **Jade—Terrell** **Terrell—Devon** **Nikki—Terrell** **Jade—Devon** **Nikki—Devon** There are 6 different combinations that can be in each tent.
Check	Look back at the problem. There are 4 children. They can each pair up with three other children. Each child's name does appear 3 times on the list. So, the answer is correct.

ANALYZE the Strategy

Refer to the problem on the previous page.

1. Suppose one of the children brings a friend camping. How does the additional child affect the possible combinations?

2. Identify another way to organize all of the possible outcomes.

3. Suppose Nikki, Jade, and Terrell go for a hike in a single file line. Make a list to show all the possible ways they can line up.

4. What is the probability that Nikki will be first in line if the children line up in random order?

PRACTICE the Strategy

EXTRA PRACTICE
See page R29.

Solve. *Make an organized list.*

5. Richard has one blue shirt and one red shirt. He has gray pants and navy pants. How many different outfits can he wear?

6. Sadie put four slips of paper into a hat. Each slip of paper has a number written on it as shown. Sadie chooses two slips of paper. How many different sums could she have?

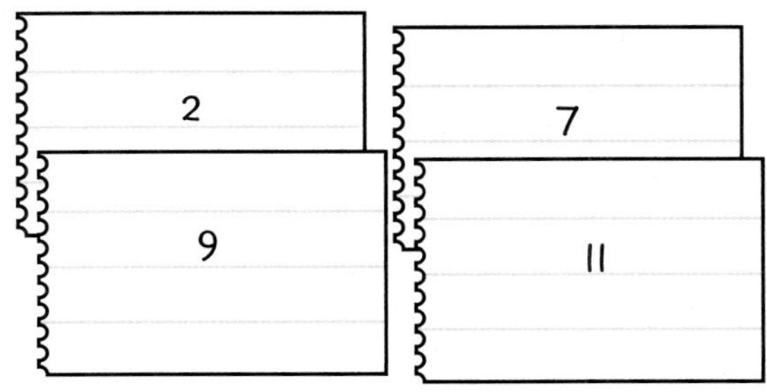

7. Yogi's mom is hanging three photographs side-by-side on a wall. How many different ways can the photographs be arranged?

8. Pari, Montana, Katie, and Leon are in line for lunch. Montana is first. How many ways could the other people be arranged behind her?

9. Jimmy put the coins shown into a piggy bank. If he chooses 2 coins at a time, what possible combinations might he choose?

10. Sandra has three animal-shaped pillows. One is a dog, another is a cat, and the third is a fish. How many different ways can she arrange her pillows?

11. Alexa needs to read a mystery, biography, or fantasy book. Then she must write a report, give a speech, or act out a scene from the book. How many different options are there?

12. **WRITING IN ►MATH** Look back at Exercise 11. Explain how you used the *make an organized list* strategy to solve the problem.

9-4 Find Points on a Grid

MAIN IDEA

I will use ordered pairs to find and name points on a grid.

Preparation for Grade 5 TEKS 5.9 The student recognizes the connection between ordered pairs of numbers and locations of points on a plane. **The student is expected to locate and name points on a coordinate grid using ordered pairs of whole numbers.**

New Vocabulary

coordinate plane
origin
***x*-axis**
***y*-axis**
ordered pair
coordinates

Vocabulary Link

The prefix *quad-* means *four.*

GET READY to Learn

The map gives the locations of several students' homes and their school. From the school, Dave lives 5 units right and 3 units up. This can be written as (5, 3).

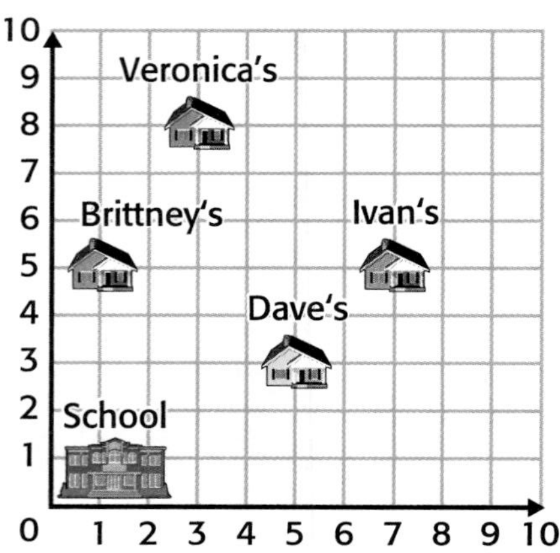

The map shown above is an example of a coordinate plane. A **coordinate plane** is formed when two number lines intersect at their zero points.

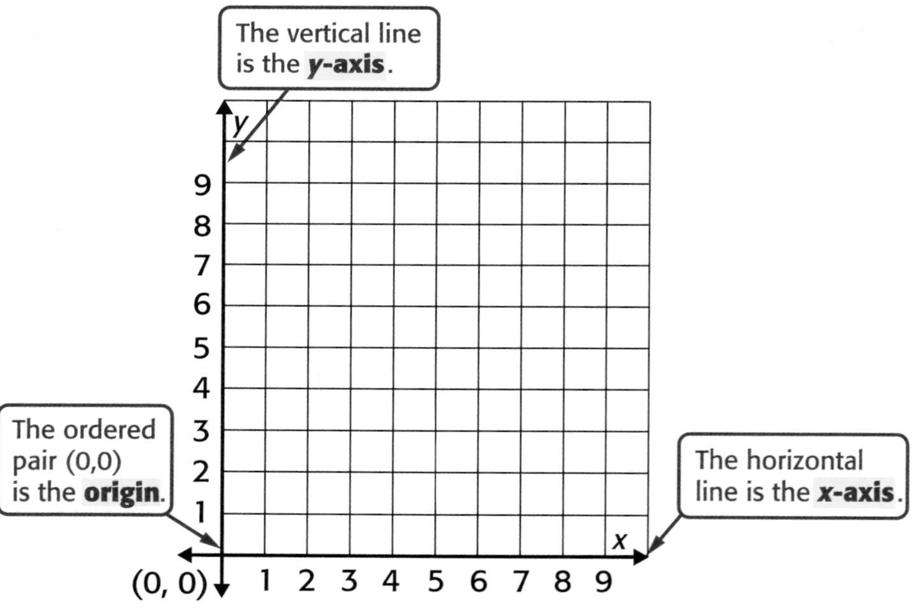

The point (5, 3) is an example of an **ordered pair**. The numbers in an ordered pair are called **coordinates**. The coordinates give the location of the point.

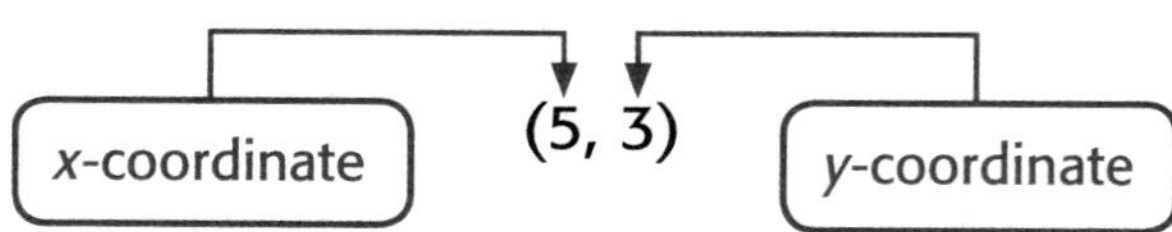

Find Ordered Pairs

1 A map of a zoo is shown. Identify the animal that is located at (5, 4).

To find (5, 4), start at (0, 0). Move right 5 units. Then, move up 4 units. The ordered pair (5, 4) locates the lions.

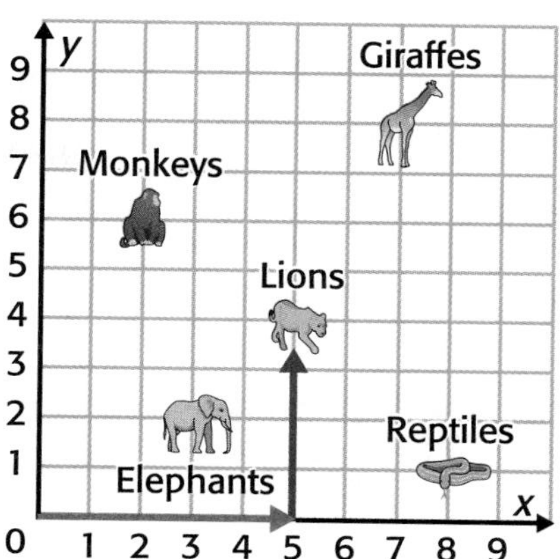

Online **Personal Tutor at** tx.gr4math.com

CHECK What You Know

Identify the building that is located at each ordered pair. See Example 1 (p. 363)

1. (6, 8) **2.** (3, 7)

3. (2, 4) **4.** (8, 6)

Identify the ordered pair for each building.
See Example 1 (p. 363)

5. Grocery Store **6.** Hospital

7. Bus Station **8.** Town Hall

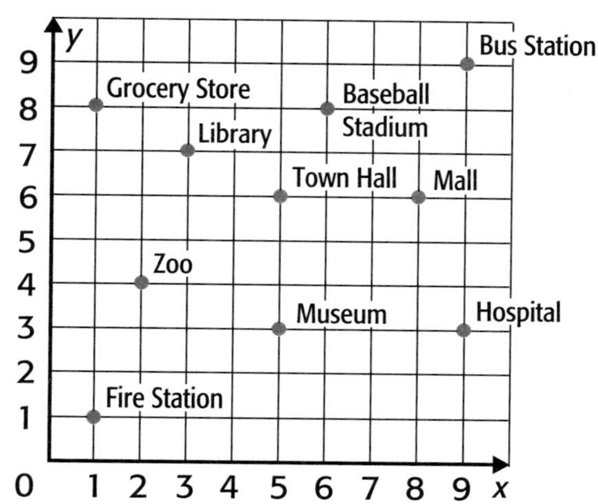

On the grid above, describe how to get from one place to another.

9. Library to the Grocery Store

10. Zoo to the Museum

11. Fabio is at the bus station. He needs to go to the town hall. How does he get there on the grid?

12. Jill is at the museum. She lives near the library. How will she get there on the grid?

13. Talk About It How does an ordered pair name a location?

Practice and Problem Solving

Identify the object that is located at each ordered pair. See Example 1 (p. 363)

14. (9, 6) **15.** (2, 8)

16. (5, 1) **17.** (1, 2)

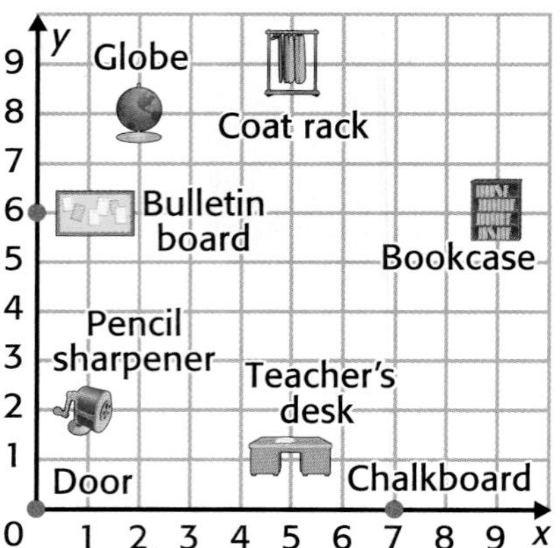

Identify the ordered pair for each object.
See Example 1 (p. 363)

18. Coat Rack **19.** Bulletin board

20. Door **21.** Chalkboard

22. Describe how to move from the ordered pair for pencil sharpener to coat rack.

Real-World PROBLEM SOLVING

Data File Map makers use latitude and longitude lines to find locations. These lines form a coordinate grid.

23. What city can be found near 29°N and 98°W?

24. What latitude and longitude lines are near Austin?

25. Name two other cities on this map and their lines of latitude and longitude.

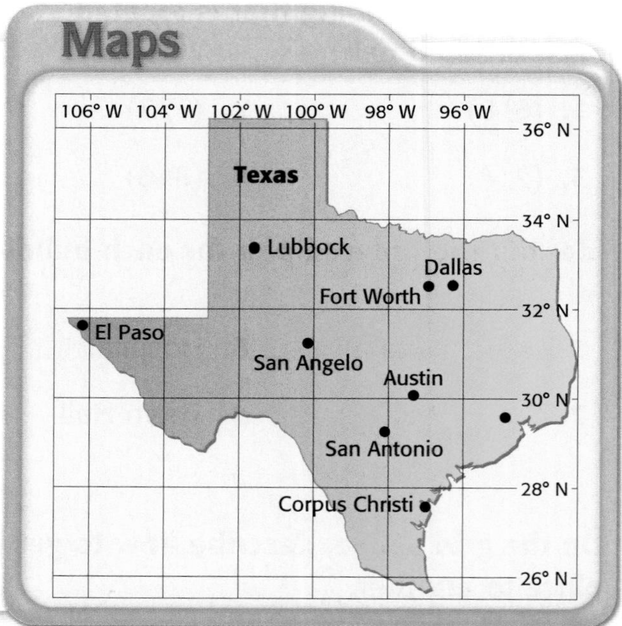

H.O.T. Problems

26. **OPEN ENDED** Draw a picture of your classroom on grid paper. Draw the location of your desk on the grid. What is the ordered pair for your location?

27. **WRITING IN MATH** How is the location of (2, 4) different from the location of (4, 2)? Explain.

Mid-Chapter Check

CHAPTER 9

Lessons 9-1 through 9-4

Write the number represented by each letter. (Lesson 9-1)

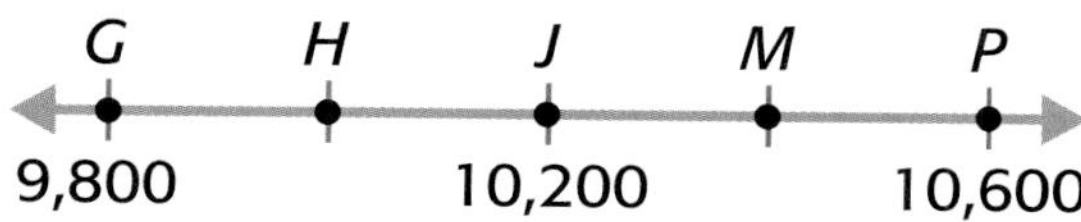

1. *H*

2. *M*

3. **TEST PRACTICE** Which number does point *K* represent? (Lesson 9-1)

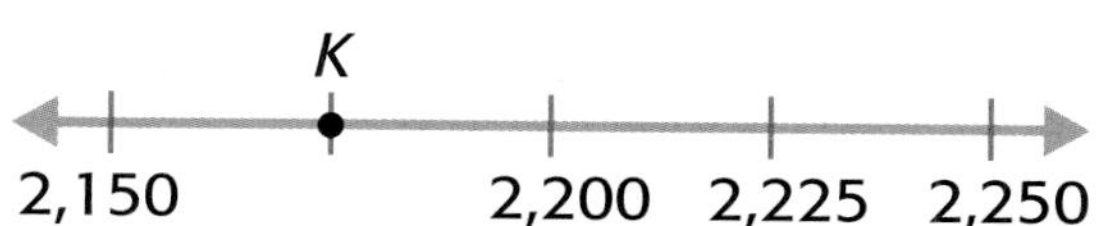

A 2,075

B 2,125

C 2,155

D 2,175

4. Describe the line segments formed by the top of the step stool. (Lesson 9-2)

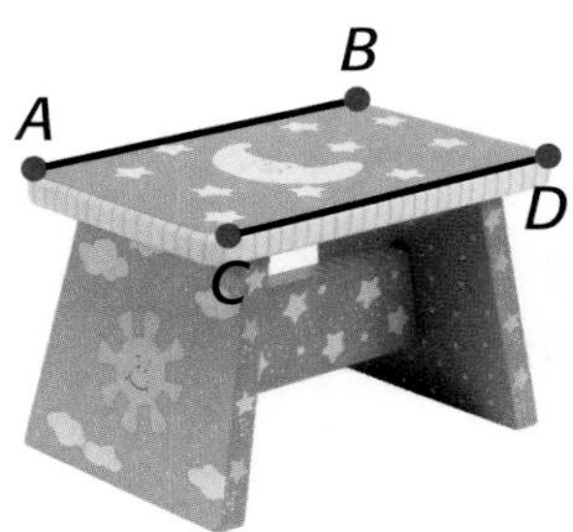

Identify each figure. (Lesson 9-2)

5.

6. *C* *D*

7. Serena has one red shirt and one white shirt. She has one blue skirt and one black skirt. How many different shirt-skirt outfits can she wear? (Lesson 9-3)

8. **TEST PRACTICE** Which ordered pair is graphed? (Lesson 9-4)

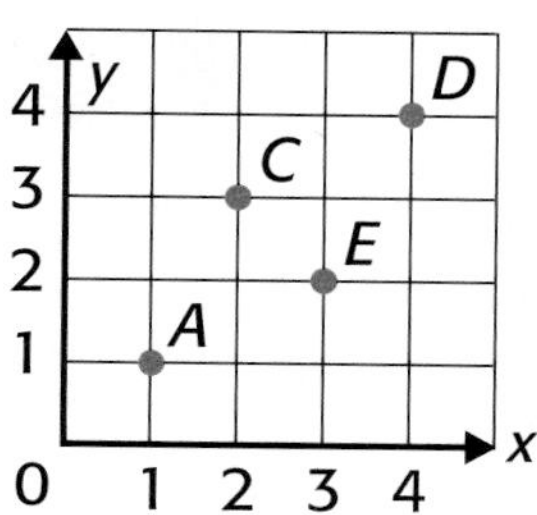

F (3, 4)

G (2, 3)

H (3, 1)

J (5, 2)

Identify the letter located at each point. (Lesson 9-4)

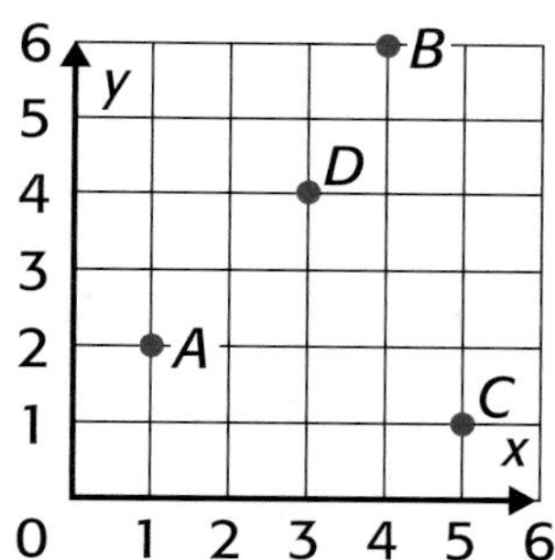

9. (1, 2)

10. (4, 6)

11. (3, 4)

12. (5, 1)

13. **WRITING IN MATH** Do the ordered pairs (2, 3) and (3, 2) give the location of the same point? Explain.

Geometry Activity for Lesson 9-5

Rotations, Reflections, and Translations

MAIN IDEA

I will demonstrate rotations, reflections, and translations using concrete models.

The student connects transformations to congruence and symmetry.
(A) **Demonstrate translations, reflections, and rotations using concrete models.**

You Will Need
pattern blocks

New Vocabulary

transform
rotation
reflection
translation

You can **transform** shapes by using rotations, reflections, and translations.

ACTIVITY

1 Demonstrate Rotations, Reflections, and Translations

Step 1 **Trace a figure.**

Trace a square pattern block onto a piece of paper.

Step 2 **Rotate (turn) a figure.**

Take the figure and turn or rotate it $\frac{1}{2}$ a turn.

Then trace it again.

This is called a **rotation**.

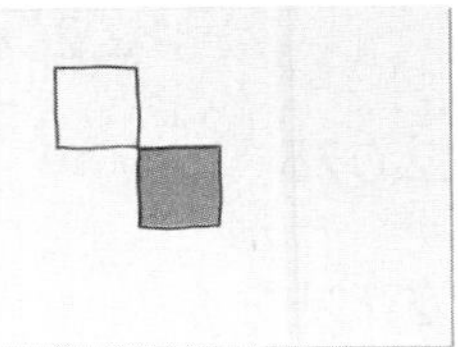

Step 3 **Show a reflection (flip).**

Now take the paper and trace the square again, making a mirror image of what you have already drawn. This is called a **reflection**.

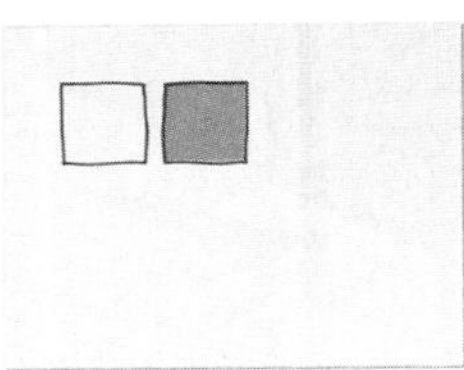

Step 4 **Show a translation (slide).**

Use the same square and trace around it again. Now move the square to the right (horizontally) and draw it again. Remember, do not turn it. This is called a **translation**.

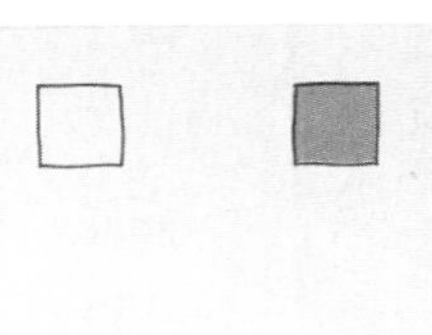

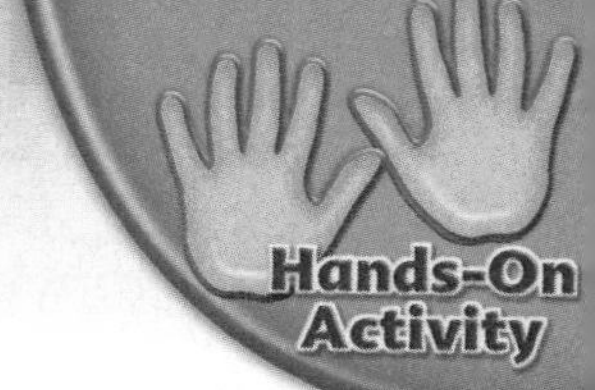

Think About It

1. What did you do to the square to demonstrate a rotation?

2. What is the difference between a rotation and a reflection?

3. Name two shapes that will look exactly the same after being reflected.

4. Describe the transformation made by figure *A* to the location of figure *B*.

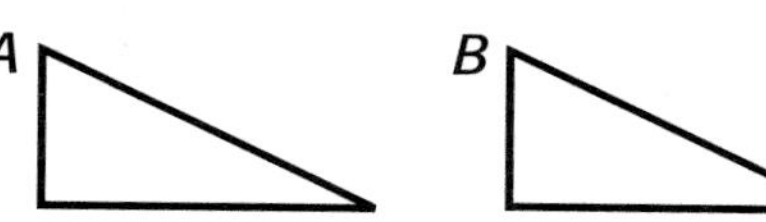

CHECK What You Know

Use each shape to demonstrate and draw the given transformation.

5. rotation

6. translation

7. reflection

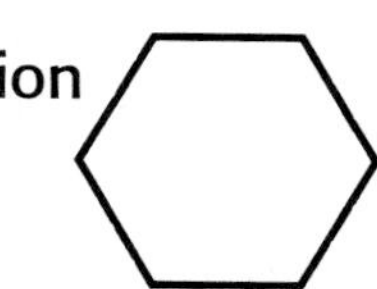

8. rotation

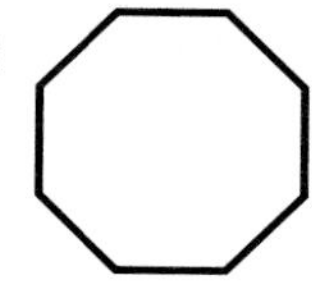

9. reflection

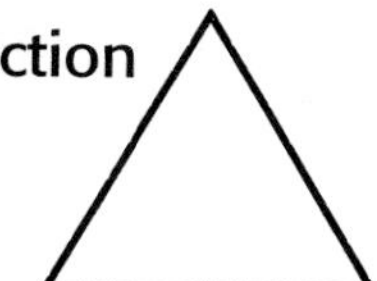

10. translation

11. Choose 3 objects from your classroom. Demonstrate each transformation. Copy and complete the table with a partner.

Object	Transformation
Crayon	Rotation
	Reflection
	Translation

12. **WRITING IN ▸MATH** In your own words, define the terms *rotation, reflection,* and *translation.*

Rotations, Reflections, and Translations

GET READY to Learn

In this picture the square has been moved. Demonstrate the movement of the square. What type of movement is shown?

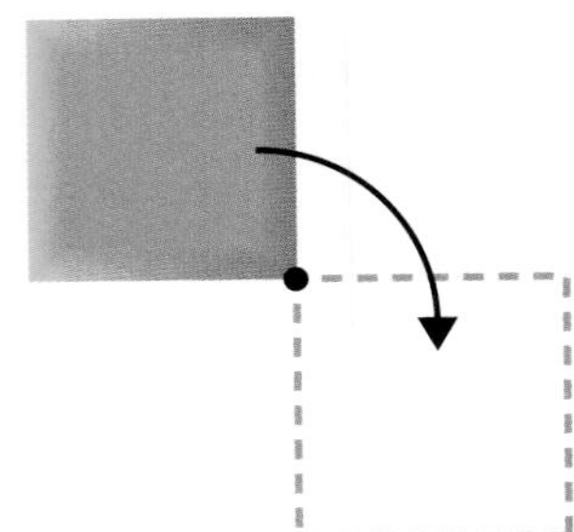

MAIN IDEA

I will demonstrate rotations, reflections, and translations using concrete models.

Targeted TEKS 4.9 The student connects transformations to congruence and symmetry. (A) **Demonstrate translations, reflections, and rotations using concrete models.**

New Vocabulary

rotation
reflection
translation
transformation

In this picture, the square was moved or transformed. When a geometric figure changes location, it has gone through a **transformation**. Three types of transformations are **rotation**, **reflection**, and **translation**.

EXAMPLE Demonstrate and Identify Transformations

1 **Demonstrate and identify the transformation that is shown in the square above.**

Take a square. Then notice where the square started.

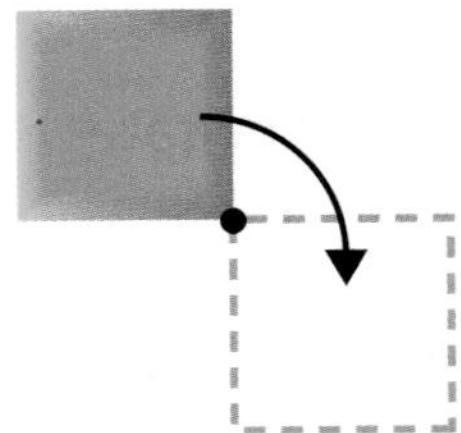

Move the square. Look at where the square ended up.

The one corner has not moved. It stayed on the same point.

So, this is an example of rotation.

KEY CONCEPT

rotation	reflection	translation
	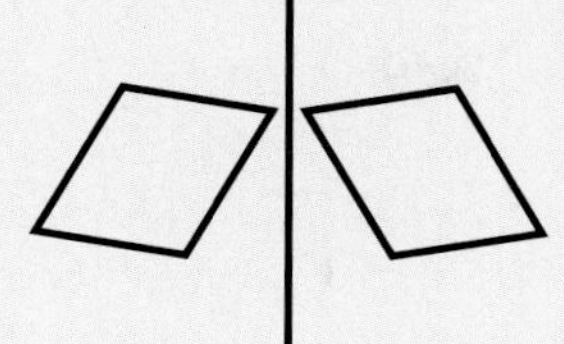	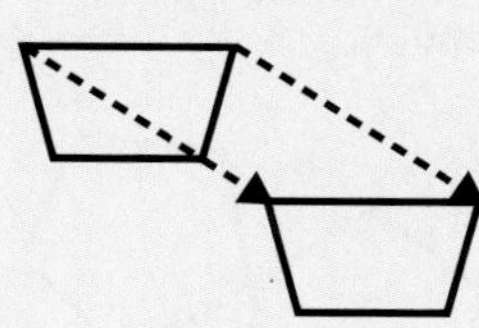
A rotation is a transformation in which a figure is rotated or turned around a point.	A reflection is a transformation that flips a figure across a line to make a mirror image of that figure.	A translation is moving a figure in a vertical, horizontal, or diagonal direction.

Real-World EXAMPLE Identify Reflections

2 **CLOTHING The T-shirt has a design of geometric shapes in a pattern. Identify the transformation of the shapes that has created this pattern.**

Notice the geometric shapes on the T-shirt.

If we fold the shirt down the middle we see that the shapes are the same just mirror images.

So, this shirt is an example of reflections.

Personal Tutor at tx.gr4math.com

EXAMPLE Identify Translations

3 **Identify the transformation. Write *rotation, reflection,* or *translation.***

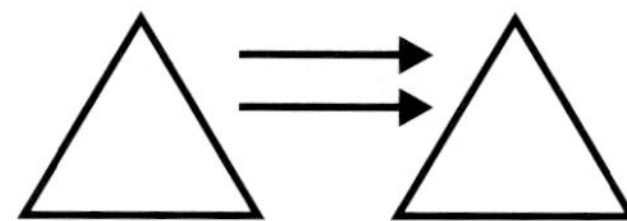

The triangle above has moved sideways. It has not turned or flipped.

So, the transformation of the triangle is a translation.

CHECK What You Know

Identify each transformation. Write *rotation, reflection,* or *translation*.

See Examples 1–3 (pp. 368–369)

1. 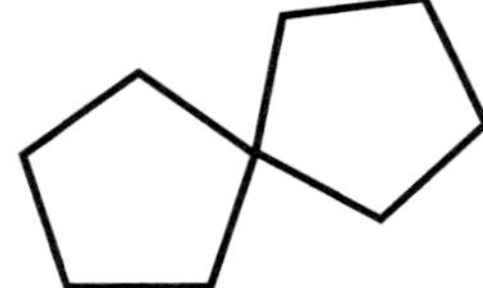

2. 

3. Miguel is designing a mosaic picture of a tree. He is using geometric shapes to create the picture. What two transformations is his mosaic an example of?

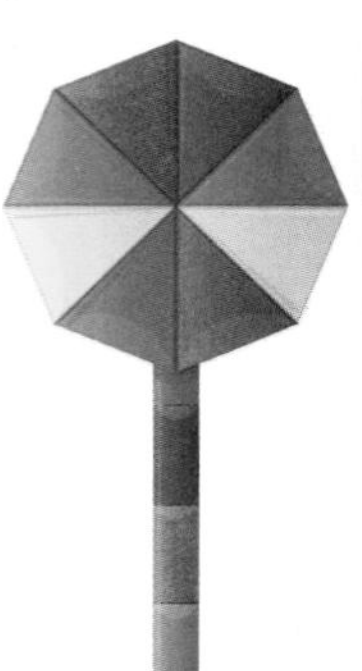

4. Talk About It The stars on the United States flag show what kind of transformation? Explain your answer.

Practice and Problem Solving

EXTRA PRACTICE See page R30.

Identify each transformation. Write *rotation, reflection,* or *translation*.

See Examples 1–3 (pp. 368–369)

5. 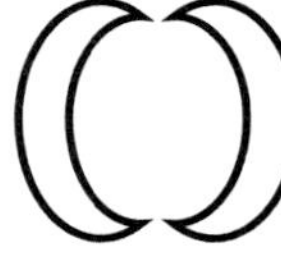

6. 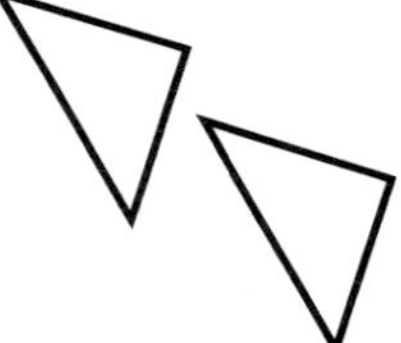

7. 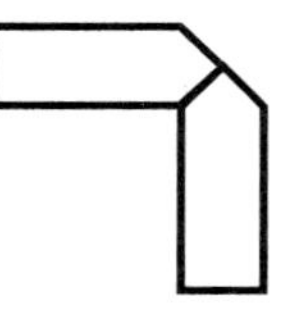

8. 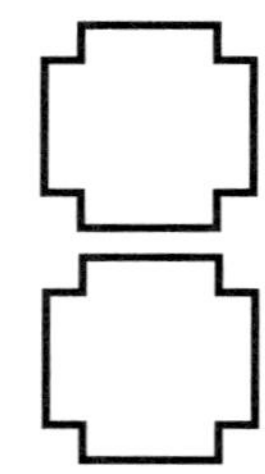

Using pattern blocks, demonstrate the following transformations by tracing.

9. translation

10. rotation

11. reflection

12. Draw a checkerboard. Show how it is an example of each transformation.

13. Eliza and José drew the picture to the right on the sidewalk with chalk. What transformations can be seen in the picture?

H.O.T. Problems

14. OPEN ENDED Draw a picture. Then draw the picture again using a transformation. Explain what transformation you demonstrated.

15. WRITING IN ▶MATH Describe how a translation can also be a reflection.

TEST Practice

16. Which of the following describes where point *J* is located? **(Lesson 9-2)**

A (1, 5)

B (2, 7)

C (5, 8)

D (8, 5)

17. Which pair of figures does **NOT** show a rotation? **(Lesson 9-5)**

F

H

G

J

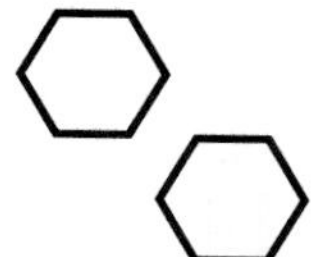

Spiral Review

Identify the place that is located at each ordered pair. **(Lesson 9-4)**

18. (5, 8)

19. (8, 3)

20. (3, 2)

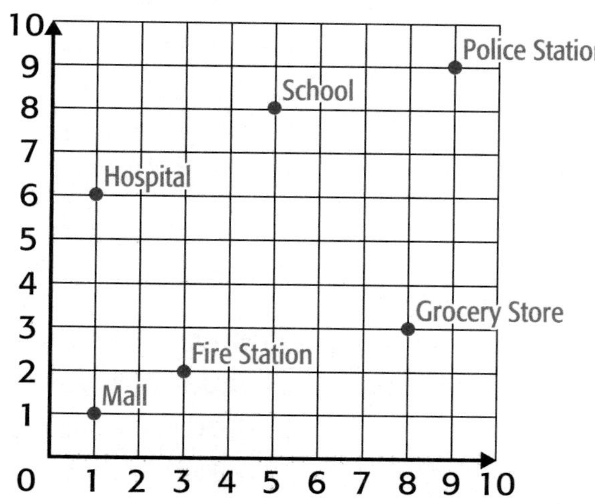

Identify the ordered pair for each building.

21. Hospital

22. Police Station

23. Mall

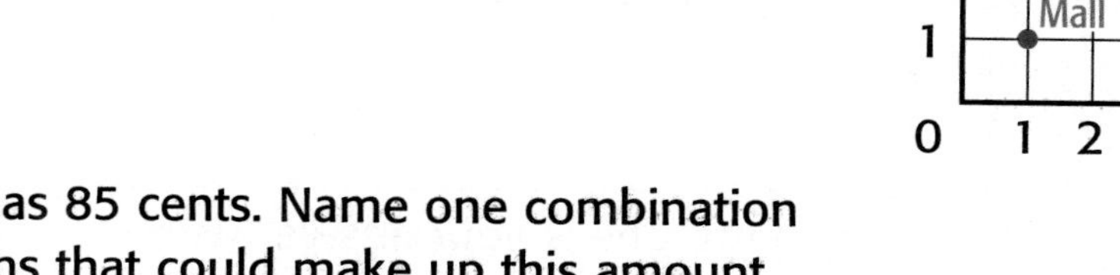

24. Dan has 85 cents. Name one combination of coins that could make up this amount.

25. Sarah purchased 5 items. If each item was the same price and she spent $45, how much did each item cost?

Problem-Solving Investigation

MAIN IDEA I will choose the best strategy to solve a problem.

Targeted TEKS 4.14 The student applies Grade 4 mathematics to solve problems connected to everyday experiences and activities in and outside of school. **(B) Solve problems that incorporate understanding the problem, making a plan, and evaluating the solution for reasonableness.** *Also addresses TEKS 4.14(C).*

P.S.I. TEAM +

CARMEN: My family ate at a restaurant. We ordered salads for $6 each, steaks for $15 each, and sandwiches for $8 each. The total cost was $43.

YOUR MISSION: Find how many of each item was ordered.

You know the cost of each item and the total cost of the meal. Find how many of each item was ordered.

Use logical reasoning to solve the problem.

Solve

At least one of each item was ordered. Add the costs.

$$\begin{array}{rl} \$15 & \text{1 steak} \\ \$\ 6 & \text{1 salad} \\ +\ \$\ 8 & \text{1 sandwich} \\ \hline \$29 & \end{array}$$

So, the cost of the other items ordered must be $43 − $29, or $14.

Since $8 + $6 is the only combination of costs that equal $14, you know that another salad and another sandwich were ordered.

So, they ordered 1 steak, 2 salads, and 2 sandwiches.

Check

Look back at the problem. Check your answer with addition.
$6 + $6 + $8 + $8 + $15 = $43
So, the answer is correct.

Mixed Problem Solving

See page R30.

Use any strategy shown below to solve. Tell what strategy you used.

PROBLEM-SOLVING STRATEGIES

- Use logical reasoning.
- Make a model.
- Make an organized list.
- Draw a picture.
- Work backward.

1. There are 6 wagons for the fall hayride. Each wagon needs 4 horses to pull it. How many horses will it take to pull all 6 wagons?

2. There are four boys and six girls in line at a movie theater. Each is carrying two food items purchased at the concession stand. How many food items do they have in all?

3. Curtis bought the meal shown below. He paid with a $20 bill and his change was $13. If the fruit juice cost $1, how much did each taco cost?

4. Macie made 70 bracelets in 3 colors. She made 22 red bracelets and 18 blue bracelets. How many bracelets were yellow?

5. Carol, Irina, Yori, and Nora are on a relay team. The fastest girl will run last. The slowest girl will run second. Irina runs faster than Carol. Nora runs first. Irina runs slower than Yori. In what order does the team run?

6. Julie sold roses at a bike club fundraiser. Use the pattern in the table below to find how many roses she had left on Friday.

Day	Started with	Ended with
Monday	96	48
Tuesday	48	24
Wednesday	24	12
Thursday	12	6
Friday	6	■

7. Amós's baseball team needs $2,500 to pay for camp. They raised $310 in April and $477 in May. They already had $1,203 saved. How much do they still need to pay for camp?

8. **Measurement** An object on Earth weighs 6 times its weight on the moon. An astronaut weighs 210 pounds on Earth. How much would he or she weigh on the moon?

9. **WRITING IN MATH** There are three rock, five country, and two oldies CDs in Mrs. Link's car. The answer is $\frac{5}{10}$. What is the question?

9-7 Congruent Figures

GET READY to Learn

Hands-On Mini Activity

Materials geomirror and pattern blocks

Step 1 Place a geomirror and a hexagon pattern block onto a sheet of paper.

Step 2 Look into the geomirror from the left side. Trace the figure you see onto the right side.

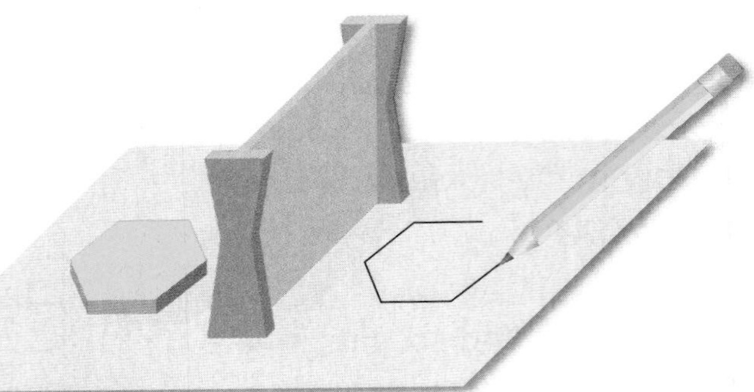

Step 3 Remove the mirror.

1. Is the figure you drew a translation, rotation, or reflection?

2. What do you notice about the size and shape of each pair of figures?

MAIN IDEA

I will identify congruent figures.

Targeted TEKS 4.9 The student connects transformations to congruence and symmetry. (B) **Use translations, reflections, and rotations to verify that two shapes are congruent.** *Also addresses TEKS 4.14(A).*

New Vocabulary

congruent

When figures have the same size and shape, they are **congruent**.

EXAMPLES Identify Congruent Figures

Concepts in Motion

Animation
tx.gr4math.com

Tell whether the figures appear to be congruent. Write *yes* or *no*. If they are, describe the movements that show their congruence.

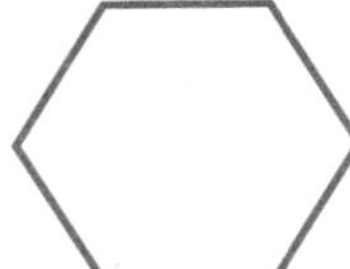

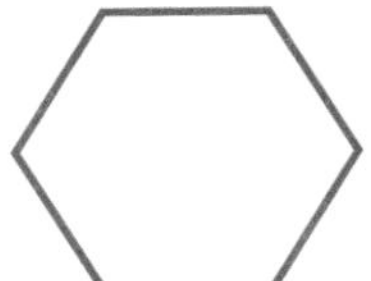

The hexagons appear to have the same size and shape. So, they are congruent.

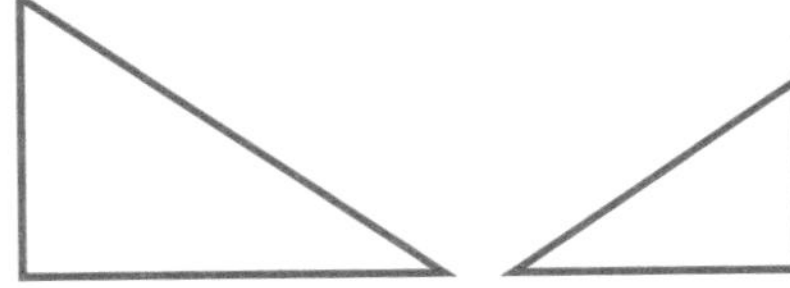

The triangles appear to have the same shape, but have a different size. So, they are not congruent.

Real-World EXAMPLE — Identify Congruent Figures

3 **SCHOOL The diagrams show the shapes and sizes of two classrooms. Are the classrooms congruent? Explain.**

Mr. Cruz's Classroom: 42 ft by 32 ft

Ms. Hale's Classroom: 42 ft by 35 ft

Both classrooms have the same shape. They are rectangles.

Both classrooms have the same length, but Ms. Hale's classroom has a greater width. So, they are not the same size.

Since the classrooms have different sizes, they are not congruent.

Personal Tutor at tx.gr4math.com

CHECK What You Know

Tell whether the figures appear to be congruent. Write *yes* or *no*. If they are, describe the movements that show the congruence. See Examples 1–3 (pp. 374–375)

1.

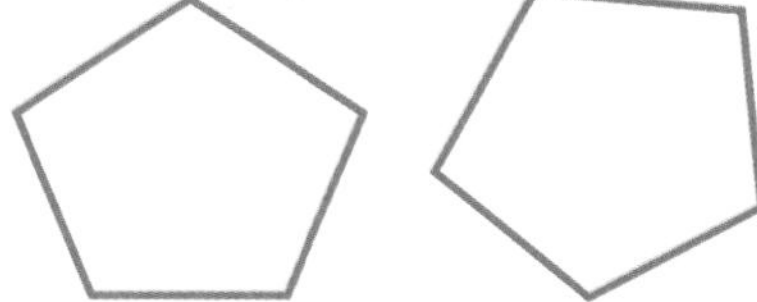

2.

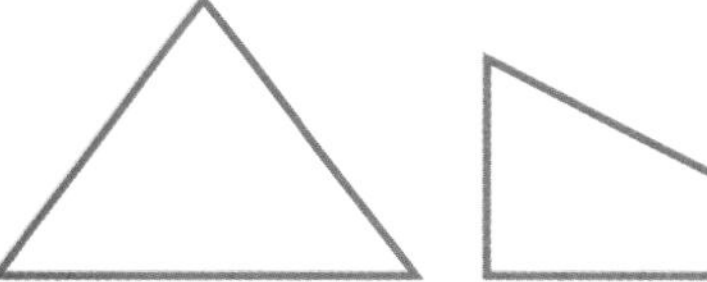

3. How many of the kitchen tiles appear to be congruent to the tile labeled *E*?

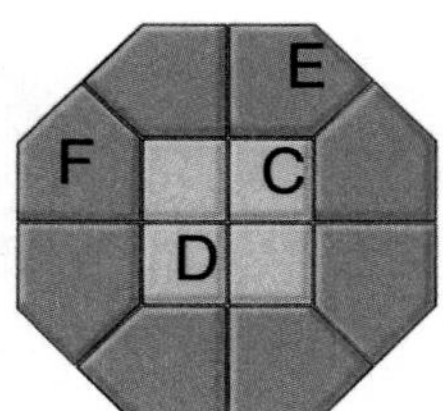

4. In the birdhouse, do the windows and door appear to be congruent? Explain.

5. Talk About It — Describe the movements that can be used to check if two figures are congruent.

Practice and Problem Solving

EXTRA PRACTICE

See page R31.

Tell whether the figures appear to be congruent. Write *yes* or *no*. If they are, describe the movements that show the congruence. See Examples 1–3 (pp. 374–375)

6. 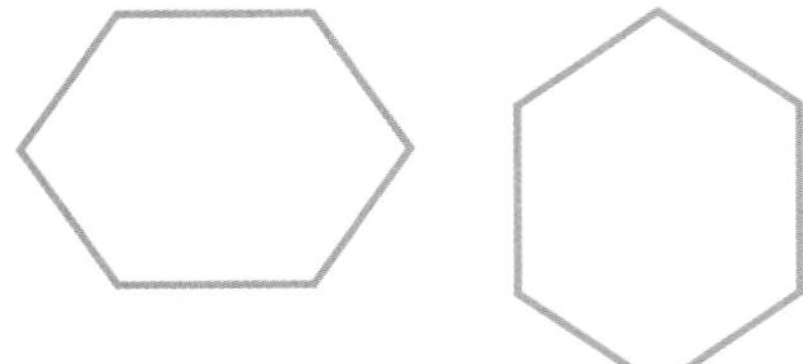

7. 

8. 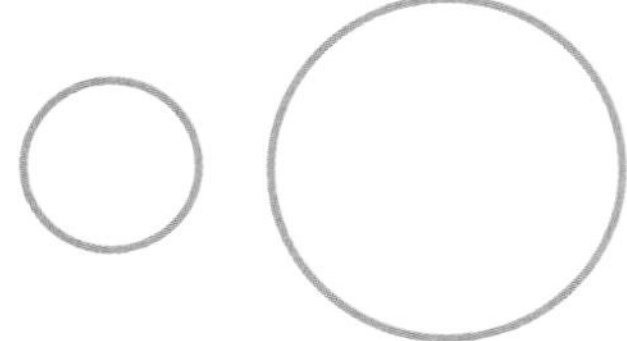

9. 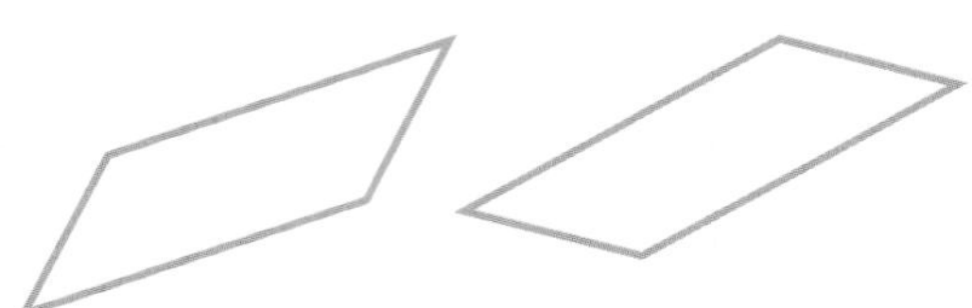

10. Tell whether the cells on a honeycomb are congruent.

11. Which figures on a soccer ball are congruent?

12. **Measurement** The television in Lin's room is 30 inches wide and 24 inches long. His friend has the same television. If the television is 30 inches wide, how long is it?

13. **Measurement** One of Paloma's picture frames is 5 inches wide and 7 inches long. She has another picture frame that is the same size. If it is 7 inches long, how wide is it?

H.O.T. Problems

14. **OPEN ENDED** Create two rectangles. Tell whether they are congruent or not congruent. Explain.

15. **FIND THE ERROR** Tammy and Jacinto are comparing their slices of pizza. Who is correct? Explain.

Tammy
Mine is larger.
Jacinto
They are congruent.

16. **WRITING IN MATH** Are all squares with one side measuring 5 inches congruent? Explain your reasoning.

Technology Activity for 9-7

Draw Congruent Figures

MAIN IDEA

I will use technology to draw congruent figures

Targeted TEKS 4.14 The students applies Grade 4 mathematics to solve problems connected to everyday experiencs and activities in and outside of school. **(D) Use tools such as** real objects, manipulatives, and **technology to solve problems.** *Also addresses TEKS 4.15(A).*

You can use pattern blocks on the *Math Tool Chest* to draw congruent geometry figures.

Petra is designing a quilt. She wants to draw congruent pentagons to use in her design. Draw any pentagon. Then draw a congruent pentagon. Use transformations to prove both figures are congruent.

- Click on the pattern blocks.
- Choose the pentagon.
- Place two on the mat.
- Use transformations to move the second.

How do you know the figures are congruent?

CHECK What You Know

Use the computer to show transformations to prove that shapes are congruent.

1. triangle

2. quadrilateral

3. hexagon

Use technology to solve.

4. Kurt wants to create a design for a book cover. He wants to draw congruent regular octagons to use in his design. Draw a regular octagon. Then draw a congruent octagon.

5. Two pictures in a magazine are to be outlined with congruent rectangles. Draw two rectangles that could be used to outline the pictures. Explain how you know that your figures are correct.

6. **Analyze** How do the geometry and measurement tools help you draw congruent figures?

Problem Solving in Geography

Latitude and Longitude

The coordinate grid system of latitude and longitude is used to find exact locations on Earth.

Latitude measures the north-south position of locations on Earth. Longitude measures the east-west position of locations on Earth. You can learn the basics of latitude and longitude using a four-quadrant grid system. The Equator represents 0 on the *x*-axis. A line called the Prime Meridian represents 0 on the *y*-axis.

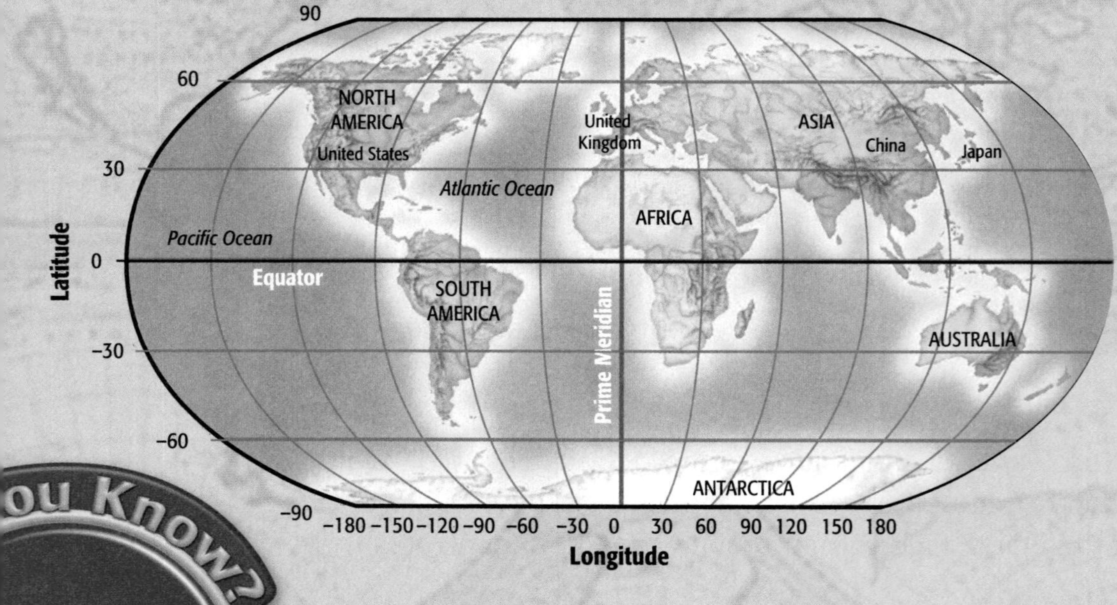

…ou Know?

…e length of … Equator is …901 miles.

Targeted TEKS 4.14 The student uses Grade 4 mathematics to solve problems connected to everyday experiences and activities in an outside of school. **(A) Identify the mathematics in everyday situations.**

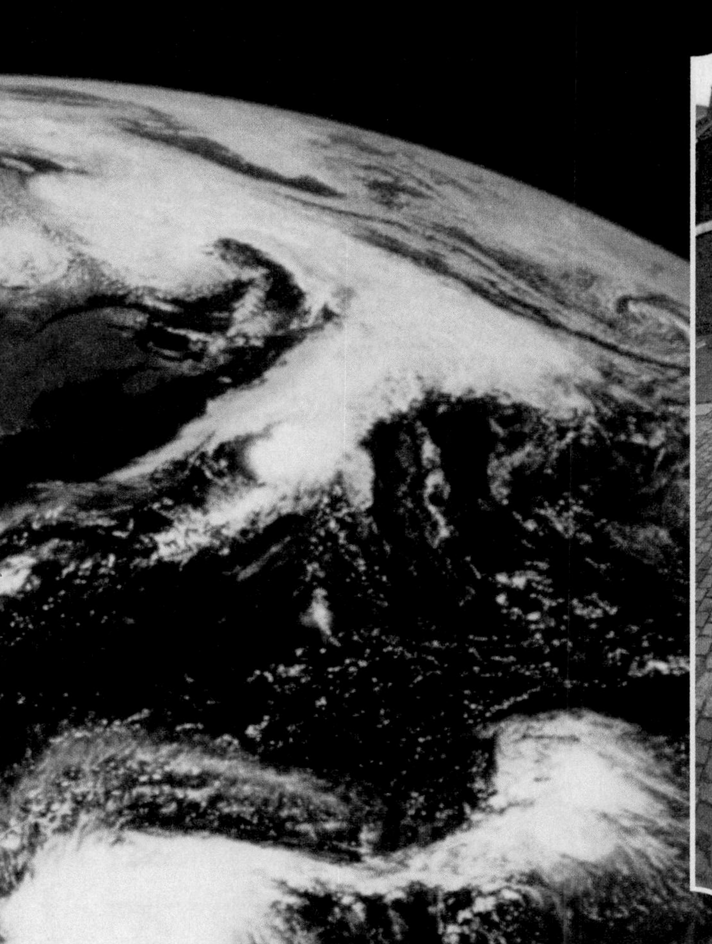

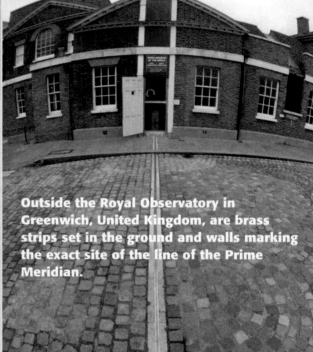

Outside the Royal Observatory in Greenwich, United Kingdom, are brass strips set in the ground and walls marking the exact site of the line of the Prime Meridian.

Real-World Math

Use the information on page 378 to solve each problem.

1. What continent is located at (30, 0)?

2. What ocean is located at (−60, 30)?

3. What continent is located at (120, −30)?

4. Identify one coordinate that represents North America.

5. What continent is closest to the point (0, 0)?

6. Suppose you are at coordinate (−60, 0). If you fly 2 units north and 5 units east, which continent would you land in?

9-8 Symmetry

GET READY to Learn

A butterfly uses its wings to fly. Look at the left side and the right side of the butterfly. When a butterfly folds its wings in half, will the two parts match?

MAIN IDEA

I will identify figures with symmetry and use reflections to check.

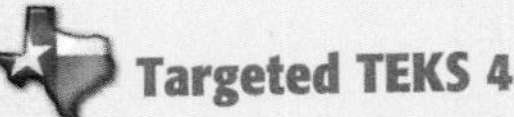

Targeted TEKS 4.9 The student connects transformations to congruence and symmetry. (C) **Use reflections to verify that a shape has symmetry.**

New Vocabulary

line symmetry
line of symmetry
bilateral symmetry

A figure has **line symmetry** if it can be folded so that the two parts of the figure match, or are congruent. This is also called **bilateral symmetry**. The fold line is a **line of symmetry**.

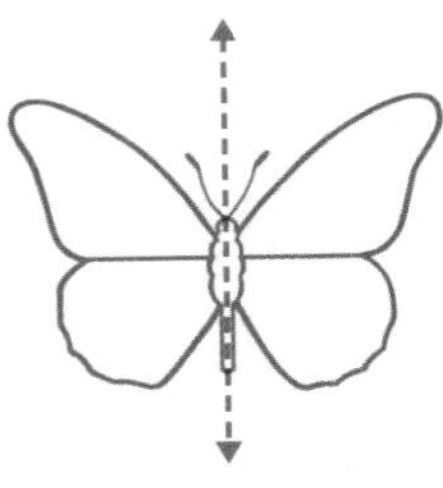

1 line of symmetry
line symmetry

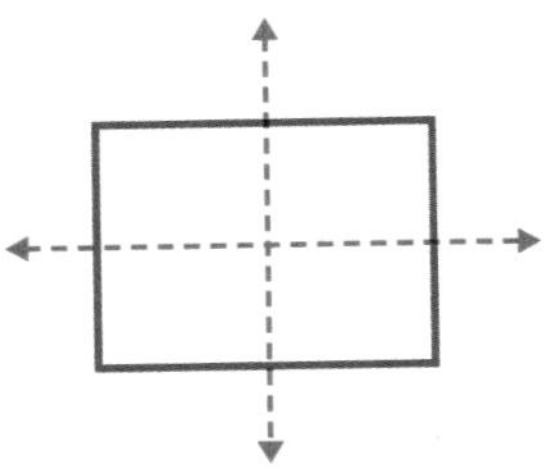

2 lines of symmetry

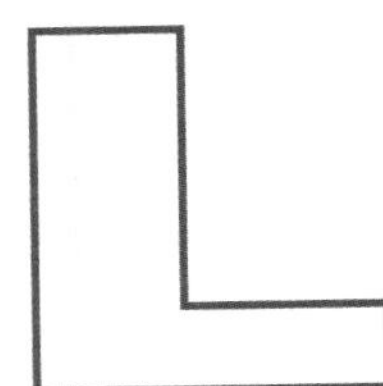

no lines of symmetry

EXAMPLES

Tell whether each figure has line symmetry. Write *yes* or *no*. Then tell how many lines of symmetry the figure has.

1

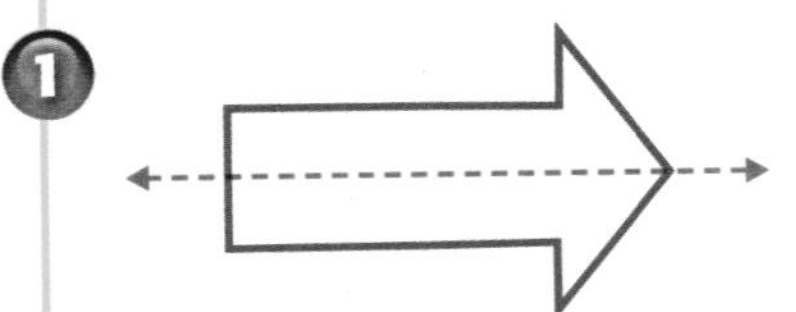

Yes; the figure has 1 line of symmetry.

2

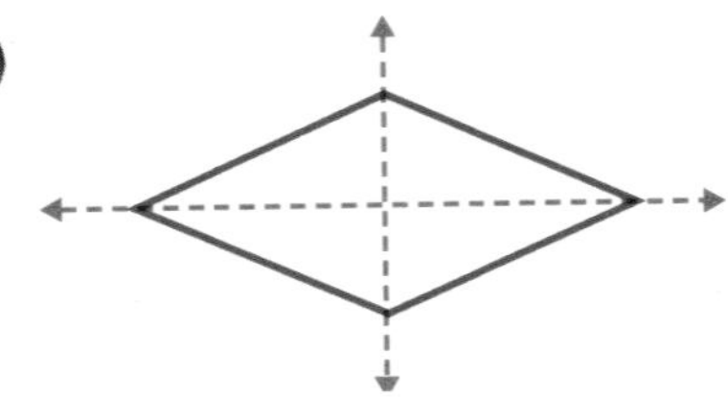

Yes; the figure has 2 lines of symmetry.

Hands-On Mini Activity

Materials geomirror and pattern blocks

You can use the reflection in a geomirror to contruct figures that have symmetry.

Step 1 Place a geomirror next to a square as shown.

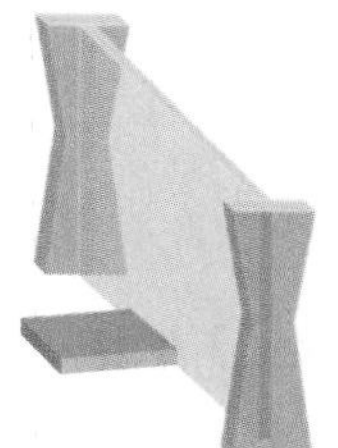

Step 2 Draw the reflection of the square as shown.

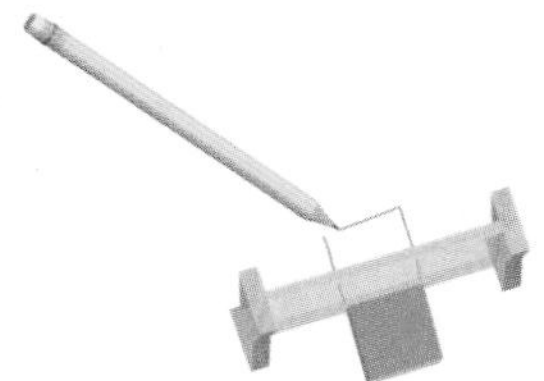

Step 3 Repeat Steps 1 and 2 with two other shapes.

1. How many lines of symmetry do the figures have? Explain.

2. What do you notice about the two sides of a figure that has symmetry? equal?

CHECK What You Know

Tell whether each figure has line symmetry. Write *yes* or *no*. Then tell how many lines of symmetry the figure has. Check by using a mirror. See Examples 1 and 2 (p. 380)

1.

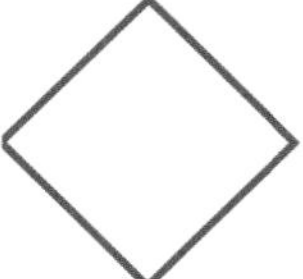

2.

3. Tell whether the snowflake shown at the right has symmetry. Explain.

4. Talk About It Describe how using a mirror can help you check for bilateral symmetry.

Practice and Problem Solving

See page R31.

Tell whether each figure has line symmetry. Write *yes* or *no*. Then tell how many lines of symmetry the figure has. Check by using a mirror. See Examples 1 and 2 (p. 380)

5. 

6. 

7. 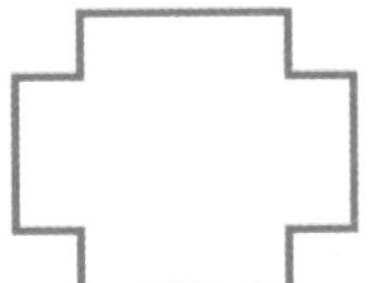

8. 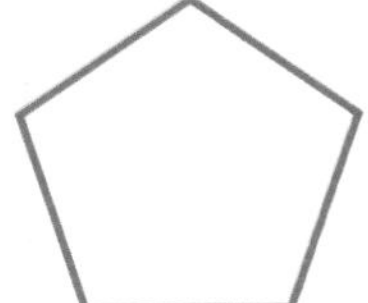

9. Does the letter C have symmetry? If it does, tell how many lines of symmetry the letter has.

10. Does a square have symmetry? If is does, tell how many lines of symmetry the shape has.

Tell whether the line is a line of symmetry. Write *yes* or *no*.

11. 

12. 

13. 

Real-World PROBLEM SOLVING

Art Lines of symmetry can be seen in many pieces of art work, such as cultural masks.

14. Sketch the mask shown and show the line of symmetry.

15. Using a sheet of grid paper, create half of a cultural mask. Then, switch papers with another student. Complete the image of the cultural mask you now have.

16. Does the cultural mask you created have rotational symmetry?

H.O.T. Problems

17. OPEN ENDED Design a plane figure that has more than 3 lines of symmetry.

18. WRITING IN ►MATH How many lines of symmetry do you think a circle has? Explain.

Reflections and Symmetry

Get Ready!

Players: 2 or 3 players

You will need: 30 index cards, paper and pencil, mirror

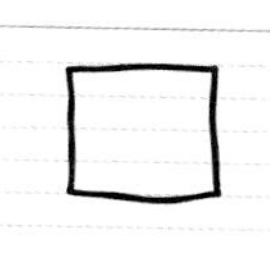
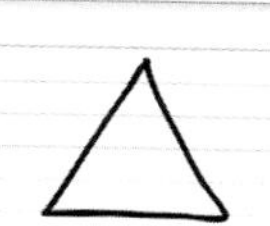

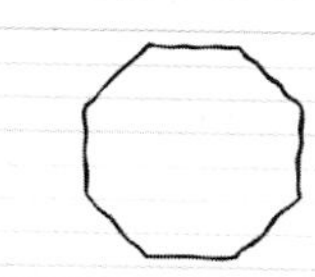

Get Set!

Draw 2-dimensional shapes on the index cards. They can be regular geometric shapes, unusual shapes (like a moon), or real objects such as a house. Make sure not all the shapes have symmetry.

Go!

- Begin with all cards face down in a stack.
- Player 1 picks a card from the stack.
- Player 1 then can use the mirror to decide if the shape is symmetrical.
- If the shape is symmetrical he or she receives a point.
- If the shape is not symmetrical the player can draw a shape using the one they picked symmetrical to receive the point.
- The player with the highest score when all the cards have been used wins.

CHAPTER 9

Study Guide and Review

FOLDABLES™ Study Organizer GET READY to Study

Be sure the following Key Vocabulary words and Key Concepts are written in your Foldable.

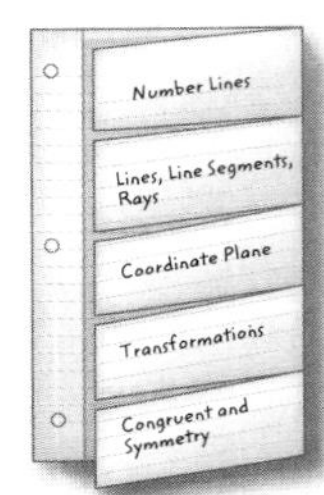

BIG Ideas

- A **number line** is a line that represents numbers as points. (pp. 351–353)

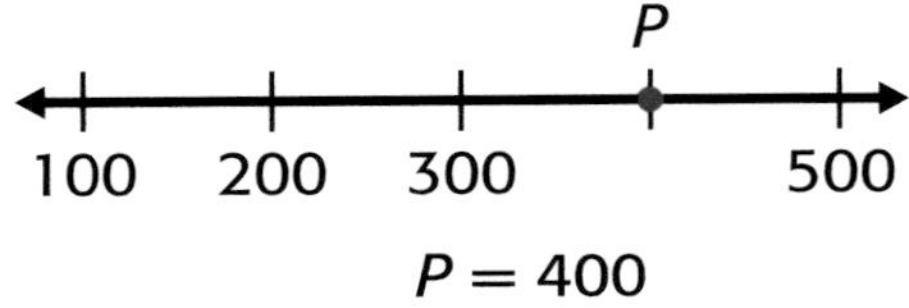

- Transformations are movements of figures such as:

Translations

Rotations

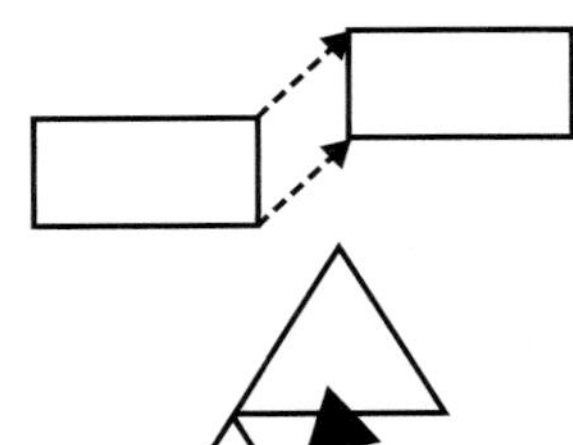

Reflections

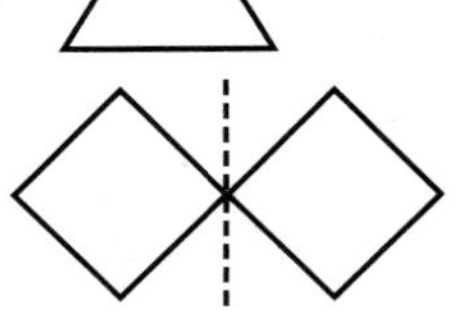

Key Vocabulary

coordinate plane (p. 362)
congruent (p. 374)
number line (p. 351)
point (p. 351)
transformation (p. 368)

Vocabulary Check

Decide which vocabulary word best completes each sentence.

1. A __?__ is formed when two number lines intersect at their zero points.

2. __?__ means to move shapes.

3. A __?__ is an exact location in space.

4. Numbers can be found represented on a __?__.

5. Figures that are the same size and shape are __?__.

Math Online Vocabulary Review at tx.gr4math.com

Lesson-by-Lesson Review

9-1 Locate Points on a Number Line (pp. 351–353)

Example 1
Write the number represented by each letter.

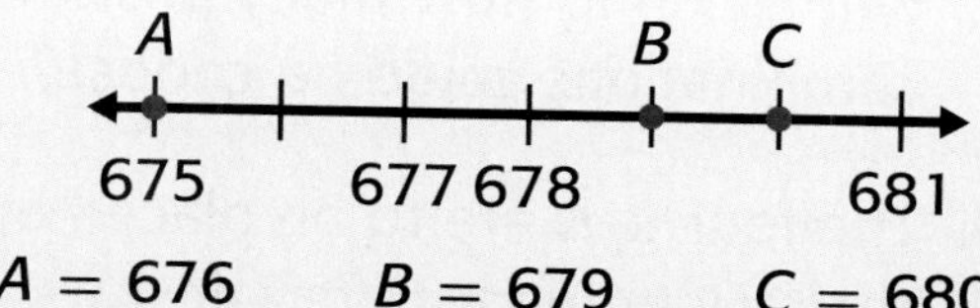

$A = 676$ $B = 679$ $C = 680$

Example 2
Write the number point *Z* represents on the number line.

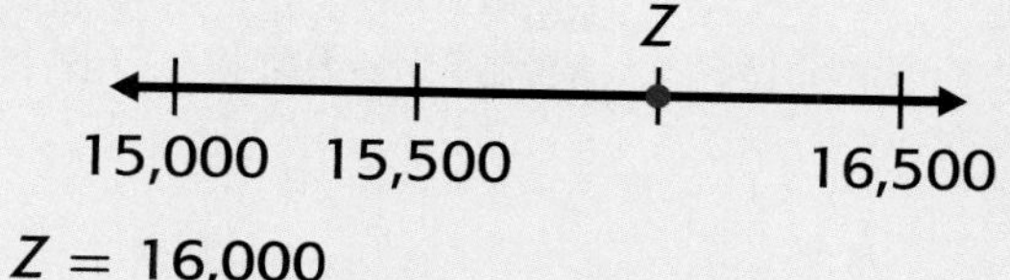

$Z = 16,000$

Write the number represented by each letter.

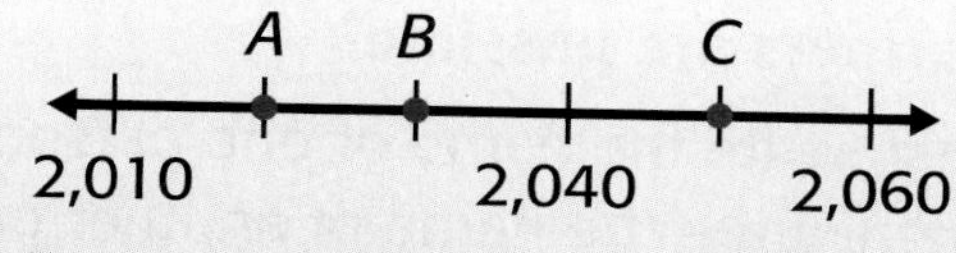

6. $A =$ **7.** $B =$ **8.** $C =$

Write the number point *W* represents on the number line.

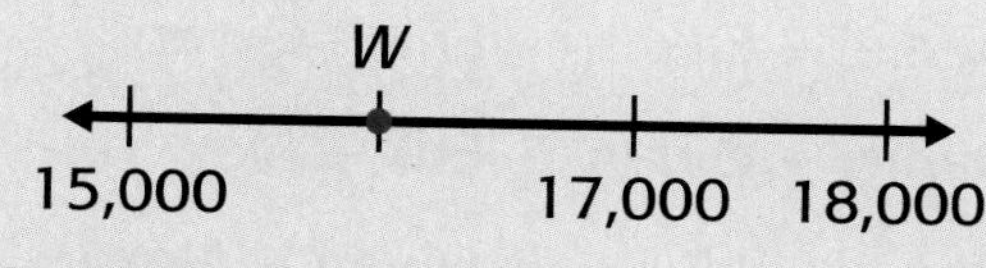

9. $W =$

9-2 Lines, Line Segments, and Rays (pp. 356–359)

Example 3
Describe the figure.

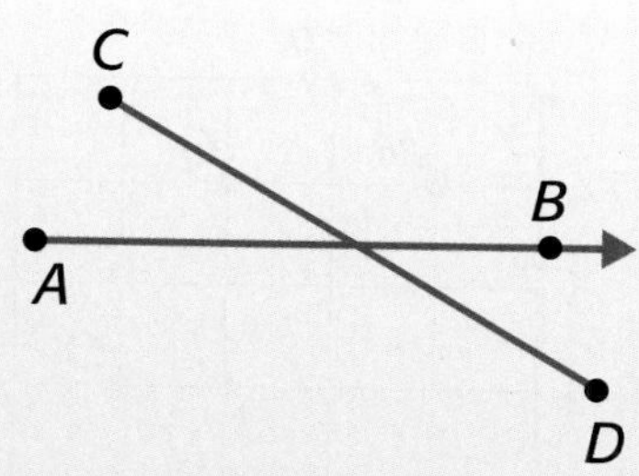

The figure shows ray *AB* and line segment *CD*. Notice that ray *AB* intersects line segment *CD*.

$\overrightarrow{AB}$ intersects $\overline{CD}$.

Identify each figure.

10.

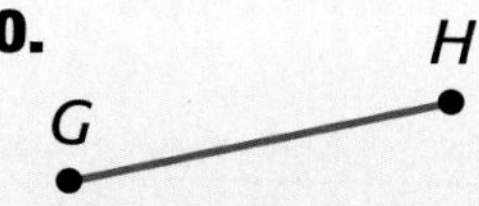

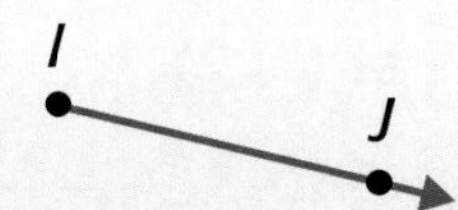

Describe the figure.

11.

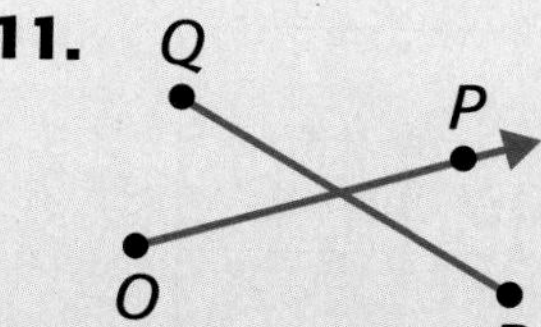

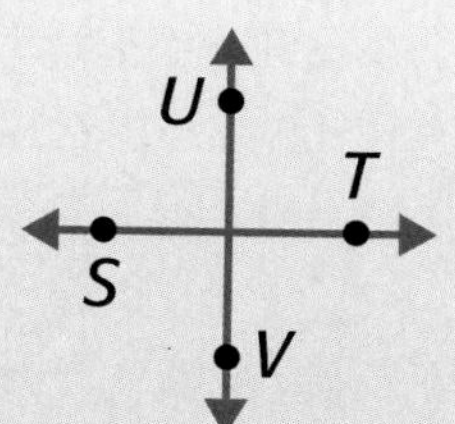

12.

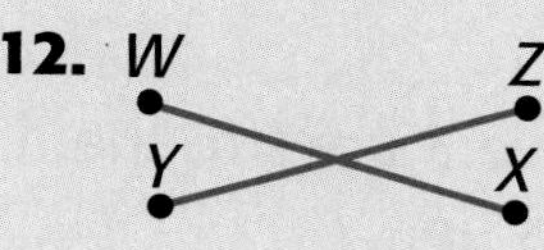

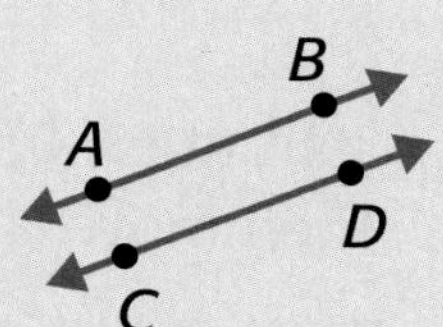

Study Guide and Review

9-3 Problem-Solving Strategy: Make an Organized List (pp. 360–361)

Example 4
Daniel, Erik, Owen, and Alek are going hiking. They will hike in pairs. How many different pairs of hiking partners are possible?

First, write the name of one person. Then, write the name of another person by the first person's name. Continue to do this with each person. Do not repeat pairs.

Daniel – Erik	Erik – Owen
Daniel – Owen	Erik – Alek
Daniel – Alek	Owen – Alek

There are 6 different pairs.

Solve. Use the *make an organized list* strategy.

13. Sergio has to find a combination for his lock. It has 2, 4, and 6 written on it. How many possible combinations could he choose?

14. The four toys are to be placed on a shelf. How many different ways can the toys be arranged?

9-4 Find Points on a Grid (pp. 362–364)

Example 5
Identify the letter that is located at (3, 2).

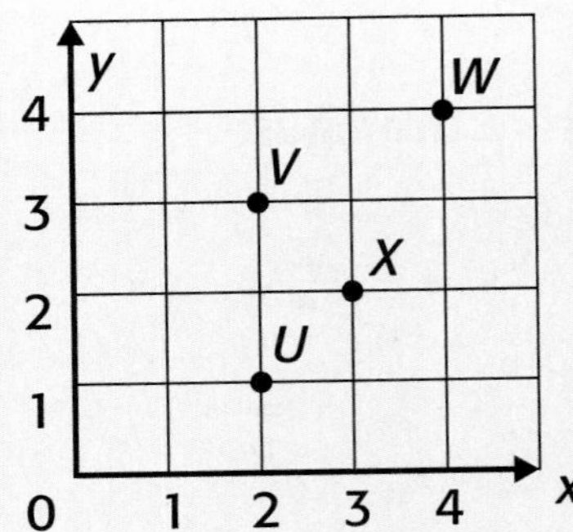

Start at (0, 0). Move 3 units to the right. Then move 2 units up.

The letter *X* is located at (3, 2).

Identify the letter that is located at each ordered pair.

15. (3, 2) **16.** (1, 4) **17.** (2, 5)

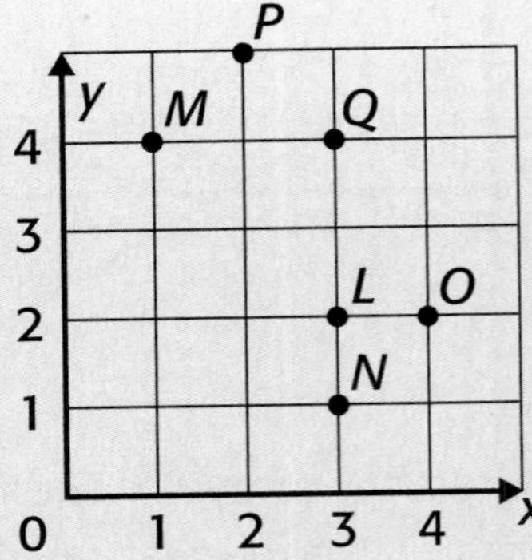

18. Describe how to move from *L* to *Q*.

9-5 Rotations, Reflections, and Translations (pp. 368–371)

Example 6

Identify each transformation. Write *rotation, reflection,* or *translation.*

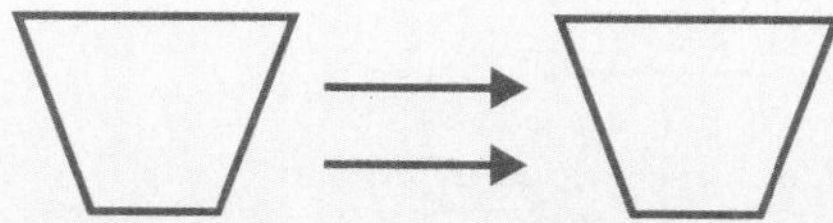

The trapezoid above has moved sideways. It has not turned or flipped.

So, the transformation of the trapezoid is a translation.

Identify each transformation. Write *rotation, reflection,* or *translation.*

19.

20.

Using pattern blocks demonstrate the following transformations by tracing.

21. reflection **22.** rotation

9-6 Problem-Solving Investigation: Choose a Strategy (pp. 372–373)

Example 7
Alberto has $5 left after buying skates for $62 and a helmet for $24. How much did he have originally?

Use the *work backward* strategy.

 $ 5 change
+ $62 amount for skates
 $67
+ $24 amount for helmet
 $91

So, Alberto had $91 originally.

Use any strategy to solve.

23. A teacher is arranging 24 desks. If she wants to group the desks in groups of 4, how many groups will she have?

24. Peter can choose a ham or turkey sandwich. He can choose an apple or orange. How many different sandwich and fruit combinations can Peter choose?

25. A house has 15 rooms. One room is the kitchen, 4 rooms are bedrooms, and 2 rooms are bathrooms. How many other rooms are there?

Study Guide and Review

9-7 Congruent Figures (pp. 374–376)

Example 8
The diagrams show the shapes and sizes of two tables. Are the tables congruent? Explain.

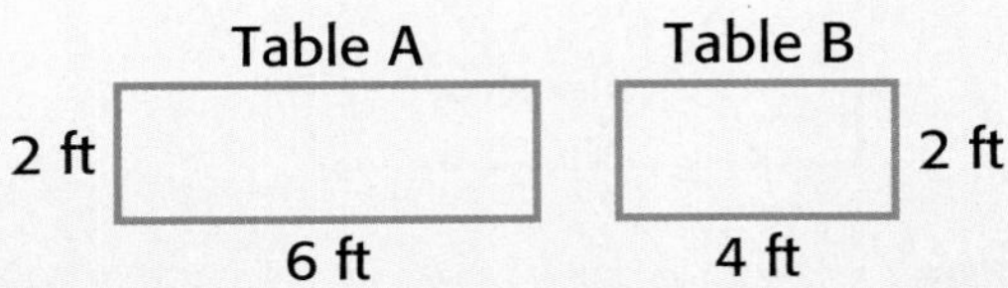

Both tables are rectangular in shape. They have the same width but do not have the same length.

Since the tables have different sizes, they are not congruent.

Tell whether the figures appear to be congruent. Write *yes* or *no*. If they do, describe the movement that shows the congruence.

26.

27.

28.

9-8 Symmetry (pp. 380–382)

Example 9
Tell whether each figure has line symmetry. Then tell how many lines of symmetry the figure has.

The figure has 0 lines of symmetry.

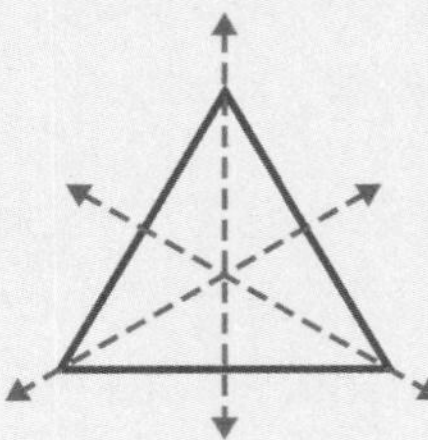

The figure has 3 lines of symmetry.

Tell whether each figure has line symmetry. Write *yes* or *no*. Then tell how many lines of symmetry the figure has.

29.

30.

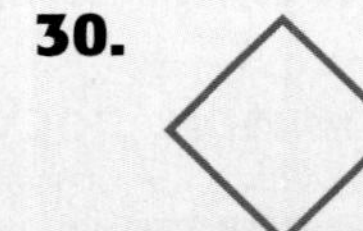

31.

32.

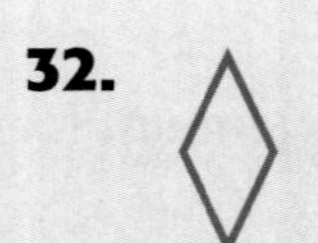

CHAPTER 9

Chapter Test

Identify each transformation. Write *rotation, reflection,* or *translation.*

1.

2.

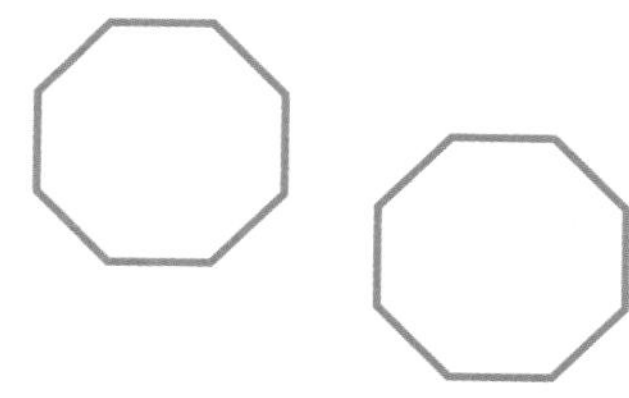

3. **TEST PRACTICE** Which number does letter *C* represent?

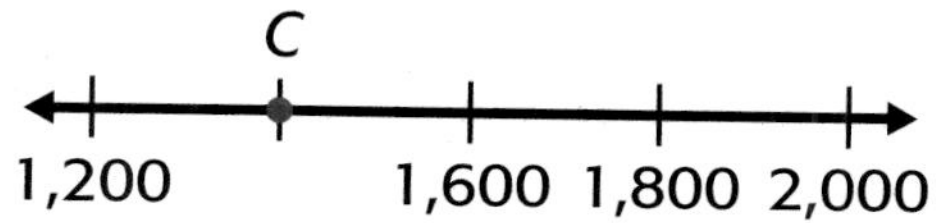

A 2,000 **C** 1,300

B 1,400 **D** 1,000

Write the number represented by each letter.

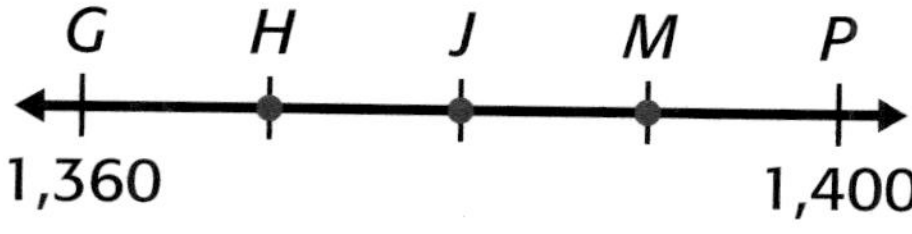

4. *H* **5.** *M*

Identify each figure.

6.

7.

Tell whether the figures appear to be congruent. Write *yes* or *no*. (Lesson 9-7)

8.

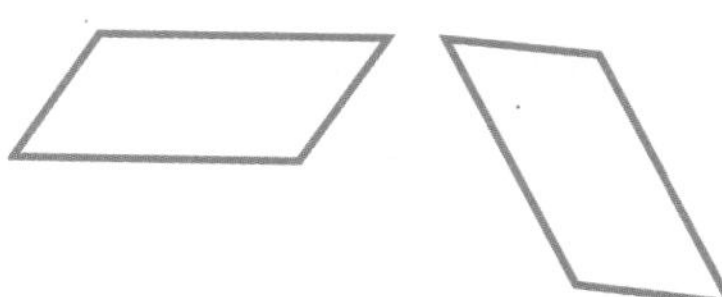

9.

10. **Measurement** Tanika's swimming pool is 8 feet wide and 12 feet long. Tanika's neighbor has the same pool. If the pool is 12 feet long, how wide is it? (Lesson 9-7)

Tell whether each figure has line symmetry. Write *yes* or *no*. Then tell how many lines of symmetry the figure has. (Lesson 9-8)

11.

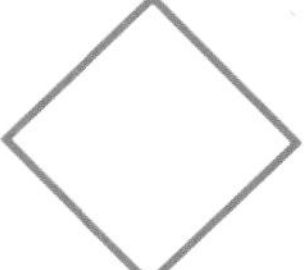

12.

13. **TEST PRACTICE** How many lines of symmetry does this figure have? (Lesson 9-8)

F 0 **H** 2

G 1 **J** 3

CHAPTER 9

Texas Test Practice

Cumulative, Chapters 1–9

Look at the map below.

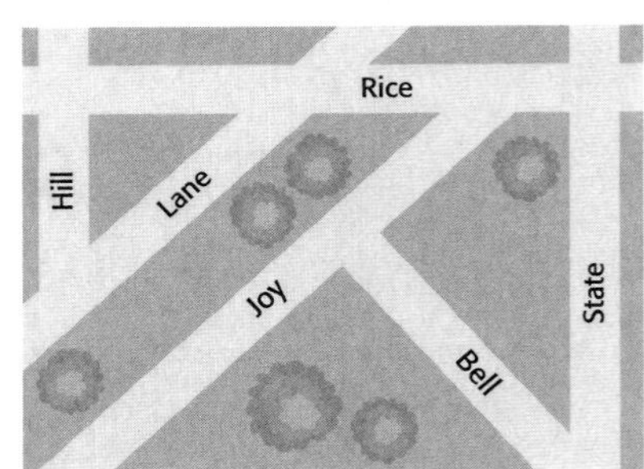

Which streets appear to be parallel to each other?

A Rice and Bell

B State and Lane

C Lane and Joy

D Hill and Rice

TEST-TAKING TIP

Think about the steps you will need to solve the problem.

Read the Test Question

You need to compare the streets to each other. See which streets intersect at some point.

Solve the Test Question

Since Lane and Joy never intersect and are going the same direction, they are parallel.

The answer is C.

Personal Tutor at tx.gr4math.com

Choose the best answer.

1. **What number on the number line does point *J* best represent?**

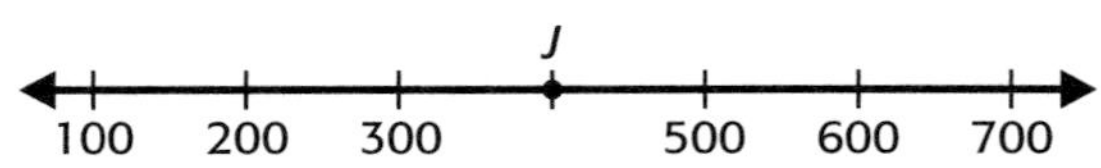

A 400

B 450

C 500

D 550

2. **Which line is perpendicular to line *D*?**

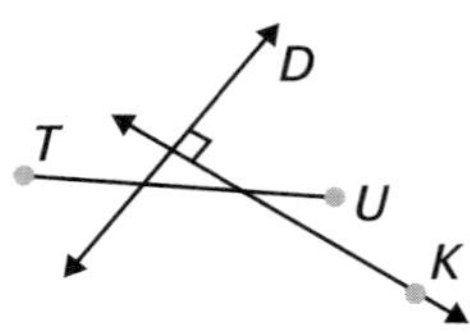

F Ray *Q*

G Line segment *TU*

H Line *S*

J Line *K*

Get Ready for the Texas Test
For test-taking strategies and more practice, see pages TX1–TX21.

3. Look at the figures below.

What is a good description of the figures?

A One is a reflection of the other.

B They are not congruent.

C They are congruent.

D They intersect.

4. How many lines of symmetry does this shape have?

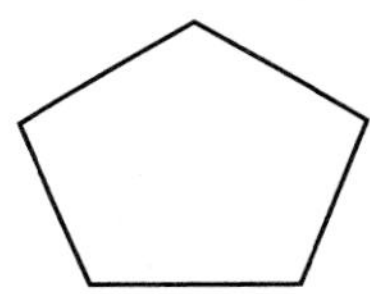

F 2   **H** 4

G 3   **J** 5

5. Justin practices the piano 30 minutes per day, 6 days per week. Which expression shows minutes he practices in 10 weeks?

A $6 \times 10 + 30$ **C** $6 \times 10 \times 30$

B $6 + 10 + 30$ **D** $30 \div 10 \times 6$

6. Evita has 3 red crayons, 2 blue crayons, and 4 green carayons. If a crayon is selected at random, what is the probability it will be blue?

F 3 out of 9   **H** 2 out of 7

G 2 out of 5   **J** 2 out of 9

7. Kai baked 15 trays of cookies for a bake sale. Each tray has 14 cookies. How many cookies did Kai bake in all?

A 200   **C** 225

B 210   **D** 240

8. In the figure below, which angle appears to be obtuse?

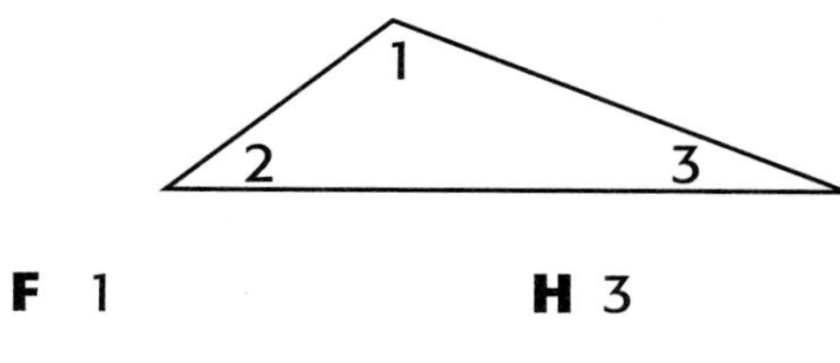

F 1   **H** 3

G 2   **J** none

9. GRIDDABLE Ryan has 3 cats: Abbey, Tally, and Whiskers. Tally weighs 5 pounds. Whiskers weighs twice as much as Tally. Abbey weighs 3 pounds less than Whiskers. How many pounds does Abbey weigh?

10. What is the value of the digit 3 in 564,327?

A 30   **C** 3,000

B 300   **D** 30,000

Measure Length, Perimeter, Area, and Temperature

BIG Idea What is perimeter?

Perimeter is the distance around a closed figure.

Example To find the perimeter of the cow pasture, you can add the lengths of the sides of the fence.

$$\begin{array}{r} 225 \text{ yd} \\ 150 \text{ yd} \\ 225 \text{ yd} \\ +\ 150 \text{ yd} \\ \hline 750 \text{ yd} \end{array}$$

So, the perimeter of the pasture is 750 yards.

What will I learn in this chapter?

- Measure length in customary and metric units.
- Estimate and determine perimeter and area.
- Relate perimeter and area.
- Use a thermometer to measure temperature and changes in temperature.
- Solve problems by working simpler problems.

Key Vocabulary

perimeter
area

Student Study Tools at tx.gr4math.com

FOLDABLES™ Study Organizer

Make this Foldable to help you organize information about geometry and measurement. Begin with a sheet of notebook paper.

1. **Fold** a sheet of paper in half.

2. **Cut** every third line on one side. Ten tabs will result.

3. **Label** each tab as shown.

ARE YOU READY for Chapter 10?

You have two ways to check prerequisite skills for this chapter.

Option 2

Math Online Take the Chapter Readiness Quiz at tx.gr4math.com.

Option 1

Complete the Quick Check below.

QUICK Check

Identify which is longer in each pair. (Prior grade)

1.

2. 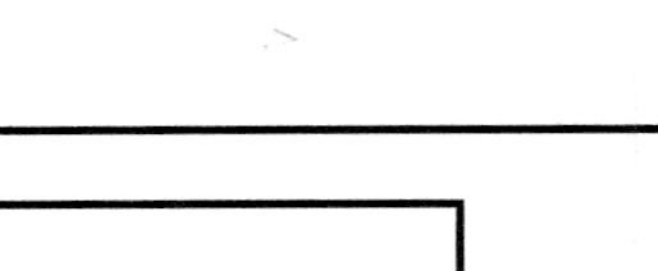

3. Ted is comparing his shoe to his mom's shoe. Which is longer?

Ted's shoe

Mom's shoe

Find the value of each expression. (Lesson 5-1)

4. $8 + 14 + 8 + 14$
5. $9 + 16 + 9 + 16$
6. 15×7
7. 12×6
8. $(2 \times 7) + (2 \times 14)$
9. $(2 \times 13) + (2 \times 9)$

Identify which sides are the same length. (Prior grade)

10. 

11. 

12. 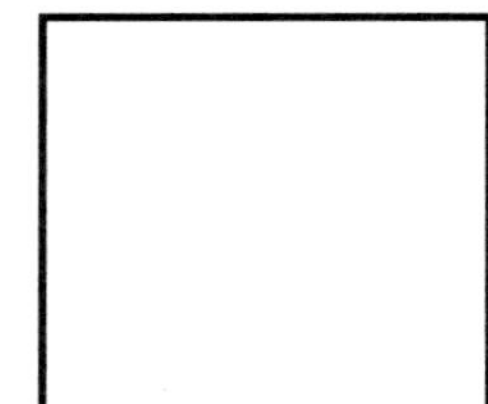

13. Mercedes is making a picture frame. It will be a square. How many sides are the same length?

Measurement Activity for Lesson 10-1

Estimate and Measure Length

In this activity, you will use a ruler to measure lengths to the nearest inch, $\frac{1}{2}$ inch, and $\frac{1}{4}$ inch.

MAIN IDEA

I will estimate and measure lengths to the nearest inch, $\frac{1}{2}$ inch, and $\frac{1}{4}$ inch.

Targeted TEKS 4.11 The student applies measurement concepts. The student is expected to estimate and measure to solve problems involving length (including perimeter) and area. . . . (A) **Estimate and use measurement tools to determine length . . . using standard units** SI (metric) and **customary.**

You Will Need
ruler

ACTIVITY

1 Find the length of the pencil to the nearest inch, $\frac{1}{2}$ inch, and $\frac{1}{4}$ inch.

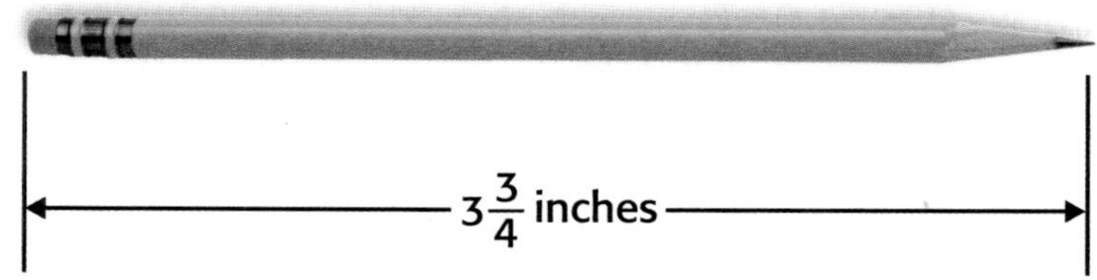

Step 1 **Copy the table.**

Object	Estimate	Whole Inch	$\frac{1}{2}$ Inch	$\frac{1}{4}$ Inch
Pencil				

Step 2 **Estimate.**

Estimate the length of the pencil. Record your estimate in the table.

Step 3 **Measure.**

Place the ruler against a side of the pencil so that the 0 on the ruler lines up with one end. Measure the length to the nearest inch, $\frac{1}{2}$ inch, and $\frac{1}{4}$ inch. Record the measurements in your table.

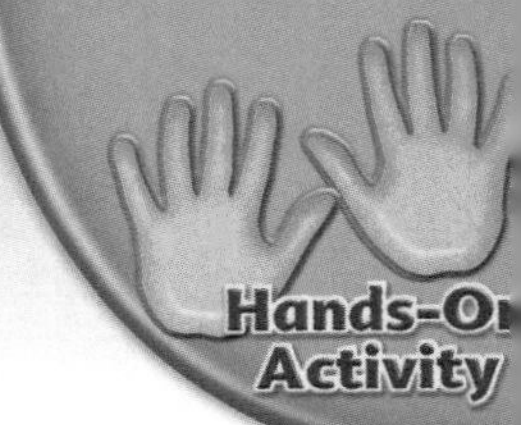

ACTIVITY

2 **Find four items in your classroom to measure to the nearest inch, $\frac{1}{2}$ inch, and $\frac{1}{4}$ inch.**

Step 1 **Select the items.**

Find four items from your classroom that are less than 12 inches long.

Step 2 **Estimate.**

Estimate their length in inches. Record your estimates in a table similar to the one in Activity 1.

Step 3 **Measure.**

Measure each object's length to the nearest inch, $\frac{1}{2}$ inch, and $\frac{1}{4}$ inch. Record the measurements in your table.

Think About It

1. Which is more accurate, measuring to the nearest inch or measuring to the nearest $\frac{1}{4}$ inch? Explain.

2. How could the length around a round object, such as a globe, be measured?

CHECK What You Know

Estimate and then measure each to the nearest inch, $\frac{1}{2}$ inch, and $\frac{1}{4}$ inch.

3. 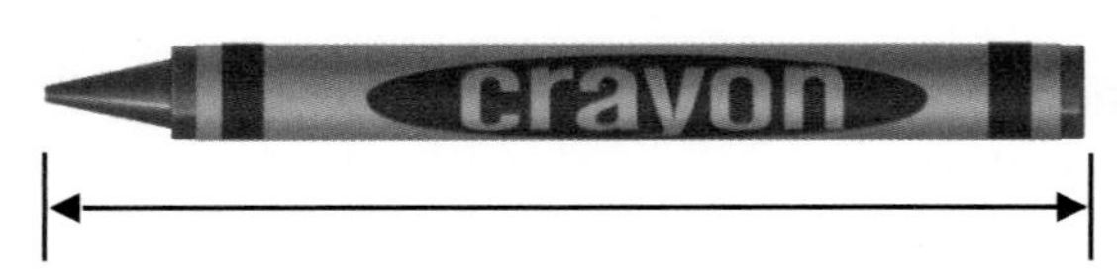

4. 

5. WRITING IN MATH Describe a situation in which measuring to the nearest $\frac{1}{4}$ inch is necessary.

10-1 Customary Units of Length

GET READY to Learn

A neon damsel marine fish is shown. How long is this fish?

MAIN IDEA

I will estimate and measure customary lengths.

Targeted TEKS 4.11 The student applies measurement concepts. The student is expected to estimate and measure to solve problems involving length (including perimeter) and area. . . . (A) **Estimate and use measurement tools to determine length . . . using standard units** SI (metric) and **customary.**

New Vocabulary

length
inch
foot
yard
customary

Length is the measurement of a line between two points. **Inch**, **foot**, and **yard** are all **customary** units of measure for length.

KEY CONCEPT — Customary Measurements

An **inch** is about the length of one paper clip.	A **foot** is about the length of a textbook.	A **yard** is about the height of a chair.
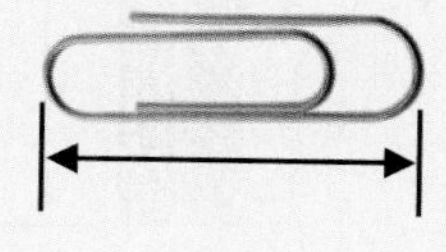		

Real-World EXAMPLE — Estimate and Measure Length

1 FISH **Estimate. Then measure the length of the neon damsel to the nearest inch, $\frac{1}{2}$ inch and $\frac{1}{4}$ inch.**

1. Estimate
Estimate by looking at the length. Compare that length to what you know about inches.

2. Measure
Using a ruler, measure the length of the fish to the nearest $\frac{1}{2}$ inch.

3. Measure
Measure the length of the fish to the nearest $\frac{1}{4}$ inch.

So, the fish is $1\frac{1}{2}$ inches long.

Real-World EXAMPLE Estimate Length

2 **SCIENCE Choose the best estimate.**

Which is the best estimate for the length of the caterpillar?

A 2 inches
B 20 inches
C 20 feet
D 2 yards

A caterpillar is small. So we would estimate inches. 20 inches is more than a foot and is too big. So, the answer will be A, 2 inches.

Online Personal Tutor at tx.gr4math.com

CHECK What You Know

Estimate. Then measure each to the nearest inch, $\frac{1}{2}$ inch, and $\frac{1}{4}$ inch. See Example 1 (p. 397)

1.

2.

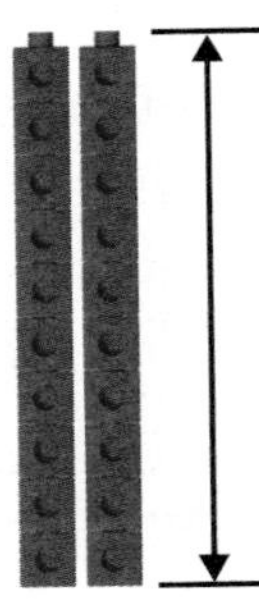

Choose the best estimate for each length. See Example 2 (p. 398)

3.

A 12 inches
B 4 feet
C 12 feet
D 4 yards

4.

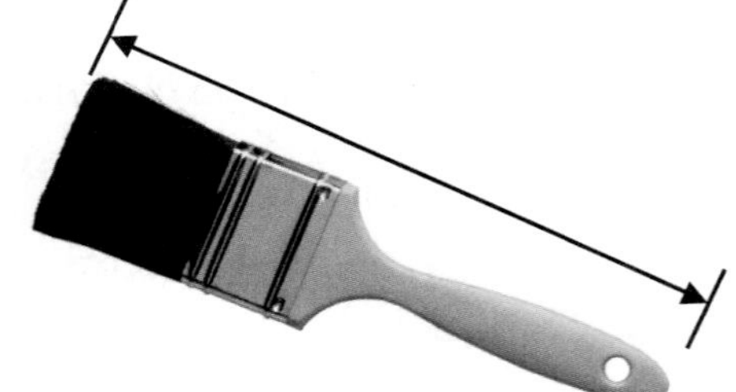

F 3 inches
G 8 inches
H 3 feet
J 8 feet

5. Dr. Franks measured Tavis's height and said he was 50 units tall. What customary unit was probably being used to measure Tavis's height?

6. Talk About It Why do you think there is more than 1 unit of measure for length?

Practice and Problem Solving

EXTRA PRACTICE See page R32.

Estimate. Then measure each to the nearest inch, $\frac{1}{2}$ inch, and $\frac{1}{4}$ inch. See Example 1 (p. 397)

7.

8.

9.

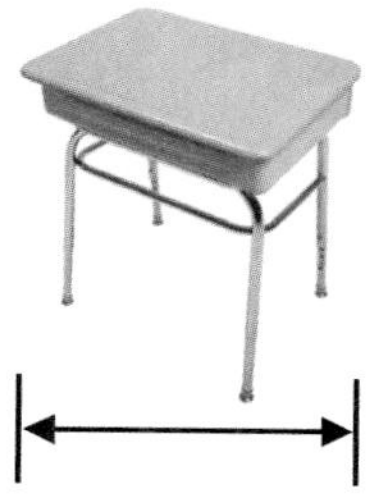

10.

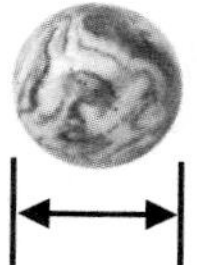

11. Patrice found a book that was $2\frac{1}{4}$ inches thick. She stacked it with another book that was the same thickness. How tall was the stack?

12. Rajeev found a stick that was $5\frac{3}{4}$ feet long. He needed one that was about 5 feet long. Is it reasonable to say that this stick will work? Explain.

Choose the best estimate for each length. See Example 2 (p. 398)

13. length of a whistle

A 2 yards

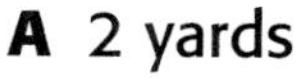

B 2 feet

C 12 inches

D 2 inches

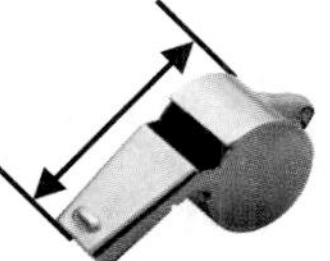

14. width of a chalkboard

F 1 foot

G 2 feet

H 1 yard

J 2 yards

H.O.T. Problems

15. OPEN ENDED Find two objects in your desk that are longer than 2 inches and shorter than 4 inches. How did you use estimation in selecting objects?

16. WRITING IN MATH List two tools used to measure length and provide a situation in which that tool would be useful.

10-2 Converting Customary Length

GET READY to Learn

Marla's dog, Cory, competes in big air competitions. Each dog jumps into water. Cory's longest jump is 21 feet. How many yards are in 21 feet?

MAIN IDEA

I will convert customary units of length.

Targeted TEKS 4.11 The student applies measurement concepts. The student is expected to estimate and measure to solve problems involving length (including perimeter) and area. . . . (B) **Perform simple conversions between different units of length, . . . within the customary measurement system.**

New Vocabulary

convert

To **convert** between units of measurement means to change the unit. When converting measurements, think about two things:

- First, the unit you are starting with and the unit you are ending with.
- Second, are you converting from a smaller unit to a larger unit or a larger unit to a smaller unit?

EXAMPLE Convert to Larger Units

1 How many yards are in 21 feet?

You know the number of feet and want to find the number of yards. Feet are a smaller unit than yards. So use division.

To convert 21 feet to yards, divide by 3.

21 ft = ■ yd ← Divide by 3 because 3 ft = 1 yd.

21 ÷ 3 = ■

21 ÷ 3 = 7 21 feet = 7 yards

So, there are 7 yards in 21 feet.

EXAMPLE Convert to Smaller Units

2 Complete. 6 yds = ■ ft

To convert 6 yards to feet, multiply by 3.

6 × 3 = ■ ← Multiply by 3 because 3 ft = 1 yd.

6 × 3 = 18 6 yds = 18 ft

So, there are 18 feet in 6 yards.

CHECK What You Know

Complete. See Examples 1 and 2 (p. 400)

1. 36 in. = ■ ft

2. 12 ft = ■ yd

3. 4 yd = ■ in.

4. 2 yd = ■ ft

5. ■ in. = 7 ft

6. 24 in. = ■ ft

7. The Costa family hiked a trail that was 2 miles in one direction. How many feet was the hike round-trip?

8. Talk About It Explain how to convert a smaller unit of measure to a larger unit of measure.

Practice and Problem Solving

Complete. See Examples 1 and 2 (p. 400)

9. 2 ft = ■ in.

10. 6 ft = ■ in.

11. ■ in. = 2 yd

12. 6 ft = ■ yd

13. ■ ft = 132 in.

14. ■ in. = 12 ft

15. 18 ft = ■ in.

16. 18 yd = ■ in.

17. ■ in. = 4 ft

18. 16 ft = ■ in.

19. 216 in. = ■ yd

20. 84 ft = ■ yd

21. Darin is 4 feet 10 inches tall. His brother is 68 inches tall. How many inches taller is Darin's brother than Darin?

22. Sumi lives 2 miles from school. Valerie lives 10,542 feet from school. Who lives closer to school? Explain your answer.

23. Cassey's mom bought 16 yards of yarn. She needs 580 inches of yarn for her art project. Does she have enough? Explain.

24. Mr. Shank used 15 feet of tape. He bought a container of tape that was 5 yards long. Did he buy enough? Explain.

H.O.T. Problems

25. OPEN ENDED Measure two objects that are at least one foot long. Convert the measurement to a smaller unit.

26. CHALLENGE Ramiro sits 5 feet from the bookshelf. Michelle sits 64 inches from the bookshelf. Who sits closer to the bookshelf?

27. WRITING IN MATH Write a real-world problem involving the conversion of customary lengths. Give your problem to a classmate to solve.

Problem-Solving Strategy

MAIN IDEA I will solve problems by solving a simpler problem.

Targeted TEKS 4.14 The student applies Grade 4 mathematics to solve problems connected to everyday experiences and activities in and out of school. (C) **Select or develop an appropriate problem-solving plan or strategy, . . . working a simpler problem, ... to solve a problem.** *Also addresses 4.14(B).*

It takes Pearl 2 minutes to ride her bike one block in her neighborhood. How long does it takes Pearl to ride the route shown in her neighborhood three times?

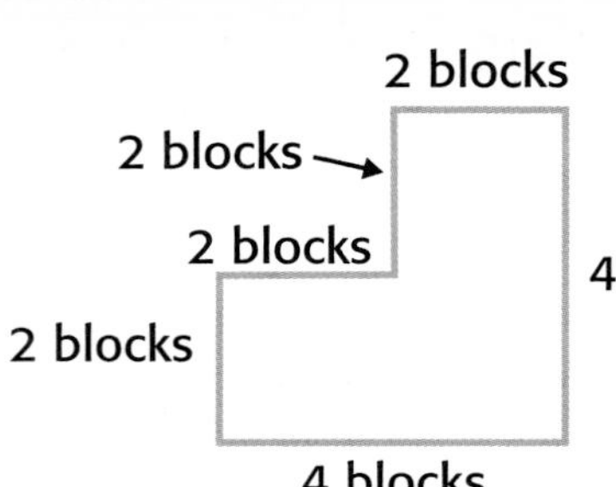

Understand	**What facts do you know?** • The length of each street in her neighborhood. • It takes Lynn 2 minutes to ride her bike 1 block. **What do you need to find?** • Find how long it will take to ride the route three times.
Plan	You can solve a simpler problem to find the answer.
Solve	First, find the number of blocks Pearl rides one time around. $\underbrace{2 + 2 + 2 + 2 + 4 + 4}_{\text{Add the distances.}} = \underbrace{16}_{\text{Total blocks}}$ Using the result, you find that Pearl rides 16 + 16 + 16 or 48 blocks when she rides three times around. Now, find how many minutes it takes her to ride three times around. $\underbrace{2}_{\text{Minutes per block}} \times \underbrace{48}_{\text{Total blocks}} = \underbrace{96}_{\text{Total minutes}}$ So, it takes Pearl 96 minutes to ride three times around.
Check	Look back at the problem. Estimate the total number of blocks times 2. $48 \times 2 \rightarrow 50 \times 2$ or 100. Since 96 is close to 100, the answer is correct.

ANALYZE the Strategy

Refer to the problem on the previous page.

1. Explain why $2 + 2 + 2 + 2 + 4 + 4$ was the first step in finding the answer to the problem.
2. Could you have used multiplication to find the number of blocks it takes Pearl to ride three times around? Explain.
3. Suppose it takes Pearl 1 minute to ride her bike one block. Would it take her less than 1 hour to ride three times around her neighborhood? Explain.
4. Look back at Exercise 3. Explain how you found the answer.

PRACTICE the Strategy

EXTRA PRACTICE
See page R33.

Solve. Use the *solve a simpler problem* strategy.

5. Marcos is making three tile pictures. He uses 310 green tiles to make each picture. He uses 50 less red tiles than green tiles for each picture. How many red and green tiles does he use in all?
6. **Measurement** Ling is putting up a wallpaper border on three walls that are 14 feet long and 12 feet tall. How many feet of wallpaper border will she use if she puts the border only at the top of the wall?
7. Violeta sells twice as much orange juice as lemonade. She charges $2 for each. She sold 10 cups of lemonade. How much did she earn in all?
8. A basketball coach is going to buy 16 basketballs. What will be the total cost of the basketballs?

9. Jerome's CD has 16 songs, and each song is 3 minutes long. Ana's CD has 14 songs, and each song is 4 minutes. Whose CD plays longer and by how much?
10. Five gardeners spent 260 hours in all planting trees. One of the gardeners spent 40 hours. The rest spent the same amount of time. How many hours did each spend on planting trees?

11. Marian is placing 72 photographs in an album. She will put the same number of photos on each of 6 pages. She can put 4 pictures in each row. How many rows will be on each page?
12. WRITING IN ▸MATH Explain how you solved Exercise 11.

Explore

Measurement Activity for 10-4

Metric Measurement of Length

Centimeters are metric units of measure for length. Each side of a base-ten unit is equal to 1 centimeter (cm).

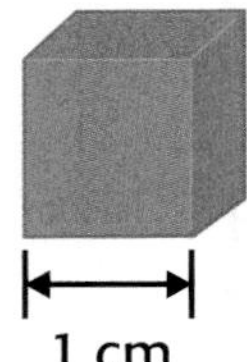

MAIN IDEA

I will estimate and measure objects to the nearest centimeter.

Targeted TEKS 4.11 The student applies measurement concepts. The student is expected to estimate and measure to solve problems involving length (including perimeter) and area. . . . (A) **Estimate and use measurement tools to determine length . . . using standard units SI (metric)** and customary.

You Will Need

metric ruler

ACTIVITY

1 Estimate and measure lengths.

Step 1 Copy the table.

Copy the table shown.

Object	Estimate	Length

Step 2 Choose four items.

Choose four items in your classroom that can be measured in centimeters.

Step 3 Estimate length.

Estimate the length of each item you selected in centimeters. Record the estimates in your table.

Step 4 Measure length.

Place the ruler against a side of one of the objects you selected so that the 0 on the ruler lines up with the edge. Measure the object's length to the nearest centimeter. Record your measurement in the table.

Think About It

1. Which of the objects you measured was the longest?
2. Which of the objects you measured was the shortest?
3. How did you estimate the length of each object?
4. Name two things in the room that would be about 100 centimeters long.

CHECK What You Know

Estimate. Then measure each line segment to the nearest centimeter.

5.

6.

7.

8.

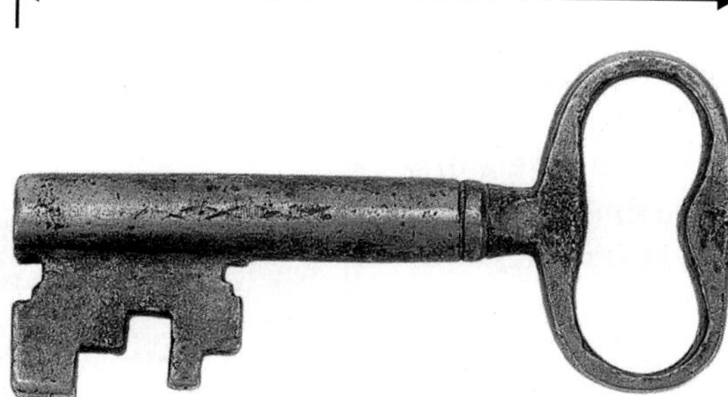

9.

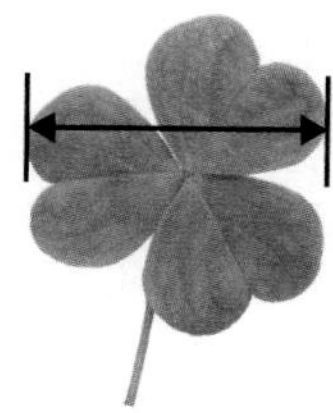

10.

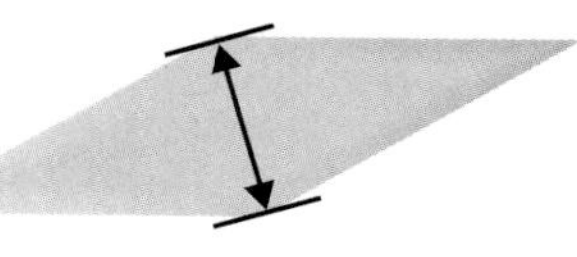

11. **WRITING IN ➤MATH** Describe the steps in measuring the length of an object using a metric ruler.

10-4 Metric Units of Length

GET READY to Learn

Doug is growing carrots in his garden. He pulled out a carrot to see if it was growing. Measure the carrot to the nearest centimeter.

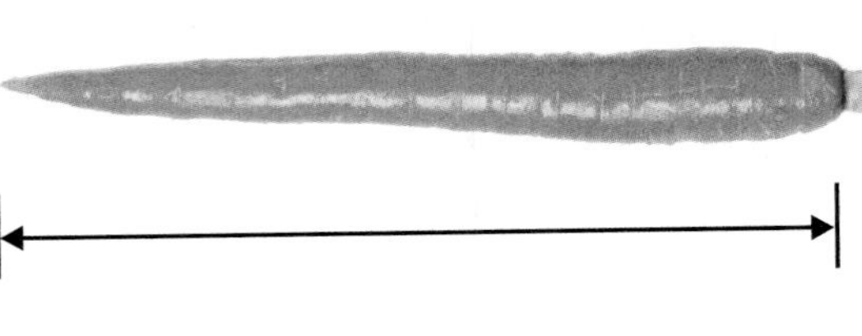

MAIN IDEA

I will estimate and measure lengths within the metric system.

Targeted TEKS 4.11 The student applies measurement concepts. The student is expected to estimate and measure to solve problems involving length (including perimeter) and area. The student uses measurement tools to measure capacity/volume and weight/mass. (A) **Estimate and use measurement tools to determine length** (including perimeter), area, capacity and weight/mass **using standard units SI (metric)** and customary.

New Vocabulary

millimeter
centimeter
meter
kilometer

A metric ruler is used to measure metric lengths. The metric units of length are the millimeter, centimeter, meter, and kilometer.

KEY CONCEPT — Metric Measurements

A **millimeter** is about as thick as 6 sheets of notebook paper.	A **centimeter** is about the width of a number on a calculator.	A **meter** is about the height of a chair.	A **kilometer** is about six city blocks.

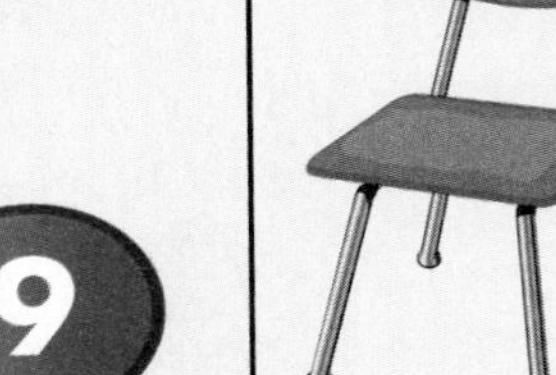

Real-World EXAMPLE — Measuring Metric Lengths

1 FOOD Measure the carrot to the nearest centimeter.

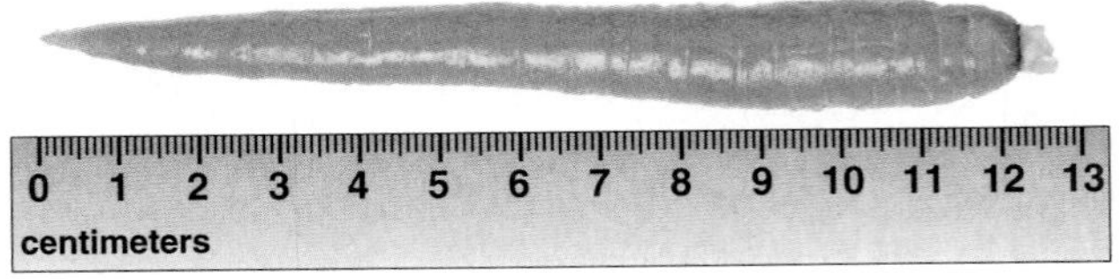

Align the 0 on the ruler with the left side of the carrot. The carrot ends before the 13-centimeter mark.

So, the carrot is almost 13 centimeters long.

Before measuring any object, always estimate the length to decide which unit of measurement is best to use.

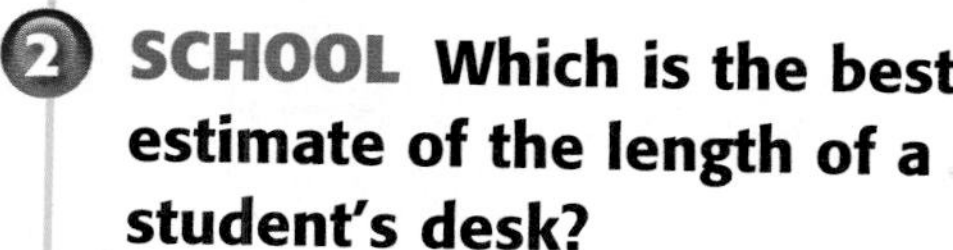

Metric Measurements of Length

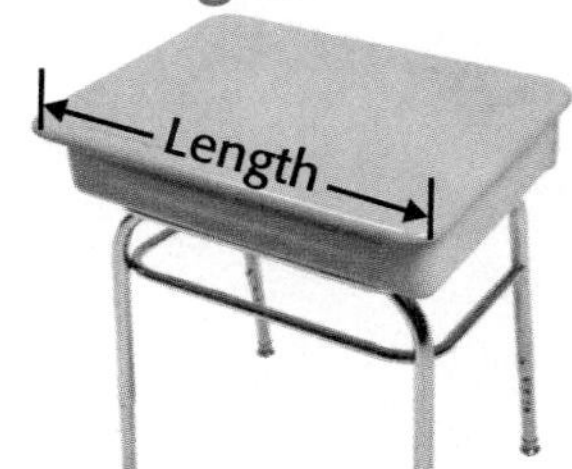

2 **SCHOOL Which is the best estimate of the length of a student's desk?**

A 5 centimeters

B 5 millimeters

C 50 centimeters

D 50 millimeters

A desk has to be high enough to sit under. 5 centimeters, 5 millimeters, and 50 millimeters are all too small. So, the answer must be C, 50 centimeters.

Online **Personal Tutor at** tx.gr4math.com

CHECK What You Know

Measure each object to the nearest centimeter. See Example 1 (p. 406)

1. 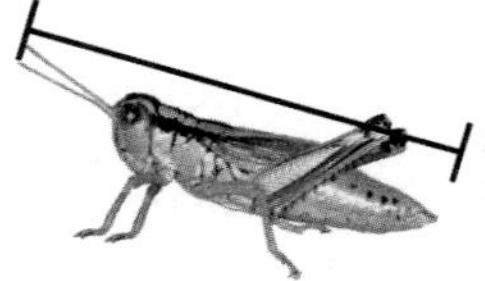

2. 

Choose the best estimate. See Example 2 (p. 407)

3. length of a canoe

A 6 centimeters **C** 6 meters

B 2 meters **D** 2 kilometers

4. width of a piece of string

A 1 millimeter **C** 1 meter

B 1 centimeter **D** 1 kilometer

5. Patty said to Lina, "I'm about 150 millimeters tall." Is Patty correct? Explain why or why not.

6. Talk About It Describe a situation when it would be appropriate to measure an object using millimeters. When is it appropriate to measure in kilometers?

Practice and Problem Solving

See page R33.

Measure each object to the nearest centimeter. See Example 1 (p. 406)

7. 

8. 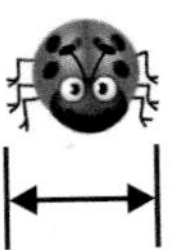

Choose the best estimate. See Example 2 (p. 407)

9. height of a cornstalk

A 2 millimeters **C** 2 meters

B 2 centimeters **D** 2 kilometers

10. length of an airport runway

A 5 millimeters **C** 5 meters

B 50 centimeters **D** 5 kilometers

11. A giraffe at the zoo is 5 meters tall. Name something else about 5 meters tall.

12. Is the distance from Boston, Massachusetts, to Los Angeles, California, about 5,000 kilometers? Explain how you know.

H.O.T. Problems

13. **OPEN ENDED** Find three things in the classroom that are longer than 10 centimeters and smaller than 100 centimeters. Estimate and determine the actual measurements.

14. **WRITING IN MATH** Explain why it would be better to measure the length of the classroom with a meter stick instead of a centimeter ruler.

Chapter 10 Mid-Chapter Check

Lessons 10-1 through 10-4

Estimate. Then measure each to the nearest inch, $\frac{1}{2}$ inch, and $\frac{1}{4}$ inch.
(Lesson 10-1)

1. 

2. 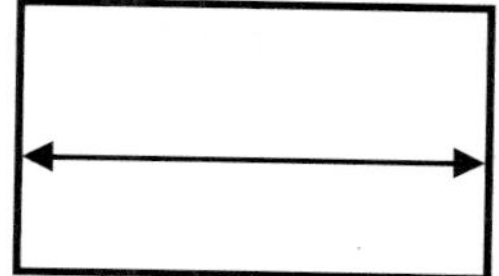

3. **TEST PRACTICE** Choose the best estimate for the height of a giraffe.
(Lesson 10-1)

A 19 inches

B 19 feet

C 19 yards

D 19 miles

Complete. (Lesson 10-2)

4. 3 feet = ■ inches

5. 2 yards = ■ feet

6. **TEST PRACTICE** Kenyi's family wants to fence in their yard. They need 80 yards of fence. How many feet of fence should they buy? (Lesson 10-2)

F 79 feet

G 96 feet

H 240 feet

J 960 feet

7. Which measurement best describes the length of a couch, 6 feet or 6 inches?

8. What is the width of the rectangle below if the length of one side of each square is 1 centimeter long? (Lesson 10-3)

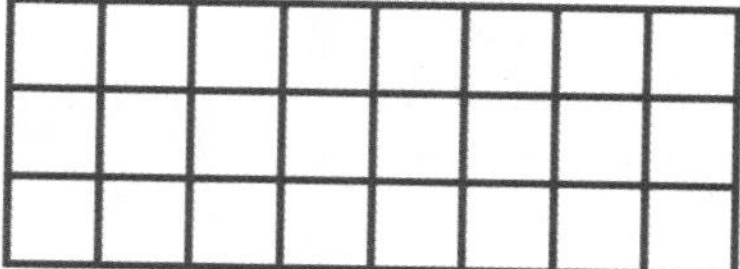

9. **TEST PRACTICE** What is the length of one side of the square shown? (Lesson 10-3)

A 2 mm

B 2 cm

C 2 m

D 2 km

10. Marcus went on a hiking trip. Which measurement best describes how far he hiked, 10 kilometers or 10 meters? (Lesson 10-4)

11. **WRITING IN ▶ MATH** Explain why 3 yards is equal to 108 inches.

10-5 Measure Perimeter

Berto is walking around a park on the path shown. How far did Berto walk?

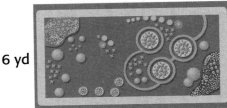

12 yd

6 yd

The distance around a figure is called the **perimeter**.

MAIN IDEA

I will find the perimeter of a polygon.

Targeted TEKS 4.11 The student applies measurement concepts. The student is expected to estimate and measure to solve problems involving length (including perimeter) and area. . . . (A) **Estimate and use measurement tools to determine length (including perimeter) . . . using standard units SI (metric)** and customary.

New Vocabulary

perimeter

KEY CONCEPT — Perimeter of a Rectangle

Words To find the perimeter of a rectangle, add the lengths of the sides. The perimeter of a rectangle also equals 2 times its length plus 2 times its width.

Symbols $P = \ell + w + \ell + w$

$P = (2\ell) + (2w)$

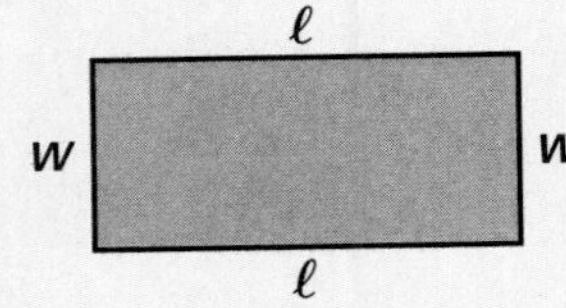

Real-World EXAMPLE — Find Perimeter

1 DISTANCE How far did Berto walk?

One Way: Use Addition	**Another Way:** Use a Formula
Add the measures of all of the sides of the figure.	Multiply the length and the width each by 2. Then add.
$P = 12 + 6 + 12 + 6$ $P = 36$	$P = (2\ell) + (2w)$ $P = (2 \times 12) + (2 \times 6)$ $P = 24 + 12$ or 36

So, Berto walked 36 yards.

You can estimate perimeter before finding the exact perimeter.

EXAMPLE Find Perimeter

2 **Find the perimeter of a square with side lengths of 6 inches.**

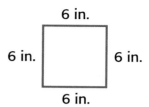

6 in.
6 in. 6 in.
6 in.

There is more than one way to find the perimeter of a square.

Estimate: $5 + 5 + 5 + 5 = 20$

One Way: **Use Addition**	Another Way: **Use a Formula**
Add the measures of all of the sides of the figure.	Multiply the length of one side by 4 because there are 4 sides of equal length.
$P = 6 + 6 + 6 + 6$ $P = 24$	$P = 4 \times \text{side length}$ $P = 4 \times 6$ $P = 24$

So, the perimeter of the square is 24 inches.

Online **Personal Tutor at** tx.gr4math.com

CHECK What You Know

Estimate. Then find the perimeter of each square or rectangle.

See Examples 1 and 2 (pp. 410–411)

1. 8 cm, 8 cm, 8 cm, 8 cm

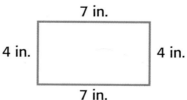

2. 7 in., 4 in., 4 in., 7 in.

3.

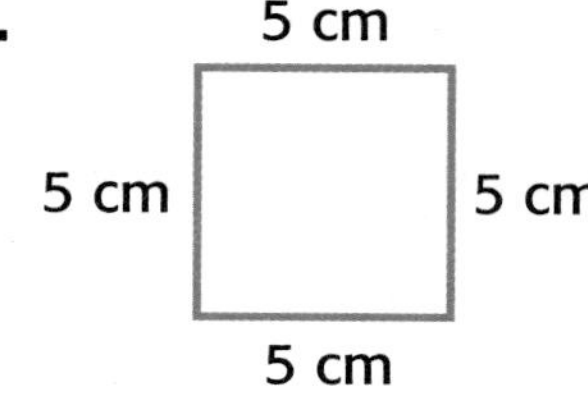

4. Luis made a drawing of his room. His drawing is shown. What is the perimeter of Luis's room?

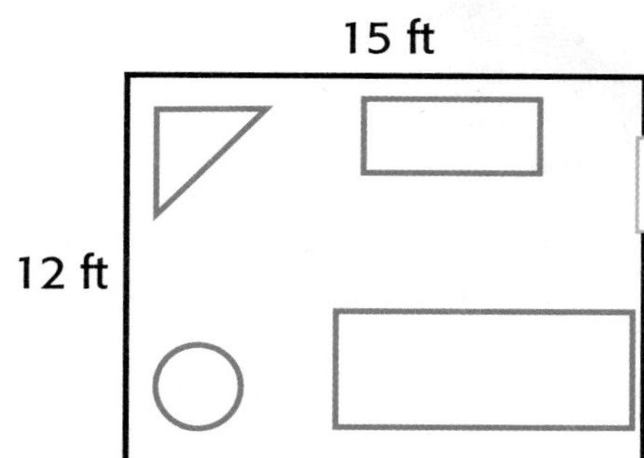

5. What is the perimeter of a square with side lengths of 4 inches?

6. Talk About It Explain the two ways to find the perimeter of a rectangle. What are the two ways to find the perimeter of a square?

Practice and Problem Solving

EXTRA PRACTICE
See page R34.

Estimate. Then find the perimeter of each square or rectangle.

See Examples 1 and 2 (pp. 410–411)

7.

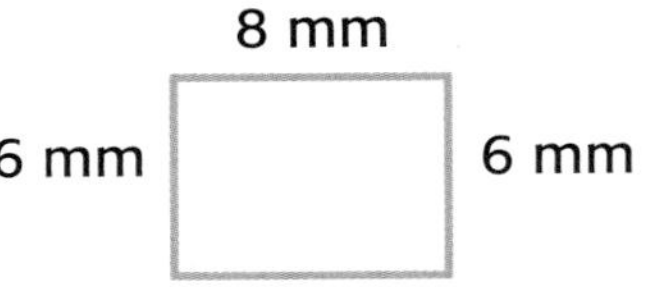

8.

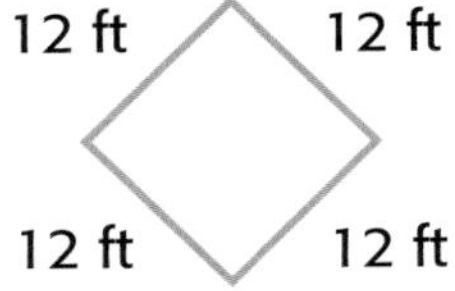

9.

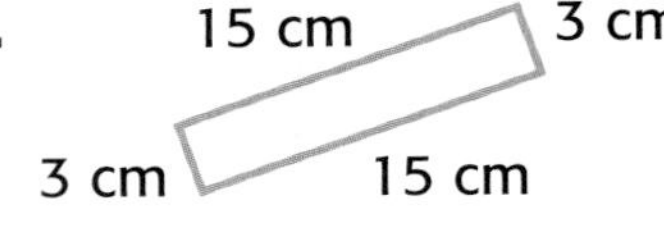

10.

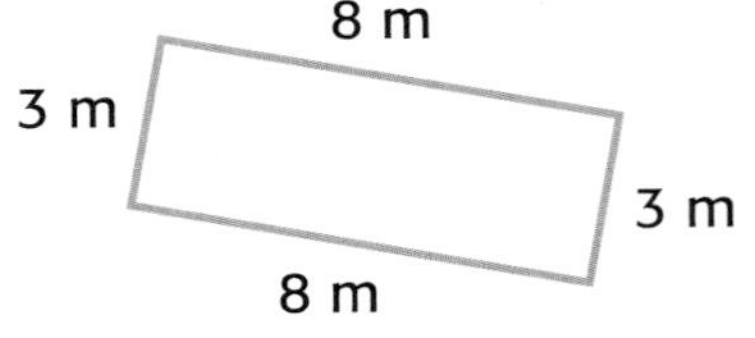

11.

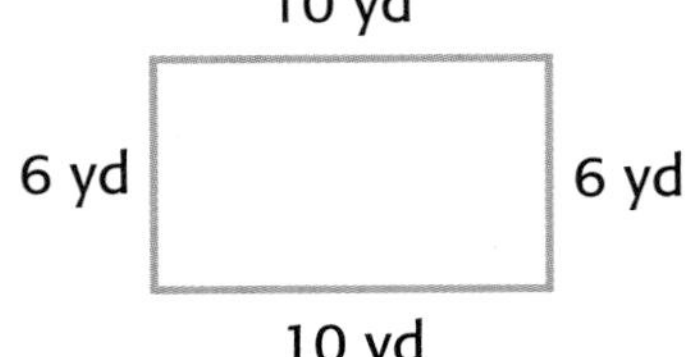

12.

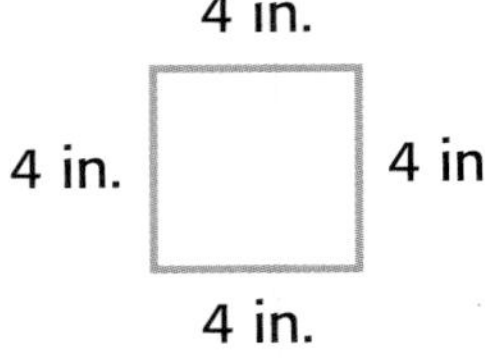

Estimate. Then find the perimeter of each rectangle in units.

13.

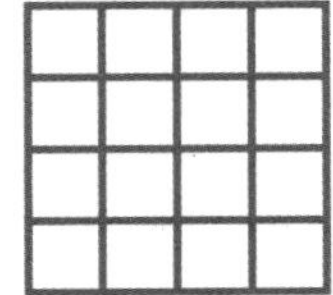

14.

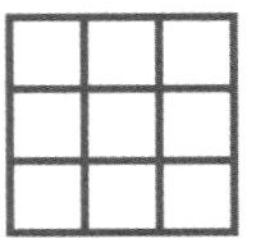

15.

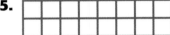

16. A baseball diamond is shaped like a square. Each side is 90 feet long. What is its perimeter?

17. A yard is 82 feet long and 45 feet wide. What is the perimeter of the yard?

Real-World PROBLEM SOLVING

Social Science The Parthenon is an ancient building in Athens, Greece. It has a rectangular base measuring about 228 feet by 101 feet.

18. What is the perimeter of the base of the Parthenon?

19. If you doubled the length of each side of the base, is the perimeter doubled? Show your work.

H.O.T. Problems

20. OPEN ENDED Locate a four-sided figure in your classroom. Use a measurement tool to find its perimeter.

21. WRITING IN MATH Suppose you double the side length of a square. Will the perimeter also double? Explain.

TEST Practice

22. What is the perimeter of the figure below if the side of each block represents 1 centimeter? **(Lesson 10-5)**

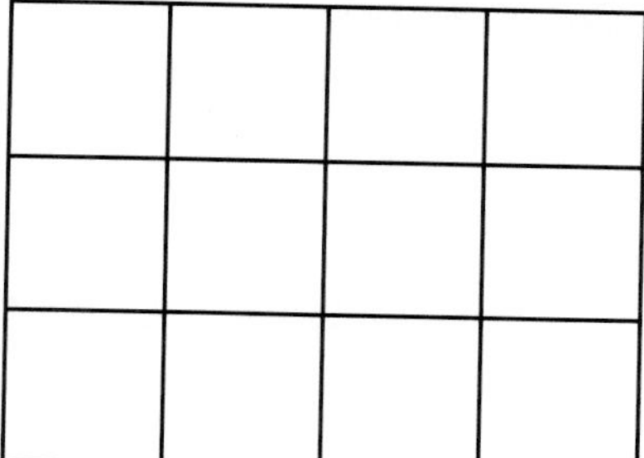

A 7 cm

B 12 cm

C 14 cm

D 20 cm

23. Choose the best unit for measuring distance across the United States. **(Lesson 10-4)**

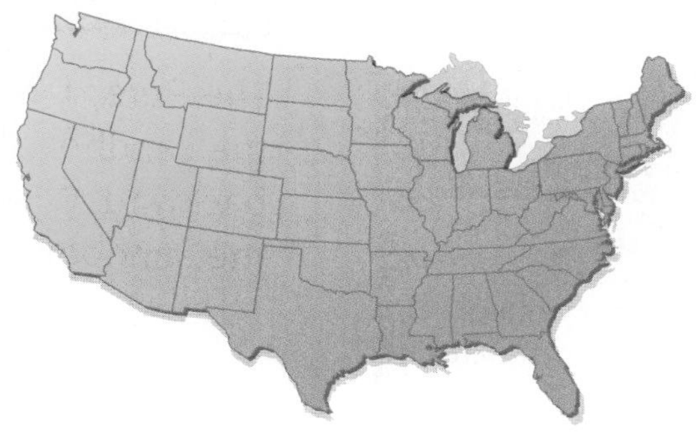

F centimeter

G meter

H decimeter

J kilometer

Spiral Review

Measure each object to the nearest centimeter. **(Lesson 10-4)**

24.

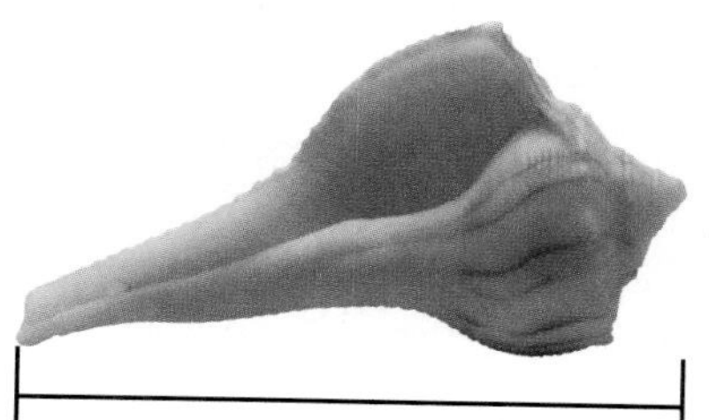

25.

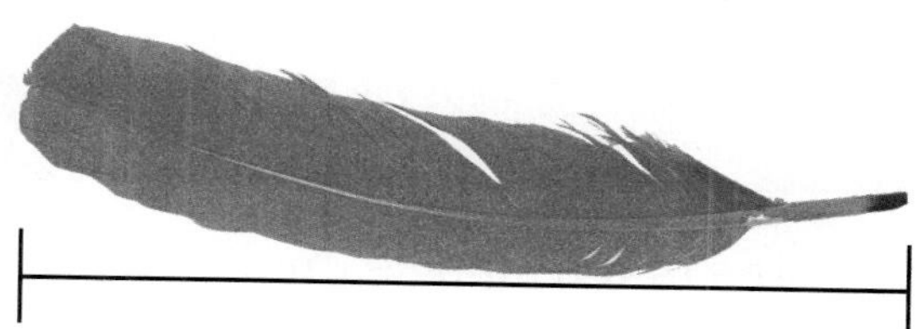

26. There are 15 girls in class and 13 boys in class. If 7 more girls came to class, how many students will there be in the class? **(Lesson 10-3)**

Complete. **(Lesson 10-2)**

27. 36 in. = ■ ft

28. 12 ft = ■ yd

29. 4 yd = ■ in.

10-6 Measure Area

MAIN IDEA

I will find the area of rectangles and squares.

Targeted TEKS 4.11 The student applies measurement concepts. The student is expected to estimate and measure to solve problems involving length (including perimeter) and area. . . . (A) **Estimate and use measurement tools to determine** length (including perimeter), **area, . . . using standard units SI (metric) and customary.**

New Vocabulary

area

square units

GET READY to Learn

The Perez family wants to put the sandbox shown in their backyard. What is the area of the sandbox?

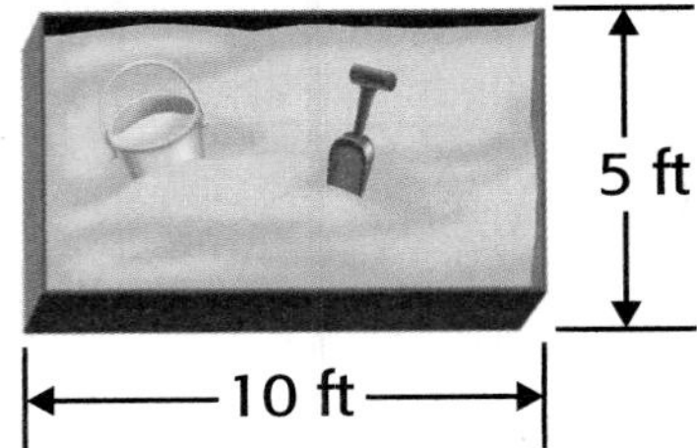

Area is the number of square units needed to cover a region or figure without any overlap. It is measured in **square units**.

Real-World EXAMPLE — Area of a Rectangle

1 SANDBOX **Find the area of the sandbox.**

One Way: Count

10 ft

5 ft

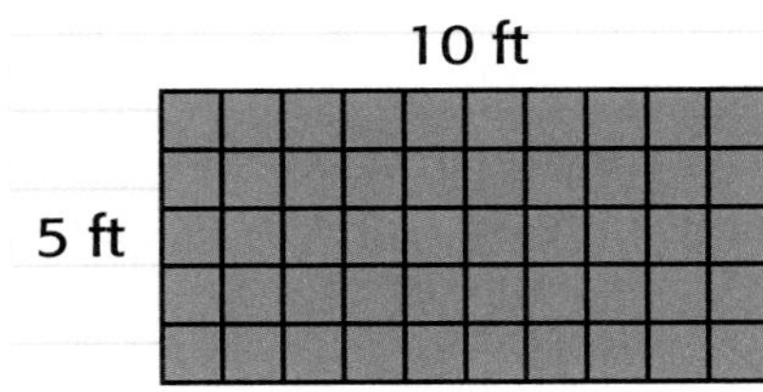

There are 50 square feet.

Another Way: Multiply

Multiply the length times the width to find the area.

$A = \text{length} \times \text{width}$

$A = \ell \times w$

$= 10 \text{ feet} \times 5 \text{ feet}$

$= 50 \text{ square feet}$

So, the area of the sandbox is 50 square feet.

KEY CONCEPT — Area of a Rectangle

Words To find the area of a rectangle, multiply the length by the width.

Formula $A = \ell \times w$

ℓ

w w

ℓ

You can also find the area of a square.

KEY CONCEPT — **Area of a Square**

Words	To find the area of a square, multiply the length of one side s by itself.
Formula	$A = s \times s$

s s s s

Real-World EXAMPLE — **Area of a Square**

Remember

Estimate before finding the exact area.
9 cm × 9 cm →
10 cm × 10 cm
10 × 10 = 100
Since 81 is close to 100, the answer is reasonable.

2 **PICTURES What is the area of the picture if its sides are 9 centimeters in length?**

9 cm
9 cm

A = side × side	Formula
A = 9 cm × 9 cm	$s = 9$
A = 81 sq cm	Multiply.

The area of the picture is 81 square centimeters.

Online **Personal Tutor at** tx.gr4math.com

CHECK What You Know

Estimate. Then find the area of each square or rectangle.

See Examples 1 and 2 (pp. 414–415)

1. 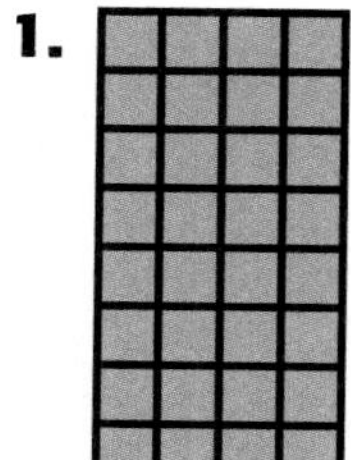

2. 6 m, 1 m

3. 3 yd, 3 yd

4. Mr. Hart is hanging a picture on a wall. The picture frame has a length of 12 inches and a width of 9 inches. How much wall space will the picture need?

5. **Talk About It** Explain two ways to find the area of a rectangle. What are two ways to find the area of a square?

Practice and Problem Solving

EXTRA PRACTICE See page R34.

Estimate. Then find the area of each square or rectangle.

See Examples 1 and 2 (pp. 414–415)

6. 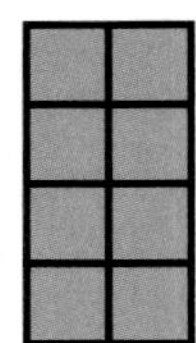

7. 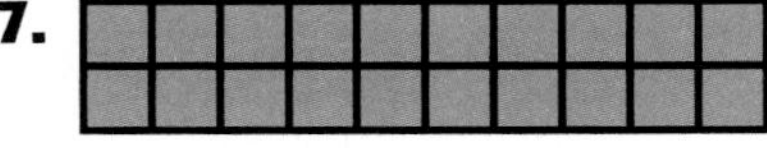

8. 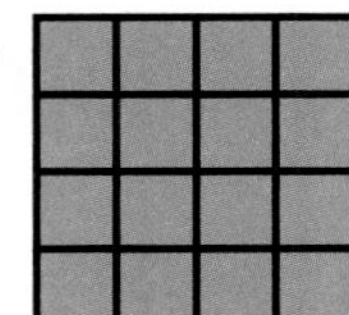

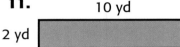

9. 6 m

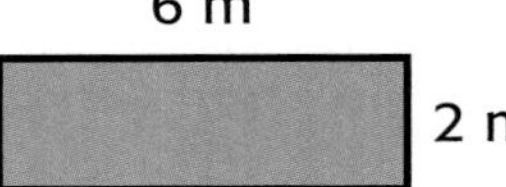

2 m

10. 8 km

8 km

11. 10 yd

2 yd

12. Each child in Mrs. Chan's class has a rectangular desk that is 15 inches long and 32 inches wide. What is the area of the top of each student's desk?

13. Ricky's computer monitor is a rectangle. The length is 15 inches and the width is 12 inches. Estimate the area of the monitor.

14. A car is 15 feet long and 6 feet wide. It is parked on a rectangular driveway with an area of 112 square feet. How much of the driveway is *not* covered by the car?

15. A rectangular playground is 40 meters by 10 meters. Its area will be covered with shredded tires. Each bag of shredded tires covers 200 square meters and costs $30. Find the total cost for this project.

H.O.T. Problems

16. OPEN ENDED Draw three rectangles that each have an area of 36 square inches, but have different perimeters.

NUMBER SENSE The area and the measure of one side of each square or rectangle is given. Find the missing sides.

17. 6 in.

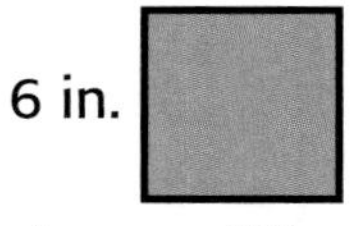

Area = 36 sq in.

18. 4 m

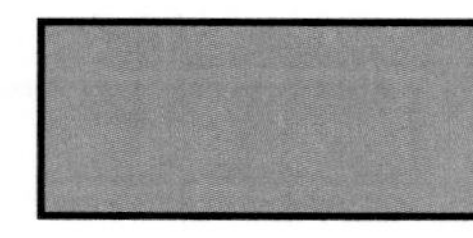

Area = 36 sq m

19. 1 cm

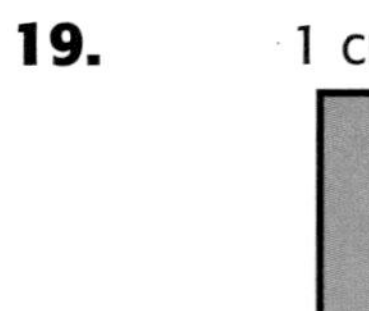

Area = 5 sq cm

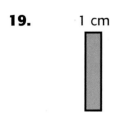

20. WRITING IN MATH A square has sides measuring 3 feet. If the sides of a square are doubled, will the area also double? Explain.

Area Guess

Find Area of Rectangles

Get Ready!

Players: 2 players

You will need: 2 metric rulers with centimeters

Get Set!

Each player makes a copy of the table shown.

Player ______			
Object	Area		Difference
	Estimated	Actual	

Go!

- Each player selects four objects in the classroom that have a rectangular surface.
- Each player estimates the area of the objects selected to the nearest square centimeter.
- Find the exact measurements and the exact areas of the objects.
- Find the differences between the estimated areas and the actual areas of the objects.
- Find the sum of the four differences.
- The player who has the least difference between the estimated and actual areas wins.

Measurement Activity for 10-6
Perimeter and Area

MAIN IDEA

I will explore perimeter and area.

 **Targeted TEKS 4.11** The student applies measurement concepts. The student is expected to estimate and measure to solve problems involving length (including perimeter) and area. . . . **(A)** **Estimate and use measurement tools to determine length (including perimeter), area, . . . using standard units SI (metric) and customary.**

You Will Need
grid paper

Animation
tx.gr4math.com

In this activity, you will explore whether rectangles with the same area can have different perimeters.

ACTIVITY **Relate Perimeter and Area**

Step 1 **Draw rectangles.**

Draw the following rectangles on grid paper.

- 1 unit by 24 units
- 2 units by 12 units
- 3 units by 8 units
- 4 units by 6 units

Step 2 **Copy and complete the table.**

Find the perimeter and area of the rectangles. Record the information on your table.

Figure	Perimeter	Area
Rectangle 1	■ units	■ square units
Rectangle 2	■ units	■ square units
Rectangle 3	■ units	■ square units
Rectangle 4	■ units	■ square units

Step 3 **Examine your table.**

What similarities and differences do you notice among the rectangles?

Is it possible for rectangles with the same area to have different perimeters?

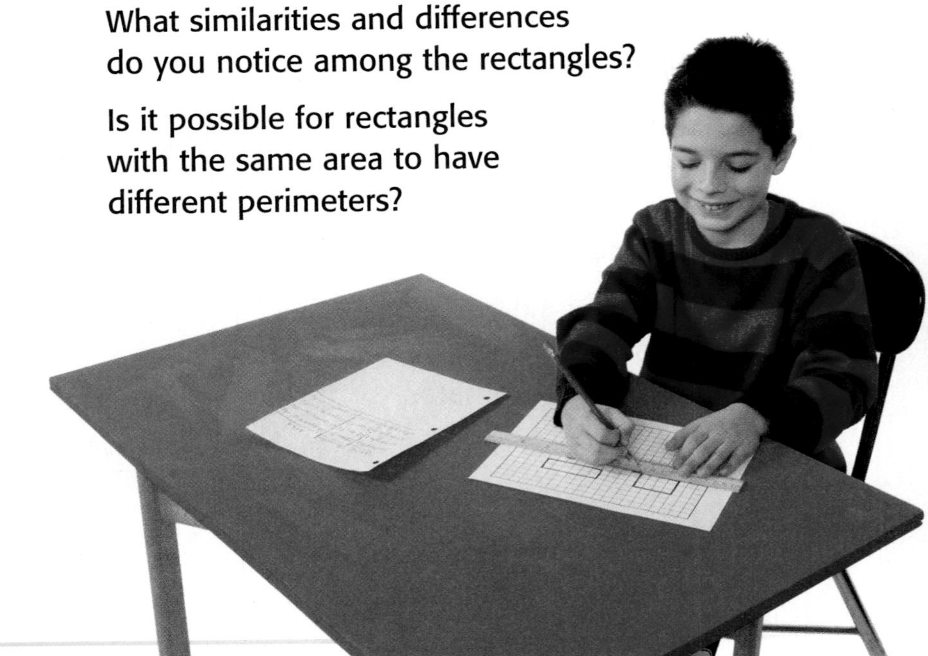

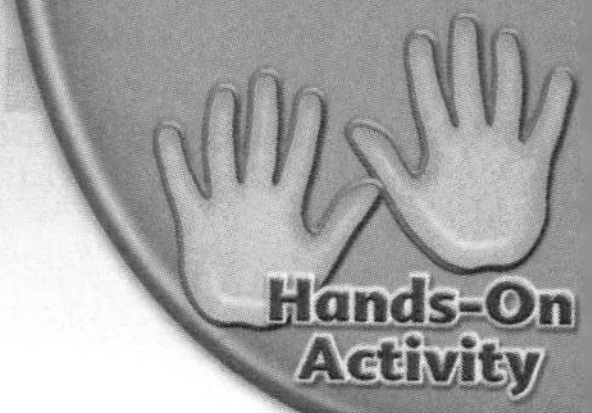

Think About It

1. Explain the difference between area and perimeter.

2. Is it possible to draw a rectangle that has an area of 24 square units and a perimeter of 24 units? Explain.

3. Is there a relationship between the area and the perimeter of a rectangle? Explain.

4. Look at the rectangles that you drew. What do you notice about the shape of the rectangle that has the greatest perimeter?

CHECK What You Know

Find the perimeter and area for each square or rectangle.

5. 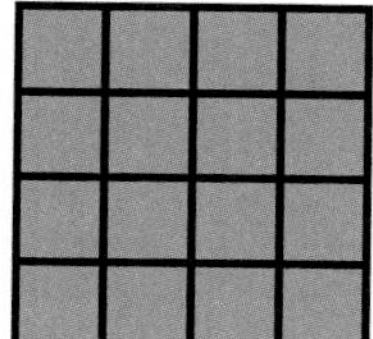

6. 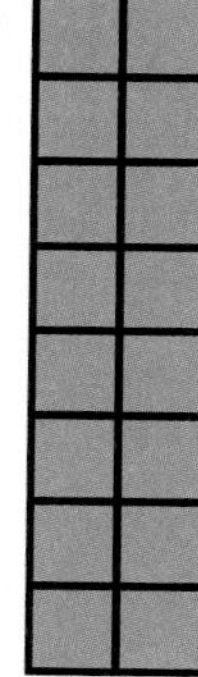

7.

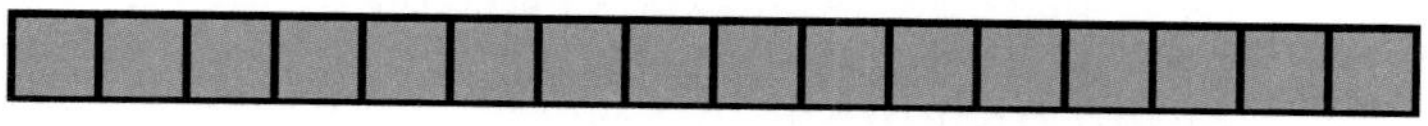

8. What do the figures in Exercises 5–7 have in common? How do these figures differ?

9. Draw two rectangles that have the same areas and the same perimeters.

10. Can rectangles that have the same perimeter have different areas? Explain.

11. **WRITING IN ►MATH** If a figure has a greater perimeter than another, does it also have a greater area? Explain your thinking.

10-7 Problem-Solving Investigation

MAIN IDEA I will choose the best strategy to solve a problem.

Targeted TEKS 4.14 The student applies Grade 4 mathematics to solve problems . . . in and outside of school. (B) **Solve problems that incorporate understanding the problem, making a plan, carrying out the plan, and evaluating the solution for reasonableness.** *Also addresses TEKS 4.14(C).*

P.S.I. TEAM +

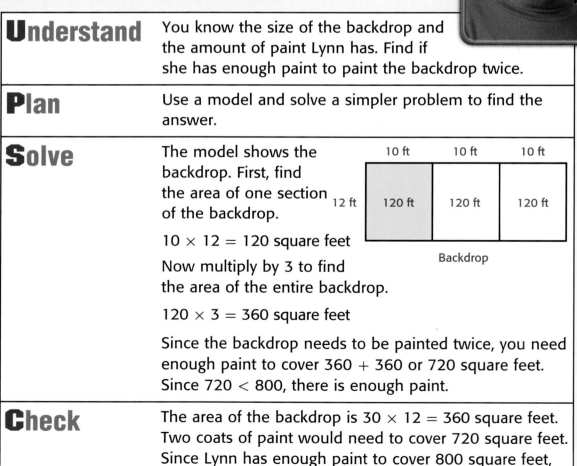

LYNN: **I am painting a backdrop that is 30 feet long and 12 feet wide for the school play. The backdrop needs two coats of paint. I have two cans of paint and each covers 400 square feet.**

YOUR MISSION: **Determine if Lynn has enough paint to paint the backdrop.**

Understand	You know the size of the backdrop and the amount of paint Lynn has. Find if she has enough paint to paint the backdrop twice.
Plan	Use a model and solve a simpler problem to find the answer.
Solve	The model shows the backdrop. First, find the area of one section of the backdrop. $10 \times 12 = 120$ square feet Now multiply by 3 to find the area of the entire backdrop. $120 \times 3 = 360$ square feet Since the backdrop needs to be painted twice, you need enough paint to cover $360 + 360$ or 720 square feet. Since $720 < 800$, there is enough paint.
Check	The area of the backdrop is $30 \times 12 = 360$ square feet. Two coats of paint would need to cover 720 square feet. Since Lynn has enough paint to cover 800 square feet, the answer is correct.

Backdrop

Mixed Problem Solving

See page R35.

Use any of the strategies shown below to solve. Tell what strategy you used.

PROBLEM-SOLVING STRATEGIES
- Act it out.
- Guess and check.
- Look for a pattern.
- Work a simpler problem.

1. **Measurement** When Jake got up, there was 4 inches of snow on the ground. By recess, one inch of the snow melted. Then, at bedtime, another 2 inches of snow had fallen. How many inches of snow were on the ground when Jake went to bed?

2. **Measurement** One seal weighs 26 pounds. The second seal weighs three times as much. How much do the baby seals weigh altogether?

3. Four numbers between 1 and 9 have a sum of 23. Each number is used once. What are the numbers?

4. A movie theater has 18 screens. About 212 people see a movie on each screen at the same time on Friday. About how many people are seeing movies in the theater at that time?

5. The table shows the amount of vegetables sold at a grocery store every four weeks. Is it reasonable to say that the store sells about 300 vegetables every week?

Vegetable	Amount
Corn	396
Onions	316
Tomatoes	489

6. Heath brought 25 trading cards to a hobby show. He received three cards for one card in three trades. Then he gave 2 cards for one card in two trades. How many cards does Heath have now?

7. Pedro bought 3 pencils for 15¢. How much would 10 pencils cost?

8. Describe the pattern below. Then find the missing number.

   20, 200, 2,000, ■, 200,000

9. **Measurement** Clarissa has 4 pictures that are the size of the one shown. How much space will they take up in her photo album?

5 in.

3 in.

10. **WRITING IN MATH** Look back at Exercise 9. Explain how you solved the problem.

10-8 Measure Temperature

GET READY to Learn

Ashton's teacher is measuring the temperature of the liquid being used in a science experiment. What is the temperature?

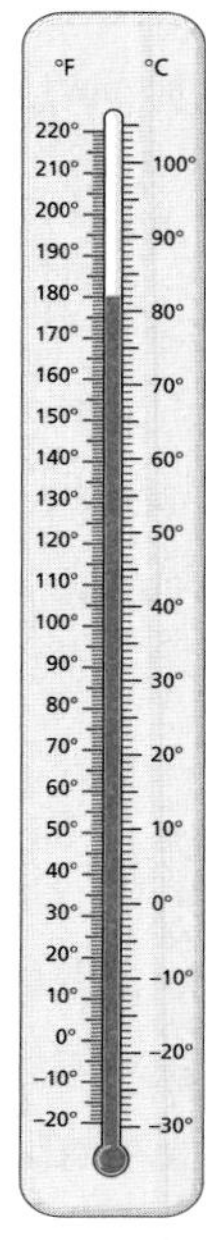

MAIN IDEA

I will measure temperature and calculate changes in temperature.

Targeted TEKS 4.12 The student applies measurements concepts. The student measures times and temperature (in degrees Fahrenheit and Celsius). **(A) Use a thermometer to measure temperature and changes in temperature.**

New Vocabulary

Fahrenheit

Celsius

Temperature can be measured in **Fahrenheit** (°F) or **Celsius** (°C).

Real-World EXAMPLE — Read a Thermometer

1 SCIENCE **Write the approximate temperature of the liquid being used in the science experiment in Fahrenheit and Celsius.**

The needle is pointing to 180 and about 82.

The °F shows the temperature in degrees Fahrenheit, and the °C shows the temperature in degrees Celsius.

So, the temperature is 180°F or about 82°C.

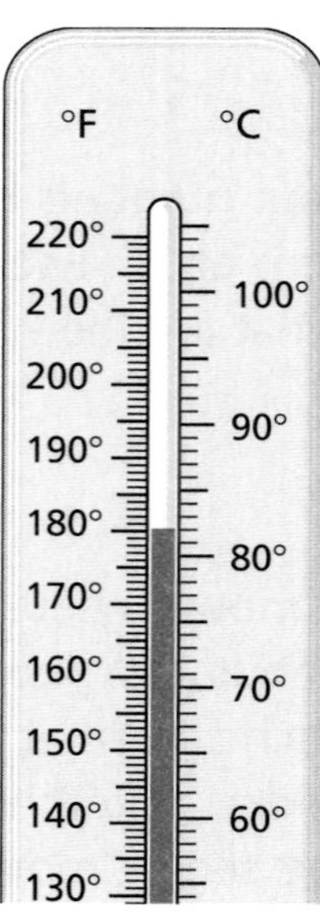

ACTIVITY

Hands-On Mini Activity

Measure and calculate changes in temperature.

1. Set a thermometer in the back of the classroom and another one outside.

2. At the end of math class, check both thermometers. Determine the temperature indoors and outdoors.

3. Which thermometer shows a warmer temperature?

4. How much warmer was the one thermometer than the other in degrees Fahrenheit? How did you find the difference?

5. How much warmer was the one thermometer than the other in degrees Celsius? How did you find the differences?

Use addition or subtraction to find changes in temperatures.

EXAMPLE Temperature Change

2 Find the change in the temperatures.

A thermometer inside reads:

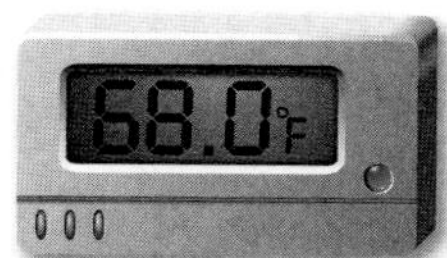

A thermometer outside reads:

84° − 68° = change in temperature

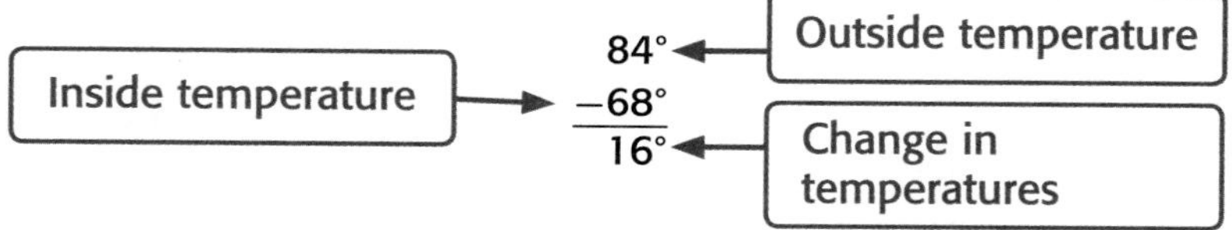

So, it is 16° F warmer outside than inside.

Personal Tutor at tx.gr4math.com

CHECK What You Know

Write the approximate temperature in degrees Fahrenheit and Celsius. See Example 1 (p. 422)

1. 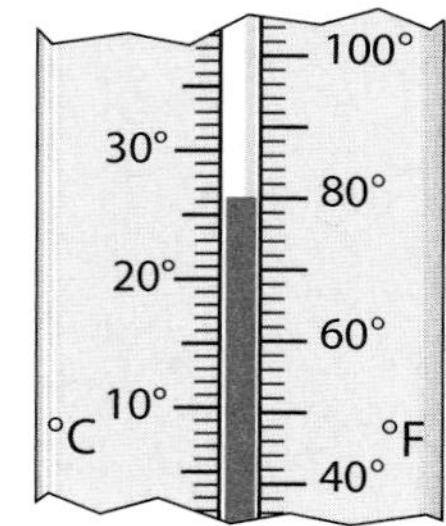

2.

Find the change in temperature. See Example 2 (p. 423)

3. 16°C to 5°C

4. 34°F to 21°F

5. The thermometer reads 15°C. Vickie decides to wear her mittens and hat. Is this a good idea? Explain how you know.

6. A normal cow's body temperature is about 101°F. About what is that in degrees Celsius?

7. When Neva woke up, the temperature was 20°C. By lunchtime, the temperature went up 6°C. Neva later found out that the high temperature for the day was 31°C. How much higher did the temperature go after Neva had lunch?

8. Talk About It The temperature outside is 16°F warmer than in the classroom. The classroom's temperature is 67°F. What is the temperature outside? Write the number sentence you used to find the answer.

Practice and Problem Solving

EXTRA PRACTICE See page R35.

Write the approximate temperature in degrees Fahrenheit and Celsius. See Example 1 (p. 422)

9. 

10. 

11. 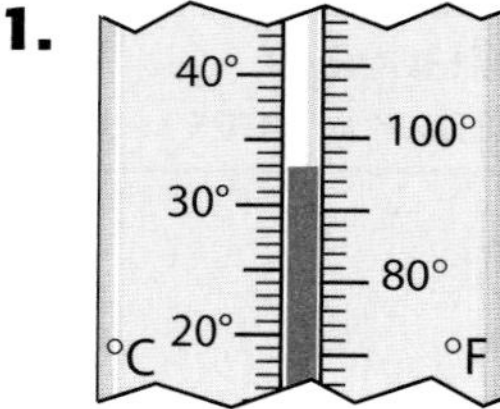

12. 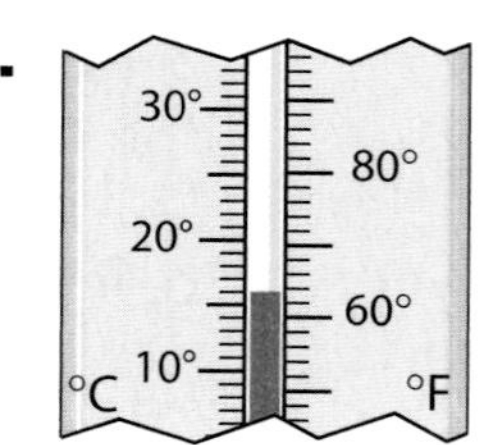

Find the change in the temperatures. See Example 2 (p. 423)

13. 0°F to 26°F

14. 18°F to 6°F

15. 15°C to 8°C

16. 87°C to 60°C

17. 212°F to 87°F

18. 75°F to 114°F

19. 31°C to 15°C

20. 47°C to 79°C

21. Two hamburgers are cooking on a grill. The grill's flame is 187°F. The flame needs to be 163°F hotter. At what temperature should the burgers cook?

22. It is 25°F outside and 46°F warmer inside. What is the temperature inside?

H.O.T. Problems

23. OPEN ENDED Research the high and low temperatures from last week. Which day experienced the greatest change in temperature?

24. FIND THE ERROR Abbie and Sashi each found the change in the temperature for today. Who is correct? Prove it.

Abbie
"The high was 55°F and the low was 42°F. The change in temperature was 13°F."

Sashi
"The high was 55°F and the low was 42°F. The change in temperature was 97°F."

25. WRITING IN MATH Write a real-world problem involving temperature. Have a classmate solve your problem.

Problem Solving in History

WALLS WITH HISTORY

Humans have built forts all over the world for thousands of years. Most forts are rectangles. There are more than 136 forts in the United States. Some forts can hold hundreds to thousands of people, while others hold less than 100. The Alamo, a fort in Texas, protected 189 soldiers. The fort protected them for 13 days against an army of 6,000 soldiers!

Some forts like Sutter's Fort are now museums or state parks. However, other forts like Fort Knox in Kentucky are still used by the military today.

Famous Forts

Fort	Size of Main Building
Fort McIntosh (Georgia)	33 yd by 33 yd
The Alamo (Texas)	148 ft by 159 ft
Stone Fort at Harper's Ferry (West Virginia)	40 ft by 100 ft
Sutter's Fort (California)	64 ft by 35 ft
Fort Clatsop (Oregon)	50 ft by 50 ft

Targeted TEKS 4.14 The student applies Grade 4 mathematics to solve problems connected to everyday experiences and activities in and outside of school. (A) **Identify the mathematics in everyday situations.**

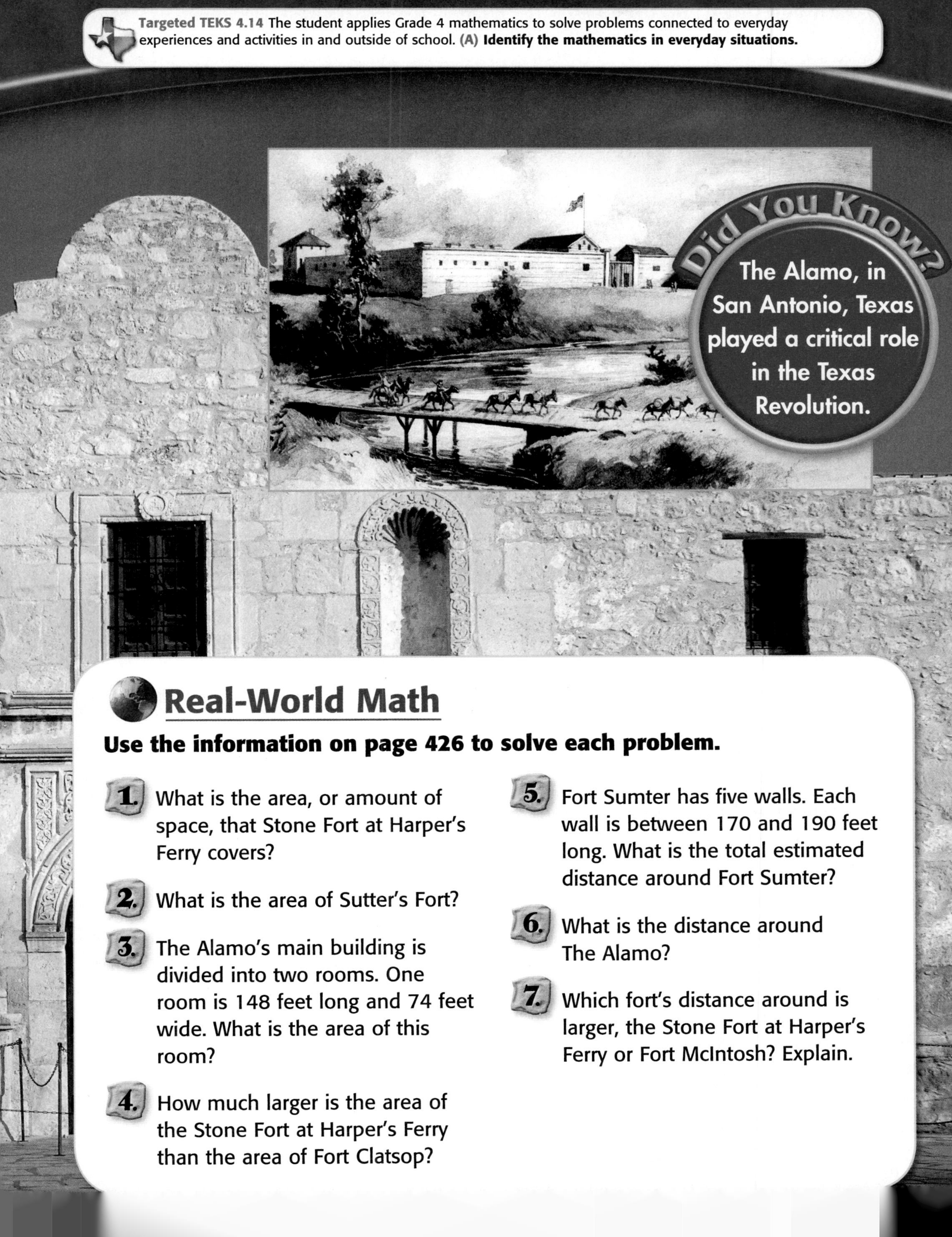

Did You Know?

The Alamo, in San Antonio, Texas played a critical role in the Texas Revolution.

Real-World Math

Use the information on page 426 to solve each problem.

1. What is the area, or amount of space, that Stone Fort at Harper's Ferry covers?
2. What is the area of Sutter's Fort?
3. The Alamo's main building is divided into two rooms. One room is 148 feet long and 74 feet wide. What is the area of this room?
4. How much larger is the area of the Stone Fort at Harper's Ferry than the area of Fort Clatsop?
5. Fort Sumter has five walls. Each wall is between 170 and 190 feet long. What is the total estimated distance around Fort Sumter?
6. What is the distance around The Alamo?
7. Which fort's distance around is larger, the Stone Fort at Harper's Ferry or Fort McIntosh? Explain.

CHAPTER 10 Study Guide and Review

Be sure the following Key Vocabulary words and Key Concepts are written in your Foldable.

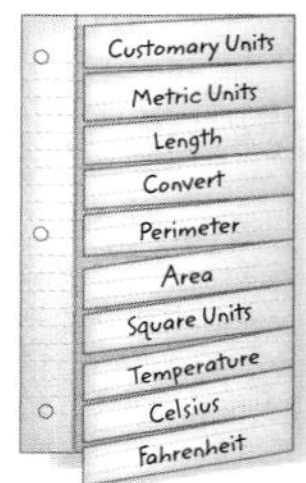

BIG Ideas

Measure Length (pp. 395–408)

- Common customary units of length are inch, foot, and yard.
- Metric units of length are millimeter, centimeter, meter, and kilometer.
- To measure the distance between two cities, you would use kilometers.

Perimeter and Area (pp. 410–419)

Perimeter is the distance around a figure.

- To find perimeter, add the lengths of the sides. $P = \ell + \ell + w + w$

Area is the number of square units needed to cover a region or figure without any overlap.

- Area of a Rectangle = length × width
- Area of a Square = side × side

Key Vocabulary

area (p. 414)
convert length (p. 400)
perimeter (p. 410)

Vocabulary Check

Choose the vocabulary word that completes each sentence.

1. The distance around a figure is the ___?___.
2. If you measure something in inches, you have measured its ___?___.
3. When you change the unit of measure, you ___?___ measurements.
4. ___?___ is the number of square units needed to cover a region or figure.

Math Online Vocabulary Review at tx.gr4math.com

Lesson-by-Lesson Review

10-1 Customary Units of Length (pp. 397–399)

Example 1

Estimate. Then measure the length of the frog below to the nearest inch, $\frac{1}{2}$ inch and $\frac{1}{4}$ inch.

The frog is 2 inches long.

Estimate. Then measure to the nearest inch, $\frac{1}{2}$ inch, and $\frac{1}{4}$ inch.

5.

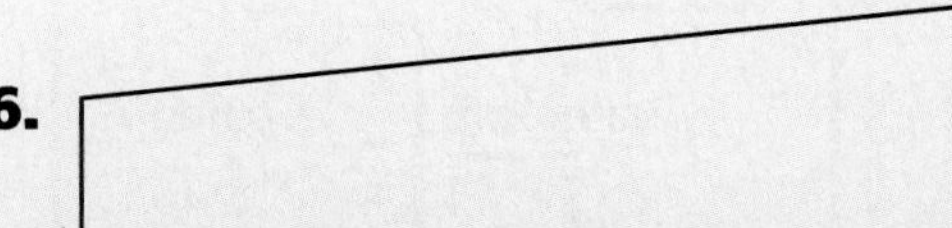

6.

7. The school supply store has index cards that are $2\frac{1}{2}$ inches wide and 3 inches long. How many inches long will four index cards be that are placed end to end?

10-2 Converting Customary Length (pp. 400–401)

Example 2

How many feet are in 3 yards?

You need to find the number of feet in 3 yards. Since a yard is a larger unit than a foot, you will use multiplication to convert.

To convert 3 yards to feet, multiply by 3.

3 yards = ■ feet

3 yards × 3 = ■ feet

Multiply by 3 since there are 3 feet in each yard.

3 × 3 = 9

So, 3 yards = 9 feet.

Complete.

8. 2 ft = ■ in.

9. 6 ft = ■ in.

10. ■ in. = 2 yd

11. How many inches long is this wagon?

12. John is making a window covering for his room. He needs 15 feet of fabric. If he buys 4 yards of fabric will he have enough? Explain.

10-3 Problem-Solving Strategy: Solve a Simpler Problem (pp. 402–403)

Example 3
Find the perimeter of the first floor of the house shown below.

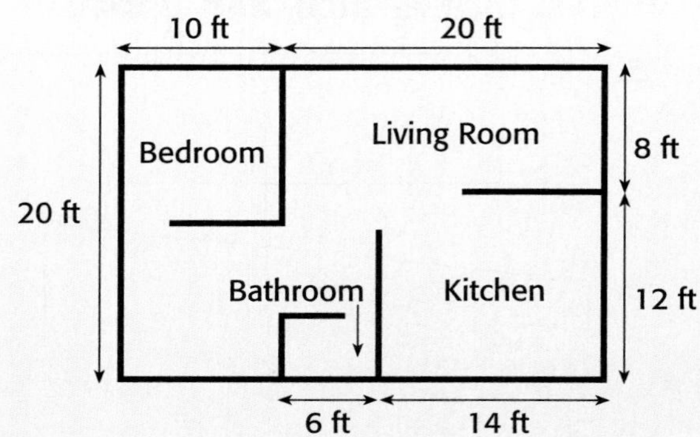

Understand

What facts do you know?

- One side measures 20 feet.
- Another side measures the sum of 10 feet and 20 feet.

What do you need to find?

- The perimeter of the house.

Plan Solve a simpler problem.

Solve Multiply the width by 2.

$20 \times 2 = 40$

Next, add 10 and 20. Then multiply the sum by 2.

$10 + 20 = 30$

$30 \times 2 = 60$

So, the perimeter is 40 + 60 or 100 feet.

Check Add all the measures

$20 + 10 + 6 + 14 + 12 + 8 + 20 + 10 = 100$

So, our answer is correct.

13. **Measurement** Mr. and Mrs. Lobo are building a fence around their rectangular yard that is 16 feet long and 14 feet wide. How much fence will they need?

14. Melisa ran two laps around the track. How many feet did she run?

15. **Measurement** Oliver is buying a border for a poster. How many inches of border will Oliver need for a poster that is 44 inches long and 28 inches wide?

16. Look at this figure. What is the length of the dashed line?

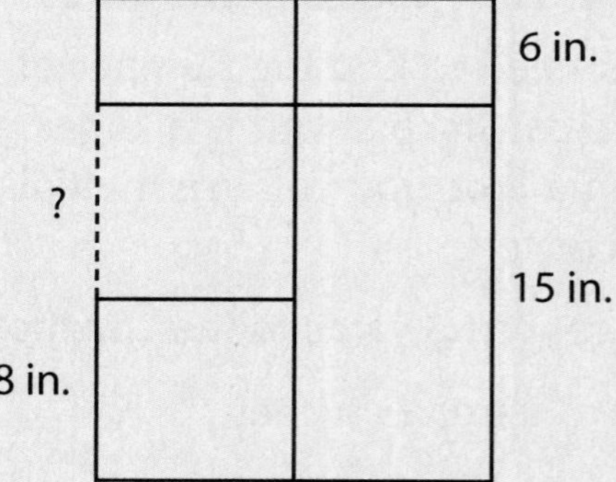

17. Sal had boxes he was stacking. Each was 2 feet high. If he stacks 3 boxes on top of a table that is 3 feet high, what will the total height be?

10-4 Metric Units of Length (pp. 406–408)

Example 4
Measure the flower to the nearest centimeter.

Align the 0 mark on the ruler to the left side of the flower. The flower ends at the 4 centimeter mark on the ruler. So, the flower is 4 centimeters long.

Measure the object to the nearest centimeter.

18.

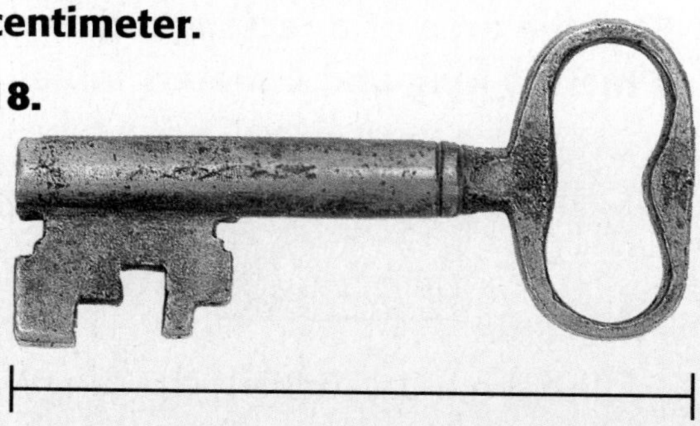

19.

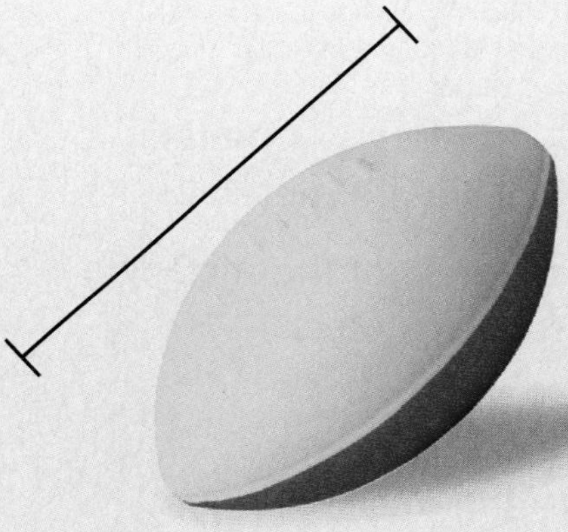

10-5 Measure Perimeter (pp. 410–413)

Example 5
Find the perimeter of the rectangle.

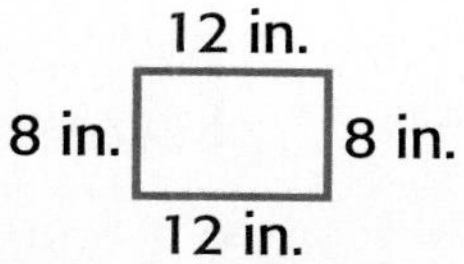

$P = \ell + w + \ell + w$
$P = 12 + 8 + 12 + 8$
$P = 24 + 16$
$P = 40$ inches

Example 6
Find the perimeter of the square.

$P = 4 \times s$
$P = 4 \times 3$
$P = 12$ centimeters

Estimate. Then find the perimeter of each square or rectangle.

20.

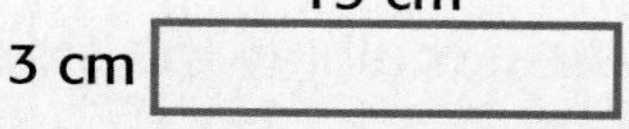

21.

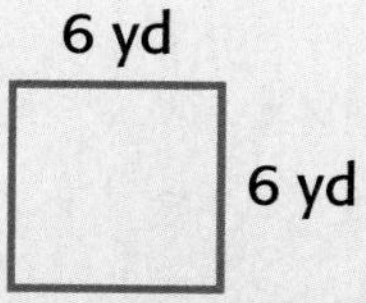

22. Measurement A poster has a length of 24 inches, and its width is 12 inches. What is the perimeter of the poster?

10-6 Measure Area (pp. 414–417)

Example 7
Find the area of a rectangle that is 7 meters long and 4 meters wide.

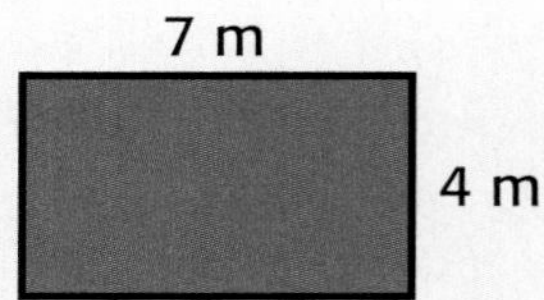

To find the area, multiply the length and the width.

$A = \ell \times w$
$A = 7$ meters $\times$ 4 meters
$A = 28$ square meters

So, the area of the rectangle is 28 square meters.

Example 8
What is the area of a square with sides that are 5 inches long?

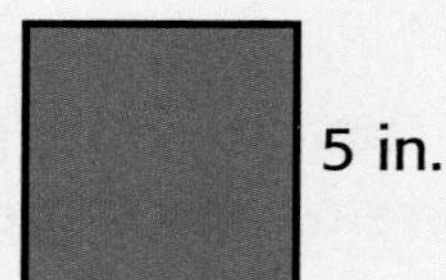

To find the area, multiply the side length by itself.

$A = s \times s$
$A = 5$ inches $\times$ 5 inches
$A = 25$ square inches

So, the area of the square is 25 square inches.

Find the area of each square or rectangle.

23. 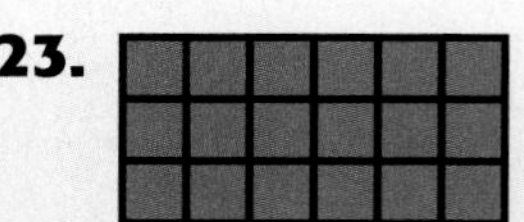

24. 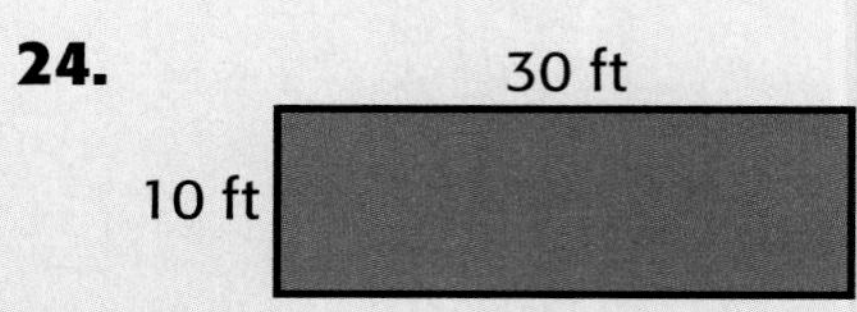

25. 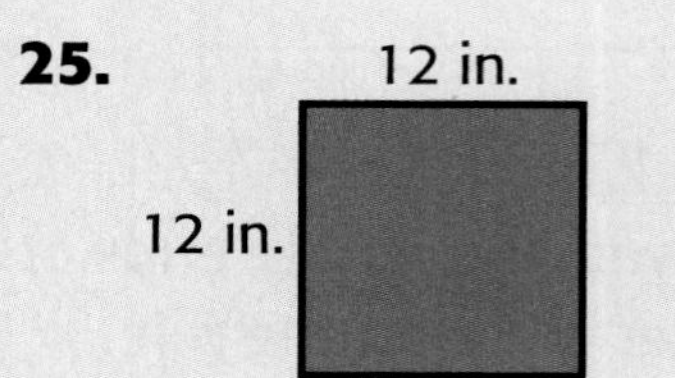

Algebra **The area and the measure of one side of each square or rectangle is given. Find the missing side.**

26. 6 in.

Area = 24 sq in.

27. 8 ft

Area = 64 sq ft

28. Rodolfo's table tennis table has an area of 45 square feet. The length is 9 feet. What is the perimeter of the table tennis table?

10-7 Problem-Solving Investigation: Choose a Strategy (pp. 420–421)

Example 9

Mr. Palmer is buying a cover for his pool table. Is it reasonable to say that a cover with an area of 30 square feet will be large enough to cover his pool table?

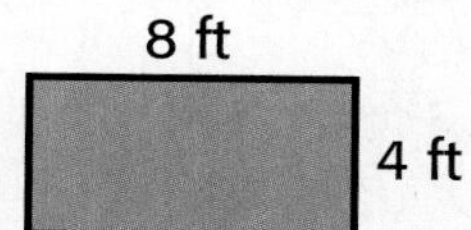

Understand

What facts do you know?

- The pool table is 8 feet by 4 feet.
- The area of the cover is 30 square feet.

What do you need to find?

- Is 30 square feet reasonable?

Plan Solve a simpler problem.

Solve $A = \ell \times w$

$A = 8 \text{ feet} \times 4 \text{ feet}$

$A = 32 \text{ square feet}$

The pool table has an area of 32 square feet. Since $30 < 32$, it is not reasonable to say that the cover is large enough.

Check $32 - 30 = 2$

So, the area of the pool table is 2 square feet larger than the cover. It is not large enough.

Use any strategy to solve.

29. Mindy is mowing the lawn. What area does she have to mow?

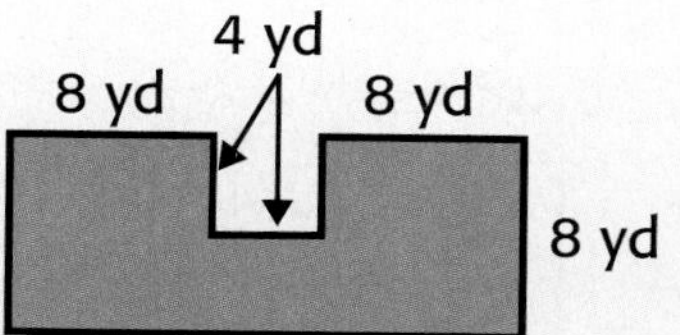

30. Measurement What is the total area of the three squares below?

31. Measurement There are six tables that measure 3 feet by 6 feet. If a room measures 25 feet by 10 feet, will the tables fit in the room?

32. A sandbox measures 12 feet by 8 feet. The area of the playground is 200 square feet. How many square feet are not used by the sandbox?

33. James bought lunch for $3. Then he paid his club $1. He earned $5 for mowing grass. He now has $25. How much did he start with?

10-8 Measure Temperature (pp. 422–425)

Example 10
Write the approximate temperature in Fahrenheit and Celsius.

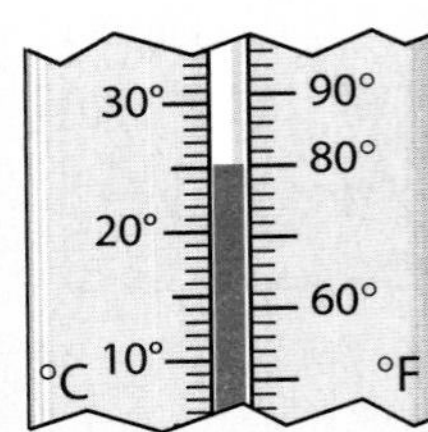

The red shows 80°F. So, it is approximately 25°C and 80°F.

Example 11
Find the change in the temperatures.

A thermometer inside reads:

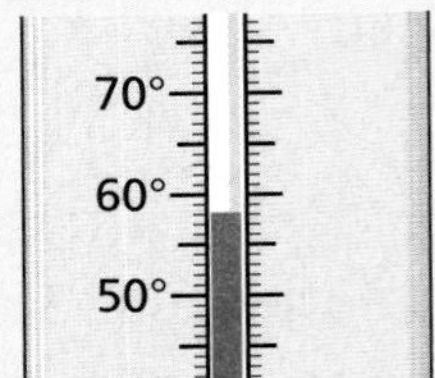

A thermometer outside reads:

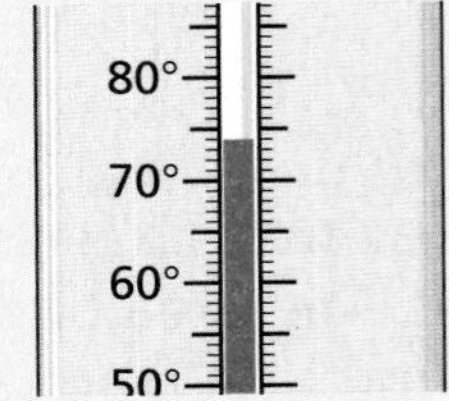

74° − 58° = change in temperature

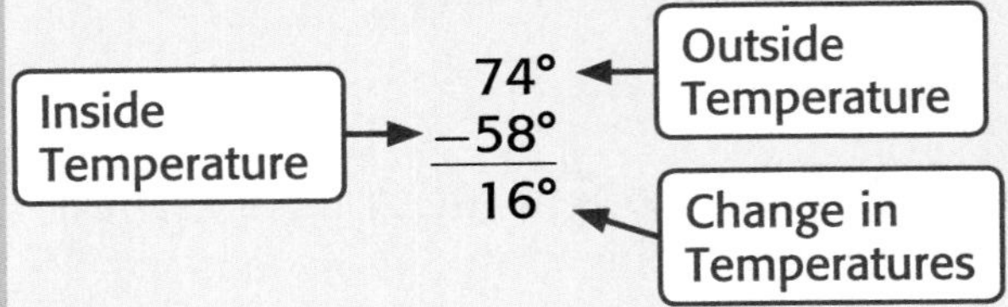

It is 16°F warmer outside than inside.

Write the approximate temperature in Fahrenheit and Celsius.

34.

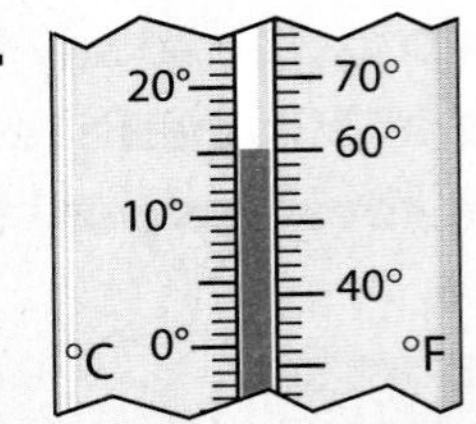

35. The thermometer reads 10°C. What type of clothing should be worn outside?

Find the change in temperature.

36.

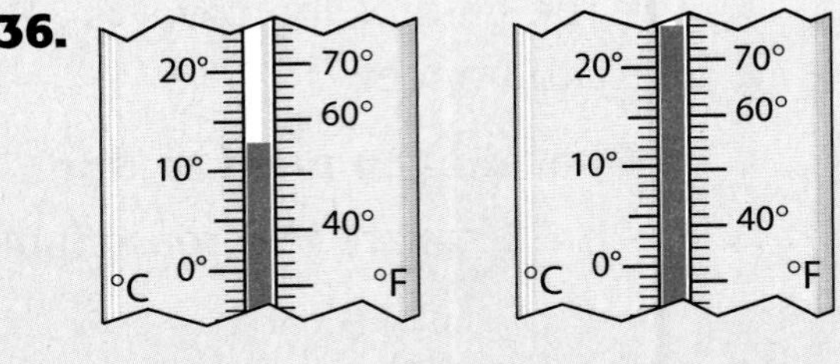

37.

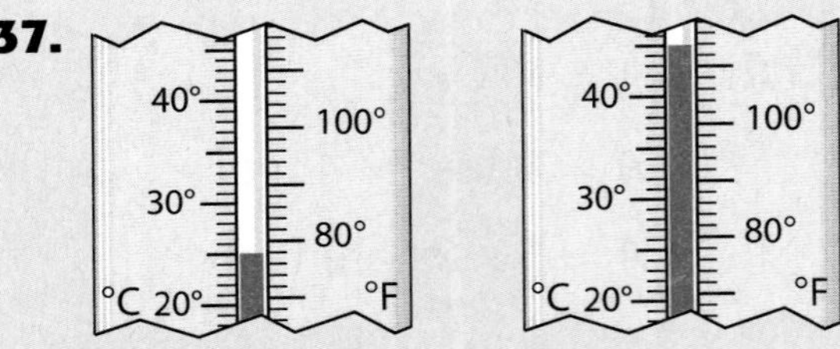

38. 2°F to 37°F

39. 95°C to 41°C

40. Abby's class is taking a field trip to the zoo. When the students arrived at school, the temperature was 80°F. When they left for the zoo, it was 95°F. How much warmer was it when they left for the zoo?

CHAPTER 10

Chapter Test

For Exercises 1 and 2, tell whether each statement is *true* or *false*.

1. Area is the distance around a figure.

2. To change units of measurement is to convert.

Choose the best estimate for each length.

3. length of a green bean, 2 inches or 2 feet

4. length of a sheep, 3 yards or 3 feet

5. Tessa's swimming pool is 13 feet long. How many inches is this?

6. A bottle of glue is about 15 centimeters tall. Name something else that has a height or width of about 15 centimeters.

7. **TEST PRACTICE** Which statement about the rectangle is true?

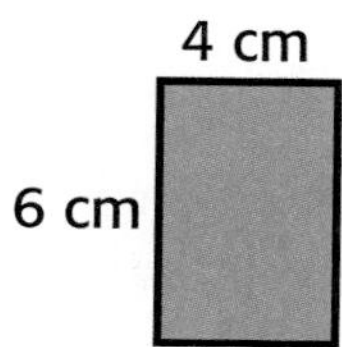

A The area is equal to the perimeter.
B The area is less than the perimeter.
C The perimeter is 20 centimeters.
D The area is 10 square centimeters.

8. Find the area of the rectangle.

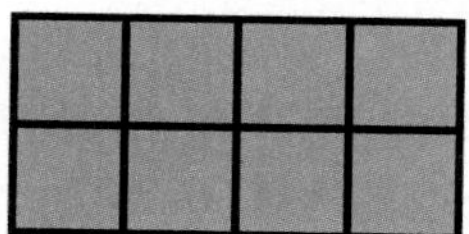

9. Brett painted 3 walls. Each wall was 9 feet tall and 12 feet long. How much wall area did he paint?

10. Which figure has the greater perimeter?

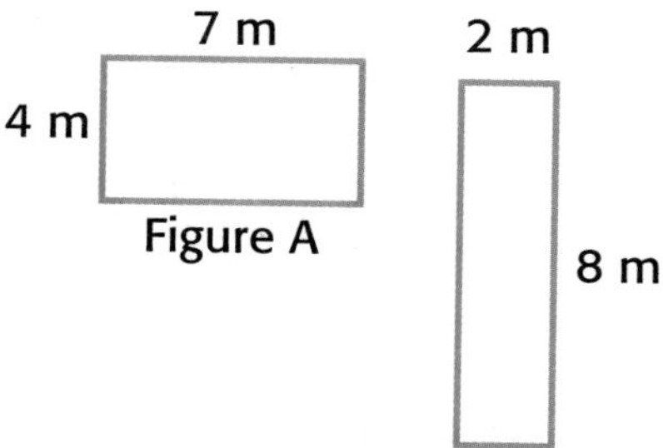

11. **Algebra** Three numbers between 1 and 8 have a sum of 20. Each number is used once. What are the numbers?

Find the change in temperature.

12. 25°C to 38°C

13. 70°F to 52°F

14. **TEST PRACTICE** Which equation represents the area (A) of the square in square inches?

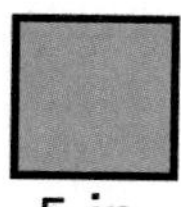

F $5 = A \times 5$
G $A = 5 \times 5$
H $A = 5 + 5$
J $A = 5 \times 4$

15. **WRITING IN MATH** Do all squares with one side of 3 inches have the same area? Explain.

Chapter 10 Texas Test Practice

Cumulative, Chapters 1–10

TEST Example

Martino is building a new deck behind his house. When completed, the deck will be 15 feet long and 22 feet wide. What is the area, in square feet, of the deck?

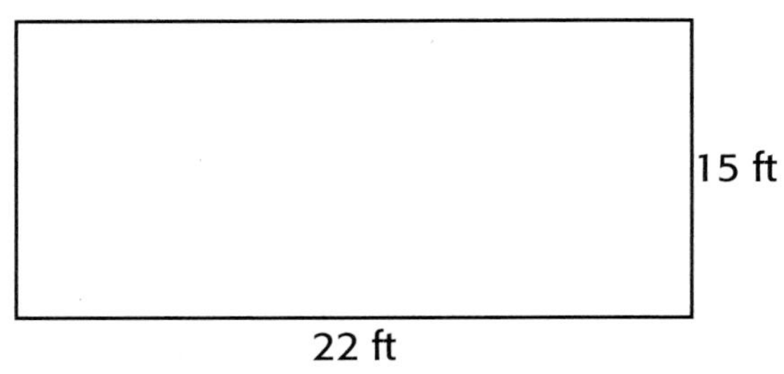

TEST-TAKING TIP

Use the correct formula to solve the problem. The formula for the area of a rectangle is length × width.

Read the Test Question

You need to find the area of the rectangular deck.

Solve the Test Question

Use the formula for the area of a rectangle.

Area = length × width
Area = 22 × 15
Area = 330

The area of the deck is 330 square feet.

Personal Tutor at tx.gr4math.com

Choose the best answer.

1. **GRIDDABLE Hanna's bedroom is shaped like a rectangle. The room is 12 feet long and 10 feet wide. What is the area, in square feet, of the room?**

2. **GRIDDABLE The soccer field behind the school is 50 meters wide and 120 meters long. What is the area, in square meters, of the soccer field?**

Get Ready for the Texas Test
For test- taking strategies and more practice, see pages TX1–TX21.

3. The map shows the distance from Lora's house to school. Use a ruler to measure the line segment. What is the distance from Lora's house to school?

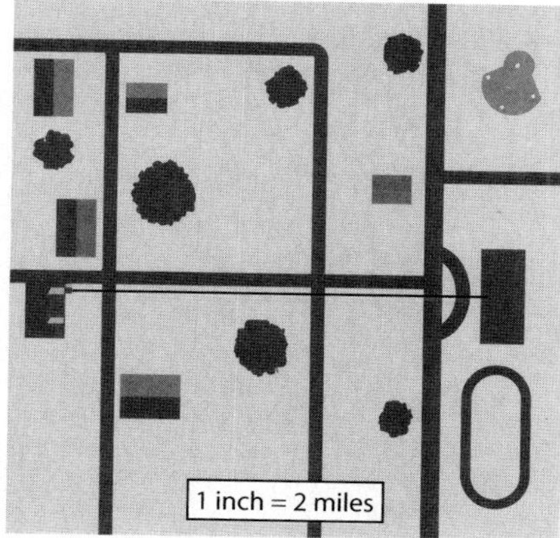

A 2 miles
B 2.5 miles
C 4.5 miles
D 5 miles

4. There are 29 students in Mr. Clark's art class. Each student needs 7 toothpicks for a project. About how many toothpicks are needed altogether?

F 175
G 190
H 210
J 225

5. Linda has 443 pennies. She wants to put them into rolls of 50 each. About how many rolls will she need?

A 9
B 10
C 11
D 12

6. A hair styling salon had 112 customers on Tuesday and 94 customers on Wednesday. How many customers were there in the two days?

F 218
G 206
H 204
J 198

7. Miss Butler has 30 students in her class. The students are arranged into groups of 5 to play a game. How many groups are there in all?

A 4
B 5
C 6
D 7

8. What temperature is shown on the thermometer?

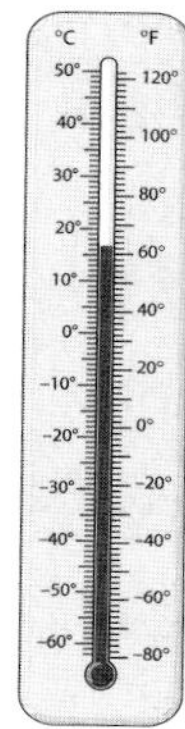

F 61°F
G 62°F
H 64°F
J 65°F

Measure Capacity, Weight/Mass, and Volume

BIG Idea How do you convert units of weight?

Multiplication converts a larger unit to a smaller unit and division converts a smaller unit to a larger unit.

Example If the total birth weight of eight pandas is 32 ounces, what would the total birth weight be in pounds?

Use division to convert ounces to pounds.

$$\begin{array}{r} 2 \\ 16\overline{)32} \\ -\underline{32} \\ 0 \end{array}$$

16 ounces = 1 pound
Divide 32 by 16 to find the birth weight in pounds.

So, the total birth weight of 8 pandas is 2 pounds.

What will I learn in this chapter?

- Estimate, measure, and convert customary units of capacity and weight.
- Estimate and measure capacity and mass within the metric system.
- Solve problems using logical reasoning.
- Measure and estimate volume in cubic units.
- Solve problems about elapsed time.

Key Vocabulary

capacity **volume**
weight **elapsed time**
mass

Student Study Tools at tx.gr4math.com

Make this Foldable to help you organize information about capacity, weight/mass, and volume. Begin with 5 sheets of $8\frac{1}{2}$" × 11" paper.

1. **Stack** 5 sheets of paper. Place each sheet $\frac{3}{4}$ inch apart.
2. **Roll** up the edge, so all tabs are the same size.
3. **Crease** and staple along the fold.
4. **Label** the tabs with the topics from each lesson.

ARE YOU READY for Chapter 11?

You have two ways to check prerequisite skills for this chapter.

Option 2

Math Online Take the Chapter Readiness Quiz at tx.gr4math.com.

Option 1

Complete the Quick Check below.

QUICK Check

Multiply or divide. (Lesson 4-5)

1. 2×8 **2.** 4×16 **3.** 8×24 **4.** 9×36

5. $4 \div 2$ **6.** $12 \div 4$ **7.** $36 \div 6$ **8.** $64 \div 8$

9. Dan shared his markers equally with three friends. If he gave his friends and himself the same number of markers, how many markers did each person get?

Compare. Write >, <, or =. (Lesson 1-4)

10. 12 ● 21 **11.** 64 ● 36 **12.** 128 ● 182

13. The table shows the number of cans collected by two fourth grade classes at Franklin Elementary School. Which class collected more cans?

Cans Collected	
Class	**Number of Cans Collected**
Mr. Santos	236
Ms. Davis	263

Write the time shown on each clock. (Prior grade)

14.

15.

16.

Measurement Activity for 11-1

Estimate and Measure Capacity

MAIN IDEA

I will estimate and measure capacity.

 **Targeted TEKS 4.11** The student applies measurement concepts . . . The student uses measurement tools to measure capacity/volume and weight/mass. (A) **Estimate and use measurement tools to determine** length (including perimeter), area, **capacity**, and weight/mass **using** standard units SI (metric) and **customary**.

You Will Need

standard measuring tools
water and food coloring

Capacity is the amount of liquid a container holds.

ACTIVITY **Measure Capacity**

Step 1 **Estimate.**

Estimate the number of cups in a pint.

Step 2 **Measure.**

Fill the cup with water and pour its contents into the pint. Repeat until the pint is full. It takes 2 cups to fill the pint. So, there are 2 cups in a pint.

Step 3 **Copy and complete the table.**

First estimate the amount each container holds. Then use water to find the exact measures. Record your results.

Container	Estimate	Actual
Pint	■ cups	■ cups
Quart	■ pints	■ pints
Gallon	■ quarts	■ quarts

Think About it

1. How many cups are in one pint?

2. How many quarts are in one gallon?

CHECK What You Know

3. ■ cups = 3 pints

4. ■ pints = 4 gallons

5. WRITING IN MATH Would it be quicker to water two large pots of flowers using a pitcher that holds one cup or one quart? Explain.

Customary Units of Capacity

MAIN IDEA

I will estimate and measure customary capacities.

Targeted TEKS 4.11 The student applies measurement concepts. . . . The student uses measurement tools to measure capacity/volume and weight/mass. (A) **Estimate and use measurement tools to determine** length (including perimeter), area, **capacity**, and weight/mass **using** standard units SI (metric) and **customary.**

New Vocabulary

capacity
fluid once
cup
pint
quart
gallon

GET READY to Learn

Jorge is filling an aquarium. He went to the kitchen to find a container to fill the aquarium. Which container should Jorge use to fill his aquarium most quickly?

1 cup 1 quart 1 gallon

The amount a container holds is its **capacity**. Different containers measure different capacities. A cup contains 8 **fluid ounces**.

1 cup = 8 fluid ounces

1 pint

1 quart

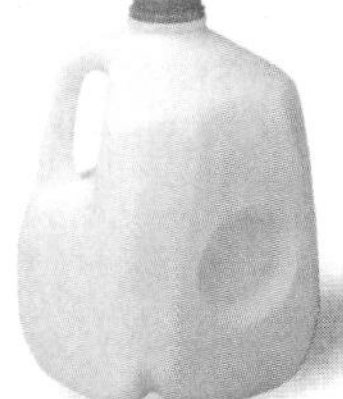

1 gallon

EXAMPLE Estimate Capacity

1 Which container should Jorge use to fill the aquarium most quickly? Use this container to find the capacity of the aquarium.

To fill the aquarium most quickly, Jorge should use the container that will hold the most liquid. Since the gallon is the largest unit, the bucket will fill the aquarium most quickly.

The capacity of the bucket is 1 gallon. Jorge used the bucket 32 times to fill the aquarium. Since 1 gallon $\times$ 32 = 32 gallons, the capacity of the aquarium is 32 gallons.

When estimating capacity, containers that have very different shapes can have similar capacities.

Real-World EXAMPLE Estimate Capacity

2 FOOD Nita is pouring salsa into a small bowl. Is the most reasonable estimate for the capacity of the bowl 8 fluid ounces, 8 cups, 8 quarts, or 8 gallons?

Use logic to eliminate the choices that are not reasonable.

The salsa is a small amount. So, you would use a small unit. Thus, 8 gallons, 8 quarts, and 8 cups are too much. The most reasonable estimate for the capacity of the bowl is 8 fluid ounces.

Online Personal Tutor at tx.gr4math.com

CHECK What You Know

Choose the most reasonable estimate for each capacity. See Examples 1 and 2 (pp. 442–443)

1.

A 1 fluid ounce
B 1 pint
C 1 quart
D 100 quarts

2.

A 4 fluid ounces
B 4 cups
C 40 cups
D 4 gallons

3.

A 1 fluid ounce
B 1 cup
C 1 pint
D 1 gallon

Estimate and then measure the capacity of each object.
See Example 1 (p. 442)

4. vase

5. small paper cup

6. Talk About It Is it possible for both of the containers shown to have a capacity of 1 pint? Explain why or why not.

Practice and Problem Solving

Choose the most reasonable estimate for each capacity. See Examples 1 and 2 (pp. 442–443)

7. 

A 12,000 fluid ounces
B 12,000 pints
C 12,000 quarts
D 12,000 gallons

8. 

A 5 fluid ounces
B 5 cups
C 5 pints
D 5 gallons

9. 

A 1 fluid ounce
B 1 cup
C 1 quart
D 1 gallon

10. 

A 8 fluid ounces
B 8 cups
C 8 pints
D 8 gallons

11. 

A 1 quart
B 10 quarts
C 100 quarts
D 1,000 quarts

12. 

A 16 gallons
B 16 quarts
C 16 fluid ounces
D 16 cups

Estimate and then measure the capacity of each object. See Example 1 (p. 442)

13. water bottle

14. juice box

15. sink

Real-World PROBLEM SOLVING

Water Some household activities and the amount of water they consume are listed in the table.

16. If Callie takes one shower each day, is it reasonable to say that she could use 210 gallons of water in one week? Explain.

17. Callie brushes her teeth three times each day. Is it reasonable to say that she uses 2 cups of water in one day? Explain.

Water Consumption

Activity	Water Used (gallons)
Take shower	15–30
Brush teeth (water running)	1–2
Wash dishes (by hand)	20
Wash dishes (in dishwasher)	9–12
Flush toilet	5–7

Source: science.enotes.com

H.O.T. Problems

18. OPEN ENDED Name two things in your classroom that would hold more than one cup.

19. WRITING IN ▶MATH A set of twins is sharing 1 pint of ice cream. Their friend, Shannon, is eating 1 cup of ice cream. Who is eating the most ice cream? Explain.

20. At bedtime the temperature was 45°F. In the morning it was 15°F cooler. What was the temperature in the morning? **(Lesson 10-8)**

A 75°F

B 60°F

C 30°F

D 15°F

21. Which of the following holds about 1 quart of water? **(Lesson 11-1)**

F

H 

G 

J 

Spiral Review

Find the change in the temperatures. (Lesson 10-8)

22. 75°F to 34°F

23. 35°C to 50°C

24. 85°F to 68°F

Write the approximate temperature in degrees Fahrenheit and Celsius. (Lesson 10-8)

25. 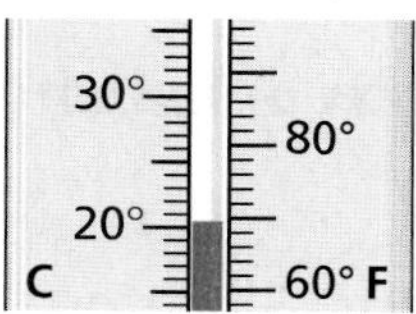

26. 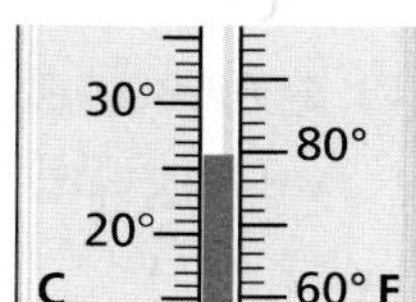

Estimate. Then measure each to the nearest inch, $\frac{1}{2}$ inch, and $\frac{1}{4}$ inch. (Lesson 10-1)

27. 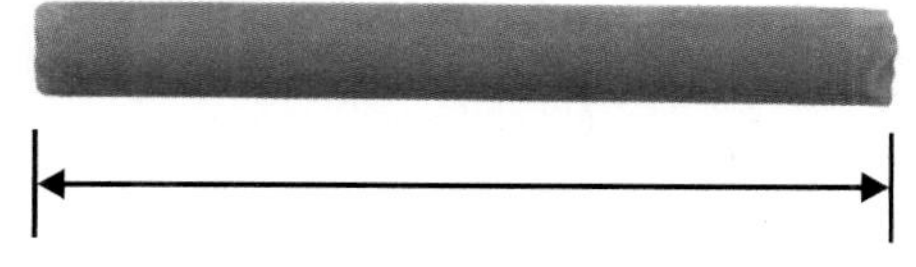

28. 

29. Tonya got money for her birthday. She got $8 from her friends, $16 from her parents, and $5 from her sister. She now has $48. How much did she have originally? **(Lesson 4-4)**

Converting Customary Capacity

GET READY to Learn

Marcus is buying a 2-gallon container of laundry detergent. How many quarts of laundry detergent is he buying?

MAIN IDEA

I will convert customary units of capacity.

Targeted TEKS 4.11 The student applies measurement concepts. . . . The student uses measurement tools to measure capacity/volume and weight/mass. (B) **Perform simple conversions between different units of** length, different units of **capacity,** and between different units of weight **within the customary measurement system.**

Use division to convert a smaller unit of measure into a larger unit of measure. Use multiplication to convert a larger unit of measure into a smaller unit of measure.

KEY CONCEPT — Customary Units of Capacity

1 cup = 8 fluid ounces (fl oz)
2 cups (c) = 1 pint
2 pints (pt) = 1 quart
4 quarts (qt) = 1 gallon (gal)
1 gallon = 128 fluid ounces

Real-World EXAMPLE — Convert Capacity

1 **MEASUREMENT If Marcus is buying 2 gallons of laundry detergent, how many quarts is he buying?**

Complete the conversion 2 gallons = ■ quarts. Since quarts are smaller than gallons, multiply.

2 gallons × 4 quarts = ■ quarts

Multiply by 4 because there are 4 quarts in each gallon.

2 gallons × 4 quarts = 8 quarts

So, there are 8 quarts in 2 gallons.

Online Personal Tutor at tx.gr4math.com

EXAMPLE Convert Capacity

2 **Complete the conversion 8 pints = ■ quarts.**

Since quarts are larger than pints, divide.

8 pints ÷ 2 quarts = ■ quarts

Divide by 2 because there are 2 pints in each quart.

8 pints ÷ 2 quarts = 4 quarts

So, there are 4 quarts in 8 pints.

CHECK What You Know

Complete. See Examples 1 and 2 (pp. 446–447)

1. 20 pt = ■ qt

2. 3 c = ■ fl oz

3. 4 qt = ■ pt

4. Taka is buying 3 gallons of milk. How many quarts of milk is she buying?

5. Talk About It Explain how to convert 6 pints to cups.

Practice and Problem Solving

EXTRA PRACTICE See page R37.

Complete. See Examples 1 and 2 (pp. 446–447)

6. 64 fl oz = ■ c

7. 6 gal = ■ qt

8. ■ gal = 20 qt

9. 5 c = ■ fl oz

10. ■ pt = 30 c

11. ■ c = 128 fl oz

Compare. Write >, <, or =.

12. 4 qt ● 10 pt

13. 10 gal ● 1,280 fl oz

14. 1 qt ● 2 c

15. Tomas is buying a 16-fluid ounce container of liquid dish soap. How many cups of dish soap is he buying?

16. Karen is buying 4 gallons of orange juice. How many quarts of orange juice is she buying?

H.O.T. Problem

17. WRITING IN MATH Write a rule for converting capacities measured in customary units.

11-3 Metric Units of Capacity

GET READY to Learn

Hands-On Mini Activity

A liter is a metric unit of capacity. This container holds a liter.

1 liter

Materials 3 different containers, liter measuring tool

Step 1 Copy the table.

Object	Estimate	Actual

Step 2 Estimate.

Select three containers. Choose one and estimate whether it has a capacity that is greater than, less than, or equal to 1 liter. Record the estimate.

Step 3 Measure.

Fill a liter measuring tool with water. Pour the water into each of the containers. Tell whether each container is greater than, less than, or equal to 1 liter. Record your results.

MAIN IDEA

I will estimate and measure capacity within the metric system.

Targeted TEKS 4.11 The student applies measurement concepts. . . . The student uses measurement tools to measure capacity/volume and weight/mass. (A) **Estimate and use measurement tools to determine** length (including perimeter), area, **capacity**, and weight/mass **using standard units SI (metric)** and customary.

New Vocabulary

liter
milliliter

In the metric system, the liter and milliliter are often used as units of measurement for capacity.

Liter (L)

A bottle about this size can hold a liter.

Milliliter (mL)

A milliliter is less than half of an eyedropper.

EXAMPLE Estimate Capacity

1 Decide whether 300 milliliters or 300 liters is the more reasonable estimate for the capacity of the mug.

Use logic to estimate the capacity of the mug.

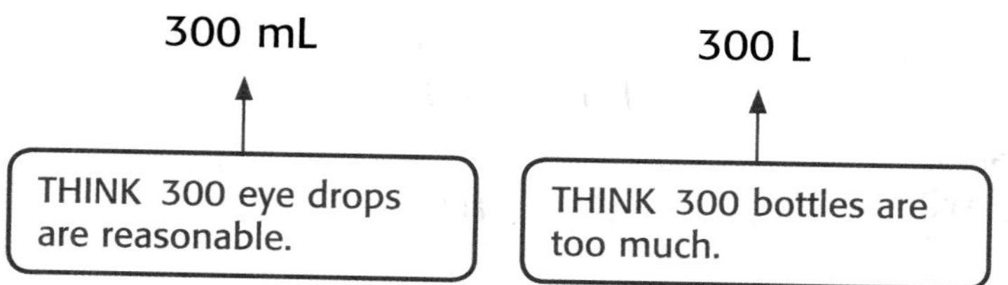

300 mL
300 L
THINK 300 eye drops are reasonable.
THINK 300 bottles are too much.

So, 300 milliliters is the more reasonable estimate.

Online **Personal Tutor at** tx.gr4math.com

CHECK What You Know

Choose the more reasonable estimate for each capacity. See Example 1 (p. 449)

1. 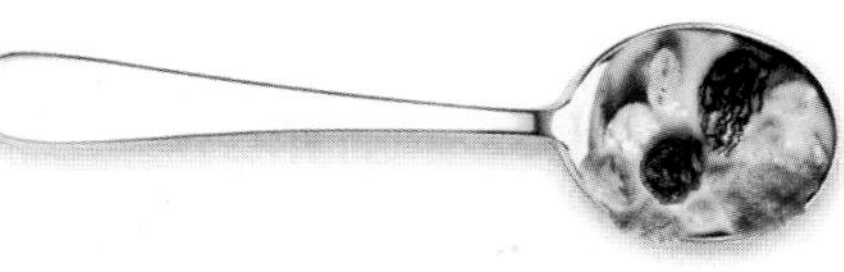

2 mL or 2 L

2. 

1 mL or 1 L

3. 

135 mL or 135 L

4. 

30 mL or 30 L

5. Jonah said he drank 3 liters of water after his soccer game. Is this a reasonable statement? Explain.

6. **Talk About It** Describe the unit of capacity that you would use to measure the capacity of a bottle of medicine.

Practice and Problem Solving

EXTRA PRACTICE
See page R37.

Choose the more reasonable estimate for each capacity.

See Example 1 (p. 449)

7.

150 mL or 150 L

8.

120 mL or 120 L

9.

500 mL or 500 L

10.

700 mL or 700 L

11.

2 mL or 2 L

12.

220 mL or 220 L

13. Jaya said that she took 4 milliliters of medicine for her cold. Is that reasonable? Explain.

14. Select three containers. Estimate and then measure whether each container has a capacity that is greater than, less than, or equal to 1 liter.

Object	Estimate	Actual

H.O.T. Problems

15. **OPEN ENDED** Identify four objects in your house that can hold more than 1 liter.

16. **CHALLENGE** Suppose you have a 4-liter bucket and a 7-liter bucket. You need 3 liters of water for an aquarium. Explain how to get 3 liters of water if neither bucket is marked.

17. **WRITING IN ▶MATH** How many milliliters are in 15 liters? Explain.

Math Online Self-Check Quiz tx.gr4math.com

18. Marco drank 64 fluid ounces of water in one day. Which of the following is equal to the amount of water Marco drank? (Lesson 11-2)

A 4 cups **C** 4 quarts

B 4 pints **D** 4 gallons

19. Which is the best estimate of the capacity of a glass of iced tea? (Lesson 11-3)

F 250 L **H** 250 lb

G 250 mL **J** 250 fl oz

Spiral Review

Complete. (Lesson 11-2)

20. 12 gal = ■ qt

21. 32 fl oz = ■ c

22. ■ pt = 18 c

Choose the most reasonable estimate for each capacity. (Lesson 11-1)

23.

A 2 fl oz **C** 2 qt

B 2 c **D** 2 gal

24.

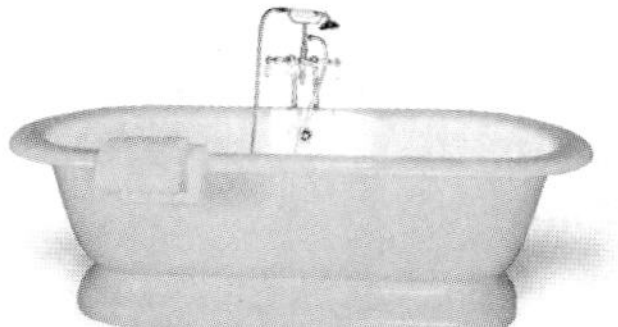

A 18 fl oz **C** 18 qt

B 18 c **D** 18 gal

Tell whether the figures appear to be congruent. Write *yes* or *no*. If they are, describe the movements that show the congruence. (Lesson 9-7)

25.

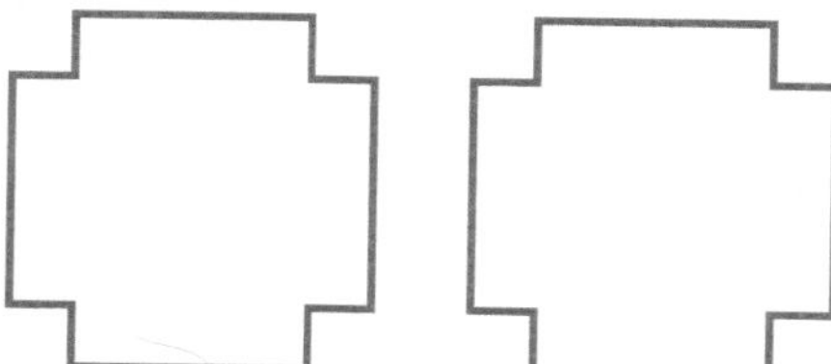

26.

Use technology to multiply. Check for reasonableness. (Lesson 6-6)

27. $\begin{array}{r} 218 \\ \times\ 3 \\ \hline \end{array}$

28. $\begin{array}{r} 896 \\ \times\ 5 \\ \hline \end{array}$

29. $\begin{array}{r} 2{,}731 \\ \times\ \quad 7 \\ \hline \end{array}$

30. Matt drank 22 fluid ounces of grape juice in one day. Is it reasonable to say that he drank more than 3 cups of grape juice that day? Explain. (Lesson 6-2)

Measurement Activity for 11-4

Estimate and Measure Weight

In this activity, you will measure the weight of objects. The **weight** of an object is how heavy it is.

MAIN IDEA

I will measure weight.

Targeted TEKS 4.11 The student applies measurement concepts. . . . The student uses measurement tools to measure capacity/ volume and weight/ mass. (A) **Estimate and use measurement tools to determine** length (including perimeter), area, capacity, and **weight**/ mass **using** standard units SI (metric) and **customary.**

You Will Need
chalkboard eraser
balance scale
glue bottle

ACTIVITY Measure Weight

Step 1 Copy the table.

Object	Estimate	Actual
Eraser		
Glue Bottle		
Math Book		
Object of your Choice		

Step 2 Estimate.

Estimate the weight of a chalkboard eraser. Record the estimate.

Step 3 Measure.

Place the eraser on one side of a balance scale. Set ounce or pound weights on the other side until the sides are balanced. Record the actual weight. Repeat Steps 2 and 3 for the other objects.

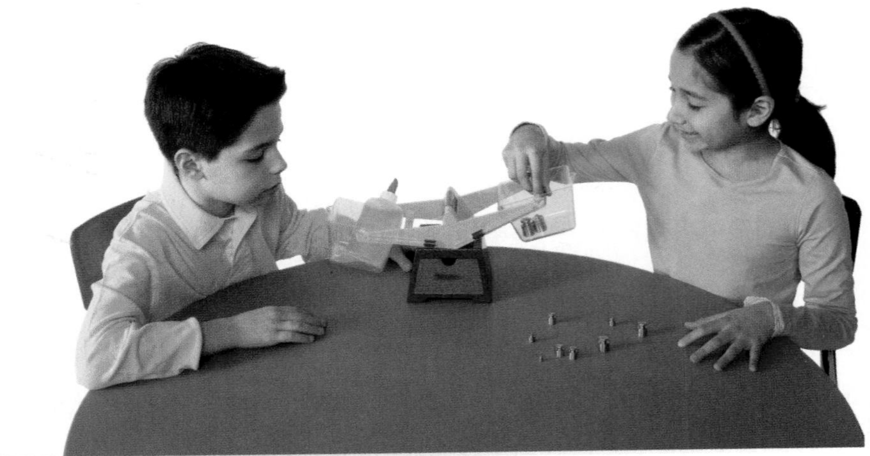

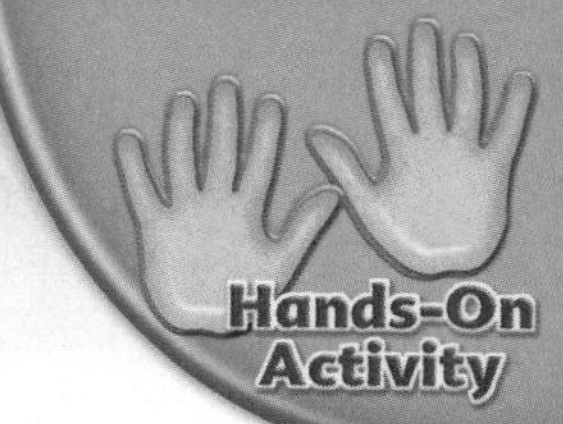

Think About It

1. Order the four objects you weighed in the Activity from greatest to least weight.
2. Use the weights of the objects you found to estimate the weight of two other objects in your classroom. Weigh the objects. Were your estimations close?
3. Is the total weight of the four objects you measured greater than 2 pounds? Explain.

CHECK What You Know

4. How many 1-ounce weights are needed to balance the scale when a 1-pound weight is in the other pan?
5. How many ounces are in two pounds?
6. How many ounces are in four pounds?

Compare. Use >, <, or =.

7. 46 ounces ● 3 pounds
8. 5 pounds ● 78 ounces
9. 96 ounces ● 6 pounds
10. 7 pounds ● 110 ounces

For Exercise 11, copy and complete the table.

Object	Estimate	Actual

11. Identify three objects in your classroom that weigh more than an eraser and less than your math book. Estimate each object's weight. Then weigh each object and record the exact weight.
12. WRITING IN ▶MATH Write a sentence that describes the relationship that is usually found between an object's size and weight.

11-4 Customary Units of Weight

GET READY to Learn

Suzie's father went to the store to buy some sugar for their favorite recipe. Suzie wondered how much the bag of sugar weighed.

MAIN IDEA

I will estimate and measure customary units of weight.

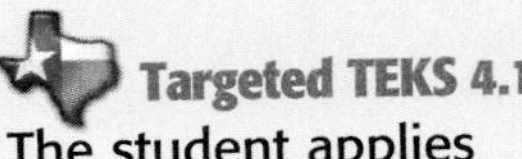

Targeted TEKS 4.11 The student applies measurement concepts. . . . The student uses measurement tools to measure capacity/volume and weight/mass. (A) **Estimate and use measurement tools to determine** length (including perimeter), area, capacity, and **weight/**mass **using** standard units SI (metric) and **customary.**

New Vocabulary

weight
ounce
pound
ton

The **weight** of an object is how heavy it is. Customary weight is measured in ounces, pounds, and tons. Ounces are the lightest, and tons are the heaviest.

1 ounce

1 pound

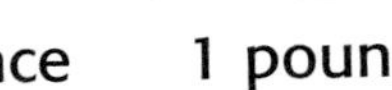

1 ton

Real-World EXAMPLE Estimate Weight

1 FOOD **Which is a more reasonable unit of measurement for the weight of each package of sugar, ounces or pounds?**

A small packet of sugar would be weighed in ounces.

A bag of sugar is much larger and would be weighed in pounds.

EXAMPLE Estimate Weight

2 Which is the most reasonable estimate for the weight of a colored pencil: 1 ounce, 1 pound, 1 ton, or 10 tons?

Compare the weight of a colored pencil to the weight of objects that you know. A colored pencil weighs less than a pineapple or one pound.

Objects that weigh less than one pound are weighed in ounces. The only option that contains ounces is 1 ounce.

Online **Personal Tutor at** tx.gr4math.com

CHECK What You Know

Choose the most reasonable estimate. See Examples 1 and 2 (pp. 454–455)

1. paper airplane

A 4 ounces **C** 4 pounds
B 40 ounces **D** 4 tons

2. helicopter

A 5 ounces **C** 5 tons
B 500 ounces **D** 500 tons

3. rabbit

A 4 ounces **C** 40 pounds
B 4 pounds **D** 4 tons

4. chair

A 5 ounces **C** 50 tons
B 50 pounds **D** 500 tons

5. Is it more reasonable to say that a fourth grade student weighs 56 ounces, 56 pounds, or 5 tons? Explain.

6. Talk About It Does an object that is small always weigh less than an object that is large? Explain.

Practice and Problem Solving

See page R38.

Choose the most reasonable estimate. See Examples 1 and 2 (pp. 454–455)

7. postcard

A 1 ounce

B 11 ounces

C 1 pound

D 1 ton

8. bed

A 20 ounces

B 20 pounds

C 200 pounds

D 20 tons

9. shell

A 4 ounces

B 4 pounds

C 400 pounds

D 4 tons

10. camper

A 3 ounces

B 3 pounds

C 300 pounds

D 3 tons

11. goldfish

A 2 ounces

B 2 pounds

C 20 pounds

D 2 tons

12. desk

A 18 ounces

B 18 pounds

C 180 pounds

D 1 ton

Real-World PROBLEM SOLVING

Data File The Texas longhorn's ancestors were the first cattle in the United States.

13. Is it reasonable to say that an adult Texas longhorn can weigh up to one ton? Explain.

14. Is it reasonable to say that a herd of eight adult Texas longhorn weigh about 800 pounds?

Texas Longhorn

H.O.T. Problem

15. **NUMBER SENSE** Estimate the weight of three objects in your desk. Then weigh them. Order the objects from greatest to least weight.

Mid-Chapter Check

Lessons 11-1 through 11-4

Choose the most reasonable estimate for each capacity. (Lesson 11-1)

1. 

A 5 pints
B 5 gallons
C 5 fluid ounces
D 5 cups

2. 

A 16 fluid ounces
B 16 cups
C 16 pints
D 16 gallons

3. Wendy is washing her mother's car. Is it reasonable to say that she will need about 16 pints of water? Explain.

4. Adamo is filling his cat's water bowl. Is it reasonable to say that he will need about 8 fluid ounces of water? Explain.

Complete. (Lesson 11-2)

5. 6 c = ■ fl oz

6. ■ gal = 8 qt

7. ■ pt = 30 c

8. 20 pt = ■ qt

Compare. Write >, <, or =. (Lesson 11-2)

9. 5 pt ● 3 qt

10. 1 c ● 7 fl oz

11. **TEST PRACTICE** Which of the comparisons is true? (Lesson 11-2)

A 4 qt > 10 pt
B 6 pt < 11 c
C 1 gal > 5 qt
D 16 oz < 2 gal

Choose the more reasonable estimate for each capacity. (Lesson 11-3)

12. 

600 L or 600 mL

13. 

3 mL or 3 L

14. **TEST PRACTICE** Which of the following is a reasonable estimate? (Lesson 11-3)

F A glass of water can hold about 10 milliliters of water.
G A swimming pool can hold about 15 liters of water.
H A bottle of juice has a capacity of 100 milliliters.
J A bucket can hold about 5 liters of water.

15. Choose the most reasonable estimate for the weight of a guinea pig. (Lesson 11-4)

A 2 pounds
B 12 pounds
C 120 pounds
D 2 tons

16. **WRITING IN MATH** Explain how units of capacity are related.

Problem-Solving Strategy

MAIN IDEA I will solve problems using logical reasoning.

Targeted TEKS 4.14 The student applies Grade 4 mathematics to solve problems connected to everyday experiences and activities in and outside of school. **(C) Select or develop an appropriate problem-solving strategy, including . . . making a table, . . . to solve a problem.** *Also addresses TEKS 4.14(B).*

Adina, Tonisha, and Carl are each writing a report. The reports are about elephants, lions, and monkeys. Adina is writing about an animal whose weight is measured in tons. Carl is writing about an animal whose average weight is 375 pounds. Which animal is each student writing a report about?

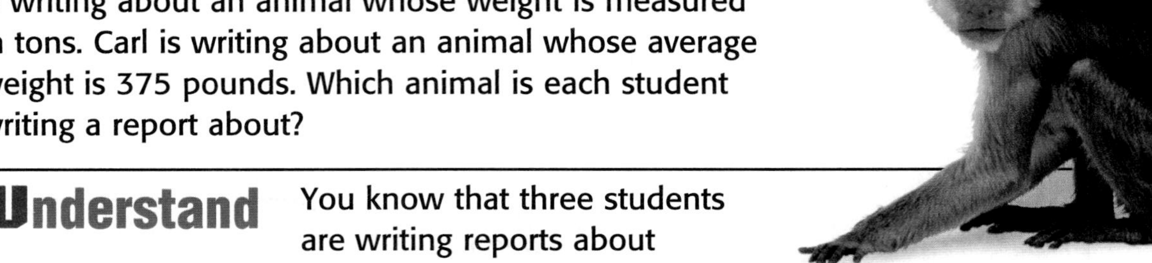

Understand

You know that three students are writing reports about animals. Adina is writing about an animal whose weight is in tons. Carl is writing about an animal whose weight is 375 pounds. You need to find which animal each student is writing a report about.

Plan

You can use logical reasoning to solve the problem.

Solve

- Adina must be writing about elephants because the other two animals' weights are in pounds.
- Carl must be writing about lions because monkeys weigh much less than 300 pounds.

Place an X in the boxes that you know cannot be correct.

	Elephant	Lion	Monkey
Adina	✓	X	X
Tonisha	X	X	✓
Carl	X	✓	X

So, Adina is writing about elephants, Tonisha is writing about monkeys, and Carl is writing about lions.

Check

Look back at the problem. The answer makes sense for the facts given in the problem. So, the answer is correct.

ANALYZE the Strategy

Refer to the problem on the previous page.

1. Explain how logical reasoning helped to solve the problem.
2. Why do you think a table was used in solving the problem?
3. Suppose a rhinoceros is being written about instead of a monkey. Would it be possible to determine which animal each person is writing about?

PRACTICE the Strategy

EXTRA PRACTICE
See page R38.

Solve. Use logical reasoning.

4. Three dogs are named Max, Sam, and Rufus. One is a collie, one is a spaniel, and one is a pug. Sam is not the collie. The spaniel's name is the longest. What are the names of each dog?
5. Hector arranges the cards in a row. The 2 is between the two odd numbered cards. The 4 has no card to its left. The 3 has cards on both sides. What is the order?

6. There are 4 people in a line. Kenzo is at the end. Juan is second in line. Carla is in front of Kenzo. Amy is first. What is the order of the people?
7. Manuella, Danny, and Tyson are wearing red, blue, and yellow T-shirts. Manuella is wearing red, and Danny is not wearing blue. What color T-shirt is each person wearing?
8. Jesse, Kata, Romeo, and Sheldon play basketball. Their numbers are 5, 7, 9, and 12. Jesse's number equals the number of letters in his name. Kata's is a two-digit number, while Romeo's number is not a prime number. What is Sheldon's number?
9. Lizzy has dogs, birds, and fish. She has twice as many dogs as birds. She has three more fish than dogs. She has two birds. How many dogs and fish does she have?

10. Copy and complete the puzzle below. Use the digits 1, 2, 3, and 4 so that each row and column has each digit lised one time.

2	3	■	1
1	4	■	2
3	■	2	4
4	■	■	3

11. **WRITING IN MATH** Explain what it means to use logical reasoning.

11-6 Converting Weights

GET READY to Learn

Leigh is buying 2 pounds of hamburger for dinner. The package she found was 32 ounces. Does 32 ounces equal 2 pounds?

MAIN IDEA

I will convert customary units of weight.

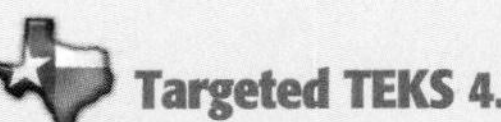

Targeted TEKS 4.11 The student applies measurement concepts … The student uses measurement tools to measure capacity/volume and weight/mass. **(B) Perform simple conversions between different units of** length, different units of capacity, and **between different units of weight within the customary measurement system.**

If converting from a larger unit to a smaller unit, multiply.
If converting from a smaller unit to a larger unit, divide.

KEY CONCEPT — Units of Weight

16 ounces (oz) = 1 pound (lb)

2,000 pounds (lb) = 1 ton (T)

EXAMPLE Convert Customary Weights

1 Do 32 ounces equal 2 pounds?

One Way	Another Way
Convert 32 ounces to pounds. Ounces are smaller than pounds. Divide.	Convert 2 pounds to ounces. Pounds are larger than ounces. Multiply.
$32 \div 16 = \blacksquare$	$2 \times 16 = \blacksquare$
Divide by 16 because there are 16 ounces in a pound.	Multiply by 16 because there are 16 ounces in a pound.
So, 32 ounces equals 2 pounds.	So, 2 pounds equals 32 ounces.

A very heavy unit of measurement is a ton. There are 2,000 pounds in one ton.

Real-World EXAMPLE — Convert Customary Weights

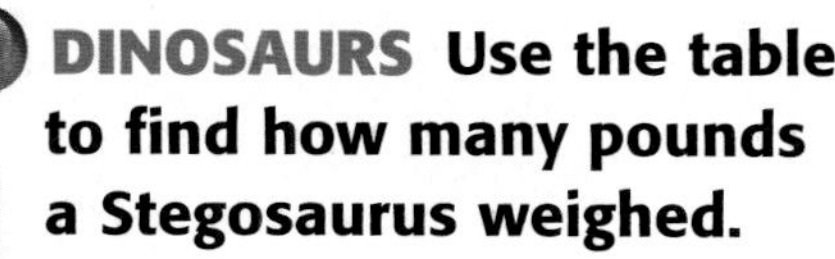

2 DINOSAURS Use the table to find how many pounds a Stegosaurus weighed.

Dinosaur Weights	
Dinosaur	**Weight (tons)**
Allosaurus	2
Megalosaurus	1
Stegasaurus	3
Supersaurus	60
Tyrannosaurus	8

To find the weight of a Stegosaurus in pounds, multiply the number of tons by 2,000.

$3 \times 2{,}000 = \blacksquare$

$3 \times 2{,}000 = 6{,}000$

THINK $3 \times 2 = 6$
$3 \times 20 = 60$
$3 \times 200 = 600$
So, $3 \times 2{,}000 = 6{,}000$

So, a Stegosaurus weighed 6,000 pounds.

Online **Personal Tutor at** tx.gr4math.com

CHECK What You Know

Complete. See Examples 1 and 2 (pp. 460–461)

1. 4 lb = ■ oz

2. 48 oz = ■ lb

3. 4,000 lb = ■ T

4. ■ T = 6,000 lb

5. ■ oz = 1 lb 4 oz

6. ■ lb = 4 T and 100 lb

7. A hippopotamus eats about 100 pounds of food a day. How many days would it take a hippo to eat one ton of food?

8. The world's largest bird egg is the ostrich egg. It weighs 64 ounces. Is the weight of the ostrich egg greater than 5 pounds? Explain.

9. Talk About It Explain why you multiply to convert a larger unit of measure to a smaller unit of measure.

Practice and Problem Solving

EXTRA PRACTICE See page R39.

Complete. See Examples 1 and 2 (pp. 460–461)

10. 1 lb = ■ oz

11. 160 oz = ■ lb

12. ■ T = 8,000 lb

13. 5 lb = ■ oz

14. ■ lb = 3 T and 600 lb

15. ■ oz = 3 lb and 6 oz

Copy and complete.

16.

Pounds	6	■	8	■
Ounces	■	112	■	144

17. A baby blue whale weighs about 3,000 pounds and can gain about 200 pounds each day. About how many days would it take a baby blue whale to gain 1 ton of weight?

18. The weight capacity of a bridge is 3 tons. Three trucks need to cross the bridge at the same time. If each truck weighs 1,800 pounds, can they safely cross at the same time? Explain.

Real-World PROBLEM SOLVING

Animals Baby animals weigh different amounts at birth.

Animal	Birth Weight
Alligator	2 ounces
Giraffe	100–150 pounds
Giant panda	3.2 to 4.6 ounces
Walrus	100–160 pounds

Source: sandiegozoo.org

19. What is the fewest number of baby walruses whose weight would equal about 1 ton?

20. An alligator nest usually contains about 30 eggs. What will the total weight of the babies be in pounds after all 30 eggs hatch?

H.O.T. Problems

21. OPEN ENDED Give two examples of objects that can be measured in tons and two examples of objects that cannot be measured in tons.

22. CHALLENGE Tiffany weighed 7 pounds 12 ounces when she was born. Her weight doubled after four months. How much did Tiffany weigh after four months?

23. WRITING IN MATH Explain how to convert 2 tons 1,265 pounds to pounds.

24. Which is the most reasonable measurement for a can of green beans? **(Lesson 11-4)**

A 13 ounces

B 130 ounces

C 13 pounds

D 13 tons

25. Russ paid $10 for dog food that costs $1.25 per pound. Which is the most reasonable estimate for the amount of dog food Russ bought? **(Lesson 11-4)**

F 8 ounces

G 8 pounds

H 80 pounds

J 8 tons

26. Which table represents the relationship between pounds and ounces? **(Lesson 11-6)**

A

Pounds	1	2	3	4
Ounces	16	32	32	144

B

Pounds	1	2	3	4
Ounces	8	16	24	32

C

Pounds	1	2	3	4
Ounces	16	24	32	40

D

Pounds	16	32	48	64
Ounces	1	2	3	4

Spiral Review

27. Greg, Liza, Erina, and Julius each play a sport. The sports they play are baseball, soccer, tennis, and volleyball. Liza uses a racquet. Julius does not play volleyball. Greg uses a mitt. Which sport does each student play? **(Lesson 11-5)**

Choose the more reasonable estimate. **(Lesson 11-4)**

28. grapes

10 ounces or 10 pounds

29. pig

50 ounces or 50 pounds

Choose the more reasonable estimate for each capacity. **(Lesson 11-3)**

30.

225 mL or 225L

31.

2 mL or 2L

11-7 Metric Units of Mass

GET READY to Learn

Hands-On Mini Activity

You can use a balance scale to find the mass of objects.

Materials balance scale, 4 different objects, gram weights

Step 1 Copy the table.

Object	Estimate	Mass (grams)

Step 2 Estimate.

Select four objects that will fit on one side of the balance scale. Choose one and estimate its mass in grams. Record the estimate.

Step 3 Measure.

Set the object on one side of the balance scale. On the other side, set gram weights until both sides are balanced. Record the actual mass. Repeat Steps 2 and 3 for the other objects.

1. Did the larger objects have a greater mass than the smaller objects?
2. Explain how a larger object can have less mass than a smaller object.

MAIN IDEA

I will estimate and measure mass and learn the difference between weight and mass.

Targeted TEKS 4.11 The student applies measurement concepts ... The student uses measurement tools to measure capacity/volume and weight/mass. (A) **Estimate and use measurement tools to determine** length (including perimeter), area, capacity and **weight/mass using standard units SI (metric)** and customary. *Also addresses TEKS 4.11(E).*

New Vocabulary

gram
kilogram
mass

Mass is the amount of matter an object has. The mass of an object is not affected by gravity. In contrast, an object's weight differs depending on gravity.

Remember

You would weigh less on the moon than you do on Earth. However, your mass is the same on Earth as it is on the moon.

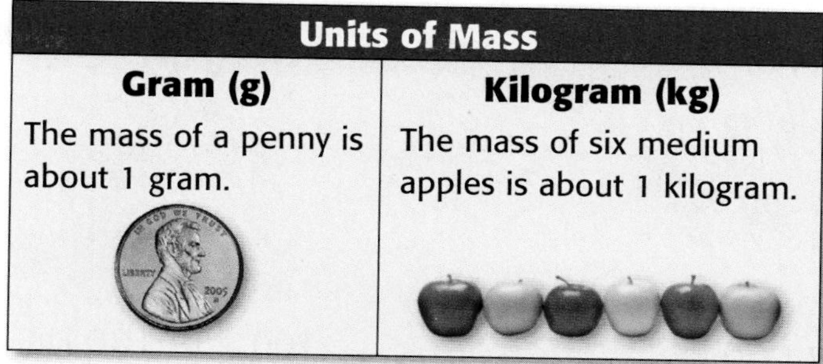

Units of Mass	
Gram (g)	**Kilogram (kg)**
The mass of a penny is about 1 gram.	The mass of six medium apples is about 1 kilogram.

You can use what you know about the gram and kilogram to estimate mass.

EXAMPLE Estimate Mass

1 Which is the more reasonable estimate for the mass of the laptop, 2 g or 2 kg?

If the laptop has a mass of 2 grams, it would have the same mass as 2 pennies. This is not a reasonable estimate. So, a reasonable estimate is 2 kg.

 **Personal Tutor at** tx.gr4math.com

CHECK What You Know

Choose the more reasonable estimate. See Example 1 (p. 465)

1. ball cap

25 g or 25 kg

2. polar bear

450 g or 450 kg

3. Is it more reasonable to say that Cheryl lifts dumbbells that have a mass of 30 grams or 30 kilograms? Explain.

4. Talk About It Explain the difference between weight and mass. Look back at Explore 11-4 if needed.

Practice and Problem Solving

Choose the more reasonable estimate. See Example 1 (p. 465)

5. stamps

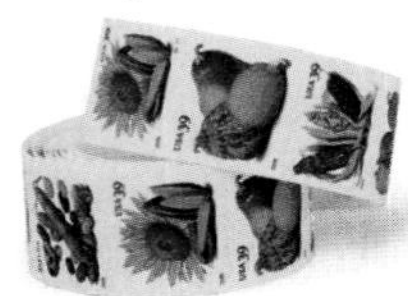

8 g or 8 kg

6. box of crayons

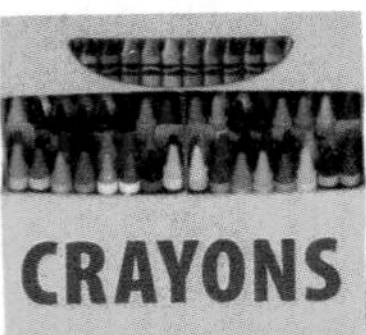

100 g or 100 kg

7. cooler

25 g or 25 kg

8. ball

20 g or 20 kg

9. tool box

30 g or 30 kg

10. trampoline

50 g or 50 kg

11. The table lists items that can be found in a classroom. Estimate and then measure the mass of each object. Copy and complete the table.

Mass of Classroom Objects		
Object	**Estimate**	**Actual**
Glue bottle	■	■
Paper clip	■	■
Pencil	■	■
Stapler	■	■

12. Tyler bought a large bag of peanuts at a baseball game. Is it more reasonable to say that the mass of the peanuts is 1 gram or 1 kilogram?

13. Alicia is buying 6 oranges that cost \$1 per kilogram. Is it reasonable to say that the cost of the oranges will be greater than \$6? Explain.

H.O.T. Problems

14. **OPEN ENDED** Name five classroom objects that have a mass greater than 1 kilogram.

15. **CHALLENGE** Which weighs more, an astronaut on Earth or the same astronaut on the Moon? Explain.

16. **NUMBER SENSE** The mass of a dime is written as 4. What metric unit was used to measure the mass of the dime? Explain.

17. **WRITING IN MATH** Write about a real-world situation in which you would have to decide which metric unit to use to measure an object's mass.

Math Online Self-Check Quiz at tx.gr4math.com

Massive Estimates

Estimate and Measure Mass

You will need: 10 index cards
pencils

Get Ready!

Players: 2 players

Get Set!

Label each index card as shown. Then label the back of each index card with the correct unit of measurement that would be used to find each object's mass.

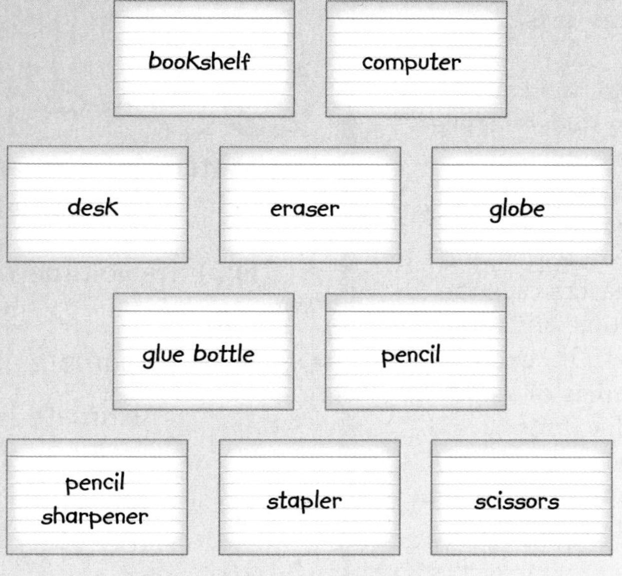

Go!

- Shuffle the cards. Lay the stack of cards face up on the table.
- Player 1 shows the object on the first card to Player 2.
- Player 2 decides whether the mass of the object would be measured in grams or kilograms.
- Player 2 keeps the card if his or her answer is correct. If Player 2 is incorrect, Player 1 keeps the card.
- Players take turns showing each other cards.
- Continue playing until all of the cards are used. The player with the most cards wins.

11-8 Estimate and Measure Volume

GET READY to Learn

Volume is the amount of space that a three-dimensional figure contains. It is measured in **cubic units**. Each side of a centimeter cube has a length of 1 centimeter. So, the volume for a rectangular prism is measured in **cubic centimeters**.

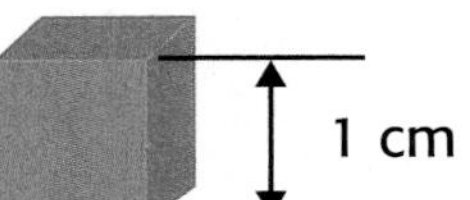

MAIN IDEA

I will measure and estimate volume in cubic units.

Targeted TEKS 4.11 The student applies measurement concepts ... The student uses measurement tools to measure capacity/volume and weight/mass. (C) **Use concrete models of standard cubic units to measure volume.** (D) **Estimate volume in cubic units.**

New Vocabulary

volume
cubic units
cubic centimeter

Hands-On Mini Activity

Materials cube and rectangular prism from the set of geometric solids, centimeter cubes

Find the volume of each three-dimensional figure.

Step 1 Estimate.

Estimate how many centimeter cubes it will take to fill the cube.

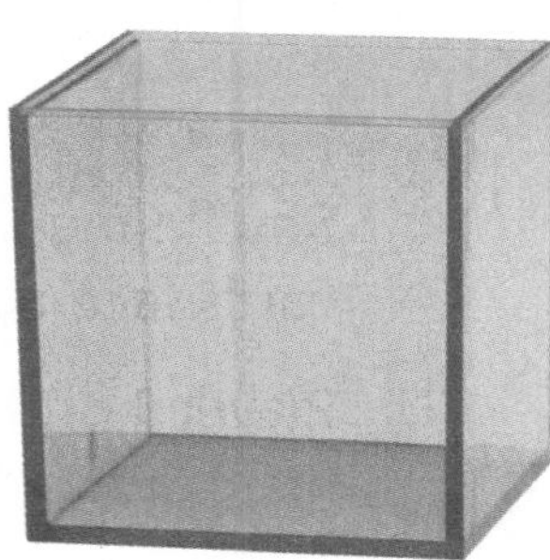

Step 2 Measure.

Place centimeter cubes inside the cube. When it is full, count the centimeter cubes. The number of centimeter cubes that the cube will hold is the volume of the cube. Compare this with your estimate.

Step 3 Apply.

Repeat steps 1 and 2 for the rectangular prism.

1. What is the volume of the rectangular prism?

2. Which has a greater volume, the prism or the cube? how much greater?

KEY CONCEPT — Volume

Volume is the number of cubic units needed to fill a three-dimensional figure.

To find volume of a figure, count the number of cubic units in the figure.

EXAMPLE Find Volume

1 Find the volume of the cube shown to the right.

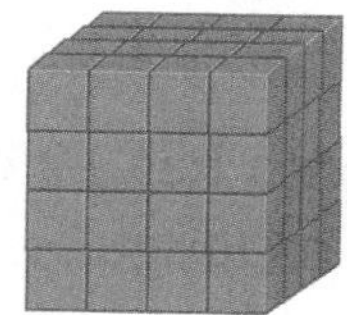

You can build a model using base-ten blocks. Then count the number of cubes it takes to make the object.

The cube shown has 4 layers. Each layer has 16 cubes.

One layer

Four layers

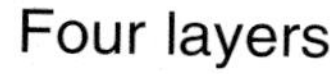

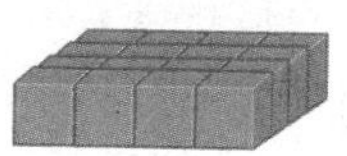

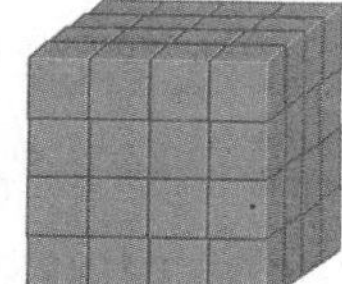

16 cubes

$4 \times 16 = 64$ cubes

So, the volume of the cube is 64 cubic units.

Online Personal Tutor at tx.gr4math.com

You can estimate to find the volume of a three-dimensional figure that has different numbers of cubes in each layer.

EXAMPLE Estimate Volume

2 Estimate the volume of the figure shown to the right.

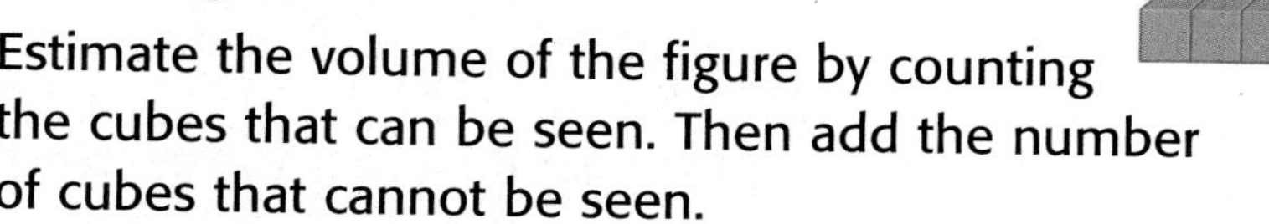

Estimate the volume of the figure by counting the cubes that can be seen. Then add the number of cubes that cannot be seen.

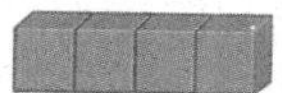

Four cubes can be seen in the top layer.

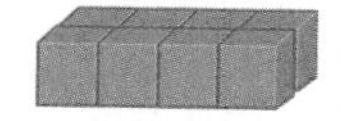

Five cubes can be seen in the bottom layer and three cubes are hidden.

So, the volume of the figure is $4 + 8$ or 12 cubic units.

CHECK What You Know

Use models to find each volume. See Example 1 (p. 469)

1. 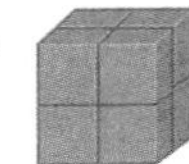

2. 

Estimate each volume. See Example 2 (p. 469)

3. 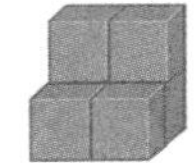

4.

5. Rona has 12 cubes. Model and describe a rectangular prism she could create that has a volume of 12 cubic units.

6. **Talk About It** The volume of a cube is 8 cubic units. What is the height of the cube? Explain how you found your answer

Practice and Problem Solving

EXTRA PRACTICE See page R40.

Use models to find each volume. See Example 1 (p. 469)

7. 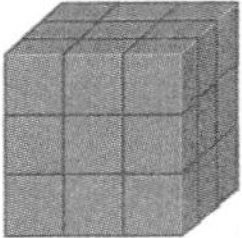

8. 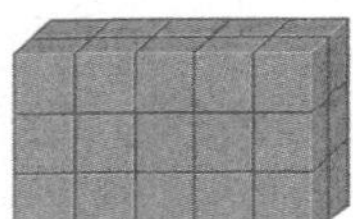

9. 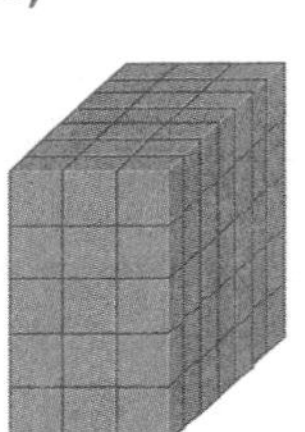

10. 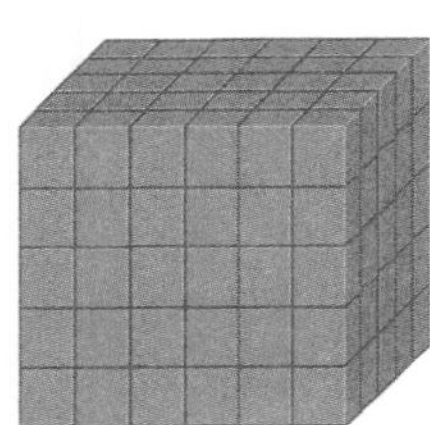

Estimate each volume. See Example 2 (p. 469)

11. 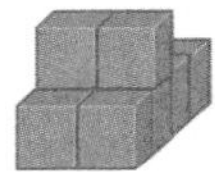

12. 

13. 

14. 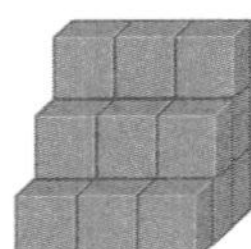

15. Find containers that are rectangular prisms or cubes. Estimate and measure the volume in cubic units.

16. Toby and Lena each have a box for their trading cards. Toby's box is 8 units long, 4 units wide, and 1 unit tall. Lena's box is 5 units long, 7 units wide, and 1 unit tall. Whose box has a volume of 32 cubic units? Explain.

17. Vijay is making a tower that is 3 units long, 4 units wide, and 5 units tall. So far he has a tower that is 3 units long, 3 units wide, and 3 units tall. What is the volume that is left to be added to the tower? Explain.

H.O.T. Problems

18. OPEN ENDED Give the dimensions of a rectangular prism that has a volume greater than 50 cubic units.

19. WHICH ONE DOESN'T BELONG? Identify the figure that does not belong with the other three. Explain.

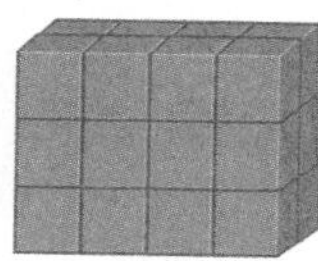

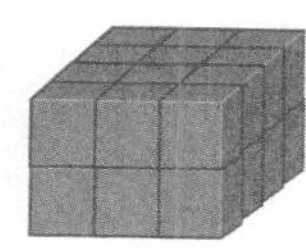

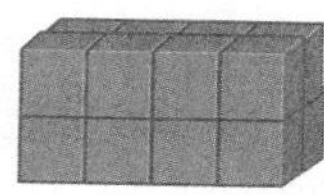

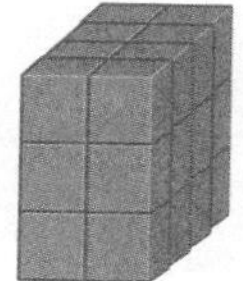

20. WRITING IN MATH Explain the difference between area and volume.

TEST Practice

21. Which of these units would best measure the mass of a watermelon? (Lesson 11-7)

A cups

B grams

C kilograms

D meters

22. Which is the best estimate for the volume of the prism? (Lesson 11-8)

F 14 cubic units

G 22 cubic units

H 77 cubic units

J 154 cubic units

Spiral Review

Choose the more reasonable estimate. (Lesson 11-7)

23. cherry

5 g or 5 kg

24. wagon

15 g or 15 kg

Complete. (Lesson 11-6)

25. 1 lb = ■ oz

26. 80 oz = ■ lb

27. 8,000 lb = ■ T

28. Alex bought a 32-ounce fruit smoothie. Minda bought a fruit smoothie that is half the size of Alex's smoothie. Tyrell's smoothie is 8 ounces less than Alex's smoothie. How many ounces is each person's smoothie? (Lesson 11-5)

Problem Solving in Science

Tide Pool Ecosystems

Tide pools are rocky areas on the edge of an ocean that are filled with sea water. Many plants and animals live there. Some animals that can be found in tide pools are starfish, mussels, and crabs. Kelp and other sea plants are also found in tide pools.

Life is tough for plants and animals that live in tide pools. Parts of the shore are covered and then uncovered as tides go in and out. The plants and animals that live in tide pools must avoid being washed away by waves, keep from drying out in the sun, and avoid predators. The tide pool ecosystem is the hardest ecosystem to recreate in an aquarium.

mussel

crab

starfish

Targeted TEKS 4.14 The student applies Grade 4 mathematics to solve problems connected to everyday experiences and activities in and outside of school. **(A) Identify the mathematics in everyday situations.**

Did You Know?

A starfish can grow back an arm if it loses one.

Aquarium

Type	Capacity (gal)	Cost
A	20	$75
B	25	$100

Real-World Math

Use the information on page 473 to solve each problem.

1. Elias has decided to buy a 20-gallon aquarium. He is going to use a one-quart container to fill the aquarium. How many times will Elias use the one-quart container to fill the 20-gallon aquarium?

2. Suppose Elias had decided to get the 25-gallon aquarium. How many times would he have needed to use his one-quart container to fill the aquarium?

3. Elias is also buying the gravel to place in the bottom of his 20-gallon aquarium. He needs one pound of gravel for every gallon of water. How many ounces of gravel will he need for the 20-gallon aquarium?

4. If Elias buys the 25-gallon aquarium, how many ounces of gravel would he have needed?

5. For the 20-gallon aquarium, the gravel costs $15. How much would Elias spend for the gravel and the aquarium?

6. For the 25-gallon aquarium, the gravel costs $18. How much would Elias spend for the gravel and the aquarium?

7. What is the difference in cost of the 20-gallon aquarium filled with gravel and the 25-gallon aquarium filled with gravel?

11-9 Problem-Solving Investigation

MAIN IDEA I will solve problems by choosing the best strategy.

Targeted TEKS 4.14 The student applies Grade 4 mathematics to solve problems .... **(B) Solve problems that incorporate understanding the problem, making a plan, carrying out the plan, and evaluating the solution for reasonableness.** *Also addresses TEKS 4.14(C).*

P.S.I. TEAM +

AIDEN: I have a video game system. Games cost $20. Felice has a different video game system. Her games cost $15. How many video games can we each buy if we each have $60?

YOUR MISSION: Find out how many games each person can buy.

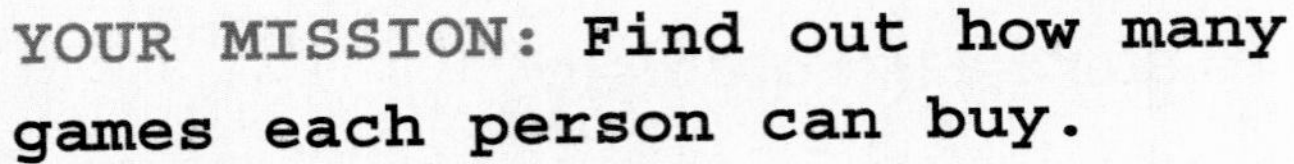

Understand Games for Aiden's game system cost $20. Games for Felice's game system cost $15. Each has $60 to spend on video games. Find how many games each person can buy.

Plan Organize the data to show the number of games and the total amount of money spent.

Solve

Aiden	
Rule: ▲ = 20■	
Games	Total ($)
1	20
2	40
3	60

Felice	
Rule: ▲ = 15■	
Games	Total ($)
1	15
2	30
3	45
4	60

Since Aiden's games cost more, he can buy only 3. Felice can buy 4.

Check Look back at the problem. Since $20 \times 3 = 60$ and $15 \times 4 = 60$, you know that the answer is correct.

Mixed Problem Solving

See page R40.

Use any strategy shown below to solve. Tell what strategy you used.

PROBLEM-SOLVING STRATEGIES
- Act it out.
- Guess and check.
- Look for a pattern.
- Work a simpler problem.
- Use logical reasoning.

1. Keisha and Andy went hiking from 9:30 A.M. until 12:00 P.M. After lunch, they hiked for another hour and 40 minutes. How many minutes did they spend hiking?

2. For every day at school that no students are absent, a teacher put 3 marbles in a jar. If the jar holds 426 marbles, how many days of no absences will it take to fill the jar?

3. A roller coaster car carries 32 people every 10 minutes. There are 572 people in line in front of Ruben. About how long will it take for him to ride the roller coaster?

4. A family spends $22 on tickets for a community play.

If there are two adults, how many children are with them?

5. Dora took 9 photos with her camera. She takes 2 more photos each day for a week. How many more days does she need to take photos to have 30?

6. Sally gave a cashier $25 for two CDs. They cost the same amount. She got $3 back. How much did each CD cost?

7. April's birthday party is being held at an arcade. Each guest will be given 16 tokens to play games. Copy and complete the table to find how many tokens are needed for 12 guests.

Guests	Tokens
2	32
4	64
6	96
8	128
10	■
12	■

8. A concert hall has 13 rows of seats. The hall has a total of 221 seats. Write a number sentence that could be used to find the number of seats in each row.

9. Myron has 2 red marbles for every one green marble. He has three times as many blue marbles as red marbles. Myron has four red marbles. How many green and blue marbles does he have?

10. WRITING IN ▸MATH Identify the problem-solving strategy you used to find the answer to Exercise 9. Explain how you found the answer.

11-10 Elapsed Time

GET READY to Learn

Hands-On Mini Activity

Materials stopwatch

You can use a stopwatch to find elapsed time.

Step 1 Copy the table.

Activity	Time	End Time	Elapsed Time
Write alphabet	■	■	■
Name 10 states	■	■	■
Jump 20 times	■	■	■

Step 2 Measure.
Write the alphabet while your partner uses a stopwatch to time you. Record the start and end times. Complete the next two activities while your partner times you. Do not reset the stopwatch between the activities. Record the start and end times.

Step 3 Copy and complete the table.
Find the elapsed time between each event. To find the elapsed times, subtract the start times from the end times. Record the results in the third column.

1. Which event took the longest time? the shortest time?

2. Select one of the elapsed times. List two more activities that might take that long.

The last column of your table gives examples of elapsed time. **Elapsed time** is the amount of time between the beginning and ending of an activity.

MAIN IDEA

I will solve problems about elapsed time.

Targeted TEKS 4.12 The student applies measurement concepts, the student measures time and temperature (in degrees Fahrenheit and Celsius) (B) **Use tools such as a clock with gears or a stopwatch to solve problems involving elapsed time.**

New Vocabulary

elapsed time

Remember

60 minutes = 1 hour

Real-World EXAMPLE Elapsed Time

1 **TRAVEL It takes Louisa one hour and 30 minutes to travel to her aunt's house. If she leaves at 4:00 P.M., what time will she get to her aunt's house?**

Add 1 hour and 30 minutes to 4:00 p.m

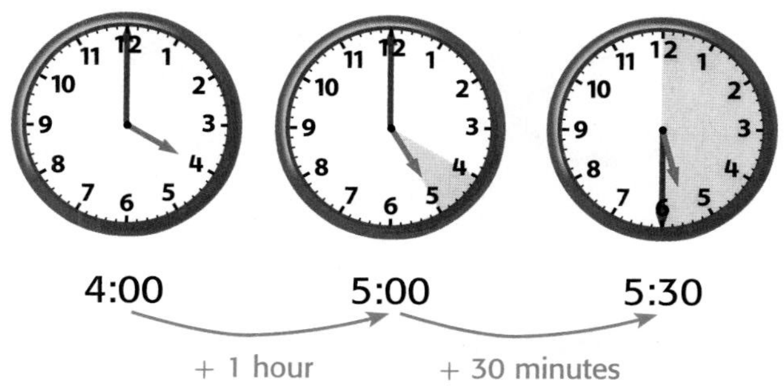

4:00 → 5:00 → 5:30

+ 1 hour   + 30 minutes

So, Louisa will get to her aunt's house at 5:30 p.m

Personal Tutor at tx.gr4math.com

CHECK What You Know

The following are movie times. Find the length of each movie. See Example 1 (p. 477)

1. Start Time End Time

2. Start Time End Time

Find each elapsed time. Use a clock if needed. See Example 1 (p. 477)

3. Julian's family went to the library at the time shown on the clock. They stay until 4:00.

4. Trisha is going to the park. She has to be home by the time shown on the clock. If it is 3:15 P.M. now, how long will she be gone?

5. Talk About It Kayla went to sleep at 9:15 P.M. and awoke at 6:30 A.M. Explain how to find how long Kayla slept.

Practice and Problem Solving

EXTRA PRACTICE See page R41.

The following are times of baseball games. Find the length of each game. See Example 1 (p. 477)

6. Start Time End Time

7. Start Time End Time

Find each elapsed time. Use a clock if needed. See Example 1 (p. 477)

8. The clock shows when Nikia began reading her book. It is 12:50 when she stops.

9. The clock shows the time Samie arrives home from school. He goes to bed at 8:30.

Real-World PROBLEM SOLVING

Science The table to the right shows the schedule of the Texas State Aquarium's daily presentations.

Daily Presentations Schedule	
Presentation	**Time**
Amazon Creature Feature	1:30 P.M.
Diver in the Water	11:30 A.M. and 1:30 P.M.
Dolphin Training Lesson	11 A.M. and 1 P.M.
Reptile Report	3 P.M.
You "Otter" Know This	10 A.M. and 4 P.M.

10. Albert first attended the Amazon Creature Feature. If the presentation ended at 2:45 P.M., how long did it last?

11. Next, Albert attended the Reptile Report. It ended at 3:45 P.M. How long was this presentation?

12. The last presentation Albert attended was You "Otter" Know This. It lasted 1 hour and 30 minutes. If it takes Albert 20 minutes to get home, did he make it home in time to eat dinner at 6 P.M.? Explain.

H.O.T. Problems

13. **CHALLENGE** Dennis earns $5 for each hour he works. One day he worked from 8:00 A.M. until 12:00 P.M., had lunch, and then worked for 3 more hours. How much money did he earn that day?

14. **FIND THE ERROR** Haley and Hidalgo are finding elapsed time. Who is correct? Explain your reasoning.

Haley
It's 10:30 a.m. In 1 hour and 45 minutes, it will be 12:15 p.m.

Hidalgo
It's 10:45 a.m. In 30 minutes it will be 11:45 p.m.

TEST Practice

15. Which of these units would best measure the mass of a box of books? (Lesson 11-8)

    A Grams
    B Kilograms
    C Liters
    D Milliliters

16. Gretchen downloaded music for 45 minutes. She began at 11:45 A.M. What time did she finish? (Lesson 11-10)

    F 11:00 A.M.
    G 12:30 P.M.
    H 11:00 P.M.
    J 12:30 A.M.

Spiral Review

17. Airports have limits on luggage weight. Is it more reasonable to say that an airport's weight limit is 35 grams or 35 kilograms? Explain. (Lesson 11-7)

Find each volume. (Lesson 11-8)

18. 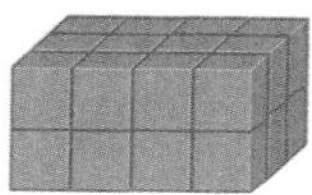

19. 

Choose the more reasonable estimate. (Lesson 11-7)

20. dog

40g or 40 kg

21. hamster

500 g or 500 kg

Study Guide and Review

FOLDABLES Study Organizer GET READY to Study

Be sure the following Key Vocabulary words and Key Concepts are written in your Foldable.

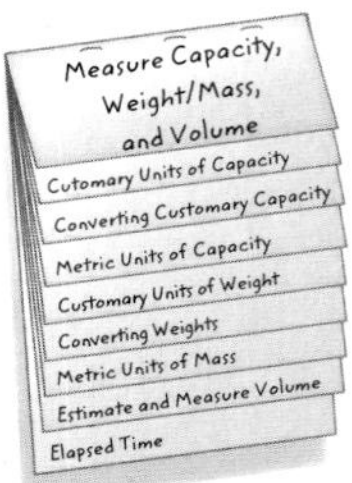

Measure Capacity, Weight/Mass, and Volume
Customary Units of Capacity
Converting Customary Capacity
Metric Units of Capacity
Customary Units of Weight
Converting Weights
Metric Units of Mass
Estimate and Measure Volume
Elapsed Time

BIG Ideas

- **Capacity** is the amount of liquid a container holds. The customary units of capacity are fluid ounces, cups, pints, gallons, and quarts. The metric units of capacity are liter and milliliter. (p. 442)
- The **weight** of an object is how heavy it is. Weight is measured in ounces, pounds, and tons. (p. 454)
- The **mass** of an object is the amount of matter it has. Mass is measured in grams and kilograms. (p. 465)
- **Volume** is the amount of space a three-dimensional figure contains. It is measured in cubic units. (p. 468)
- **Elapsed time** is the amount of time between the beginning and ending of an activity. (p. 476)

Key Vocabulary

capacity (p. 442)
elapsed time (p. 476)
mass (p. 465)
volume (p. 468)
weight (p. 454)

Vocabulary Check

Complete each sentence with the correct vocabulary word.

1. ___?___ is the amount of matter an object has.
2. The ___?___ of an object is how heavy it is.
3. ___?___ is the amount of time between the beginning and end of an activity.
4. ___?___ is measured in grams and kilograms.
5. ___?___ is the amount of space that a three-dimensional figure contains.
6. ___?___ is measured in ounces, pounds, and tons.
7. The amount of liquid a container holds is its ___?___.

Math Online Vocabulary Review at tx.gr4math.com

Lesson-by-Lesson Review

11-1 Customary Units of Capacity (pp. 442–445)

Example 1

Carrie is pouring fruit juice into a punch bowl. Is the most reasonable estimate for the capacity of the bowl 2 fluid ounces, 2 cups, 2 quarts, or 2 gallons?

Use logic to eliminate the choices that are not reasonable.

The capacity of a punch bowl is greater than 2 fluid ounces or 2 cups. Then consider 2 quarts or 2 gallons. 2 quarts is still not large enough. So, 2 gallons is the most reasonable estimate for the capacity of the bowl.

Choose the most reasonable estimate.

8. Pablo is filling a watering can with water. Is the most reasonable estimate for the capacity of the watering can 10 ounces, 10 cups, 10 quarts, or 10 gallons?

9. Lila is pouring guacamole into a bowl. Is the most reasonable estimate for the capacity of the bowl 12 fluid ounces, 12 cups, 12 pints, or 12 quarts?

10. Paul is filling a gas tank of a car. Is the most reasonable estimate for the capacity of the gas tank 12 cups, 12 pints, 12 quarts, or 12 gallons?

11-2 Converting Customary Capacity (pp. 446–447)

Example 2

Complete the conversion 3 c = ■ fl oz.

Since fluid ounces are smaller than cups, multiply.

3 cups × 8 fluid ounces = ■

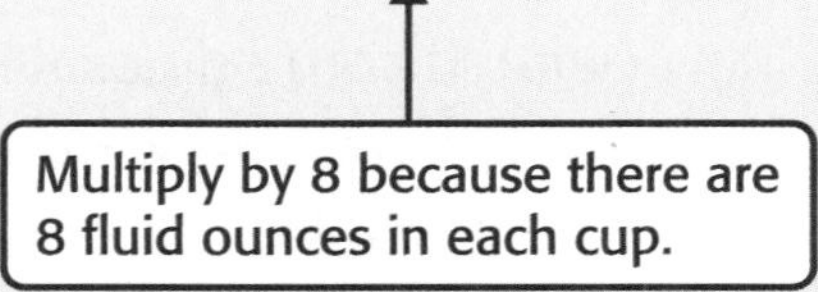

Multiply by 8 because there are 8 fluid ounces in each cup.

$3 \times 8 = 24$

So, there are 24 fluid ounces in 3 cups.

Complete.

11. 16 fl oz = ■ c **12.** 2 gal = ■ qt

13. ■ pt = 12 qt **14.** ■ pt = 18 c

Compare

15. 5 qt ● 10 pt **16.** 2 cups ● 18 fl oz

17. Chen is buying a 16-fluid ounce container of spaghetti sauce. How many cups of spaghetti sauce is he buying?

11-3 Metric Units of Capacity (pp. 448–451)

Example 3
Decide whether 700 mL or 700 L is the more reasonable estimate for the capacity of a bottle of salad dressing.

Salad
Dressing

Use logic to estimate the capacity of the bottle of salad dressing.

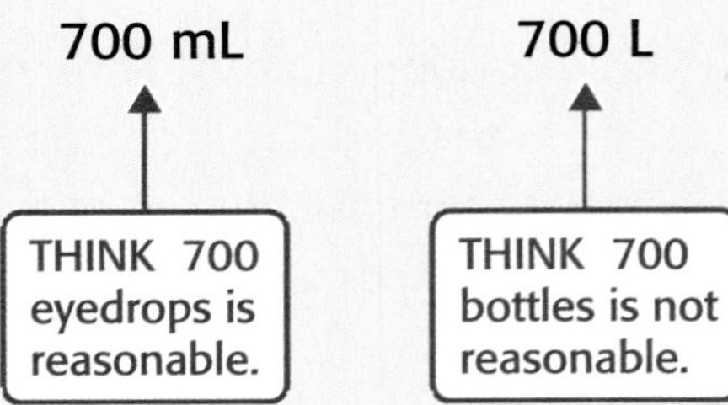
700 mL
700 L
THINK 700 eyedrops is reasonable.
THINK 700 bottles is not reasonable.

So, 700 mL is a more reasonable estimate.

Choose the more reasonable estimate for each capacity.

18. 

265 mL or 265 L

19. 

6 mL or 6 L

20. 

800 mL or 800 L

21. Carina said that her father took 6 liters of medicine for his cold. Is that reasonable? Explain.

11-4 Customary Units of Weight (pp. 454–456)

Example 4
Which is the most reasonable estimate for the weight of a pencil case: 1 ounce, 1 pound, 10 pounds, or 10 tons?

Compare the weight of a pencil case to the weight of objects that you know. A pencil case weighs more than a strawberry or 1 ounce. A pencil case weighs less than 10 pineapples or 10 pounds. Tons weigh more than pounds, so the answer is 1 pound.

Choose the most reasonable estimate.

22. table

A 8 ounces
B 80 pounds
C 800 pounds
D 8 tons

23. Ravi claimed some dinosaurs weighed 3 tons. Is Ravi's claim reasonable? Explain.

24. Annie claims her basketball weighs 50 lbs. Is Annie's claim reasonable?

11-5 Problem-Solving Strategy: Use Logical Reasoning (pp. 458–459)

Example 5

Chris, Sayra, Mark, and Ebony competed in a race. Chris came in third place. Ebony was faster than Mark. Sayra won the race. Which order did Chris, Sayra, Mark, and Ebony finish the race in?

Understand

You know that Chris came in third place. Ebony was faster than Mark. Sayra won the race. You need to find the order that Chris, Sayra, Mark, and Ebony finished the race in.

Plan You can use logical reasoning to solve the problem.

Solve Since Sayra won the race, she came in first place.

Chris came in third place.

Since Ebony was faster than Mark, she came in second place. This means that Mark came in fourth place.

So, the order that each person finished was Sayra, Ebony, Chris, and Mark.

Check Look back at the problem. The answer makes sense for the facts given in the problem. So, the answer is correct.

25. The Ruiz family is on a bike ride. Each person is riding either a bicycle or a tricycle. There are 5 members in the family and 11 wheels. The number of bicycles is four times the number of tricycles. How many tricycles and bicycles are there?

26. Felix, Laura, and Suki packed lunches that contain a peanut butter sandwich, a turkey sandwich, and a bologna sandwich. Laura's sandwich is shown. Suki's sandwich had bologna on it. Which sandwiches did each person get in their lunch?

27. Rhonda, Jordan, and Mala were born in September, December, and June. Jordan's birthday is during the winter. The number of letters in Mala's name matches the number of letters in her birth month. In what months was each person born?

28. Bella has a brother named Ricardo and a sister named Rosa. The ages of the three children are 3, 5, and 10. Bella is twice as old as Ricardo. What are the ages of the children?

11-6 Converting Weight (pp. 460–463)

Example 6
Shawn is buying 3 pounds of flour. The package he found was 32 ounces. Do 32 ounces equal 3 pounds?

Convert 32 ounces to pounds. Ounces are smaller than pounds. Divide.

$$32 \div 16 = 2$$

Divide by 16 because there are 16 ounces in a pound.

So, 32 ounces does not equal 3 pounds.

Complete.

29. 2,000 lb = ■ T **30.** 32 oz = ■ lb

31. 16 oz and 1 lb = ■ lb

32. 1 lb = ■ oz

33. ■ lb = 3 T

34. ■ lb = 2 T and 2 lbs

35. Marita uses 7 ounces of clay to make a vase. How many pounds of clay will she need to make 4 vases?

36. A sandwich shop uses 2 ounces of ham on a club sandwich. If 20 club sandwiches are made in one day, how many pounds of ham will be used?

11-7 Metric Units of Mass (pp. 464–466)

Example 7
Which is the more reasonable estimate for the mass of the digital music player: 500 g or 500 kg?

If the digital music player has a mass of 500 kilograms it would have the same mass as 3,000 apples. This is not a reasonable estimate.

So, a reasonable estimate for the mass of the digital music player is 500 g.

Choose the more reasonable estimate.

37. pencil

4 g or 4 kg

38. dog

20 g or 20 kg

39. chair

15 g or 15 kg

40. scissors

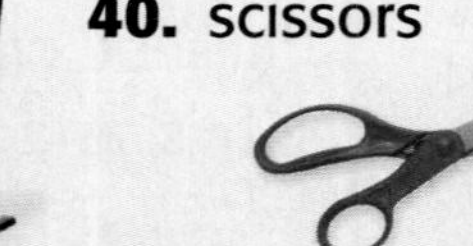

50 g or 50 kg

41. Is it more reasonable to say that the mass of a medium tub of popcorn is 1 gram or 1 kilogram?

11-8 Estimate and Measure Volume (pp. 468–471)

Example 8

Use models to find the volume of the cube shown to the right.

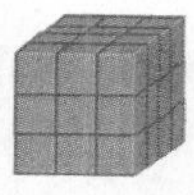

The cube shown has 3 layers. Each layer has 9 cubes.

One layer   Three layers

So, the volume of the cube is 27 cubic units.

Use models to find each volume.

42. 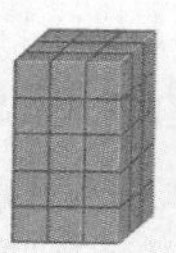

43. 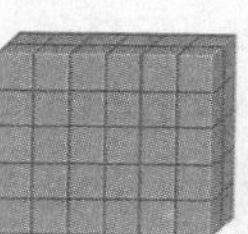

Estimate each volume.

44.

45. 

11-9 Problem-Solving Investigation: Choose a Strategy (pp. 474–475)

Example 9

Jamal's school is going to see a play. There are 230 seats in the theatre. If every class has 25 students, how many classes can see the play at the same time?

You know that there are 230 seats in the theatre and 25 students in each class. You need to find how many classes can see the play at the same time.

Divide the number of seats in the theatre by the number of students in each class.

230	÷	25	=	9 R5
seats in theater		students per class		

So, 9 classes can see the play at the same time.

Adding 25 nine times equals 225. So, the answer is correct.

Use any strategy to solve.

46. Kelsey has a week to catch 30 insects for science class. Yesterday she caught 3. The insects she caught today are shown below. If she catches 5 more each day for 4 days, how many more will she need to catch to have 30?

47. Bobby went to the grocery store on Tuesday and tomatoes were $1 each. Jessica went to the store on Wednesday and the price of tomatoes had increased to $2 each. If both spend $12 on tomatoes, how many did each buy?

Study Guide and Review

11-10 Elapsed Time (pp. 476–479)

Example 10
Laua started working on her homework at the time shown on the first clock below. She finished her homework at the time shown on the second clock below. How long did it take Laua to complete her homework?

You can find the elapsed time by counting the hours and minutes between 4:45 P.M. and 6:00 P.M.

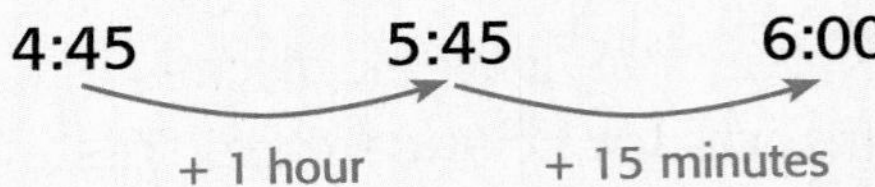

So, it took Laua 1 hour and 15 minutes to complete her homework.

Example 11
What time will it be in 3 hours and 45 minutes?

Add 3 hours and 45 minutes to 12:15.

12:15 → 1:15 → 2:15 → 3:15 → 4:00

+ 1 hour, + 1 hour, + 1 hour, + 45 minutes

So, in 3 hours and 45 minutes it will be 4:00.

The following are times of football games. Find the length of each game.

48. Start Time / End Time

49. Start Time / End Time

Find each elapsed time. Use a clock if needed.

50. Franklin walked in the park from 2:10 P.M. until the time shown on the clock.

51. Delia left the store at 7:05 P.M. The clock shows when she arrived home.

CHAPTER 11 Chapter Test

For Exercises 1 and 2, tell whether each statement is *true* or *false*.

1. Weight is the amount of matter an object has.

2. Elapsed time is the amount of time between the beginning and end of an activity.

Choose the most reasonable estimate for each capacity.

3.

A 6 fluid ounces
B 6 cups
C 6 quarts
D 6 gallons

4.

A 1 fluid ounce
B 1 cup
C 1 pint
D 1 quart

Choose the most reasonable estimate.

5. microscope

A 7 tons
B 70 pounds
C 7 pounds
D 7 ounces

6. bald eagle

A 8 ounces
B 8 pounds
C 80 pounds
D 8 tons

7. **TEST PRACTICE** Which of the comparisons is false?

A 3 qt > 2 pt
B 10 pt < 25 c
C 2 gal > 6 qt
D 16 oz < 3 c

8. Pete, Suzanne, and Monica are playing soccer. Their jersey numbers are 4, 7, and 13. Suzanne's number equals the number of letters in her name. Pete's is a two-digit number. What is Monica's number?

Complete.

9. ■ lb = 4 T

10. 80 oz = ■ lb

Choose the more reasonable estimate.

11. ruler

20 g or 20 kg

12. picture

10 g or 10 kg

Use models to find each volume.

13.

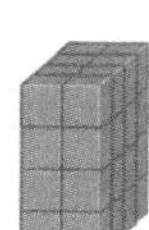

14.

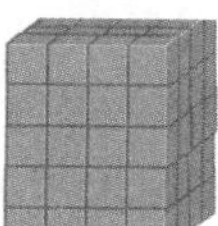

15. **TEST PRACTICE** Tim took a nap from 4:15 P.M. to 5:30 P.M. How much time passed?

F 1 hour
G 1 hour 15 minutes
H 1 hour 30 minutes
J 1 hour 45 minutes

16. Find the elapsed time. What time will it be in 4 hours and 40 minutes?

17. **WRITING IN MATH** Explain how to find elapsed time.

Texas Test Practice

Cumulative, Chapters 1–11

Which unit of measure would be most reasonable to use when finding the capacity of a thermos?

A fluid ounces **C** quarts
B cups **D** gallons

TEST-TAKING TIP

You can eliminate incorrect answer choices by thinking of real world examples.

Read the Test Question

You need to find the most reasonable unit for measuring the capacity of a thermos.

Solve the Test Question

Look at the answer choices. Eliminate the ones that are not reasonable for measuring the capacity of a thermos.

Eight fluid ounces equals one cup. So, fluid ounces are too small.
Since a cup equals eight fluid ounces, cups are a reasonable unit of measurement.
A quart is equal to the capacity of a small pitcher of lemonade. So, a quart is too large.
A gallon is equal to the capacity of a jug of milk. So, a gallon is too large.

So, the correct answer is B.

 **Personal Tutor at** tx.gr4math.com

Choose the best answer.

1. **Which unit of measure would be most reasonable to use when finding the capacity of cleaning solution a contact lens holds?**

   A gram **C** liter
   B kilogram **D** milliliter

2. **Which unit of measure would be most reasonable to use when finding the capacity of bubble solution that a bottle of bubbles holds?**

   F fluid ounce **H** pint
   G cup **J** quart

Get Ready for the Texas Test
For test-taking strategies and more practice, see pages TX1–TX21.

3. How many edges does a rectangular prism have?

A 4

B 6

C 8

D 12

4. Isabel exercises every three days. If she exercised on Monday and Thursday, what are the next two days she will exercise?

F Sunday and Tuesday

G Sunday and Wednesday

H Friday and Monday

J Saturday and Monday

5. Which term best describes the picture below?

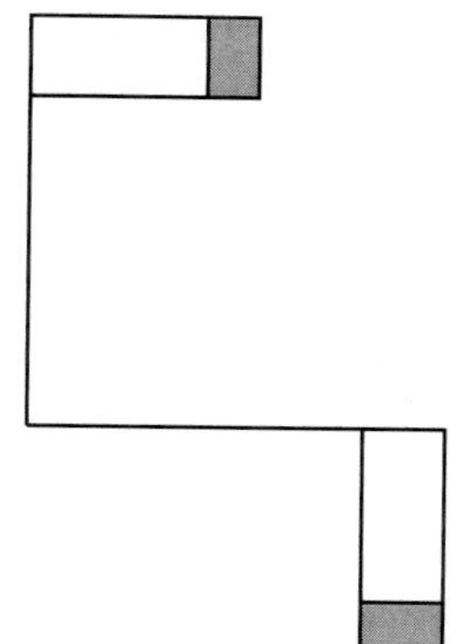

A dilation

B reflection

C rotation

D translation

6. Which rule best describes the pattern of numbers below?

4, 7, 10, 13, 16, 19, 22

F add 3

G add 4

H subtract 3

J subtract 4

7. The weight of a small puppy is best measured in what units?

A milligrams

B grams

C pounds

D kilograms

8. Percy is flying to his grandparent's house. It takes 25 minutes to drive to the airport. He needs to arrive at least 1 hour before his plane leaves. What other information is needed for Percy to arrive at the airport on time?

F the time the plane leaves

G how fast he drives

H the distance he will fly

J the amount of time he will fly

9. How many lines of symmetry does the figure have?

A 0

B 1

C 2

D 4

10. GRIDDABLE A landscaper orders 3 tons of mulch. How many pounds are there in 3 tons?

CHAPTER 12

Describe and Compare Fractions

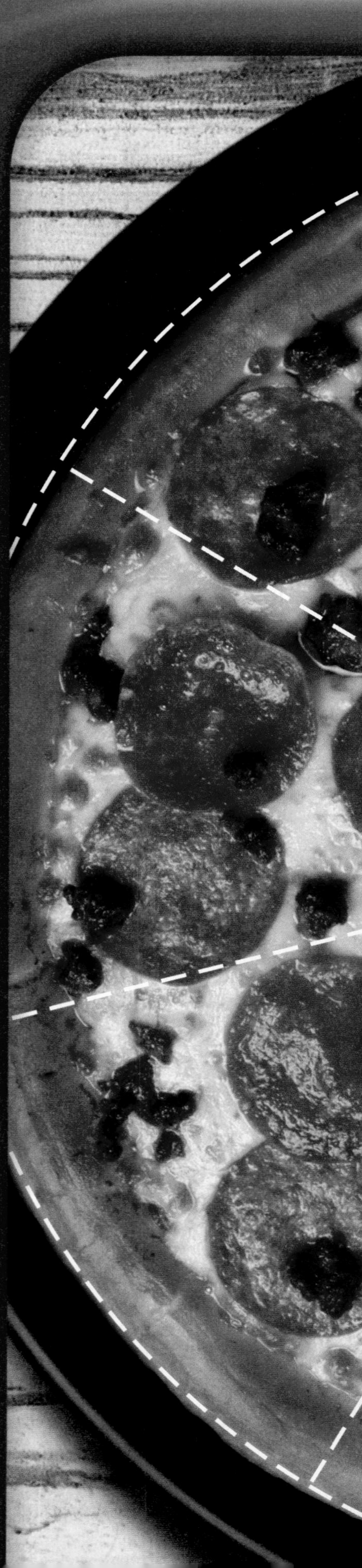

BIG Idea What is a fraction?

A **fraction** is a number that names part of a whole or part of a set.

Example If you have a pizza that is cut into eight pieces, each piece would be *one-eighth* or *one of eight* pieces.

or

What will I learn in this chapter?

- Identify, read, and write fractions.
- Identify and find equivalent fractions.
- Compare and order fractions.
- Solve problems by drawing a picture.

Key Vocabulary

fraction

numerator

denominator

equivalent fractions

mixed number

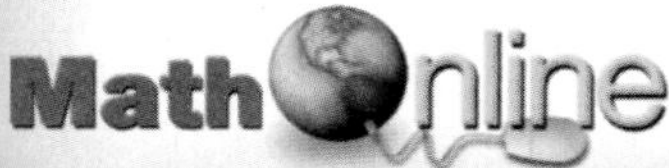

Student Study Tools at tx.gr4math.com

FOLDABLES™ Study Organizer

Make this Foldable to help you organize information about fractions. Begin with one sheet of $8\frac{1}{2}'' \times 11''$ paper.

1. **Fold** the paper into thirds as shown.
2. **Open** and fold down 1 inch from the top.
3. **Unfold** and draw lines along the folds.
4. **Label** as shown. Record what you learn.

ARE YOU READY for Chapter 12?

You have two ways to check prerequisite skills for this chapter.

Option 2

Math Online Take the Chapter Readiness Quiz at tx.gr4math.com.

Option 1

Complete the Quick Check below.

QUICK Check

Write the word that names the equal parts in each whole. Write *halves*, *thirds*, *fourths*, and *fifths*. (Prior grade)

1. 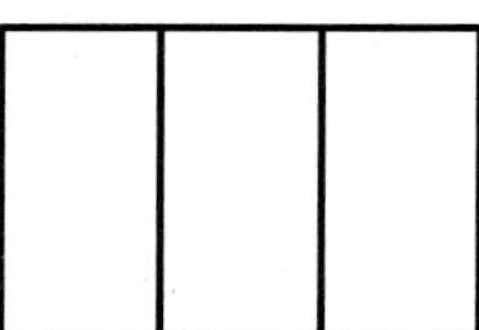

2. 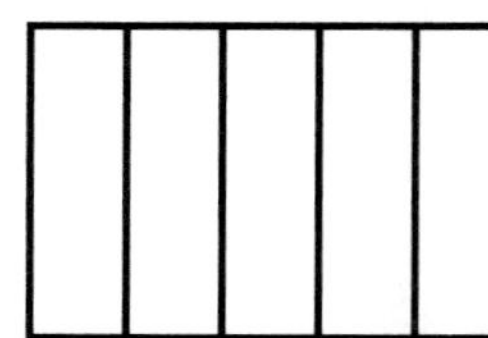

3. 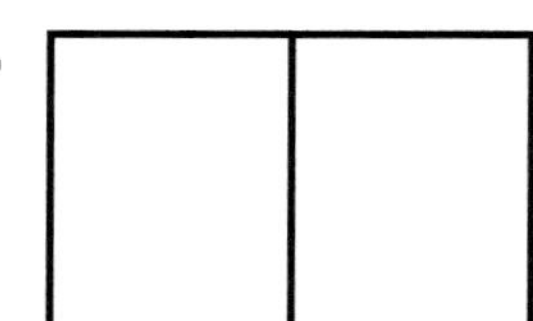

4. 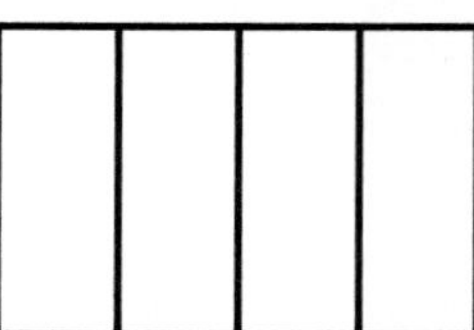

Divide. (Lesson 5-5)

5. 16 ÷ 4 **6.** 48 ÷ 8 **7.** 24 ÷ 3 **8.** 36 ÷ 6

9. 72 ÷ 9 **10.** 64 ÷ 8 **11.** 42 ÷ 6 **12.** 56 ÷ 8

13. Tyree downloaded 120 songs in 10 days. He downloaded the same number of songs each day. How many songs did he download each day?

List the factors of each number. (Lesson 5-9)

14. 12 **15.** 30 **16.** 45 **17.** 21

18. Write the factor of 36 that is missing from the list 1, 2, 3, 4, 6, ■, 12, 18, 36.

12-1 Parts of a Whole

MAIN IDEA

I will identify, write, and read fractions for parts of a whole.

Targeted TEKS 4.2 **The student describes and compares fractional parts of whole objects** or sets of objects.

New Vocabulary

fraction
numerator
denominator

GET READY to Learn

Some of the pieces of pizza have pepperoni. Some have just cheese. You can use a fraction to describe the pizza and the toppings.

A **fraction** is a number that names part of a whole or part of a set. In a fraction, the **numerator** tells the number of equal parts. The **denominator** tells the number of equal parts in all.

pieces with pepperoni → 3 ← numerator
total number of pieces → 4 ← denominator

Real-World EXAMPLE

1 FOOD **Suppose Molly and her mom made the pizza shown. What fraction of the pizza is pepperoni?**

Write pepperoni slices → 4
total slices in all → 6

Read *four-sixths* or *four divided by six*

So, $\frac{4}{6}$ of the whole pizza is pepperoni.

EXAMPLE Write and Read Fractions

2 **What fraction of the figure is shaded?**

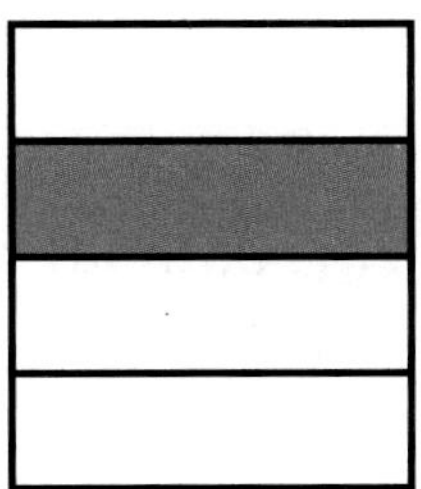

Write parts shaded → 1
total equal parts in all → 4

Read *one-fourth* or *one divided by four*

So, $\frac{1}{4}$ of the whole figure is shaded.

You can use different pictures to show the same part of a whole.

Remember

The denominator is always the bottom number in a fraction. Remember that **d** in **d**enominator could stand for **d**own.

Real-World EXAMPLE — Draw a Fraction Model

3 GARDENS **The students at Watson Elementary School are making a garden. They will plant vegetables in $\frac{1}{3}$ of the whole garden. Draw a picture to show this fraction.**

One Way: Use a Rectangle	Another Way: Use a Circle
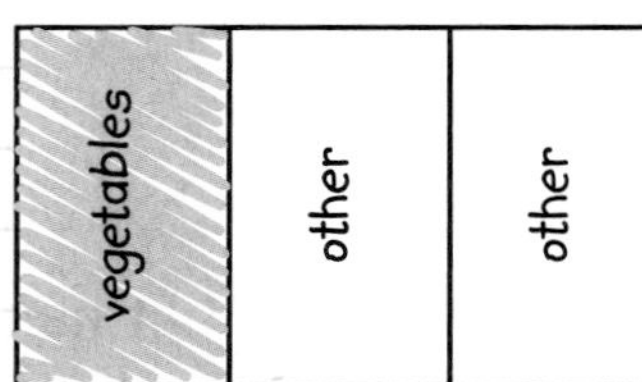	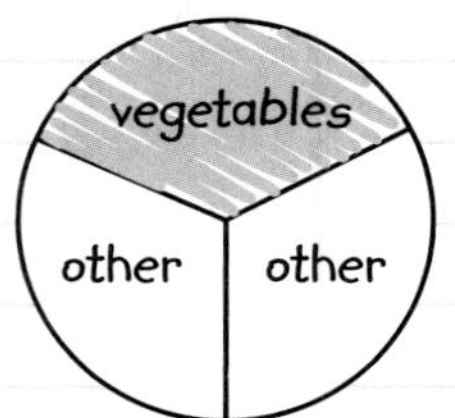
Divide a rectangle into 3 equal parts. Shade one part to show one-third.	Divide a circle into 3 equal parts. Shade one part to show one-third.

Online Personal Tutor at tx.gr4math.com

CHECK What You Know

Write the fraction that names part of the whole. See Examples 1 and 2 (p. 493)

1. 

part left

2. 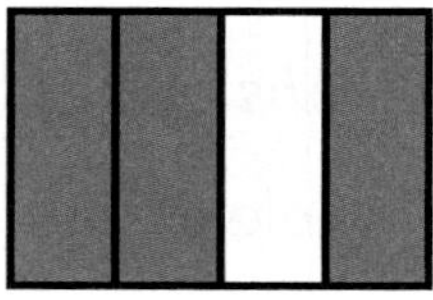

part shaded

3. 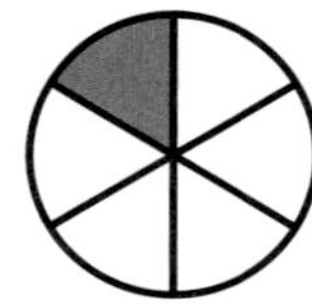

part not shaded

Draw a picture and shade part of it to show the fraction. See Example 3 (p. 494)

4. $\frac{1}{4}$

5. $\frac{2}{3}$

6. $\frac{5}{8}$

7. A birthday cake is cut into 8 equal pieces. Arnaldo ate one piece. The guests ate the remaining pieces. What fraction of the whole cake did the guests eat?

8. Talk About It What part of a fraction is the denominator? What does the denominator mean?

 Math Online Extra Examples at tx.gr4math.com

Practice and Problem Solving

Write the fraction that names part of the whole. See Examples 1 and 2 (p. 493)

9. 
part left

10. 
part filled

11. 
part filled

12. 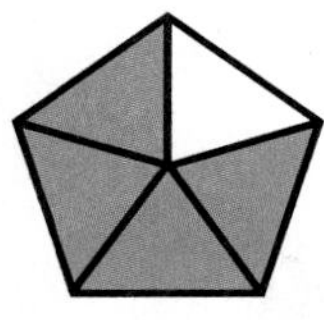
part shaded

13. 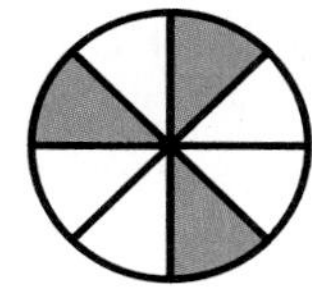
part not shaded

14. 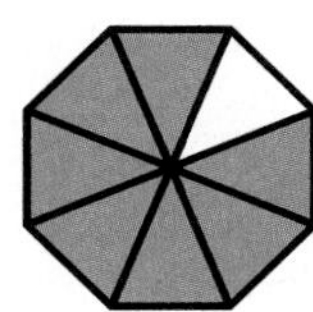
part not shaded

Draw a picture and shade part of it to show the fraction. See Example 3 (p. 494)

15. $\frac{3}{5}$ **16.** $\frac{3}{6}$ **17.** $\frac{7}{8}$ **18.** $\frac{4}{10}$

Alphabet flags are used by ships at sea to send short messages. Write the fraction for the part of each flag that is blue.

19. 
Letter C

20. 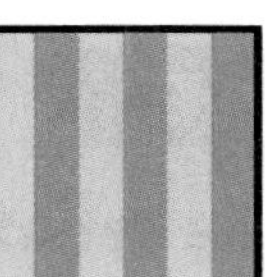
Letter G

21. 
Letter N

22. 
Letter Z

For Exercises 23–25, use the recipe shown.

23. What is the total number of cups of ingredients needed to make one batch of the party mix?

24. What fraction of the ingredients is pretzels?

25. What fraction of the ingredients is peanuts and raisins?

Recipe for: Party Mix
1 cup peanuts
3 cups rice cereal
2 cups pretzels
2 cups raisins
Makes: one batch

H.O.T. Problems

26. OPEN ENDED Name two different real-world items that can show the fraction $\frac{2}{3}$.

27. WRITING IN ▶MATH If the denominator of $\frac{2}{5}$ was increased from 5 to 10, would it be greater or less than $\frac{2}{5}$? Explain.

12-2 Parts of a Set

MAIN IDEA

I will identify, read, write, and model fractions for parts of a set.

Targeted TEKS 4.2 The student describes and compares fractional parts of whole objects **or sets of objects.**

GET READY to Learn

A set of toy cars has two red cars, one green car, and one blue car. What fraction of the cars is green?

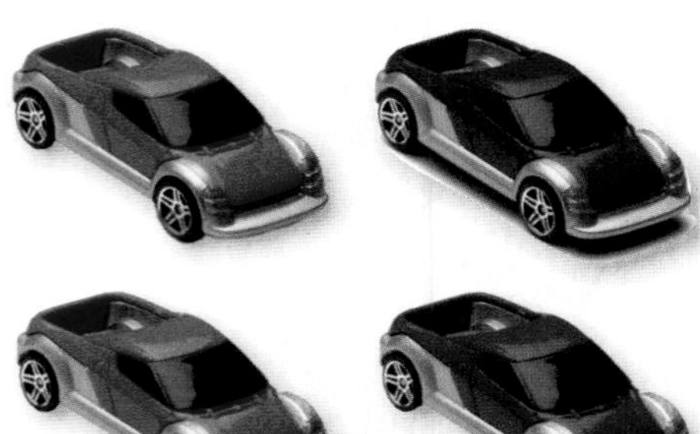

A set is a group of objects. In Lesson 12-1, you learned to use a fraction to name part of a whole. Fractions can also be used to name part of a set.

Real-World EXAMPLE

1 CARS What fraction of the set of cars is green?

Write green cars → $\frac{1}{4}$ ← numerator
total cars → ← denominator

Read *one-fourth* or *one divided by four*

So, $\frac{1}{4}$ of the set of cars is green.

EXAMPLE Write and Read Fractions

2 What fraction of the set of stars is *not* green?

Write stars *not* green → $\frac{2}{5}$
total stars →

Read *two-fifths* or *two divided by five*

So, $\frac{2}{5}$ of the set of stars are *not* green.

Online **Personal Tutor at** tx.gr4math.com

You have learned that fractions can be used to name part of a whole and part of a set. Another way of looking at fractions is as division of whole numbers by whole numbers.

Remember

Recall that a quotient is the answer to a division problem.

Real-World EXAMPLE Fraction as a Quotient

3 FOOD Tammy and three friends went to a pancake breakfast. They ordered and shared three pancakes equally. What part of the pancakes did each receive?

Draw a picture to show the division.

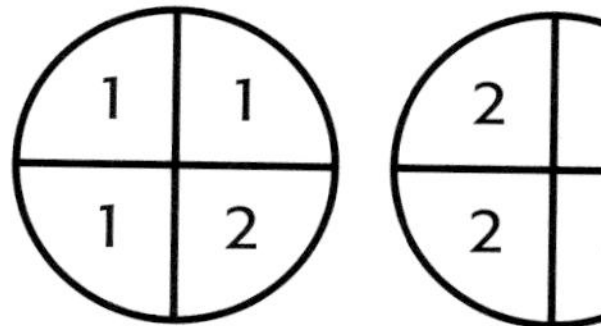

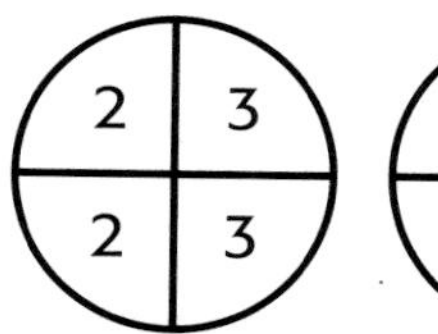

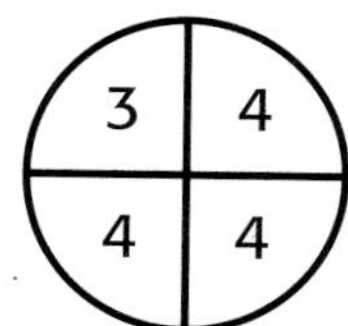

Three pancakes are divided among 4 people. So, each person receives 3 divided by 4 or $\frac{3}{4}$ of the pancakes.

CHECK What You Know

Write the fraction for the part of the set that is yellow. Then write the fraction for the part that is *not* yellow. See Examples 1 and 2 (p. 496)

1.  

2. 

Write the fraction that names the part of the set of vegetables.
See Examples 1 and 2 (p. 496)

3. *not* red peppers

4. *not* corn

5. *not* green peppers

6. Five chimpanzees are sharing four bananas equally. What part of the bananas does each receive?
See Example 3 (p. 497)

7. 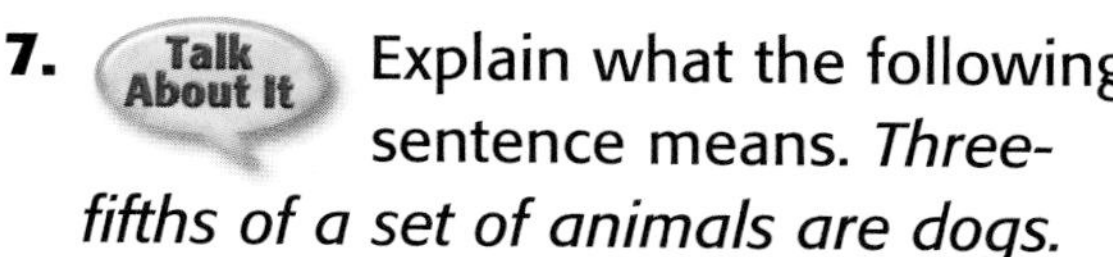
Talk About It Explain what the following sentence means. *Three-fifths of a set of animals are dogs.*

Practice and Problem Solving

See page R42.

Write the fraction for the part of the set that is blue. Then write the fraction for the part that is *not* blue. See Examples 1 and 2 (p. 496)

8.   

9. 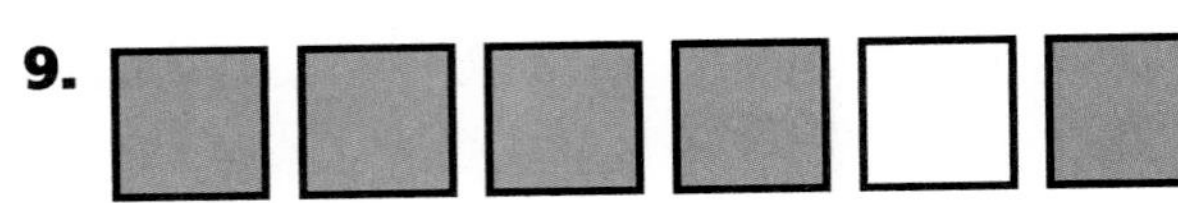

10. 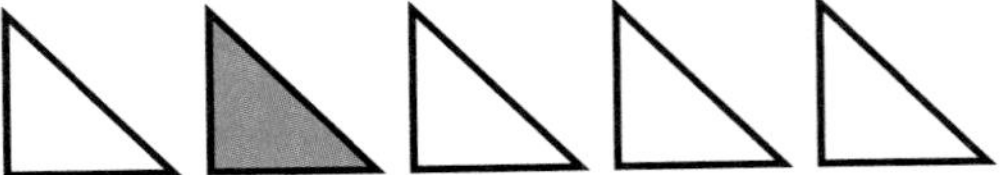

11. 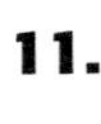 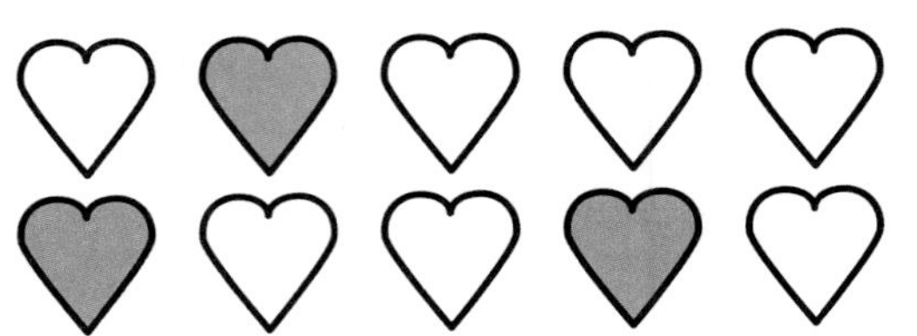

Write the fraction that names the part of the set of shapes. See Example 2 (p. 496)

12. *not* circles

13. *not* squares

14. *not* triangles

15. *not* red

16. *not* yellow

17. *not* blue

18. Eight people are sharing five apples equally. What part of an apple does each receive? See Example 3 (p. 497)

19. Twelve elephants are sharing nine bales of hay equally. What part of a bale of hay does each receive? See Example 3 (p. 497)

Real-World PROBLEM SOLVING

Data File The state mammal of Texas is the armadillo.

20. Suppose 10 armadillos are traveling together. If 4 of them are adult females and 3 are babies, what fraction are adult males?

21. Suppose 12 armadillos live in a burrow and 5 leave. What fractional part of the armadillos is left?

Armadillos

 Math Online **Self-Check Quiz at** tx.gr4math.com

H.O.T. Problems

22. **OPEN ENDED** Draw a set of objects that shows the fraction $\frac{3}{5}$.

23. **FIND THE ERROR** Three-eighths of a set of fruit are oranges. What part is *not* oranges? Who is correct, Sonja or Jairo?

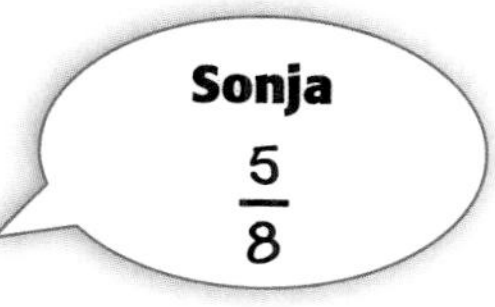

24. **WRITING IN MATH** Write a problem that involves identifying a fraction that describes part of a group.

TEST Practice

25. Which figure shows $\frac{2}{5}$? (Lesson 12-1)

A 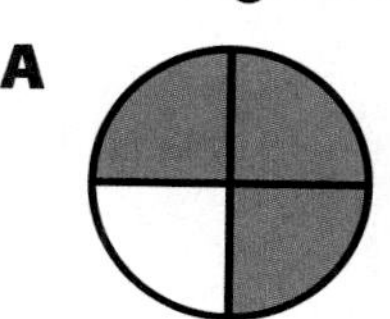

C 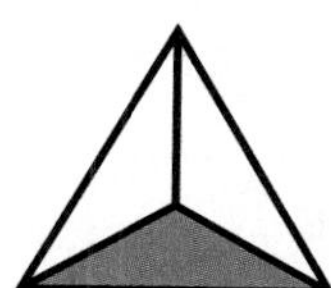

B 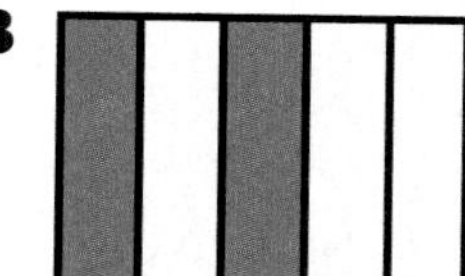

D 

26. Stephen walks his dog 4 days each week. His brother walks the dog the other days. What fraction names the part of a week Stephen's brother walks the dog? (Lesson 12-2)

F $\frac{3}{7}$

H $\frac{4}{7}$

G $\frac{1}{2}$

J $\frac{3}{4}$

Spiral Review

Draw a picture and shade part of it to show the fraction. (Lesson 12-1)

27. $\frac{2}{5}$

28. $\frac{1}{6}$

29. $\frac{4}{10}$

30. Estimate and measure the weight of two objects in your bookbag. (Lesson 11-4)

31. Maurice left for school at 8:30 A.M. He arrived at 9:05 A.M. How long did it take him to get to school? Use a clock if needed. (Lesson 11-10)

12-3 Problem-Solving Strategy

MAIN IDEA I will solve problems by drawing a picture.

Targeted TEKS 4.14 The student applies Grade 4 mathematics to solve problems connected to everyday experiences and activities in and outside of school. **(C) Select or develop an appropriate problem-solving plan or strategy,** including **drawing a picture, . . . to solve a problem.** *Also addresses TEKS 4.14(B).*

Brandi and her mom are at a pet store. The pet store has 15 reptiles. One-third of the reptiles are turtles. Two are snakes, and the rest are lizards. How many of each reptile are there?

Understand

What facts do you know?

- There are 15 reptiles at the store.
- One-third are turtles.
- Two are snakes.
- The rest are lizards.

What do you need to find?

- Find the number of each reptile.

Plan

Draw a picture to solve the problem.

Solve

- Draw 15 circles. Since the fraction $\frac{1}{3}$ is used, place the circles in 3 equal groups.

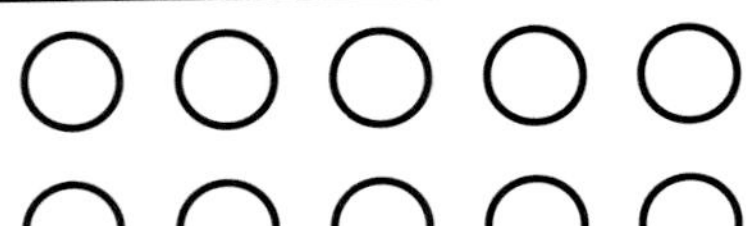

- To show the turtles, shade $\frac{1}{3}$ of the circles. That is, one of the three equal groups. So, there are 5 turtles. There are 2 snakes, so shade 2 circles to show the snakes.

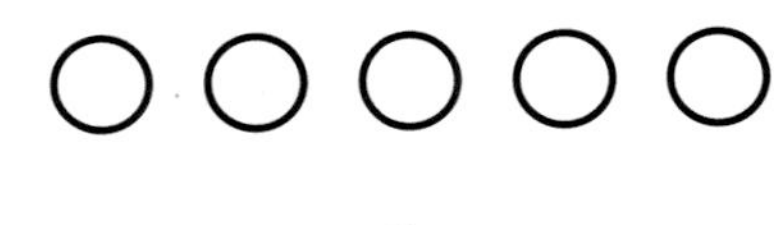

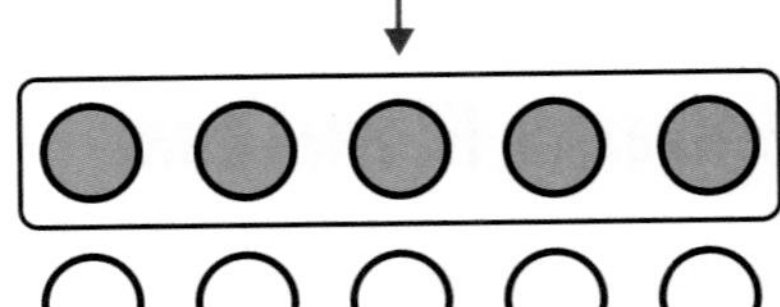

- There are 8 circles not shaded. This is the number of lizards.

So, there are 5 turtles, 2 snakes, and 8 lizards at the pet store.

Check

Look back at the problem. 5 turtles + 2 snakes + 8 lizards = 15 reptiles. The pet store has 15 reptiles. So, the answer is correct.

ANALYZE the Strategy

Refer to the problem on the previous page.

1. Explain why you used 15 circles.
2. You know that $\frac{1}{3}$ of the reptiles are turtles. Explain why 5 circles were shaded to show the number of turtles.
3. If the pet store had 24 reptiles, how many of the reptiles would be lizards?
4. Check your answer to Exercise 3. How do you know that it is correct?

PRACTICE the Strategy

EXTRA PRACTICE
See page R42.

Solve. Use the *draw a picture* strategy.

5. There are three trees in a backyard. The second tree is half as tall as the first. The third tree is taller than the second tree and shorter than the first tree. The total height of the trees is 24 feet. Find the height of each tree.

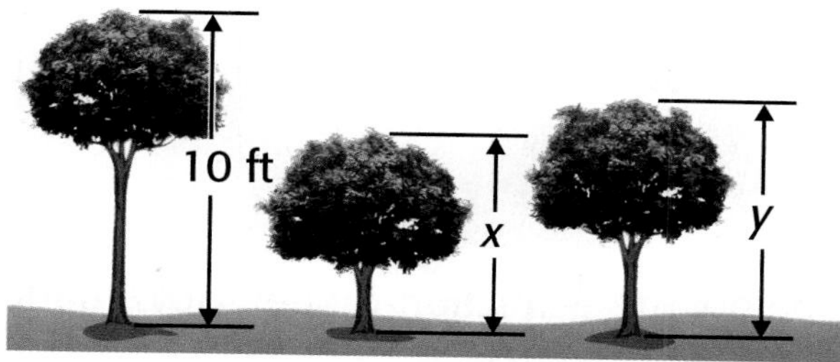

6. Pam and three other students are waiting in a line. Lakita is ahead of Pam. Sanjay is third in line. Rob is behind Sanjay. In what order are the students standing?

7. Emil bought his mom a dozen roses. Some of the roses are shown below. The rest are white. Which color were there the most of? How many roses were that color?

8. There are 22 students in Ms. Lane's class. Half of them packed their lunches. Eight students are buying pizza. The rest are buying salads. How many students are buying salads?

9. The table shows how long Adam and Kenya rode their bikes. Who biked longer? How much longer?

Biking Schedule	
Name	**Time Spent Biking**
Adam	$\frac{1}{3}$ of an hour
Kenya	15 minutes

10. There are 16 books on a shelf. One-fourth of the books are about animals. Two are adventure. The rest are mystery. How many are mystery books?

11. **WRITING IN MATH** Look back at Exercise 10. Explain how you used the *draw a picture* strategy to solve the problem.

Explore

Math Activity for 12-4

Equivalent Fractions

MAIN IDEA

I will identify equivalent fractions.

Targeted TEKS 4.2 The student describes and compares fractional parts of whole objects or sets of objects. (A) **Use concrete objects and pictorial models to generate equivalent fractions.**

You Will Need

fraction models

New Vocabulary

equivalent fractions

Animation
tx.gr4math.com

Fractions that represent the same amount are **equivalent fractions**.

ACTIVITY

1 Identify two fractions that are equivalent to $\frac{1}{3}$.

Step 1 **Model $\frac{1}{3}$.**

Start with 1 whole. Then, use the $\frac{1}{3}$ fraction model to show $\frac{1}{3}$.

1

$\frac{1}{3}$

Step 2 **Find a fraction equivalent to $\frac{1}{3}$.**

Using $\frac{1}{6}$ fraction models, place them below the $\frac{1}{3}$ fraction model. How many $\frac{1}{6}$ fraction models are used?

1

$\frac{1}{3}$

$\frac{1}{6}$ $\frac{1}{6}$

Step 3 **Find another fraction equivalent to $\frac{1}{3}$.**

Use $\frac{1}{12}$ fraction models to equal the length of the $\frac{1}{3}$ fraction model. Count the number of $\frac{1}{12}$ fraction models.

1

$\frac{1}{3}$

$\frac{1}{6}$ $\frac{1}{6}$

$\frac{1}{12}$ $\frac{1}{12}$ $\frac{1}{12}$ $\frac{1}{12}$

So, $\frac{1}{3}$, $\frac{2}{6}$, and $\frac{4}{12}$ are equivalent fractions.

Hands-On Activity

ACTIVITY

2 **Identify equivalent fractions.**

Step 1 Draw three identical number lines that show zero and one.

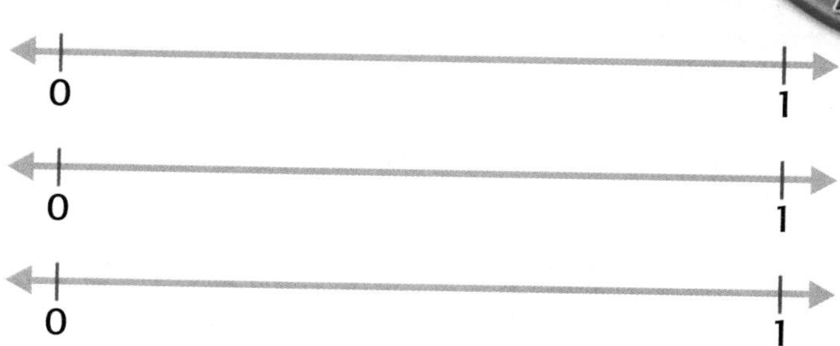

Step 2 Divide the first number line into fourths. Divide the second number line into eighths. Divide the third number line into sixteenths.

Notice that $\frac{1}{4} = \frac{2}{8} = \frac{4}{16}$.

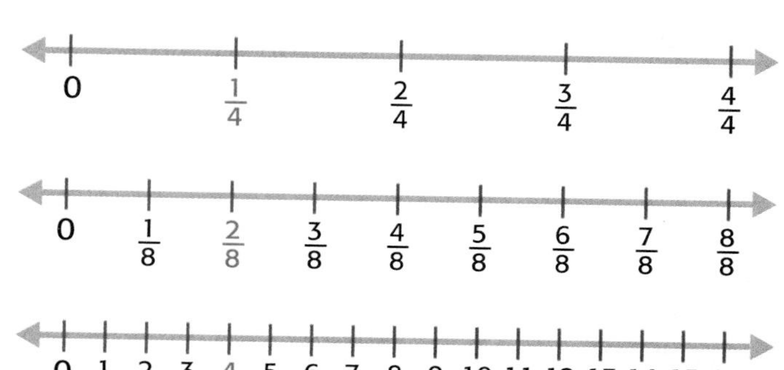

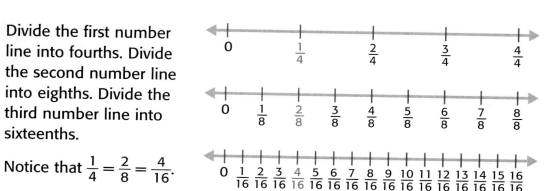

Think About It

1. **Algebra** Copy and complete $\frac{1}{3} = \frac{■}{9} = \frac{■}{15}$.
2. Refer to Activity 2. Find two fractions equivalent to $\frac{3}{4}$.

CHECK What You Know

Determine whether each pair of fractions is equivalent. Use fraction models or number lines.

3. $\frac{2}{4}$ and $\frac{6}{12}$
4. $\frac{6}{8}$ and $\frac{5}{10}$
5. $\frac{2}{3}$ and $\frac{3}{5}$
6. $\frac{9}{12}$ and $\frac{3}{4}$

Find two equivalent fractions for each fraction. Use fraction models or number lines.

7. $\frac{1}{5}$
8. $\frac{2}{6}$
9. $\frac{4}{8}$
10. $\frac{2}{12}$
11. **WRITING IN MATH** Explain what it means for two fractions to be equivalent.

12-4 Equivalent Fractions

GET READY to Learn

Megan has 8 fish in an aquarium. Four fish are green. So, Megan says that $\frac{4}{8}$ of the fish are green. Megan could use another fraction to represent $\frac{4}{8}$.

MAIN IDEA

I will find equivalent fractions.

 **Targeted TEKS 4.2** The student describes and compares fractional parts of whole objects or sets of objects. (A) **Use concrete objects and pictorial models to generate equivalent fractions.** *Also addresses TEKS 4.10.*

New Vocabulary

equivalent fractions

The fraction models below show that $\frac{4}{8}$ is the same as $\frac{1}{2}$. Fractions that represent the same amount are **equivalent fractions**.

1			
$\frac{1}{2}$			
$\frac{1}{8}$	$\frac{1}{8}$	$\frac{1}{8}$	$\frac{1}{8}$

Vocabulary Link

prefixes The prefix *equi-* means *equal*.

EXAMPLE Find Equivalent Fractions

1 **Find three fractions that are equivalent to $\frac{4}{8}$.**

To find equivalent fractions, you can use multiplication or division.

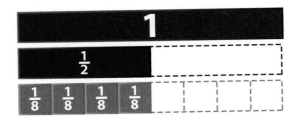

One Way: Multiply		Another Way: Divide	
$\frac{4 \times 2}{8 \times 2} = \frac{8}{16}$	Multiply the numerator and the denominator by the same number, 2.	$\frac{4 \div 2}{8 \div 2} = \frac{2}{4}$ $\frac{2 \div 2}{4 \div 2} = \frac{1}{2}$	Divide the numerator and the denominator by the same number, 2.

So, $\frac{8}{16}$, $\frac{2}{4}$, or $\frac{1}{2}$ are equivalent to $\frac{4}{8}$.

EXAMPLE Use Concrete Models

2 **Dale has $\frac{3}{4}$ of his book completed. Luanda has the same amount of her book completed. Use fraction models to find an equivalent fraction.**

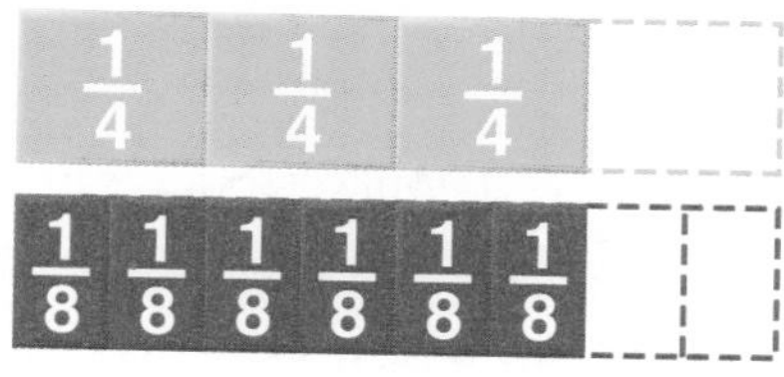

$$\frac{3}{4} = \frac{6}{8}$$

So, $\frac{6}{8}$ is an equivalent fraction to $\frac{3}{4}$.

EXAMPLE Draw a Picture to Model

3 **Find an equivalent fraction to $\frac{8}{24}$.**

Draw a model.

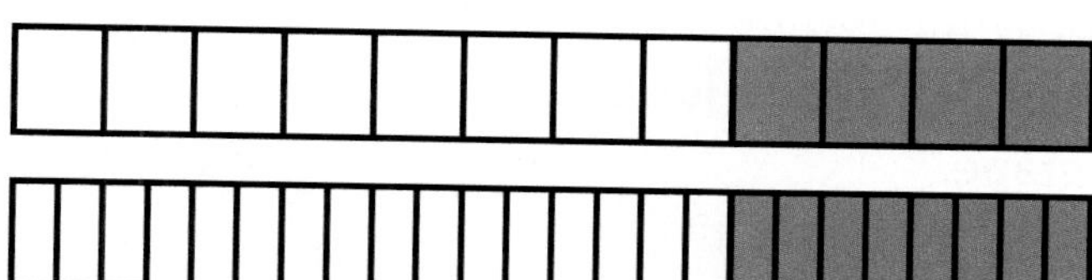

So, $\frac{4}{12}$ is an equivalent fraction.

Online Personal Tutor at tx.gr4math.com

EXAMPLE Fractions on a Number Line

4 **Write the letter on the number line that best represents $\frac{2}{8}$. Find an equivalent fraction.**

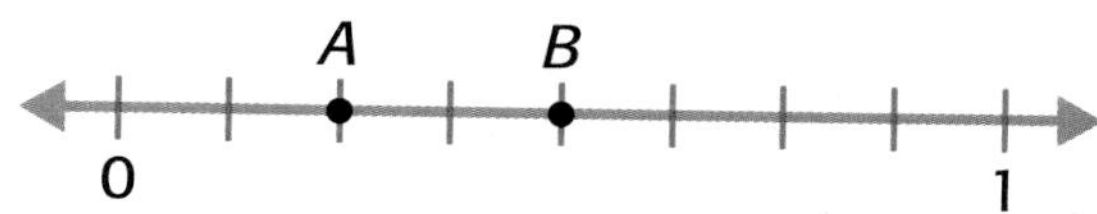

The number line is divided into eighths.

So, $A = \frac{2}{8}$. An equivalent fraction would be $\frac{1}{4}$.

CHECK What You Know

Write the fraction for the part that is shaded. Then find an equivalent fraction. See Example 1 (p. 504)

1. 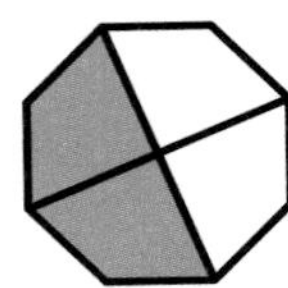

2. 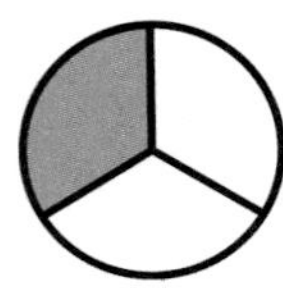

3. 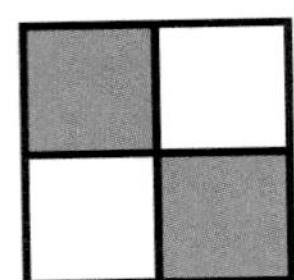

Use models to find an equivalent fraction for each fraction.
See Examples 2 and 3 (p. 505)

4. $\frac{1}{4}$ **5.** $\frac{4}{6}$ **6.** $\frac{1}{5}$ **7.** $\frac{8}{10}$ **8.** $\frac{1}{3}$

9. Write the letter on the number line below that best represents $\frac{6}{10}$. Then find an equivalent fraction. See Example 4 (p. 505)

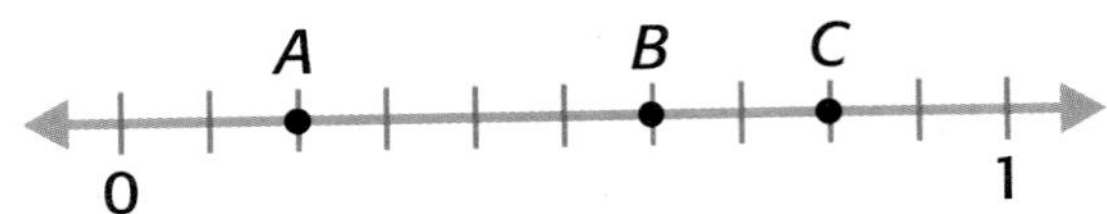

10. Javier has 4 juice boxes. Three are grape flavored. Write two fractions that describe the part of the juice boxes that is grape.

11. Talk About It Tell why $\frac{3}{4}$, $\frac{6}{8}$, and $\frac{9}{12}$ are equivalent fractions. Give an example of another set of three equivalent fractions.

Practice and Problem Solving

EXTRA PRACTICE See page R43.

Write the fraction for the part that is shaded. Then find an equivalent fraction. See Example 1 (p. 504)

12. 

13. 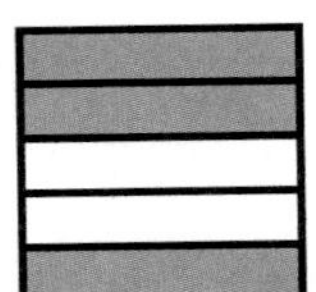

14. 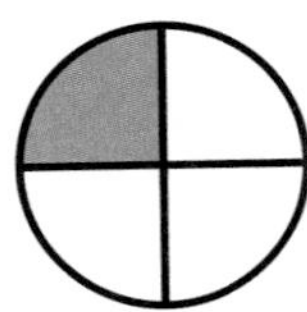

15. 

16. 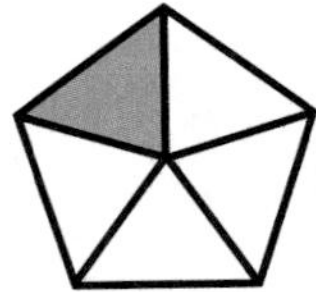

17. 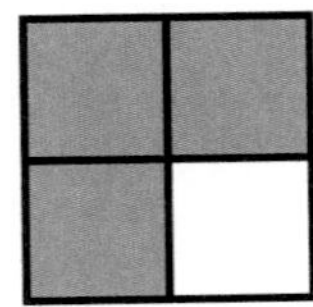

Use models to find an equivalent fraction for each fraction.
See Examples 2 and 3 (p. 505)

18. $\frac{2}{7}$ **19.** $\frac{2}{5}$ **20.** $\frac{6}{10}$ **21.** $\frac{2}{12}$ **22.** $\frac{2}{3}$

Write the letter on the number line. Then find an equivalent fraction that best represents the given fraction. See Example 4 (p. 505)

23. 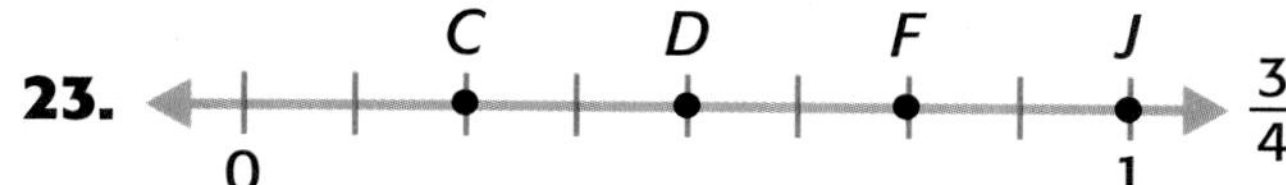

$\frac{3}{4}$

24. 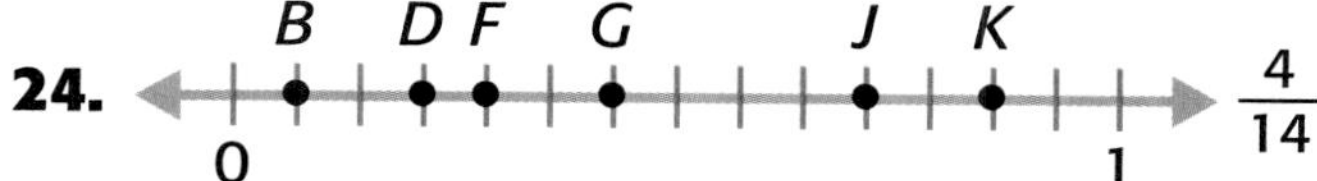

$\frac{4}{14}$

25. A roller coaster has 16 cars. Six of the cars are green. Write two fractions for the part of the cars that is green.

26. **Measurement** Lucas ran $\frac{1}{2}$ mile. Candace ran $\frac{4}{6}$ mile. Did they run the same distance? Explain.

Real-World PROBLEM SOLVING

Science Giraffes grow to a height of about 20 feet. Their neck is about $\frac{2}{5}$ their total height. Giraffes spend about $\frac{5}{6}$ of a day eating.

27. What fraction of a day does a giraffe spend eating? Write another fraction that represents this amount.

28. What fraction of the total height is the length of a giraffe's neck? Write a fraction equivalent to this fraction.

H.O.T. Problems

29. **OPEN ENDED** Write a fraction equivalent to $\frac{2}{5}$. Write a fraction equivalent to $\frac{3}{6}$. Which fraction represents a greater amount? Explain.

30. **FIND THE ERROR** Rachel and Miguel are finding a fraction equivalent to $\frac{6}{18}$. Who is correct? Explain.

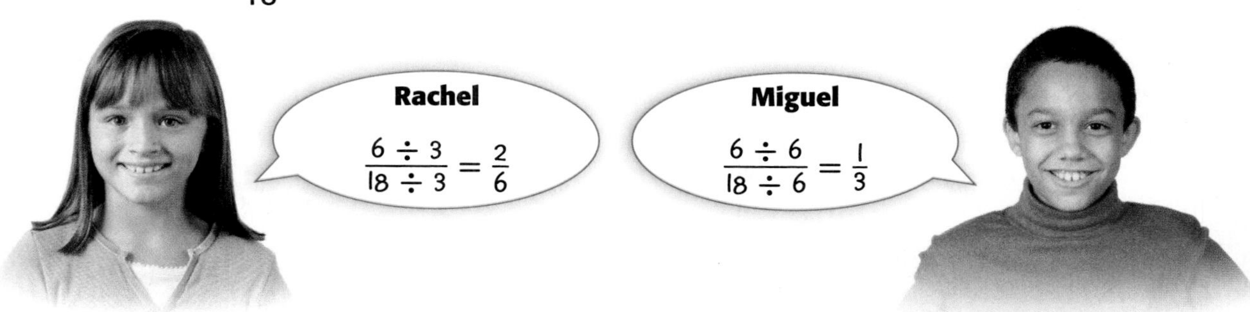

Rachel
$\frac{6 \div 3}{18 \div 3} = \frac{2}{6}$
Miguel
$\frac{6 \div 6}{18 \div 6} = \frac{1}{3}$

31. **WRITING IN MATH** Can you always find an equivalent fraction for a fraction? Explain.

Fractions Made Equal

Make Equivalent Fractions

Get Ready!

Players: 2

You will need: 10 index cards

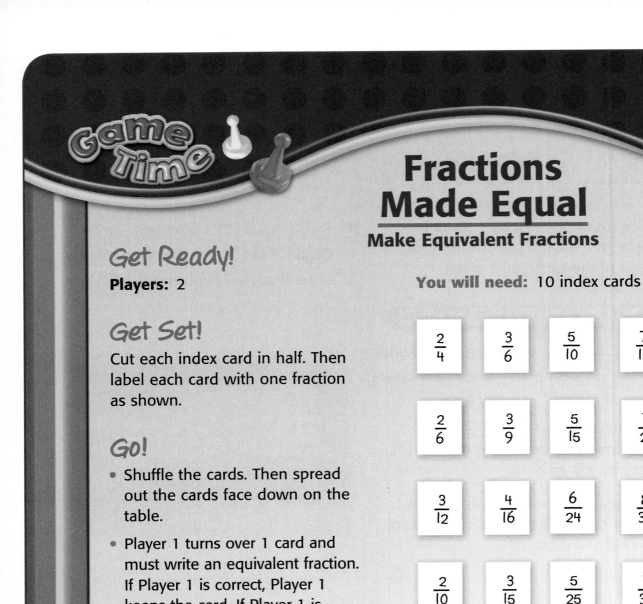

Get Set!

Cut each index card in half. Then label each card with one fraction as shown.

$\frac{2}{4}$	$\frac{3}{6}$	$\frac{5}{10}$	$\frac{7}{14}$
$\frac{2}{6}$	$\frac{3}{9}$	$\frac{5}{15}$	$\frac{7}{21}$
$\frac{3}{12}$	$\frac{4}{16}$	$\frac{6}{24}$	$\frac{8}{32}$
$\frac{2}{10}$	$\frac{3}{15}$	$\frac{5}{25}$	$\frac{7}{35}$
$\frac{2}{12}$	$\frac{3}{18}$	$\frac{5}{30}$	$\frac{6}{36}$

Go!

- Shuffle the cards. Then spread out the cards face down on the table.
- Player 1 turns over 1 card and must write an equivalent fraction. If Player 1 is correct, Player 1 keeps the card. If Player 1 is incorrect, the card is put back.
- Player 2 takes a turn.
- Play continues in the same way. The player with the most cards wins.

CHAPTER 12 Mid-Chapter Check

Lessons 12-1 through 12-4

Write the fraction that names the shaded part of the whole. (Lesson 12-1)

1. 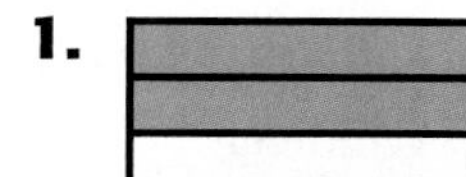

2. 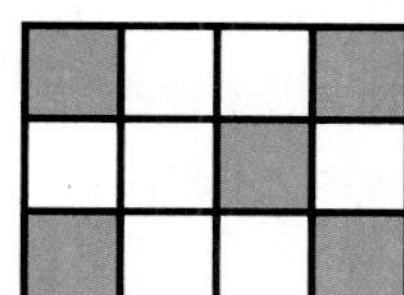

Draw a picture and shade part of it to show the fraction. (Lesson 12-1)

3. $\frac{1}{8}$

4. $\frac{3}{7}$

5. The flag of Italy is shown. What fraction of the flag is green? (Lesson 12-1)

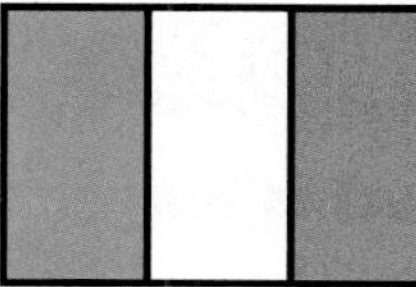

6. **TEST PRACTICE** What fraction of the hearts is shaded? (Lesson 12-2)

A $\frac{4}{10}$

B $\frac{1}{2}$

C $\frac{5}{9}$

D $\frac{6}{10}$

7. Draw a picture that represents the statement below. (Lesson 12-2)

Three of the five leaves are shaded.

8. There are 3 red apples, 6 green apples, and 1 yellow apple on a table. Of the apples, what fraction is green? (Lesson 12-2)

Write the fraction that names the part of the set of smile faces. (Lesson 12-2)

9. red

10. green

11. Janey is planting 12 trees in her yard. There are 5 maple trees and the rest are oak. What fraction of the trees is oak? (Lesson 12-3)

12. Galeno spent $\frac{1}{2}$ of his money on a movie ticket and $\frac{1}{4}$ of his money on a snack. He had $8 before the movie. How much money does he have now? (Lesson 12-3)

Find an equivalent fraction for each fraction. (Lesson 12-4)

13. $\frac{1}{3}$

14. $\frac{4}{5}$

15. $\frac{1}{2}$

16. $\frac{4}{5}$

17. Yang's mom used 12 of the 20 stamps she had bought. Yang said that she used $\frac{3}{5}$ of the stamps. Is Yang correct? Explain. (Lesson 12-4)

18. **WRITING IN MATH** Is $\frac{1}{4}$ of the rectangle green? Explain why or why not. (Lesson 12-1)

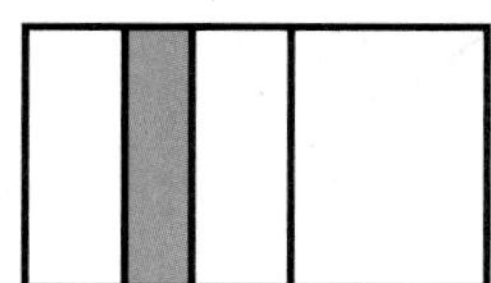

12-5 Compare and Order Fractions

GET READY to Learn

Ramon has an insect collection. The table shows the lengths of four insects in his collection. Which is longer, a field cricket or a whirligig beetle?

Insect	Length (in.)
Mosquito	$\frac{1}{4}$
Field cricket	$\frac{5}{8}$
Whirligig beetle	$\frac{3}{8}$
Lightning bug	$\frac{1}{2}$

MAIN IDEA

I will compare and order simple fractions.

Targeted TEKS 4.2 The student describes and compares fractional parts of whole objects or sets of objects.
(C) **Compare and order fractions using concrete objects and pictorial models.** *Also addresses TEKS 4.10.*

To compare fractions, you can use models, number lines, and equivalent fractions.

Real-World EXAMPLES Compare Fractions

1 SCIENCE **Which insect is longer, a field cricket or a whirligig beetle?**

You can use fraction models to compare $\frac{5}{8}$ and $\frac{3}{8}$.

$\frac{1}{8}$	$\frac{1}{8}$	$\frac{1}{8}$	$\frac{1}{8}$	$\frac{1}{8}$				$\frac{5}{8}$ Field cricket
$\frac{1}{8}$	$\frac{1}{8}$	$\frac{1}{8}$						$\frac{3}{8}$ Whirligig beetle

The models show that $\frac{5}{8} > \frac{3}{8}$.

So, the field cricket is longer than the whirligig beetle.

2 SCIENCE **Which is longer, a mosquito or lightning bug?**

You need to compare $\frac{1}{4}$ and $\frac{1}{2}$.

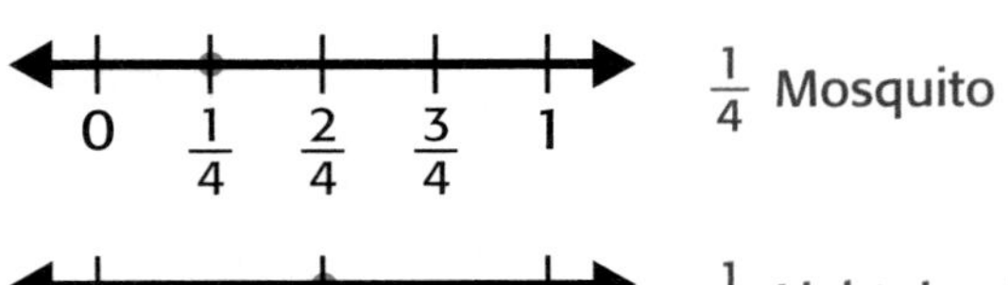

$\frac{1}{4}$ Mosquito

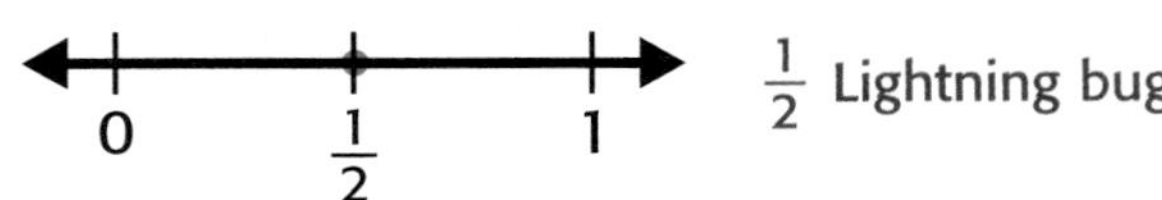

$\frac{1}{2}$ Lightning bug

So, the lightning bug is longer than the mosquito.

EXAMPLE Order Fractions

3 **Order $\frac{2}{3}$, $\frac{1}{2}$, and $\frac{7}{12}$ from least to greatest.**

One Way: Number Lines

Use a number line.

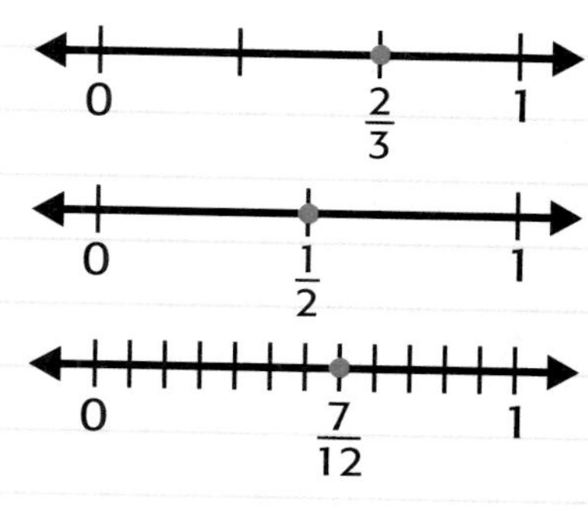

$\frac{1}{2} < \frac{7}{12} < \frac{2}{3}$

Another Way: Equivalent Fractions

Find equivalent fractions with the same denominator.

$\frac{2 \times 4}{3 \times 4} = \frac{8}{12}$ $\frac{1 \times 6}{2 \times 6} = \frac{6}{12}$

Compare the numerators. Order from least to greatest.

$\frac{6}{12}, \frac{7}{12}, \frac{8}{12}$

↓ ↓ ↓

$\frac{1}{2}, \frac{7}{12}, \frac{2}{3}$

So, the order from least to greatest is $\frac{1}{2}, \frac{7}{12}, \frac{2}{3}$.

Online Personal Tutor at tx.gr4math.com

CHECK What You Know

Use models to compare. Write <, >, or =. See Examples 1 and 2 (p. 510)

1.

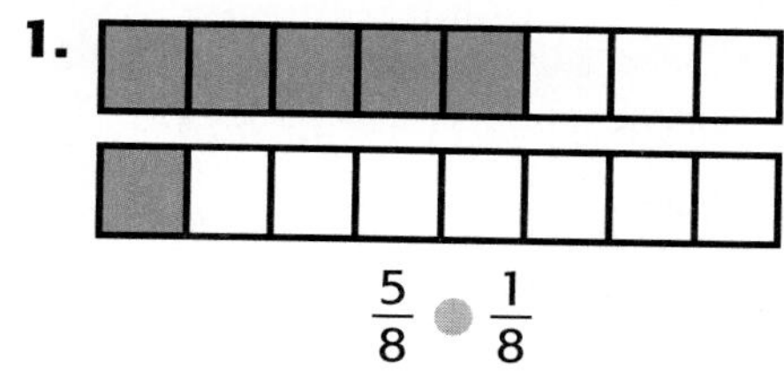

$\frac{5}{8}$ ● $\frac{1}{8}$

2.

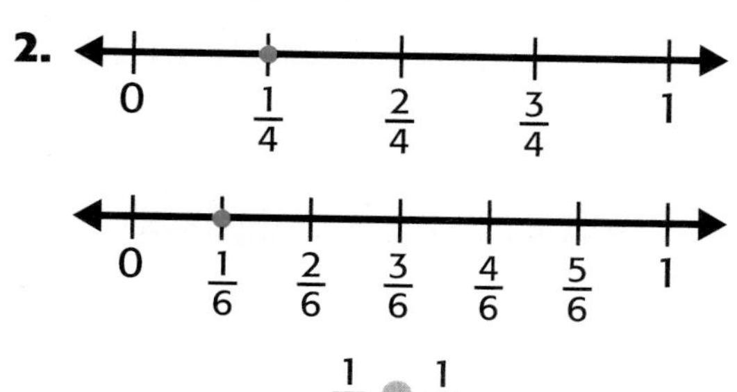

$\frac{1}{4}$ ● $\frac{1}{6}$

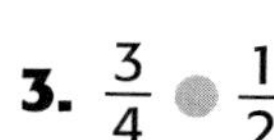

3. $\frac{3}{4}$ ● $\frac{1}{2}$

4. $\frac{3}{6}$ ● $\frac{3}{4}$

Use models to order from least to greatest. See Example 3 (p. 511)

5. $\frac{3}{8}, \frac{2}{6}, \frac{4}{8}$

6. $\frac{1}{16}, \frac{7}{8}, \frac{3}{4}$

7. Griff worked for $\frac{1}{3}$ of an hour. Sasha worked for $\frac{3}{12}$ of an hour. Who worked longer?

8. Talk About It Explain how to compare the fractions $\frac{7}{12}$ and $\frac{2}{6}$.

Practice and Problem Solving

EXTRA PRACTICE
See page R43.

Use models to compare. Write <, >, or =. See Examples 1 and 2 (p. 510)

9.

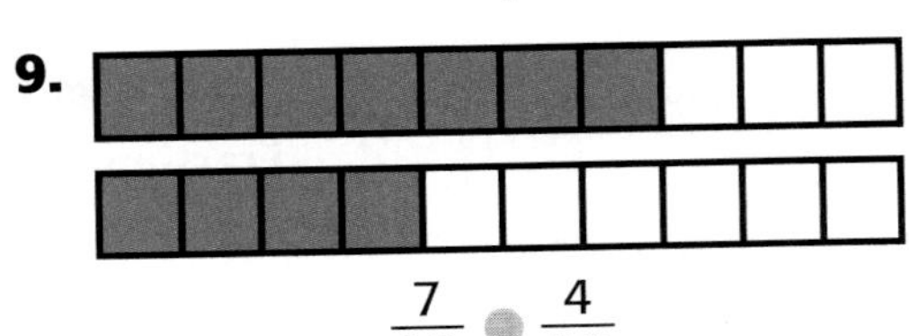

$\frac{7}{10}$ ● $\frac{4}{10}$

10.

$\frac{4}{8}$ ● $\frac{1}{4}$

11.

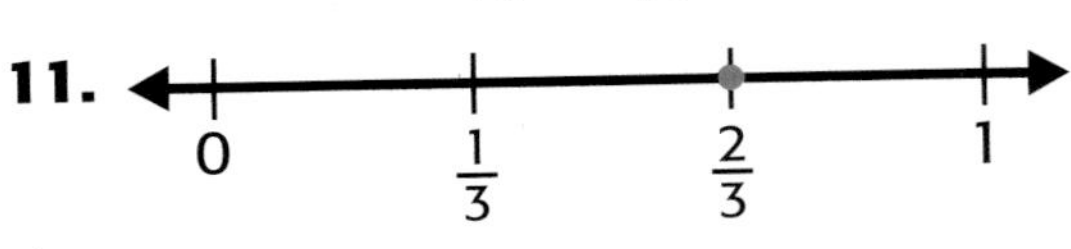

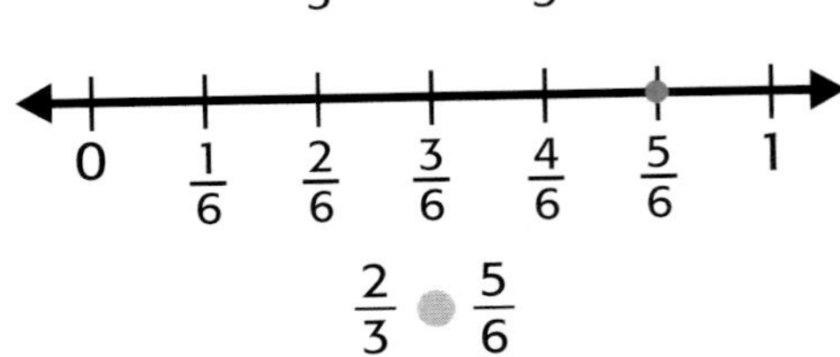

$\frac{2}{3}$ ● $\frac{5}{6}$

12.

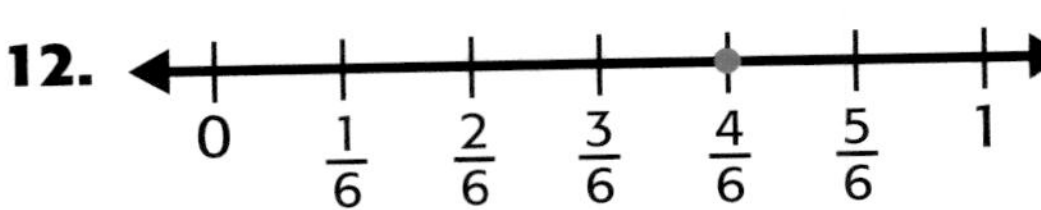

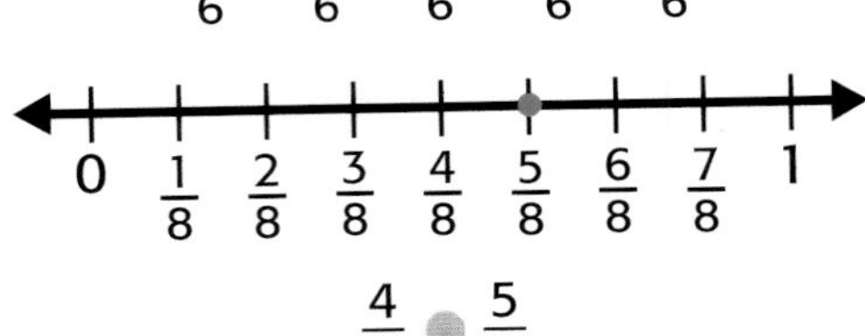

$\frac{4}{6}$ ● $\frac{5}{8}$

13. $\frac{2}{6}$ ● $\frac{1}{3}$

14. $\frac{3}{5}$ ● $\frac{5}{6}$

15. $\frac{4}{5}$ ● $\frac{8}{10}$

16. $\frac{2}{3}$ ● $\frac{5}{9}$

17. $\frac{4}{10}$ ● $\frac{1}{2}$

18. $\frac{5}{8}$ ● $\frac{2}{3}$

Use models to order from least to greatest. See Example 3 (p. 511)

19. $\frac{4}{6}, \frac{1}{3}, \frac{3}{3}$

20. $\frac{3}{4}, \frac{2}{3}, \frac{7}{8}$

21. $\frac{3}{10}, \frac{3}{4}, \frac{3}{5}$

22. Which meat makes up most of Mr. Collin's sandwich?

23. Statistics Allison took a survey. Find the favorite weekend activity.

Favorite Weekend Activities

Activity	Fraction of Friends
Movie	$\frac{2}{6}$
Mall	$\frac{1}{4}$
Basketball	$\frac{5}{12}$

ADMIT ONE ADMIT ONE

24. Vani ate $\frac{1}{4}$ of the carrots in the bag. Enrique ate $\frac{3}{12}$ of the carrots in the bag. Who ate more carrots?

25. Measurement Suzanne practiced volleyball for $\frac{2}{3}$ hour on Saturday. She practiced for $\frac{1}{6}$ hour on Sunday. Which day did she practice longer?

26. The table shows how much time each student needs to finish an art project. Does Simón need more or less time than Phil? Explain.

Student	Time
Simón	$\frac{4}{12}$ hour
Phil	$\frac{3}{4}$ hour

H.O.T. Problems

27. OPEN ENDED Write three fractions that are *not* greater than $\frac{1}{2}$.

28. WHICH ONE DOESN'T BELONG? Identify the set of fractions that does not belong with the other three sets. Explain.

$\frac{1}{4}, \frac{5}{8}, \frac{15}{16}$ | $\frac{2}{9}, \frac{1}{3}, \frac{1}{2}$ | $\frac{2}{5}, \frac{1}{2}, \frac{7}{10}$ | $\frac{3}{4}, \frac{1}{2}, \frac{2}{12}$

29. CHALLENGE Identify a fraction that is greater than $\frac{150}{300}$.

30. WRITING IN MATH Explain how to decide if $\frac{3}{4}$ is greater than or less than $\frac{3}{5}$.

TEST Practice

31. What fraction is best represented by point *M* on the number line? (Lesson 12-5)

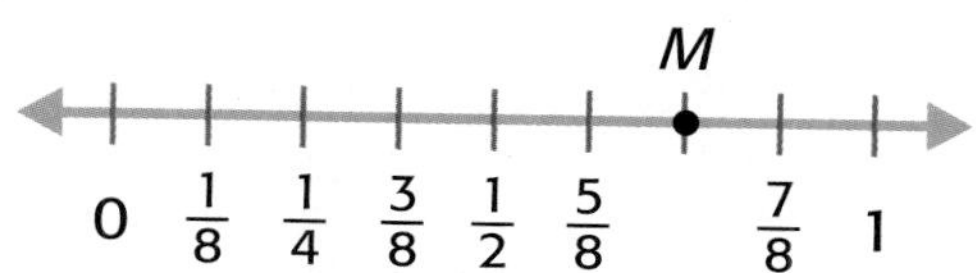

A $\frac{1}{4}$

B $\frac{3}{8}$

C $\frac{1}{2}$

D $\frac{3}{4}$

32. Which set of fractions is ordered from greatest to least? (Lesson 12-7)

F $\frac{3}{5}, \frac{6}{15}, \frac{2}{10}$

G $\frac{2}{10}, \frac{3}{5}, \frac{6}{15}$

H $\frac{2}{10}, \frac{6}{15}, \frac{3}{5}$

J $\frac{6}{15}, \frac{3}{5}, \frac{2}{10}$

Spiral Review

33. Toya has 8 coins in her piggy bank. One-fourth of the coins are quarters. Three of the coins are dimes. The rest of the coins are pennies. How many pennies does Toya have? (Lesson 12-3)

Choose the appropriate measurement tool. Then find the perimeter of the item. (Lesson 12-3)

34. shelf

35. triangle pattern block

36. math book cover

Find each product. (Lesson 6-4)

37. 37×4

38. 51×7

39. 85×9

No BONES about it . . .

Every human has a skeleton made up of bones. Your skeletal system is very important. Not only does it protect your internal organs, but it also allows you to stand up and walk. Without a skeleton you would be nothing but skin and guts!

Humans are born with 350 bones in their body. But, by the time you are 25, you will have only about 200 bones. This is because some of the bones join together to make a single bone.

The smallest bone is in the ear. It can be as small as $\frac{1}{10}$ of an inch. The largest bone, the femur, is located in the thigh. It is about $\frac{1}{4}$ of your height.

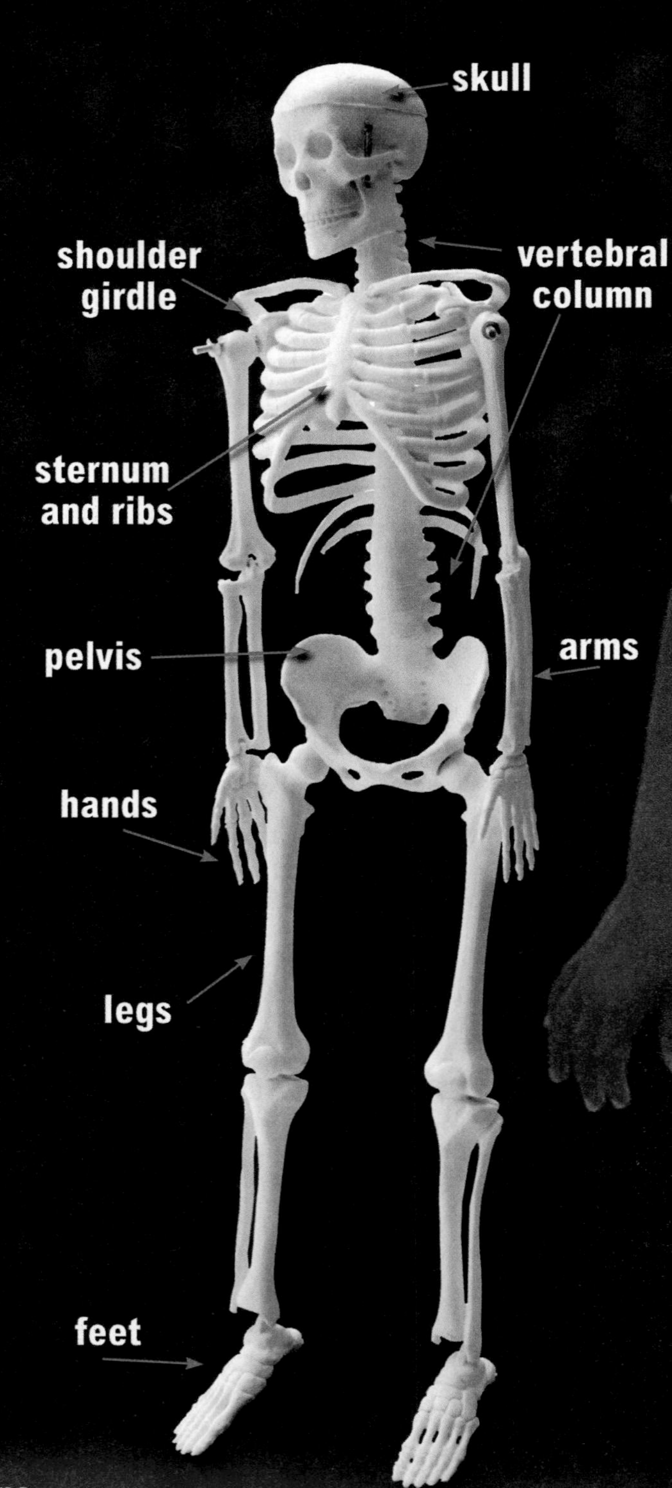

Did You Know?

Of the bones in your skeleton, about $\frac{3}{20}$ are found in your spine.

Targeted TEKS 4.14 The student applies Grade 4 mathematics to solve problems connected to everyday experiences and activities in and outside of school. **(A) Identify the mathematics in everyday situations.**

Adult Human Skeleton

Body Part	Approximate Number of Bones
Skull	20
Middle ears	6
Throat	1
Shoulder girdle	4
Sternum and ribs	25
Vertebral column	25
Arms	6
Hands	50
Pelvis	4
Legs	8
Feet	50

Source: www.answers.com

Problem Solving

Use the information on pages 514 and 515 to solve each problem.

1. What fraction of the bones in an adult human is located in the skull? Write in simplest form.
2. Which two body parts contain $\frac{1}{2}$ of the bones in an adult human? Explain your reasoning.
3. Which body part contains $\frac{1}{25}$ of the bones in an adult human?
4. What fraction of the bones at birth does a human have when an adult?
5. Are more bones located in the skull or in the spine?
6. The backbone is approximately 28 inches. What fraction of a foot is 28 inches? Write as a mixed number.
7. Use your height to find the length of your femur in inches.

12-6 Mixed Numbers

GET READY to Learn

Nyoko is selling pies at a bake sale. Each pie has 5 slices. Each slice of pie is sold separately. There are 7 slices left. What fraction of the pies are left?

MAIN IDEA

I will write mixed numbers and improper fractions.

Targeted TEKS 4.2 The student describes and compares fractional parts of whole objects or sets of objects. (B) **Model fraction quantities greater than one using concrete objects and pictorial models.** *Also addresses TEKS 4.10.*

New Vocabulary

mixed number

improper fraction

A **mixed number** has a whole number part and a fraction part. An **improper fraction** has a numerator that is greater than or equal to its denominator.

Mixed Numbers			Improper Fractions		
$1\frac{1}{2}$	$2\frac{3}{4}$	$3\frac{5}{6}$	$\frac{3}{2}$	$\frac{11}{4}$	$\frac{23}{6}$

Real-World EXAMPLE

1 FOOD What fraction of a pie does Nyoko have left?

Each pie has 5 slices. There are 7 slices left.

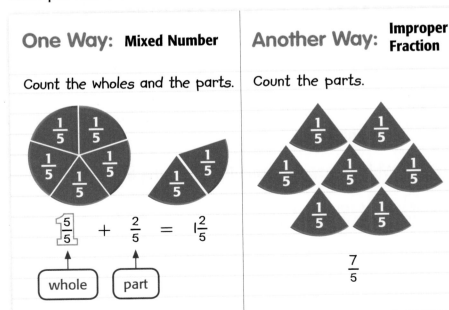

One Way: Mixed Number

Count the wholes and the parts.

$\frac{1}{5}$ $\frac{1}{5}$ $\frac{1}{5}$ $\frac{1}{5}$ $\frac{1}{5}$ $\frac{1}{5}$ $\frac{1}{5}$

$\frac{5}{5} + \frac{2}{5} = 1\frac{2}{5}$

whole part

Another Way: Improper Fraction

Count the parts.

$\frac{1}{5}$ $\frac{1}{5}$ $\frac{1}{5}$ $\frac{1}{5}$ $\frac{1}{5}$ $\frac{1}{5}$ $\frac{1}{5}$

$\frac{7}{5}$

So, $1\frac{2}{5}$ or $\frac{7}{5}$ of a pie is left.

You can change from a mixed number to an improper fraction. You can also change from an improper fraction to a mixed number.

EXAMPLES Mixed Number to Improper Fraction

2 Write $1\frac{3}{8}$ as an improper fraction.

$1\frac{3}{8} = 1 + \frac{3}{8}$ Write the mixed number as the sum of a whole and part.

$= \frac{8}{8} + \frac{3}{8}$ Write the whole number as a fraction.

$= \frac{8 + 3}{8}$ Add.

$= \frac{11}{8}$

Remember

The fraction bar stands for *divided by*. So, $\frac{11}{8}$ means *11 divided by 8*.

3 Write $\frac{11}{8}$ as a mixed number.

Divide the numerator by the denominator.

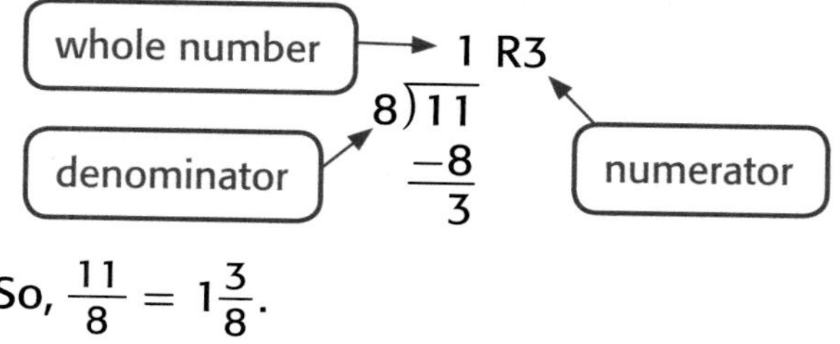

So, $\frac{11}{8} = 1\frac{3}{8}$.

Online Personal Tutor at tx.gr4math.com

You can show improper fractions and mixed numbers on a number line.

EXAMPLE Use a Number Line

4 Identify point *A* as a mixed number and improper fraction.

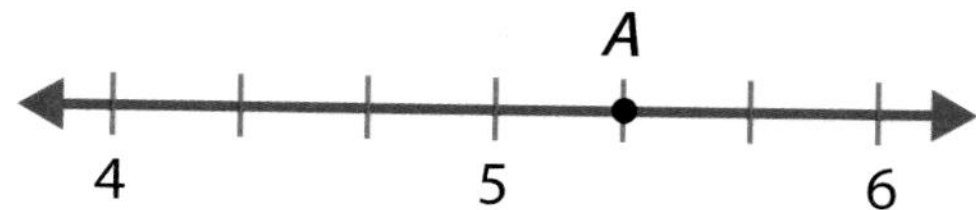

Each interval on the number line is one-third. So, point *A* is $5\frac{1}{3}$.

A
4 5 $5\frac{1}{3}$ 6

$5\frac{1}{3} = \frac{3}{3} + \frac{3}{3} + \frac{3}{3} + \frac{3}{3} + \frac{3}{3} + \frac{1}{3}$

$= \frac{3 + 3 + 3 + 3 + 3 + 1}{3} = \frac{16}{3}$

So, Point *A* is $5\frac{1}{3}$ or $\frac{16}{3}$.

CHECK What You Know

Write a mixed number and an improper fraction for each model.
See Example 1 (p. 516)

1. 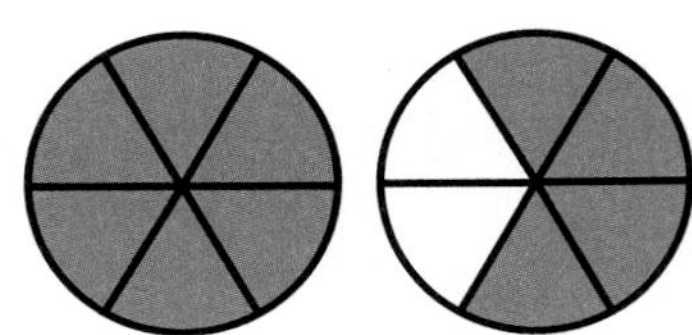

2. 

3. 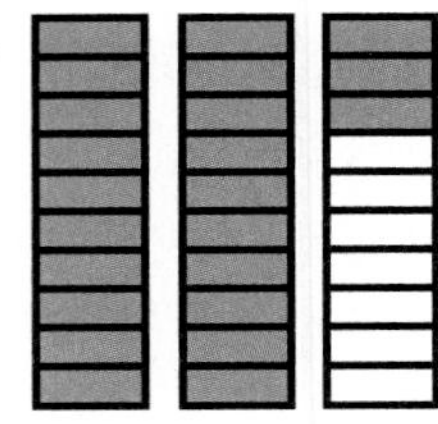

Write each as an improper fraction or a mixed number. Use models if needed. See Examples 2 and 3 (p. 517)

4. $1\frac{2}{5}$

5. $2\frac{3}{4}$

6. $\frac{9}{4}$

7. $\frac{13}{3}$

Identify each point. Write as a mixed number and an improper fraction. See Example 4 (p. 517)

8. 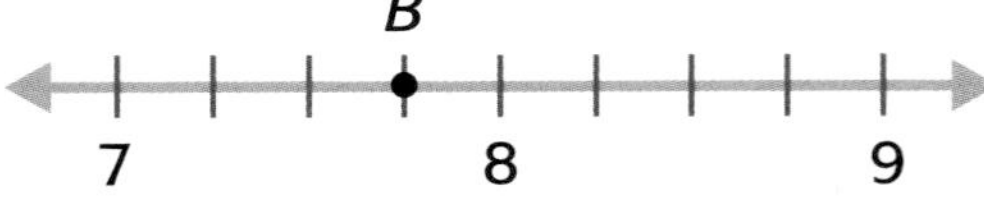

9. 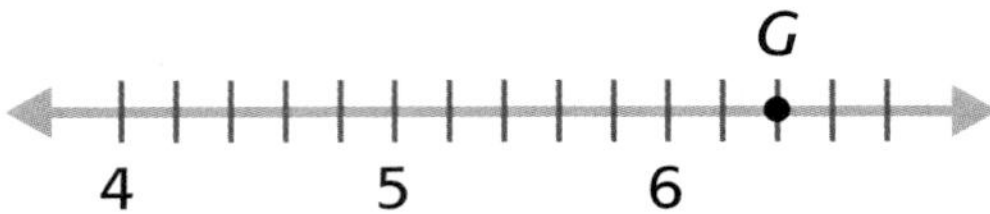

10. Andrew has $1\frac{3}{8}$ orange slices and Sheri has $1\frac{4}{16}$ orange slices. Who has more orange slices?

11. 

Explain how to compare $2\frac{3}{5}$ and $\frac{17}{5}$.

Practice and Problem Solving

EXTRA PRACTICE
See page R44.

Write a mixed number and an improper fraction for each model.
See Example 1 (p. 516)

12. 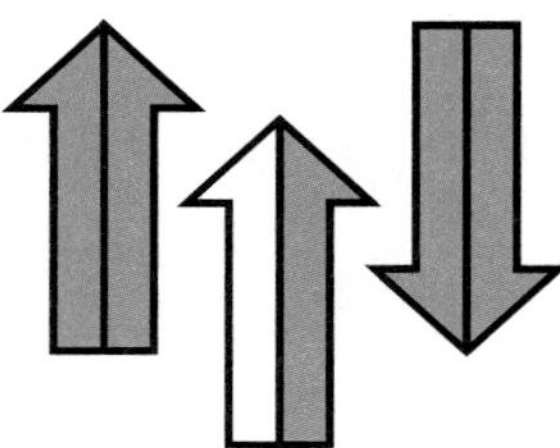

13. 

14. 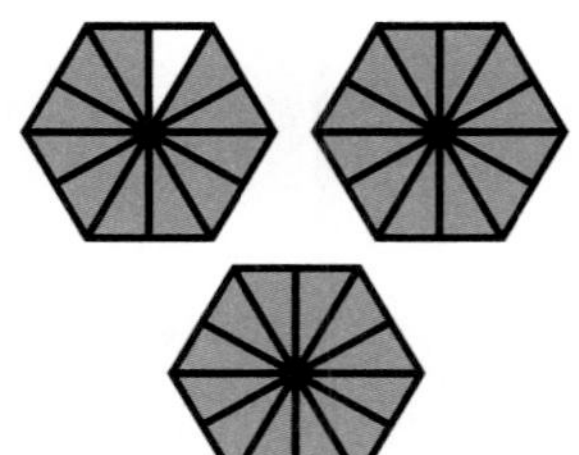

Write each as a improper fraction or a mixed number. Use models if needed. See Example 2 (p. 517)

15. $1\frac{3}{4}$

16. $2\frac{7}{10}$

17. $6\frac{7}{8}$

18. $8\frac{5}{8}$

19. $\frac{7}{3}$

20. $\frac{17}{5}$

21. $\frac{45}{8}$

22. $\frac{50}{6}$

Identify each point. Write as a mixed number and an improper fraction. See Example 4 (p. 539)

23. 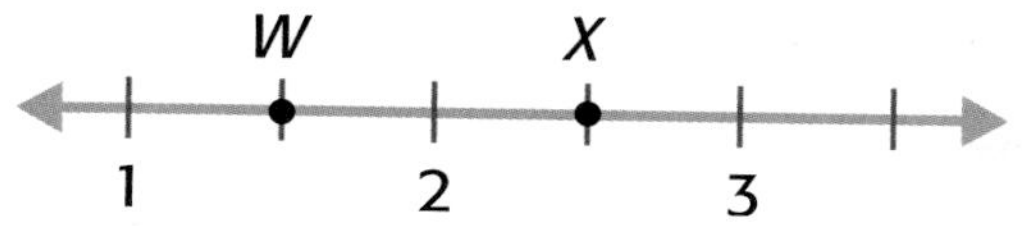

24. 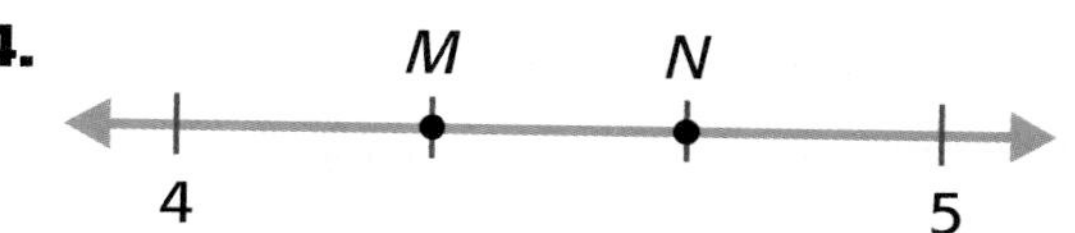

25. Ray needs $1\frac{1}{2}$ cups of flour for pancakes and $1\frac{3}{4}$ cups of sugar for banana bread. Does Ray need more sugar or more flour?

26. Elio drank $2\frac{3}{5}$ cups of water after the first half of the soccer match and $2\frac{4}{6}$ cups of water after the second half. When did he drink more water?

Real-World PROBLEM SOLVING

Travel A diagram of a horseback riding tour is shown. There are resting stops along the trail.

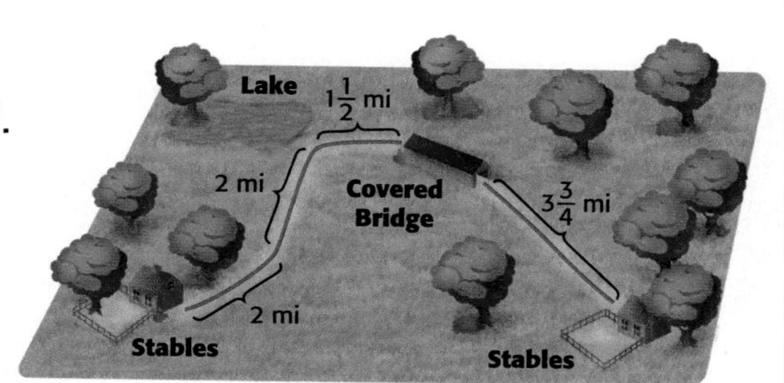

27. Joaquin and his family started at the stables on the left. They are at the covered bridge. How many miles of the trail have they traveled?

28. Joaquin reached the end of the trail in 2 hours and 15 minutes. Write the amount of time he spent on the trail as an improper fraction in simplest form.

H.O.T. Problems

29. OPEN ENDED Name an improper fraction that can be written as a whole number.

30. FIND THE ERROR Heather and Wesley are writing $4\frac{3}{5}$ as an improper fraction. Who is correct? Explain.

Heather

$4\frac{3}{5} = \frac{23}{5}$

Wesley

$4\frac{3}{5} = \frac{20}{5}$

31. WRITING IN MATH Compare fraction, mixed number, and improper fraction.

12-7 Problem-Solving Investigation

MAIN IDEA I will choose the best strategy to solve a problem.

Targeted TEKS 4.14 The student applies Grade 4 mathematics to solve problems connected to everyday experiences and activities in and outside of school. **(B) Solve problems that incorporate understanding the problem, making a plan, carrying out the plan, and evaluating the solution for reasonableness.** *Also addresses TEKS 4.14(C).*

P.S.I. TEAM +

ANICA: **My class visited the zoo. I learned that one-sixth of the animals at the zoo are reptiles. There are 420 animals at the zoo. How many animals are reptiles?**

YOUR MISSION: **Find how many animals are reptiles.**

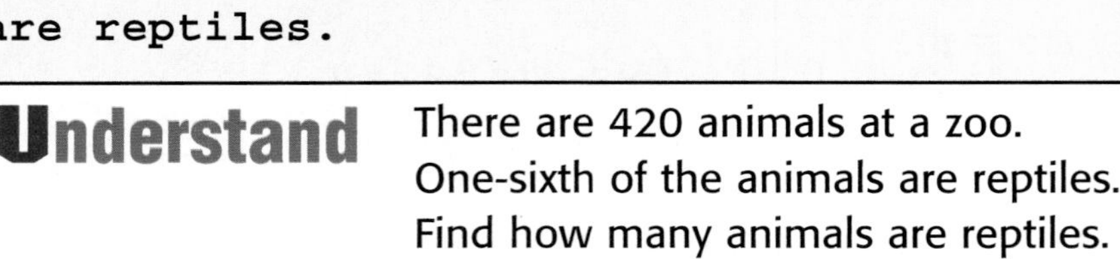

Understand

There are 420 animals at a zoo.
One-sixth of the animals are reptiles.
Find how many animals are reptiles.

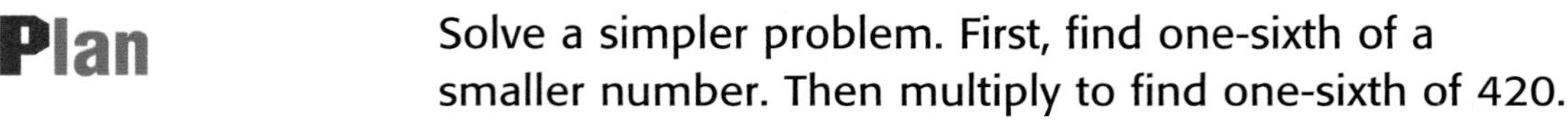

Plan

Solve a simpler problem. First, find one-sixth of a smaller number. Then multiply to find one-sixth of 420.

Solve

First, find one-sixth of 42.

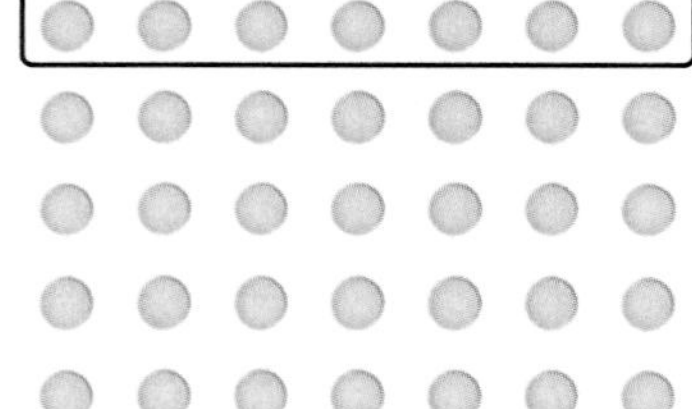

There are 42 counters in 6 equal rows. One of the six equal groups is circled.

So, one-sixth of 42 equals 7. Now multiply.

$$\begin{array}{r} 42 \\ \times\ 10 \\ \hline 420 \end{array}$$

THINK What number can you multiply 42 by to equal 420? Then multiply 7 by the same number.

$$\begin{array}{r} 7 \\ \times\ 10 \\ \hline 70 \end{array}$$

So, 70 of the animals at the zoo are reptiles.

Check

Since $70 \times 6 = 420$, then 70 is one-sixth of 420. The answer is correct.

Mixed Problem Solving

Use any strategy shown below to solve. Tell what strategy you used.

PROBLEM-SOLVING STRATEGIES

- Guess and check.
- Look for a pattern.
- Work a simpler problem.
- Use logical reasoning.
- Draw a picture.

1. A chef wants to cook an 8-pound turkey. It takes 20 minutes per pound to fully cook. What time should the chef start cooking the turkey if it needs to be done at 5:00 P.M?

2. After Malcolm buys three packages of stickers like the one shown, the number of stickers in his collection will double. How many stickers will he have?

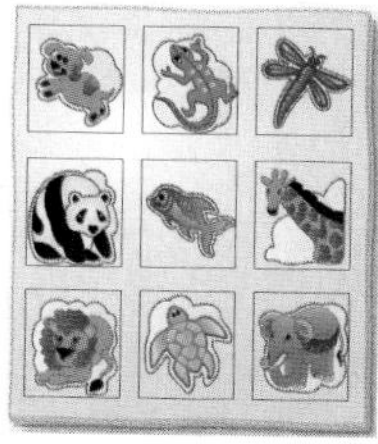

3. Dario and three of his friends shared the cost of renting a rowboat. It cost $12 an hour, and they used the boat for 3 hours. How much did each friend pay?

4. A geometric pattern is shown. What is the next figure in the pattern?

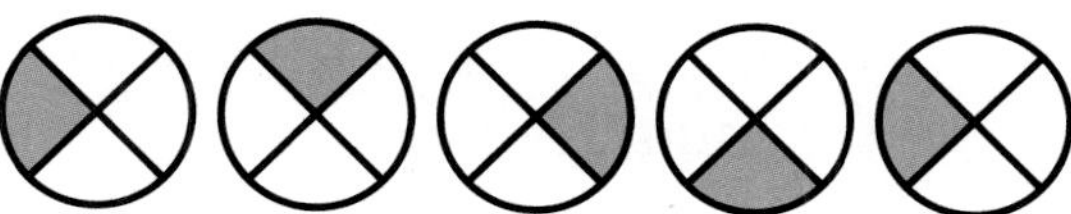

5. Mei has some coins. She has 3 more quarters than nickels and 2 more dimes than quarters. If Mei has 4 nickels, how much money does she have?

6. A customer buys small, medium, and large sweatshirts. The total cost is $68. How many of each size were bought?

7. Daisy exercises for 30 minutes 2 times a day. If she keeps up this schedule for 30 days, how many minutes will she exercise in all?

8. Randall's goal is to run one mile the first week and double the number of miles each week for the next 6 weeks. How many miles will he run the sixth week?

9. Find the area of the fifth figure in the pattern shown.

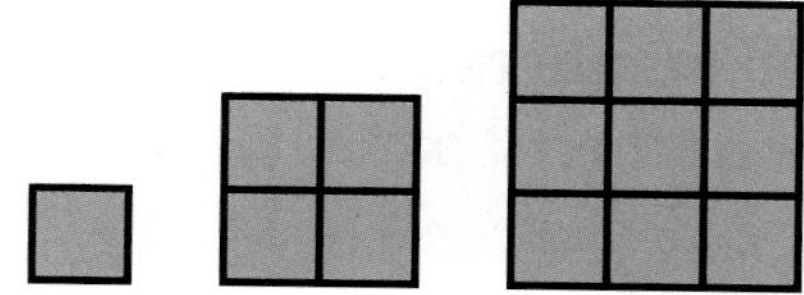

10. WRITING IN ▸MATH Write a few sentences to explain what it means to solve a problem by solving a simpler problem.

CHAPTER 12

Study Guide and Review

FOLDABLES Study Organizer GET READY to Study

Be sure the following Key Vocabulary words and Key Concepts are written in your Foldable.

Parts of a Whole	Parts of a Set	Equivalent Fractions

BIG Ideas

- A **fraction** names part of a whole or part of a set. (p. 493)

  $\frac{4}{5}$ ← numerator / ← denominator

- **Equivalent fractions** represent the same amount. (p. 504)

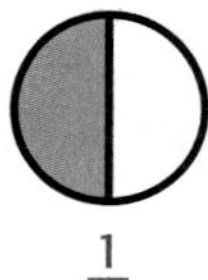

$\frac{1}{2}$

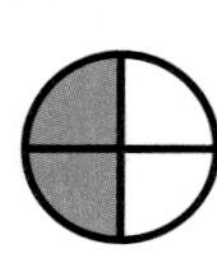

$\frac{2}{4}$

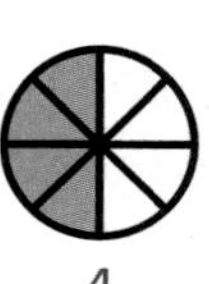

$\frac{4}{8}$

- **Mixed numbers** have a whole number and a fractional part.

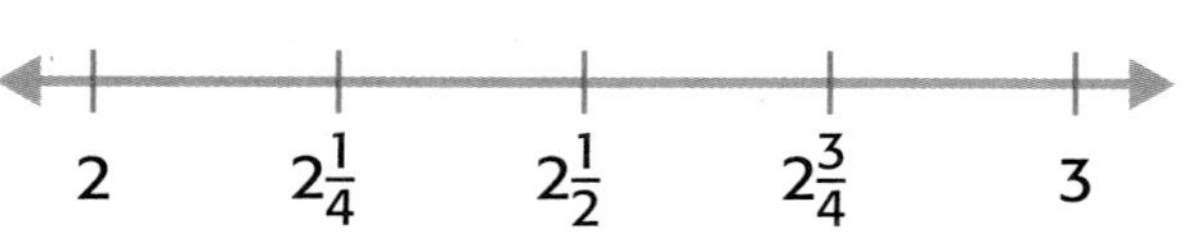

Key Vocabulary

denominator (p. 493)
equivalent fraction (p. 504)
fraction (p. 493)
mixed number (p. 516)
numerator (p. 493)

Vocabulary Check

Complete each sentence with the correct vocabulary word.

1. In the fraction $\frac{3}{4}$, the 4 is the ___?___.

2. A number that names part of a whole or part of a set is a(n) ___?___.

3. A(n) ___?___ has a whole number part and a fraction part.

4. In the fraction $\frac{3}{4}$, the 3 is the ___?___.

5. Fractions that represent the same amount are ___?___.

6. In a fraction, the ___?___ is the top number and the ___?___ is the bottom number.

Math Online Vocabulary Review at tx.gr4math.com

Lesson-by-Lesson Review

12-1 Parts of a Whole (pp. 493–495)

Example 1
What fraction of the figure is shaded?

Write parts shaded ⟶ 5
total parts in all ⟶ 8

Read *five-eighths* or
five divided by eight

So, $\frac{5}{8}$ of the figure is shaded.

Write the fraction that names part of the whole.

7. 

part shaded

8. 

part shaded

Draw a picture and shade part of it to show the fraction.

9. $\frac{2}{3}$

10. $\frac{5}{6}$

11. What fraction of the waffle is missing?

12-2 Parts of a Set (pp. 496–499)

Example 2
What fraction of the crayons shown is *not* red?

Write crayons not red ⟶ 3
total crayons ⟶ 5

Read *three-fifths* or
three divided by five

So, $\frac{3}{5}$ of the crayons are *not* red.

Write the fraction that names the part of the set of shapes.

12. *not* purple

13. *not* green

14. *not* orange

15. *not* red

16. *not* yellow

17. *not* a sun

18. There are five cars. Two-fifths of the cars are blue. Draw a picture to show the set.

12-3 Problem-Solving Strategy: Draw a Picture (pp. 500–501)

Example 3
Marcela has 24 crayons. Of them, $\frac{1}{3}$ are blue. Four are yellow, and the rest are green. How many crayons are green?

Understand

What facts do you know?

- There are 24 crayons.
- $\frac{1}{3}$ are blue.
- 4 are yellow.
- The rest are green.

What do you need to find?

Find how many crayons Marcela has of each color.

Plan Draw a picture.

Solve Divide 24 equal parts. Shade $\frac{1}{3}$ to show the blue crayons. Shade 4 to show the yellow crayons.

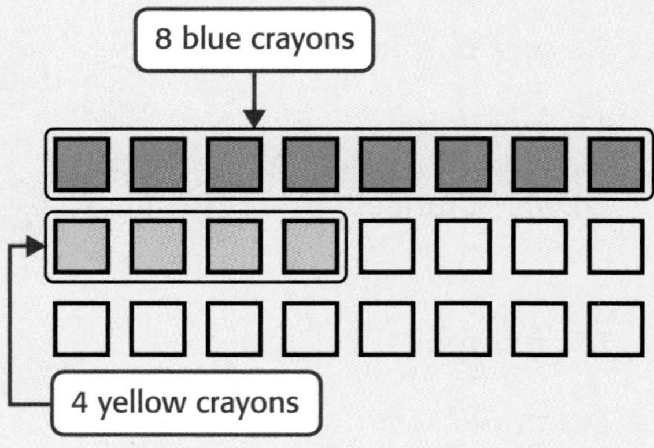

There are 12 parts left. So, 12 of the crayons are green.

Check Since $8 + 4 + 12 = 24$ crayons, the answer makes sense.

19. The 24 students in Ms. Cameron's class are working on final art projects. One-half of them are painting. Eight of the students are making a clay sculpture. The rest of the students are making sketches. How many students are making sketches?

20. Serefina took part in the activities listed. How long did she eat a snack?

Serefina's Activities	
Activity	**Time Spent**
Read a book	$\frac{1}{2}$ of an hour
Watch TV	20 minutes
Eat a snack	rest of the hour

21. Of 15 cars, 7 are blue and $\frac{1}{5}$ are red. The rest of the cars are black. How many cars are black?

22. Jeff had 28 grapes. He ate $\frac{1}{2}$ of them for lunch. Then he ate 10 more as a snack. How many are left?

23. Marisa has a marble collection. One-fourth of her 16 marbles are blue. Her red marbles are shown below. The rest of the marbles are green. How many of the marbles are green?

12-4 Equivalent Fractions (pp. 504–508)

Example 4

Find two fractions equivalent to $\frac{4}{6}$.

One Way: Multiply

$\frac{4 \times 2}{6 \times 2} = \frac{8}{12}$ Multiply the numerator and the denominator by the same number, 2.

Another Way: Divide

$\frac{4 \div 2}{6 \div 2} = \frac{2}{3}$ Divide the numerator and the denominator by the same number, 2.

So, $\frac{8}{12}$ and $\frac{2}{3}$ are equivalent to $\frac{4}{6}$.

Find an equivalent fraction for each fraction.

24. $\frac{1}{5}$ **25.** $\frac{1}{3}$ **26.** $\frac{1}{4}$

27. $\frac{6}{8}$ **28.** $\frac{7}{14}$ **29.** $\frac{9}{12}$

Write an equivalent fraction for each amount.

30. Dave hit 4 out of 8 baseballs.

31. Teresa's team won 9 out of 12 tennis matches.

32. Lara ate 4 out of 8 carrot sticks.

12-5 Compare and Order Fractions (pp. 510–513)

Example 5

Dakota has a red and a blue pencil. The red pencil is $\frac{1}{2}$ of a foot long. The blue pencil is $\frac{3}{8}$ of a foot long. Which pencil is longer?

You can use number lines to compare the length of the pencils.

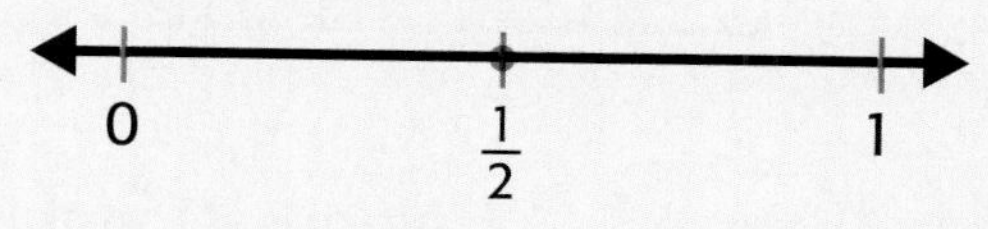

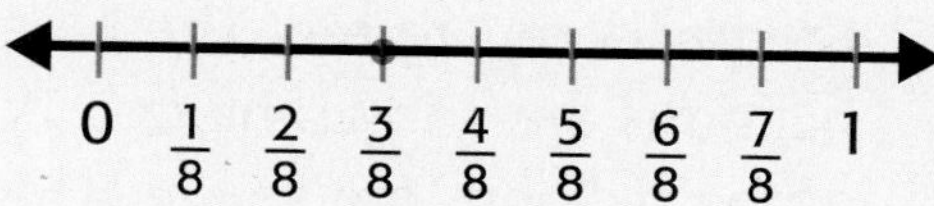

So, the red pencil is longer than the blue pencil.

Use models to compare. Write <, >, or =.

33.

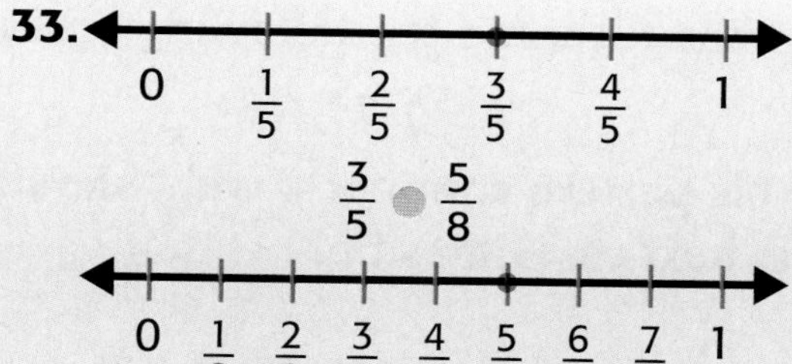

34. $\frac{4}{5}$ ● $\frac{8}{10}$ **35.** $\frac{6}{6}$ ● $\frac{5}{6}$

Use models to order from the least to the greatest.

36. $\frac{2}{3}, \frac{3}{7}, \frac{4}{35}$ **37.** $\frac{1}{4}, \frac{3}{16}, \frac{7}{8}$

38. Patrick took $\frac{3}{4}$ of an hour to finish a test. José took $\frac{3}{8}$ of an hour to finish. Who took longer to finish the test?

CHAPTER 12

Study Guide and Review

12-6 Mixed Numbers (pp. 516–519)

Example 6

A fourth grade class had a pizza party. The amount of pizza eaten can be represented as $3\frac{1}{5}$. Write the amout of the pizza eaten as an improper fraction.

$3\frac{1}{5} = \frac{5}{5} + \frac{5}{5} + \frac{5}{5} + \frac{1}{5}$

$= \frac{5 + 5 + 5 + 1}{5}$

$= \frac{16}{5}$

So, $3\frac{1}{5} = \frac{16}{5}$.

Write a mixed number and an improper fraction for each model.

39. 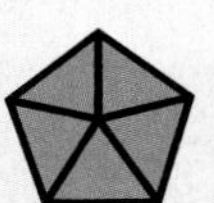 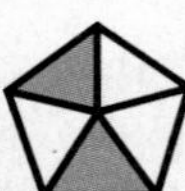

40. 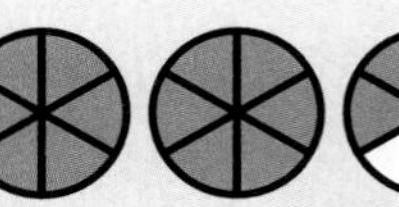

Write each as an improper fraction or a mixed number.

41. $\frac{18}{4}$

42. $\frac{32}{8}$

43. $2\frac{3}{4}$

44. $3\frac{7}{8}$

12-7 Problem-Solving Investigation: Choose a Strategy (pp. 520–521)

Example 7

Charlie runs track daily and records his time in seconds. In the last four days he has recorded the following times:

27, 24, 21, 18

If his pattern continues, what should his next two times be?

Look for a pattern in the times. Then extend to solve the problem.

Notice that each of Charlie's times goes down by three. So, the pattern is subtract 3.

27, 24, 21, 18, 15, 12

−3 −3 −3 −3 −3

So, Charlie's next two times will be 15 and 12 seconds.

Use any strategy to solve.

45. Kellie earned $35 a day for chopping wood. If she earned a total of $245, how many days did she chop wood?

46. Draw the next figure in the pattern.

47. There are 12 balloons. One-third of the balloons are red. The blue balloons are shown below. The rest of the balloons are yellow. How many of the balloons are yellow?

CHAPTER 12

Chapter Test

For Exercises 1 and 2, tell whether each statement is *true* or *false*.

1. An improper fraction has a numerator that is less than its denominator.
2. To find an equivalent fraction, multiply or divide the numerator and denominator by the same number.

Find an equivalent fraction for each fraction.

3. $\frac{3}{12}$
4. $\frac{24}{40}$
5. $\frac{1}{5}$
6. $\frac{1}{3}$
7. Madison and Alan each ate the amount of apple pie shown. How much of one whole apple pie is left?

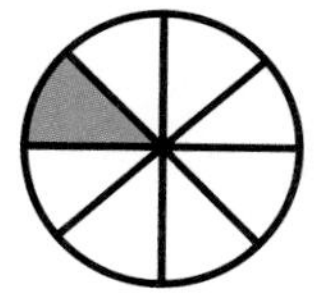

8. **TEST PRACTICE** Which fraction is NOT equivalent to the shaded area of the circle?

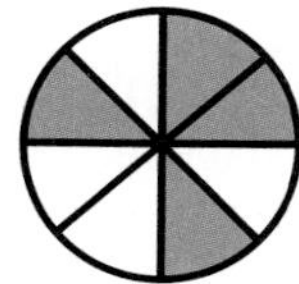

A $\frac{1}{2}$ **C** $\frac{4}{8}$

B $\frac{2}{4}$ **D** $\frac{7}{12}$

Compare. Write <, >, or =.

9. $\frac{2}{4} \bullet \frac{3}{4}$
10. $\frac{4}{10} \bullet \frac{1}{2}$

Write each mixed number as an improper fraction.

11. $2\frac{3}{4}$
12. $4\frac{5}{12}$
13. There are 12 fish in Nicolas's aquarium. One-half of the fish are goldfish. Four of the fish are tetras. The rest of the fish are rainbow fish. How many of the fish are rainbow fish?

Identify these points on the number line.

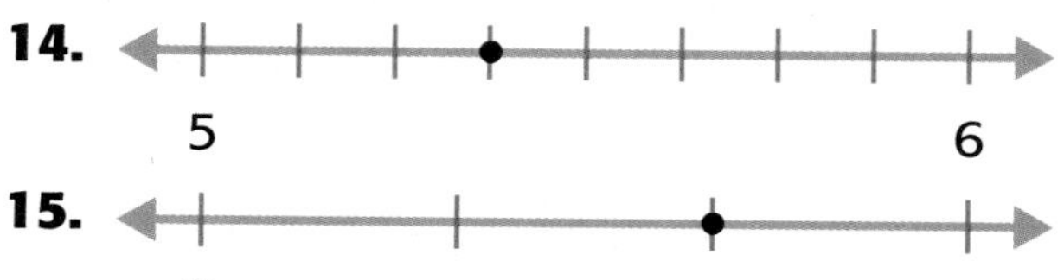

16. Abby read $\frac{3}{10}$ of a book on Saturday. Then she read $\frac{4}{10}$ of the book on Sunday. What fraction of the book does Abby still have to read?
17. **TEST PRACTICE** Identify the improper fraction below that is NOT equivalent to $2\frac{4}{5}$.

F $\frac{28}{10}$ **H** $\frac{5}{14}$

G $\frac{42}{15}$ **J** $\frac{56}{20}$

18. **WRITING IN MATH** Explain how $\frac{2}{7}$ and $\frac{6}{21}$ are equivalent fractions.

CHAPTER 12

Texas Test Practice

Cumulative, Chapters 1–12

TEST Example

Santos answered 8 out of 10 questions on a quiz correctly. Which fraction is equivalent to $\frac{8}{10}$?

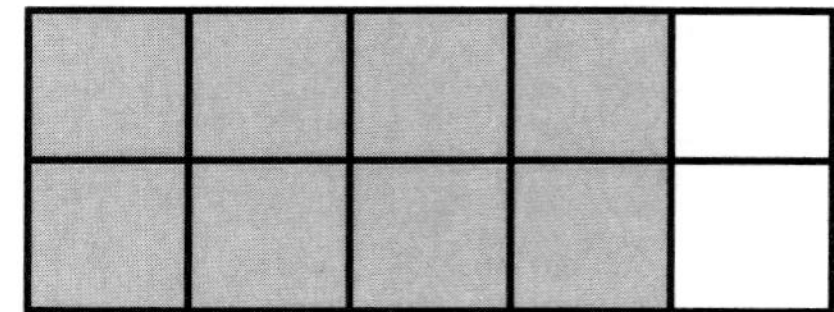

A $\frac{4}{5}$

B $\frac{3}{4}$

C $\frac{5}{6}$

D $\frac{2}{3}$

TEST-TAKING TIP

Draw a model that is equivalent to $\frac{8}{10}$.

Read the Test Question

You need to find a fraction that is equivalent to $\frac{8}{10}$.

Solve the Test Question

You can divide both the numerator and denominator by 2 to find an equivalent fraction. You can also draw another model to find an equivalent fraction.

$$\frac{8 \div 2}{10 \div 2} = \frac{4}{5}$$

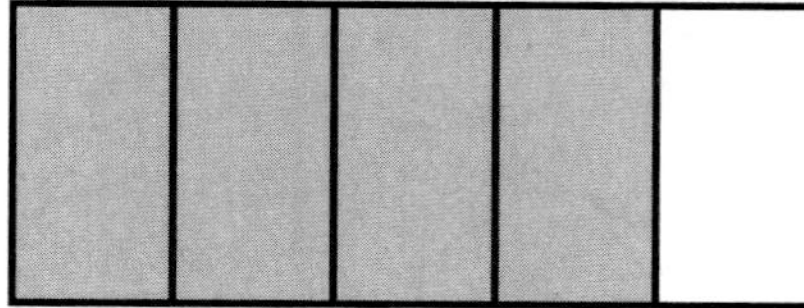

The answer is A.

 **Personal Tutor at** tx.gr4math.com

Choose the best answer.

1. **Which fraction is equivalent to $\frac{1}{3}$?**

   A $\frac{2}{4}$

   B $\frac{5}{12}$

   C $\frac{3}{9}$

   D $\frac{2}{8}$

2. **Which fraction is equivalent to $\frac{8}{12}$?**

   F $\frac{1}{4}$

   G $\frac{2}{3}$

   H $\frac{3}{4}$

   J $\frac{3}{5}$

Get Ready for the Texas Test
For test-taking strategies and more practice, see pages TX1–TX21.

3. **Megan's dog is $3\frac{1}{2}$ years old. Which point best represents $3\frac{1}{2}$ on the number line?**

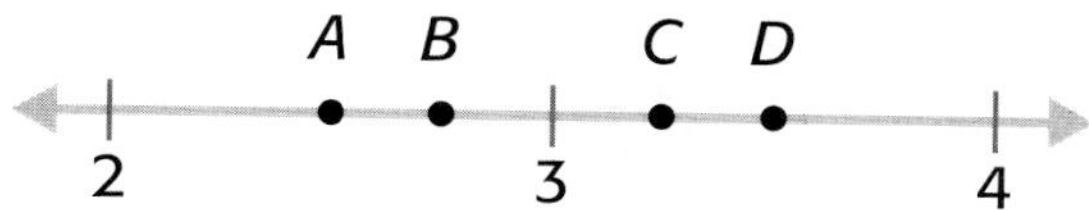

A point *A**
B point *B*
C point *C*
D point *D*

4. **Which expression is shown by the model?**

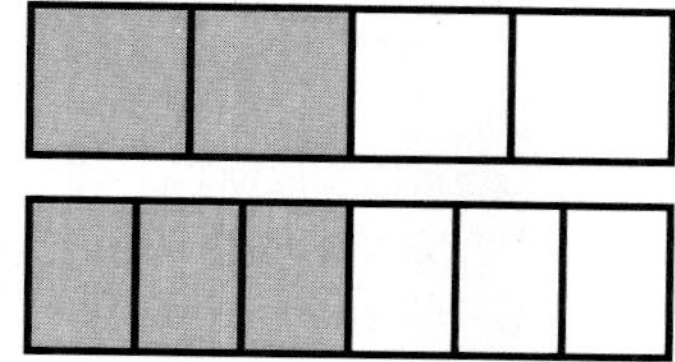

F $\frac{2}{4} = \frac{3}{6}$
G $\frac{2}{4} > \frac{3}{6}$
H $\frac{2}{4} < \frac{3}{6}$
J $\frac{2}{4} + \frac{3}{6}$

5. **GRIDDABLE A vegetable garden is 8 yards long and 55 yards wide. What is the area, in square yards, of the garden?**

6. **There are 60 members in the choir. They will be arranged into 5 equal rows for a concert. How many rows will there be?**

A 11
B 12
C 13
D 15

7. **Look at the figures. Which fraction is shown by the shaded part of the figures?**

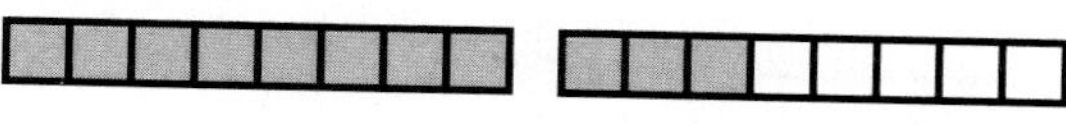

F $1\frac{1}{4}$
G $1\frac{1}{2}$
H $1\frac{3}{8}$
J $1\frac{5}{8}$

8. **The temperature has increased by 12 degrees since this morning. What is the current temperature?**

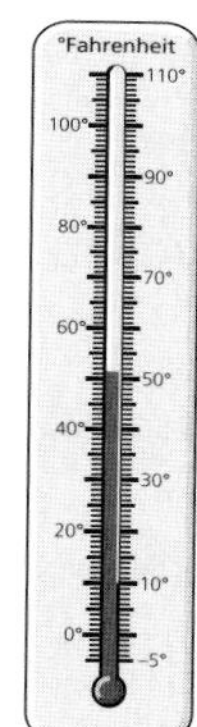

Morning Temperature

A 51°F
B 53°F
C 63°F
D 64°F

9. **Shane has 58 postcards. He wants to store them in an album that holds 6 cards per page. About how many pages will he need for the album?**

F 7
G 8
H 9
J 10

Use Place Value to Represent Decimals

BIG Idea What are decimals?

Decimals are numbers that use place value and a decimal point to show part of a whole.

Example There are 10 dimes in a dollar. One dime is $\frac{1}{10}$ of a dollar. There are 100 pennies in a dollar. One penny is $\frac{1}{100}$ of a dollar.

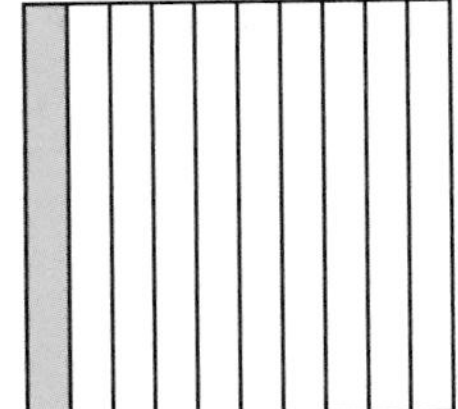

One dime is $\frac{1}{10}$ of a dollar.

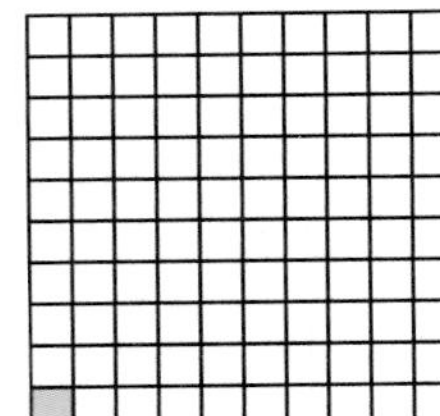

One penny is $\frac{1}{100}$ of a dollar.

What will I learn in this chapter?

- Identify, read, write, and model decimals.
- Relate decimals, fractions, and mixed numbers.
- Compare and order decimals.
- Solve problems by making a model.

Key Vocabulary

decimal
decimal point
tenth
hundredth

Student Study Tools at tx.gr4math.com

FOLDABLES™ Study Organizer

Make this Foldable to help you organize information about decmials. Begin with one sheet of 11″ × 17″ paper.

1. **Fold** the short sides so they meet in the middle.

2. **Fold** again so the top meets the bottom.

3. **Unfold** and cut as shown to make four tabs.

4. **Label** the outside of each tab as shown.

ARE YOU READY for Chapter 13?

You have two ways to check prerequisite skills for this chapter.

Option 2

Math Online Take the Chapter Readiness Quiz at tx.gr4math.com.

Option 1

Complete the Quick Check below.

QUICK Check

Write a fraction to describe the part that is green. (Lesson 12-1)

1. 

2. 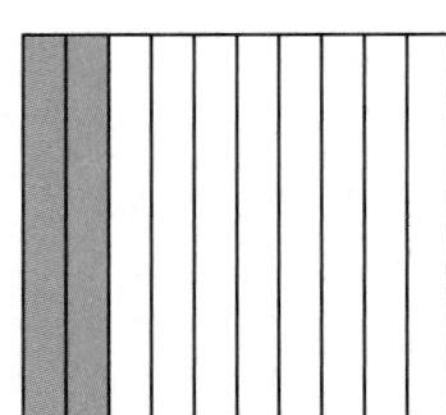

3. 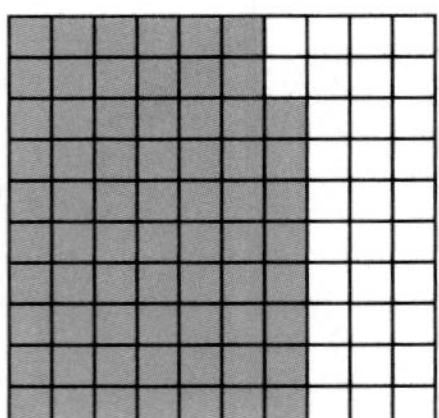

Write each as a fraction. (Lessons 12-1 and 12-2)

4. four-tenths

5. eight-tenths

6. twenty-hundredths

7. On Tuesday, seven-tenths of an inch of rain fell. Write the amount of rain that fell as a fraction.

Algebra Copy and complete. (Lesson 12-4)

8. $\frac{1}{5} = \frac{■}{10}$

9. $\frac{4}{5} = \frac{■}{10}$

10. $\frac{1}{2} = \frac{■}{10}$

11. $\frac{1}{4} = \frac{■}{100}$

12. $\frac{2}{5} = \frac{■}{100}$

13. $\frac{1}{2} = \frac{■}{100}$

14. In Salvador's aquarium, $\frac{4}{10}$ of the fish are yellow and $\frac{6}{10}$ are blue. Are there more blue or yellow fish in Salvador's aquarium? Explain how you know.

Explore

Math Activity for 13-1
Fractions and Decimals

MAIN IDEA

I will use models to show tenths and hundredths.

 **Targeted TEKS 4.2** The student describes and compares fractional parts of whole objects or sets of objects. **(D) Relate decimals to fractions that name tenths and hundredths using concrete objects and pictorial models.** *Also addresses TEKS 4.1(B).*

You Will Need
tenths grid
hundredths grid

Interactive Lab
tx.gr4math.com

A fraction shows part of a whole. A decimal also shows a part of a whole. A **decimal** is a number that uses place value, numbers, and a decimal point to show part of a whole.

one whole

$\frac{1}{1} = 1.0$

decimal point

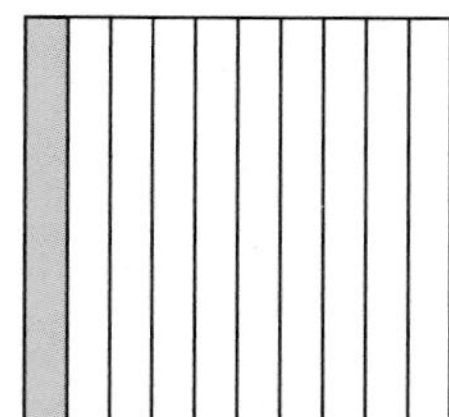

one **tenth**

$\frac{1}{10} = 0.1$

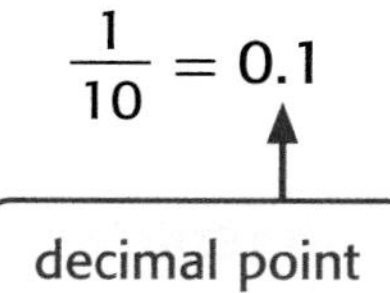

decimal point

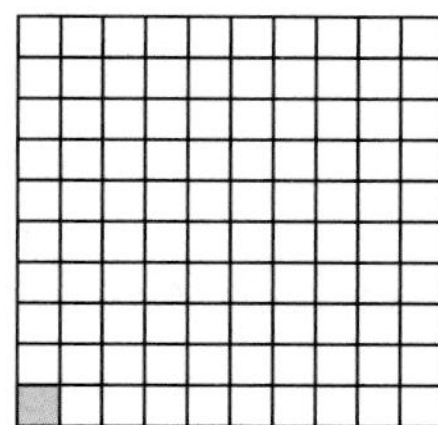

one **hundredth**

$\frac{1}{100} = 0.01$

decimal point

ACTIVITY

1 Create a model for 4 tenths.

Step 1 **Use a tenths grid.**
Shade in 4 of the 10 parts to show 4 tenths.

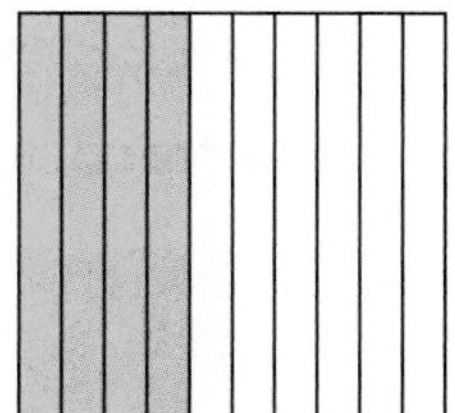

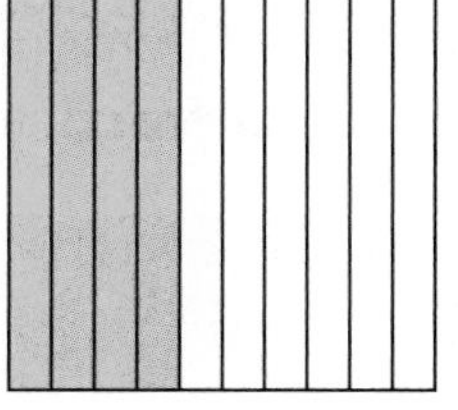

Step 2 **Use a hundredths grid.**
Shade 40 of the 100 parts to show 40 hundredths.

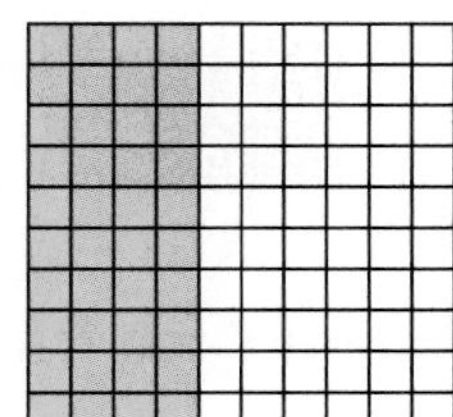

Step 3 **Compare.**
Compare the grids. Write the fraction for each shaded part.

Step 4 **Write decimals.**
How is 4 tenths written as a decimal?
How is 40 hundredths written as a decimal?

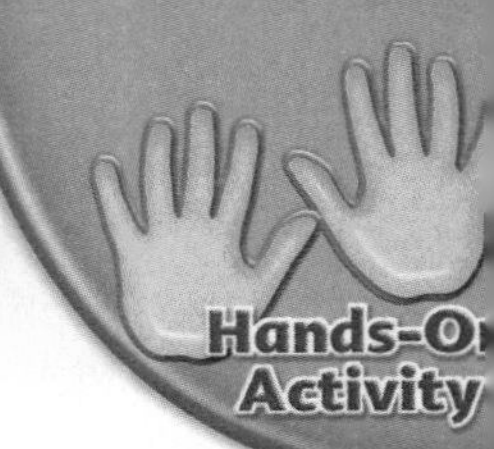

ACTIVITY

2 Model 77 hundredths using coins.

Step 1 **Use pennies.**
One penny is $\frac{1}{100}$ of a dollar. Count out 7 pennies to represent 7 hundredths or $\frac{7}{100}$.

Step 2 **Use dimes.**
One dime is $\frac{1}{10}$ of a dollar. Count out 7 dimes to represent 7 tenths or $\frac{7}{10}$.

Step 3 **Combine the coins.**
Combine the dimes and pennies to represent $\frac{77}{100}$ or 0.77.

Think About It

1. Do $\frac{4}{10}$, $\frac{40}{100}$, 0.4, and 0.40 represent the same number? Explain.
2. Is 0.02 greater than 0.2? Support your answer with models.
3. Is 0.3 greater than 0.30? Explain.

CHECK What You Know

Write a fraction and a decimal for each shaded part.

4. 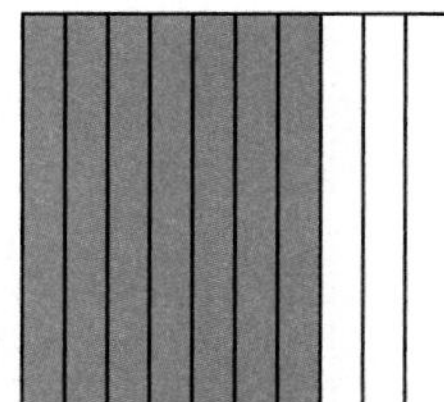

5. 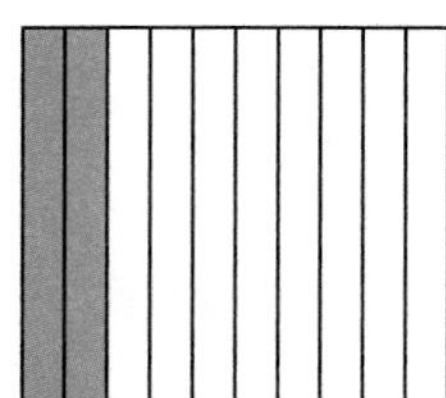

6. 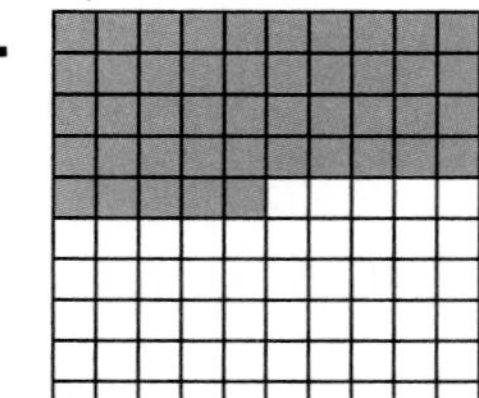

7. 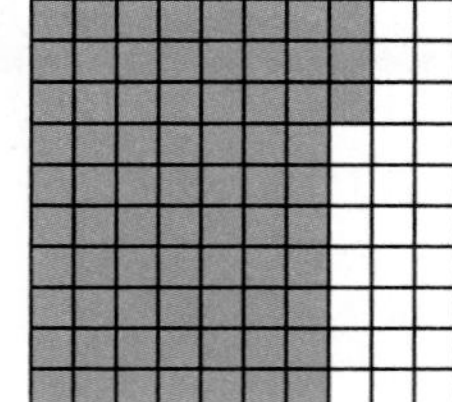

Model each fraction. Then write as a decimal.

8. $\frac{1}{10}$
9. $\frac{3}{10}$
10. $\frac{60}{100}$
11. $\frac{82}{100}$

Model each decimal. Then write as a fraction.

12. 0.5
13. 0.75
14. 0.30
15. 0.25

16. **WRITING IN ▶MATH** Explain how to write a fraction with a denominator of 10 as a decimal.

13-1 Tenths and Hundredths

MAIN IDEA

I will identify, read, and write tenths and hundredths as decimals and fractions.

Targeted TEKS 4.1 The student uses place value to represent whole numbers and decimals. (B) **Use place value to read, write, compare, and order decimals involving tenths and hundredths, including money, using concrete objects and pictorial models.** *Also addresses TEKS 4.2(D).*

New Vocabulary

decimal
decimal point
tenth
hundredth

GET READY to Learn

It costs 85 cents for a child to ride the light rail system. Can you write this part of a dollar as a fraction and as a decimal?

A **decimal** is a number that uses place value and a **decimal point** to show part of a whole.

EXAMPLE Read and Write Decimals

1. **MONEY Write 85 cents as a fraction and as a decimal.**

The amount 85 cents means 85 pennies out of 1 dollar.

One Way: Create Models

Draw a hundredths model. Shade 85 out of 100 parts to show 85 cents.

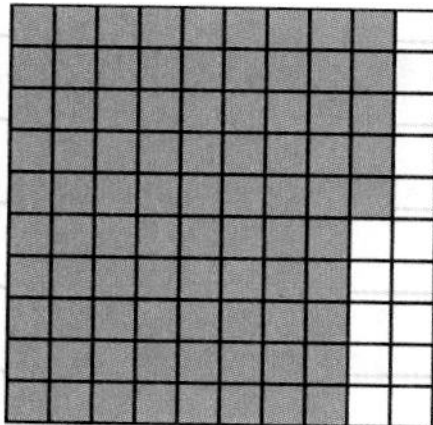

Read eighty-five hundredths

Write $\frac{85}{100}$ or 0.85

Another Way: Place Value

Hundreds	Tens	Ones	Tenths	Hundredths
		0.	8	5

Read eighty-five hundredths

Write $\frac{85}{100}$ or 0.85

So, 85 cents is $\frac{85}{100}$ as a fraction and 0.85 as a decimal.

Some decimals can be written as **tenths** and **hundredths**.

EXAMPLE Write Tenths and Hundredths

2 **Write $\frac{5}{10}$ as two different decimals.**

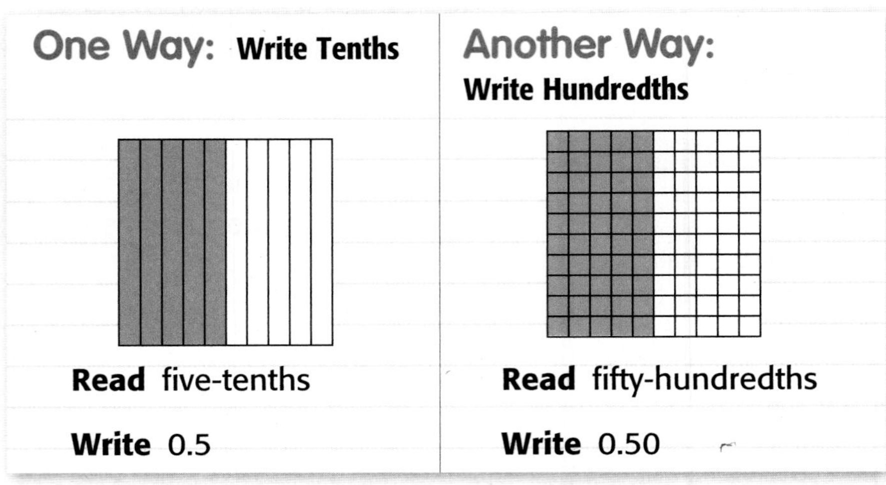

One Way: Write Tenths
Read five-tenths
Write 0.5
Another Way: Write Hundredths
Read fifty-hundredths
Write 0.50

The decimals 0.5 and 0.50 are equivalent decimals.

Online **Personal Tutor at** tx.gr4math.com

CHECK What You Know

Write a fraction and a decimal for each shaded part. See Example 1 (p. 535)

1. 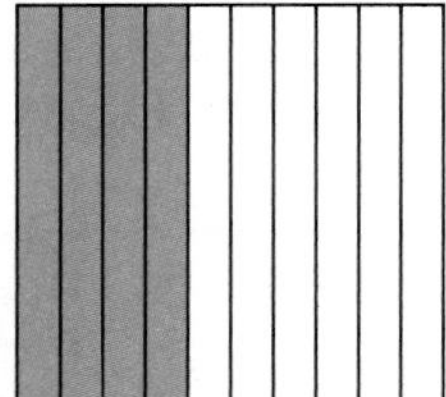

2. 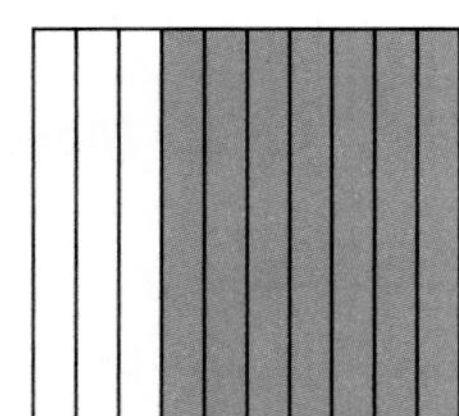

3. 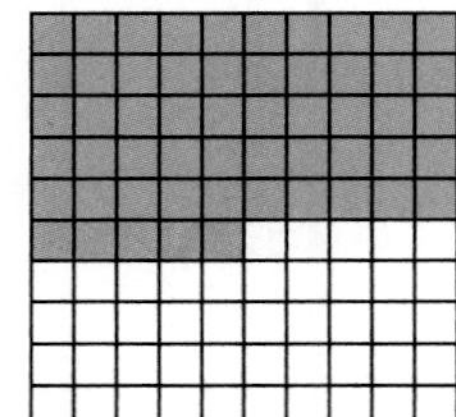

Model each number. Then write as a fraction and as a decimal. See Example 1 (p. 535)

4. one-tenth
5. twenty-five hundredths
6. seven hundredths

Model each fraction. Then write as a decimal. See Example 2 (p. 536)

7. $\frac{6}{10}$
8. $\frac{9}{10}$
9. $\frac{10}{100}$
10. $\frac{69}{100}$

11. **Measurement** A baby owl weighs about twenty-three hundredths of a kilogram. Write this amount as a fraction and decimal.

12. Talk About It Shade all of the boxes along the outer edge of a hundredths grid. Write a fraction and decimal for the shaded area part. Why is it not 0.40?

Math Online **Extra Examples at** tx.gr4math.com

Practice and Problem Solving

EXTRA PRACTICE See page R45.

Write a fraction and a decimal for each shaded part. See Example 1 (p. 535)

13. 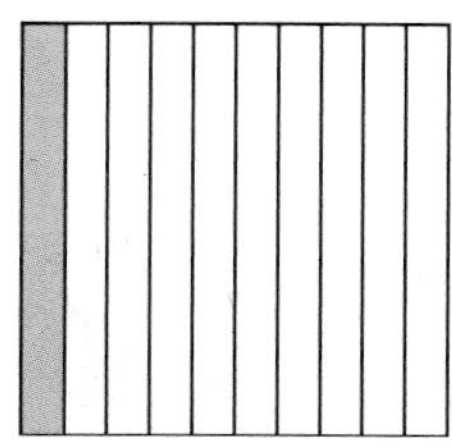

14. 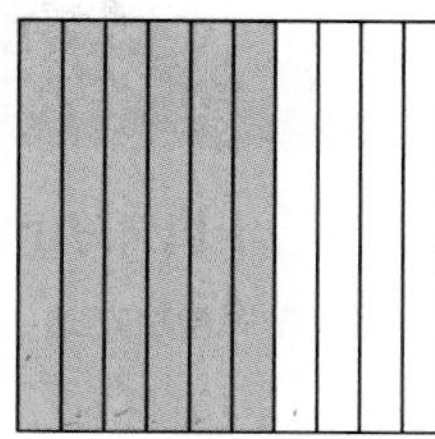

15. 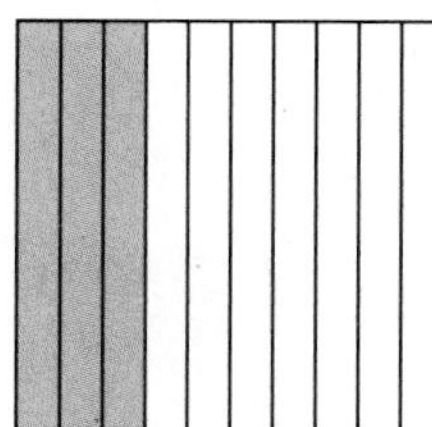

16. 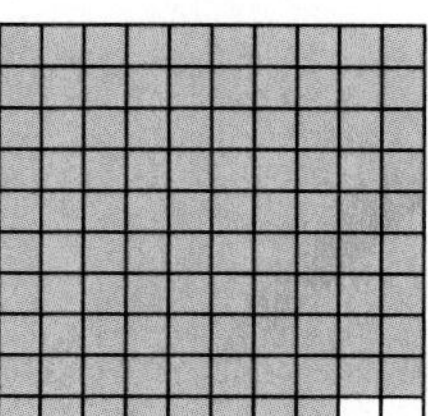

17. 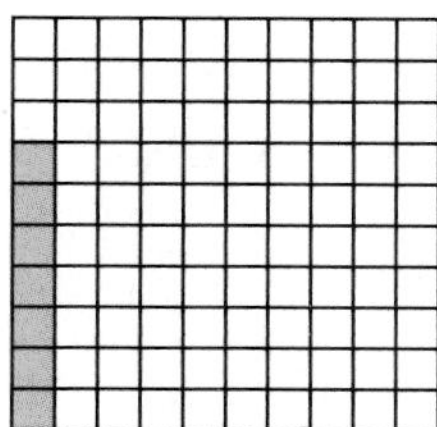

18. 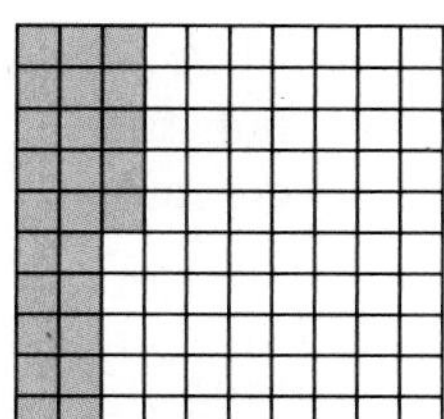

Model each number. Then write as a fraction and as a decimal. See Example 1 (p. 535)

19. sixty-two hundredths

20. two-tenths

21. thirty-five hundredths

22. eight-tenths

23. fourteen-hundredths

24. six-tenths

Model each fraction. Then write as a decimal. See Example 2 (p. 536)

25. $\frac{22}{100}$

26. $\frac{2}{100}$

27. $\frac{2}{10}$

28. $\frac{50}{100}$

29. $\frac{75}{100}$

30. $\frac{80}{100}$

31. Measurement On Monday, it snowed $\frac{6}{10}$ of an inch.

32. Measurement A car traveled $\frac{3}{10}$ of a mile in 18 seconds.

33. Each state has a representation of $\frac{2}{100}$ in the U.S. Senate.

34. Cody learned that $\frac{4}{10}$ of the students in his class are left handed.

H.O.T. Problems

35. OPEN ENDED Write a fraction whose decimal value is between $\frac{2}{10}$ and $\frac{25}{100}$. Write the fraction and its decimal equivalent.

36. CHALLENGE Decide whether the following sentence is true or false. Explain. *The fraction* $\frac{6}{1,000}$ *equals 0.006.*

37. WRITING IN MATH Write a summary statement about decimals equivalent to fractions that have denominators of 10 and 100.

Relate Mixed Numbers and Decimals

GET READY to Learn

Giant saguaro (*sah-WAH-ro*) cacti are found in Arizona and Mexico. A saguaro's growth is slow. It takes about 30 years for one to grow $2\frac{5}{10}$ feet tall and start flowering.

MAIN IDEA

I will identify, read, and write decimals greater than 1.

Targeted TEKS 4.2 The student describes and compares fractional parts of whole objects or sets of objects. **(D) Relate decimals to fractions that name tenths and hundredths using concrete objects and pictorial models.** *Also addresses TEKS 4.1(B).*

Review Vocabulary

mixed number a number named by a whole number and a fraction; *Example:* $2\frac{1}{2}$ **(Lesson 12–7)**

A mixed number like $2\frac{5}{10}$ is a fraction greater than one. You can write mixed numbers as decimals.

EXAMPLE Mixed Numbers as Decimals

1 Write $2\frac{5}{10}$ as a decimal.

One Way: Create Models

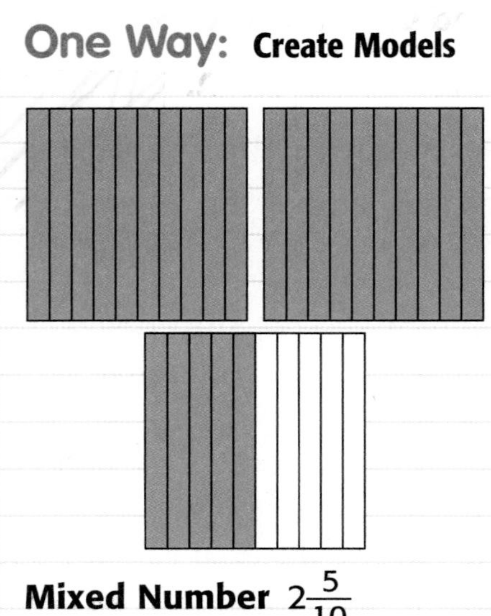

Mixed Number $2\frac{5}{10}$

Read two and five-tenths

Write 2.5

Another Way: Place Value

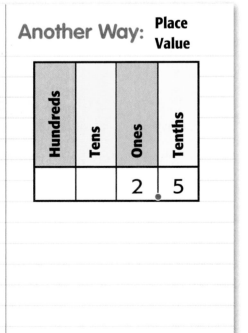

Hundreds	Tens	Ones	Tenths
		2.	5

So, $2\frac{5}{10}$ as a decimal is 2.5.

Remember
When reading a decimal, the word *and* represents the decimal.

2 **MEASUREMENT** **The length of an iguana is $1\frac{9}{100}$ yards. Write $1\frac{9}{100}$ as a decimal.**

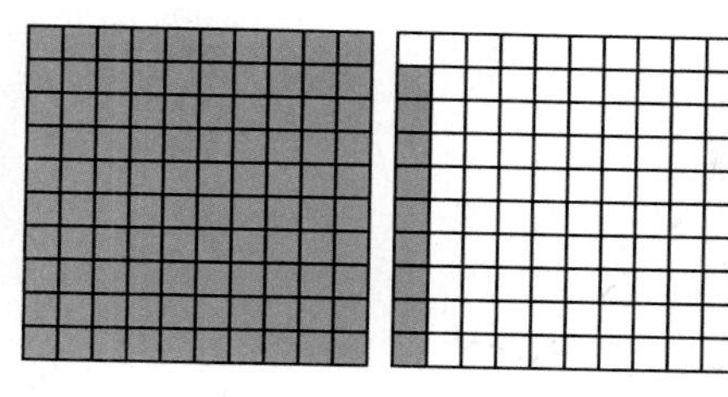

Hundreds	Tens	Ones	Tenths	Hundredths
		1.	0	9

Mixed Number $1\frac{9}{100}$

Read one and nine hundredths

Write 1.09

Online Personal Tutor at tx.gr4math.com

CHECK What You Know

Write each as a mixed number and decimal. See Examples 1 and 2 (pp. 538–539)

1\.

2\. 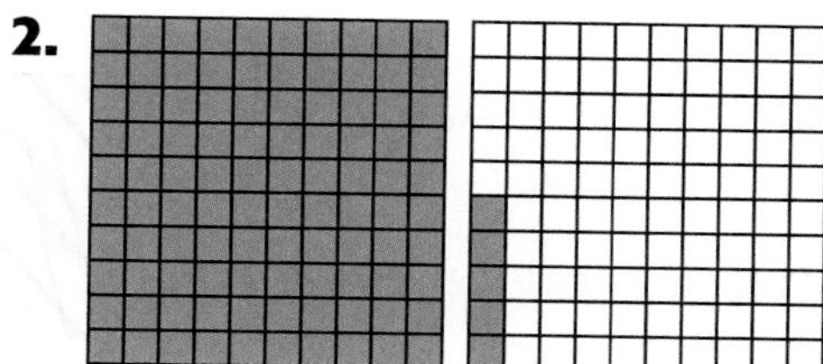

3\. twelve and three tenths

4\. twelve and three hundredths

5\. three and six tenths

6\. sixteen and thirty-two hundredths

Model each mixed number. Then write as a decimal. See Examples 1 and 2 (pp. 538–539)

7\. $5\frac{3}{10}$

8\. $12\frac{5}{10}$

9\. $6\frac{50}{100}$

10\. $24\frac{8}{100}$

11\. Jodi ran the 100-meter dash in 14.6 seconds. Tyra ran the 100-meter dash in 14.64 seconds. Write each girl's time as a mixed number.

12\. **Talk About It** Do $8\frac{5}{10}$, $8\frac{1}{2}$, and 8.5 name the same amount? Explain your reasoning.

Practice and Problem Solving

EXTRA PRACTICE See page R45.

Write each as a mixed number and decimal. See Examples 1 and 2 (pp. 538–539)

13. 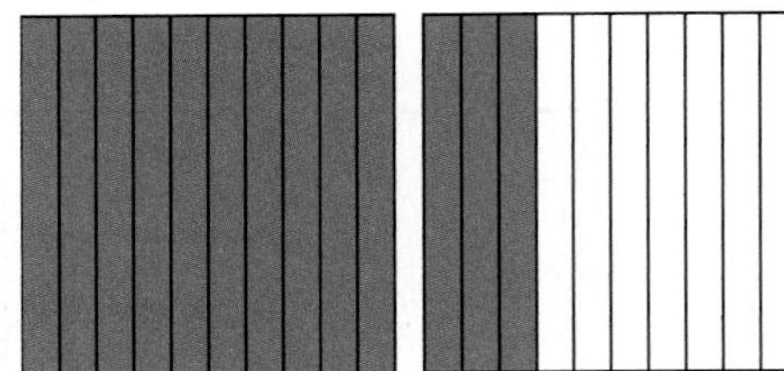

14. 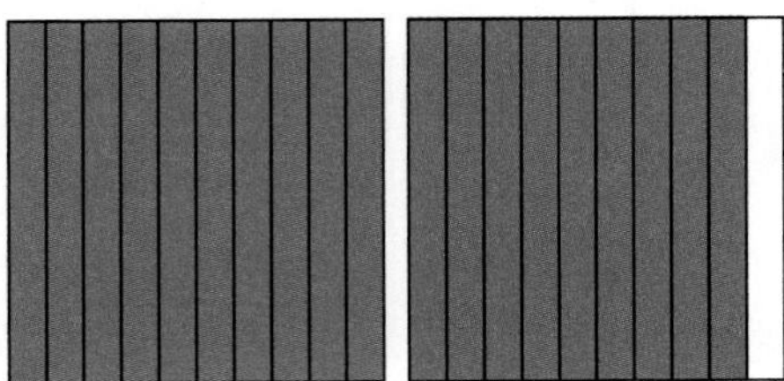

15. 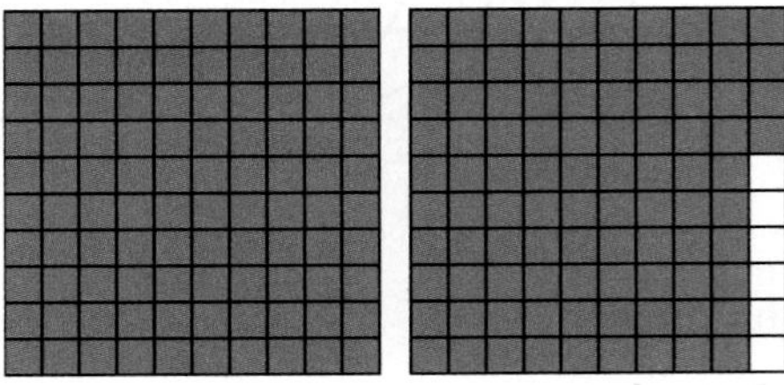

16. 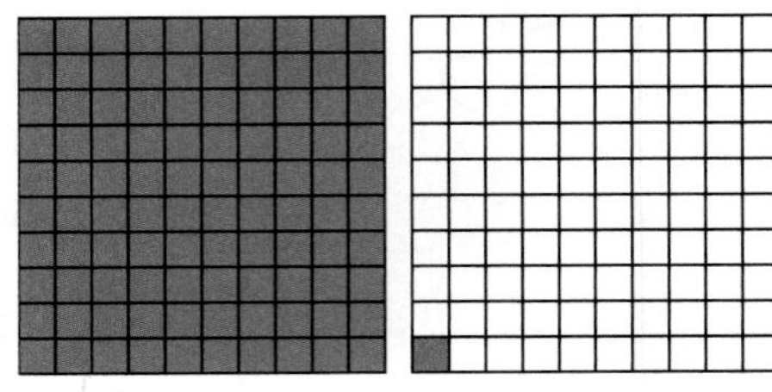

17. one and five tenths

18. sixteen and seven tenths

19. nineteen and one hundred hundredths

20. fifty-six and one hundredth

Model each mixed number. Then write as a decimal. See Examples 1 and 2 (pp. 538–539)

21. $2\frac{5}{10}$

22. $6\frac{6}{10}$

23. $50\frac{1}{10}$

24. $78\frac{8}{10}$

25. $10\frac{16}{100}$

26. $60\frac{2}{100}$

27. $5\frac{25}{100}$

28. $22\frac{75}{100}$

29. Measurement Aaron has grown $3\frac{4}{10}$ feet since he was born. Write a decimal to show how many feet Aaron has grown.

30. Measurement Coastal Plains received 5.52 inches of rain. Write a mixed number to show the number of inches Coastal Plains received.

31. Measurement Kevin lives $2\frac{6}{10}$ miles from the library. Write a decimal to show how many miles Kevin lives from the library.

32. Measurement Ramona's paper airplane flew 3.05 meters. Write a mixed number to show how many meters the airplane flew.

33. Measurement A moose is one of the world's tallest mammals. Write a decimal to show how tall a moose is.

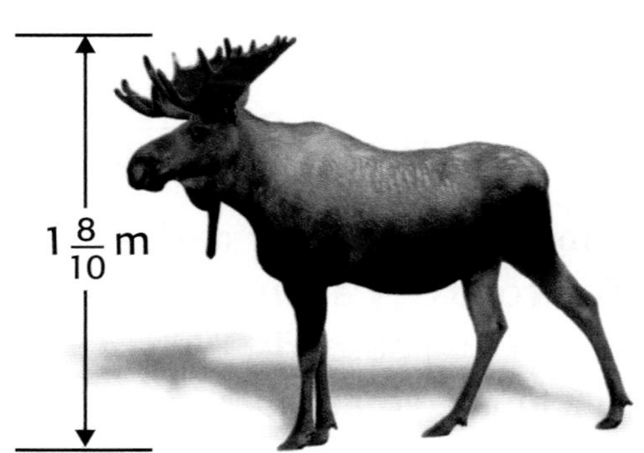

Math Online Self-Check Quiz at tx.gr4math.com

H.O.T. Problems

34. OPEN ENDED Write a mixed number and decimal that are less than five and eight tenths.

35. FIND THE ERROR Brianna and Nick are writing $2\frac{3}{4}$ as a decimal. Who is correct? Explain your reasoning.

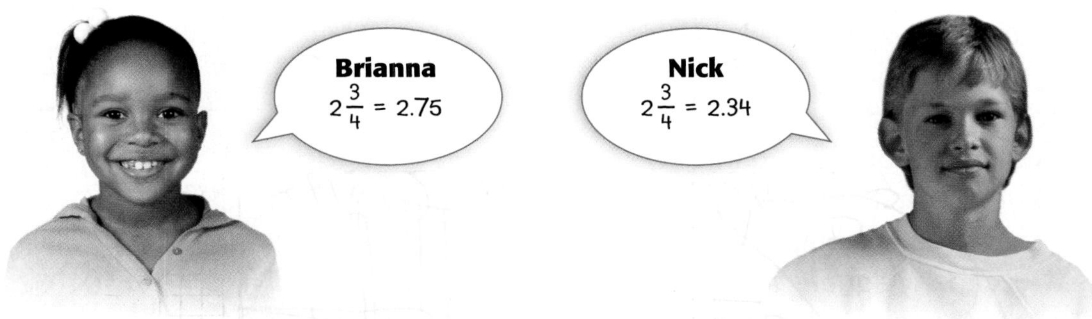

36. WRITING IN ▸MATH Are $2\frac{4}{8}$ and 2.5 equivalent? Explain.

TEST Practice

37. Which number represents the shaded parts of the figure? (Lesson 13-1)

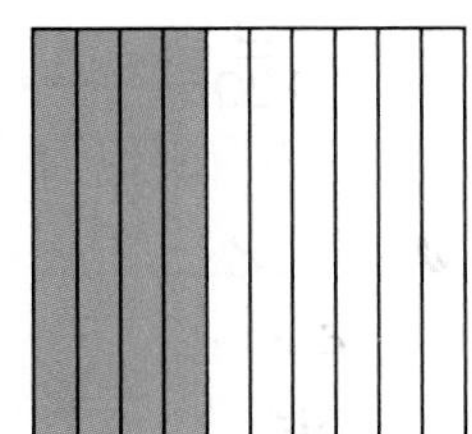

A 0.04

B 0.4

C 4.0

D 4.4

38. Which of the following is seven and seven hundredths? (Lesson 13-2)

F 0.77

G 7.07

H 7.7

J $7\frac{7}{10}$

Spiral Review

Model each number. Then write as a fraction and as a decimal. (Lesson 13-1)

39. five tenths

40. fifty-six hundredths

41. Justino read $\frac{16}{10}$ books this week. How many books did he read written as a mixed number?

42. Select two containers. Estimate and then measure whether each container has a capacity that is greater than, less than, or equal to 2 liters.

13-3 Problem-Solving Strategy

MAIN IDEA I will solve problems by making a model.

Targeted TEKS 4.14 The student applies Grade 4 mathematics to solve problems connected to everyday experiences and activities in and outside of school. **(C) Select or develop an appropriate problem-solving plan or strategy,** including **drawing a picture, . . .** to solve a problem. *Also addresses TEKS 4.14(B).*

Luisa's mom has asked her to find seating for 22 guests for her birthday party. They have an oval table that can seat 10 people. They also have square tables that each seat 4 people. How many square tables are needed to seat the guests?

Understand

What facts do you know?

- An oval table seats 10 people.
- There will be 22 guests altogether.
- Each square table seats 4 people.

What do you need to find?

- The number of square tables needed to seat the guests.

Plan

You can make a model to see how many tables are needed.

Solve

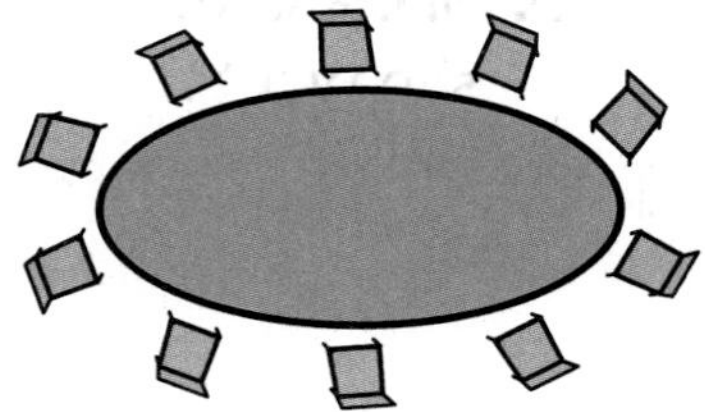

The oval table can seat 10 people.
$22 - 10 = 12$

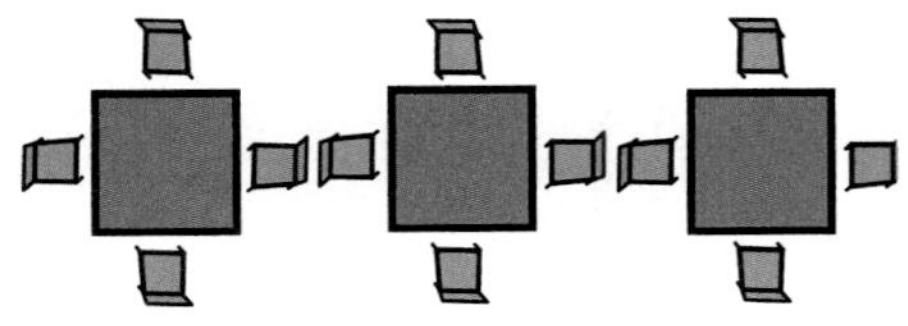

12 people will sit at square tables.
$12 - 12 = 0$

So, three is the fewest number of square tables needed to seat the guests.

Check

Look back at the problem. The fewest number of square tables needed is 3. This makes sense because $22 - 10 - (3 \times 4) = 0$. So, the answer is correct.

ANALYZE the Strategy

Refer to the problem on the previous page.

1. Explain how a model was used to find the fewest number of tables.

2. Explain another strategy you could use to solve Luisa's problem.

3. Suppose there were 30 guests. How many square tables would be needed?

4. Look back to Exercise 3. Check your answer. How do you know that it is correct? Show your work.

PRACTICE the Strategy

Solve. Use the *make a model* strategy.

5. Eileen opened 8 boxes of clay for her project. Each box had 4 sticks of gray clay and half as many sticks of red clay. How many sticks of clay were there in all?

6. Cesar is making a model of the longest bridge in the table for a school project. The scale he is using is one inch equals 200 feet. How many inches long will the model be?

Bridges	
Bridge	**Length (ft)**
Drawbridge	4,200
Suspension Bridge	3,478
Cable-Stayed Bridge	2,310

7. Katia is painting her living room. The room has 3 walls that are 16 feet long and 9 feet tall. A gallon of paint covers 150 square feet. How many gallons should she buy to cover all 3 walls?

8. Every day Marvin runs 3,200 meters around the school track. How many times does he run around the track?

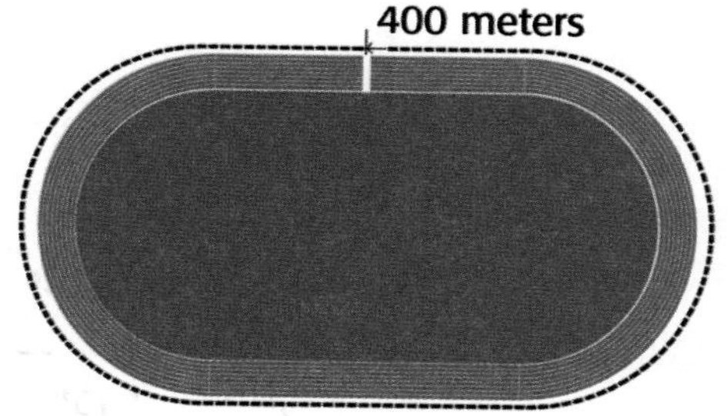

9. Mariana rode her bike 5 miles. Then she went back to get her brother. They rode together for 17 miles. How far did Mariana go altogether?

10. A volleyball court measures 18 meters by 9 meters. A basketball court measures 29 meters by 15 meters. How many volleyball courts could be placed in a basketball court?

11. WRITING IN ►MATH The bottom layer of a pyramid-shaped display has four boxes. There is one less box in each layer. There are four layers. The answer is 10. What is the question?

13-4 Locate Fractions and Decimals on a Number Line

GET READY to Learn

Antón is trying to find $4\frac{1}{4}$ on the number line. He knows that the point is between 4 and 5.

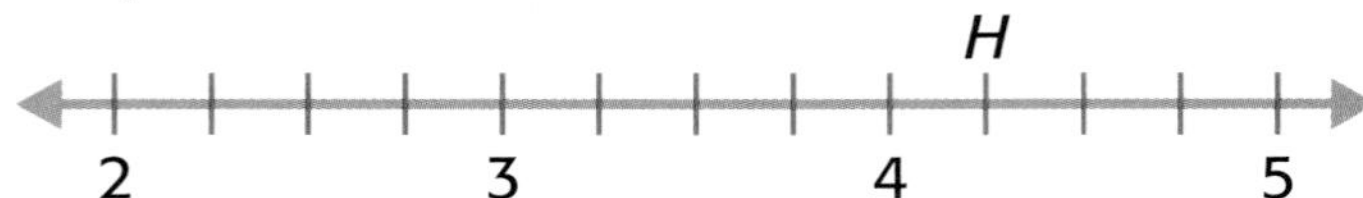

Fractions and decimals can be found on number lines. Use the markings between the whole numbers to determine the fraction or decimal value of a certain point on a number line.

MAIN IDEA

I will find points on a number line.

The student recognizes the connection between numbers and their properties and points on a line. **Locate and name points on a number line using** whole numbers, **fractions such as halves and fourths, and decimals such as tenths.**

EXAMPLE Locate Points on a Number Line

1 Locate $4\frac{1}{4}$ on the number line.

To find $4\frac{1}{4}$, first find 4. Then, find the $\frac{1}{2}$ mark between 4 and 5.

Finally, find the $\frac{1}{4}$ mark halfway between 4 and $4\frac{1}{2}$.

Points on a number line can be represented by a letter. So, $H = 4\frac{1}{4}$ or 4.25.

EXAMPLE Name Points on a Number Line

2 Name the point *N* as a decimal.

Locate *N* on the number line.

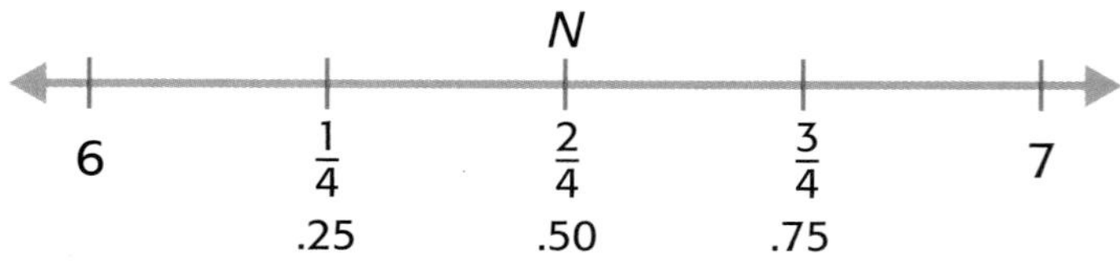

Since *N* is between 6 and 7, you know *N* is a fraction or decimal. The three marks between 6 and 7 let you know it will have a denominator of 4. Make equivalent fractions to determine the decimal. So, *N* is $6\frac{2}{4}$ or 6.5

CHECK What You Know

Locate the given fraction on the number line. Write as a decimal. See Example 1 (p. 544)

1. $10\frac{7}{10}$

2. $10\frac{2}{10}$

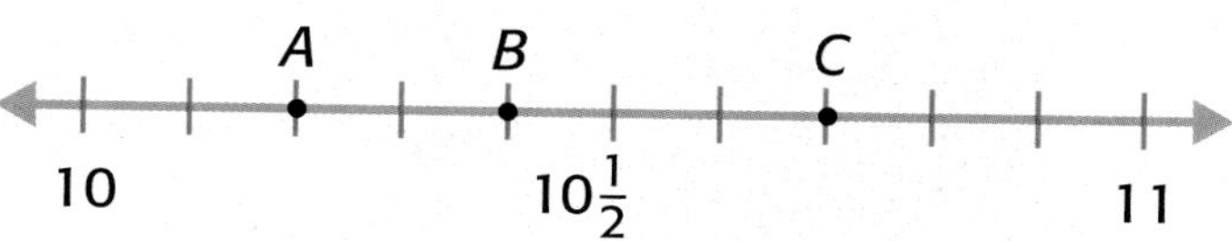

Name the point *N* represents on the number line. See Example 2 (p. 544)

3. $N =$

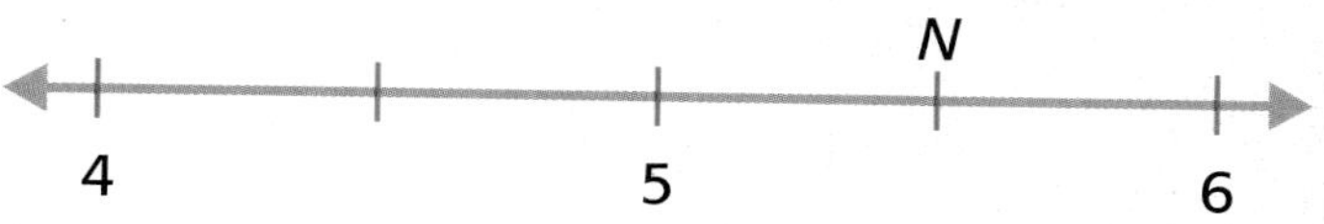

4. Selma is measuring a book with a centimeter ruler. The book ends at the fourth mark between 14 and 15. How many centimeters long is the book?

5. Talk About It Explain the difference between finding $\frac{1}{2}$ on a number line and finding the halfway point on a number line.

Practice and Problem Solving

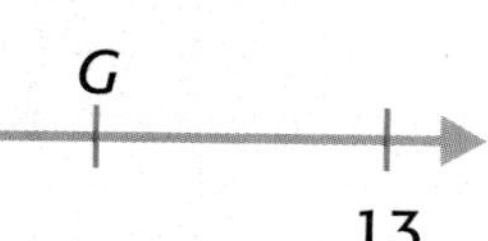

Locate the given fraction on the number line. Write as a decimal. See Example 1 (p. 544)

6. $12\frac{1}{2}$

7. $12\frac{3}{4}$

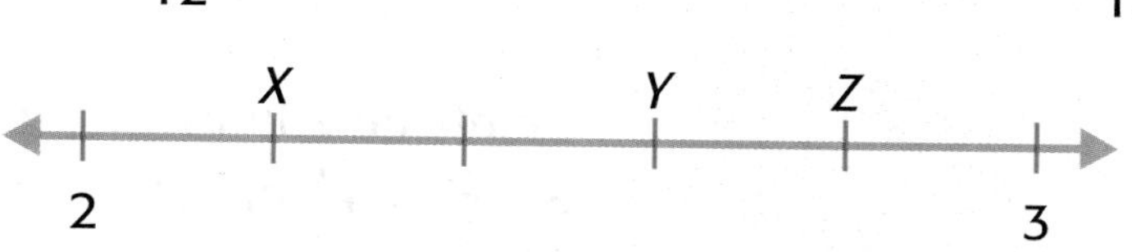

8. $2\frac{3}{5}$

9. $2\frac{1}{5}$

Name the point *N* represents on each number line. See Example 2 (p. 544)

10. $N =$

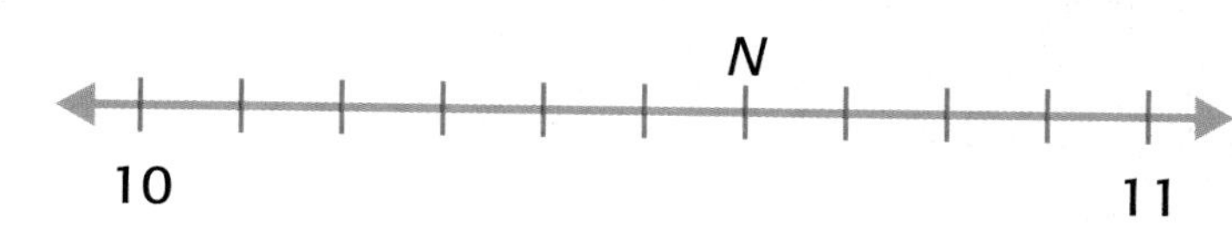

11. $N =$

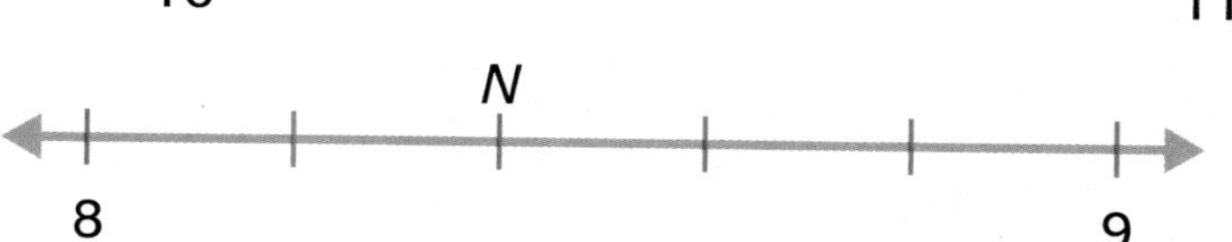

H.O.T. Problems

12. OPEN ENDED Create a number line that has four points plotted. One point must be $12\frac{3}{4}$.

13. WRITING IN ▶MATH Explain how to plot 2.5 on a number line.

Compare and Order Decimals

GET READY to Learn

The table shows the results from a skateboarding competition. Who has the higher score, Doria or Elise?

Skateboarding Results

Name	Score
Doria	79.7
Lina	79.2
Holly	78.9
Elise	79.5
Jane	78.8

MAIN IDEA

I will compare and order decimals.

Targeted TEKS 4.1 The student uses place value to represent whole numbers and decimals. **(B) Use place value to** read, write, **compare, and order decimals involving tenths and hundredths, including money, using concrete objects and pictorial models.** *Also addresses TEKS 4.10.*

Vocabulary Link

order

Everyday Use select desired items

Math Use to arrange in a logical pattern

To compare decimals, you can use a number line or place value.

Real-World EXAMPLE Compare Decimals

1 SCORES Who has the higher score, Doria or Elise?

Doria has a score of 79.7, while Elise has a score of 79.5.

One Way: Number Line

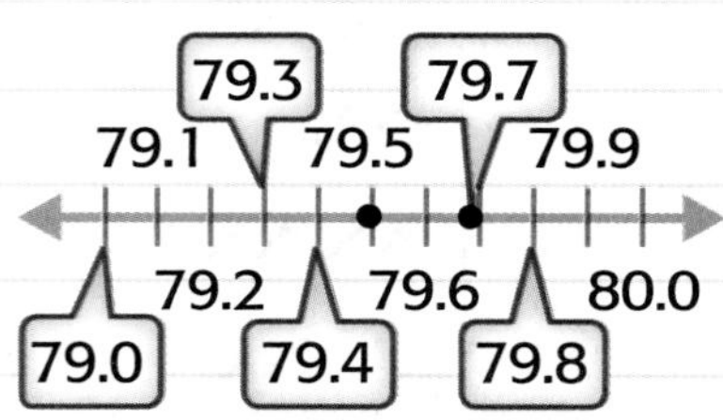

79.7 is to the right of 79.5. So, 79.7 > 79.5.

Another Way: Create Models

All of the numbers begin with 79, so you can create models for each decimal. Then compare and order the models.

Another Way: Place Value

Line up the decimal points. Then compare the digits in each place value position.

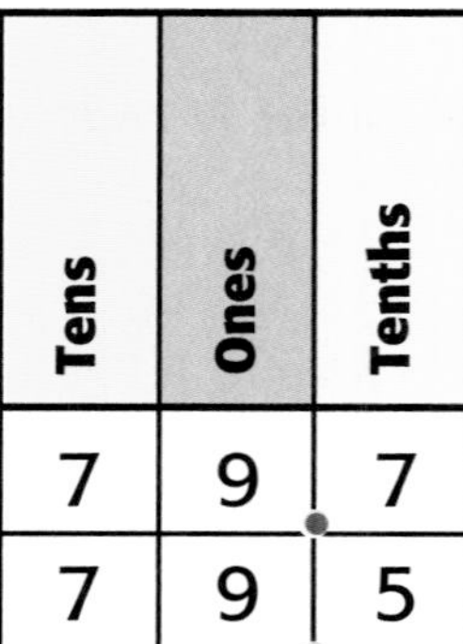

Tens	Ones	Tenths
7	9	7
7	9	5

In the tenths place, 7 > 5. So, 79.7 is greater than 79.5.

So, Doria has the higher score.

You can also order decimals.

EXAMPLE **Order Decimals**

2 Order 9.86, 9.8, 9.92, and 9.09 from greatest to least.

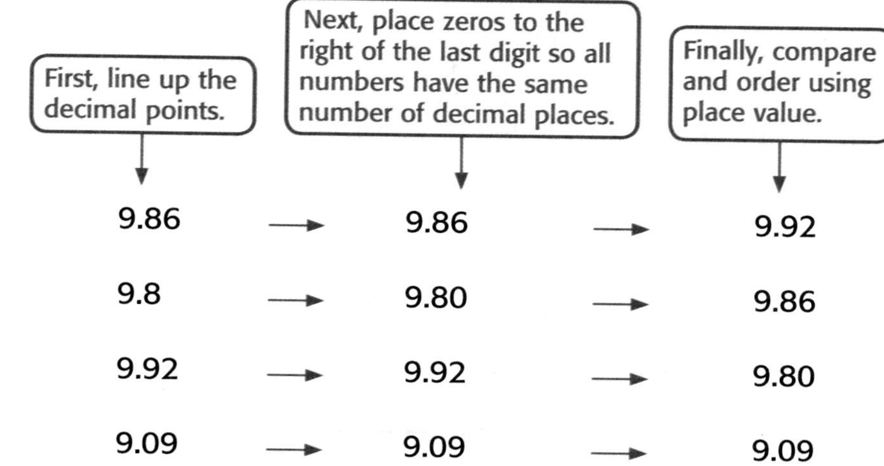
First, line up the decimal points.
Next, place zeros to the right of the last digit so all numbers have the same number of decimal places.
Finally, compare and order using place value.
9.86 → 9.86 → 9.92
9.8 → 9.80 → 9.86
9.92 → 9.92 → 9.80
9.09 → 9.09 → 9.09

The order from greatest to least is 9.92, 9.86, 9.8, and 9.09.

Online **Personal Tutor at** tx.gr4math.com

CHECK What You Know

Compare. Write >, <, or =. Use models if needed. See Example 1 (p. 546)

1. 0.2 ● 0.6 **2.** 12.07 ● 1.207 **3.** 5.60 ● 5.6

Order from greatest to least. Use models if needed. See Example 2 (p. 547)

4. **3.2, 4.5, 3.9, 4.1** **5.** **0.12, 1.2, 1.21, 12.0** **6.** $6.52, $5.62, $6.50, $5.60

Use the number line to compare and order.

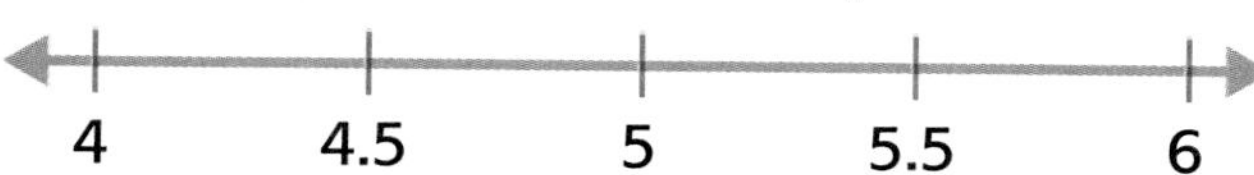
4
4.5
5
5.5
6

7. 5.7, 5.2, 4.7, 4.2 **8.** 4.2, 4.8, 6.2, 5.8

9. **Measurement** Four friends are going to different summer camps. The table shows the distance between each camp and their hometown. Order the distances from least to greatest.

Traveling to Camp	
Name	**Distance (mi)**
Bill	64.25
Sami	42.5
Angel	64.87
Irena	42.35

10. Talk About It Tell how to order 5.5, 5.3, 5.4, and 5.0 from greatest to least.

Practice and Problem Solving

EXTRA PRACTICE See page R47.

Compare. Write >, <, or =. See Example 1 (p. 546)

11. 0.74 ● 7.4 **12.** 16.33 ● 16.3 **13.** 0.56 ● 0.58 **14.** 0.8 ● 0.80

15. 1 ● 0.09 **16.** 0.90 ● 0.9 **17.** 82.6 ● 82.60 **18.** 1.06 ● 1.05

Order from greatest to least. Use models if needed. See Example 2 (p. 547)

19. 0.4, 0.42, 0.54 **20.** 0.08, 0.80, 0.82 **21.** $12.50, $1.25,$ $12.05

22. $19.62, $19.56, $19.60 **23.** 0.5, 0.55, 0.6 **24.** 68.16, 81.6, 68.1

Use the number line to compare and order.

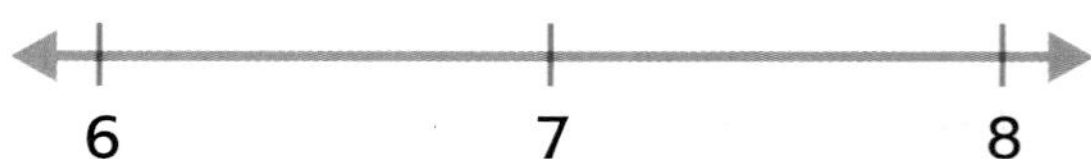

25. 6.3, 8.1, 7.5, 7.7 **26.** 7.5, 6.2, 7.75, 6.25

27. Marlon averages 5.6 rebounds per game. Tina averages 5.9 rebounds per game. Bret averages 4.3 rebounds per game. Who averages the most rebounds? Explain.

28. **Measurement** The table shows the distances Seth biked. Did he bike more the first weekend or the last weekend?

Distance Biked in July	
Weekend	**Distance (mi)**
1	3.25
2	3.5
3	3
4	3.6

29. **Measurement** Rita ran the 100-meter dash four times, which is timed in seconds. Her times were 16.25, 15.36, 16.55, and 15.23. What was her slowest time?

H.O.T. Problems

30. **OPEN ENDED** Draw a number line that contains two whole numbers. Divide the number line in tenths. Identify the location of three decimals on the number line.

31. **NUMBER SENSE** What number is halfway between 4.36 and 4.48 on a number line?

32. **WRITING IN MATH** Write a real-world problem about comparing or ordering decimals.

Mid-Chapter Check

Chapter 13

Lessons 13-1 through 13-5

Write a fraction and a decimal for each shaded part. (Lesson 13-1)

1.

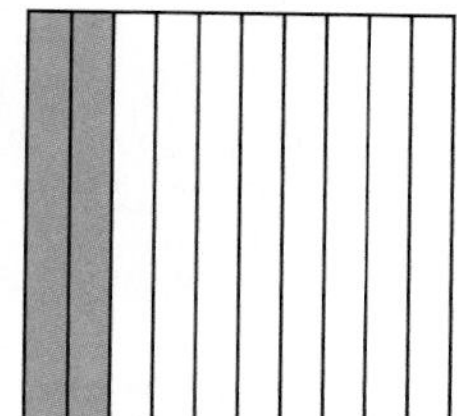

2.

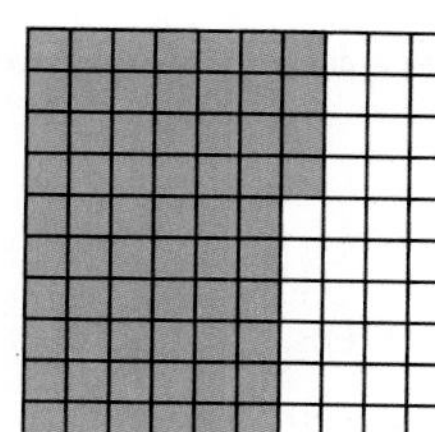

Write each fraction as a decimal. (Lesson 13-1)

3. $\frac{7}{10}$

4. $\frac{34}{100}$

Write as a fraction and as a decimal. (Lesson 13-1)

5. three-fourths

6. one-fifth

7. **TEST PRACTICE** Which of the following is *six and six hundredths*? (Lesson 13-1)

A 0.66

B 6.06

C 6.6

D $6\frac{6}{10}$

Write each as a decimal. (Lesson 13-2)

8. $9\frac{1}{4}$

9. $10\frac{3}{5}$

10. $7\frac{1}{5}$

11. $2\frac{3}{4}$

Write each as a mixed number and decimal. (Lesson 13-2)

12. seven and three-fourths

13. two and six-tenths

14. **TEST PRACTICE** Which number represents the shaded parts of the figure? (Lesson 13-2)

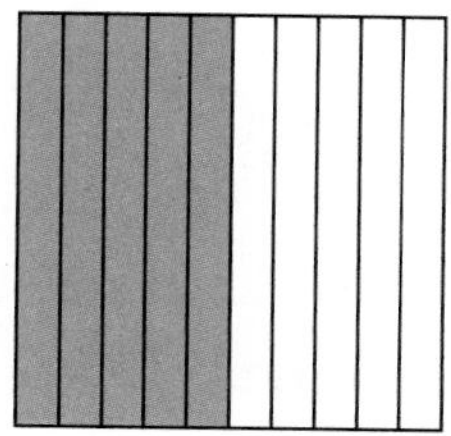

F 0.05

G 0.5

H 5.0

J 5.5

Solve. Use the *make a model* strategy. (Lesson 13-3)

15. Dasan has 18 coins. One half are nickels. One third are dimes. The rest are quarters. How much are Dasan's coins worth?

Name the points *N* and *P* represent on the number line. (Lesson 13-4)

16.

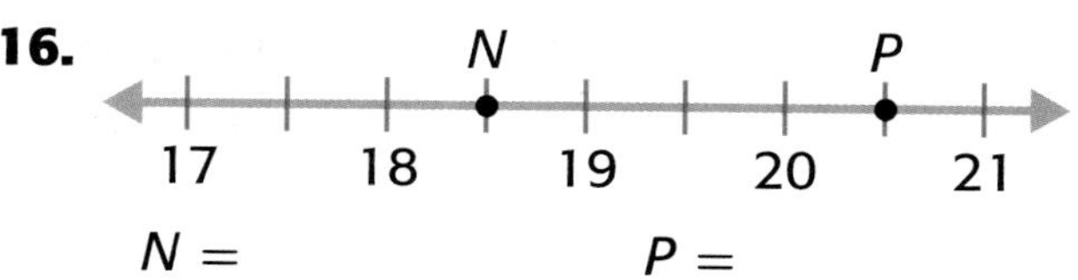

$N =$ $P =$

Compare. Write >, <, or =. (Lesson 13-5)

17. 6.4 ● 6.4

18. 13.09 ● 1.309

Order from greatest to least. (Lesson 13-5)

19. 1.2, 2.5, 1.9, 2.1

20. 0.32, 3.2, 1.31, 13.0

21. **WRITING IN MATH** Explain why $\frac{3}{10}$ and $\frac{30}{100}$ are equal.

13-6 Problem-Solving Investigation

MAIN IDEA I will choose the best strategy to solve a problem.

Targeted TEKS 4.14 The student applies Grade 4 mathematics to solve problems connected to everyday experiences and activities in and outside of school. (B) **Solve problems that incorporate understanding the problem, making a plan, carrying out the plan, and evaluating the solution for reasonableness.** *Also addresses TEKS 4.14(C).*

P.S.I. TEAM +

SANDEEP: **My father and I each ate $\frac{1}{4}$ of a pizza. My brother ate 1 more slice than I did and twice as many as my mother. She ate 2 slices.**

YOUR MISSION: **Find the number of slices of pizza Sandeep's family ate.**

Understand	You know how much pizza each person ate. Find the total number of slices of pizza the family ate.
Plan	Use logical reasoning to determine the answer.
Solve	Start with what is known. • Mother: 2 slices • Brother: twice as much as his mother or $2 \times 2 = 4$ slices • Sandeep: 1 less slice than his brother or 3 slices • Father: 3 slices So, Sandeep's family ate $2 + 4 + 3 + 3 = 12$ slices of pizza.
Check	Look back at the problem. Sandeep and his father → $\frac{1}{4}$ of $12 = 3$ Sandeep's brother → $3 + 1 = 4$ Sandeep's mother → $4 \div 2 = 2$. $3 + 3 + 4 + 2 = 12$. So, the answer is correct.

Mixed Problem Solving

See page R47.

Use any strategy shown below to solve. Tell what strategy you used.

PROBLEM-SOLVING STRATEGIES
- Look for a pattern.
- Work a simpler problem.
- Use logical reasoning.
- Draw a picture.
- Make a model.

1. Gina cut an apple into 8 slices and ate 3 of them. Rudy cut an apple into 4 slices and ate 2 of them. If the apples were the same size, who ate more?

2. Sarah's dad gave her the money shown. He gave $7 to each of her two brothers. He had $16 left. How much money did Sarah's dad start with?

3. Craig paid $75 for a snowboard that he used 32 times. Diego paid twice as much as Craig but used his board 82 times. Who got a better deal per use? Explain.

4. Felicia is building a garden. The garden will have an area of 48 square feet. Give three possible dimensions.

5. What is the rule for the pattern shown? What number comes next?

   5, 13, 10, 18, 15, . . .

6. **Measurement** Adriano's driveway is rectangular in shape. The area of the driveway is 345 square feet. The length is shown. What is the width of the driveway?

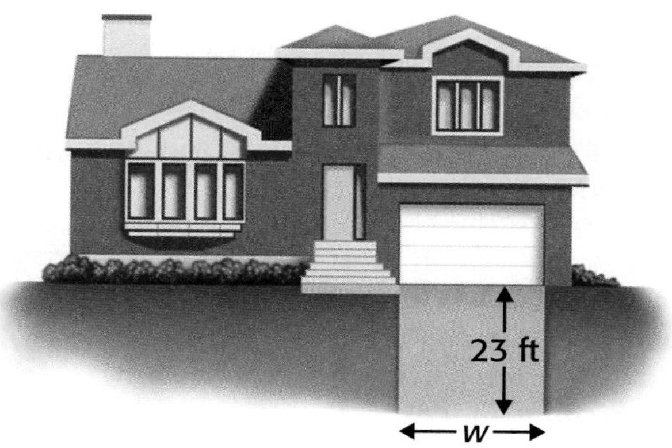

7. Paige and Mustafa were in a snow skiing competition. Paige earned a score of 88.6, while Mustafa earned a score of 88.59. Who won? Explain.

8. Alani started her homework at 4:25 P.M. She stopped at 5:15 P.M. to eat dinner. She started her work again at 5:50 P.M. She then worked another 15 minutes and finished. How many minutes did she do her homework?

9. **WRITING IN MATH** The sum of Roman and his younger sister's age together equals 24. Roman's age is twice the amount of his sister's. How old is Roman and his sister? Explain how you found your answer.

Fraction and Decimal Equivalents

GET READY to Learn

Nicole and Austin's family is taking a trip. Nicole says that the odometer shows they have driven 0.5 mile. Austin says $\frac{1}{2}$ mile. Can they both be correct?

MAIN IDEA

I will learn about fractions and decimal equivalents.

Targeted TEKS 4.2 The student describes and compares fractional parts of whole objects or sets of objects.
(D) **Relate decimals to fractions that name tenths and hundredths using concrete objects and pictorial models.**
Also addresses TEKS 4.10.

When a fraction and a decimal name the same amount, they are fraction and decimal equivalents.

EXAMPLE Fraction and Decimal Equivalents

1 **Determine whether 0.5 and $\frac{1}{2}$ are equivalent.**

Use tenths and hundredths grids to model that 0.5 and $\frac{1}{2}$ name the same amount.

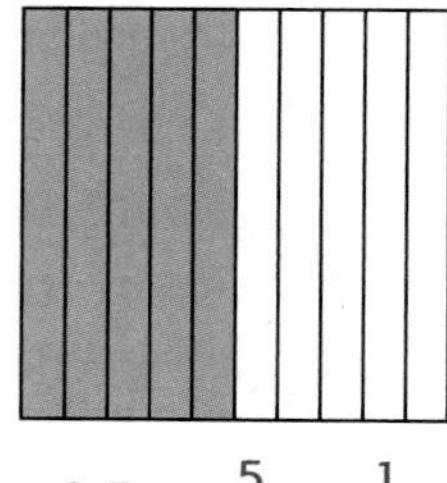

$0.5 = \frac{5}{10} = \frac{1}{2}$

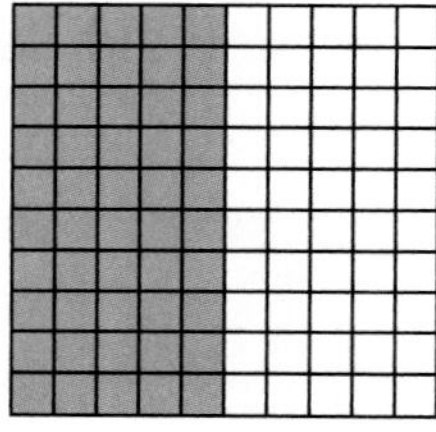

$0.50 = \frac{50}{100} = \frac{1}{2}$

The number lines also show that they name the same amount.

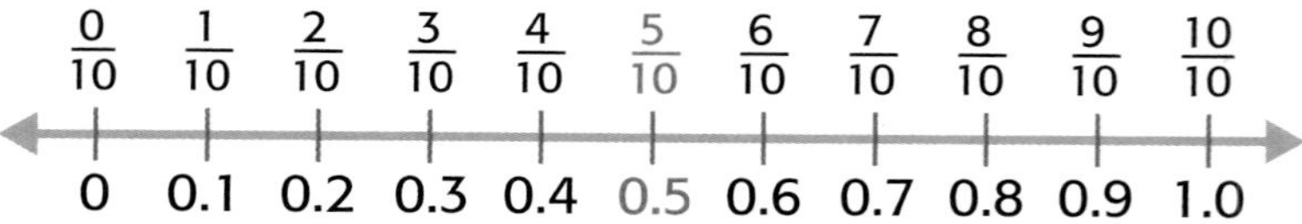

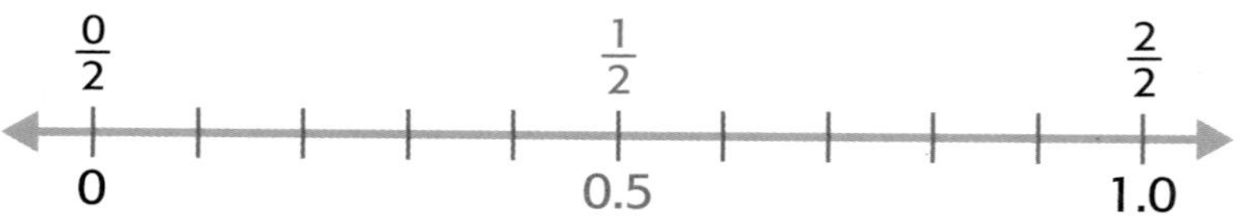

So, 0.5 and $\frac{1}{2}$ are equivalent.

To find a decimal that is equivalent to a fraction, it helps to write the fraction with a denominator of 10 or 100.

EXAMPLE **Find Fraction and Decimal Equivalents**

2 **Write a fraction and decimal to describe the shaded part of the model.**

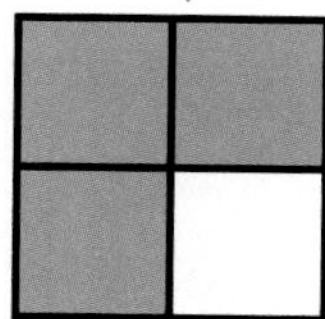

$$\frac{3 \times 25}{4 \times 25} = \frac{75}{100}$$ ← THINK What number can you multiply the denominator by to get 100?

$\frac{75}{100} = 0.75$ Write $\frac{75}{100}$ as a decimal.

So, $\frac{3}{4}$ and 0.75 describe the shaded part of the model.

Online **Personal Tutor at** tx.gr4math.com

Here are some common fraction and decimal equivalents.

KEY CONCEPT **Fraction-Decimal Equivalents**

$\frac{1}{2} = 0.5$	$\frac{1}{4} = 0.25$	$\frac{2}{4} = 0.5$	$\frac{3}{4} = 0.75$
$\frac{1}{5} = 0.2$	$\frac{2}{5} = 0.4$	$\frac{3}{5} = 0.6$	$\frac{4}{5} = 0.8$

CHECK What You Know

Write a fraction and decimal to describe the shaded part of each model. See Examples 1 and 2 (pp. 552–553)

1. 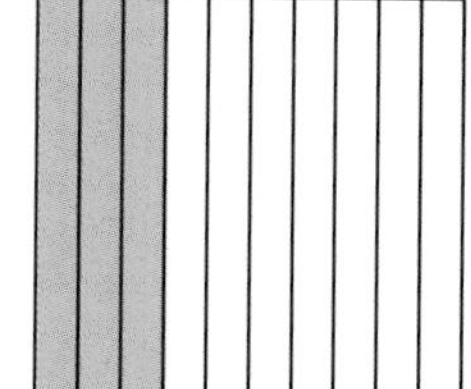

2. 

3. 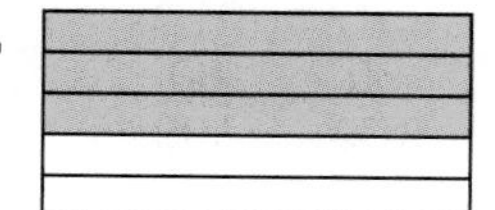

4. 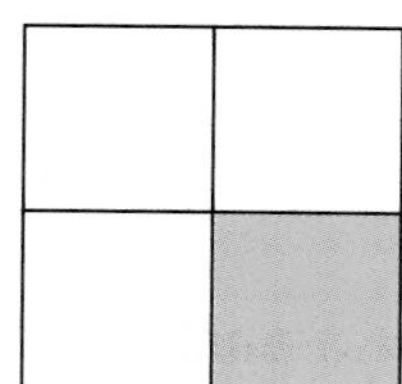

Model each fraction. Then write as a decimal. See Example 2 (p. 553)

5. $\frac{6}{10}$

6. $\frac{6}{100}$

7. $\frac{2}{4}$

8. $\frac{4}{5}$

9. Lupe got 20 out of 25 questions correct on a quiz. Write her score as a decimal and a fraction.

10. 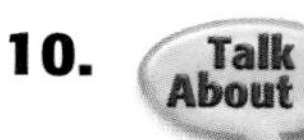

What do you notice about $\frac{3}{4}$, $\frac{6}{8}$, and $\frac{12}{16}$?

Practice and Problem Solving

Write a fraction and decimal to describe the shaded part of each model. See Examples 1 and 2 (pp. 552–553)

11. 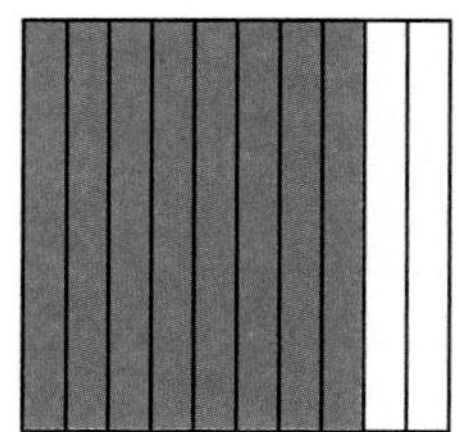

12. 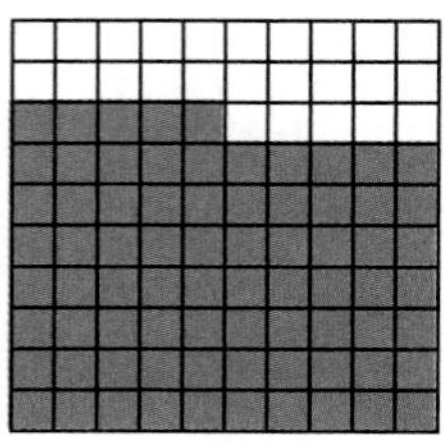

13. 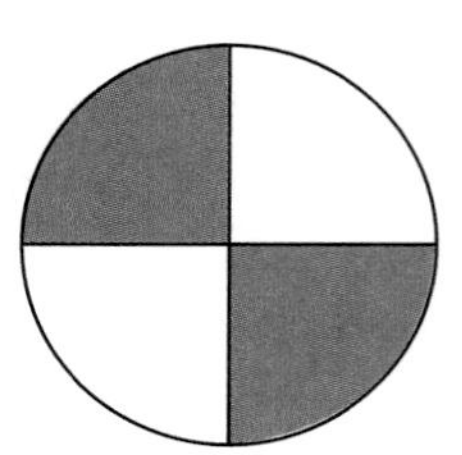

14. 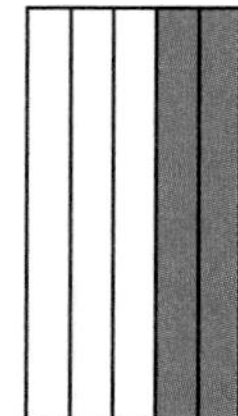

15. 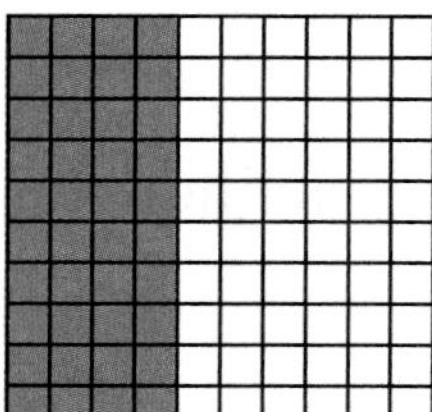

16. 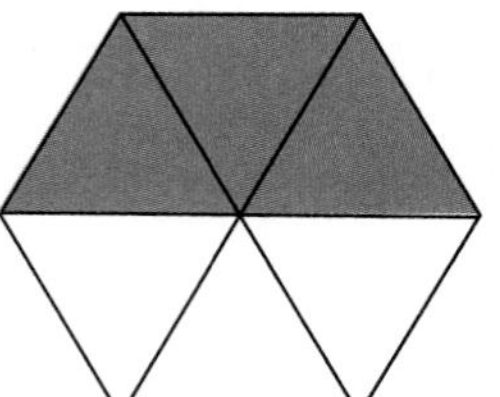

17. 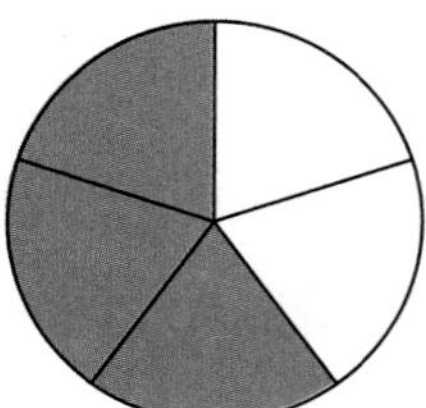

18. 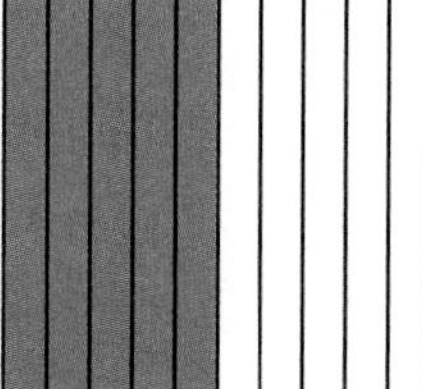

Model each fraction. Then write as a decimal. See Example 2 (p. 553)

19. $\frac{78}{100}$ **20.** $\frac{4}{10}$ **21.** $\frac{3}{5}$ **22.** $\frac{35}{100}$

23. $\frac{1}{4}$ **24.** $\frac{4}{5}$ **25.** $\frac{7}{25}$ **26.** $\frac{1}{10}$

Recreate the number line using decimal equivalents. See Example 1 (p. 552)

27. 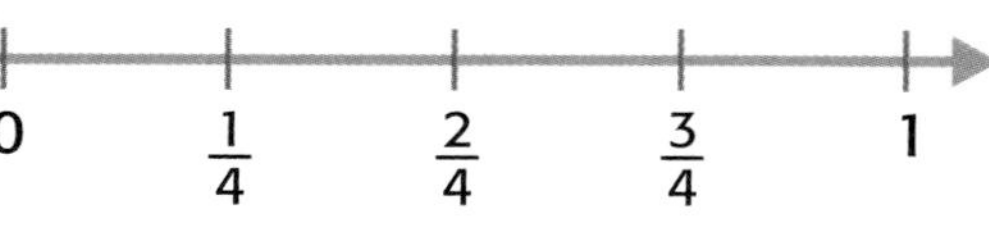

28. 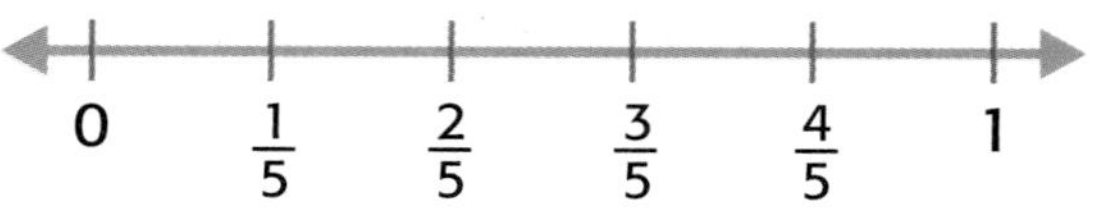

29. 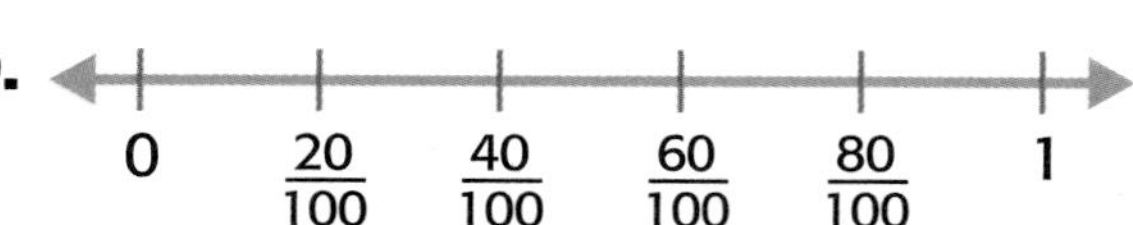

30. 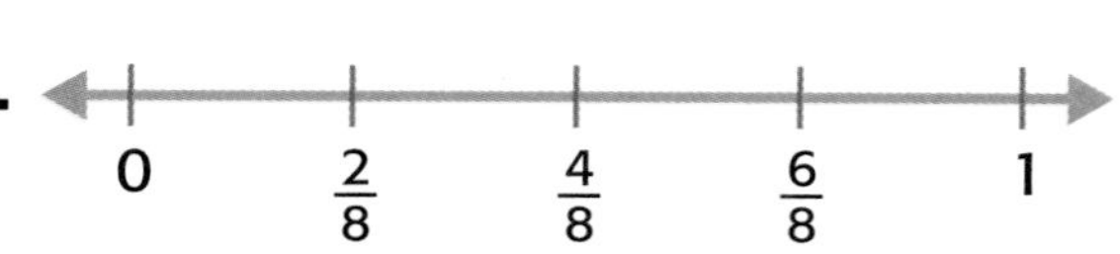

Write each amount as a fraction and a decimal.

31. Measurement Diana swam 3 out of 4 laps.

32. Vince read 6 out of 10 pages in a chapter of a book.

33. Robin ate 8 out of her 10 orange slices.

34. Cathy has completed 18 out of 20 math problems.

35. Maya has painted 1 out of 4 walls of her bedroom.

36. Jack has opened 3 out of 10 of his birthday presents.

H.O.T. Problems

37. OPEN ENDED Create a model and shade in a fraction of it. Write two fractions and a decimal to describe the shaded area of the model.

38. CHALLENGE Talia collects stuffed frogs. She has 25 frogs, and $\frac{2}{25}$ of them are multicolored. The rest are green. How many green frogs are in her collection? Explain how you found your answer.

39. WRITING IN MATH Demetri is completing $0.\blacksquare = \frac{5}{50}$. Explain how he can find the correct answer.

TEST Practice

40. Look at the number line and detemine which order of numbers correctly shows the location of the points. (Lesson 13-5)

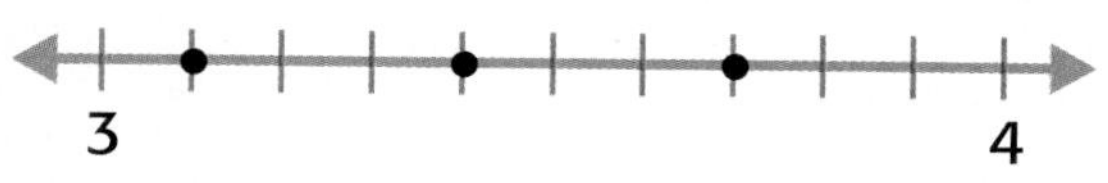

A 3.1, 3.3, $3\frac{7}{10}$

B 3.1, $3\frac{4}{10}$, 3.7

C 3.01, 3.04, $3\frac{7}{100}$

D $3\frac{1}{10}$, 3.1, $3\frac{4}{10}$

41. Which of the number sentences is false? (Lesson 13-5)

F $\frac{1}{4} = 0.25$

G $0.5 = \frac{4}{8}$

H $1.2 = 1\frac{1}{4}$

J $0.2 = 0.20$

Spiral Review

42. Elliott's age and his brother's age have a sum of 15. Elliott's age is twice as much as his brother's. How old are the boys? (Lesson 13-6)

Compare. Write >, <, or =. (Lesson 13-5)

43. 0.70 ● 0.07

44. 8.75 ● 8.7

45. 19.70 ● 19.7

Identify these quadrilaterals as *square, rhombus, rectangle, parallelogram,* or *trapezoid.* (Lesson 8-6)

46.

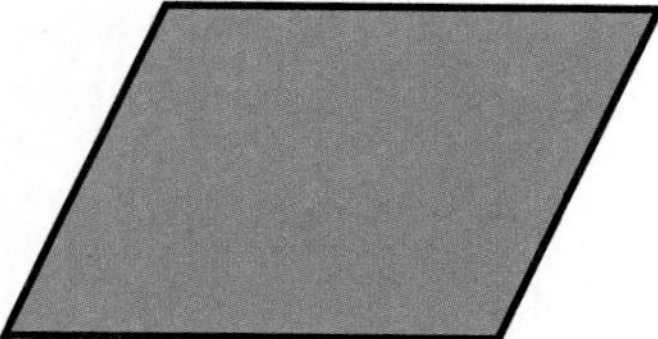

47.

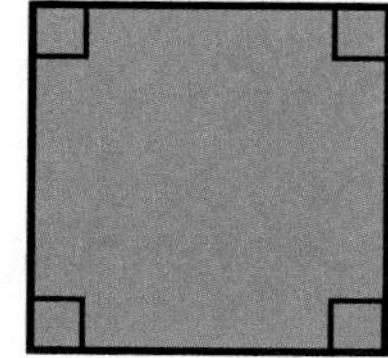

Estimate. Check your estimate. (Lesson 7-4)

48. $153 \div 3$

49. $347 \div 5$

50. $618 \div 8$

Problem Solving in Music

Decimal Note-ation

Like numbers, musical notes are a universal language. Musical notes are based on fractions. The most common musical notes include whole, half, quarter, eighth, and sixteenth notes. These values represent the duration of the notes. The durations of the notes are not specific; they are relative to the other notes. For example, a one-eighth note is twice as long as a one-sixteenth note, a one-fourth note is twice as long as a one-eighth note, and so on.

Did You Know?

Beethoven was the first musician to use the one-hundred twenty-eighth note.

Targeted TEKS 4.14 The student applies Grade 4 mathematics to solve problems connected to everyday experiences and activities in and outside of school. **(A) Identify the mathematics in everyday situations.**

Musical Notes and Equivalent Fractions		
Note	**Notation**	**Fractional Equivalent**
Whole		$\frac{1}{1}$
Half		$\frac{1}{2}$
Quarter		$\frac{1}{4}$

Real-World Math

Use table above to answer each problem.

Write the value of each musical note as a decimal.

1.

2.

3. 

4. Refer to Exercises 1–3. Draw a number line that shows these values.

Write the value of each musical note as a mixed number. Then write each mixed number as a decimal.

5. 

6. 

7. 

8. Draw three musical notes that represent a value of 2.5.

9. Draw four musical notes that represent a value of $2\frac{1}{4}$.

Decimals, Fractions, and Mixed Numbers

GET READY to Learn

The table shows the number of inches Walter has grown over four years. At what age did Walter grow the most inches? the fewest inches?

Walter's Change in Growth	
Age	Growth (in.)
7	2.5
8	$2\frac{1}{4}$
9	2.0
10	$2\frac{3}{4}$

MAIN IDEA

I will compare and order decimals, fractions, and mixed numbers.

Targeted TEKS 4.2 The student describes and compares fractional parts of whole objects or sets of objects. (D) **Relate decimals to fractions that name tenths and hundredths using concrete objects and pictorial models.** *Also addresses TEKS 4.1(B), 4.10.*

To compare fractions and decimals, you can write the fractions as decimals and then compare.

Real-World EXAMPLE

1 MEASUREMENT At what age did Walter grow the most inches? the fewest inches?

Step 1 Write $2\frac{1}{4}$ and $2\frac{3}{4}$ as decimals.

$2\frac{1}{4} = 2.25$ $\quad$ $2\frac{3}{4} = 2.75$

Step 2 Compare 2.5, $2\frac{1}{4}$, 2.0, and $2\frac{3}{4}$.

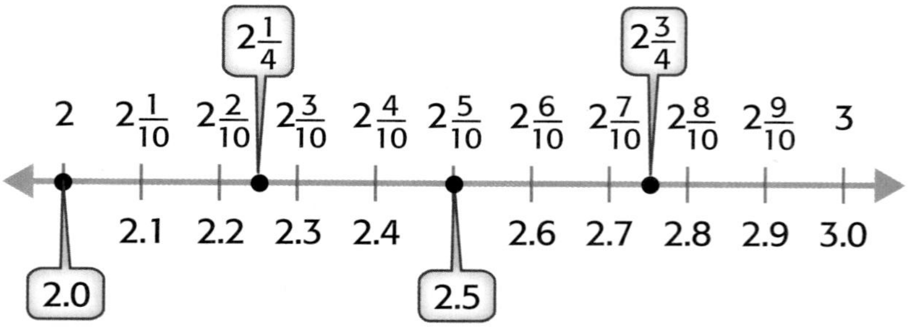

The order from greatest to least is $2\frac{3}{4}$, 2.5, $2\frac{1}{4}$, and 2.0. So, Walter grew the most when he was 10 and the least when he was 9.

Personal Tutor at tx.gr4math.com

CHECK What You Know

Use a number line or model to compare. Write <, >, or =. See Example 1 (p. 558)

1. 1.25 ● $1\frac{1}{4}$ **2.** 9.2 ● $9\frac{2}{10}$ **3.** $3\frac{3}{100}$ ● 3.3 **4.** 6.6 ● $6\frac{5}{10}$

Use a number line to order from greatest to least. See Example 1 (p. 558)

5. 6.34, $6\frac{1}{4}$, 6.5, and $6\frac{21}{100}$

6. $6\frac{1}{5}$, 6.48, $6\frac{4}{10}$, and 6.12

7. Which plant food produced a plant with highest growth? Explain.

Plant Food	Feed Me!	Magic Touch	Feed Booster	Garden Growth
Plant Growth (in.)	$3\frac{7}{10}$	3.1	$3\frac{1}{2}$	3.36

8. Talk About It Is the number sentence $5.5 = 5\frac{3}{6} = \frac{44}{8}$ true? Explain.

Practice and Problem Solving

EXTRA PRACTICE See page R48.

Use a number line or model to compare. Write <, >, or =. See Example 1 (p. 558)

9. 7 ● $6\frac{9}{10}$ **10.** 3.03 ● $3\frac{3}{100}$ **11.** $\frac{16}{4}$ ● 4 **12.** 8.2 ● 8

13. 5.3 ● 5.03 **14.** $4\frac{1}{10}$ ● 4.1 **15.** 12.5 ● $12\frac{2}{5}$ **16.** 15.36 ● 15.4

Use a number line to order from greatest to least. See Example 1 (p. 558)

17. $10\frac{1}{2}$, 10.9, $10\frac{36}{100}$, 10.75

18. 5.71, $5\frac{67}{100}$, $4\frac{5}{10}$, 4.75

19. $\frac{5}{10}$, $\frac{3}{4}$, 0.38, $\frac{25}{100}$, $\frac{1}{1}$

20. $\frac{4}{5}$, 2.25, $2\frac{3}{4}$, 2.77

Write the letter that represents each mixed number or decimal.

See Example 1 (p. 558)

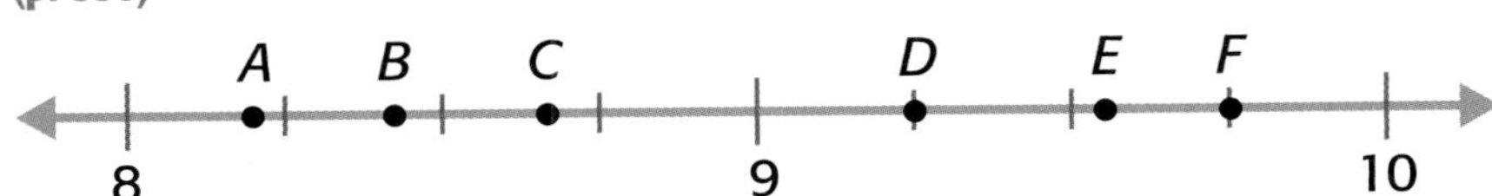

21. $9\frac{6}{10}$ **22.** 8.2 **23.** $8\frac{2}{5}$ **24.** $9\frac{1}{4}$

25. The table at the right shows the amount of rainfall Capitol City received during three months. Order the amounts of rain received from greatest to least.

Month	Rainfall (in.)
March	$2\frac{89}{100}$
April	3.25
May	$3\frac{2}{10}$

H.O.T. Problems

26. **FIND THE ERROR** Alicia and Leonardo are identifying the number point *C* represents. Who is correct? Explain.

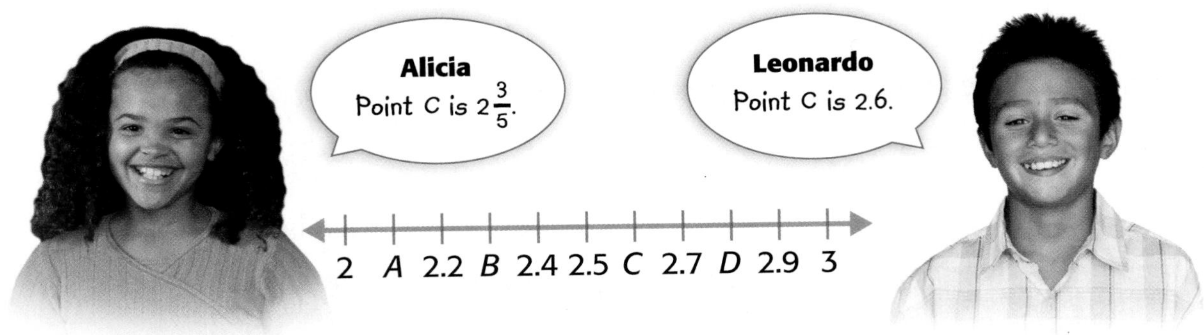

27. **WHICH ONE DOESN'T BELONG?** Identify the number that does not belong with the others. Explain.

three and five tenths	$3 + 0.5$	$3\frac{1}{2}$	3.05

TEST Practice

28. Which fraction means the same as 0.25? **(Lesson 13-7)**

A $\frac{2}{10}$ **C** $\frac{2}{5}$

B $\frac{1}{4}$ **D** $\frac{5}{10}$

29. Which letter represents the number closest to 3.6? **(Lesson 13-7)**

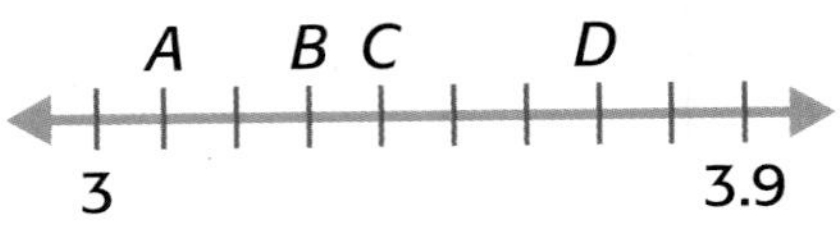

F *A* **H** *C*

G *B* **J** *D*

Spiral Review

Model each fraction. Then write as a decimal. **(Lesson 13-7)**

30. $\frac{4}{10}$ 31. $\frac{35}{100}$ 32. $\frac{4}{5}$

33. Enrico went to a movie. It started at 3:25 P.M. and lasted 135 minutes. What time was the movie over? **(Lesson 13-6)**

Order from greatest to least. Use models if needed. **(Lesson 13-5)**

34. 1.5, 1.8, 1.2, 2.1 35. 3.2, 2.3, 3.23, 2.32 36. $7.80, $8.78, $7.88, $8.70

Math Online Self-Check Quiz at tx.gr4math.com

Fraction and Decimal Game

Compare Decimals to Fractions

Get Ready!

Players: 2

You Will Need: 10 index cards

Get Set!

On each index card, write a statement using $>$, $<$, or $=$. Write 5 true statements and 5 false statements. A few examples are shown to the right.

$0.25 < \frac{1}{3}$	$0.5 > \frac{10}{20}$
$0.75 = \frac{3}{4}$	$0.8 < \frac{75}{100}$

Go!

- Shuffle the cards.
- Spread out the cards face down on a desk.
- Player 1 turns over an index card and must say whether the statement is true or false.
- Player 1 keeps the card if the answer is correct, and draws again. If Player 1 is wrong, the index card is put back. Player 2 takes a turn.
- The player who collects the most cards, wins.

CHAPTER 13

Study Guide and Review

Be sure the following Key Vocabulary words and Key Concepts are written in your Foldable.

Fractions and Decimals | Compare and Order Decimals | Relate Mixed Numbers and Decimals | Decimals, Fractions, and Mixed Numbers

BIG Ideas

Read, Write, and Model Decimals (pp. 533–545)

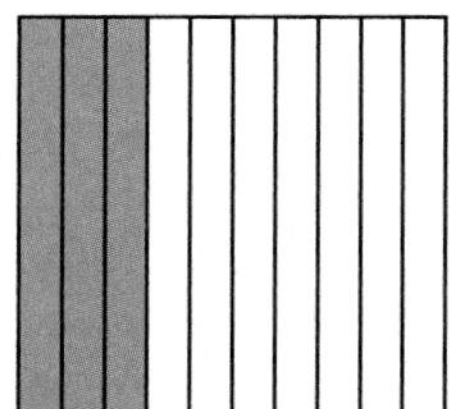

three-tenths

$\frac{3}{10}$ or 0.3

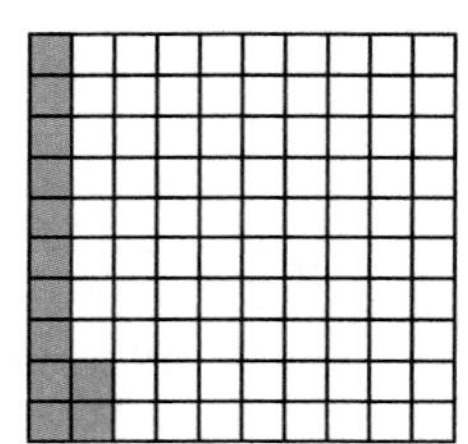

twelve-hundredths

$\frac{12}{100}$ or 0.12

Compare and Order Decimals (pp. 546–548)

- You can compare and order decimals, fractions, and mixed numbers using a number line.

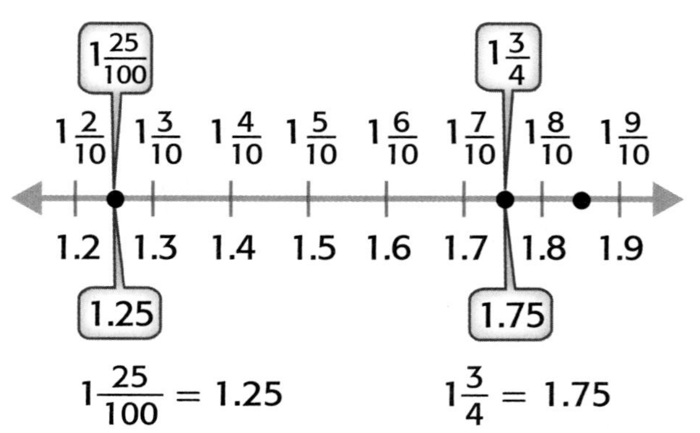

$1\frac{25}{100} = 1.25$ $1\frac{3}{4} = 1.75$

Key Vocabulary

decimal (p. 535)
decimal point (p. 535)
hundredth (p. 536)
tenth (p. 536)

Vocabulary Check

Complete each sentence with the correct vocabulary word.

1. In 0.56, the __?__ is between the 0 and 5.
2. A(n) __?__ is a number that uses place value, numbers, and a decimal point to show part of a whole.
3. The underlined digit in 1.<u>3</u>6 is in the __?__ place.
4. Since the number 0.36 has a 6 in the __?__ place, the fraction is written as $\frac{36}{100}$.
5. The underlined digit in 0.4<u>2</u> is in the __?__ place.
6. The __?__ is always directly to the right of the ones place.

Math Online Vocabulary Review at tx.gr4math.com

Lesson-by-Lesson Review

13-1 Tenths and Hundredths (pp. 535–537)

Example 1

Write eight tenths as two different decimals.

Write tenths

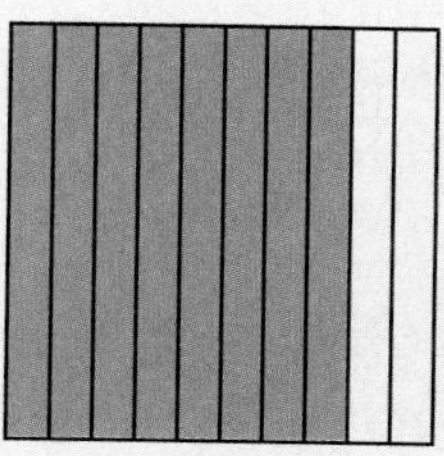

eight-tenths
0.8

Write hundredths

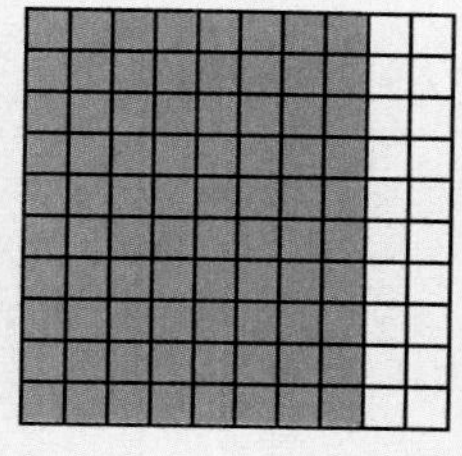

eighty hundredths
0.80

The decimals 0.8 and 0.80 are equivalent decimals.

7. Write a fraction and a decimal for the shaded part.

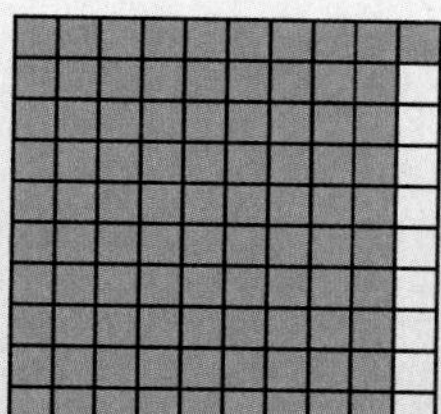

Write as a fraction and as a decimal.

8. three tenths

9. twenty-two hundredths

Write each fraction as two different decimals.

10. $\frac{1}{10}$

11. $\frac{60}{100}$

13-2 Relate Mixed Numbers and Decimals (pp. 538–541)

Example 2

Write $7\frac{52}{100}$ as a decimal.

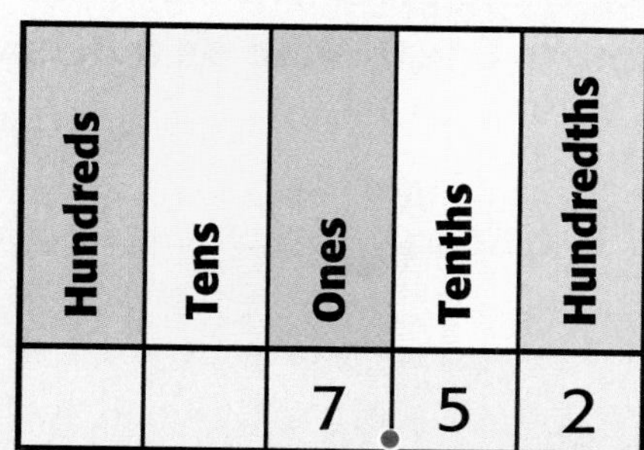

Hundreds	Tens	Ones	Tenths	Hundredths
		7	5	2

Mixed Number $7\frac{52}{100}$

Read seven and fifty-two hundredths

Write 7.52

Write each as a mixed number and decimal.

12. forty-six and seven tenths

13. fifty-one and three hundredths

Write each as a decimal.

14. $30\frac{3}{100}$

15. $7\frac{8}{10}$

16. A Burmese python is eight and twenty-three hundredths meters long. Write its length as a mixed number.

CHAPTER 13

Study Guide and Review

13-3 Problem-Solving Strategy: Make a Model (pp. 542–543)

Example 3
Leo jogged 3 miles. Then he jogged back to his house to get his skateboard. He rode his skateboard for 2 miles. How far did Leo travel?

You can draw a model.

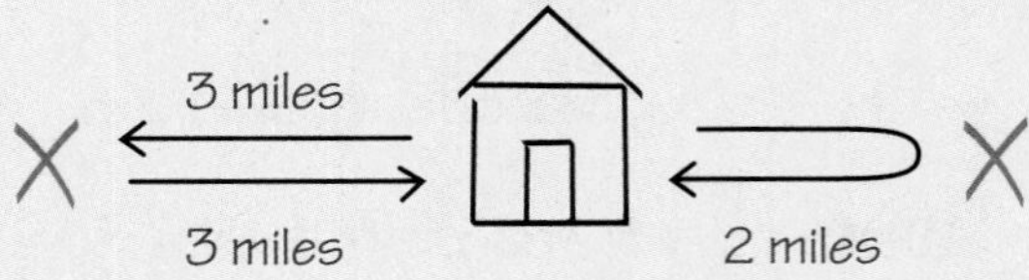

jogging route skateboard route

3 mi + 3 mi + 2 mi = 8 mi

So, Leo traveled 8 miles.

Check Work backward to check.
8 − 2 − 3 − 3 = 0 ✓

17. There are 12 coins in a piggy bank that equal $2. What could be the coins?

18. Raul paid $12.50 for a shirt and socks. The socks cost $1.75. How much was the shirt?

19. One-fourth of 36 houses receive 1 newspaper each day. The rest of the houses receive 2 newspapers each day. How many newspapers are delivered each day?

20. Raven wants to arrange 18 square tables into one larger rectangular-shaped table with the least perimeter possible. How many tables will be in each row?

13-4 Locate Fractions and Decimals on a Number Line (pp. 544–545)

Example 4
Locate 4.5 on the number line.

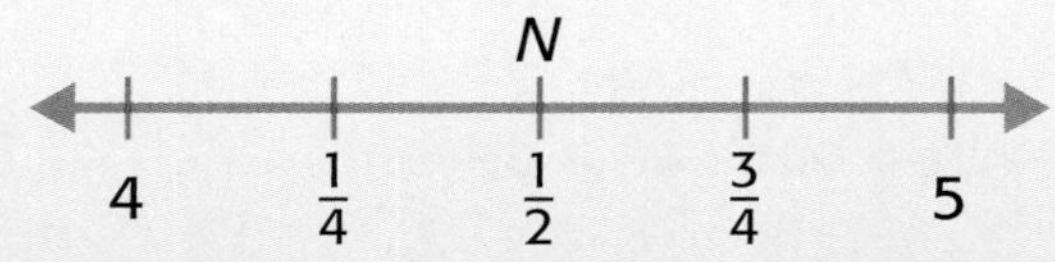

To find 4.5, first find 4. Then, find the $\frac{1}{2}$ mark between 4 and 5.

Points on a number line can be represented by a letter.

So, $N = 4\frac{1}{2}$ or 4.5.

Locate the given fraction on the number lines. Write as a decimal.

21. $5\frac{9}{10}$

N Y

5 $5\frac{1}{2}$ 6

22. $16\frac{1}{2}$

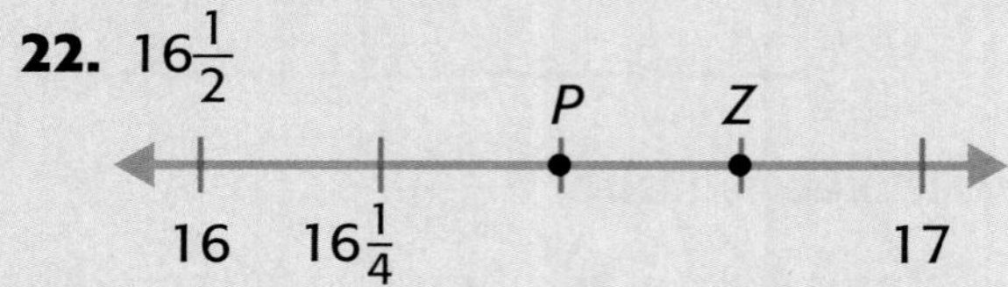

13-5 Compare and Order Decimals (pp. 546–548)

Example 5
Compare 7.26 and 7.62.

Hundreds	Tens	Ones	Tenths	Hundredths
		7	2	6
		7	6	2

Since the ones column has the same digits, compare the tenths place.

6 > 2. So, 7.62 > 7.26.

Compare. Write >, <, or =.

23. 6.50 ● 6.5
24. 2.06 ● 2.05
25. 0.58 ● 0.59
26. 0.78 ● 0.87

Order from greatest to least.

27. 54.06, 54.6, 54.04, 54.4

28. 80.17, 80.2, 80.3, 80.36

29. 4.3, 4.25, 4.4, 4.56

30. India has 2.04 percent of the world's coral reefs and Fiji has 3.52 percent. Which country has a greater percentage of the world's coral reefs?

13-6 Problem-Solving Investigation: Choose a Strategy (pp. 550–551)

Example 6
What is the rule for the pattern 0, 3, 6, 9, 12, ■? What number comes next?

Each number is 3 more than the number before it

0, 3, 6, 9, 12, ■
+3 +3 +3 +3

So, the rule is +3.

Use the rule, +3, to find the next number in the pattern. So, the next number in the pattern is 12 + 3 or 15.

Use any strategy to solve.

31. Steph is making a necklace with 15 beads. One third of the beads are red. The rest are black. How many are black?

32. Jonathan has a $20 bill. He buys a puzzle for $12.69. What will his change be?

33. Andrea pays the train fare of $2.75. What coins can Andrea use to pay for the fare using quarters, dimes, and nickels?

34. A biologist collected samples of bark from 258 trees. She took 4 samples from each tree. How many samples did she take in all?

13-7 Fraction and Decimal Equivalents (pp. 552–555)

Write a fraction and decimal to describe the shaded area.

Example 7

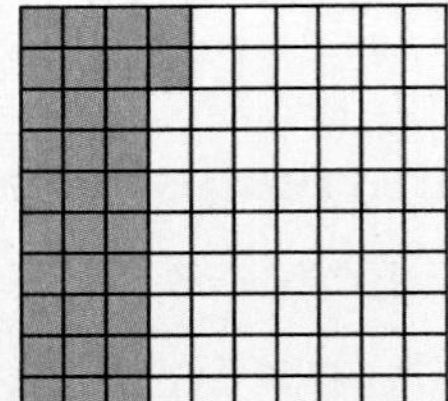

Thirty-two squares are shaded. So, that is $\frac{32}{100}$ or 0.32.

Example 8

Three triangles are shaded. So, that is $\frac{3}{6}$ or 0.5.

Write a fraction and decimal to describe the shaded area.

35.

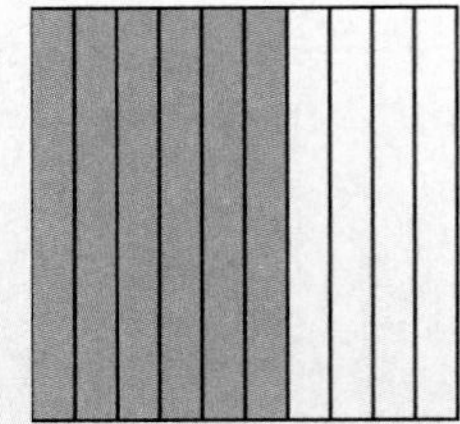

36.

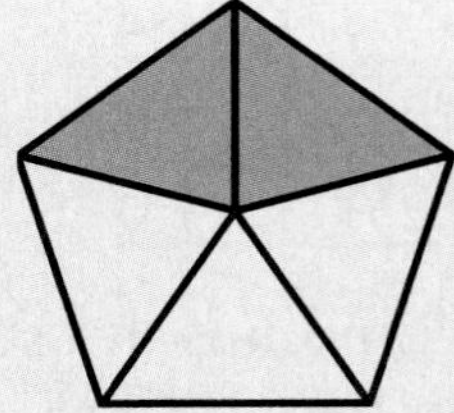

37. Della gave her brother part of a sandwich and said, "Here is your $\frac{1}{2}$ of the sandwich." Her brother said, "Actually, you ate $\frac{2}{4}$ of it." Who is correct? Explain.

13-8 Decimals, Fractions, and Mixed Numbers (pp. 558–561)

Example 9
Order 6.34, $6\frac{1}{4}$, 6.5, and $6\frac{21}{100}$ from greatest to least.

Write the fractions as decimals. Then, compare.

$6\frac{1}{4} = 6.25$ $\qquad$ $6\frac{21}{100} = 6.21$

The order is 6.5, 6.34, $6\frac{1}{4}$, $6\frac{21}{100}$.

Order from greatest to least.

38. $9\frac{1}{2}$; 9.9; $9\frac{36}{100}$; 9.75

39. 54.71; $54\frac{67}{100}$; $5\frac{5}{10}$; 56.75

40. Some of the greatest distances ever jumped in a long-jump competition are $\frac{89}{10}$ meters, $\frac{895}{100}$ meters, 8.99 meters, and $\frac{896}{100}$ meters. Order these distances from greatest to least.

Chapter 13 Chapter Test

For Exercises 1 and 2, tell whether each statement is *true* or *false*.

1. To compare fractions and decimals, you can write the fractions as decimals and then compare.

2. Some decimals can be represented as more than one equivalent fraction.

Compare. Write <, >, or =.

3. 1.75 ● $1\frac{3}{4}$

4. $3\frac{2}{100}$ ● 3.2

5. Write a fraction and a decimal for the shaded part.

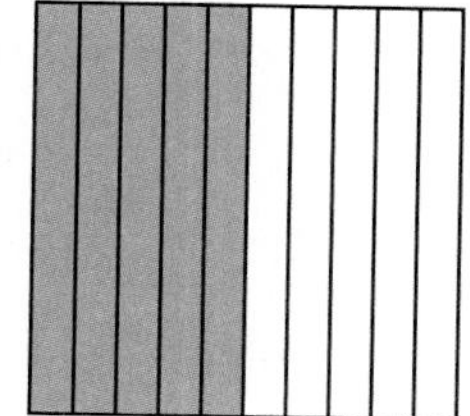

6. **TEST PRACTICE** Which of the number sentences is false?

A $\frac{1}{4} = 0.25$

B $0.75 = \frac{6}{8}$

C $1.2 = 1\frac{1}{4}$

D $0.2 = 0.20$

7. A teacher is arranging 24 desks in a classroom in even rows. How many desks should be placed in each row so that the teacher has the smallest perimeter to walk around?

Write as a fraction and as a decimal.

8. nine tenths

9. twenty hundredths

Write each as a decimal.

10. $4\frac{7}{10}$

11. $18\frac{65}{100}$

Write a fraction and a decimal to describe the shaded part of the model.

12.

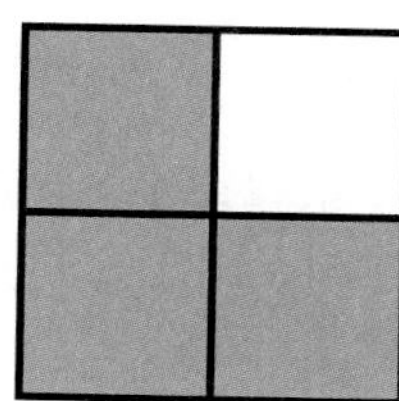

13.

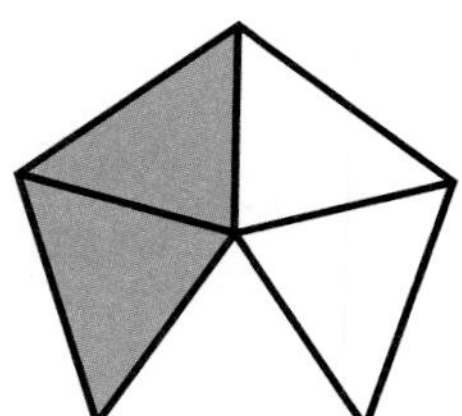

Order from greatest to least.

14. 7.8; 7.78; 8.78; 8.7

15. $\frac{3}{4}$; 2.25; $2\frac{3}{4}$; 1.75

16. 9.3; $9\frac{1}{4}$; $9\frac{3}{4}$; 9.5

17. **TEST PRACTICE** Look at the number line. Which order of numbers correctly shows the location of the points?

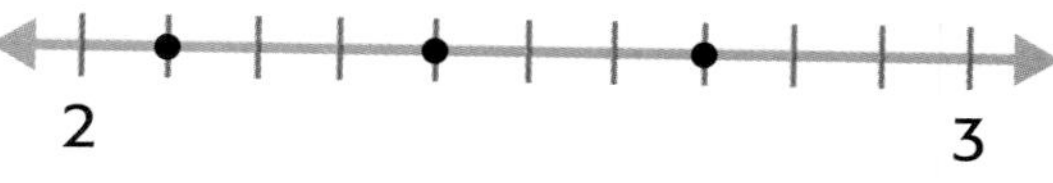

F 2.1, 2.2, $2\frac{7}{10}$

G 2.1, $2\frac{4}{10}$, 2.7

H 2.01, 2.04, $2\frac{7}{100}$

J $2\frac{1}{10}$, 2.1, $2\frac{4}{10}$

18. **WRITING IN MATH** Claire was given the following Exercise: $\frac{7}{10} = 0.\blacksquare$. Explain how you would find the correct answer.

CHAPTER 13

Texas Test Practice

Cumulative, Chapters 1–13

TEST Example

On the number line below, what number does point *M* represent?

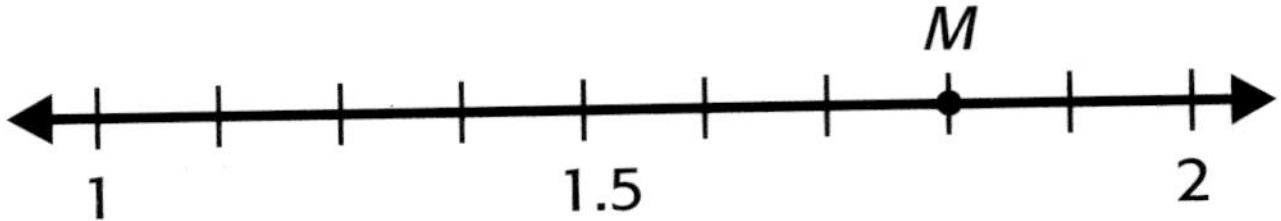

A 1.8

B 1.2

C 1.88

D 1.6

Read the Test Question

You need to find the number that point *M* represents.

Solve the Test Question

The number line is divided into tenths. It begins with 1 and ends with 2. The number 1.5 is marked.

Count on to find point *M*: 1.5, 1.6, 1.7, 1.8.

So, point *M* represents 1.8.

The answer is A.

Online **Personal Tutor at** tx.gr4math.com

TEST-TAKING TIP

You can relate decimals with money. Use the digits to the right of the decimal point as amounts less than 1.

Choose the best answer.

1. **On the number line below, what number does point *H* represent?**

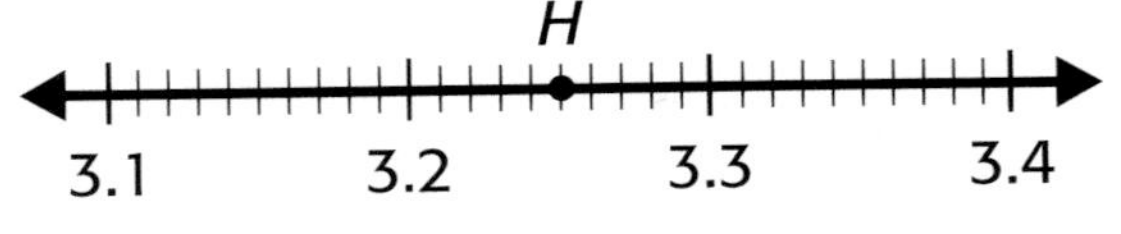

A 3.2

B 3.24

C 3.25

D 3.29

2. **On the number line below, what number does point *K* represent?**

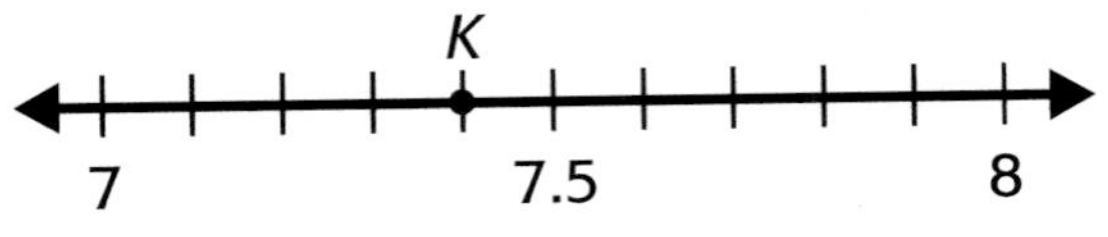

F 7.3

G 7.45

H 7.35

J 7.4

3. Which decimal is the same as $\frac{4}{5}$?

A 0.75
B 0.7
C 0.8
D 0.85

4. The clock below shows what time school ends. Volleyball practice begins 1 hour 15 minutes after school ends. At what time does volleyball practice begin?

F 3:30
G 3:45
H 4:00
J 4:15

5. What fraction means the same as 0.35?

A $\frac{35}{100}$
B $\frac{3}{10}$
C $\frac{35}{50}$
D $\frac{25}{80}$

6. There are 17 boxes of crayons in the closet. Each box contains 24 crayons. How many crayons are there altogether?

F 372
G 386
H 404
J 408

7. Which symbol makes the number sentence true?

1.453 _____ 1.428

A <
B >
C =
D +

8. GRIDDABLE What number comes next in the pattern below?

2, 7, 12, 17, 22, 27, __

9. Hannah's reading class begins at the time shown. This is 1 hour 30 minutes after school begins. At what time does school begin?

F 8:30
G 8:45
H 9:00
J 9:15

10. What solid figure has two circular faces?

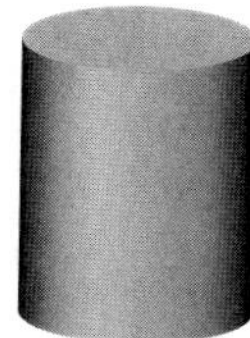

A cone
B cylinder
C prism
D sphere

Add and Subtract Decimals

BIG Idea How do I subtract decimals?

You can use models to subtract decimals.

Example One butterfly has a wingspan of 0.33 feet, and another has a wingspan of 0.25 feet. The model shows that the wingspan of the first butterfly is 0.33 − 0.25 or 0.08 feet longer than the other.

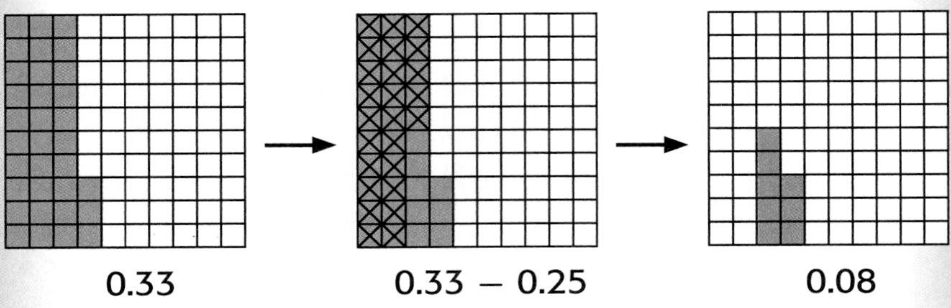

What will I learn in this chapter?

- Round decimals.
- Estimate decimal sums and differences.
- Add and subtract simple decimals.
- Solve problems by working backward.

Key Vocabulary

decimal

decimal point

estimate

sum

difference

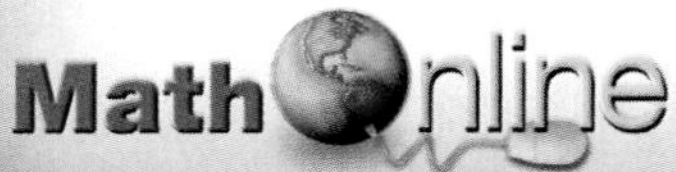

Student Study Tools at tx.gr4math.com

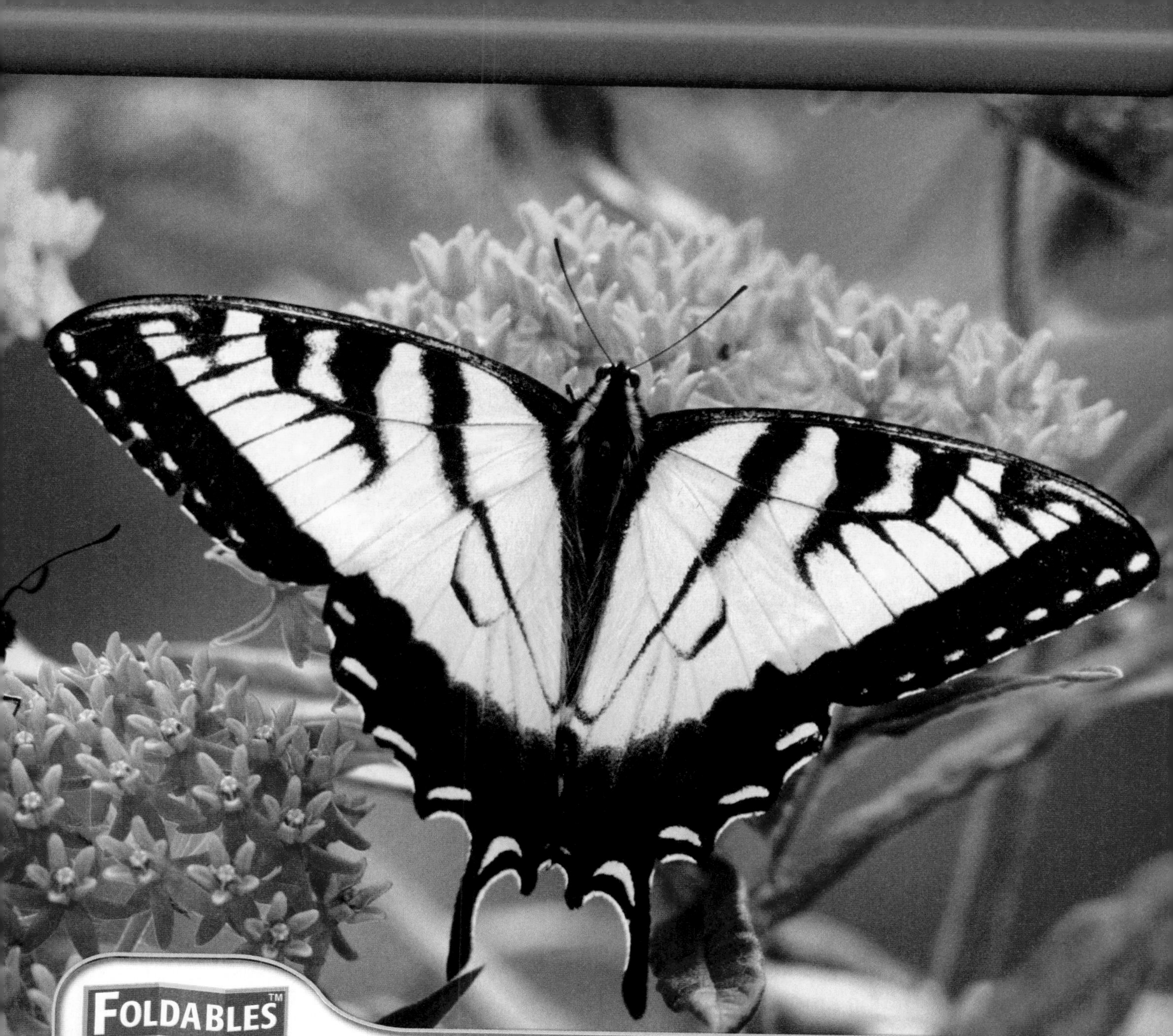

FOLDABLES™ Study Organizer

Make this Foldable to help you organize information about decimals. Begin with one sheet of $8\frac{1}{2}'' \times 11''$ paper.

1. **Fold** the paper lengthwise about 3 inches from the bottom.

2. **Fold** the paper in thirds.

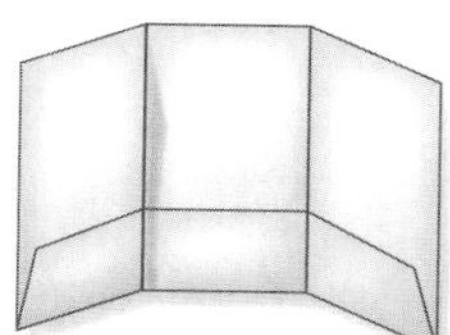

3. **Open** and staple the edges to form 3 pockets.

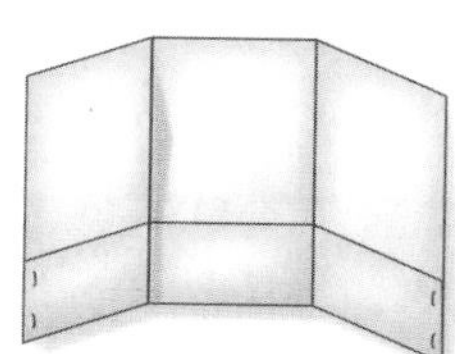

4. **Label** as shown. Place two index cards in each pocket.

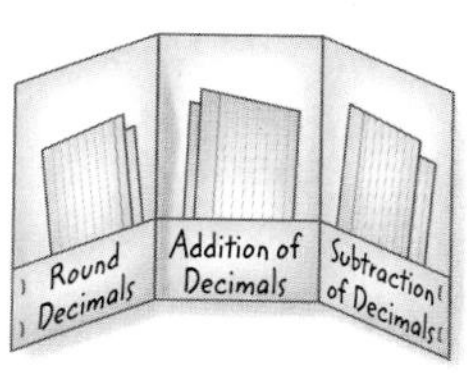

ARE YOU READY for Chapter 14?

You have two ways to check prerequisite skills for this chapter.

Option 2

Math Online Take the Chapter Readiness Quiz at tx.gr4math.com.

Option 1

Complete the Quick Check below.

QUICK Check

Round each number to the indicated place value. (Lesson 1-6)

1. 852; hundreds

2. 2,614; tens

3. 26,703; ten thousands

4. Farah has $1,363 in her bank account. To the nearest thousand, how much money does she have in her account?

Write a decimal for the shaded part of each figure. (Lesson 12-1)

5.

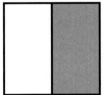

6.

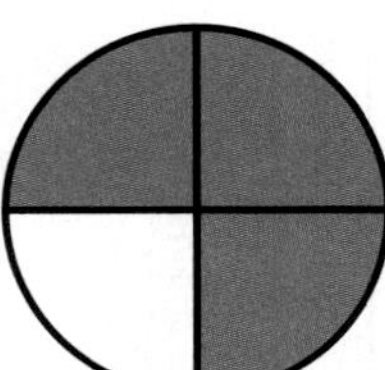

7.

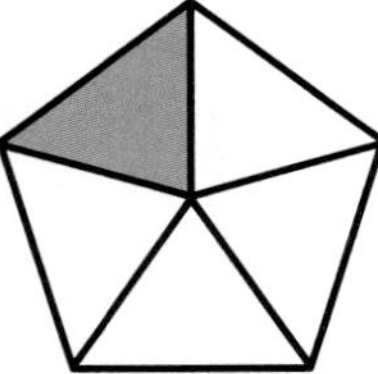

8. Tim ate part of the sandwich shown. Write a decimal to represent the amount of the sandwich Tim ate.

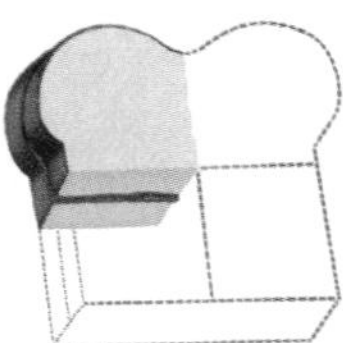

Graph each decimal on a number line. (Lesson 13-4)

9. 0.15

10. 0.38

11. 1.75

12. What decimal does the letter *D* represent?

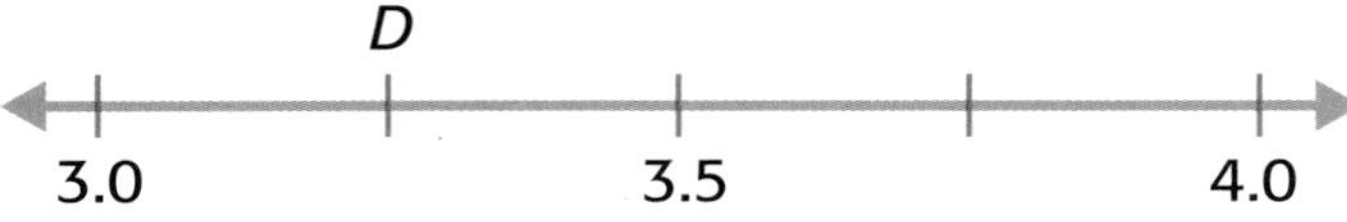

14-1 Round Decimals

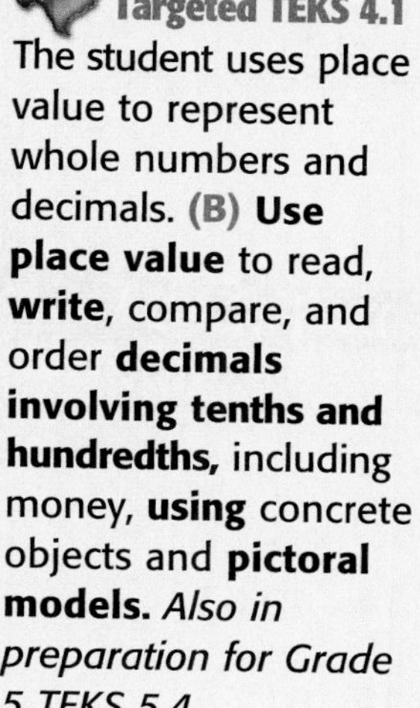

MAIN IDEA

I will round decimals.

Targeted TEKS 4.1 The student uses place value to represent whole numbers and decimals. **(B) Use place value** to read, **write**, compare, and order **decimals involving tenths and hundredths,** including money, **using** concrete objects and **pictoral models.** *Also in preparation for Grade 5 TEKS 5.4.*

GET READY to Learn

Yellowstone National Park has 2.22 million acres of land. What is 2.22 rounded to the nearest whole number?

You can use a number line or models to round a two-place decimal like 2.22.

Real-World EXAMPLE Round Decimals

1 PARKS Round 2.22 to the nearest whole number.

One Way: Use a Number Line

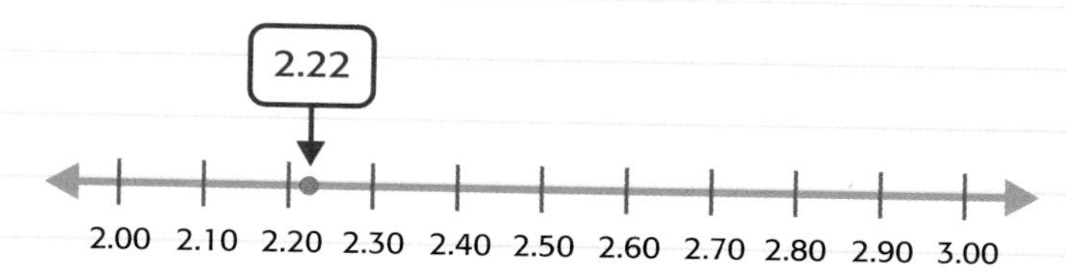

2.22 is between 2 and 3. It is closer to 2.
So, round 2.22 to 2.

Another Way: Use Concrete Models

Use hundredths grids to show the amount.

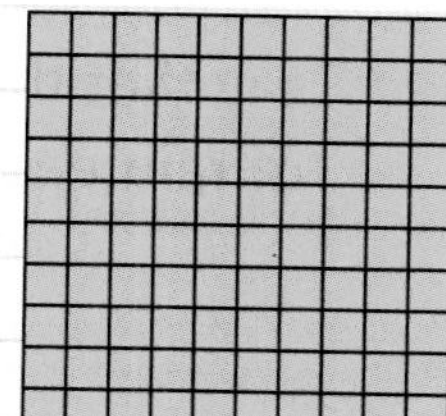 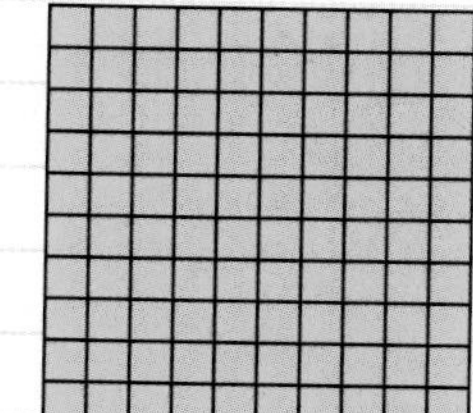 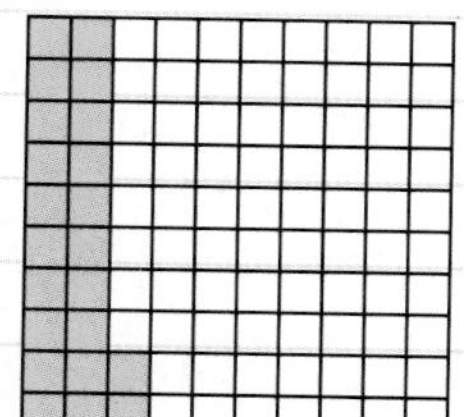

There are three grids, but the third is not half filled. It is closer to 2 than 3.

So, round 2.22 to 2.

Review Vocabulary

decimal and **decimal point** A decimal is a number that uses place value and a decimal point to show part of a whole. **(Lesson 12-1)**

CHECK What You Know

Round to the nearest whole number. Use number lines and models.
See Example 1 (p. 573)

1. 3.24 **2.** 9.87 **3.** 36.61 **4.** 83.14

5. 4.13 **6.** 8.45 **7.** 25.94 **8.** 67.28

9. **Measurement** Use the table to round the length of each bird to the nearest tenth of a foot.

World's Smallest Birds	
Bird	**Length (feet)**
Pygmy parrot	0.29
Bee hummingbird	0.20
Gouldian finch	0.33
New Zealand wren	0.29

10. Talk About It How is rounding decimals similar to rounding whole numbers? How is it different?

Practice and Problem Solving

EXTRA PRACTICE See page R49.

Round to the nearest whole number. Use number lines and models.
See Example 1 (p. 573)

11. 1.54 **12.** 6.38 **13.** 31.72 **14.** 49.63

15. 54.37 **16.** 59.72 **17.** 64.26 **18.** 81.48

19. 2.58 **20.** 7.31 **21.** 37.54 **22.** 42.07

23. 55.70 **24.** 63.05 **25.** 79.49 **26.** 97.33

For Exercises 27–28, round to the nearest whole number.

27. Caley wants to buy a shirt for $22.53. About how much money will she need to buy the shirt?

28. **Measurement** A city in the country of Peru receives only 0.09 inch of rainfall each year. Is it reasonable to say that the city receives about 1 inch of rain each year? Explain.

H.O.T. Problems

OPEN ENDED Give a reasonable rounded estimate for each decimal.

29. 23.81 pounds **30.** 30.85 feet **31.** 16.37 miles per gallon

32. WRITING IN MATH Explain how to find the greatest decimal in tenths that rounds to 75. What is the decimal?

Match Up

Round Decimals

Get Ready!

Players: 2 players

Get Set!

Cut each index card in half. Then label each card with one decimal as shown.

Go!

- Shuffle the cards. Then spread the cards out face down.
- Player 1 turns over two cards.
- If one decimal equals the other decimal after being rounded to the tenths place, Player 1 keeps the cards. Player 1 continues by choosing two more cards.
- If one decimal does not equal the other decimal after being rounded to the tenths place, the cards are turned over and Player 2 takes a turn.
- Continue playing until all matches are made. The player with the most cards wins.

You will need: 10 index cards

0.13	0.1	38.54	38.5
0.15	0.2	38.56	38.6
2.14	2.4		
2.46	2.5		
8.73	8.7		
8.77	8.8		
12.31	12.3		
12.35	12.4		

Estimate Decimal Sums and Differences

GET READY to Learn

Martina is going white water rafting with her family. During their first day, they will travel 6.5 miles before lunch and 8.7 miles after lunch. About how far will they travel on their first day?

MAIN IDEA

I will use rounding to estimate sums and differences.

Targeted TEKS 4.3 The student adds and subtracts to solve meaningful problems involving whole numbers and decimals. (B) **Add and subtract decimals** to the hundredths place **using** concrete objects and **pictorial models.**

Review Vocabulary

estimate When you do not need an exact answer, you can estimate. (Lesson 1-6)

To estimate the sum of decimals, you can round each decimal to the nearest whole number and then add.

KEY CONCEPT — Estimate Decimal Sums

Words To estimate the sum of two or more decimals, round each decimal to the nearest whole number. Then add.

Example

\$7.8	⟶	\$8
+ \$4.20	⟶	+ \$4
		\$12

Real-World EXAMPLE — Estimate Sums

1 **TRAVEL About how far will Martina and her family travel on their first day?**

You need to estimate 6.5 + 8.7. Round each addend to the nearest whole number. Use a number line.

6 6.5 7 8 8.7 9

Then add.

6.50	⟶	7	Round 6.5 to 7.
+ 8.7	⟶	+ 9	Round 8.7 to 9.

So, Martina and her family will travel about 16 miles.

Remember

When rounding to the nearest whole number, think about the whole number that comes before and after the number to be rounded.

KEY CONCEPT — Estimate Decimal Differences

Words To estimate the difference of two decimals, round each decimal to the nearest whole number. Then subtract.

Example

$$\begin{array}{r} \$28.75 \\ -\ \$13.49 \\ \hline \end{array} \longrightarrow \begin{array}{r} \$29 \\ -\ \$14 \\ \hline \$15 \end{array}$$

Real-World EXAMPLE — Estimate Differences

2 **Neela wants to buy a cell phone that costs \$37.99. She has \$45.25. About how much money will she have left to buy ring tones after she buys the phone?**

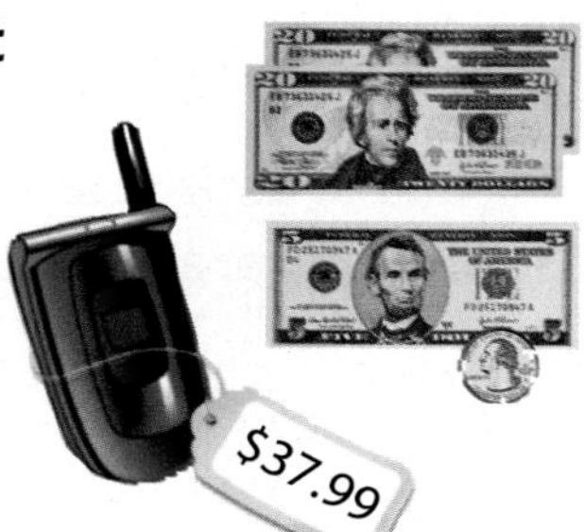

Estimate \$45.25 − \$37.99

Round each decimal to the nearest whole number. Then subtract.

$$\begin{array}{r} \$45.25 \\ -\ \$37.99 \\ \hline \end{array} \longrightarrow \begin{array}{r} \$45 \\ -\ \$38 \\ \hline \end{array}$$

Round \$45.25 to \$45.
Round \$37.99 to \$38.

$$\begin{array}{r} {\scriptstyle 3\ 15} \\ \$\not{4}\not{5} \\ -\ \$38 \\ \hline \$\ \ 7 \end{array}$$

So, Neela will have about \$7 left to buy ring tones.

 **Personal Tutor at** tx.gr4math.com

CHECK What You Know

Estimate. Round to the nearest whole number. Use models if needed. See Examples 1 and 2 (pp. 576–577)

1. $\begin{array}{r} 1.5 \\ +\ 2.3 \\ \hline \end{array}$

2. $\begin{array}{r} 5.4 \\ -\ 3.61 \\ \hline \end{array}$

3. $\begin{array}{r} 24.9 \\ +\ 9.8 \\ \hline \end{array}$

4. 62.8 − 9.5

5. \$8.75 + \$3.25

6. 46.37 − 7.3

7. Hakan is running in a charity run that is 3.12 miles long. Hakan has run 1.2 miles so far. About how many miles does he have left to run?

8. 

Explain how you could use estimation to find a reasonable sum for 2.1 and 3.3.

Practice and Problem Solving

EXTRA PRACTICE See page R49.

Estimate. Round to the nearest whole number. Use models if needed.

See Examples 1 and 2 (pp. 576–577)

9. $2.5 + 4.8$

10. $9.8 + 8.2$

11. $8.5 + 11.7$

12. $19.6 + 2.4$

13. $\$17.50 + \$6.25$

14. $28.49 + 12.83$

15. $9.7 - 7.2$

16. $5.2 - 4.6$

17. 34.5 – 5.4

18. 29.7 – 8.9

19. \$49.54 – \$25.15

20. 78.29 – 39.85

Algebra **Estimate by rounding to the nearest whole number. Then compare. Use >, <, or =.**

21. 18.34 + 3.67 ● 12.29 + 7.95

22. 14.58 – 6.91 ● 21.62 – 12.19

23. The hawk moth is the fastest flying insect. It can fly up to 33.3 miles per hour. A hornet can fly up to 13.3 miles per hour. About how much faster can the moth fly than the hornet?

24. Amit is buying some action figures for \$12.29. He is also buying a pack of trading cards for \$1.25. If he pays with a 20 dollar bill, about how much change will he get back?

25. Oscar is 4.3 feet tall. The giant ragwood plant is 8.9 feet tall. Is 8 – 4 a reasonable estimate of the difference in Oscar's and the plant's height to the nearest whole number? Explain.

26. On Monday, Paco ran one mile in 7.58 minutes. On Tuesday, he ran one mile in 8.23 minutes. Is 7.6 + 8.2 a reasonable estimate of the combined times to the nearest tenth? Explain.

Real-World PROBLEM SOLVING

Science The table to the right shows the speeds in which planets travel during their orbits, or trips around the sun.

Orbital Speeds of Planets

Planet	Speed (miles per second)
Mercury	29.75
Venus	21.76
Earth	18.51
Mars	14.51
Jupiter	8.12

27. To the nearest whole number, what is the difference between the fastest and slowest orbital speeds of the planets listed?

28. About how much faster does Mercury travel than Earth?

29. Earth's orbital speed is faster than two other planets on the table. About how much faster does Earth travel than each of these planets?

H.O.T. Problems

30. OPEN ENDED Write an addition and a subtraction problem that involves decimals and results in an estimated answer of $12.

31. CHALLENGE Estimate 32.4 + 21.5 + 17.95 to the nearest whole number.

32. WRITING IN ➤ MATH Explain how you would estimate the difference of 9 and 5.52.

TEST Practice

33. The deepest plant root is 393.7 feet deep. What is the total depth of the root rounded to the nearest whole number? (Lesson 14-1)

A 300 feet

B 390 feet

C 394 feet

D 400 feet

34. On Friday, Noah drove 166.5 miles. On Saturday, he drove 68.4 miles. On Sunday, he drove 72.75 miles. Approximately how many miles did Noah drive in three days? (Lesson 14-2)

F 200 miles

G 210 miles

H 300 miles

J 310 miles

Spiral Review

Round to the nearest whole number. (Lesson 14-1)

35. 28.5 **36.** 43.4 **37.** 84.2

Use a number line to compare. Write >, <, or =. (Lesson 13-8)

38. $3 \bullet 2\frac{7}{10}$ **39.** $7.03 \bullet 7\frac{3}{100}$ **40.** $\frac{25}{5} \bullet 5$

41. Identify the pattern in the shapes at the right. Continue the pattern by drawing the next four shapes. (Lesson 8-3)

42. Algebra The table shows a pattern. Identify the rule. Then find the missing numbers. (Lesson 5-8)

Rule: ■				
Input	3	4	5	■
Output	7	9	■	13

14-3 Problem-Solving Strategy

MAIN IDEA I will solve problems by working backward.

Targeted TEKS 4.14 The student applies Grade 4 Mathematics to solve problems connected to everyday experiences and activities in and outside of school. **(C) Select or develop an appropriate problem-solving plan or strategy, working backwards to solve a problem.** *Also addresses TEKS 4.14(B).*

Rey has lacrosse practice in the evenings. He gets home from school and eats a snack for 15 minutes. Then he spends 1 hour doing his homework. It takes him 15 minutes to get to practice. Practice is at 5 P.M. What time does Rey get home from school?

Understand

What facts do you know?

- Rey eats a snack for 15 minutes.
- He works on homework for 1 hour.
- It takes 15 minutes to get to practice at 5 P.M.

What do you need to find?

- What time Rey gets home from school.

Plan

Work backward to solve the problem.

Solve

Start with the end result. Then work backward one step at a time.

5 P.M. (practice starts) − 15 minutes (time to get to practice) = 4:45 P.M.

4:45 P.M. − 1 hour (homework) = 3:45 P.M.

3:45 P.M. − 15 minutes (time spent eating) = 3:30 P.M.

So, Rey gets home from school at 3:30 P.M.

Check

Look back at the problem.
15 minutes + 1 hour + 15 minutes = 1 hour and 30 minutes.
He gets home at 3:30 P.M. One hour and 30 minutes later is 5 P.M.
The answer is correct.

ANALYZE the Strategy

Refer to the problem on the previous page.

1. Explain why 15 minutes was subtracted from 5 P.M. in the first step of solving the problem.

2. Suppose practice started at 4:30 P.M. What time would Rey get home from school?

3. Suppose it takes Rey 45 minutes to complete his homework. What time would he get home from school?

4. Look back to Exercise 3. Check your answer. How do you know it is correct? Explain.

PRACTICE the Strategy

EXTRA PRACTICE
See page R50.

Solve. Use the *work backward* strategy.

5. Debbie bought a movie ticket. She then let her friend borrow $3. She now has $7. How much money did she have originally?

6. Adrian volunteers at an animal shelter. It takes him 20 minutes to walk each dog shown. It takes him 15 minutes to give each dog a bath. He finished walking and bathing the dogs at 6 P.M. What time did he start?

7. A number is multiplied by 3. Next, 8 is subtracted from the product. Then, the difference is divided by 4. The result is 7. What is the number?

8. Susana jogs a mile in 8 minutes. She warms up for 10 minutes. She stretches for 5 minutes after she jogs. She jogs 2 miles, including warming up and stretching. She finishes at 8 A.M. What time does she start?

9. Nadina has two times as many pennies as dimes. The number of quarters she has is shown below. She has 4 more dimes than quarters. How much money does she have?

10. A number is divided by 3. Next, 25 is added to the quotient. Then, the sum is multiplied by 4. The result is 116. What is the number?

11. **WRITING IN MATH** Explain how you used the *work backward* strategy to solve Exercise 10.

Math Activity for 14-4
Addition of Decimals

You can use grid paper to explore adding decimals.

MAIN IDEA

I will use models to add decimals.

Targeted TEKS 4.3 The student adds and subtracts to solve meaningful problems involving whole numbers and decimals. **(B) Add and subtract decimals to the hundredths place using concrete objects and pictorial models.**

You Will Need
grid paper
colored pencil

Interactive Lab
tx.gr4math.com

ACTIVITY

Use models to add decimals. Find 1.5 + 0.29.

Step 1 **Model 1.5.**

To show 1.5, shade one whole 10-by-10 grid and $\frac{50}{100}$ of a second grid.

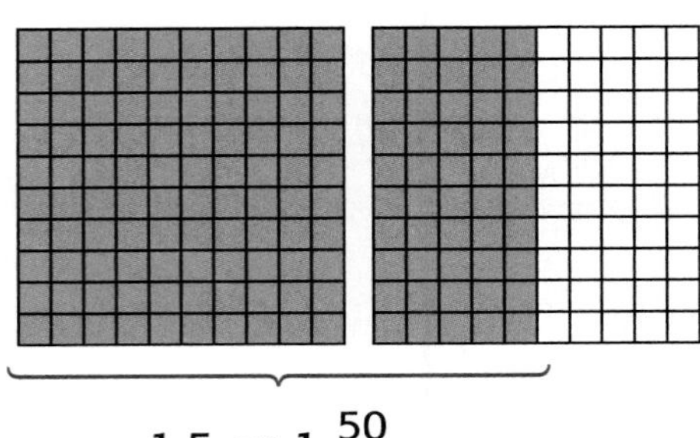

1.5 or $1\frac{50}{100}$

Step 2 **Model 0.29.**

To show 0.29, shade $\frac{29}{100}$ of the second grid using a different color.

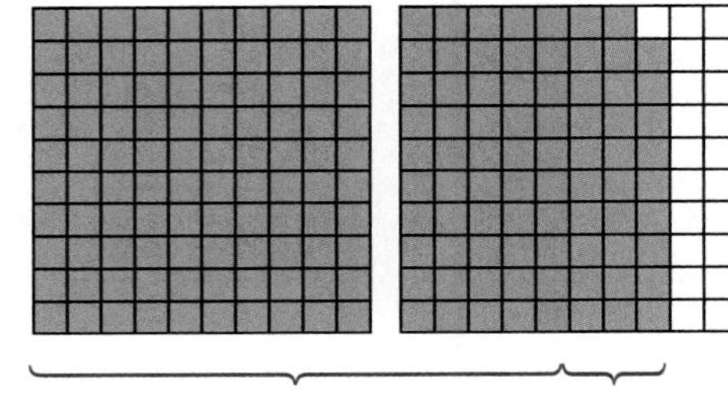

1.5

0.29 or $\frac{29}{100}$

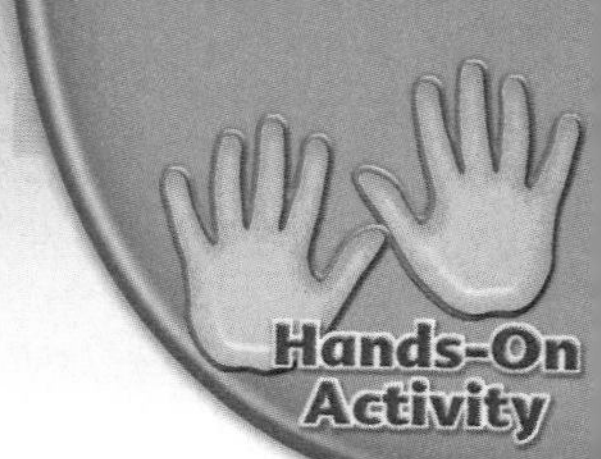

Step 3 **Add the decimals.**

Count the total number of shaded squares. Write as a decimal.

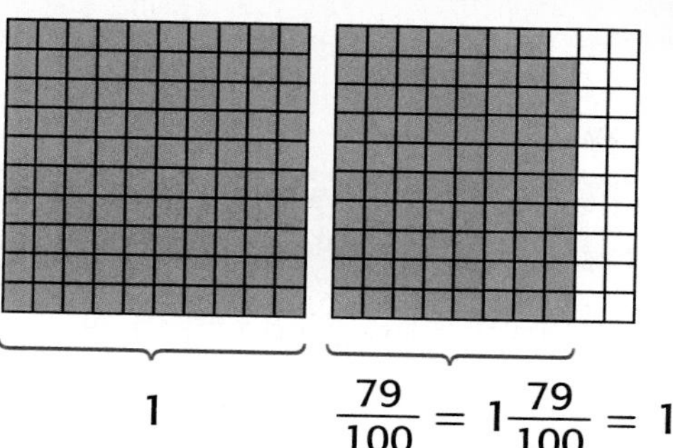

$1 \quad \frac{79}{100} = 1\frac{79}{100} = 1.79$

Think About It

1. Why did you draw two 10-by-10 grids to show 1.5?
2. Why did you shade 50 squares of the second grid?
3. Why did you shade 29 squares of the second grid?
4. How did you find the sum of the decimals?

CHECK What You Know

Add. Use the models.

5. 1.15 + 0.57

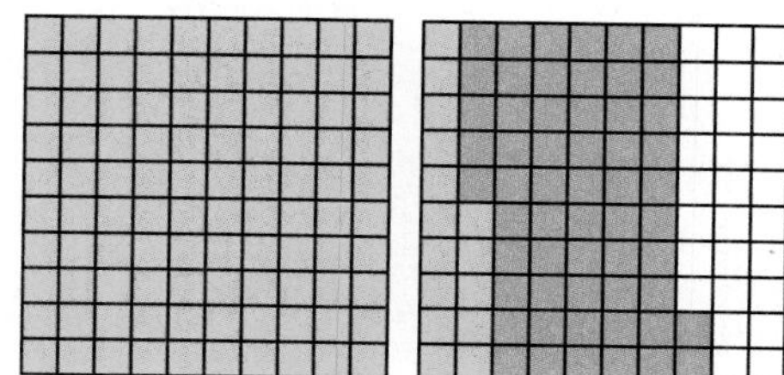

6. 0.25 + 0.46

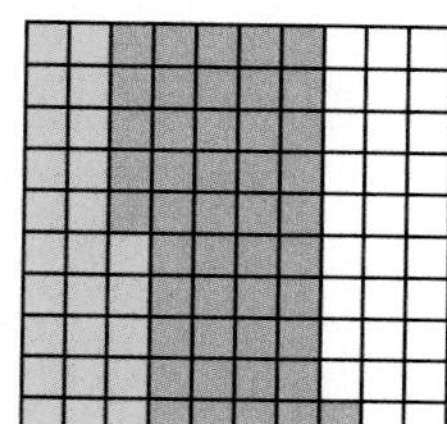

Add. Use models if needed.

7. $\begin{array}{r} 0.45 \\ +\ 0.30 \\ \hline \end{array}$

8. $\begin{array}{r} 0.16 \\ +\ 0.58 \\ \hline \end{array}$

9. $\begin{array}{r} 1.12 \\ +\ 1.50 \\ \hline \end{array}$

10. $\begin{array}{r} 0.19 \\ +\ 1.62 \\ \hline \end{array}$

11. $\begin{array}{r} 1.09 \\ +\ 1.58 \\ \hline \end{array}$

12. $\begin{array}{r} 1.42 \\ +\ 0.26 \\ \hline \end{array}$

13. 0.44 + 1.39

14. 1.28 + 2.10

15. 2.05 + 1.9

16. **WRITING IN MATH** Write the steps to use to find 2.34 + 1.76.

14-4 Add Decimals

MAIN IDEA

I will add decimals.

Targeted TEKS 4.3 The student adds and subtracts to solve meaningful problems involving whole numbers and decimals. (B) **Add and subtract decimals to the hundredths place using concrete objects and pictorial models.**

GET READY to Learn

Darlene practiced the flute 1.5 hours on Saturday. On Sunday, she practiced 2.3 hours. How long did she practice during the two days?

In the previous Explore Activity, you used models to add decimals. You can also use paper and pencil to add decimals.

Real-World EXAMPLE Add Decimals

1 **MEASUREMENT How many hours did Darlene practice the flute during the two days?**

One Way: Use Models

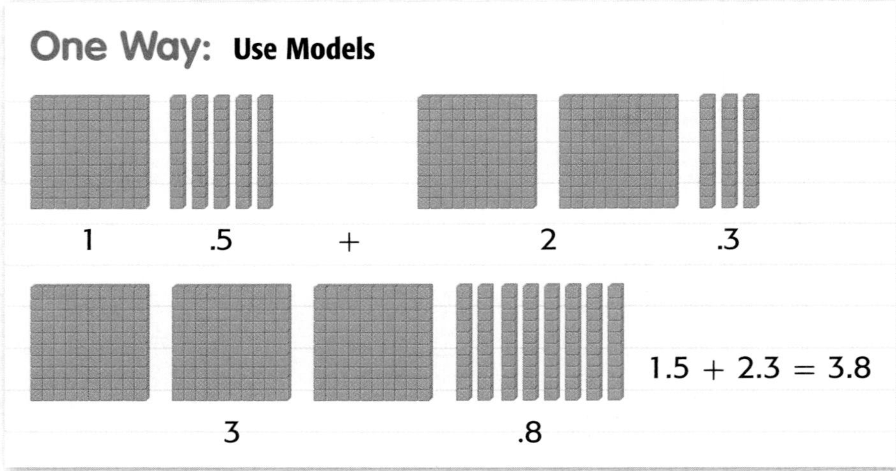

Another Way: Paper and Pencil

Step 1 Line up the decimal points.

$$\begin{array}{r} 1.5 \\ +\ 2.3 \\ \hline \end{array}$$

Step 2 Add.

$$\begin{array}{r} 1.5 \\ +\ 2.3 \\ \hline 3.8 \end{array}$$

Add the digits in each place value. Then bring down the decimal point.

So, Darlene practiced a total of 3.8 hours.

Real-World EXAMPLE Add Decimals

2 **ANIMALS The pygmy shrew is one of the smallest mammals. It weighs 1.72 grams. The spiny pocket mouse is also very small. It weighs 16.35 grams. What is the total weight of these?**

You need to find 1.72 + 16.35. **Estimate** 2 + 16 = 18

Step 1 Line up the decimal points.

$$\begin{array}{r} 1.72 \\ +\ 16.35 \\ \hline \end{array}$$

Step 2 Add.

$$\begin{array}{r} \scriptstyle 1 \\ 1.72 \\ +\ 16.35 \\ \hline 18.07 \end{array}$$

Add the digits in each place value. Regroup if necessary.

So, the total weight of the mammals is 18.07 grams.

Check for reasonableness

The sum of 18.07 is close to the estimate of 18.
So, the answer is reasonable. ✓

Remember

Line up the decimal points before you add to make sure you are adding the same place values together.

Online **Personal Tutor at** tx.gr4math.com

CHECK What You Know

Add. Use models or pictures if needed. See Examples 1 and 2 (pp. 584–585)

1. $\begin{array}{r} 1.4 \\ +\ 0.7 \\ \hline \end{array}$

2. $\begin{array}{r} 4.72 \\ +\ 3.9 \\ \hline \end{array}$

3. $\begin{array}{r} 9.8 \\ +\ 7.33 \\ \hline \end{array}$

4. 4.82 + 6.27

5. \$25.85 + \$8.49

6. 54.90 + 38.41

For Exercises 7 and 8, use the poster shown.

Medieval Era
Adults $48.95
Children $33.95

7. Andre has his birthday dinner at Medieval Era, a dinner theatre with knights jousting. What is the total cost for Andre and his father?

8. Suppose Andre's mother is also going to his birthday dinner. What is the total cost?

9. Talk About It Why is it important to line up the decimal points before you add?

Practice and Problem Solving

EXTRA PRACTICE See page R50.

Add. Use models or pictures if needed. See Examples 1 and 2 (pp. 584–585)

10. $0.7 + 0.2$

11. $0.4 + 0.6$

12. $1.1 + 0.39$

13. $5.1 + 7.56$

14. $8.76 + 6.95$

15. $7.09 + 4.68$

16. $\$9.82 + \$5.33$

17. $\$12.33 + \$5.79$

18. 47.28 + 36.05

19. \$51.20 + \$29.75

20. 3.21 + 14.7 + 9.35

21. The ostrich lays the largest bird egg in the world. It weighs 1.8 kg. The emu lays the second largest bird egg in the world. It weighs 0.82 kg. What is the combined weight of the two bird eggs?

22. Two bones in a leg are the femur and tibia. The average adult male femur is 19.88 inches long. The tibia is 16.94 inches long. How long is the average adult male's leg?

Real-World PROBLEM SOLVING

Data File The Bentsen-Rio Grande Valley State Park features The World Birding Center headquarters. One bird that can be found there is the Great Horned Owl.

23. Suppose one owl weighed 1.3 kg and another weighed 1.7 kg. How much do they weigh together?

24. Another bird found in the Birding Center is the white tipped dove, which weighs about 0.02 kg. If an owl that weighed 1.5 kg and a dove that weighed 0.02 kg were both weighed together, how much would they weigh?

The Great Horned Owl average weight 1.5 kg

H.O.T. Problems

25. WHICH ONE DOESN'T BELONG? Three of the decimals shown below have a sum equal to 14.04. Identify the number that does not belong with the other three.

1.15	2.57	5.03	6.44

26. WRITING IN MATH Explain how to find the sum of 136.28 and 264.57.

CHAPTER 14

Mid-Chapter Check

Lessons 14-1 through 14-4

Round to the nearest whole number. (Lesson 14-1)

1. 4.55 **2.** 25.24

3. 8.58 **4.** 36.34

5. **Measurement** A bald eagle's nest is 2.4 meters wide. How wide is its nest to the nearest whole number? (Lesson 14-1)

6. **TEST PRACTICE** The height of a monster truck is 15.4 feet. What is the height of the truck rounded to the nearest whole number? (Lesson 14-1)

A 14 **C** 15.4

B 15 **D** 16

Estimate. Round to the nearest whole number. (Lesson 14-2)

7. $\begin{array}{r} 2.4 \\ +\ 3.8 \\ \hline \end{array}$ **8.** $\begin{array}{r} 9.4 \\ -\ 5.82 \\ \hline \end{array}$

Algebra **Estimate by rounding to the nearest whole number. Then compare. Use >, <, or =.** (Lesson 14-2)

9. 13.73 + 8.04 ● 9.8 + 12.52

10. 46.91 − 19.8 ● 53.4 − 20.26

11. Tamika Catchings, a WNBA player, scores an average of 19.2 points per game. About how many points would Tamika score in two games? (Lesson 14-2)

12. A number is divided by 4. Next, 8 is added to the quotient. Then, the sum is multiplied by 2. The result is 28. What is the number? (Lesson 14-3)

13. **Measurement** Bruno is going on vacation and needs to leave for the airport at 1 P.M. What time does Bruno need to wake up? (Lesson 14-3)

Task	Time to Complete (hours)
Clean house	3.25
Eat lunch	0.75
Pack suitcase	1.5

Add. Use models or pictures if needed. (Lesson 14-4)

14. 14.5 + 7.8 **15.** 37.08 + 19.56

16. **TEST PRACTICE** Brad buys a movie ticket for $4.75, a pretzel for $1.50, and a soda for $2.25. How much money did Brad spend? (Lesson 14-4)

F $8.50 **H** $9

G $8.75 **J** $9.25

Algebra **Describe the pattern. Then identify the missing numbers.** (Lesson 14-4)

17. 0.8, 1.6, ■, 3.2, ■, ■

18. 1.23, 3.25, ■, ■, 9.31, ■

19. **WRITING IN MATH** Tell whether 40 is a reasonable estimate for the sum of 28.4 + 14.68. Explain.

Problem Solving in History

Olympic Games

The Olympic games have been taking place since ancient times.

There are currently summer and winter games. Each season occurs every four years and includes different sports. There are over one hundred summer events including cycling, gymnastics, swimming and diving, and track and field, among others. A highlight of the summer games has always been the gymnastic events. These events mix strength, agility, style, and grace. Some of the events that take place in the gymnastic competition are floor exercise, horizontal bar, parallel bars, pommel horse, rings, and vault. Gymnasts are scored on a scale of one to ten, with ten being a perfect score and very difficult to earn.

Recent Olympic Games Men's Individual Scores

Gymnast	Floor	Horse	Rings	Vault	Parallel Bars	High Bar	Total Score
Paul Hamm (U.S.)	9.73	9.70	9.59	9.14	9.84	9.84	57.84
Kim Dae-Eun (Korea)	9.65	9.54	9.71	9.41	9.78	9.73	57.82
Yang Tae-Young (Korea)	9.51	9.65	9.73	9.70	9.71	9.48	57.78

Recent Olympic Games Women's Individual Scores

Gymnast	Vault	Uneven Bars	Beam	Floor	Total Score
Carly Patterson (U.S.)	9.38	9.58	9.73	9.71	38.34
Svetlana Khorkina (Russia)	9.46	9.73	9.46	9.56	38.21
Zhang Nan (China)	9.33	9.46	9.66	9.60	38.05

* All scores have been rounded to the nearest hundredth.

Targeted TEKS 4.14 The student applies Grade 4 mathematics to solve problems connected to everyday experiences and activities in and outside of school. **(A) Identify the mathematics in everyday situations.**

Did You Know

As of January 1, 1999, trampoline became a gymnastic event at the Olympic games.

Real-World Math

Use the information on the previous page to solve each problem.

1. A summer Olympic games will be taking place in London, England, in the year 2012. What years will the four previous Olympic games have been held?

2. What is the top female gymnast's total score rounded to the nearest whole number?

3. How much higher is Paul Hamm's score in the parallel bars than the vault when both scores are rounded to the nearest tenth?

4. What is the sum of Carly Patterson's two highest event scores when rounded to the nearest tenth?

5. Kim Dae-Eun's scores were higher than Paul Hamm's scores in two of the events. Identify the events. Find the difference in their scores for each event to the nearest tenth.

6. The gymnasts that earn the top three total scores win gold, silver, and bronze medals. Suppose the scores were rounded to the tenths place. Would this scoring change the medals that were given out to the male athletes? Explain.

7. Which place value would the female gymnast's scores have to be rounded to in order to have a three-way tie for gold? Explain.

Problem-Solving Investigation

MAIN IDEA I will choose the best strategy to solve a problem.

Targeted TEKS 4.14 The student applies Grade 4 mathematics to solve problems connected to everyday experiences and activities in and outside of school. (B) **Solve problems that incorporate understanding the problem, making a plan, carrying out the plan, and evaluating the solution for reasonableness.** *Also addresses TEKS 4.14(C).*

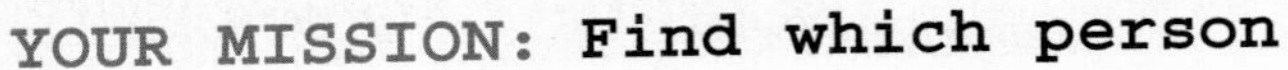

JENNIFER: My friends and I all have different kinds of pets. Among the three of us, we have a lizard, a cat, a gerbil, and a snake. I do not have a cat. Rondell's pet is not a gerbil or a snake. Lorena's two pets are not lizards. My pet does not begin with the letters s or g.

YOUR MISSION: Find which person owns each pet.

Understand	You know the clues for each person's pet. You need to find which person owns each pet.
Plan	Make a table to show what you know. Then use logical reasoning to find which person owns each pet.
Solve	Make a table. Write *yes* or *no* for each fact that you are given. Once you write yes in the table, you can write no in the rest of the boxes in that row and column.

	Cat	Gerbil	Lizard	Snake
Jennifer	No	No	Yes	No
Lorena	No	Yes	No	Yes
Rondell	Yes	No	No	No

So, Jennifer owns a lizard. Lorena owns a gerbil and a snake. Rondell owns a cat.

Check	Look back at the problem. The solution matches the facts given in the problem. So, the answer is correct.

Mixed Problem Solving

Use any strategy shown below to solve. Tell what strategy you used.

PROBLEM-SOLVING STRATEGIES
- Work a simpler problem.
- Use logical reasoning.
- Draw a picture.
- Make a model.
- Work backward.

1. Reina is going bowling. Which route would be the shortest? Explain.

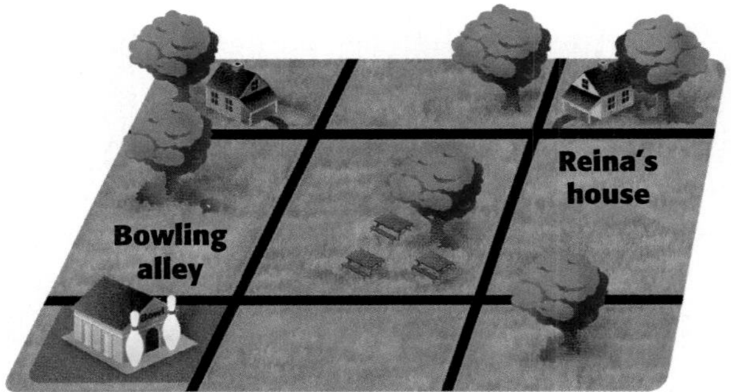

2. Students voted for a new mascot. Six out of ten students voted for a tiger. There are 300 students. How many students voted for a tiger?

3. A number is divided by 3. Then the quotient is subtracted from 20. The result is 8. What is the number?

4. Haley's comet can be seen from Earth about every 76 years. The next time it can be seen will be in 2062. When could the comet last be seen?

5. Dean bought three comic books for $6. At the same price, how much would 10 comic books cost?

6. Laurie spent 30 minutes on math homework. She spent half as much time doing her science homework. She spent 5 minutes longer on her reading homework than her science homework. How much time did Laurie spend on her homework?

7. The toy car below cost $2.50. At the same price, how many toy cars can Domingo buy with $10?

8. A type of bacteria doubles in number every 12 hours. After 2 days, there are 48 bacteria. How many bacteria were there at the beginning of the first day?

9. The product of two numbers is 24. Their difference is 5. What are these two numbers?

10. Audrey biked the trail below. Find the value of *y*.

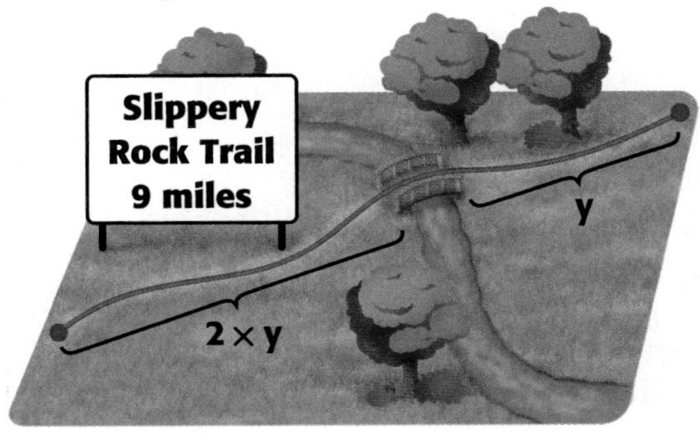

11. **WRITING IN ▶MATH** The two busiest subway systems in the world have 3.1 and 2.84 billion passengers each year. The answer is 5.94 billion. What is the question?

Math Activity for 14-6
Subtraction of Decimals

You can use grid paper to explore subtracting decimals.

MAIN IDEA

I will use models to subtract decimals.

Targeted TEKS 4.3 The student adds and subtracts to solve meaningful problems involving whole numbers and decimals. **(B)** Add and **subtract decimals to the hundredths place using concrete objects and pictorial models.**

You Will Need
grid paper
colored pencil

Use models to find 2.75 − 1.15.

Step 1 Model 2.75.

To show 2.75, shade two whole grids and $\frac{75}{100}$ of a third grid.

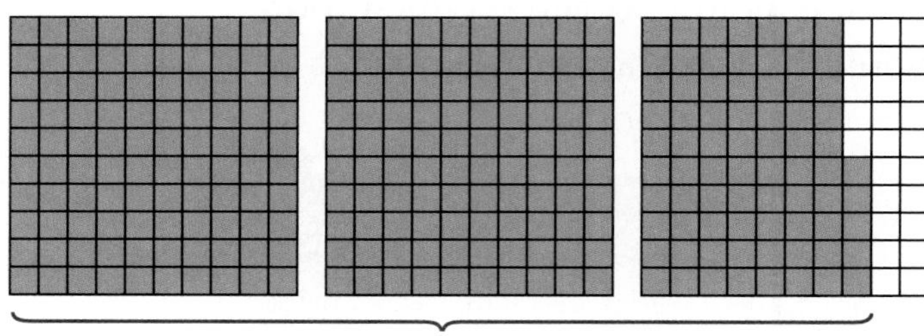

2.75 or $2\frac{75}{100}$

Step 2 Subtract 1.15.

To subtract 1.15, cross out 1 whole grid and 15 squares of the third grid.

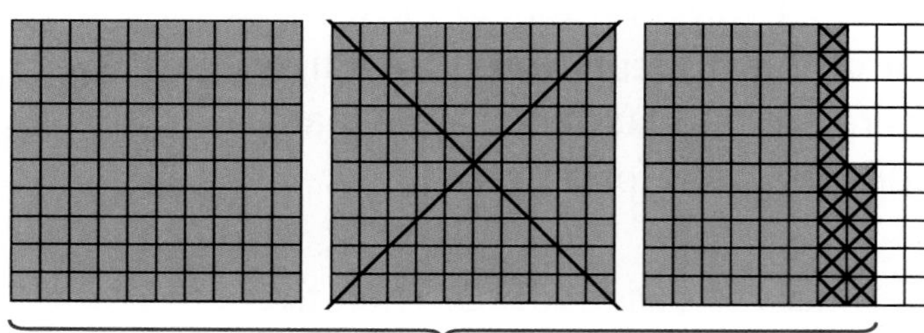

2.75 − 1.15 or $1\frac{15}{100}$

Interactive Lab
tx.gr4math.com

Hands-On Activity

Step 3 **Find the difference.**

Count the number of shaded squares left.

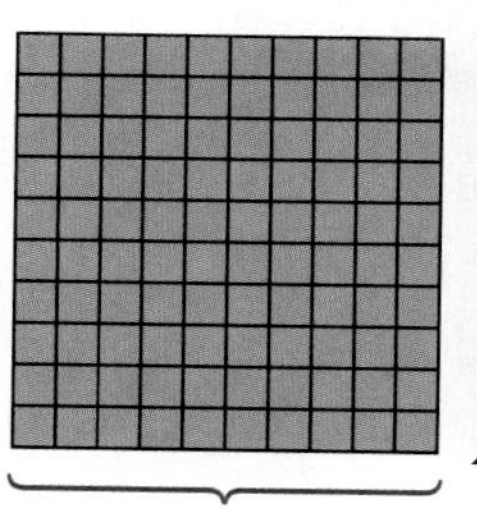
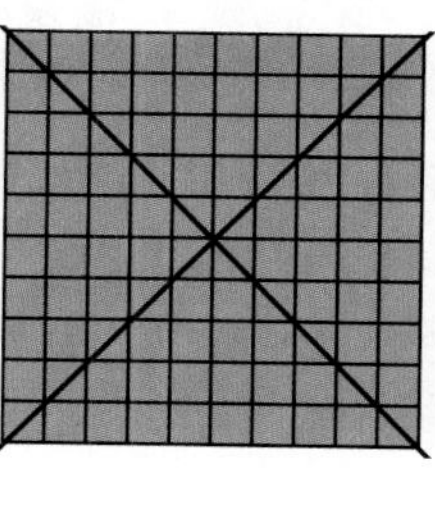
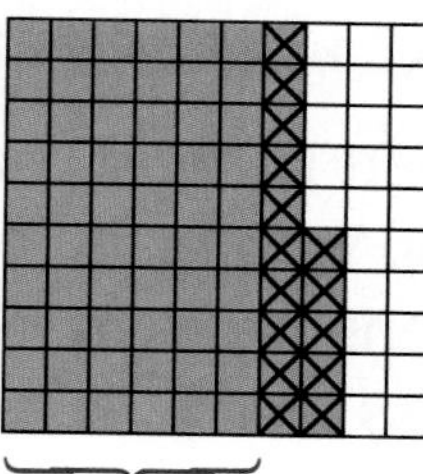

1 $\frac{60}{100} = 1\frac{60}{100} = 1.6$

Think About It

1. How did you model 2.75?
2. How did you model subtracting 1.15 from 2.75?
3. How did you find the difference?

CHECK What You Know

Subtract. Use the models.

4. 1.46 − 0.34

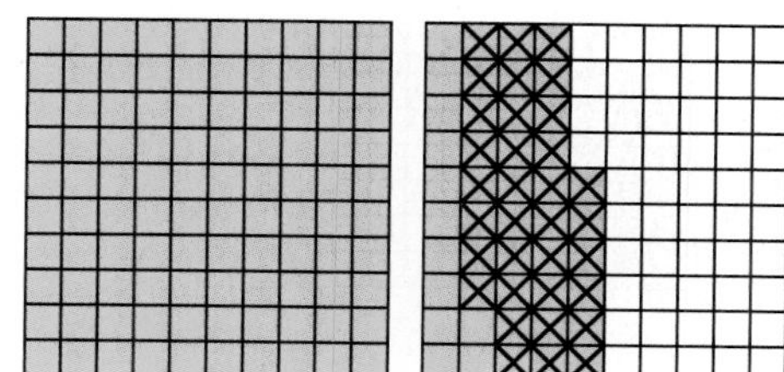

5. 2.8 − 1.23

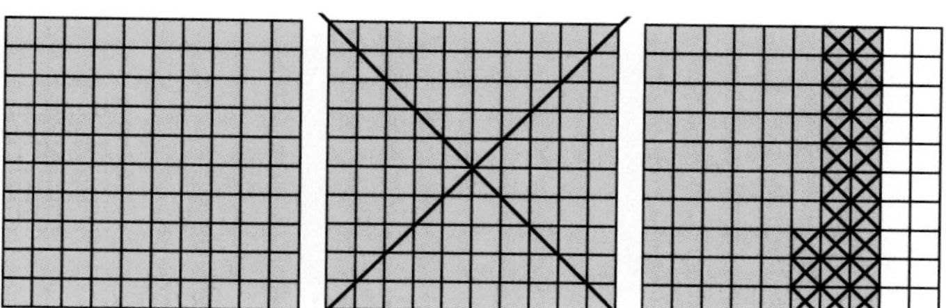

Subtract. Use models if needed.

6. $\begin{array}{r} 0.55 \\ -\ 0.29 \\ \hline \end{array}$

7. $\begin{array}{r} 0.99 \\ -\ 0.46 \\ \hline \end{array}$

8. $\begin{array}{r} 1.4 \\ -\ 1.11 \\ \hline \end{array}$

9. $\begin{array}{r} 2.6 \\ -\ 1.09 \\ \hline \end{array}$

10. $\begin{array}{r} 2.81 \\ -\ 1.29 \\ \hline \end{array}$

11. $\begin{array}{r} 3.77 \\ -\ 1.08 \\ \hline \end{array}$

12. 2.98 − 1.84

13. 3.45 − 2.73

14. 3.93 − 2.94

15. WRITING IN ▶MATH Explain how to find 3.46 − 2.62.

14-6 Subtract Decimals

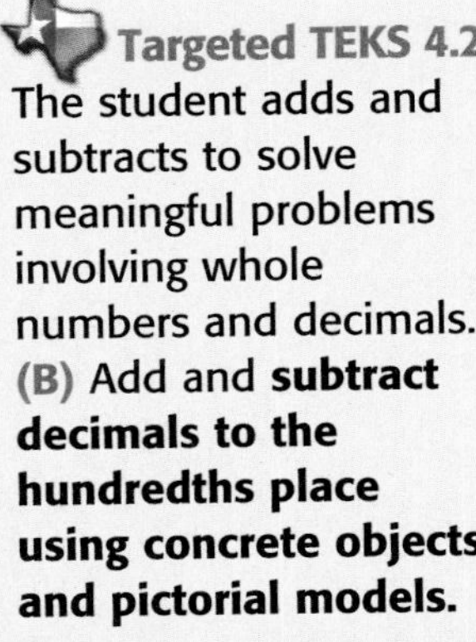

MAIN IDEA

I will use models to subtract decimals.

Targeted TEKS 4.2 The student adds and subtracts to solve meaningful problems involving whole numbers and decimals. (B) Add and **subtract decimals to the hundredths place using concrete objects and pictorial models.**

GET READY to Learn

Albert Einstein was a very intelligent man who made many important scientific discoveries. His brain had a mass of 1.23 kilograms. This is less than the mass of an average adult male brain, which has a mass of about 1.4 kilograms. What is the difference in mass?

In the previous Explore Activity, you used models to subtract decimals.

Real-World EXAMPLE Subtract Decimals

1 **MEASUREMENT What is the difference in mass between Albert Einstein's brain and the mass of an average adult male brain?**

Step 1 Draw a model of 1.4 on a hundredths grid.

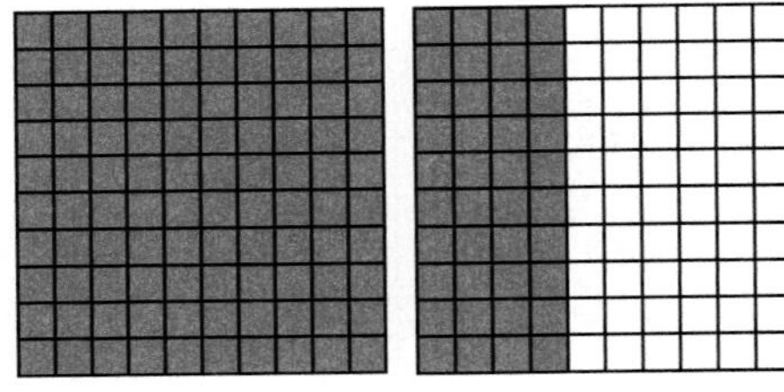

Step 2 Subract 1.23.

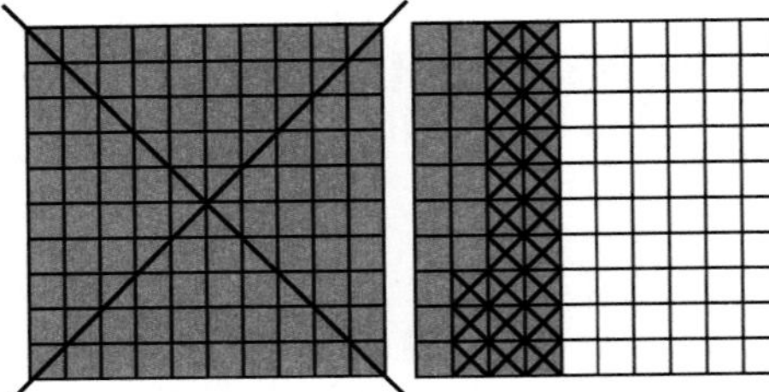

$1.4 - 1.23 = 0.17$

So, Einstein's brain had a mass of 0.17 kilogram less than the mass of an average adult male brain.

You can also use paper and pencil to solve.

Real-World EXAMPLE — Subtract Decimals

2 MEASUREMENT The average rock python is 24.6 feet long. The average king cobra is 17.7 feet long. How much longer is the rock python than the king cobra?

Subtract 24.6 − 17.7 to find how much longer the rock python is than the king cobra.

Estimate 24.6 − 17.7 ⟶ 25 − 18 = 7

Step 1 Line up the decimal points.

$$\begin{array}{r} 24.6 \\ -\ 17.7 \\ \hline \end{array}$$

Step 2 Subtract.

$$\begin{array}{r} {\scriptstyle 13\ 16} \\ 2\not{4}.\not{6} \\ -\ 17.7 \\ \hline 6.9 \end{array}$$

Subtract. Regroup if necessary.

So, the average rock python is 6.9 feet longer than the average king cobra.

Check for reasonableness

The answer, 6.9, is close to the estimate of 7. So, the answer is reasonable. ✓

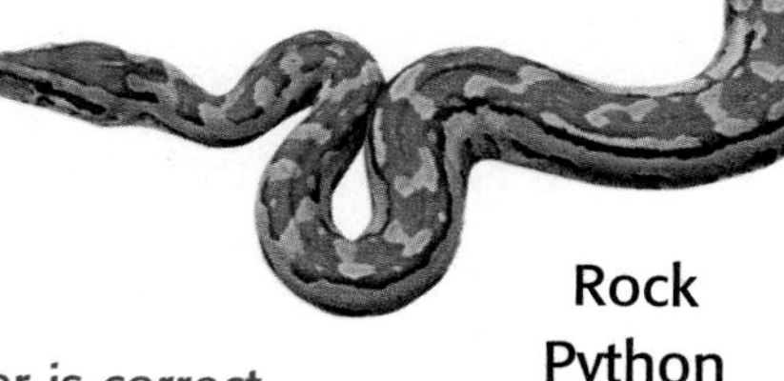

Rock Python

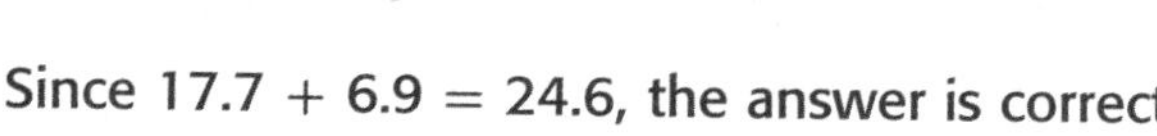

Since 17.7 + 6.9 = 24.6, the answer is correct.

Online Personal Tutor at tx.gr4math.com

CHECK What You Know

Subtract. Use models if needed. See Examples 1 and 2 (pp. 594–595)

1. $\begin{array}{r} 1.4 \\ -\ 1.0 \\ \hline \end{array}$

2. $\begin{array}{r} 0.8 \\ -\ 0.49 \\ \hline \end{array}$

3. $\begin{array}{r} \$1.67 \\ -\ \$0.58 \\ \hline \end{array}$

4. 4.67 − 2.36

5. \$8.72 − \$2.95

6. 25.74 − 12.08

7. The height of the tallest woman in the world is 7.58 feet. The height of the tallest man in the world is 8.92 feet. How much taller is the tallest man than the tallest woman?

8. Talk About It Explain how subtracting decimals is similar to subtracting whole numbers. How is it different?

Practice and Problem Solving

EXTRA PRACTICE
See page R51.

Subtract. Use models if needed. See Examples 1 and 2 (pp. 594–595)

9. $\begin{array}{r} 2.7 \\ -1.4 \\ \hline \end{array}$

10. $\begin{array}{r} 5.5 \\ -3.8 \\ \hline \end{array}$

11. $\begin{array}{r} 7.2 \\ -0.9 \\ \hline \end{array}$

12. $\begin{array}{r} 4.6 \\ -1.45 \\ \hline \end{array}$

13. $\begin{array}{r} 6.84 \\ -3.56 \\ \hline \end{array}$

14. $\begin{array}{r} \$9.67 \\ -\$7.05 \\ \hline \end{array}$

15. $\begin{array}{r} 11.92 \\ -8.87 \\ \hline \end{array}$

16. $\begin{array}{r} \$19.38 \\ -\$14.55 \\ \hline \end{array}$

17. $\begin{array}{r} 21.80 \\ -15.91 \\ \hline \end{array}$

18. $25.09 – $12.40

19. 34.94 – 28.17

20. 56.87 – 38.05

For Exercises 21 and 22, use the table.

21. How many more people play tennis in the most popular state than in the least popular state?

22. What is the total number of people in Florida, Texas, and New York who play tennis?

Most Popular States for Tennis	
State	**Number of Players (millions)**
California	3.2
Florida	1.4
Illinois	1.0
New York	1.7
Texas	1.4

23. Julina is buying pet supplies. She has $25.50. She buys cat food for $8.99, a collar for $4.79, and cat toys for $3.25. How much money will Julina have left?

24. The average American eats 57.4 kilograms of fresh fruit and 67.2 kilograms of fresh vegetables each year. What is the difference in the yearly amount of fruit and vegetables an American eats?

Real-World PROBLEM SOLVING

Science The table at the right shows the heights of different dinosaurs.

25. What is the difference in height between the two shortest dinosaurs?

26. How much taller is a Tyrannosaurus than a Araucanoraptor?

27. Which two dinosaurs have a height difference of 1.45 feet?

Dinosaur Heights	
Dinosaur	**Height (feet)**
Abrictosaurus	1.3
Araucanoraptor	2.75
Bagaceratops	1.5
Microvenator	2.5
Supersaurus	66.0
Triceratops	9.5
Tyrannosaurus	23.0

H.O.T. Problems

28. FIND THE ERROR Morgan and Lloyd are finding 46.27 − 28.16. Who is correct? Explain.

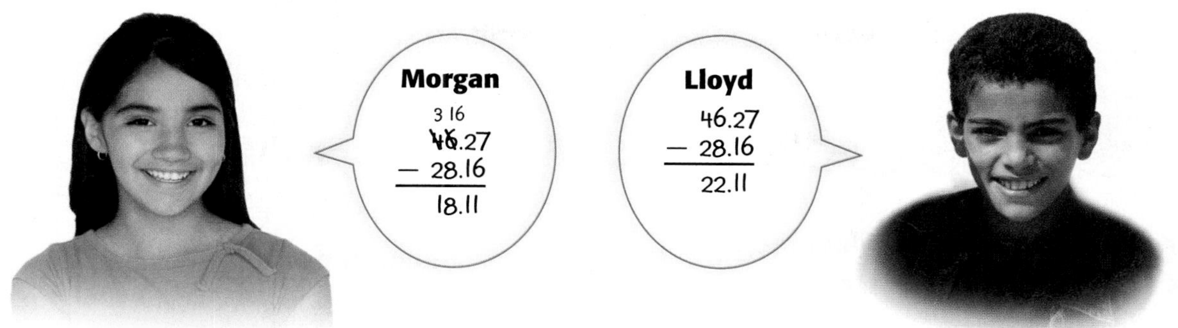

29. OPEN ENDED A number is subtracted from 24.84. The difference is greater than 9 and less than 10. What is the number?

TEST Practice TAKS 1

30. At the school store, Benito bought a package of pens for $1.34 and a set of map pencils for $2.78. What was the total cost? (Lesson 14-4)

A $1.44

B $3.02

C $4.02

D $4.12

31. Sandy and her father have $100. They buy a fishing pole for $39.95 and cooking gear for $29.39. Which additional item could they buy? (Lesson 14-6)

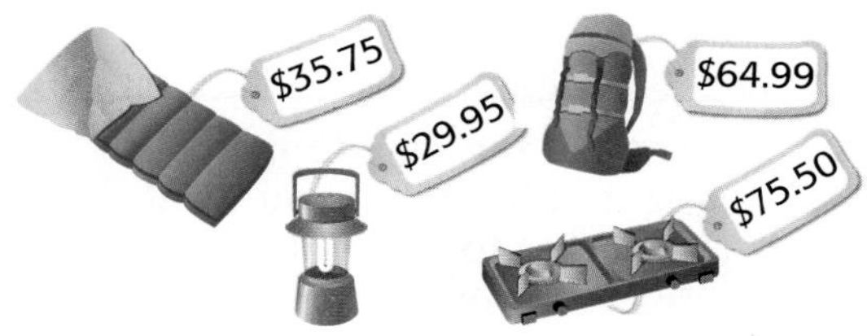

F Backpack

G Camp stove

H Lantern

J Sleeping bag

Spiral Review

Add. Use concrete objects or pictorial models. (Lesson 14-4)

32. 0.75 + 0.62

33. 4.49 + 0.76

34. 8.40 + 6.87

35. Mila volunteers at a food bank at 9 A.M. It takes 30 minutes to drive to the food bank, 20 minutes to eat breakfast, and 45 minutes to get ready in the morning. What is the latest time she can set her alarm to wake up? (Lesson 14-3)

Estimate. Round to the nearest whole number. (Lesson 14-2)

36. 2.5 + 4.3

37. 8.4 − 5.7

38. 22.9 + 5.4

CHAPTER 14

Study Guide and Review

FOLDABLES™ Study Organizer GET READY to Study

Be sure the following Key Vocabulary words and Key Concepts are written in your Foldable.

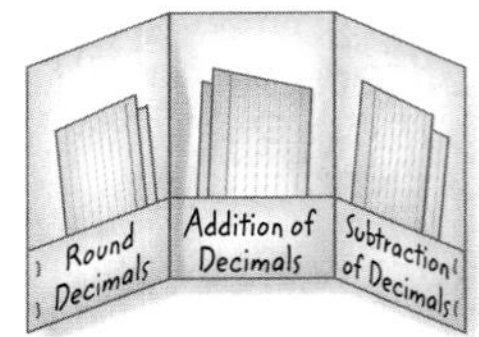

BIG Ideas

Round Decimals (p. 573)

- Round 4.36 to the nearest whole number.

4.36

Look at the digit to the right of the place you want to round to. Since it is less than 5, round down.

So, 4.36 rounds to 4.

Estimate Sums and Differences (p. 576)

- Round each addend to the nearest whole number, then add.

$8.6 + 7.2 \longrightarrow 9 + 7 = 16$

Add and Subtract Decimals (pp. 584, 594)

Find 1.27 + 0.36.

$$\begin{array}{r} 1.27 \\ +\ 0.36 \\ \hline 1.63 \end{array}$$

Find 0.78 − 0.45.

$$\begin{array}{r} 0.78 \\ -\ 0.45 \\ \hline 0.33 \end{array}$$

Key Vocabulary

decimal (pp. 557, 593)
decimal point (pp. 557, 593)
difference (pp. 70, 598)
estimate (pp. 36, 598)
sum (pp. 64, 598)

Vocabulary Check

Complete each sentence with the correct vocabulary word.

1. The answer to an addition problem is the ___?___.
2. A(n) ___?___ is a period separating the ones and the tenths in a number.
3. A(n) ___?___ indicates about how much.
4. The answer to a subtraction problem is the ___?___.
5. A(n) ___?___ is a number with one or more digits to the right of the decimal point.
6. A(n) ___?___ is a number that is close to an exact amount.

Lesson-by-Lesson Review

14-1 Round Decimals (pp. 573–575)

Example 1
Round 12.16 to the nearest tenth.

One Way: Use a Number Line

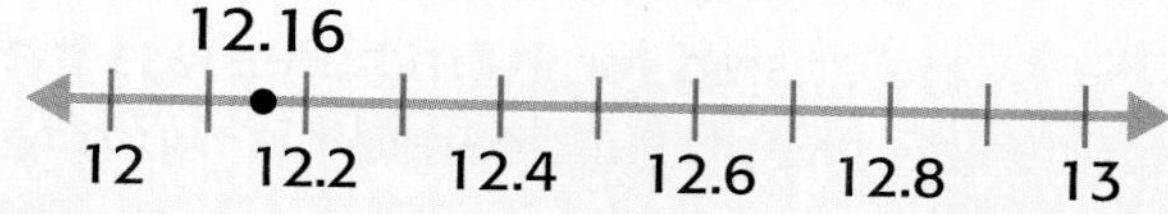

12.16
12
12.2
12.4
12.6
12.8
13

12.16 is closer to 12.2 than 12.1.

Another Way: Use Place Value

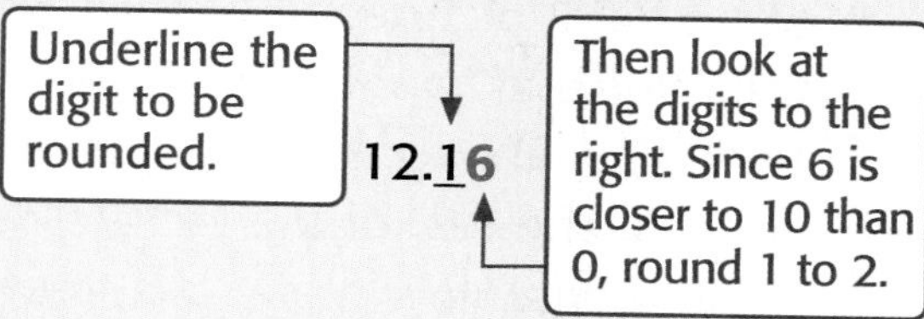

Underline the digit to be rounded.
12.16
Then look at the digits to the right. Since 6 is closer to 10 than 0, round 1 to 2.

So, round 12.16 up to 12.2.

Round to the nearest whole number.

7. 4.12 **8.** 3.65

9. 12.40 **10.** 69.95

11. Measurement Marni hiked 3.65 miles on Saturday. About how many miles did she hike?

12. A baby panda weighs 4.36 ounces. About how many ounces does the baby panda weigh?

13. Travis spent $5.32 at lunch. About how much did he spend?

14. 7.45 **15.** 9.81

16. 32.78 **17.** 44.54

14-2 Estimate Decimal Sums and Differences (pp. 576–579)

Example 2
Estimate 8.63 + 6.15.

$$\begin{array}{r} 8.63 \\ +\ 6.15 \\ \hline \end{array} \rightarrow \begin{array}{r} 9 \\ +\ 6 \\ \hline 15 \end{array}$$

Round 8.63 to 9.
Round 6.15 to 6.

So, 8.63 + 6.15 is about 15.

Example 3
Estimate 25.25 – 12.76.

$$\begin{array}{r} 25.25 \\ -\ 12.76 \\ \hline \end{array} \rightarrow \begin{array}{r} 25 \\ -\ 13 \\ \hline 12 \end{array}$$

Round 25.25 to 25.
Round 12.76 to 13.

So, 25.25 – 12.76 is about 12.

Estimate. Round to the nearest whole number.

18. $\begin{array}{r} 4.88 \\ +\ 14.56 \\ \hline \end{array}$ **19.** $\begin{array}{r} 35.15 \\ -\ 14.93 \\ \hline \end{array}$

20. $\begin{array}{r} 9.51 \\ +\ 7.43 \\ \hline \end{array}$ **21.** $\begin{array}{r} 99.65 \\ -\ 24.67 \\ \hline \end{array}$

22. A basketball costs $17.95. It is on sale for $9.99. About how much less is the sale price than the original price?

14-3 Problem-Solving Strategy: Work Backward (pp. 580–581)

Example 4

Felipe's basketball team is having a car wash. It takes 10 minutes to wash a car. Felipe's team finished washing 12 cars at 5 P.M. What time did the car wash start?

Understand

What facts do you know?

- It takes 10 minutes to wash a car.
- Felipe's team finished washing 12 cars at 5 P.M.

What do you need to find?

- The time the car wash started.

Plan Work backward.

Solve Start with the end result. Then work backward.

12	×	10	=	120
cars		minutes to wash 1 car		minutes to wash 10 cars

5 P.M. − 120 minutes = 3 P.M.

120 min = 2 hr

The car wash started at 3 P.M.

Check It took 120 minutes or 2 hours to wash the cars. Two hours before 5 P.M. is 3 P.M. So, the answer is correct.

23. A number is added to 3. The sum is multiplied by 5. The result is 45. What is the number?

24. Howard is doing his chores. He swept the floor for 20 minutes. He dusted for 10 minutes less than he swept. He cleaned his room for 45 minutes longer than he dusted. How long did it take Howard to clean his room?

25. Alana took 18 pictures of animals. She took 2 pictures of gorillas. She took twice as many pictures of penguins. She took 6 pictures of giraffes. The rest of the pictures are of sea lions. How many pictures did Alana take of sea lions?

26. Harrison, Colin, and Ruthie's favorite colors are red, blue, and green. Colin likes blue the best. Ruthie does not like green. What is Harrison's favorite color?

27. A number is divided by 7. Nine is added to the quotient. Then 5 is subtracted from the sum. The result is 9. What is the number?

14-4 Add Decimals (pp. 584–586)

Example 5

Find 2.7 + 12.38.

Step 1 Line up the decimal points.

$$\begin{array}{r} 2.70 \\ +\ 12.38 \\ \hline \end{array}$$

Place a zero in the hundredths place.

Step 2 Add.

$$\begin{array}{r} \scriptstyle 1 \\ 2.70 \\ +\ 12.38 \\ \hline 15.08 \end{array}$$

Add the digits in each place value.

Regroup if necessary.

So, 2.7 + 12.38 = 15.08.

Add. Use estimation to check for reasonableness.

28. $\begin{array}{r} 3.6 \\ +\ 0.8 \\ \hline \end{array}$

29. $\begin{array}{r} 6.82 \\ +\ 4.7 \\ \hline \end{array}$

30. 5.03 + 18.9

31. 34.82 + 8.31

32. **Measurement** The first flight of an airplane covered a distance of 17.96 kilometers. The plane's second flight covered a distance of 19.57 kilometers. What is the total distance covered by the two flights?

14-5 Problem-Solving Investigation: Choose a Strategy (pp. 590–591)

Example 6

There are 27 plants in a garden. There are twice as many tomato as cucumber plants and three more pepper than cucumber plants. There are 9 pepper plants. How many of each kind of plant is in the garden?

You can use logical reasoning to solve the problem.

There are 9 pepper plants.

There are 3 more pepper than cucumber plants. So, the number of cucumber plants is 9 − 3 or 6.

There are twice as many tomato as cucumber plants. So, the number of tomato plants is 2 × 6 or 12.

Check

9 + 6 + 12 = 27 So, the answer is correct.

Use any strategy to solve.

33. Lani is putting up a tent for camping. The tent has four corners. Each corner needs three stakes. How many stakes does Lani need?

34. Edwin is buying the books shown. How much will the books cost?

35. Use the symbols +, −, ×, or ÷ to make the following math sentence true. Use each symbol only once.

3 ■ 4 ■ 6 ■ 1 = 18

Study Guide and Review

14-6 Subtract Decimals (pp. 594–597)

Example 7

A spider is one of the slowest moving animals. It travels at a speed of 1.2 miles per hour. A sloth is even slower. It travels at a speed of 0.07 miles per hour. How much faster is a spider than a sloth?

To find out how much faster a spider is than a sloth, subtract 0.07 from 1.20.

Step 1 Line up the decimal points.

$$\begin{array}{r} 1.20 \\ -\ 0.07 \\ \hline \end{array}$$

Step 2 Subtract. Regroup if needed.

$$\begin{array}{r} {\scriptstyle 1\,10} \\ 1.\not{2}\not{0} \\ -\ 0.07 \\ \hline 1.13 \end{array}$$

Subtract the digits in each place. Regroup.

The model shows 1.20 − 0.07 = 1.13.

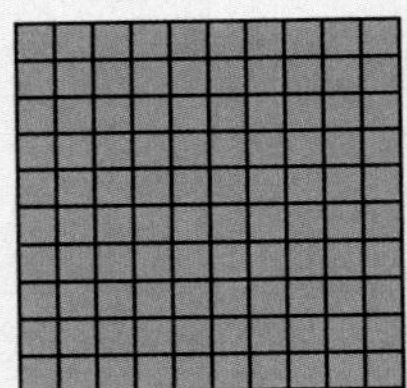

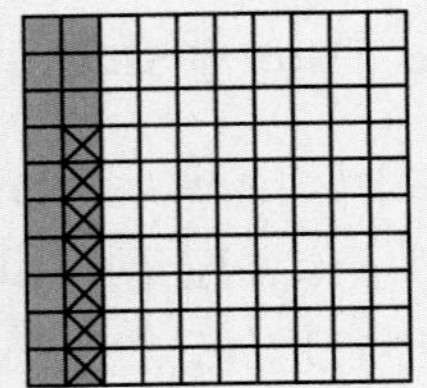

So, a spider is 1.13 miles per hour faster than a sloth.

Check

You can use addition to check.

$$\begin{array}{r} 1.13 \\ +\ 0.07 \\ \hline 1.20 \end{array}$$

So, the answer is correct. ✓

Subtract. Check your answer.

36. $\begin{array}{r} 2.6 \\ -\ 0.7 \\ \hline \end{array}$

37. $\begin{array}{r} 8.3 \\ -\ 1.5 \\ \hline \end{array}$

38. $\begin{array}{r} 6.9 \\ -\ 3.81 \\ \hline \end{array}$

39. $\begin{array}{r} 8.57 \\ -\ 5.9 \\ \hline \end{array}$

40. 26.08 − 16.4

41. 59.81 − 41.26

42. The longest space walk was 8.93 hours long. The second longest space walk was 8.48 hours long. How much longer was the longest space walk than the second longest space walk?

For Exercises 43 and 44, use the table. It shows the snakes that have the longest fangs.

Snakes' Fangs

Snake	Fang Length (cm)
Australian Taipan	1.8
Black Mamba	2.5
Bushmaster	3.8
Diamondback Rattlesnake	2.5
Gaboon Viper	5.1

Source: *Scholastic Book of World Records*

43. What is the difference in length of the Gaboon Viper's and Black Mamba's fangs?

44. Which two snakes have the greatest difference in length of fangs? What is the difference?

CHAPTER 14

Chapter Test

Estimate. Round to the nearest whole number.

1. 26.7 − 9.09 **2.** \$31.56 + \$5.01

3. San Francisco receives an average of 2.9 inches of rain in November. It receives an average of 3.6 inches of rain in December. About how much rainfall does San Francisco receive during these two months?

4. Eva has four coins. Two are the same. One coin is a nickel. One coin is worth ten cents. The other two coins equal 50¢. What coins does Eva have?

Subtract. Check your answer.

5. $\begin{array}{r} 6.9 \\ -\ 2.48 \\ \hline \end{array}$ **6.** $\begin{array}{r} 74.64 \\ -\ 12.8 \\ \hline \end{array}$

7. Marie is 4.25 feet tall. Marie's brother is 3.5 feet tall. How much taller is Marie than her brother?

8. **TEST PRACTICE** What is 67.34 rounded to the nearest tenth?

A 67 **C** 67.34

B 67.3 **D** 68

Add. Check for reasonableness.

9. 4.97 + 8.4

10. 6.26 + 29.4

Round to the nearest tenth.

11. 3.05 **12.** 84.72

13. Hermán rode 16.72 kilometers on his bike. After he rested, he rode another 11.35 kilometers. How many kilometers did he ride altogether?

14. **TEST PRACTICE** Raymond and his father are planning a camping trip. The advertisement for a campsite is shown below.

If Raymond and his father have \$45 to spend on a campsite, how many nights will they be able to stay?

F 2 **H** 4

G 3 **J** 5

Solve for the missing number.

15. ■ + 1.2 = 3.6

16. 2.8 + ■ = 4.5

17. A number is subtracted from 15. The difference is multiplied by 4. Then the product is divided by 8. The result is 3. What is the number?

18. **WRITING IN ►MATH** Explain how to estimate 12.46 + 34.9 by rounding each number to the nearest whole number.

CHAPTER 14

Texas Test Practice

Cumulative, Chapters 1–14

GRIDDABLE Jena jogged 2.5 miles on Wednesday and 3.25 miles on Friday. How many miles did she jog in all during the two days?

TEST-TAKING TIP

Write the answer in the answer boxes on the top line. Then grid in 5, the decimal point, and 75.

Read the Test Question

You need to add to find the total number of miles that Jena jogged on Wednesday and Friday.

Solve the Test Question

Write a 0 after 2.5 since the decimals 2.5 and 2.50 are equivalent. Then line the numbers up at the decimal point. Add the decimals to find the total number of miles jogged.

$$\begin{array}{r} 2.50 \\ +\ 3.25 \\ \hline 5.75 \end{array}$$

Jena jogged 5.75 miles in all during the two days.

 **Personal Tutor at** tx.gr4math.com

Choose the best answer.

1. **GRIDDABLE The Parker family drove 57.2 miles during the first hour and 62.9 miles during the second hour of a family trip. How far did the family drive in the first two hours?**

2. **Samuel is 54.3 inches tall. Nela is 52.6 inches tall. How much taller is Samuel than Nela?**

   A 2.3 inches **C** 2.1 inches

   B 1.3 inches **D** 1.7 inches

Get Ready for the Texas Test
For test-taking strategies and more practice, see pages TX1–TX21.

3. **What is 0.6 + 0.8 as shown below?**

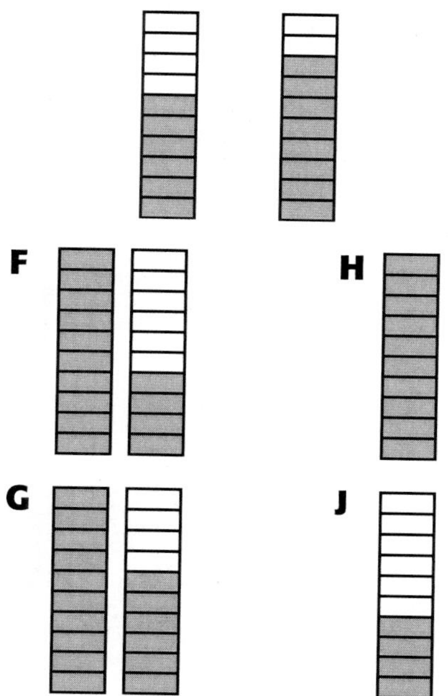

4. **What is 125.618 rounded to the nearest tenth?**

A 125.6
B 125.61
C 125.62
D 125.7

5. **What is the perimeter of the room with the dimensions shown below?**

F 37 feet
G 312 feet
H 74 feet
J 288 feet

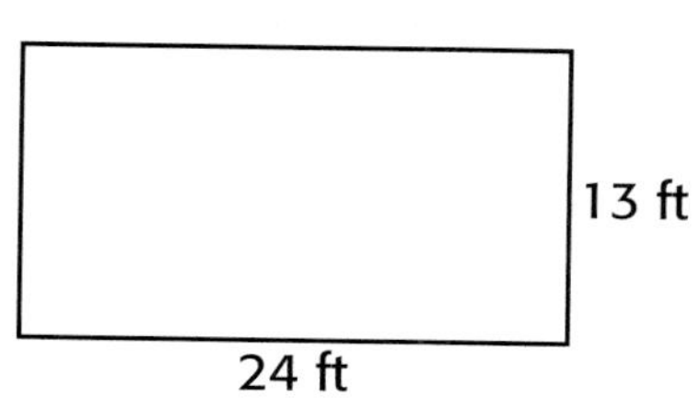

6. **Missy put 14 stickers on each page of a 22-page album. How many stickers are in the album in all?**

A 288
B 308
C 312
D 324

7. **GRIDDABLE One bag of apples weighs 7.23 pounds, and another bag weighs 6.45 pounds. How much do the two bags of apples weigh together?**

8. **Roberto earns $39.75 each week mowing lawns. About how much will he earn in 5 weeks?**

F $180
G $190
H $200
J $210

9. **What number makes this equation true?**

$$54 \div \blacksquare = 9$$

A 5
B 6
C 7
D 8

Get Ready for the Texas Test

It's almost time for the Texas Test. And you may have many questions about it. Here are some answers to help you get ready.

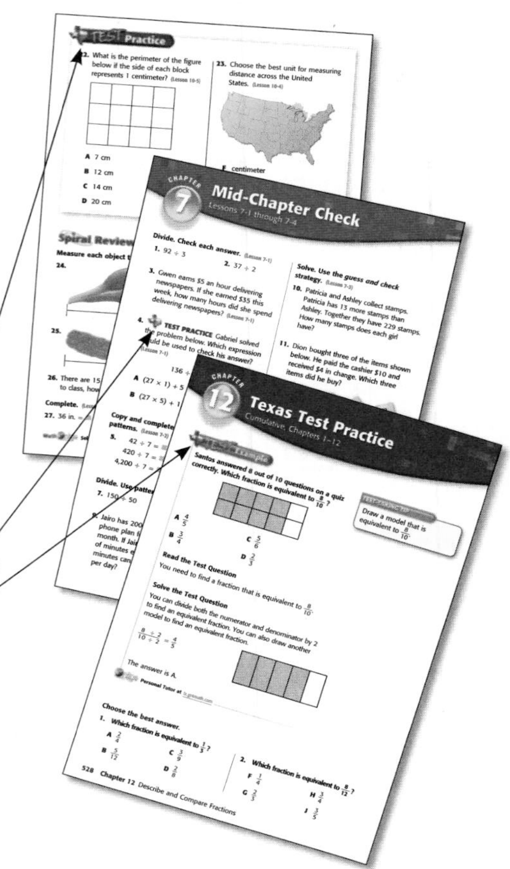

Should I study for the test?

The good news is that you've been studying all along for the test—a little bit every day. Here are some of the ways your textbook has been preparing you.

- **Every Day** Many lessons had practice questions that are similar to the questions on the test.
- **Every Week** The Mid-Chapter Check and Practice Test had several practice questions.
- **Every Month** The Texas Test Practice pages at the end of each chapter had even more questions similar to those on the Texas Test.

Can I still review before the test?

Absolutely! The following pages contain even more practice for each test objective.

Tips for SUCCESS

Before the Test

- Go to bed early the night before the test.
- Eat breakfast.

During the Test

- Make sure that the number of the question on the answer sheet matches the number of the question on which you are working in your test booklet.
- Answer questions you are sure about first.
- If you do not know the answer to a question, skip it and go back to that question later.
- Read each problem carefully.
- Underline key words.
- Watch for key words like NOT. Also look for order words like *least, greatest, first,* and *last.*

Whatever you do...

- Don't try to do it all in your head.
- Don't rush.
- Don't give up. Some problems may seem hard to you, but you may be able to figure out what to do if you read each question carefully or try another strategy.

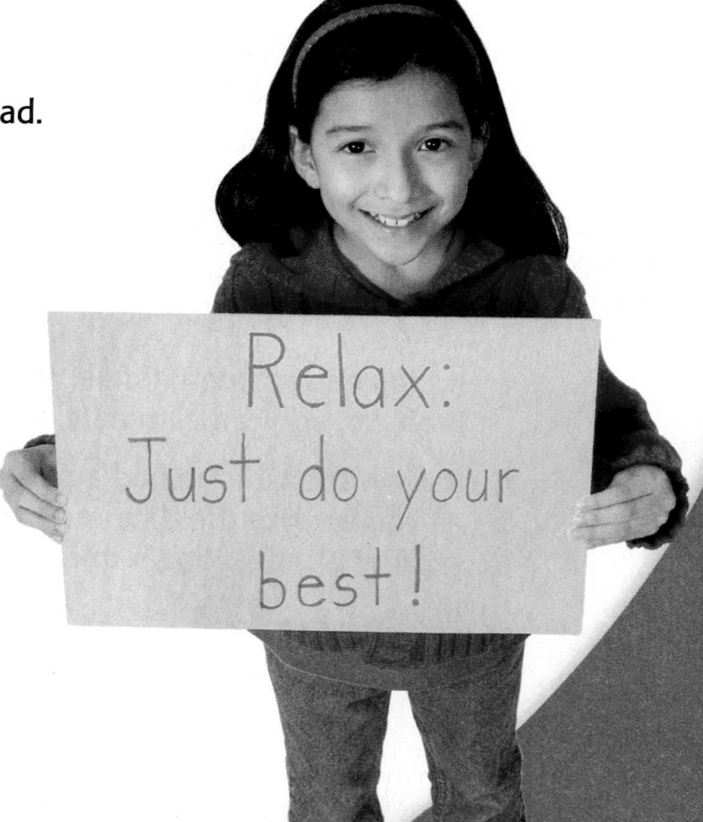

Multiple-Choice Questions

Incomplete shading
Ⓐ Ⓑ Ⓒ Ⓓ
Too light shading
Ⓐ Ⓑ Ⓒ Ⓓ
Correct shading
Ⓐ Ⓑ Ⓒ Ⓓ

Multiple-choice questions are the most common type of question on the Texas Test. You are asked to choose the best answer from four possible answers.

To record a multiple-choice answer, you will be asked to shade in a bubble that is a circle. Always make sure that your shading is dark enough and completely covers the bubble.

1 The table shows the number of hours it took four students to read two different books.

Student	*Charlotte's Web* (hours to read)	*Sounder* (hours to read)
Lisa	9	27
Jason	15	45
Torres	6	18
Monique	12	36

What is the relationship between the number of hours it took the students to read *Charlotte's Web* and the number of hours it took to read *Sounder*?

A It took 18 more hours to read *Sounder* than *Charlotte's Web.*

B It took 30 less hours to read *Sounder* than *Charlotte's Web.*

C It took 3 times as many hours to read *Sounder* as *Charlotte's Web.*

D It took 2 times as many hours to read *Sounder* as *Charlotte's Web.*

STRATEGY

Elimination Can you eliminate any of the choices?

It took each student longer to read *Sounder* than *Charlotte's Web*. So, you can eliminate choice B.

Review the table to find a pattern in the remaining choices. As you analyze the data more, you will see that it took each student 3 times longer to read *Sounder.*

$9 \times 3 = 27$ $15 \times 3 = 45$ $6 \times 3 = 18$ $12 \times 3 = 36$

So, the correct choice is C.

Griddable Questions

Griddable questions are another type of question on the Texas Test. For griddable questions, you mark your answer on a grid printed on your answer sheet.

The grid contains a row of four boxes at the top—three for numbers and one for the decimal point. Below the boxes are three columns of bubbles. An example of a grid is shown below.

TEST Example

2 **The bar graph shows the top speeds of roller coasters in the United States. How much faster in miles per hour is the speed of the roller coaster in New Jersey than the speed of the roller coaster in Texas?**

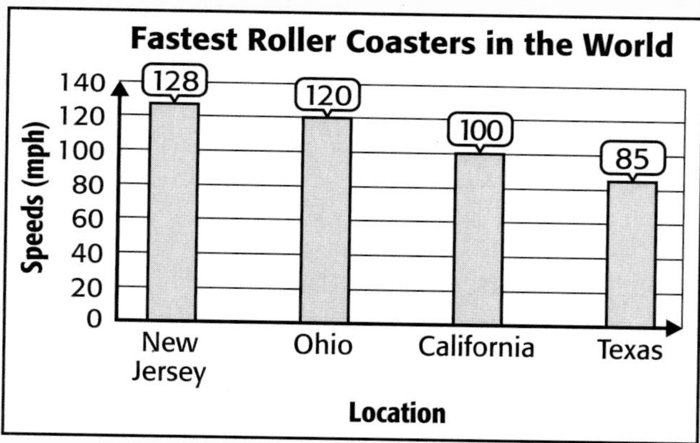

Source: Roller Coaster Database

Record your answer and fill in the bubbles on your answer document. Be sure to use the correct place value.

Remember

- Write only one digit in each answer box.
- Do not write any digits outside the answer boxes.
- Fill in only one bubble for every answer box that you have written in. Be sure not to fill in a bubble under a blank answer box.

You need to find the difference between the speeds for New Jersey and Texas. Read the graph to find the speeds for these two locations. Then subtract Texas' speed from New Jersey's speed.

$$128 - 85 = 43$$

Fill in the grid so that a 4 is placed in the tens place and a 3 is placed in the ones place.

	4	3	.
0	0	0	
1	1	1	
2	2	2	
3	3	●	
4	●	4	
5	5	5	
6	6	6	
7	7	7	
8	8	8	
9	9	9	

Practice by Objective

Objective 1: The student will demonstrate an understanding of numbers, operations, and quantitative reasoning.

DIRECTIONS
Read each question. Then fill in the correct answer on your answer document. If a correct answer is not here, mark the letter for "Not here."

QUICK Practice

1. What is the smallest possible number you can make with the digits 5, 2, 8, 6, and 4? 4.1(A)

A 25,468
B 24,685
C 24,568
D 24,586

2. Mrs. Henderson brought 42 boxes of raisins to her daughter's class. She gave 33 of the boxes away to the students. How many boxes of raisins were left? 4.3(A)

F 8 **H** 10
G 9 **J** 11

3. There are 14 buses at Millwood Elementary School. Each bus holds up to 56 students. How many students in all can be transported by the buses? 4.4(D)

A 784 **C** 660
B 762 **D** 644

QUICK Review

STRATEGY Arrange the digits to make the smallest possible number.

Place the smallest digit in the ten thousands place. Place the second smallest digit in the thousands place, and so on.

For more help with using place value, see page 17.

STRATEGY Subtract to find the number of boxes Mrs. Henderson has left over.

Subtract:
42 − 33 = ______

For more help with using subtraction to solve problems, see page 72.

STRATEGY Multiply to find the total number of students.

Multiply:

$$\begin{array}{r} 56 \\ \times\ 14 \\ \hline \end{array}$$

For more help with using multiplication to solve problems, see page 252.

QUICK Practice

4. GRIDDABLE A pizza is cut into 8 equal slices. How many slices would you have to eat to have eaten $\frac{1}{4}$ of the pizza yourself? 4.2(A)

			.
0	0	0	
1	1	1	
2	2	2	
3	3	3	
4	4	4	
5	5	5	
6	6	6	
7	7	7	
8	8	8	
9	9	9	

5. What fraction is shown by the model? 4.2(B)

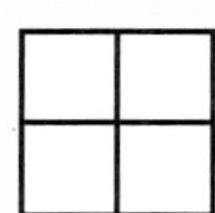
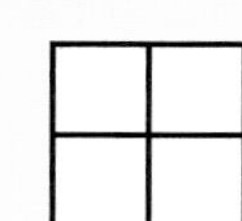
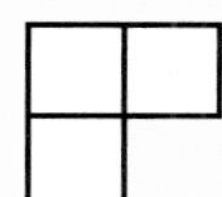

F $\frac{4}{11}$

G $\frac{4}{12}$

H $\frac{11}{4}$

J $\frac{12}{4}$

6. What fraction is represented by the shaded part of the figure below? 4.2(A)

A $\frac{2}{6}$

B $\frac{4}{6}$

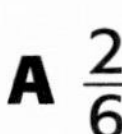

C $\frac{5}{7}$

D $\frac{2}{7}$

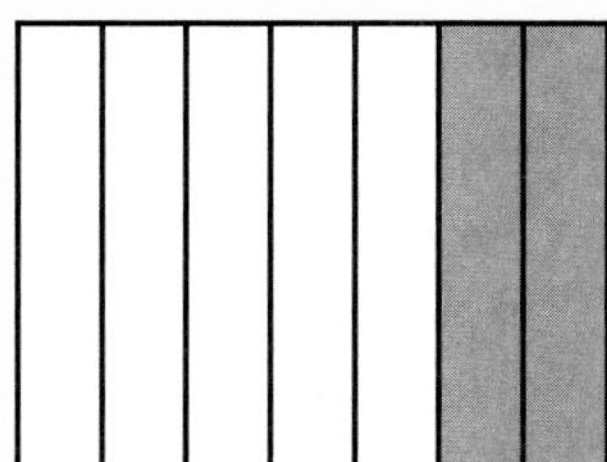

QUICK Review

STRATEGY Find a fraction with denominator 8 that is equivalent to $\frac{1}{4}$.

What numerator will result in two equivalent fractions?

$\frac{■}{8} = \frac{1}{4}$

For more help with finding equivalent fractions, see page 504.

STRATEGY Count the number of whole units and fractional units.

How many whole units are there? What fraction of a whole unit is shown?

For more help with modeling fractions greater than one, see page 516.

STRATEGY Compare the number of shaded parts to the total number of parts.

How many parts are there in the figure? How many of them are shaded?

For more help with writing fractions from models, see page 493.

Practice on Your Own

Objective 1

7. Josh counted 29 desks in each of 3 classrooms in the 4th grade hall. If there are 8 classrooms in the 4th grade hall, about how many desks are there in all? 4.5(A)

F 240

G 250

H 200

J 180

8. Which number sentence best models the pattern of tiles below? 4.4(A)

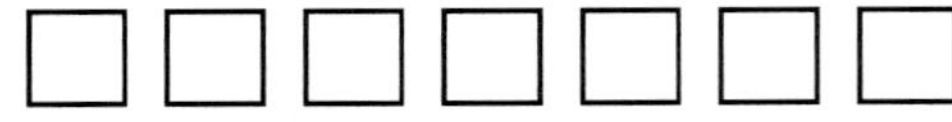

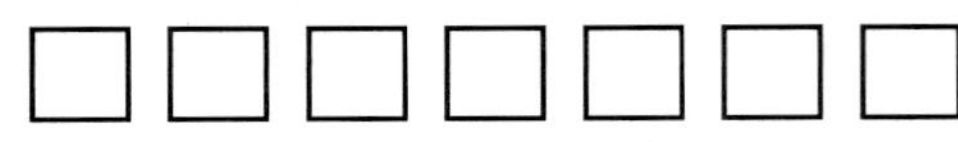

A $7 + 7 = 14$

B $3 \times 7 = 21$

C $3 + 7 = 10$

D $3 + 3 + 3 = 9$

9. Which symbol makes a true number sentence? 4.2(C)

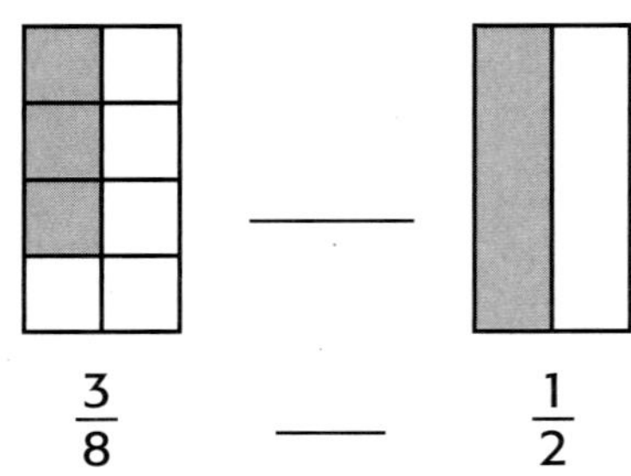

$\frac{3}{8}$ ____ $\frac{1}{2}$

F <

G >

H =

J +

10. The model is shaded to represent $\frac{24}{100}$. Which decimal is equivalent to $\frac{24}{100}$? 4.2(D)

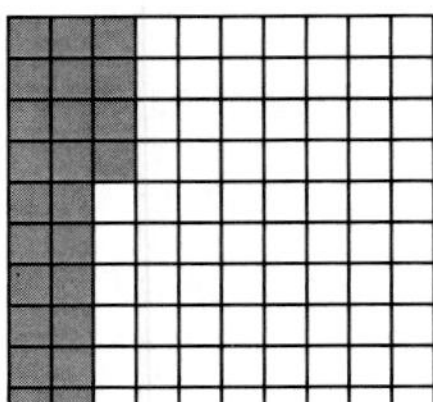

A 0.2

B 0.22

C 0.24

D 2.4

11. The bookstore sells pencils for $2 for each box. About how much would 5 boxes of pencils cost? 4.5(B)

F $5

G $10

H $12

J $15

12. $11 \times 12 =$ 4.4(C)

A 132

B 120

C 122

D 144

13. Fifty-four students are to be divided into 6 equal teams for the school field day activities. How many students will be on each team? 4.4(E)

F 6

G 7

H 8

J 9

Practice by Objective

Objective 2: The student will demonstrate an understanding of patterns, relationships, and algebraic reasoning.

DIRECTIONS
Read each question. Then fill in the correct answer on your answer document. If a correct answer is not here, mark the letter for "Not here."

QUICK Practice

1. In which number sentence does 5 make the equation true? 4.6(B)

A $28 \div 7 = \blacksquare$ **C** $\blacksquare \div 2 = 10$

B $45 \div \blacksquare = 9$ **D** $36 \div \blacksquare = 6$

2. Look at the pattern. What object comes next? 4.7(A)

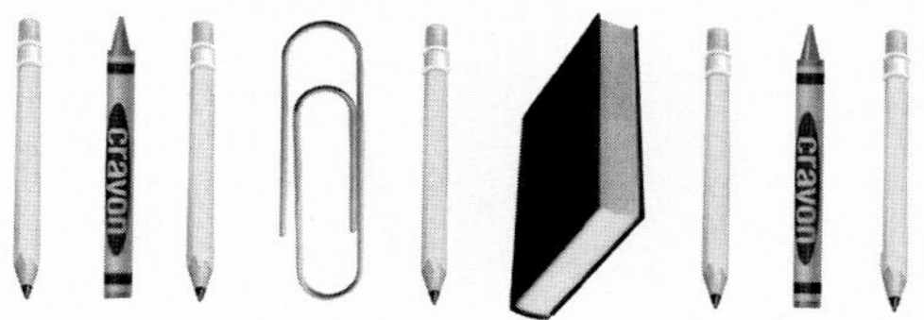

F

H 

G 

J 

3. Eggs are sold 12 to a carton. Which of the following could be the number of eggs purchased by different customers? 4.7(A)

A 36, 60, 72 **C** 24, 48, 62

B 12, 36, 44 **D** 10, 20, 30

QUICK Review

STRATEGY Determine which equation is true when 5 is inserted in the box.

Replace each box with 5. Which one results in a true number sentence?

For more help with completing number sentences, see page 210.

STRATEGY Look for a pattern in the objects to find the next object.

How are the objects repeating in the pattern? If the pattern is extended, what object comes next?

For more help with extending patterns, see page 194.

STRATEGY Generate ordered pairs to find the number of eggs in different numbers of cartons.

Continue the pattern of ordered pairs: (1, 12), (2, 24), (3, 36), and so on.

For more help with generating ordered pairs, see page 198.

QUICK Practice

4. Which number sentence does NOT belong in the same fact family with the others? 4.6(B)

F $24 \div 6 = 4$

G $4 \times 6 = 24$

H $4 + 6 = 10$

J $6 \times 4 = 24$

QUICK Review

READING HINT A *fact family* is a group of related math facts.

Which number sentence could NOT be modeled by the array below?

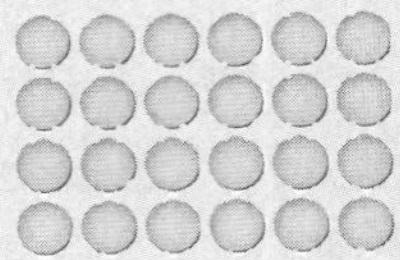

For more help with identifying fact families, see page 137.

5. Juan walks at the park every morning for exercise. The table shows the total number of miles he has walked after different numbers of days.

Morning Walks	
Number of Days	**Number of Miles**
1	6
2	12
3	18
4	24

If Juan walks the same distance each day, how many miles will he have walked after a week? 4.7(A)

A 35 miles

B 40 miles

C 42 miles

D 44 miles

STRATEGY Find the relationship between the number of days Kurt walks and the number of miles.

How many miles does Juan walk each day? How many miles will he have walked in 7 days?

For more help with modeling the relationship between ordered pairs, see page 210.

Practice on Your Own

6. Look at the number sentences below.

$532 \times 10 = 5{,}320$

$75 \times 10 = 750$

$1{,}248 \times 10 = 12{,}480$

$49 \times 10 = 490$

What is 35×10? 4.6(C)

F 35

G 350

H 305

J 3,050

7. The table shows the numbers that were put into a machine and the different numbers that came out of the machine.

In	Out
2	5
4	7
6	9
8	11
10	13
12	15

Based on the information in the table, what happened to each number that was put into the machine? 4.7(A)

A It was multiplied by 3.

B It was divided by 3.

C It had 3 subtracted from it.

D It had 3 added to it.

8. When you multiply a number by 100, you move the decimal point of the number 2 places to the right.

$630 \times 100 = 63{,}000$

What is 409×100? 4.6(C)

F 49,000

G 40,900

H 4,900

J 4,090

9. What rule best describes the pattern of ordered pairs? 4.7(A)

(1, 10) (2, 20) (3, 30)

(4, 40) (5, 50) (6, 60)

A Add 10.

B Add 9.

C Multiply by 10.

D Divide by 10.

10. Binta has 11 pages of stickers in a binder with 12 stickers on each page. She calculates that she has $11 \times 12 = 132$ stickers in all. Which number sentence can she use to check her calculation? 4.6(B)

F $11 + 12 = 23$

G $11 \times 11 = 121$

H $132 \div 12 = 11$

J $132 \div 10 = 12$

Practice by Objective

Objective 3: The student will demonstrate an understanding of geometry and spatial reasoning.

DIRECTIONS
Read each question. Then fill in the correct answer on your answer document. If a correct answer is <u>not here</u>, mark the letter for "Not here."

QUICK Practice

1. Look at the solid figures below. Which figure has exactly two faces? 4.8(C)

A 

C 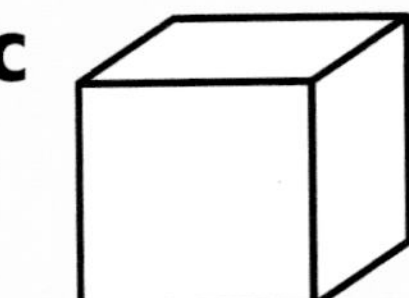

B 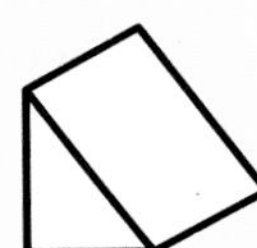

D 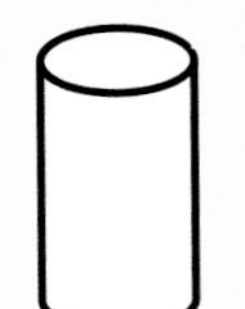

2. What types of angles are formed by two perpendicular lines? 4.8(A)

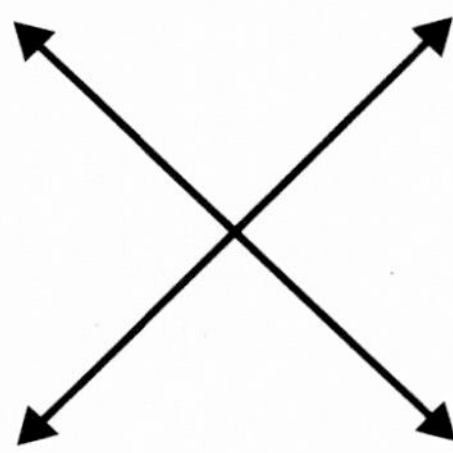

F acute angles
G obtuse angles
H right angles
J straight angles

QUICK Review

READING HINT A *face* is a flat surface of a solid figure.

Which figure shown has exactly two flat surfaces?

For more help with describing solid figures, see page 315.

STRATEGY Recall the meaning of each type of angle and choose the correct term.

Right angles have a measure of 90 degrees. For example, the corner of a room is a right angle.

For more help with identifying right angles, see page 324.

QUICK Practice

3. Look at the pairs of figures below. Which pair shows two rotated, congruent figures? 4.9(B)

A

B

C

D

QUICK Review

READING HINT A *rotation* is a turn. Two figures are *congruent* if they have the same size and shape.

Which pair shows a figure and the result after turning the figure? The figures should both have the same size and shape.

For more help with using rotations to verify congruent figures, see page 374.

4. GRIDDABLE How many lines of symmetry does a square have? 4.9(C)

			.
0	0	0	
1	1	1	
2	2	2	
3	3	3	
4	4	4	
5	5	5	
6	6	6	
7	7	7	
8	8	8	
9	9	9	

READING HINT A *line of symmetry* is a line that divides a figure into two overlapping halves.

How many ways can you fold a square to have two overlapping images?

For more help with identifying lines of symmetry, see page 380.

Practice on Your Own

Objective 3

5. Which pair of figures shows a reflection? 4.9(C)

F

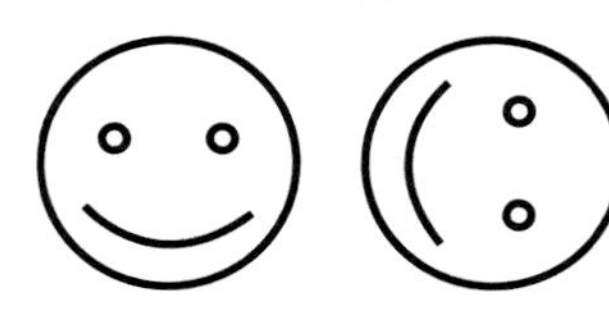

G

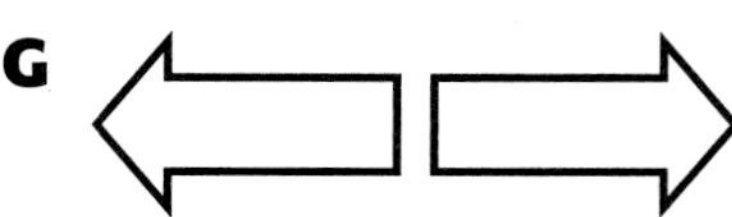

H

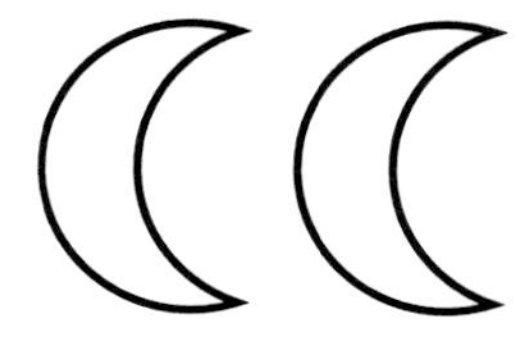

J

6. Which number is best represented by point *Q* on the number line? 4.10(A)

A 3.1

B 3.3

C 3.5

D 3.6

7. Look at the pictures below. Which picture models parallel lines? 4.8(B)

F

G

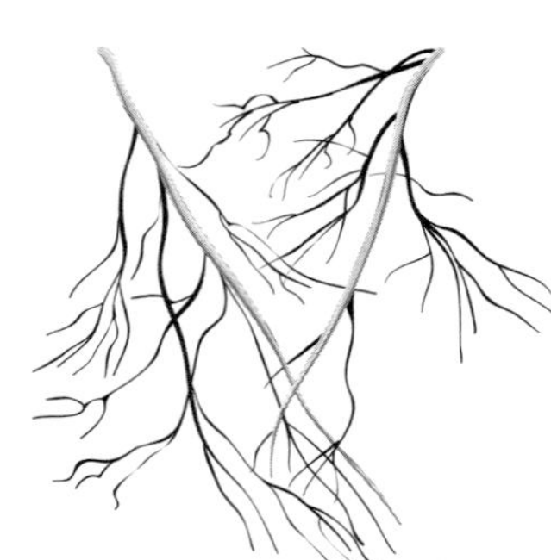

H

J

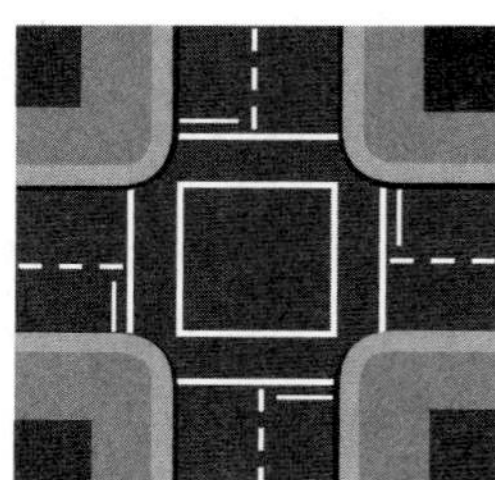

8. Which quadrilateral has 2 pairs of parallel opposite sides and 4 right angles? 4.8(C)

A parallelogram

B rectangle

C square

D trapezoid

Practice by Objective

Objective 4: The student will demonstrate an understanding of the concepts and uses of measurement.

DIRECTIONS
Read each question. Then fill in the correct answer on your answer document. If a correct answer is <u>not here</u>, mark the letter for "Not here."

QUICK Practice

1. Which of the following is the best estimate of the capacity of a pitcher of lemonade? 4.11(B)

   A 2 quarts
   B 2 cups
   C 2 grams
   D 2 kilograms

STRATEGY Eliminate answer choices that do not make sense.

You can eliminate the two answer choices that measure weight. Which of the two remaining answer choices is most reasonable?

For more help with estimating capacity, see page 442.

2. Molly's patio has the dimensions shown below.

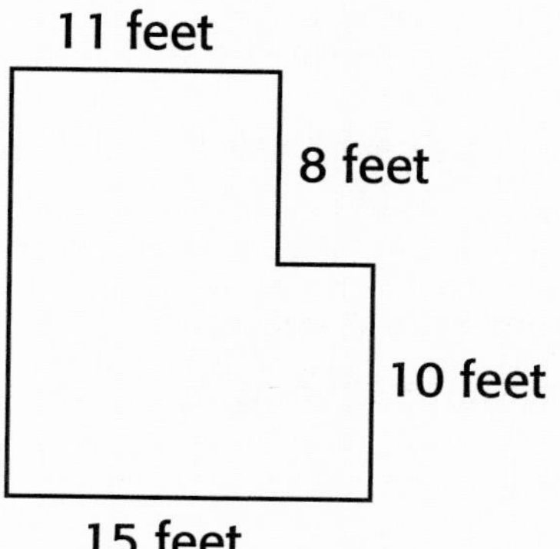

What is the area of the patio? 4.12(A)

F 270 square feet
G 256 square feet
H 238 square feet
J 220 square feet

STRATEGY Divide the patio into two sections. Then find the combined area of the two sections.

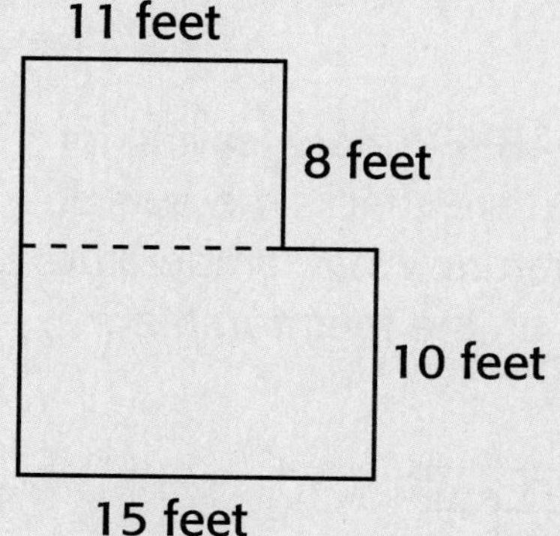

For more help with finding the area of complex figures, see page 414.

QUICK Practice

3. About how much does a large dog weigh? **4.11(A)**

A 50 ounces

B 50 grams

C 50 tons

D 50 pounds

QUICK Review

STRATEGY Choose the most reasonable estimate for the weight of a large dog.

Which answer choices can you eliminate as being unreasonable?

For more help with estimating weight, see page 454.

---

4. Suki got home from basketball practice 2 hours 15 minutes after school ended. She returned home at the time shown on the clock. At what time did school end? **4.12(A)**

F 2:15 P.M.

G 2:30 P.M.

H 2:45 P.M.

J 3:00 P.M.

STRATEGY Subtract 2 hours 15 minutes from the time shown on the clock.

What time is shown on the clock? What time is 2 hours 15 minutes earlier than this?

For more help with solving problems involving time, see page 476.

---

5. GRIDDABLE Before leaving for school, Taye checks the outside temperature. What temperature is shown on the thermometer? **4.12(A)**

			.
⓪	⓪	⓪	
①	①	①	
②	②	②	
③	③	③	
④	④	④	
⑤	⑤	⑤	
⑥	⑥	⑥	
⑦	⑦	⑦	
⑧	⑧	⑧	
⑨	⑨	⑨	

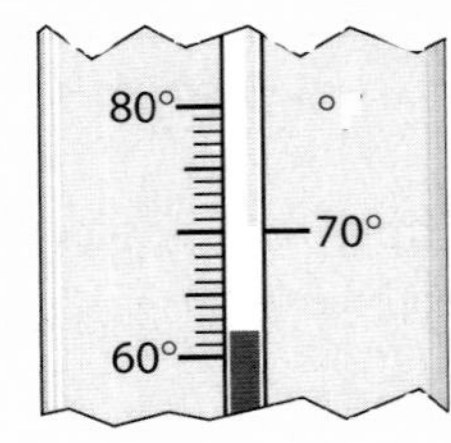

STRATEGY Record your answer carefully in the grid being careful to put the decimal point in the proper place. Place one digit in each block.

What temperatures are represented by the marks on the thermometer?

For more help with reading temperature, see page 422.

Practice on Your Own

Objective 4

6. Gina wants to use her computer to enlarge a picture. Use the ruler on the Mathematics Chart to measure the dimensions of the picture.

What is the area of the picture before Gina enlarges it? 4.12(A)

A 28 square centimeters

B 44 square centimeters

C 48 square centimeters

D 56 square centimeters

7. What is the perimeter of a soccer field with the dimensions shown below? 4.12(A)

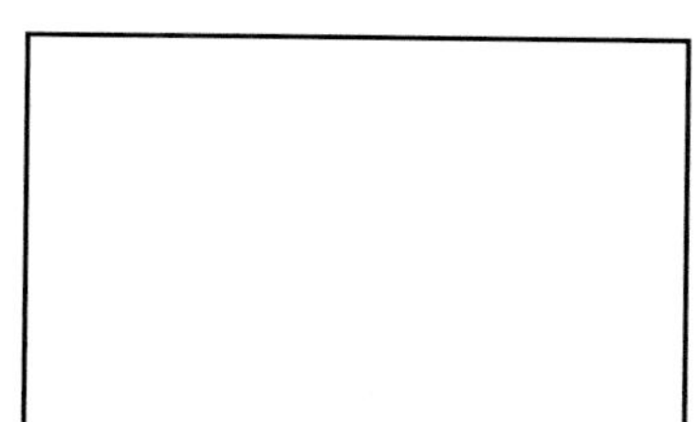

F 185 meters

G 290 meters

H 325 meters

J 370 meters

8. Which of the following objects has a weight of about 2 pounds? 4.11(A)

A 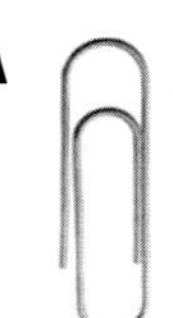

C 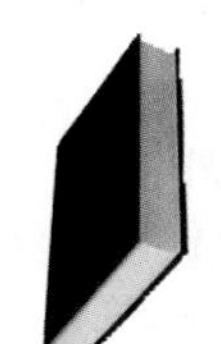

B 

D 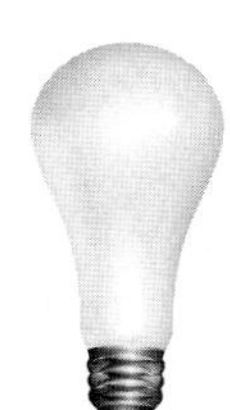

9. Which of the following objects has a capacity of about 1 gallon? 4.11(B)

F  

H  

G  

J  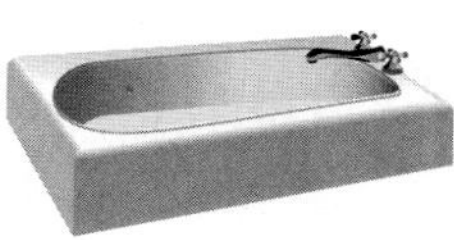

10. Which of the following is the best estimate for the weight of a car? 4.11(A)

A 1,900 tons

B 1,900 ounces

C 1,900 grams

D 1,900 kilograms

Practice by Objective

Objective 5: The student will demonstrate an understanding of probability and statistics.

DIRECTIONS
Read each question. Then fill in the correct answer on your answer document. If a correct answer is <u>not here</u>, mark the letter for "Not here."

QUICK Practice

1. A piggy bank contains 1 quarter, 3 dimes, 2 nickels, and 2 pennies. If Lindsay picks a coin without looking, what is the probability she will pick a dime? 4.13(B)

A 3 out of 5 **C** 5 out of 8
B 3 out of 8 **D** 5 out of 3

2. Danielle has 2 red pencils, 1 blue pencil, 1 green pencil, 2 yellow pencils, and 1 brown pencil in her desk. If she takes 2 colored pencils from her desk at the same time, which colors could she NOT take? 4.13(A)

F red and red
G green and brown
H blue and blue
J yellow and blue

QUICK Review

READING HINT The *probability* of an event is the chance that it will happen. Compare the number of ways the event can happen to the total number of possible outcomes.

How many coins are there in the piggy bank? How many of them are dimes?

For more help with determining the probability of an event, see page 120.

STRATEGY Make a list of the number of each color pencil in the desk.

How many of each color pencil are there in the drawer? Which combination of colors could Danielle NOT pick at the same time?

For more help with listing outcomes of a probability experiment, see page 116.

QUICK Practice

3. Refer to the bar graph below. It shows the number of absent students each day last week at Reggie's school.

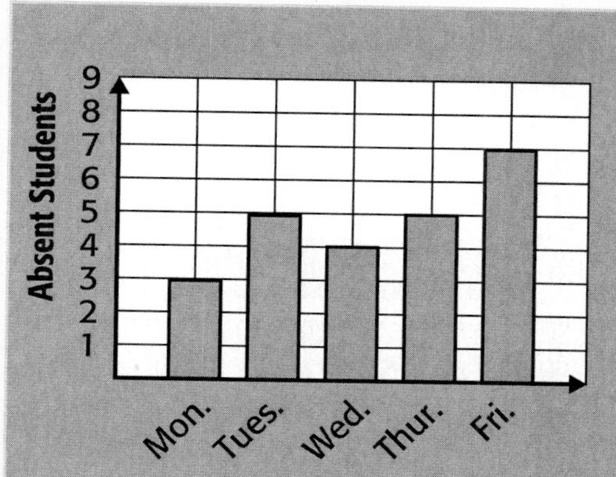

How many students were absent on Thursday and Friday combined last week? 4.13(C)

A 5 students
B 7 students
C 11 students
D 12 students

QUICK Review

STRATEGY Find the bars that represent Thursday and Friday. Find the heights of the two bars.

What are the heights of the bars that represent Thursday and Friday? How many absent students were there on these two days?

For more help with interpreting bar graphs, see page 100.

4. Each player in a game spins the spinner below on his or her turn. What is the probability that Carla will spin an odd number on her next turn? 4.13(B)

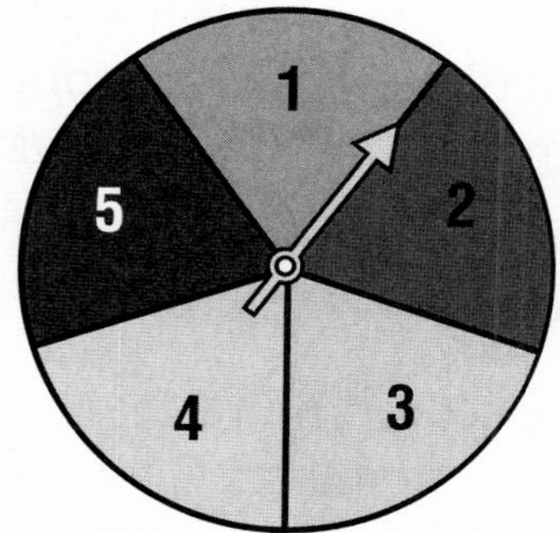

F 3 out of 5
G 3 out of 2
H 2 out of 5
J 2 out of 3

STRATEGY Compare the number of favorable outcomes to the total number of possible outcomes.

How many spaces are there on the spinner? How many of them represent odd numbers?

For more help with determining the probability of an event, see page 120.

Practice on Your Own

Objective 5

5. To play a board game, each player rolls a number cube and chooses a card at random from a deck. There are red and green cards in the deck.

How many possible outcomes are there on each turn? 4.13(A)

A 12 **C** 24
B 16 **D** 48

6. Refer to the rules for the game in Exercise 5. What is the probability that Eduardo will roll a 3 and select a red card on his next turn? 4.13(B)

F 1 out of 8 **H** 1 out of 16
G 1 out of 12 **J** 1 out of 24

7. Suppose Kathi tosses a coin and records the result. Then she tosses a second coin and records the result. Let H represent a coin landing on heads, and let T represent a coin landing on tails. Which of the following shows all of the possible outcomes? 4.13(A)

A HT, TH, TT
B HH, HT, TH
C HH, HT, TH, TT
D HH, HT, TH, HTH, TT

8. Look at the bar graph below. It shows the number of points scored by 4 players in a basketball game.

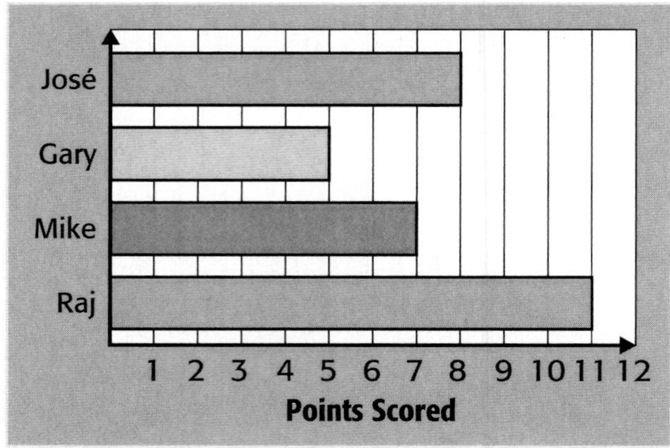

Which player scored 8 points in the game? 4.13(C)

F José

G Gary

H Mike

J Raj

9. Refer to the bar graph in Exercise 8. Which of the following conclusions can you make about the players? 4.13(C)

A José scored the greatest number of points in the game.

B Raj scored more than twice as many points as Gary.

C Gary and Mike scored fewer than 10 points combined.

D The four players scored 30 points altogether.

Practice by Objective

Objective 6: The student will demonstrate an understanding of mathematical processes and tools used in problem solving.

DIRECTIONS
Read each question. Then fill in the correct answer on your answer document. If a correct answer is not here, mark the letter for "Not here."

QUICK Practice

1. The table below shows how many baseball cards five friends have.

Name	Number of Baseball Cards
Tam	59
Marty	76
Pedro	62
Kyle	70
Luis	54

Since Marty has more cards than anyone else, he gives 6 of his baseball cards to Luis. Which statement is NOT true after Marty gives 6 of his cards to Luis? 4.14(A)

A Marty and Kyle have the same number of baseball cards.

B Luis no longer has the fewest number of baseball cards.

C Marty still has the most baseball cards.

D Pedro still has more baseball cards than Luis.

QUICK Review

STRATEGY Change the values in the table to show how many cards each person has now.

How many cards will Marty have after giving 6 of them to Luis? How many cards will Luis have?

For more help with identifying mathematics in everyday situations, see page 42.

QUICK Practice

QUICK Review

2. There are 105 students in 15 groups on a field trip. Each group has the same number of students in it. How could you find how many students there are in each group? 4.14(C)

F Add 105 and 15.

G Subtract 15 from 105.

H Multiply 15 by 105.

J Divide 105 by 15.

STRATEGY Choose an appropriate problem solving method.

What operation would you use to find equal numbers of groups?

For more help with developing a problem solving plan, see page 98.

3. What is the area of the figure below? 4.14(C)

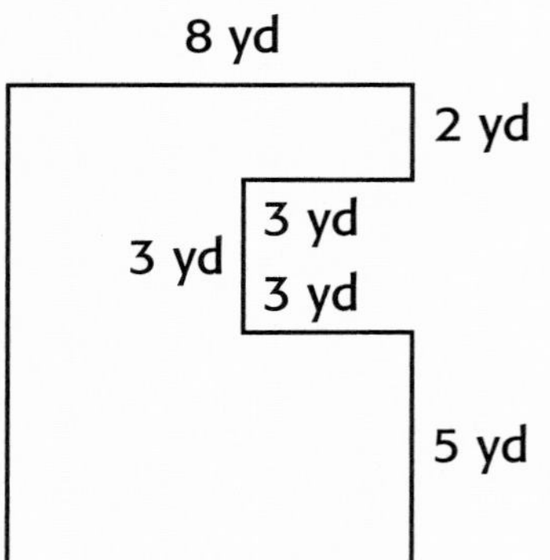

A 60 square yards

B 65 square yards

C 71 square yards

D 74 square yards

STRATEGY Break the problem into simpler parts to make solving it easier.

How can you divide the figure into parts that are all rectangles?

For more help with breaking a problem into simpler parts, see page 402.

4. The 4th graders need to raise more than $248 to take first place in the school fundraiser. Which inequality shows the amounts they can raise to take first place? 4.15(B)

F ■ $\geq$ 248 **H** ■ $>$ 248

G ■ $\leq$ 248 **J** ■ $<$ 248

READING HINT The phrase *more than* means greater than.

Will the 4th graders take first place if they raise $248? if they raise $249?

For more help with using symbols to represent mathematical reasoning, see page 60.

Practice on Your Own

5. The figure below has an area of 324 square inches. What is the area of the non-shaded part of the figure? 4.14(B)

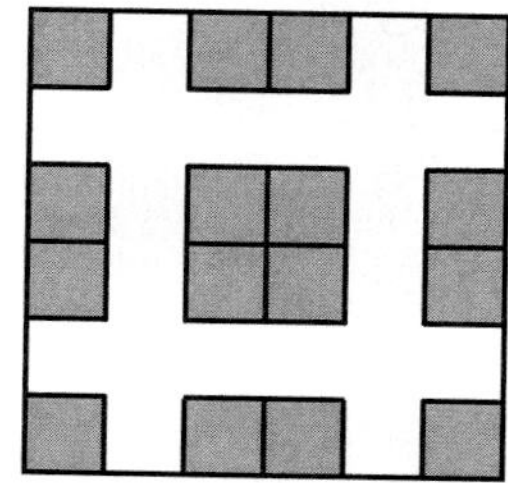

A 180 square inches
B 174 square inches
C 162 square inches
D 144 square inches

6. Kelly is saving money from her babysitting jobs. She wants to buy an arts and crafts paint kit for $18. What information is needed to find how much more Kelly needs to save? 4.14(C)

F How often Kelly gets paid
G How much Kelly has saved so far
H How much Kelly earns for each job
J How many different paint kits the store has

7. Adrian, Emily, Irva, and Oscar are all *zeeps*. None of Danny, Heather, Michael, Roberto, or Zoe is a *zeep*. Which of the following students would be a *zeep*? 4.16(A)

A Terry
B Chow
C Allison
D Paula

8. There are 273 students going on a field trip. The students will travel on buses that hold 48 people each. Which of the following is the most reasonable number of buses that will be needed? 4.14(B)

F 6 buses
G 5 buses
H 4 buses
J 3 buses

9. Mrs. Ames baked 120 cookies for a bake sale. After putting the same number of cookies on each of 16 plates, she had 8 cookies left over. How could you find how many cookies are on each plate? 4.14(C)

A Add 16 and 8 and subtract the sum from 120.
B Divide 120 by 8 and subtract 16.
C Divide 16 by 8 and subtract the quotient from 120.
D Subtract 8 from 120 and divide the difference by 16.

10. Suppose Matt tosses a beanbag onto the game board below. What is the probability that the beanbag will land on a shaded space? 4.14(B)

F 20 out of 32
G 18 out of 32
H 16 out of 32
J 12 out of 32

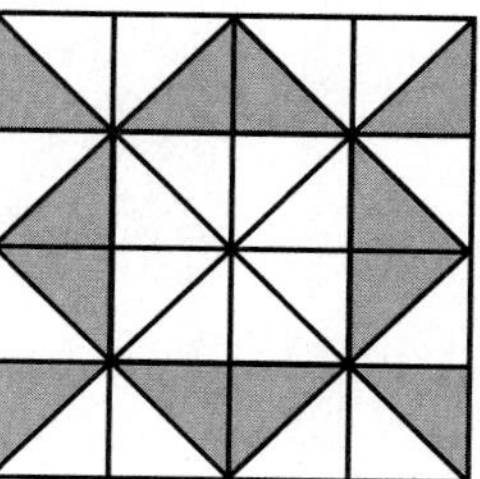

End-of-Year Projects

End-of-Year Projects

Projects

Application of TEKS 4.3(A), 4.4(C), 4.4(D), 4.4(E), 4.6(A), 4.6(B), 4.8(A), 4.8(B),4.8(C), 4.14(A), 4.14(B), 4.15(B), 4.16(B)

Make a Game

Let's make new games.

Getting Started

Day 1 Choose the Subject

- Choose one of the chapters you covered in math class this year. This will be what you make your game about.
- Determine the part of the chapter you want to focus on, such as multiplication facts, attributes of two-dimensional figures, or parts of a set.

Day 2 Brainstorm Ideas

- With your group, determine what facts, figures, or important vocabulary you want to make a part of your game.
- Discuss different ways that this game can be played.
- Design several alternative ways to play the game.

- Discuss a point system.
  - How many points can you earn and the rules to earn them?
  - Can you lose points? How?

Day 3 Rules and Regulations

- Choose one of the alternative games that were designed on Day 2.
- Write rules for the game.
- Decide if there are going to be any regulations like fouls in soccer, or penalties in football.
- Write clear instructions for the game, making sure to include any rules or regulations that may affect the scoring and outcome of the game. Give some examples of how to play and score the game.

Day 4 Create and Practice

- Review the instructions for the game, listing any items that you will need to make, such as pictures of shapes or flash cards.
- Make all items that are needed to play the game.
- Make a score card or board to keep track of the score.
- Practice your game and make sure that it works.

Day 5 Presentation Day

- Present the instructions along with the rules for the game to the class.
- Ask for volunteers to play your game.
- Play and enjoy.

Wrap Up

- How would the game have been different if you played the games using one of your alternative ways?
- Could you use this game for another area in math? Describe what changes would need to be made.
- Are there instructions that you would change?

PROJECT 2

Application of TEKS 4.1(B), 4.3(A), 4.3(B), 4.4(D), 4.13, 4.14(A), 4.14(D), 4.15(A), 4.16(A), 4.16(B)

Plan a Family Celebration

Plan a celebration for your family. It can be a known holiday, special event, or create your own holiday.

Getting Started

Day 1 Decide What to Celebrate

- Decide on a special occasion for your family, for example, family reunion, Independence Day, or "Juneteenth."
- Choose the day and time you will have this celebration.
- Calculate the number of days and hours that you have until the celebration.
- Create a time line to help organize how you will prepare for the celebration.

Day 2 The Number Makes a Difference

- Think carefully about the number of people you want to invite.
- Plan a meal that will generously feed everyone.
- Using cookbooks and family recipes, decide the foods for the celebration.
- Double the recipes.
- Calculate the amounts of each ingredient.
- Calculate a total for all food items.

Day 3 What's the Cost?

- Use the list of ingredients as a shopping list.
- Using the Internet or advertisements from a grocery store, determine the cost of each item.
- Add the amounts together to find the total cost for the recipes.
- Choose any other food items that you might need. Determine the cost and add to your other cost.

Day 4 What Else Do I Need to Buy?

- Make a list of any nonfood items that may be needed.
- Research the cost for these items.
- Make a table to show the amount spent on food and nonfood items.
- Determine the total cost for food and nonfood items.
- Write an equation for the amount spent on each person.

Day 5 Presentation Day

- Present your celebration to the class. Use your time line to describe your plan.
- Share what you will serve, the total cost for each item, and the amount spent for each individual.
- Explain your reasoning for the total cost.

Wrap Up

- Why did you choose this celebration?
- Did the prices of the foods help you decide what you would have at your celebration?
- Would you like your family to use your plan for this celebration?

Have you ever wanted to design a community? When city planners construct a new development, they create a model of the development. Then that development becomes a community.

Getting Started

Day 1 Where Do You Live?

- Research your community. What interesting information can you find?
- Find the total area of the land used for your community.
- Find the area used for parks and recreation.
- Determine the amount of area used for housing.

Day 2 Make It Better

- Think about what makes your community a nice place to live.
- Survey the class for ideas on how to improve communities.
- Place your data on a bar graph to show what you found.

Day 3 Various Viewpoints

- Talk with other students. Find out if their surveys showed similar data. If not, explain why.
- Research the cost of one idea from the survey.
- Decide 3 ways that you can raise money to improve your community.

Day 4 Map It Out

- Using a map of your community, examine the scale of the map. The scale is a chosen distance that represents an actual distance.
- Recreate the map of your community using a different scale than what is shown in the map.
- Look at your classmates' maps. What do you notice about the scales and the size of the maps?

Day 5 Presentation Day

- Present your maps, survey, and other information about your community to the class.
- Is there anything you wanted to add to your community that no one else thought of?

Wrap Up

- Would you change the way you scaled your map next time?
- How can you work toward the goal of getting the things you want to add to your community?
- Who can help you achieve your goals?

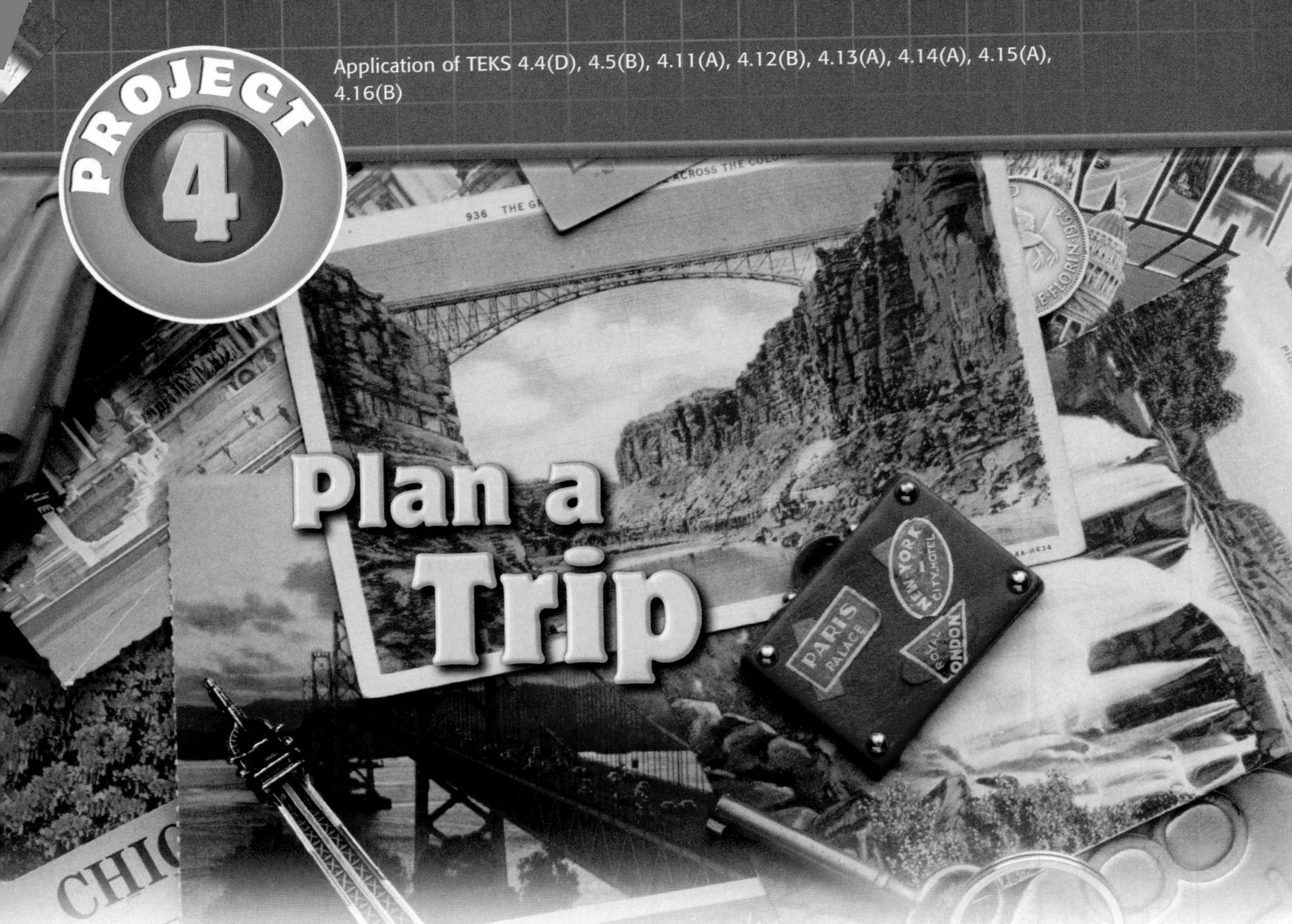

Groups of students plan a road trip in which they determine destination, cost, and route for trip.

Getting Started

Day 1 Plan the Trip

- Plan a trip that includes at least 3 states and is about 500 miles from home.
- Examine a map or atlas to determine all possible combinations of states that fit within the bounds of this trip.
- Choose the path for your trip. Find the distance to your destinations. Add all the distances to determine the total miles to your final destination.
- Multiply by 2 to determine the total round-trip mileage.
- Estimate all costs for the trip.
- Create a table to organize and display this data.

Day 2 Research Items Needed for Your Trip

- Estimate how many hours the trip to your final destination will take if you travel 65 miles per hour.
- Determine how many stops for gas you will need to make if your car gets 30 miles per gallon and holds 18 gallons of gas.
- Write an equation to determine how much you will spend on gas for the entire trip if gas costs $2.25 per gallon.
- Place the cost of the gas in the table from Day 1.

Day 3 What To Do When You Get There?

- Research what you would like to do when you get to your final destination.
- Design a calendar for the week. Account for how each hour is spent.
- Draw a clock next to each event to show the time it will occur. Write the elapsed time for each event.
- Research prices on the places you will go and the food you will eat. Add these figures to the table that was created on Day 1.

Day 4 What Is the Cost?

- Research prices for the hotel. Place this on the table from Day 1.
- Calculate the total cost of the trip using the table from Day 1.
- Finally, prepare a poster showing the information about your trip. Be ready to present it to the class.

Day 5 Presentation Day

- Present your trip to the class.
- Include a summary of where you went, your calendar, the total cost, and the poster.

Wrap Up

- How many places did your group choose from?
- Why did you choose this destination?
- Did the costs of places help you decide where you wanted to go?
- The next time your family goes on a trip, would you suggest that they plan ahead?

Student Handbook

Built-In Workbooks

Reference

How to Use the Student Handbook

A Student Handbook is the additional skill and reference material found at the end of books. The Student Handbook can help answer these questions.

What If I Need More Practice?

You, or your teacher, may decide that working through some additional problems would be helpful. The **Extra Practice** section provides these problems for each lesson so you have ample opportunity to practice new skills.

What If I Forget a Vocabulary Word?

The **English-Spanish Glossary** provides a list of important, or difficult, words used throughout the textbook. It provides a definition in English and Spanish as well as the page number(s) where the word can be found.

What If I Need to Find Something Quickly?

The **Index** alphabetically lists the subjects covered throughout the entire textbook and the pages on which each subject can be found.

What If I Forget Measurement Conversions or Multiplication Facts?

Inside the back cover of your math book is a list of measurement conversions that are used in the book. You will also find a multiplication table inside the back cover.

Extra Practice

Lesson 1-1

Pages 17–19

Write the value of the underlined digit.

1. 1,<u>6</u>37 **2.** <u>3</u>7,904 **3.** 56,5<u>7</u>2 **4.** <u>2</u>09,631

Write each number in word form and in expanded form.

5. 2,493 **6.** 6,319 **7.** 7,085 **8.** 9,160

9. 28,482 **10.** 71,045 **11.** 523,608 **12.** 347,281

Write each number in standard form and in expanded form.

13. fifty-six thousand, seven hundred twenty

14. two hundred thirty-four thousand, eight hundred three

Lesson 1-2

Pages 22–25

Write each number in word form and in expanded form.

1. 9,005 **2.** 19,860 **3.** 26,010 **4.** 360,508

5. 408,040 **6.** 26,053,107 **7.** 730,000,520 **8.** 800,530,700

Write each number in standard form and in expanded form.

9. nine million, twenty-four thousand, ten

10. six hundred thirty-five million, eight hundred fifty-seven thousand, five

11. Write in word form and in standard form.
300,000 + 20,000 + 1,000 + 50 + 8

Lesson 1-3

Pages 26–27

Solve. Use the *four-step plan*.

1. Mrs. Beal's students earned a class party. An extra large pizza cost $28. If she bought 3 pizzas, how much did she spend?

2. Carisa can draw 3 pictures in the morning and 3 pictures in the afternoon. If she draws for 5 days, how many pictures can she make?

3. Tom watched 45 movies this year. Each movie was two hours long. How many hours did he spend watching movies this year?

4. A basketball game has 4 quarters. If 5 players each score 2 points during each quarter, how many total points are scored?

Lesson 1-4

Pages 28–30

Compare. Use >, <, or =.

1. 9,719 ● 9,791
2. 3,780 ● 3,080
3. 34,925 ● 34,952
4. 89,629 ● 89,635
5. 47,283 ● 42,283
6. 72,036 ● 72,300
7. 325,614 ● 235,614
8. 758,438 ● 758,438
9. 7,863,403 ● 7,863,304
10. 9,604,138 ● 9,064,946

Copy and complete to make the number sentence true.

11. 4,■58 < 4,859
12. 34,199 = 3■,199
13. 214,166 > 2■4,166
14. 5,877,820 > 5,877,8■0

Lesson 1-5

Pages 32–35

Order the numbers from greatest to least.

1. 1,443; 1,434; 1,444; 1,344
2. 6,519; 6,600; 3,941; 4,872
3. 19,400; 9,400; 19,004; 10,440
4. 52,951; 49,384; 51,954; 52,865
5. 85,610; 85,185; 85,611; 85,625
6. 94,846; 49,846; 84,694; 46,948
7. 275,391; 2,086,344; 258,983
8. 361,259; 361,084; 61,999; 846,465
9. 568,208; 559,876; 59,986; 58,869
10. 768,635; 792,456; 741,056; 78,318
11. 3,849,257; 38,492,570; 38,492,057
12. 4,608,056; 4,608,942; 4,608,924

Lesson 1-6

Pages 36–39

Round each number to the given place-value position.

1. 136; ten
2. 274; hundred
3. 485; ten
4. 518; ten
5. 749; hundred
6. 920; hundred
7. 1,236; ten
8. 3,521; thousand
9. 4,845; hundred
10. 6,437; thousand
11. 8,146; ten
12. 9,942; hundred

Lesson 1-7

Pages 40–41

Use the *four-step plan* to solve.

1. Lisa lives 7 miles from school. She bikes to school and back every day. How many miles does she bike in 1 school week?
2. A chicken runs 5 miles an hour. An ostrich runs 40 miles an hour. How many hours would it take a chicken to run the same distance it took an ostrich to run in two hours?
3. Aaron bought a shirt that cost $27 and a hat that cost $3. How much change will he receive if he pays with two $20 bills?
4. A bag of 15 oranges costs $20. Oranges that are sold individually cost $2. Is it cheaper to buy 15 oranges in a bag or 15 oranges sold individually? Explain.

Lesson 2-1

Pages 55–57

Copy and complete each number sentence. Identify the property or rule used.

1. $20 - ■ = 0$
2. $14 + 37 = ■ + 14$
3. $7 + (4 + 8) = (7 + 4) + ■$
4. $197 + 0 = ■$
5. $233 - ■ = 233$
6. $72 + 9 = ■ + 72$
7. $(14 + 3) + 8 = 14 + (3 + ■)$
8. $863 + 44 = ■ + 863$
9. $21 + (■ + 9) = (21 + 17) + 9$
10. $541 - ■ = 0$

Lesson 2-2

Pages 58–61

Estimate. Round to the indicated place value.

1. 43 + 29; tens
2. 664 + 49; tens
3. 1,329 + 755; hundreds
4. 9,488 + 2,061; thousands
5. $341.63 + $299.82; hundreds
6. 59 – 34; tens
7. 859 – 42; tens
8. 2,495 – 468; hundreds
9. $6,295 – $1,402; thousands
10. 37,423 – 18,196; ten thousands

Lesson 2-3

Pages 62–63

Use the *act it out* strategy to solve.

1. Nina bought a CD that cost $11.99. She gave the cashier a $20 bill. About how much change should she get back?
2. Carlos wants to buy a new football that costs $32. He earns $6 every week delivering newspapers. How many weeks will it take to save enough money for the ball?
3. The 29 students in Jin's science class are riding in vans on a field trip. Each van can hold 8 students. How many vans will be needed?
4. Mika spends about 1 hour 5 minutes practicing the piano each day, Monday through Friday. About how many hours does she practice in 4 weeks?

Lesson 2-4

Pages 64–68

Find each sum. Check your work by estimating.

1. 456 + 233
2. 681 + 528
3. $387 + $ 43
4. 5,678 + 2,431
5. 36,047 + 13,726
6. $ 67 + $384
7. 60,483 + 98,218
8. $328 + $673
9. 357,816 + 93,402
10. 56,735 + 82,239
11. $9,456 + $ 331
12. $6,789 + $4,351
13. Amanda bowls 179 in her first game. Then she bowls 234 in her second game. What is her total score for the two games?
14. Mario's family is going on vacation. They will travel 1,258 miles on their way there. They are going to take a different route home, so they will travel 1,596 miles. How many miles will they travel in all?

Extra Practice

Lesson 2-5

Pages 72–75

Subtract. Use addition or estimation to check your answer.

1. 721 − 563
2. \$807 − \$328
3. 926 − 644
4. \$1,766 − \$ 819
5. 9,663 − 5,201
6. \$6,741 − \$3,983
7. \$245 − \$ 76
8. 55,788 − 34,223
9. 71,864 − 49,667

Lesson 2-6

Pages 76–77

Solve. Use any strategy.

1. Mr. Lee spent about \$23 on paintbrushes, \$50 dollars on paint, and \$15 on colored chalk. How much did he spend on art supplies?
2. Tia is hanging lights around her window. The window is a square with sides that are 28 inches. How many inches of lights will Tia need?
3. The cats in the animal shelter eat 18 pounds of food each day. How many pounds of food do the cats eat each week?
4. Casey has \$6. He buys a sandwich for \$2, a salad for \$1, and milk for \$1. How much money will he have left?

Lesson 2-7

Pages 80–83

Subtract. Use addition to check.

1. 800 − 567
2. \$400 − \$298
3. 1,000 − 703
4. 3,600 − 1,695
5. 5,000 − 2,367
6. \$9,000 − \$4,890
7. 7,000 − 5,804
8. 6,400 − 3,166
9. 9,600 − 1,879
10. 7,000 − 4,386
11. \$47 − \$28
12. 8,600 − 7,621
13. \$2,200 − \$883

Lesson 3-1

Pages 95–97

Organize each set of data in a tally chart and a frequency table.

1. George recorded the types of pets that his classmates have. His recordings are shown at the right.

Pets		
cat	cat	dog
cat	dog	lizard
dog	fish	bird
bird	dog	fish

2. Tina conducted a survey to find out the favorite sports of the children in the park. Her recordings are shown at the right.

Favorite Sports		
soccer	baseball	football
soccer	basketball	football
football	football	basketball
basketball	soccer	tennis

Lesson 3-2

Pages 98–99

Solve. Use the *make a table* strategy.

1. Akira mailed invitations to his birthday party. The postage to mail each invitation was 39¢. Akira paid about $2 in all for postage. How many invitations did he send?

2. During the soccer season, for every 3 penalty kicks he took, Jamil scored on 2 of them. If he scored on 12 penalty kicks, how many penalty kicks did he take?

3. Nick earns $7 an hour walking dogs. He works the same number of hours each week. Nick earns $252 in 1 month. How many hours does he work each week?

4. Maria bought some six-packs of soda. She bought 48 cans of soda in all. How many six-packs of soda did she buy?

Lesson 3-3

Pages 100–102

For Exercises 1–4, use the graph shown.

1. Which animal has the longest life span?

2. Which animal has a life span of 70 years?

3. Which animal has a life span that is 45 years longer than a gorilla's life span?

4. How many years would three generations of humans last?

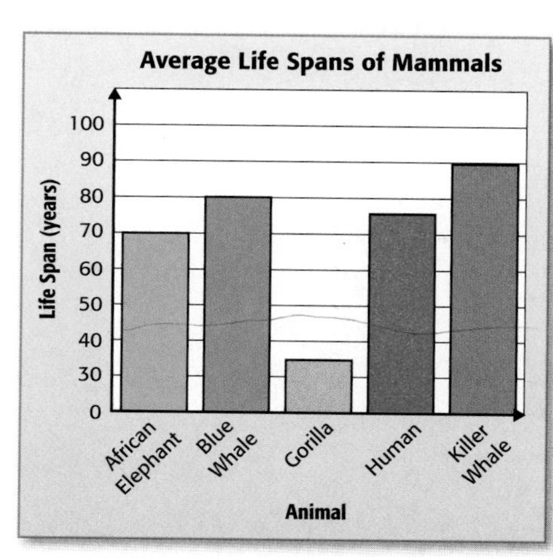

Lesson 3-4

Pages 104–107

Use the graph to answer the exercises.

1. Which fruit did the farm produce the most of?
2. Which fruit did the farm produce the least of?
3. How many more pounds of strawberries were produced than pounds of plums?
4. Which two fruits added together equal the amount of the fruit that the farm produced the most of?

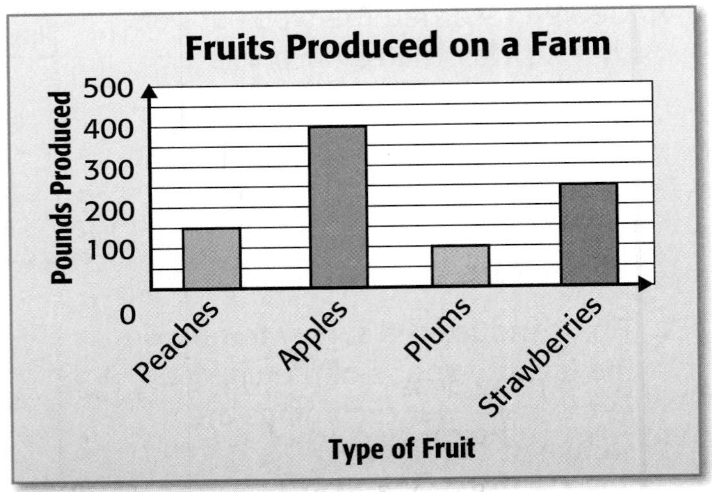

Lesson 3-5

Pages 110–111

Use any strategy to solve. Tell what strategy you used.

1. Luis has an aquarium with 47 fish. There are 12 orange fish, 13 blue fish, 9 white fish, and 8 yellow fish. The rest of the fish are red. How many are red?
2. There were 45 action, 60 comedy, 25 drama, and 50 mystery movies rented from a video store in one day. How many more comedies than dramas were rented?

Lesson 3-6

Pages 116–119

1. Draw a grid to find the number of possible outcomes if a coin is tossed and a 0–5 number cube is rolled.
2. Draw a tree diagram to find the number of possible outcomes if a spinner with three equal sections labeled 1, 2, and 3, is spun twice.

Lesson 3-7

Pages 120–123

Two spinners are divided into four equal parts. The grid shows the possible outcomes when each spinner is spun once.

Second Spinner

First Spinner	Red (R)	Blue (B)	Yellow (Y)	Green (G)
Red (R)	RR	RB	RY	RG
Blue (B)	BR	BB	BY	BG
Yellow (Y)	YR	YB	YY	YG
Green (G)	GR	GB	GY	GG

1. How many possible outcomes are there?
2. What is the probability of spinning two different colors?
3. What is the probability of spinning yellow on the first spin?
4. What is the probability of spinning blue on either the first or second spin?
5. What is the probability of spinning a primary color on the first spin?

Lesson 4-1

Pages 137–139

Copy and complete each fact family.

1. $3 \times 8 = ■$ $\quad 8 \times ■ = 24$
   $24 \div ■ = 3$ $\quad 24 \div 3 = ■$
2. $9 \times ■ = 72$ $\quad 8 \times ■ = 72$
   $72 \div 9 = ■$ $\quad 72 \div 8 = ■$

Divide. Use a related multiplication fact.

3. $27 \div 3 = ■$
4. $54 \div 9 = ■$
5. $36 \div 6 = ■$
6. $88 \div 11 = ■$
7. $32 \div 8 = ■$
8. $50 \div 5 = ■$

Lesson 4-2

Pages 140–143

Identify the property shown by each number sentence.

1. $7 \times 4 = 4 \times 7$
2. $0 \div 15 = 0$
3. $3 \times (4 \times 5) = (3 \times 4) \times 5$
4. $24 \div 1 = 24$
5. $36 \div 36 = 1$
6. $(5 \times 8) \times 6 = 5 \times (8 \times 6)$

Copy and complete each number sentence. Identify the property used.

7. $6 \div ■ = 1$
8. $16 \times ■ = 0$

Lesson 4-3

Pages 144–147

Multiply or divide.

1. 3×8 **2.** 5×5 **3.** 4×7 **4.** 2×9

5. 9×4 **6.** 2×7 **7.** 3×6 **8.** 12×3

9. $27 \div 3$ **10.** $32 \div 4$ **11.** $30 \div 5$ **12.** $15 \div 3$

13. $45 \div 5$ **14.** $28 \div 4$ **15.** $24 \div 4$ **16.** $45 \div 3$

Lesson 4-4

Pages 148–149

Tell which operation you would use to solve each problem. Then solve.

1. Sanjay and 3 of his teammates together scored 52 points in a basketball game. They each scored the same number of points. How many points did each boy score?

2. Sherri jogged 9 miles last week, which is 3 times as many miles as her sister and half as much as her brother. How many miles did her sister and brother jog?

3. There are 6 rows of desks in a classroom. There are 7 desks in each row. How many desks are in the classroom?

4. Roger earns $75 a week delivering papers. How much does he earn in one month?

Lesson 4-5

Pages 150–152

Multiply or divide.

1. 9×6 **2.** 6×8 **3.** 7×7 **4.** 8×10

5. 5×8 **6.** 9×5 **7.** 6×10 **8.** 7×9

9. $42 \div 6$ **10.** $48 \div 6$ **11.** $90 \div 10$ **12.** $56 \div 7$

13. $35 \div 5$ **14.** $81 \div 9$ **15.** $36 \div 6$ **16.** $72 \div 8$

Lesson 4-6

Pages 156–159

Multiply or divide.

1. $\begin{array}{r} 3 \\ \times 11 \\ \hline \end{array}$

2. $\begin{array}{r} 4 \\ \times 12 \\ \hline \end{array}$

3. $\begin{array}{r} 11 \\ \times 6 \\ \hline \end{array}$

4. 8×12

5. 7×11

6. 4×12

7. $11\overline{)88}$

8. $11\overline{)110}$

9. $12\overline{)48}$

10. $120 \div 12$

11. $99 \div 11$

12. $96 \div 12$

Lesson 4-7

Pages 160–161

Use any strategy to solve. Tell what strategy you used.

1. Manuel earns $4 for every 3 dozen cookies he sells. How much will Manuel earn if he sells 9 dozen cookies? 12 dozen cookies?

2. Laura has 24 jazz CDs and 7 country CDs. She has 2 times as many pop CDs as country CDs. How many CDs does she have in all?

3. Kim wants to buy a snowboard that costs $160. She has $88 in the bank. If she earns $6 an hour babysitting, how many hours will Kim have to work to earn enough money to buy the snowboard?

4. An art gallery has paintings on display in 7 rooms. There are 12 paintings in each room. How many paintings are on display in the art gallery?

Lesson 4-8

Pages 162–165

Multiply.

1. $6 \times 3 \times 4$

2. $5 \times 7 \times 3$

3. $8 \times 2 \times 5$

4. $9 \times 3 \times 2$

5. $6 \times 4 \times 5$

6. $9 \times 1 \times 4$

7. $8 \times 4 \times 3$

8. $3 \times 3 \times 12$

9. $10 \times 3 \times 5$

10. $6 \times 11 \times 1$

11. $9 \times 4 \times 2$

12. $12 \times 2 \times 4$

Extra Practice

Lesson 4-9

Pages 166–169

Find all of the factors of each number.

1. 36 **2.** 18 **3.** 16

4. 35 **5.** 11 **6.** 24

7. 48 **8.** 40 **9.** 23

Identify the first six multiples for each number.

10. 4 **11.** 7 **12.** 6

13. 12 **14.** 8 **15.** 9

16. 10 **17.** 1 **18.** 3

Lesson 5-1

Pages 183–185

Find the value of each expression if ▲ = 6 and ■ = 7.

1. ■ + 5 **2.** ▲ − 3 **3.** ■ + 9

4. 7 + ▲ **5.** ■ − 2 **6.** 14 − ▲

7. (▲ − 2) + 9 **8.** 16 − (■ + 5) **9.** 5 + (6 + ▲)

Write an expression for each situation.

10. five less than ●

11. the sum of ◆ and seventeen

12. ★ minus twenty-four

13. fifty-one subtracted from ▲

Lesson 5-2

Pages 188–191

Solve each equation mentally.

1. 4 + ■ = 12 **2.** 7 + ■ = 18 **3.** ■ − 8 = 6 **4.** 18 − 13 = ■

5. 9 − ■ = 2 **6.** ■ + 14 = 22 **7.** 8 + ■ = 18 **8.** 7 + 6 = ■

Write and solve an equation for each situation.

9. Twelve less than a number is sixteen. What is the number?

10. Eight subtracted from a number equals thirteen. What is the number?

11. The sum of nine and a number is twenty-eight. Find the number.

12. A number plus eleven equals twenty-five. What is the number?

Lesson 5-3

Pages 192–193

Identify any missing or extra information. Then solve if possible.

1. Monkeys at the zoo eat 9 bananas and 4 apples each day. How many pieces of fruit do the monkeys eat in one week?

2. Sandra has $21. She wants to buy cans of tennis balls for $4 each. There are 3 tennis balls in each can. How many cans can she buy?

3. Marco has soccer practice 3 days a week. He has 17 teammates. Practice lasts for 2 hours each day. How many hours does Marco practice soccer each week?

4. Kayla earns $5 per hour. She is saving to buy a new game that costs $36. How many weeks will Kayla have to work to earn enough money for the game?

Lesson 5-4

Pages 194–196

Find the rule and find the next number in each pattern.

1. 3, 7, 11, 15, 19, ■
2. 27, 22, 17, 12, 7, ■
3. 2, 5, 3, 6, 4, ■
4. 5, 1, 7, 3, 9, ■

5. Sara jogs on a track five days a week. What is the rule for the pattern shown in the table?

Distance Jogged					
Day	1	2	3	4	5
Laps	8	16	24	32	40

6. Trevor practices the guitar every day. What is the rule for the pattern shown in the table.

Time Spent Practicing							
Day	1	2	3	4	5	6	7
Minutes	45	90	135	180	225	270	315

Lesson 5-5

Pages 198–201

Write an equation that describes the pattern. Then use the equation to find the next three numbers.

1.

Rule: ■						
Input (▲)	4	6	10	14	20	24
Output (■)	13	15	19	■	■	■

2.

Rule: ■						
Input (▲)	11	15	19	23	27	31
Output (■)	4	8	12	■	■	■

3.

Rule: ■						
Input (▲)	$24	$32	$40	$48	$56	$64
Output (■)	$16	$24	$32	■	■	■

4.

Rule: ■						
Input (▲)	$16	$19	$22	$25	$28	$31
Output (■)	$27	$30	$33	■	■	■

5. The amounts an ice arena charges for people to ice skate are shown. How much would it cost for 20, 25, and 30 people to ice skate?

Skaters	Cost ($)
5	$30
10	$60
15	$90
20	■
25	■
30	■

Lesson 5-6

Pages 204–207

Find the value of each expression if ▲ = 4 and ■ = 8.

1. ■ ÷ 4

2. 6 × ▲

3. ■ ÷ ▲

4. ▲ ÷ ▲

5. ■ × 7

6. 5 × ▲

7. (▲ × 4) ÷ ■

8. 32 ÷ (■ ÷ ▲)

9. (■ ÷ 2) × 9

Write an expression for each situation.

10. a number divided by 5

11. The product of 3 and a number

12. a number divided by 10

13. 9 times a number

A tennis coach has 8 cans of tennis balls. Each can contains 3 tennis balls.

14. Define a symbol. Then write an expression for the number of tennis balls the coach has.

15. If the coach bought 3 more cans of tennis balls, how many tennis balls will the coach have?

Lesson 5-7

Pages 208–209

Use any strategy to solve. Tell what strategy you used.

1. Ty wants to buy posters that cost $7 each. He has $50. How many posters can he buy?

2. Ian is eating pizza with 5 of his friends. They ordered 3 pizzas. If each pizza is cut into 6 slices, how many slices can each person have?

3. A vine in the park grows 2 inches every week. The vine is 13 inches tall now. How many inches tall will the vine be in 2 weeks? 4 weeks? 8 weeks?

4. Amy is putting photos in an album. Each page in the album can hold 4 photos. There are 32 pages in the album. How many photos can Amy put in the album?

Lesson 5-8

Pages 210–213

Write an equation that describes the pattern. Then use the equation to find the next three numbers.

1.

Input (▲)	Output (■)
2	12
4	24
6	36
8	■
10	■
12	■

2.

Input (▲)	Output (■)
21	3
28	4
35	5
42	■
49	■
56	■

3.

Input (▲)	Output (■)
3	12
6	24
9	36
12	■
15	■
18	■

4.

Input (▲)	Output (■)
18	2
36	4
54	6
72	■
90	■
108	■

5. The table shows the cost of concert tickets. How many people can attend the concert for $132?

Total Cost	Input(▲)	$22	$44	$66	$88	$110	$132
Tickets	Output(■)	2	4	6	■	■	■

Lesson 6-1

Pages 227–229

Multiply. Use basic facts and patterns.

1. 4×5
4×50
4×500
$4 \times 5{,}000$

2. 3×7
3×70
3×700
$3 \times 7{,}000$

3. 8×6
8×60
8×600
$8 \times 6{,}000$

4. 3×9
3×90
3×900
$3 \times 9{,}000$

5. 5×6
5×60
5×600
$5 \times 6{,}000$

6. 7×4
7×40
7×400
$7 \times 4{,}000$

Multiply. Use mental math.

7. 7×80

8. 60×6

9. 90×3

10. 500×7

11. 9×400

12. $8{,}000 \times 5$

13. Jerome read a 9-page chapter in a book. If there are about 200 words on each page, how many words did he read?

14. A Galapagos turtle has the longest life span of any reptile. It can live up to 3×50 years. How many years can a Galapagos turtle live?

Lesson 6-2

Pages 230–231

Decide whether each answer is reasonable. Explain your reasoning.

1. Ebony practices the guitar 30 minutes every day. Is it reasonable to say that she practices the guitar more than 200 minutes each week?

2. The soccer fields in a park are each 130 yards long. Is it reasonable to say that 3 soccer fields are a total of 390 feet long?

3. The chickens on a farm produce about 4,200 eggs per week. Is it reasonable to say that the chickens produce 600 eggs each day?

4. Aman's album can hold 12 stamps on each page. There are 200 pages in the album. Is it reasonable to say that Aman's album can hold 24,000 stamps?

Lesson 6-3

Pages 232–235

Estimate each product by rounding or using compatible numbers.

1. $\begin{array}{r} 584 \\ \times\ 3 \\ \hline \end{array}$

2. $\begin{array}{r} 484 \\ \times\ 5 \\ \hline \end{array}$

3. $\begin{array}{r} 723 \\ \times\ 8 \\ \hline \end{array}$

4. 3 × 692

5. 6 × $472

6. 9 × $460

7. 7 × 1,986

8. 8 × $5,420

9. 5 × 6,752

10. 3 × $478

11. 6 × $9,810

12. 8 × 3,755

13. Earth travels through space at a rate of about 19 miles per second. About how many miles does Earth travel in 8 seconds?

14. A certain type of centipede has 178 legs. About how many legs would four of these centipedes have in all?

Lesson 6-4

Pages 236–238

Multiply. Check for reasonableness.

1. $\begin{array}{r} 18 \\ \times\ 6 \\ \hline \end{array}$

2. $\begin{array}{r} 28 \\ \times\ 5 \\ \hline \end{array}$

3. $\begin{array}{r} \$17 \\ \times\ 9 \\ \hline \end{array}$

4. 2 × 99

5. 6 × 25

6. 7 × $43

7. 5 × 73

8. 4 × $86

9. 9 × 39

10. 3 × $92

11. 8 × 78

12. 7 × $56

13. An armadillo sleeps 10 hours each day. How many hours does an armadillo sleep in a week?

14. Lisa plays the piano for 45 minutes during each of her piano lessons. If Lisa has three lessons each week, how many minutes does she play the piano each week?

Lesson 6-5

Pages 240–241

Use any strategy to solve. Tell what strategy you used.

1. Jesse bikes 56 miles each week. How many miles does Jesse bike in four weeks?

2. Movie tickets are $7 for adults and $3 for children. What is the total cost if three adults and five children go to the theater?

3. Rita is making muffins. There are 36 muffins in each batch. How many muffins will be in 3 batches of muffins? How many muffins will be in 7 batches of muffins?

4. At the zoo, the big cats are in a row. The lions are last. The jaguars are to the left of the tigers. The cheetahs are to the left of the jaguars. In what order are the big cats?

Lesson 6-6

Pages 242–245

Use technology to multiply. Check for reasonableness.

1. 127 × 2

2. $284 × 4

3. 419 × 3

4. $524 × 4

5. 360 × 5

6. 493 × 6

7. 671 × 5

8. 734 × 6

9. $897 × 9

10. 8 × $563

11. 7 × 481

12. 9 × 934

13. There are about 365 days in one year. How many days are in 5 years?

14. A city in Hawaii receives about 45 inches of rain each year. How many inches of rain would this city receive in 8 years?

Lesson 6-7

Pages 248–249

Multiply.

1. $\begin{array}{r} 18 \\ \times 30 \\ \hline \end{array}$

2. $\begin{array}{r} 24 \\ \times 50 \\ \hline \end{array}$

3. $\begin{array}{r} 48 \\ \times 90 \\ \hline \end{array}$

4. $\begin{array}{r} 47 \\ \times 60 \\ \hline \end{array}$

5. $\begin{array}{r} 75 \\ \times 40 \\ \hline \end{array}$

6. $\begin{array}{r} 56 \\ \times 90 \\ \hline \end{array}$

7. $\begin{array}{r} 64 \\ \times 30 \\ \hline \end{array}$

8. $\begin{array}{r} \$49 \\ \times 60 \\ \hline \end{array}$

9. $\begin{array}{r} 85 \\ \times 70 \\ \hline \end{array}$

10. $\begin{array}{r} \$28 \\ \times 30 \\ \hline \end{array}$

11. $\begin{array}{r} 92 \\ \times 70 \\ \hline \end{array}$

12. $\begin{array}{r} 63 \\ \times 90 \\ \hline \end{array}$

13. How many hours are in a month that is 30 days long?

14. A certain type of whale is 60 feet long. What is this whale's length in inches?

Lesson 6-8

Pages 252–255

Multiply.

1. $\begin{array}{r} 17 \\ \times 25 \\ \hline \end{array}$

2. $\begin{array}{r} 56 \\ \times 33 \\ \hline \end{array}$

3. $\begin{array}{r} \$84 \\ \times 42 \\ \hline \end{array}$

4. $\begin{array}{r} 62 \\ \times 55 \\ \hline \end{array}$

5. $\begin{array}{r} 74 \\ \times 93 \\ \hline \end{array}$

6. $\begin{array}{r} \$65 \\ \times 48 \\ \hline \end{array}$

7. $\begin{array}{r} 36 \\ \times 56 \\ \hline \end{array}$

8. $\begin{array}{r} 49 \\ \times 77 \\ \hline \end{array}$

9. $\begin{array}{r} \$44 \\ \times 83 \\ \hline \end{array}$

10. $\begin{array}{r} 64 \\ \times 95 \\ \hline \end{array}$

11. $\begin{array}{r} \$58 \\ \times 17 \\ \hline \end{array}$

12. $\begin{array}{r} 75 \\ \times 73 \\ \hline \end{array}$

13. An anaconda can be about 29 feet long. How many inches long would this snake be?

14. One of the longest space shuttle flights lasted 17 days and almost 9 hours. How many hours did this flight last in all?

Extra Practice

Lesson 7-1

Pages 269–271

Divide. Draw a picture to help. Check each answer.

1. 36 ÷ 3 **2.** 60 ÷ 5 **3.** 54 ÷ 3

4. 70 ÷ 5 **5.** 98 ÷ 7 **6.** 91 ÷ 7

7. 79 ÷ 3 **8.** 66 ÷ 4 **9.** 95 ÷ 7

10. It takes 87 cups of milk to make three pounds of butter. How many cups of milk are needed to make one pound of butter?

11. Damon is dividing 48 grapes equally amongst two of his friends and himself. How many grapes will each person get?

Lesson 7-2

Pages 272–275

Copy and complete each set of patterns.

1. 48 ÷ 6 = ■
480 ÷ 6 = ■
4,800 ÷ 6 = ■

2. 63 ÷ 9 = ■
630 ÷ 9 = ■
6,300 ÷ 9 = ■

3. $40 ÷ 8 = ■
$400 ÷ 8 = ■
$4,000 ÷ 8 = ■

4. 72 ÷ 9 = ■
720 ÷ 9 = ■
7,200 ÷ 6 = ■

5. $27 ÷ 3 = ■
$270 ÷ 3 = ■
$2,700 ÷ 3 = ■

6. 35 ÷ 7 = ■
350 ÷ 7 = ■
3,500 ÷ 7 = ■

Divide. Use patterns.

7. 420 ÷ 6 **8.** 300 ÷ 5 **9.** $280 ÷ 7

10. $210 ÷ 3 **11.** 5,600 ÷ 7 **12.** 7,200 ÷ 8

13. 8,100 ÷ 9 **14.** 1,600 ÷ 4 **15.** 3,000 ÷ 6

16. $2,700 ÷ 3 **17.** 4,500 ÷ 9 **18.** 5,400 ÷ 9

19. Nina slept about 240 hours last month. If she slept 8 hours each night, how many days were in last month?

20. Sam has 270 minutes left on his phone card. How many 30-minute phone calls can he make?

Lesson 7-3

Pages 276–277

Solve. Use the *guess and check* strategy.

1. Ren bought 5 CDs for $55. One of the CDs cost $5 more than the others. How much did each CD cost?
2. Carmen has 49 more mystery novels than adventure novels. She has 223 novels in all. How many mystery novels and adventure novels does Carmen have?
3. The chickens on a farm eat 3 times as much grain as the turkeys do per week. The chickens and turkeys eat a total of 52 pounds of grain every week. How much grain do the chickens and turkeys each eat every week?
4. A toy store has at least 10 wagons and at least 10 tricycles on sale. There are a total of 89 wheels. How many tricycles and how many wagons are on sale?

Lesson 7-4

Pages 278–280

Estimate. Use compatible numbers.

1. 242 ÷ 4
2. 510 ÷ 7
3. 433 ÷ 5
4. 476 ÷ 8
5. $537 ÷ 6
6. 298 ÷ 4
7. 337 ÷ 8
8. $259 ÷ 5
9. 1,244 ÷ 6
10. 2,240 ÷ 3
11. $6,580 ÷ 9
12. 8,256 ÷ 9
13. Kareem is saving his money to buy a video game system that costs $145. If Kareem saves the same amount of money each month for 5 months, about how much does he need to save each month to buy the video game system?
14. Michelle and her family are moving. They will travel 1,160 miles to their new home. If they drive an equal distance each day for three days, about how many miles will they drive each day?

Lesson 7-5

Pages 282–285

Divide. Use estimation to check.

1. $7\overline{)47}$
2. $8\overline{)39}$
3. $9\overline{)71}$
4. $6\overline{)33}$
5. $5\overline{)44}$
6. $8\overline{)62}$
7. $9\overline{)25}$
8. $6\overline{)45}$
9. $5\overline{)127}$
10. $9\overline{)284}$
11. $5\overline{)438}$
12. $9\overline{)872}$
13. 554 ÷ 8
14. 462 ÷ 9
15. 368 ÷ 6
16. 659 ÷ 8
17. Cindy has 96 pictures to put in an album. If she places 4 pictures on each page, how many pages will she use?
18. Booker and his mother are baking 90 muffins for a bake sale. If there are 6 muffins in each pan, how many pans of muffins do they need to bake?

Lesson 7-6

Pages 286–287

Use any strategy to solve. Tell what strategy you used.

1. What is the next number in the pattern 4, 14, 44, 134, ▒?
2. Cristina has 7 coins with a value of $0.81. What are the coins?
3. There are 9 seals at a zoo. Altogether, the seals eat about 720 fish each day. About how many fish does each seal eat every day?
4. A plant produces about 45 new flowers every 2 weeks. After 8 weeks, how many flowers will the plant have produced?
5. At the drugstore, pencils are on sale for 8 for $4. Pens are on sale for 3 for $6. How much do 24 pencils and 12 pens cost?
6. Mei hiked for 20 minutes every morning from her campsite to the lake. She hiked back to the campsite every afternoon. Mei hiked for a total of 8 hours to and from the lake. How many days was Mei at camp?

Lesson 7-7

Pages 288–290

Divide. Use estimation to check.

1. $3\overline{)693}$ **2.** $2\overline{)764}$ **3.** $7\overline{)875}$ **4.** $4\overline{)936}$

5. $2\overline{)529}$ **6.** $3\overline{)956}$ **7.** $4\overline{)875}$ **8.** $6\overline{)921}$

9. $3\overline{)677}$ **10.** $6\overline{)758}$ **11.** $5\overline{)697}$ **12.** $9\overline{)938}$

13. $539 \div 2$ **14.** $964 \div 8$ **15.** $855 \div 7$ **16.** $687 \div 4$

17. There are 6 rows of vegetables in Ian's garden. If there is a total of 132 plants, how many plants are in each row?

18. There are 132 rooms and 6 floors in the White House. If each floor has the same number of rooms, how many rooms would each floor have?

Lesson 7-8

Pages 292–294

Divide. Use estimation to check.

1. $3\overline{)315}$ **2.** $4\overline{)837}$ **3.** $4\overline{)\$432}$ **4.** $9\overline{)976}$

5. $3\overline{)625}$ **6.** $4\overline{)438}$ **7.** $2\overline{)414}$ **8.** $7\overline{)756}$

9. $3\overline{)\$317}$ **10.** $5\overline{)542}$ **11.** $3\overline{)\$617}$ **12.** $9\overline{)914}$

13. $625 \div 2$ **14.** $839 \div 4$ **15.** $\$611 \div 3$ **16.** $823 \div 4$

17. A boat for a whale watching company sailed 4 times in one day. If 428 tourists sailed that day, how many tourists sailed on each boat?

18. Kuni did 321 jumping jacks in three days. If she did the same number of jumping jacks each day, how many jumping jacks did she do each day?

Lesson 7-9

Pages 298–301

Use a calculator to divide.

1. $2\overline{)3{,}664}$
2. $3\overline{)4{,}671}$
3. $5\overline{)5{,}847}$
4. $6\overline{)7{,}248}$
5. $4\overline{)6{,}184}$
6. $8\overline{)9{,}872}$
7. $7\overline{)9{,}256}$
8. $6\overline{)57{,}888}$
9. $8\overline{)18{,}816}$
10. $9\overline{)33{,}786}$
11. $7\overline{)25{,}984}$
12. $6\overline{)23{,}678}$
13. 3,896 ÷ 2
14. 9,634 ÷ 8
15. 9,478 ÷ 4
16. 59,510 ÷ 5
17. 130,681 ÷ 8
18. 267,651 ÷ 9
19. 178,486 ÷ 7
20. 165,785 ÷ 5
21. The total weight of two giraffes is 7,054 pounds. If each giraffe weighs the same amount, how much does each giraffe weigh?
22. An elephant can eat about 3,080 pounds of food in one week. How many weeks would it take an elephant to eat 12,320 pounds of food?

Lesson 8-1

Pages 315–317

Tell the number of faces, edges, and vertices. Then identify each figure.

1. 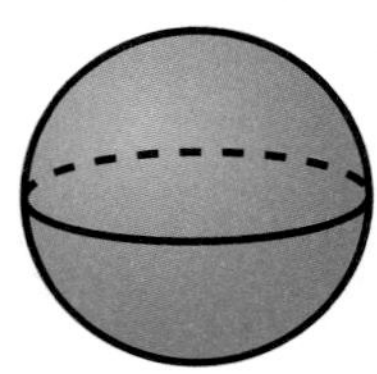
2. 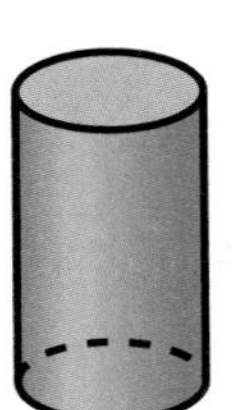
3. 
4. 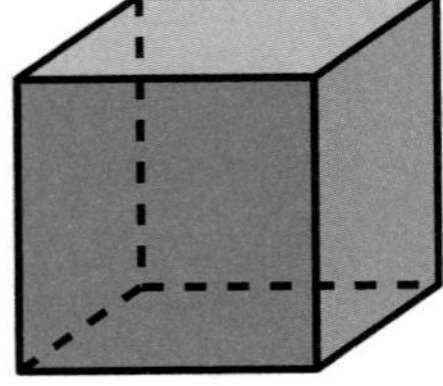
5. 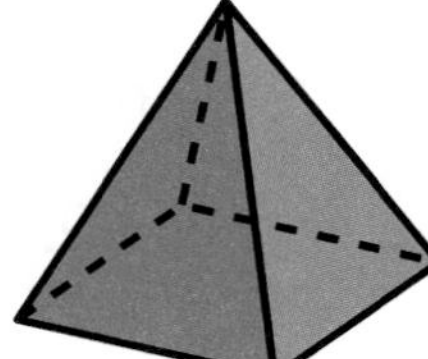
6. 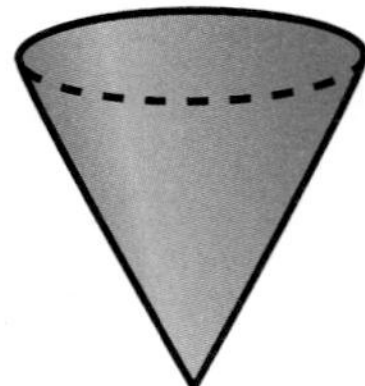
7. This solid has 1 face, 0 edges, and 1 vertex. What solid is it?
8. This solid has 6 faces, 12 edges, and 8 vertices. What solid is it?

Lesson 8-2

Pages 318–321

Identify each polygon.

1. 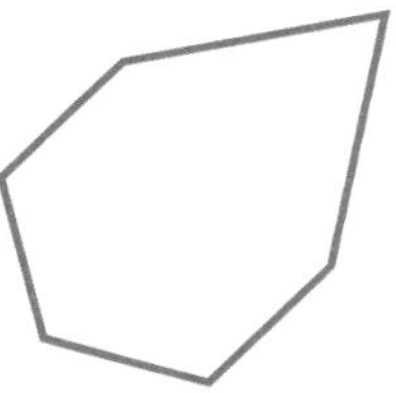

2. 

3. 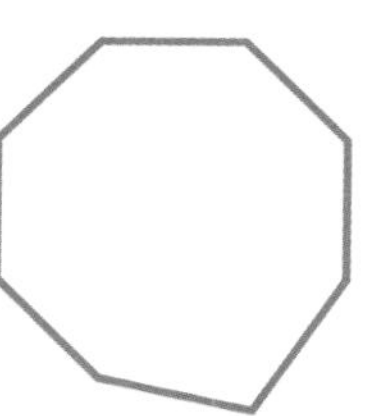

Tell whether each shape is a polygon.

4. 

5. 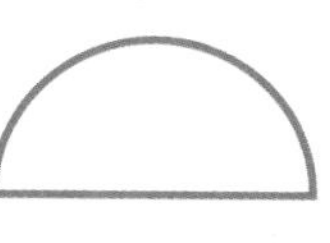

6. 

7. Identify the polygon that forms each side of the tent.

8. Identify the polygon that is formed by the chalk board.

Lesson 8-3

Pages 322–323

Solve. Use the *look for a pattern* strategy.

1. What is the pattern of the shapes below? What would the next 4 shapes be?

2. Describe the pattern below. Then find the missing number.
6, 18, 54, __, 486.

3. A flowering plant produces 15 seeds on the first day of spring. On the second day, it produces 23 seeds. On the third day, it produces 31 seeds. Describe the pattern. How many seeds will the plant produce on the sixth day?

4. Copy and complete the table. What is the pattern?

Input	Output
3	21
5	35
7	■
■	56

Extra Practice

Lesson 8-4

Pages 324–326

Write the measure of the angle in degrees and as a fraction of a full turn.

1. 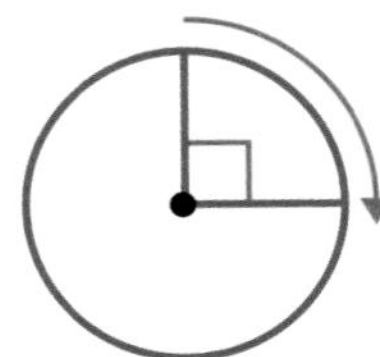

2. 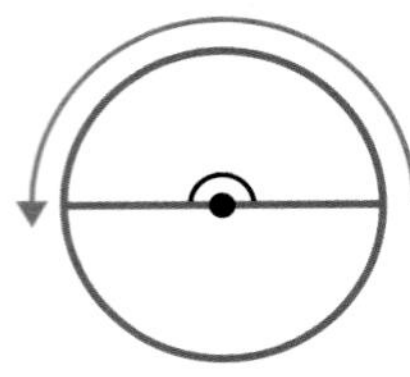

3. 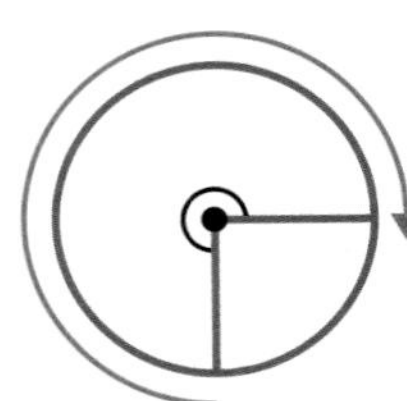

Classify each angle as *right, acute,* or *obtuse*.

4. 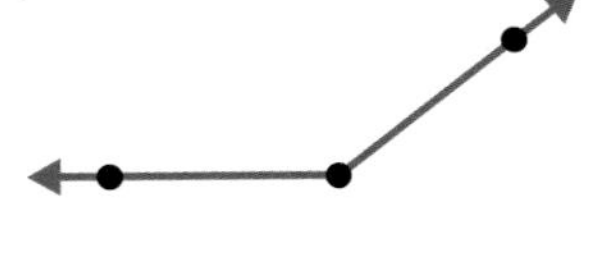

5. 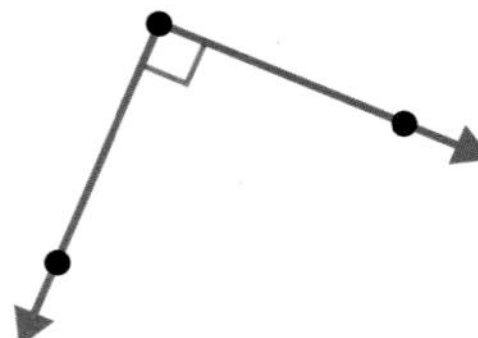

6. 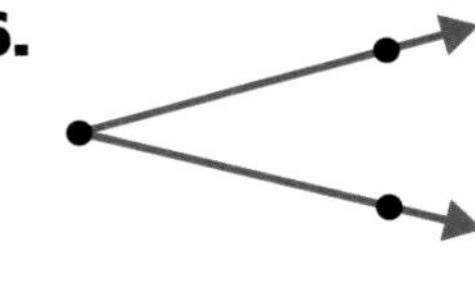

Lesson 8-5

Pages 328–331

Classify each triangle. Use *isosceles, equilateral,* or *scalene* and *acute, right,* or *obtuse*.

1. 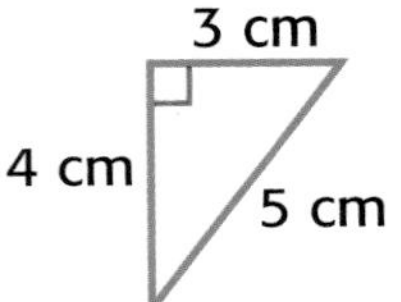

2. 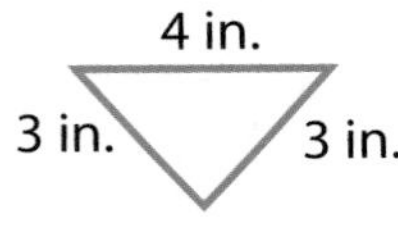

3. 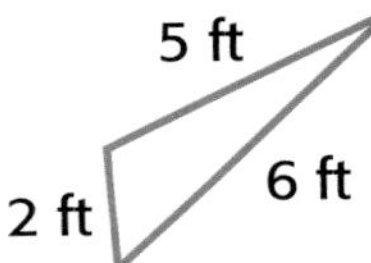

4. 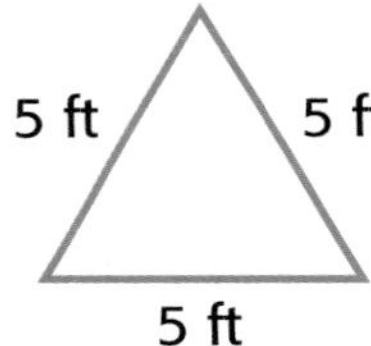

5. 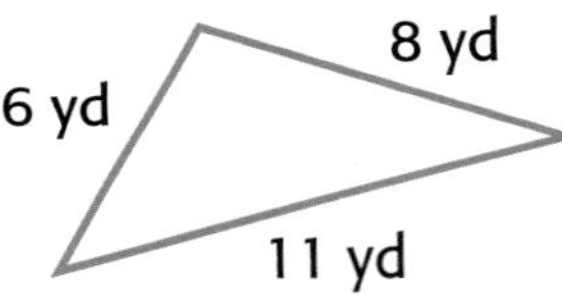

6. 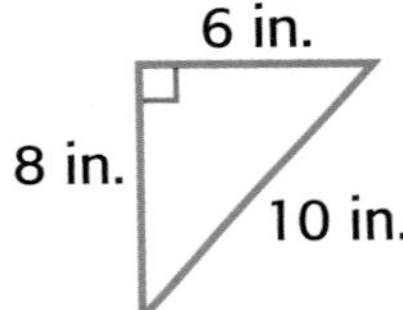

7. Don draws an isosceles triangle with the two equal sides having a total length of 16 inches. The lengths of all three sides equal 21 inches. What is the length of each side of the triangle?

8. Crystal draws a scalene triangle with a side that equals 7 inches in length. A second side has a length of 9 inches. If the sum of the lengths of all three sides equals 28 inches, what is the length of the third side?

Lesson 8-6

Pages 332–335

Classify each quadrilateral in as many ways as possible.

1. 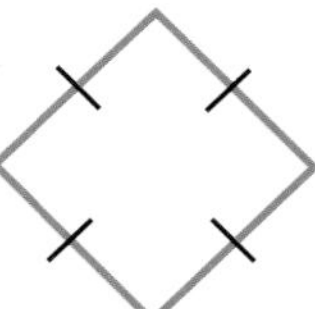

2. 

3. 

4. 

5. 

6. 

7 A quadrilateral has exactly one pair of parallel sides. What is the quadrilateral?

8 A quadrilateral has 4 right angles, with opposite sides parallel. All sides are equal in length. What is the quadrilateral?

Lesson 8-7

Pages 336–337

Use any strategy to solve. Tell what strategy you used.

1. A number is multiplied by 4, then 9 is subtracted from the product. The result is 19. What was the original number?

2. Identify 10 bills worth $49 using $1, $5, and $10 bills.

3. The polygons below form a pattern. How many sides will the eighth polygon have?

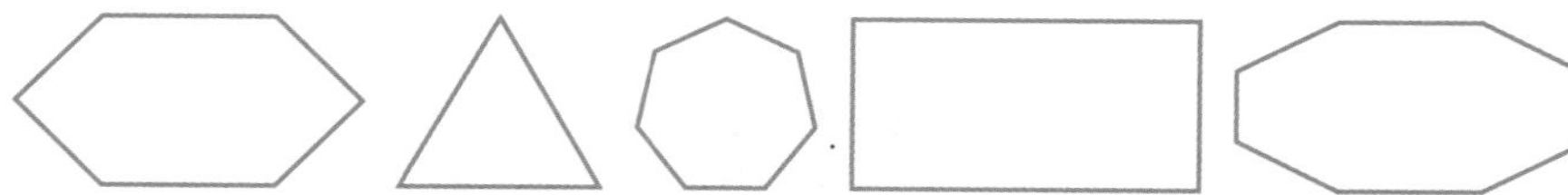

4. For every 30 minutes that Julia swims, she rests for 15 minutes. In 3 hours of swimming, how many minutes will she rest?

Extra Practice

Extra Practice

Lesson 9-1

Pages 351–353

Write the number represented by each letter.

1.

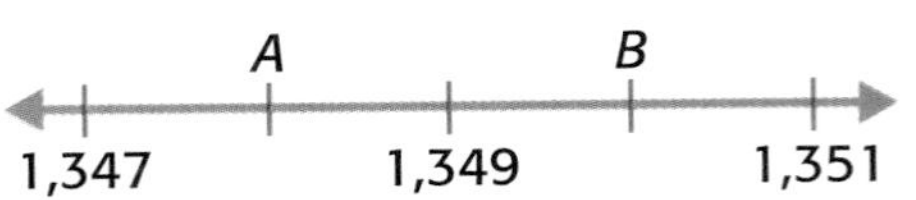

$A =$ $B =$

2.

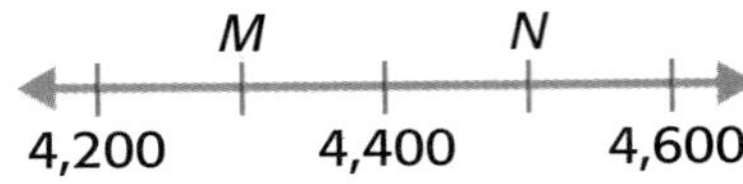

$M =$ $N =$

3.

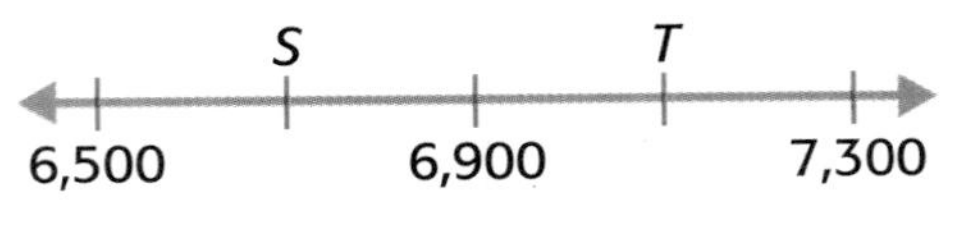

$S =$ $T =$

4.

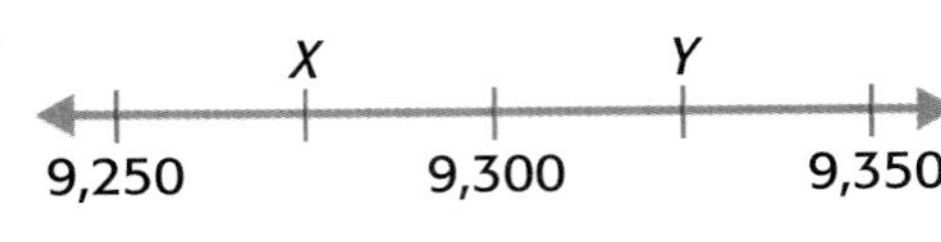

$X =$ $Y =$

Write the number *X* best represents on each number line.

5.

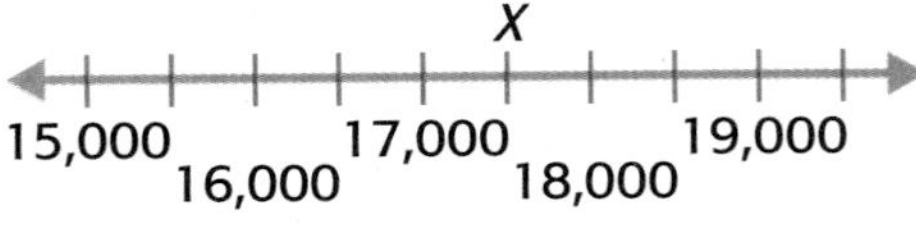

6.

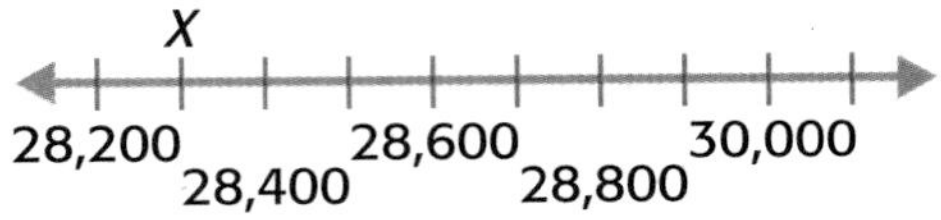

Lesson 9-2

Pages 356–359

Identify each figure.

1.

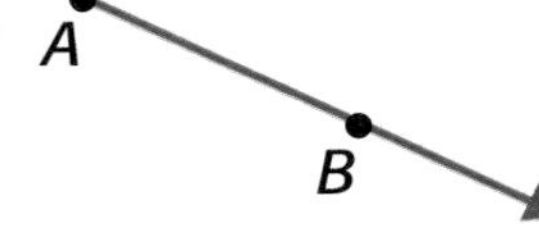

2.

3.

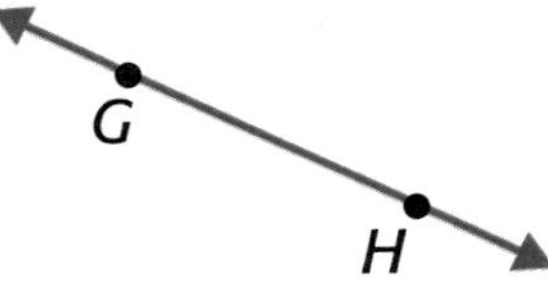

Describe the figure.

4.

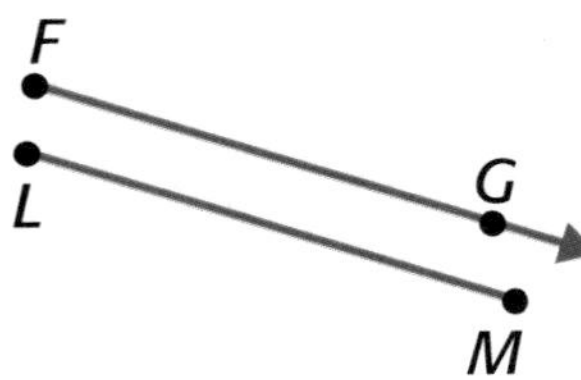

5.

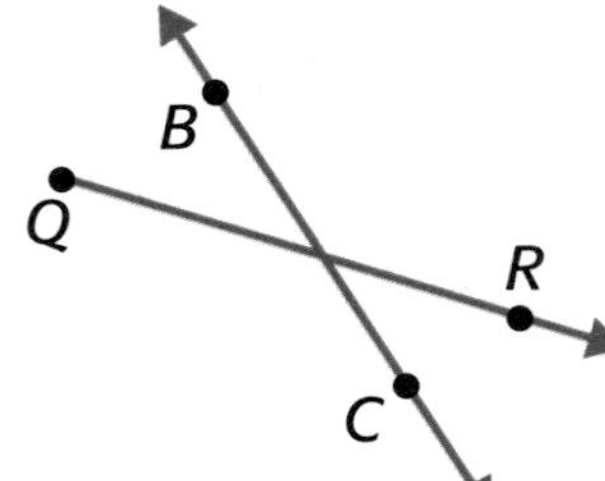

6.

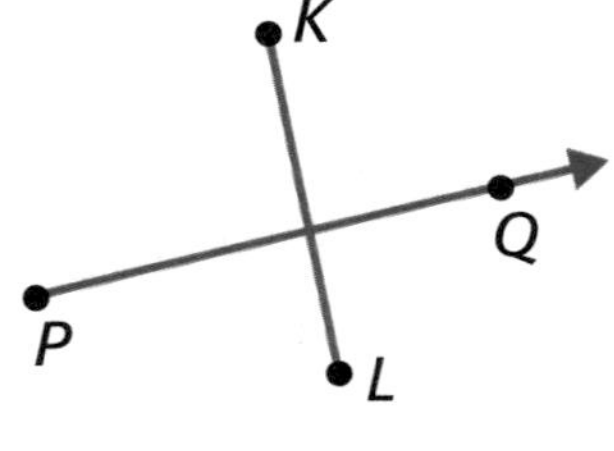

Lesson 9-3

Pages 360–361

Solve. Use the *make an organized list* strategy.

1. Jim has 1 blue jacket, 1 green jacket, and 1 brown jacket. He has 1 tan hat and 1 black hat. How many different combinations can he wear?

2. Lee, Diego, Tara, and Irena will ride the Ferris wheel. Two people can sit in each car. What pairs are possible for the four friends to ride the Ferris wheel?

Lesson 9-4

Pages 362–364

Identify the letter that is located at each ordered pair.

1. (2, 4)
2. (3, 4)
3. (7, 6)
4. (4, 2)
5. (2, 1)
6. (4, 0)
7. (7, 3)
8. (4, 7)
9. (0, 0)

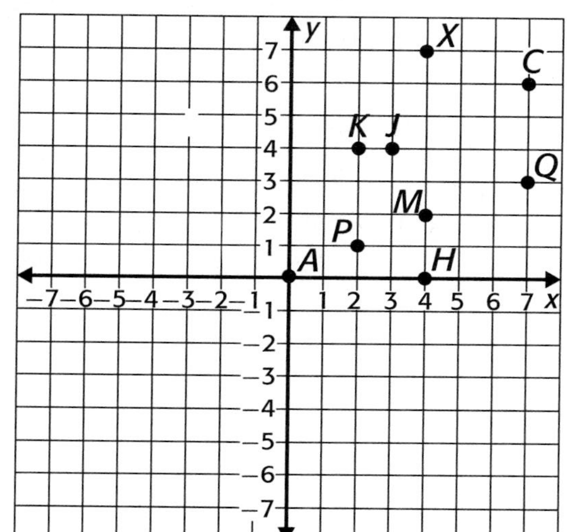

10. Describe how to move from the ordered pairs for *H* to *C*.

11. Describe how to move from the ordered pairs of *P* to *K*.

Lesson 9-5

Pages 368–371

Identify each transformation. Write *rotation, reflection,* or *translation*.

1. 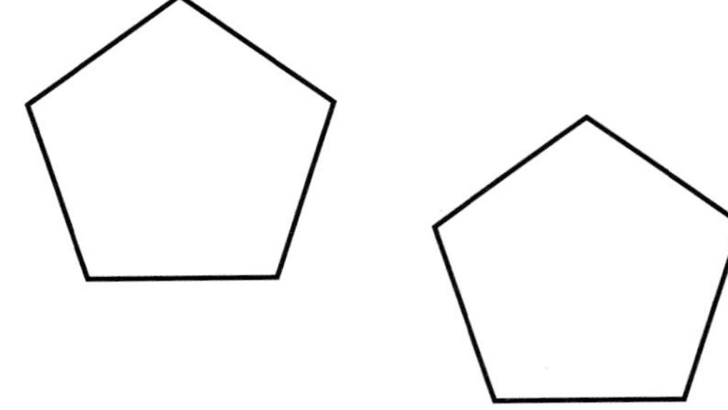

2. 

3. 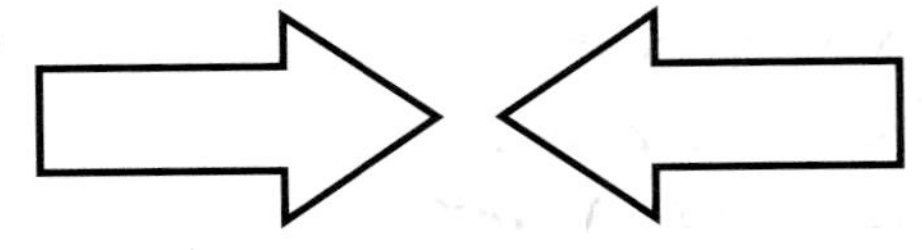

4. 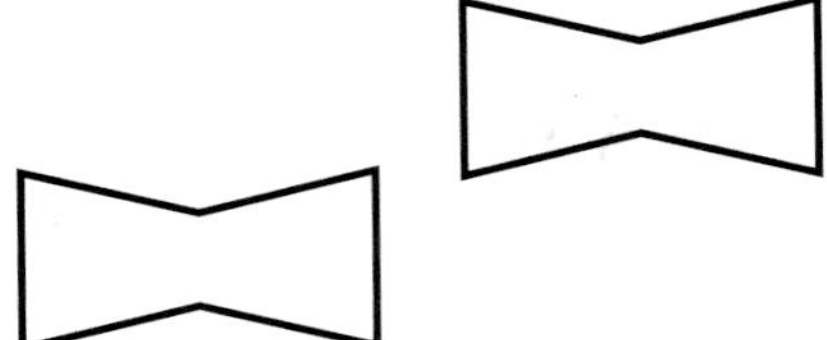

5. Identify a shape that looks exactly the same when it is rotated, reflected, and translated.

6. The command *about face* means face the opposite direction. Identify the transformation that describes this command.

Lesson 9-6

Pages 372–373

Use any strategy to solve. Tell what strategy you used.

1. Natalie is thinking of two numbers with a sum of 13 and a product of 36. What are the two numbers?

2. The fish at the pet store eat 28 jars of food every week. How many jars of food will the fish eat in 4 weeks? in 6 weeks? in 8 weeks?

3. Ramón saves $15 every week to buy a skateboard. The skateboard costs $105. How many weeks will it take him to save half as much as he needs to buy the skateboard?

4. Every fourth grader washed 4 cars at the car wash. The fourth graders washed 284 cars in all. About how many fourth grade students are there?

Lesson 9-7

Pages 374–377

Tell whether the figures appear to be congruent. Write *yes* or *no*.

1. 

2. 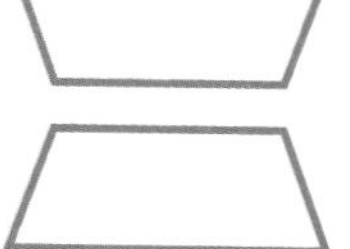

3. 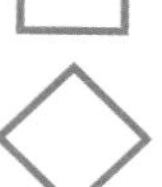

4. 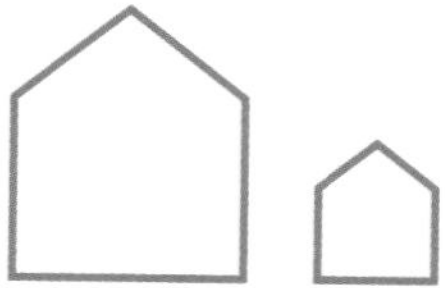

5. 

6. 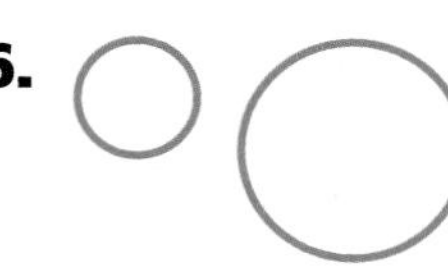

7. Jeff's pool is 6 feet wide and 9 feet long. His neighbor has the same pool. If the pool is 9 feet long. How wide is it?

8. Monifa has a poster that is 3 feet long and 2 feet wide. Her friend has the same poster. if the poster is 3 feet long, how wide is it?

Lesson 9-8

Pages 380–383

Tell whether each figure has line symmetry. Write *yes* or *no*. Then tell how many lines of symmetry the figure has.

1. 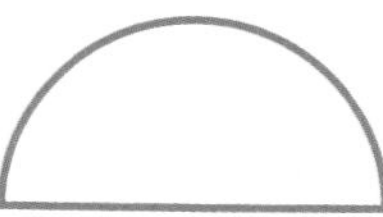

2. 

3. 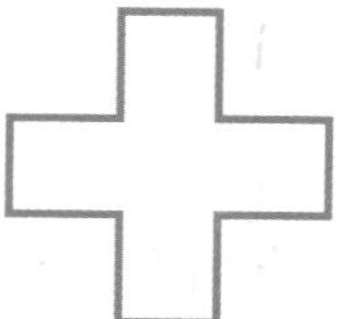

Tell whether the line is a line of symmetry, Write *yes* or *no*.

4. 

5. 

6. 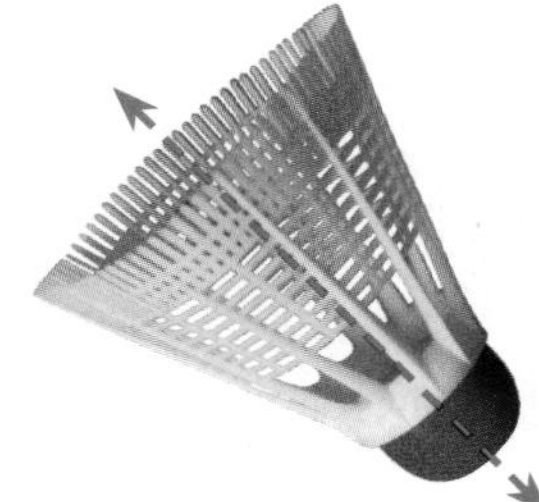

7. Does the letter X have line symmetry? If it does, tell how many lines of symmetry the letter has.

8. Does an isosceles triangle have line symmetry? If it does tell how many lines of symmetry the shape has.

Extra Practice

Lesson 10-1

Pages 397–399

Estimate. then measure each to the nearest inch, $\frac{1}{2}$ inch, and $\frac{1}{4}$ inch.

1. 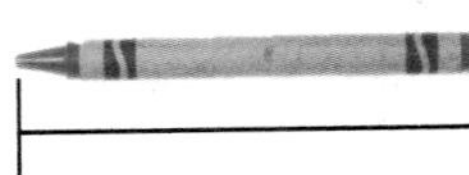

2. 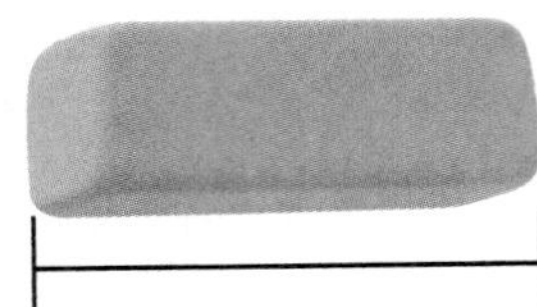

3. 

4. 

Choose the best estimate.

5. 

A. 2 inches
B. 2 feet
C. 22 feet
D. 2 yards

6. 

A. 14 inches
B. 140 inches
C. 14 feet
D. 14 yards

Lesson 10-2

Pages 400–401

Complete.

1. 24 in. = ■ ft
2. 3 ft = ■ in.
3. 15 ft = ■ yd
4. ■ ft = 48 in.
5. ■ yd = 24 ft
6. ■ in. = 5 ft
7. A sign at an amusement park says that a person must be 52 inches tall in order to ride a roller coaster. If Kwam is 4 feet 6 inches tall, is he tall enough to ride the roller coaster?
8. A python at a zoo is 6 yards 2 feet long. A cobra at the same zoo is 17 feet long. Which snake is longer? Explain.

Lesson 10-3

Pages 402–403

Solve. Use the *solve a simpler problem* strategy.

1. Mark painted a mural on each of the 4 walls of his room. It took him 6 hours and 25 minutes for each wall. How long did it take him to finish?

2. Anita bought a sandwich for $3, a salad for $2, a glass of juice for $1, and a cookie for $1. How much did she spend for lunch?

3. The price of oranges at Super Mart is 6 for $1.14. The price of oranges at Food Palace is 9 for $1.89. Which is the better value? How much does each orange cost at each store?

4. Tony's house is 8 blocks from school. His house is 12 blocks from the park. If Tony walks to and from school every day, and then walks to and from the park each day after school, how many blocks does he walk during the school week?

Lesson 10-4

Pages 406–408

Measure each object to the nearest centimeter.

1. 

2. 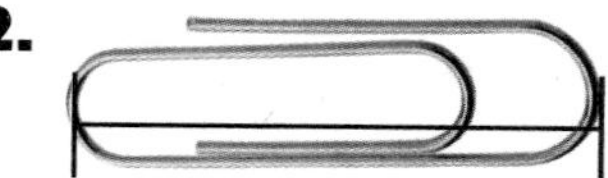

3. 

Choose the best estimate.

4. 

A 1 millimeter **C** 1 meter
B 1 centimeter **D** 1 kilometer

5. 

A 26 millimeters **C** 26 meters
B 26 centimeters **D** 26 kilometers

Extra Practice

Lesson 10-5

Pages 410–413

Find the perimeter of each figure.

1.
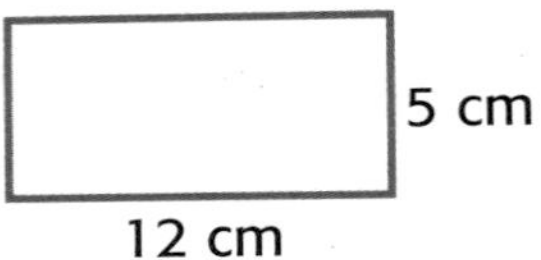

2.
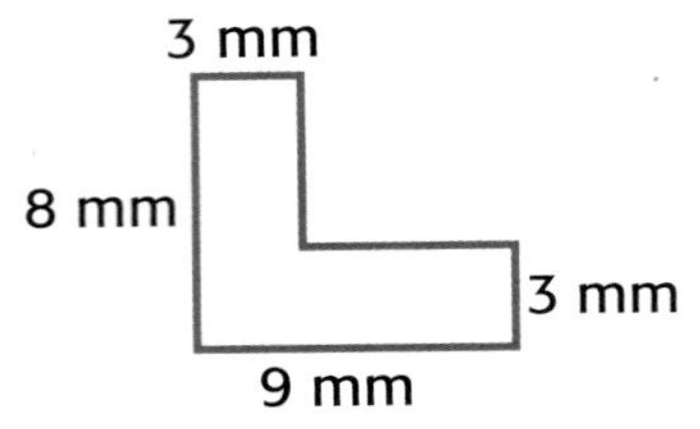

3.
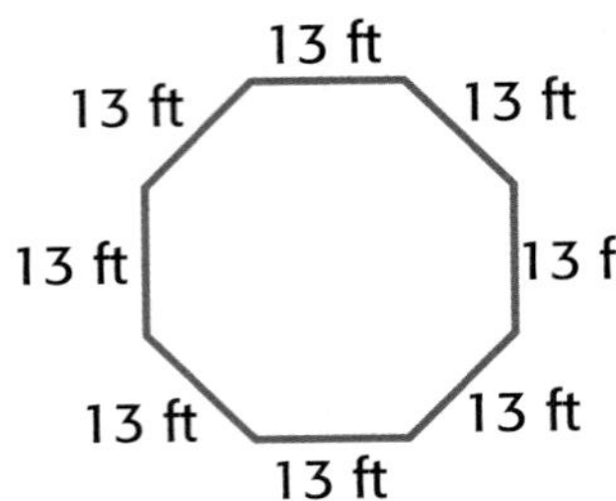

Find the perimeter of each rectangle in units.

4.

5.
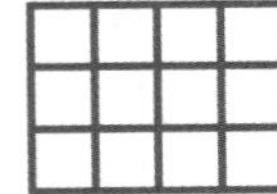

6.
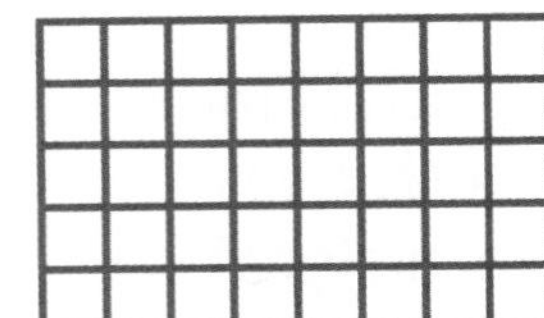

Lesson 10-6

Pages 414–417

Find the area of each figure.

1.
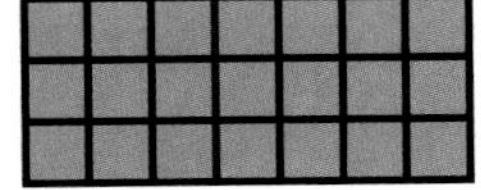

2.
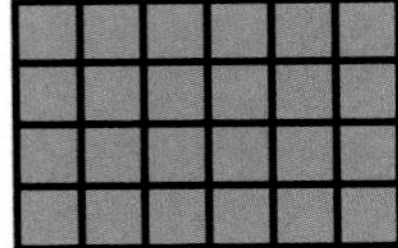

3.
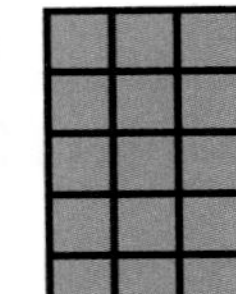

4.
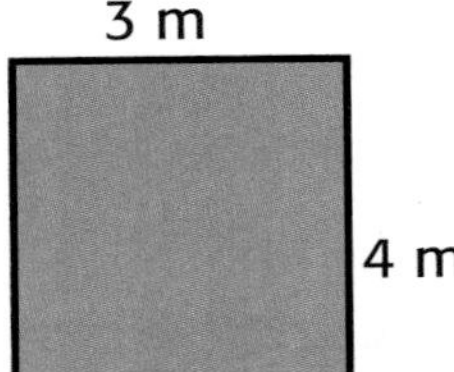

5.
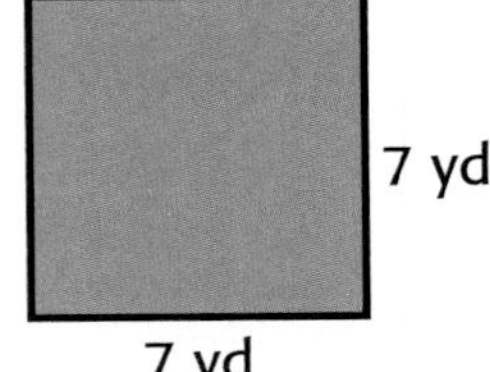

6.
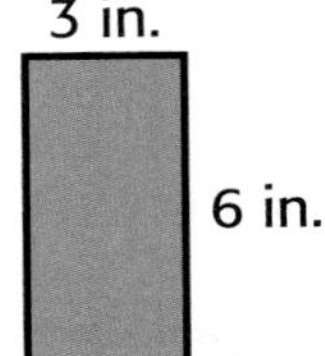

Lesson 10-7

Pages 420–421

Use any strategy to solve. Tell what strategy you used.

1. The perimeter of a rectangular yard is 20 meters. What are the possible lengths of the sides?

2. Stella bought 5 pencils for 25¢. How much would she pay for 15 pencils?

3. Each bunch of flowers has 12 tulips and 23 daisies. There are 6 bunches of flowers. How many flowers are there in all?

4. There are 324 apples at a market. There are 68 fewer apples than oranges and 127 more apples than limes. How many limes and oranges are there?

Lesson 10-8

Pages 422–425

Write the approximate temperature in Fahrenheit and Celsius.

1.
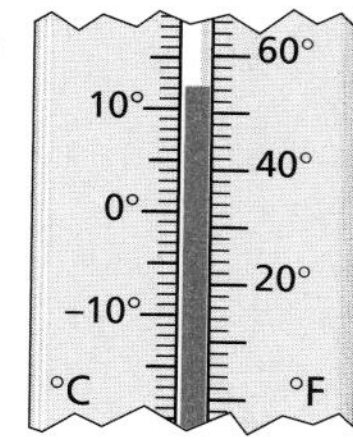

2.
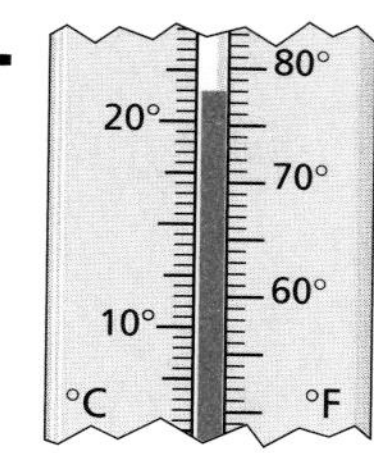

3.
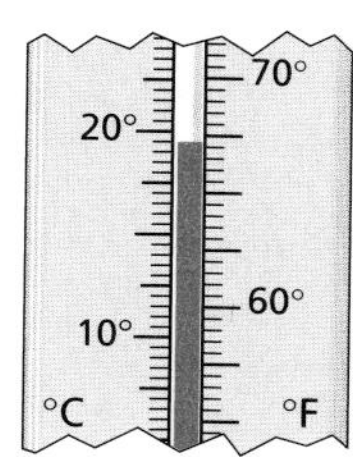

4.
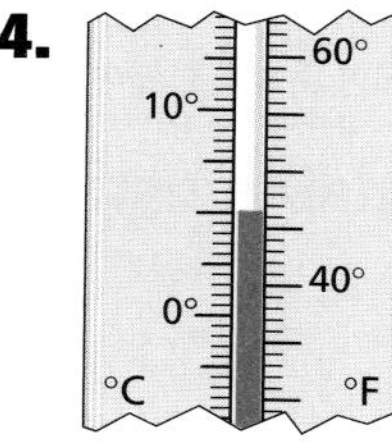

5. The thermometer reads 2° Celsius. Would Gabrielle go swimming or build a snowman? Explain.

6. An average person's body temperature is about 99° Fahrenheit. About how many degrees Celsius is this temperature?

Lesson 11-1

Pages 442–445

Choose the most reasonable estimate.

1.

A 15 fluid ounces
B 15 pints
C 15 quarts
D 15 gallons

2.

A 2 fluid ounces
B 20 fluid ounces
C 2 quarts
D 2 gallons

3.

A 6 fluid ounces
B 6 cups
C 6 pints
D 6 quarts

4.

A 6 fluid ounces
B 60 fluid ounces
C 6 cups
D 6 pints

5.

A 1 fluid ounce
B 1 cup
C 1 quart
D 1 gallon

6.

A 1 fluid ounce
B 1 cup
C 1 pint
D 1 quart

Lesson 11-2

Pages 446–447

Complete.

1. 6 c = ■ pt
2. 32 fl oz = ■ c
3. 8 qt = ■ pt
4. 2 gal = ■ qt
5. ■ fl oz = 5 c
6. 10 pt = ■ c

Compare. Write >, <, or =.

7. 3 qt ● 1 gal
8. 3 c ● 4 fl oz
9. 3 qt ● 5 pt

Lesson 11-3

Pages 448–451

Choose the more reasonable estimate.

1. 

   11 mL   11 L

2. 

   710 mL   710 L

3. 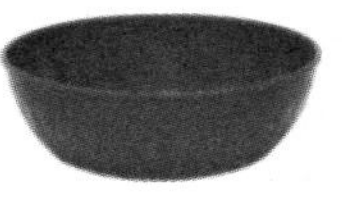

   1 mL   1 L

4. 

   235 mL   235 L

Lesson 11-4

Pages 454–456

Choose the most reasonable estimate.

1. 

   A 8 ounces
   B 80 pounds
   C 8 pounds
   D 8 tons

2. 

   A 70 ounces
   B 7 pounds
   C 700 pounds
   D 7 tons

3. 

   A 8 ounces
   B 8 pounds
   C 80 pounds
   D 8 tons

4. 

   A 1 ounce
   B 10 ounces
   C 1 pound
   D 10 pounds

Lesson 11-5

Pages 458–459

Solve. Use logical reasoning.

1. There are four buildings on a block. The bank is not next to the musuem or the school. The school is not first. What is the order of the buildings?

2. A group of 3 adults and 7 students rode a ferry. The cost for the entire group was $35. If the cost for a student to ride was $2.50, what was the cost for an adult?

3. The Bears won 18 games. The Lions won one game for every three games the Bears won. The Sharks won 8 more games than the Lions. How many games did the Lions win?

4. Mr. Myers is thinking of a number between 20 and 30. The number is not even and not divisible by 3. What could the number be?

Lesson 11-6

Pages 460–463

Complete.

1. 2 lb = ■ oz
2. 4,000 lb = ■ T
3. 64 oz = ■ lb
4. 2 T = ■ lb
5. 1 lb and 2 oz = ■ oz
6. 3 T and 400 lb = ■

Copy and complete.

Pounds	■	5	■	8	■
Ounces	48	■	96	■	160

Lesson 11-7

Pages 464–467

Choose the more reasonable estimate.

1. 

4 g   4 kg

2. 

350 g   350 kg

3. 

250 g   250 kg

3. 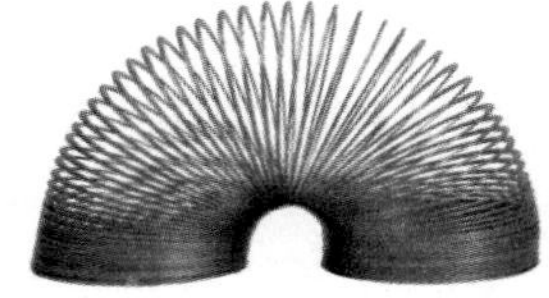

300 g   300 kg

Lesson 11-8

Pages 468–471

Use models to find each volume.

1.

2.

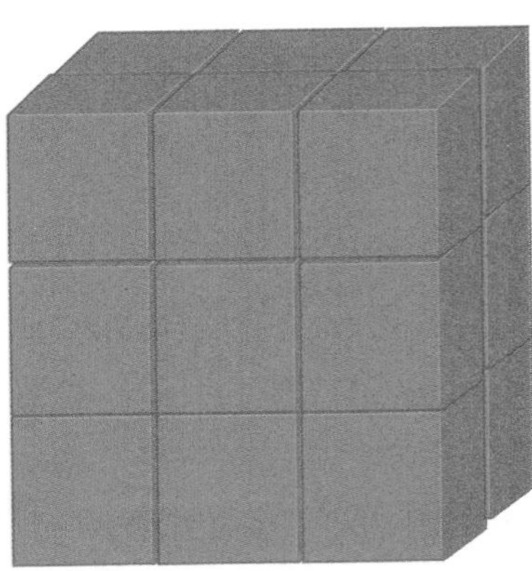

Estimate each volume.

3.

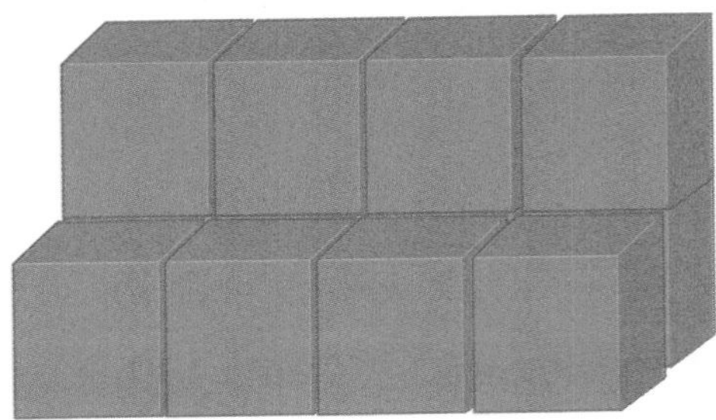

4.

5. Brady's suitcase is 6 units long, 2 units wide, and 2 units tall. Shelly's suitcase is 8 units long, 2 units wide, and 1 unit tall. Whose suitcase has a greater volume? Explain.

Lesson 11-9

Pages 474–475

Use any strategy to solve. Tell what strategy you used.

1. Mike makes $4 an hour babysitting. Omar makes $6 an hour gardening. How many hours will Mike have to work to make the same amount that Omar makes in 8 hours?

2. Suna wants to make 5 bracelets and 3 necklaces. She plans to use 3 shells for every bracelet and 4 shells for every necklace. How many shells does she need?

3. Evan has twice as many pairs of mittens as boots. He has 6 times as many pairs of socks as boots. He has 18 pairs of socks. How many pairs of boots and mittens does he have?

4. Sam is replacing the wheels on 6 bicycles. He is also replacing the wheels on 4 tricycles and 3 wagons. How many wheels is Sam replacing in all?

Lesson 11-10

Pages 476–479

The following are times of tennis matches. Find the elapsed time.

1. Start Time　　End Time

2. Start Time　　End Time

Find each elapsed time. Use a clock if needed.

3. The clock shows when Lydia started ice skating.

It is 12:45 when she stops.

4. The clock shows when Helki's hockey practice started.

It is 6:30 when it stops.

Lesson 12-1

Pages 493–495

Write the fraction that names part of the whole.

1. 

2. 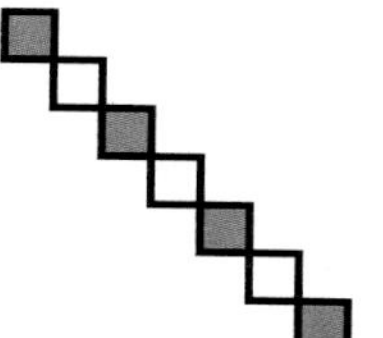

3. 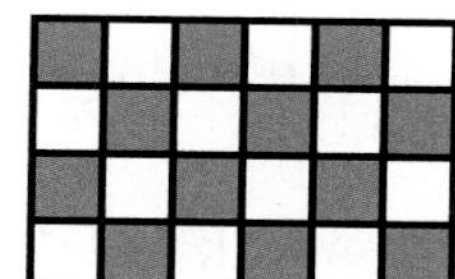

4. 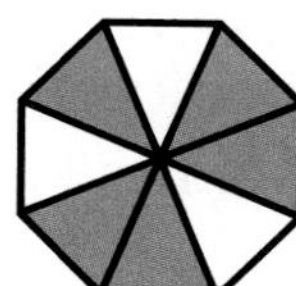

5. 

6. 

Draw a picture and shade part of it to show the fraction.

7. $\frac{3}{7}$　　8. $\frac{6}{7}$　　9. $\frac{2}{10}$　　10. $\frac{4}{5}$　　11. $\frac{7}{8}$

12. Amy's mom used 3 stamps out of a book of 20 stamps. What fraction of the book of stamps was used?

13. Kono drank 5 out of 8 ounces of a glass of water. What fraction of the glass of water was left?

Lesson 12-2

Pages 496–499

Write the fraction for the part of the set that is blue. Then write the fraction for the part that is *not* blue.

1.

2. 

3.

4. 

5. 

6.

7. Three people are sharing 2 sandwiches equally. What part of a sandwich does each peson receive?

8. Four dogs are sharing 3 cups of dog food equally. What part of a cup of the dog food does each dog receive?

Lesson 12-3

Pages 500–501

Solve. Use the *draw a picture* strategy.

1. Four dogs are standing in a row. The great dane is ahead of the poodle. The terrier is not next to the poodle. The collie is next to the terrier and is not first. What is the order of the dogs?

2. There are 30 children at the park. $\frac{1}{2}$ are playing soccer. $\frac{1}{3}$ are playing football. The rest are on the swings. How many children are on the swings?

3. There are 16 CDs on a shelf. $\frac{1}{4}$ of the CDs are jazz. 5 are classical music, and 3 are blues. The rest are pop music. How many CDs are pop music?

4. There are 4 books on display. The cookbook is next to the history book but not next to the art book or the novel. The art book is third. What is the order of the books?

Lesson 12-4

Pages 504–507

Write the fraction for the part that is shaded. Then find an equivalent fraction.

1. 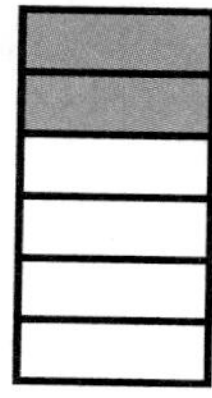

2. 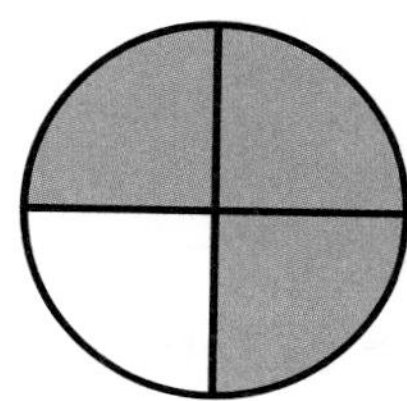

3. 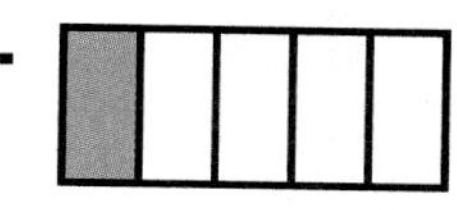

Use models to find an equivalent fraction for each fraction.

4. $\frac{3}{12}$ 5. $\frac{4}{10}$ 6. $\frac{1}{4}$ 7. $\frac{4}{6}$ 8. $\frac{3}{7}$

9. $\frac{6}{18}$ 10. $\frac{3}{8}$ 11. $\frac{6}{9}$ 12. $\frac{1}{2}$ 13. $\frac{4}{20}$

14. There are 6 pieces of fruit in a bowl. Three pieces of the fruit are apples. Write two fractions that describe the part of the fruit that is not an apple.

15. Tracy has 8 toys in her toy box. Two of the toys are stuffed animals. Write two fractions that describe the part of the toys that are stuffed animals.

Lesson 12-5

Pages 510–513

Use models to compare. Write <, >, or =.

1. 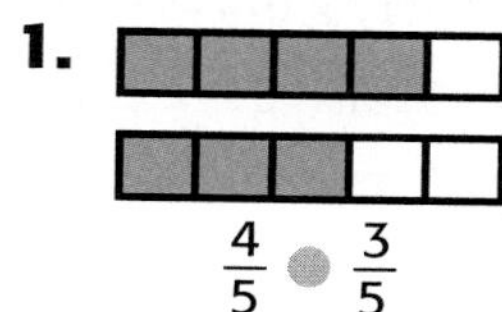

$\frac{4}{5}$ ● $\frac{3}{5}$

2. 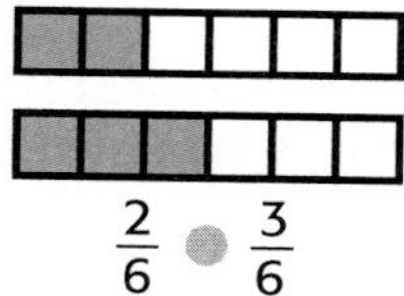

$\frac{2}{6}$ ● $\frac{3}{6}$

3. 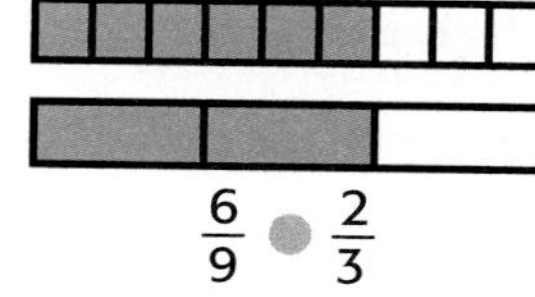

$\frac{6}{9}$ ● $\frac{2}{3}$

4. 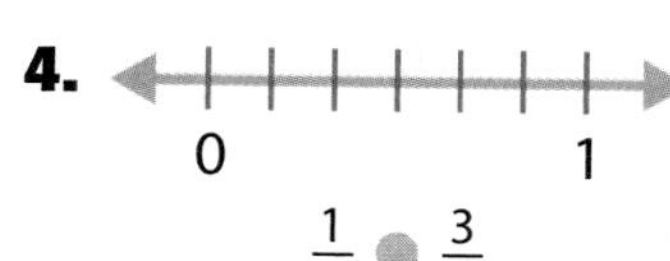

$\frac{1}{3}$ ● $\frac{3}{6}$

5. 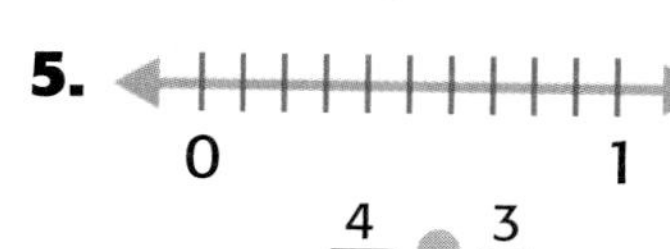

$\frac{4}{10}$ ● $\frac{3}{5}$

6. 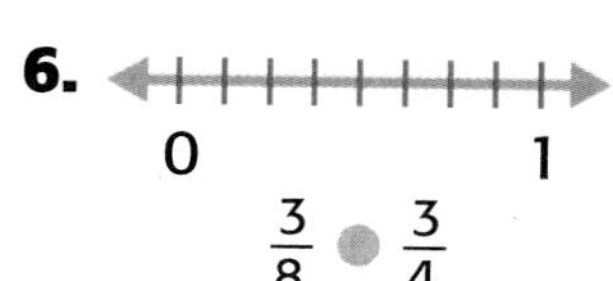

$\frac{3}{8}$ ● $\frac{3}{4}$

7. $\frac{2}{5}$ ● $\frac{1}{6}$ 8. $\frac{6}{9}$ ● $\frac{5}{10}$ 9. $\frac{3}{8}$ ● $\frac{1}{2}$

10. $\frac{7}{8}$ ● $\frac{7}{12}$ 11. $\frac{5}{5}$ ● $\frac{4}{5}$ 12. $\frac{3}{9}$ ● $\frac{9}{12}$

13. Terrence ate $\frac{1}{3}$ of the grapes in a bag. Shelly ate $\frac{2}{4}$ of the grapes in a bag. Who ate less grapes?

14. Mark jogged $\frac{4}{7}$ of a mile. Christy jogged $\frac{3}{5}$ of a mile. Who jogged a longer distance?

Lesson 12-6

Pages 516–519

Write a mixed number and an improper fraction for each model.

1.   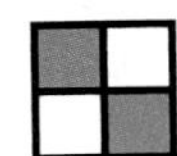

2. 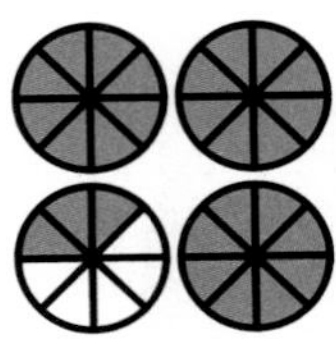

3. 

Write each as an improper fraction or a mixed number. Use models to help.

4. $3\frac{2}{3}$

5. $3\frac{1}{4}$

6. $3\frac{3}{10}$

7. $\frac{21}{4}$

8. $\frac{17}{8}$

9. $\frac{37}{7}$

10. Kelsey walked $1\frac{3}{5}$ miles and jogged $1\frac{5}{12}$ miles. Did Kelsey walk or jog a greater distance?

11. Roberto drank $2\frac{3}{6}$ cups of orange juice and $2\frac{2}{3}$ cups of water in one day. Did Roberto drink more orange juice or more water?

Lesson 12-7

Pages 520–521

Use any strategy to solve. Tell what strategy you used.

1. There are 20 fish in an aquarium. $\frac{1}{5}$ of the fish are blue. $\frac{1}{4}$ of the fish are red. The rest are yellow. How many yellow fish are there?

2. Ramona started reading at 4:20. She stopped reading at 5:15. For how many minutes did she read?

3. Ten students are in the library. Three students leave the library as 5 students go in. How many students are in the library now?

4. Juan has 9 coins that equal 85¢. None of them are pennies. What are the coins?

Lesson 13-1

Pages 535–537

Write a fraction and a decimal for each shaded part.

1. 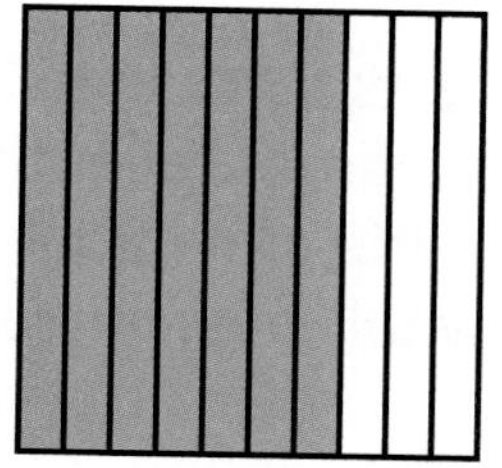

2. 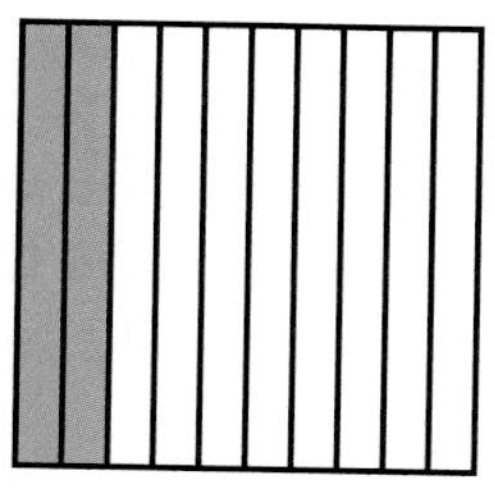

3. 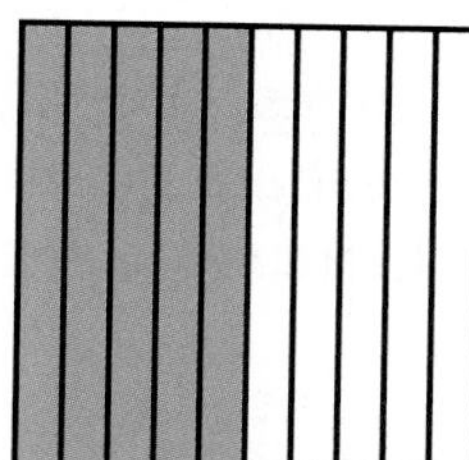

4. 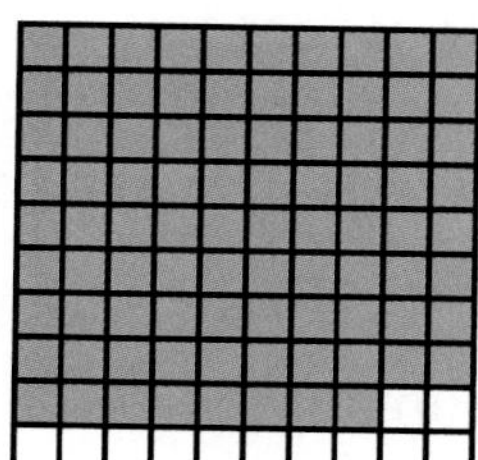

5. 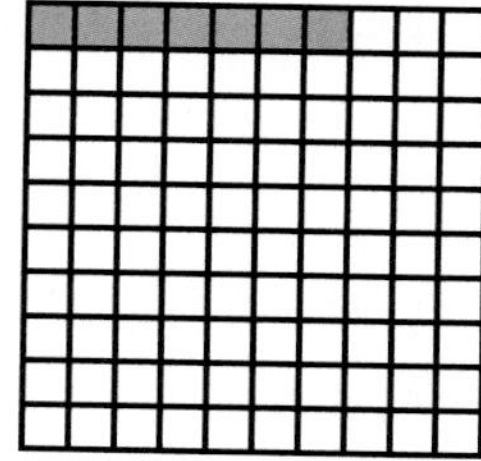

6. 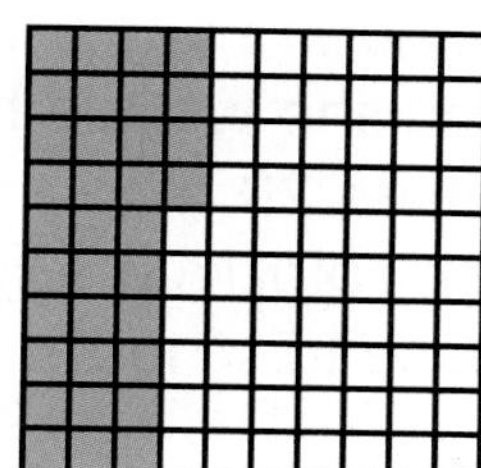

7. Cheri spent sixty-five hundredths of a dollar on a candy bar. Write this amount as a fraction and decimal.

8. Ted knocked down seven out of ten bowling pins. Write this amount as a fraction and decimal.

Lesson 13-2

Pages 538–541

Write each as a mixed number and decimal.

1.  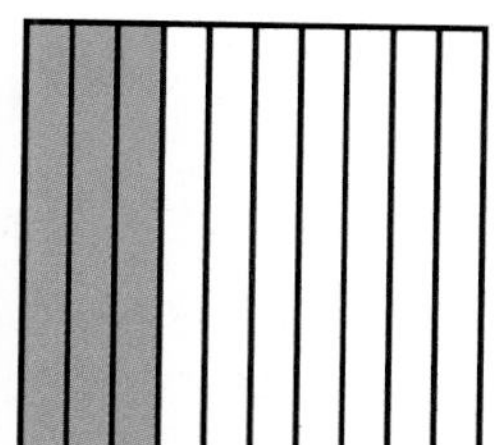

2. 

Model each mixed number, then write as a decimal.

3. $4\frac{6}{10}$ **4.** $36\frac{33}{100}$ **5.** $83\frac{45}{100}$ **6.** $99\frac{8}{10}$

7. $15\frac{74}{100}$ **8.** $75\frac{3}{10}$ **9.** $62\frac{87}{100}$ **10.** $24\frac{5}{10}$

11. An American bison can weigh $2\frac{2}{10}$ tons. Write a decimal to show. how many tons an American bison can weigh.

12. A lily blossom can reach a width of 1.5 feet. Write a mixed number to show how many feet the width of a lily blossom can reach.

Lesson 13-3

Pages 542–543

Solve. Use the *make a model* strategy.

1. Marcus has 20 coins. One fourth are dimes. One fifth are nickels. The rest are quarters. How much are Marcus's coins worth?

2. There are 3 plants in a garden. The first plant is 3 times taller than the second and 2 times taller than the third. The plants are a total of 22 feet tall. How tall is each plant?

3. Emily walked halfway home from school. She walked back 3 blocks to find the book she had dropped. Then she walked home. She walked 20 blocks in all. How many blocks is it from Emily's house to school?

4. Simon is hanging wallpaper on 3 walls of his room. Each wall is 10 feet wide and 8 feet tall. Each roll of wallpaper covers 40 square feet. How many rolls of wallpaper does Simon need?

Lesson 13-4

Pages 544–545

Name each point as a fraction and decimal.

1.

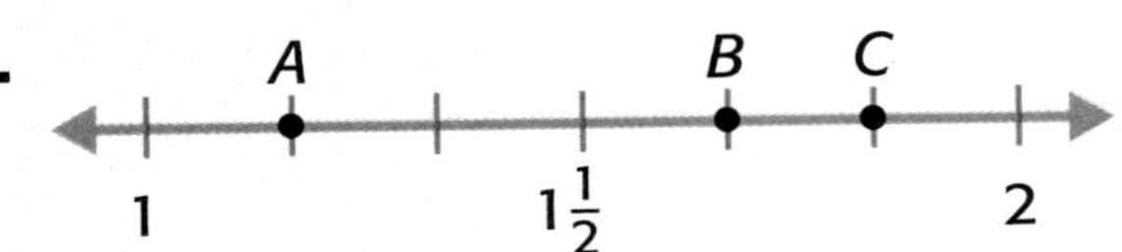

$A =$ $B =$ $C =$

2.

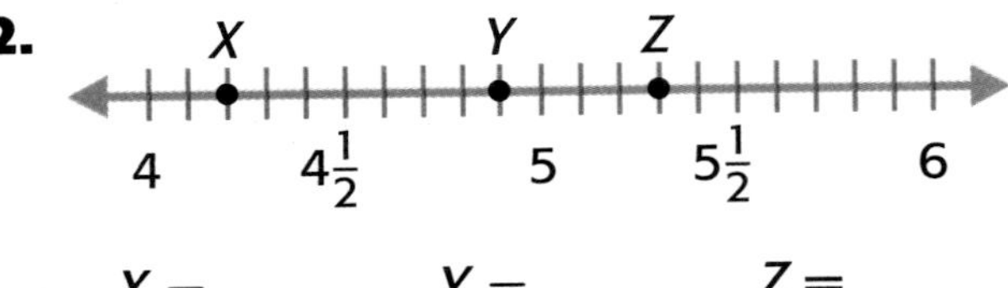

$X =$ $Y =$ $Z =$

Name the point *N* represent on a number line.

3.

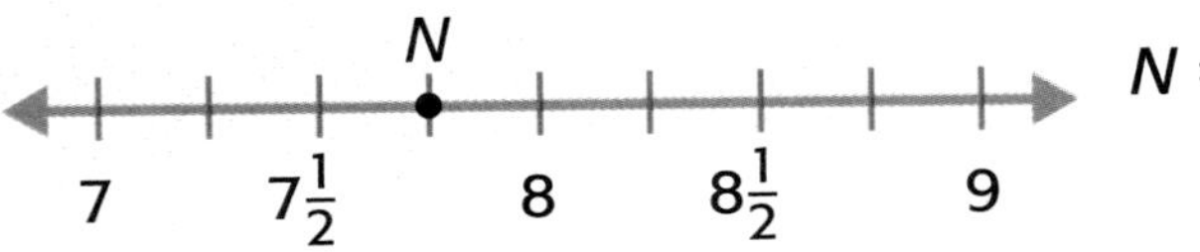

$N =$

4. Latisha is measuring her height. The top of her head reaches the eighth mark out of 11 marks between 1 feet and 5 feet. How many feet tall is Latisha?

5. A zookeeper measured the length of a newborn kangaroo. The kangaroo end at the fourth mark out of nine marks between 0 inches and 1 inch. How many inches long is the kangaroo?

Lesson 13-5

Pages 546–548

Compare. Write <, >, or =.

1. 6.7 ● 0.67 **2.** 3.96 ● 3.09 **3.** 55.5 ● 55.50

4. 9.2 ● 9.22 **5.** 1.20 ● 1.19 **6.** 64.6 ● 68.4

7. 13.80 ● 13.8 **8.** 0.67 ● 0.76 **9.** 4.91 ● 4.9

Order from greatest to least.

10. 2.08, 2.98, 2.88

11. 53.03, 53.33, 53.13

12. 65.02, 6.86, 6.5

13. 0.78, 0.87, 0.08

Use the number line to compare and order.

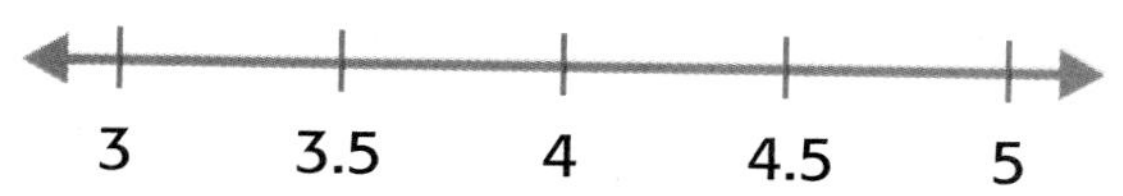

14. 3.4, 4.3, 4.7, 3.8

15. 4.0, 3.9, 3.3, 4.2

16. The amount of rainfall in a city was 5.13 inches in February and 4.08 inches in March. Then the city received 4.75 inches in April and 4.62 inches in May. Which month had the most rainfall? the least?

17. A gymnast earned a score of 9.5 on the vault and 9.75 on the rings. Then the gymnast earned a 9.52 on the uneven bars and a 9.8 on the parallel bars. Which event did the gymnast earn the greatest score? the least score?

Lesson 13-6

Pages 550–551

Use any strategy to solve. Tell what strategy you used.

1. A basement is rectangular in shape. One wall is 16 feet long. If the area is 304 square feet, what is the length of the other walls?

2. What is the next number in the pattern? What is the rule?

8, 5, 12, 9, 16, 13, 20, 17

3. Bina began her chores at 3:30 P.M. She stopped at 4:20 to walk her dog. She started her chores again at 5:15 and stopped at 5:45. How long did Bina do her chores?

4. A pepperoni pizza is cut into 10 slices. A veggie pizza the same size is cut into 6 slices. Which is greater: 4 slices of pepperoni pizza or 3 slices of veggie pizza?

Extra Practice

Lesson 13-7

Pages 552–555

Write a fraction and a decimal to describe the shaded part of each model.

1. 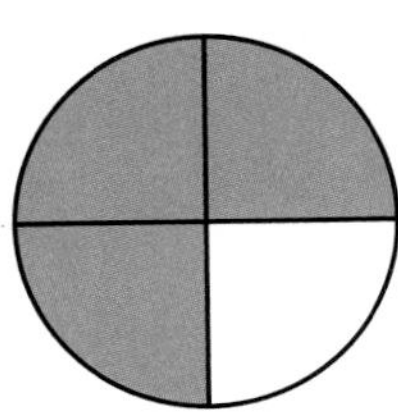
2. 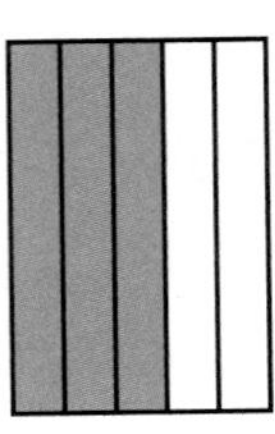
3. 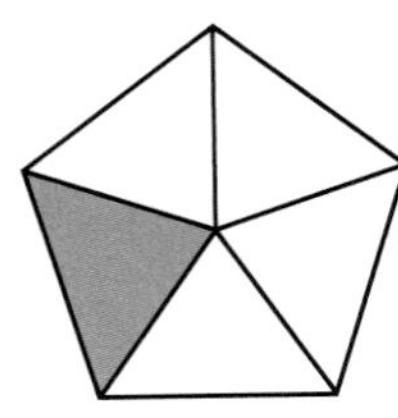
4. 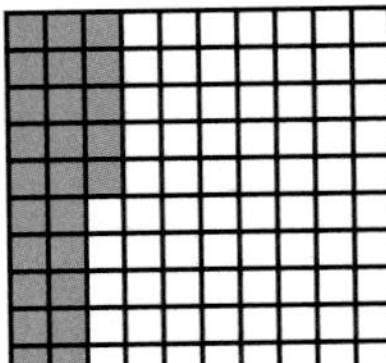
5. 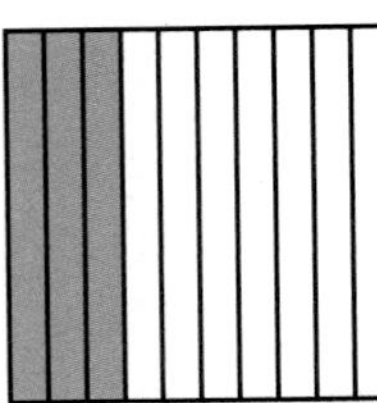
6. 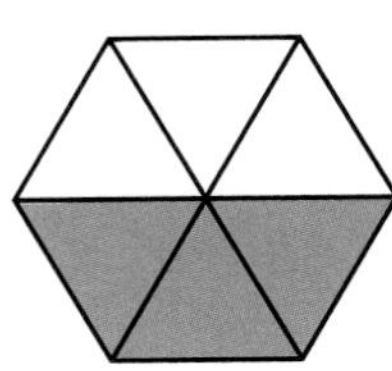

Model each fraction. Then write as a decimal.

7. $\frac{2}{5}$
8. $\frac{7}{10}$
9. $\frac{35}{100}$

Write each amount as a fraction and a decimal.

10. Sharon ate 2 out of 10 pizza slices.
11. Booker blew out 3 out of 4 candles on a cake.

Lesson 13-8

Pages 558–561

Use a number line to compare. Write <, >, or =.

1. $\frac{25}{5}$ ● 4
2. 12.34 ● 12.3
3. $6\frac{1}{2}$ ● 6.89
4. $8\frac{1}{10}$ ● 8.75
5. 72.07 ● 72.70
6. 52 ● 5.02
7. $\frac{1}{4}$ ● 0.18
8. $\frac{68}{100}$ ● $\frac{8}{10}$
9. $\frac{25}{100}$ ● 0.25

Use a number line to order from greatest to least.

10. $67\frac{2}{100}$, 67.0, 67.70
11. 50.80, $50\frac{4}{10}$, $50\frac{4}{5}$
12. $33\frac{25}{100}$, $33\frac{2}{3}$, 33.3
13. $\frac{70}{100}$, 0.75, $\frac{4}{10}$
14. A grasshopper is 7.6 centimeters long and a giant water bug is $12\frac{70}{100}$ centimeters long. A praying mantis is 30.5 centimeters long and a goliath bettle is $11\frac{4}{10}$ centimeters long. Which insect is the longest? the shortest?
15. The four largest bird nests in the world are $2\frac{1}{10}$, 1.4, $2\frac{40}{100}$, and 1.80 meters in diameter. Order the diameters of the bird nests from greatest to least.

Lesson 14-1

Pages 573–575

Round to the nearest whole number. Use number lines and models.

1. 19.8 **2.** 46.21 **3.** 73.81 **4.** 32.41

5. 55.79 **6.** 38.11 **7.** 82.7 **8.** 25.5

9. 28.27 **10.** 66.8 **11.** 24.55 **12.** 12.3

13. 16.72 **14.** 93.39 **15.** 47.11 **16.** 33.76

17. 29.28 **18.** 73.64 **19.** 51.82 **20.** 85.83

21. The world's tallest ferris wheel is located in Texas. It has a height of 64.6 meters. About how tall is this ferris wheel?

22. The average temperature of a city in Alaska is 9.8 degrees Fahrenheit. About how cold is the average temperature of this city?

Lesson 14-2

Pages 576–579

Estimate. Round to the nearest whole number. Use number lines and models.

1. 4.7 + 2.1

2. 5.3 + 4.2

3. \$14.96 + \$23.17

4. 17.67 + 23.78

5. 9.8 − 3.7

6. 13.3 − 7.2

7. 26.2 − 14.8

8. \$25.8 − \$16.2

9. 27.8 − 14.7

10. \$38.91 − 26.78

11. 59.5 − 23.12

12. \$83.32 − \$54.86

Estimate by rounding to the nearest whole number.

13. 3.72 + 5.18 ● 6.35 + 2.53

14. 17.83 − 4.59 ● 19.27 − 6.01

15. A saltwater crocodile can measure 9.2 meters in length. An American alligator can measure 3.9 meters in length. About how much longer is the saltwater crocodile?

16. Carla is buying a book for \$6.89 and a magazine for \$2.25. If she pays with a 10 dollar bill, about how much change will she receive?

Lesson 14-3

Pages 580–581

Solve. Use the *work backward* strategy.

1. Omar has \$3.75 left from lunch. He bought a taco for \$1.60, a salad for \$2.45, and milk for \$0.95. How much money did he have before lunch?

2. Allison raked leaves for 45 minutes. She took a break for 15 minutes and then pulled weeds for half an hour. She finished her yard work at 8:30. What time did she start?

3. What is the least number of coins worth 25¢ or less that could be used to make \$3.49? What are the coins?

4. A number is divided by 4. Next, 7 is subtracted from the quotient. Then, the difference is multiplied by 3. The result is 15. What is the number?

Lesson 14-4

Pages 584–586

Add. Use concrete objects or pictorial models.

1. $\begin{array}{r} 0.5 \\ +0.7 \\ \hline \end{array}$

2. $\begin{array}{r} 0.8 \\ +\ 0.7 \\ \hline \end{array}$

3. $\begin{array}{r} 2.3 \\ +\ 0.15 \\ \hline \end{array}$

4. $\begin{array}{r} 6.4 \\ +\ 9.34 \\ \hline \end{array}$

5. $\begin{array}{r} 7.65 \\ +\ 9.38 \\ \hline \end{array}$

6. $\begin{array}{r} \$7.25 \\ +\$6.49 \\ \hline \end{array}$

7. $\begin{array}{r} 14.79 \\ +\ 5.55 \\ \hline \end{array}$

8. $\begin{array}{r} 11.46 \\ +\ 4.93 \\ \hline \end{array}$

9. 22.48 + 18.67

10. 17.99 + 12.99

11. 42.52 + 21.84

12. 6.4 + 3.6 + 2.8

13. 5.2 + 8.3 + 7.4

14. 6.6 + 4.7 + 9.9

15. During a snowstorm, 2.75 inches of snow fell before noon. Then another 3.29 inches fell by 5 P.M. What is the total amount of snow that fell by 5 P.M.?

16. Amilia and her dad are buying school supplies. They are buying a pack of pencils for \$2.85, notebook paper for \$1.29, and a bottle of glue for \$1.99. How much will all of the school supplies cost?

Lesson 14-5

Pages 590–591

Use any strategy to solve. Tell what strategy you used.

1. There are two numbers whose product is 48 and difference is 8. What are the numbers?
2. A number is multiplied by 3. The product is subtracted from 50. The result is 11. What is the number?
3. A flower shop is selling 5 roses for $4. How much would 12 roses cost?
4. Dion surveyed 500 students to find out their favorite color. Blue was the favorite color of 7 out of 10 students. How many students' favorite color is blue?

Lesson 14-6

Pages 594–597

Subtract. Use models if needed.

1. $4.8 - 2.3$
2. $6.9 - 3.3$
3. $8.3 - 2.7$
4. $5.2 - 2.8$
5. $3.78 - 1.44$
6. $7.56 - 4.43$
7. \$9.45 − \$2.06
8. $8.55 - 4.38$
9. $12.61 - 8.75$
10. \$19.23 − \$12.86
11. \$26.74 − \$16.95
12. $48.03 - 27.12$
13. 54.50 − 46.72
14. 38.04 − 23.60
15. 41.93 − 15.98

For Exercises 16–17, use the table.

16. What is the difference in depth of the Baltic Sea and the Yellow Sea?
17. What is the difference between the deepest and shallowest bodies of water listed on the table?

Shallowest Oceans and Seas

Ocean or Sea	Depth (meters)
Baltic Sea	54.8
Hudson Bay	92.9
North Sea	93.8
Persian Gulf	99.9
Yellow Sea	36.8

Glossary/Glosario

Math Online A mathematics multilingual glossary is available at www.tx.gr4math.com/multilingual_glossary. The glossary includes the following languages.

Arabic	Cantonese	Korean	Tagalog
Bengali	English	Russian	Urdu
Brazilian Portuguese	Haitian Creole	Spanish	Vietnamese
	Hmong		

Cómo usar el glosario en español:

1. Busca el término en inglés que desees encontrar.
2. El término en español, junto con la definición, se encuentran en la columna de la derecha.

English / Español

A

acute angle (p. 325) An *angle* with a measure greater than 0° and less than 90°.

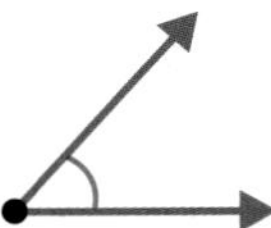

ángulo agudo Un *ángulo* que mide más de 0° y menos de 90°.

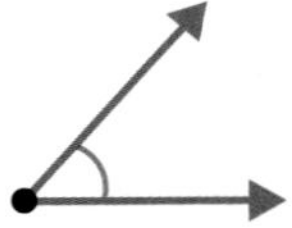

acute triangle (p. 329) A *triangle* with all three *angles* less than 90°.

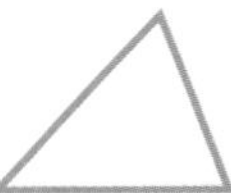

triángulo acutángulo Un *triángulo* cuyos tres *ángulos* miden menos de 90°.

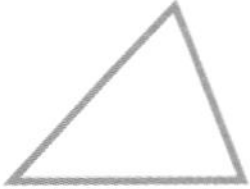

addend (p. 55) Any numbers being added together.

sumando Cualquier número que se suma a otro.

add (adding, addition) (p. 55) An operation on two or more *addends* that results in a *sum*.

$$9 + 3 = 12$$

sumar (sumando, adición) Operación en dos o más *sumandos* que resulta en una *suma*.

$$9 + 3 = 12$$

algebra (p. 183) A branch of mathematics that uses symbols, usually letters, to explore relationships between quantities.

álgebra Rama de las matemáticas que usa símbolos, generalmente letras, para explorar relaciones entre cantidades.

angle (p. 324) A figure that is formed by two *rays* with the same *endpoint*.

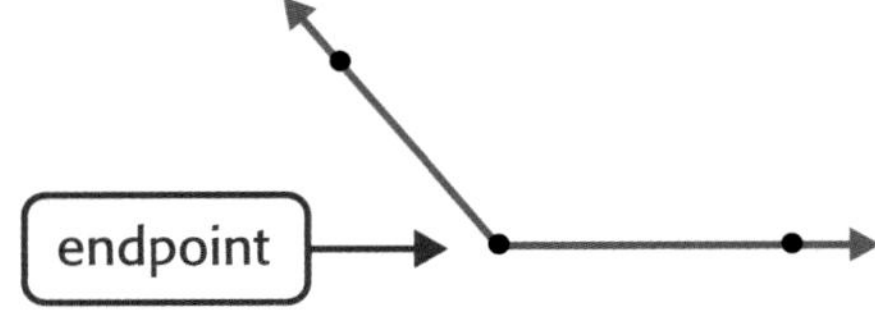

ángulo Figura formada por dos *rayos* con el mismo *extremo*.

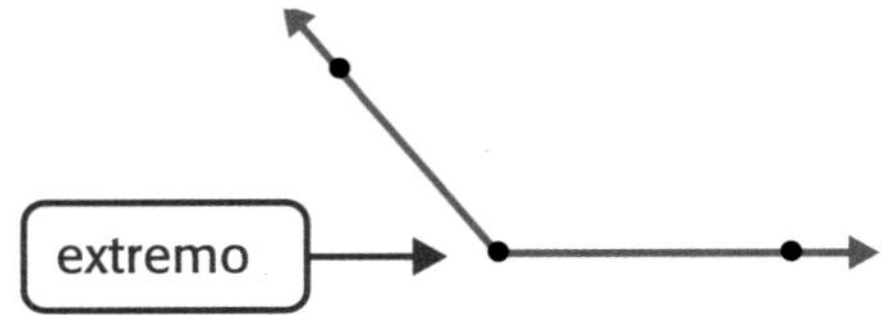

area (p. 414) The number of *square units* needed to cover the inside of a region or plane figure without any overlap.

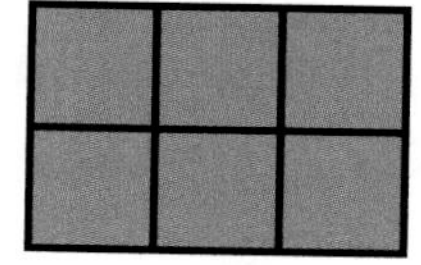

area = 6 square units

Associative Property of Addition (p. 55) The property states that the grouping of the *addends* does not change the *sum*.

$(4 + 5) + 2 = 4 + (5 + 2)$

Associative Property of Multiplication (p. 140) The property that states that the grouping of the *factors* does not change the *product*.

$3 \times (6 \times 2) = (3 \times 6) \times 2$

área El número de *unidades cuadradas* necesarias para cubrir el interior de una región o figura plana.

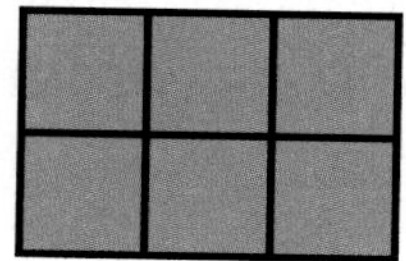

área = 6 unidades cuadrados

propiedad asociativa de la adición Propiedad que establece que la agrupación de los *sumandos* no altera la *suma*.

$(4 + 5) + 2 = 4 + (5 + 2)$

propiedad asociativa de la multiplicación Propiedad que establece que la agrupación de los *factores* no altera el *producto*.

$3 \times (6 \times 2) = (3 \times 6) \times 2$

B

balance (p. 186) An equation is balanced if both sides of the equals sign have the same value.

bar graph (p. 100) A graph that compares *data* by using bars of different lengths or heights to show the values.

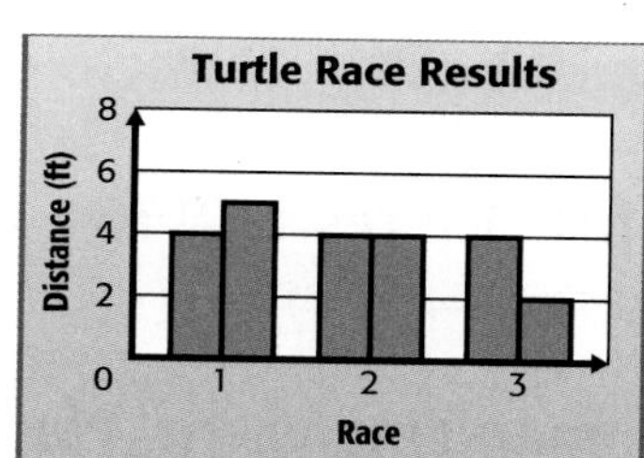

bilateral symmetry (p. 380) The property of a figure that allows it to be folded so the two halves match exactly.

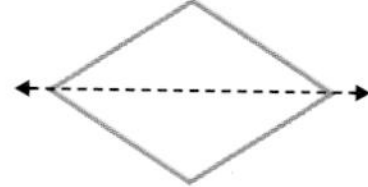

equilibrar Una ecuación está equilibrada si ambos lados del signo de igualdad tienen el mismo valor.

gráfica de barras Gráfica que compara los *datos* usando barras de distintas longitudes o alturas para mostrar los valores.

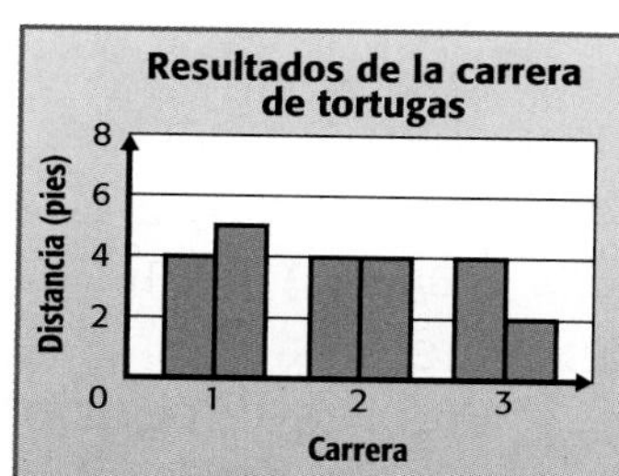

simetría bilateral Propiedad de una figura que le permite ser doblada de manera que las mitades se correspondan exactamente.

C

circle A closed figure in which all points are the same distance from a fixed point, called the center.

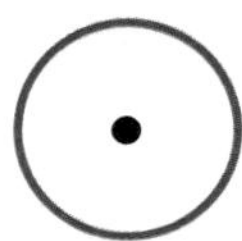

círculo Figura cerrada en la cual todos los puntos equidistan de un punto fijo llamado centro.

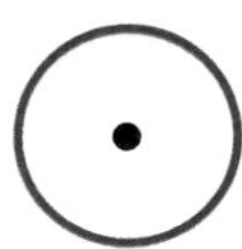

Commutative Property of Addition (p. 55) The property that states that the order in which two numbers are added does not change the *sum*.

$12 + 15 = 15 + 12$

propiedad conmutativa de la adición Propiedad que establece que el orden en el cual se suman dos o más números no altera la *suma*.

$12 + 15 = 15 + 12$

Commutative Property of Multiplication (p. 140) The property that states that the order in which two numbers are multiplied does not change the *product*.

$7 \times 2 = 2 \times 7$

propiedad conmutativa de la multiplicación Propiedad que establece que el orden en el cual se multiplican dos o más números no altera el *producto*.

$7 \times 2 = 2 \times 7$

compatible numbers Numbers in a problem or related numbers that are easy to work with mentally.

720 and 90 are compatible numbers for division because $72 \div 9 = 8$.

números compatibles Números en un problema o números relacionados con los cuales es fácil trabajar mentalmente.

720 y 90 son números compatibles en la división porque $72 \div 9 = 8$.

complex figure A shape that is made up of two or more shapes.

figura compleja Figura compuesta por dos o más formas.

composite number A whole number that has more than two factors.

12 has the factors 1, 2, 3, 4, 6, and 12.

número compuesto Número entero con más de dos factores.

12 tiene los factores 1, 2, 3, 4, 6 y 12.

cone (p. 315) A three-dimensional figure with a curved surface, a circular base, and one *vertex*.

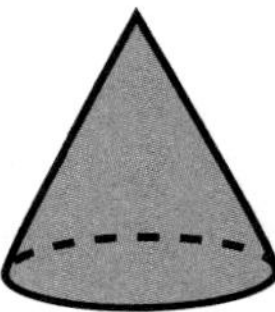

cono Figura tridimensional con una superficie curva, una base circular y un *vértice*.

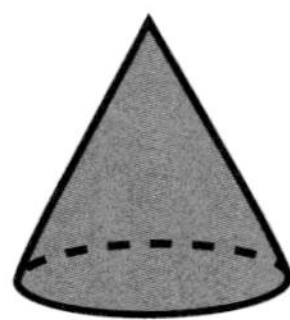

Glossary/Glosario

congruent figures (p. 374) Two figures having the same size and the same shape.

coordinate (p. 362) One of two numbers in an *ordered pair*.

In (1, 5), the 1 is the number on the *x*-axis. The 5 is on the *y*-axis.

coordinate plane or grid (p. 362) A graph that displays a set of points and gives the position of a point on a line.

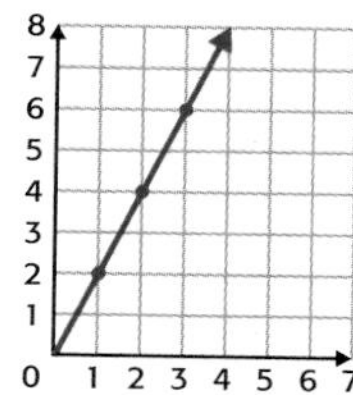

cube (p. 315) A three-dimensional figure with six *congruent* square *faces*.

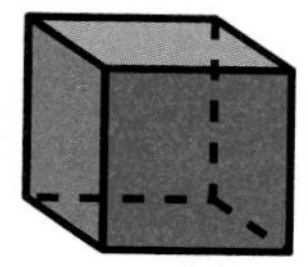

cylinder (p. 315) A three-dimensional figure having two *parallel congruent* circular bases and a curved surface connecting the two bases.

D

data (p. 95) Numbers or symbols, sometimes collected from a *survey* or experiment, to show information. Datum is singular; data is plural.

decimal equivalents (p. 552) Decimals that represent the same number.

0.3 and 0.30

figuras congruentes Dos figuras con la misma forma y el mismo tamaño.

coordenada Uno de los dos números de un *par ordenado*.

(1, 5) El 1 es el número en el eje *x* y el 5 está en el eje *y*.

gráfica de coordenadas o cuadriculado Gráfica que representa un conjunto de puntos y da, en términos numéricos, la posición de un punto sobre una recta.

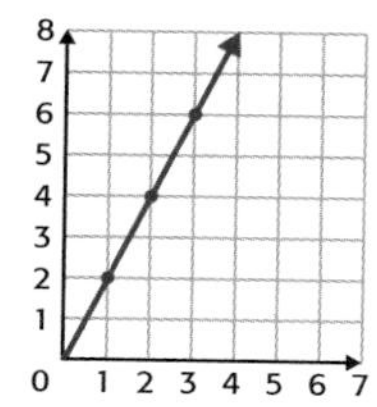

cubo Figura tridimensional con seis *caras* cuadradas *congruentes*.

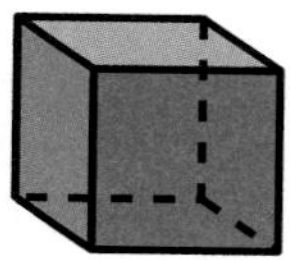

cilindro Figura tridimensional que tiene dos bases circulares *paralelas* y *congruentes* y una superficie curva que las une.

datos Números o símbolos que muestran información, algunas veces reunidos de una *encuesta* o un experimento.

decimales equivalentes Decimales que representan el mismo número.

0.3 y 0.30

decimal (p. 535) A number that uses *place value,* numbers, and a *decimal point* to show part of a whole.

decimal point (p. 535) A period separating the ones and the *tenths* in a decimal number.

0.8 or $3.77

denominator (p. 493) The bottom number in a *fraction*.

In $\frac{5}{6}$, 6 is the denominator.

diameter A *line segment* that connects two points on a circle and passes through the center of a *circle*.

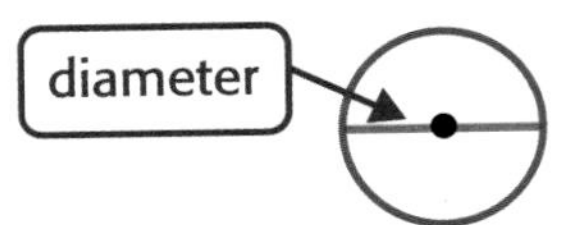

digit (p. 17) A symbol used to write numbers. The ten digits are 0, 1, 2, 3, 4, 5, 6, 7, 8, and 9.

Distributive Property of Multiplication (p. 156, 250) To multiply a *sum* by a number, multiply each *addend* by the number and add the *products*.

$$4 \times (1 + 3) = (4 \times 1) + (4 \times 3)$$

division (divide) (p. 135) An operation on two numbers in which the first number is split into the same number of equal groups as the second number.

dividend (p. 136) A number that is being divided.

$3\overline{)19}$ 19 is the dividend

divisor (p. 135) The number by which the *dividend* is being divided.

$3\overline{)19}$ 3 is the divisor

decimal/divisor

decimal Número con uno o más dígitos a la derecha del *punto decimal*, tales como 8.37 ó 0.05.

punto decimal Punto que separa las unidades de las *décimas* en un número decimal.

0.8 ó $3.77

denominador El número inferior en una *fracción*.

$\frac{5}{6}$ 6 es el denominador.

diámetro Un *segmento de recta* que pasa por el centro de un *círculo*.

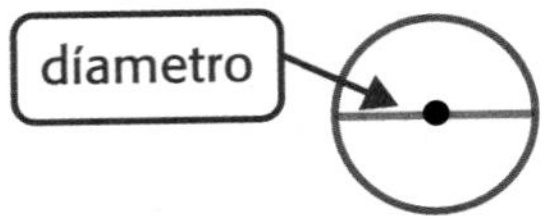

dígito Símbolo que se usa para escribir números. Los diez dígitos son 0, 1, 2, 3, 4, 5, 6, 7, 8 y 9.

propiedad distributiva de la multiplicación Para multiplicar una *suma* por un número, puedes multiplicar cada *sumando* por el número y sumar los *productos.*

$$4 \times (1 + 3) = (4 \times 1) + (4 \times 3)$$

división (dividir) Operación en dos números en que el primer número se separa en tantos grupos iguales como indica el segundo número.

dividendo El número que se divide.

$3\overline{)19}$ 19 es el dividendo

divisor El número entre el cual se divide el *dividendo*.

$3\overline{)19}$ 3 es el divisor

double bar graph (p. 105) A *bar graph* that compares two related groups of *data*.

E

edge (p. 315) The *line segment* where two *faces* of a *solid figure* meet.

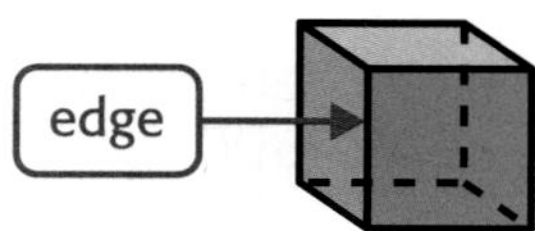

endpoint (p. 356) The point at either end of a *line segment* or the point at the beginning of a ray.

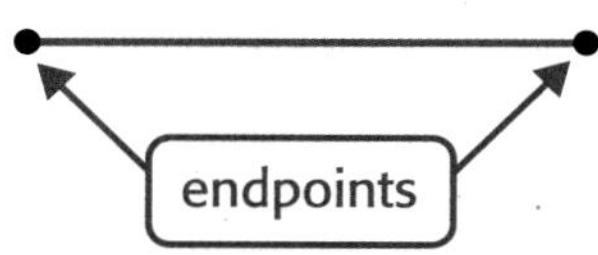

elapsed time (p. 476) The amount of time that has passed from beginning to end.

equation (p. 186) A sentence that contains an equals sign (=), showing that two *expressions* are equal.

equilateral triangle (p. 328) A *triangle* with three *congruent* sides.

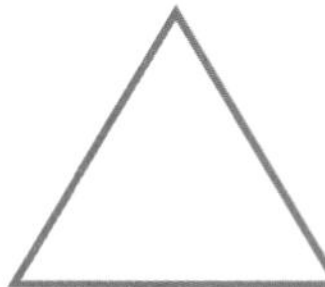

equivalent fractions (p. 502) *Fractions* that represent the same number

$$\frac{3}{4} = \frac{6}{8}$$

gráfica de barras dobles *Gráfica de barras* que compara dos grupos de *datos* relacionados.

arista El *segmento de recta* donde concurren dos *caras* de una *figura sólida.*

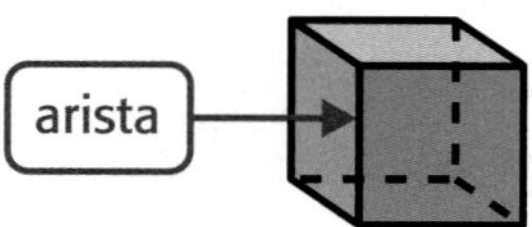

punto final El punto en cualquiera de los dos lados en que termina un *segmento de recta* o el punto al principio de un rayo.

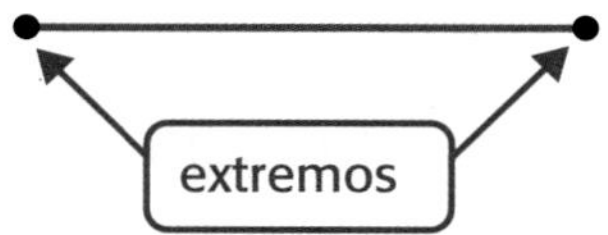

tiempo transcurrido Cantidad de tiempo que ha pasado entre el principio y el fin.

ecuación Enunciado matemático que contiene el signo de igualdad, =, el que indica que el lado izquierdo del signo de igualdad tiene el mismo valor que el lado derecho.

triángulo equilátero *Triángulo* con tres lados *congruentes*.

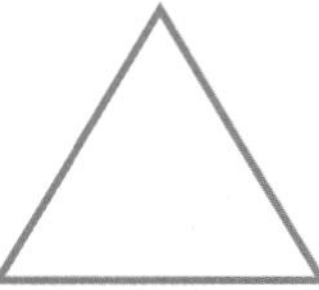

fracciones equivalentes *Fracciones* que representan el mismo número.

$$\frac{3}{4} = \frac{6}{8}$$

Glossary/Glosario

estimate (p. 36, 58) A number close to an exact value. An estimate indicates *about* how much.

47 + 22 is about 50 + 20 or 70.

expanded form/expanded notation (p. 18) The representation of a number as a sum that shows the value of each digit.

536 is written as 500 + 30 + 6.

expression (p. 183) A combination of numbers, variables, and at least one operation.

estimación Número cercano a un valor exacto. Una estimación indica *aproximadamente* cuánto.

47 + 22 es aproximadamente 50 + 20; ó 70.

forma desarrollada/notación desarrollada Representación de un número como una suma que muestra el valor de cada dígito.

536 se escribe como 500 + 30 + 6.

expresión Combinación de números, variables y por lo menos una operacion.

F

face (p. 315) The flat part of a three-dimensional figure.

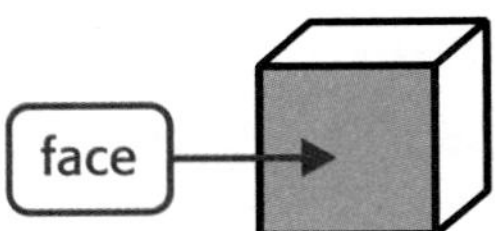

fact family (p. 137) A group of related facts using the same numbers.

5 + 3 = 8	5 × 3 = 15
3 + 5 = 8	3 × 5 = 15
8 − 3 = 5	15 ÷ 3 = 5
8 − 5 = 3	15 ÷ 5 = 3

factor (p. 135, 166) A number that divides a whole number evenly. Also a number that is multiplied by another number.

fraction (p. 493) A number that represents part of a whole or part of a set.

$\frac{1}{2}, \frac{1}{3}, \frac{1}{4}, \frac{3}{4}$

frequency table (p. 95) A table for organizing a set of *data* that shows the number of times each result has occurred.

cara Parte llana de una figura tridimensional.

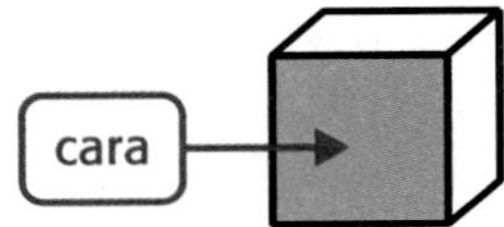

familia de operaciones Grupo de operaciones relacionadas que usan los mismos números.

5 + 3 = 8	5 × 3 = 15
3 + 5 = 8	3 × 5 = 15
8 − 3 = 5	15 ÷ 3 = 5
8 − 5 = 3	15 ÷ 5 = 3

factor Número que divide exactamente a otro número entero. También es un número multiplicado por otro número.

fracción Número que representa parte de un todo o parte de un conjunto.

$\frac{1}{2}, \frac{1}{3}, \frac{1}{4}, \frac{3}{4}$

tabla de frecuencias Tabla para organizar un conjunto de *datos* que muestra el número de veces que ha ocurrido cada resultado.

Glossary/Glosario

function A relationship in which one number depends on another number.

función Relación en que una cantidad depende de otra cantidad.

function table A table of ordered pairs that is based on a rule.

tabla de funciones Tabla de pares ordenados que se basa en una regla.

G

grid (p. 120) A group of horizontal and vertical lines, that intersect, forming squares.

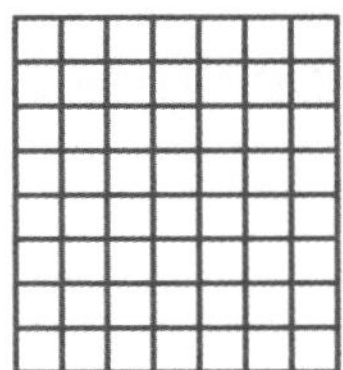

cuadriculdo Grupo de rectas horizontales y verticales que se intersecan formando cuadrados.

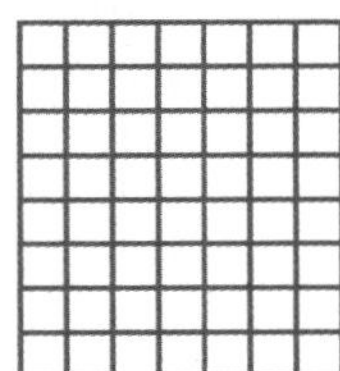

H

hexagon (p. 318) A *polygon* with six sides and six *angles*.

hexágono *Polígono* con seis lados y seis *ángulos*.

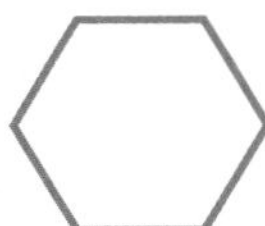

hundredth (p. 536) A place value position. One of one hundred equal parts.

In the number 0.05, 5 is in the hundredths place.

centésima Un valor de posición. Una parte de cien partes iguales.

En el número 4.57, 7 está en el lugar de las centésimas.

I

Identity Property of Addition (p. 55) For any number, zero plus that number is the number.

$3 + 0 = 3$ or $0 + 3 = 3$

propiedad de identidad de la adición Para todo numero, cero más el numero es el número.

$3 + 0 = 3$ ó $0 + 3 = 3$

Identity Property of Multiplication (p. 140) If you multiply a number by 1, the product is the same as the given number.

$8 \times 1 = 8 = 1 \times 8$

propiedad de identidad de la multiplicación Si multiplicas un número por 1, el producto es igual al número dado.

$8 \times 1 = 8 = 1 \times 8$

imposible/denominador común

impossible An event that cannot happen. It has a probability of zero.
It is impossible to choose yellow.

imposible Un evento que no puede suceder, cuya probabilidad es cero.

improper fraction (p. 516) A fraction with a *numerator* that is greater than or equal to the *denominator*.

$\frac{17}{3}$ or $\frac{5}{5}$

fracción impropia Fracción con un *numerador* mayor que o igual al *denominador*.

$\frac{17}{3}$ ó $\frac{5}{5}$

intersecting lines (p. 357) *Lines* that meet or cross at a point.

rectas secantes *Rectas* que se intersecan o cruzan entre sí.

is greater than > (p. 28) An inequality relationship showing that the number on the left of the symbol is greater than the number on the right.

$5 > 3$ 5 is greater than 3

es mayor que > Relación de desigualdad que muestra que el número a la izquierda del símbolo es mayor que el número a la derecha.

$5 > 3$ 5 es mayor que 3

is less than < (p. 28) The number on the left side of the symbol is smaller than the number on the right side.

$4 < 7$ 4 is less than 7

es menor que < El número a la izquierda del símbolo es más pequeño que el número a la derecha.

$4 < 7$ 4 es menor que 7

isosceles triangle (p. 328) A *triangle* with at least 2 sides of the same length.

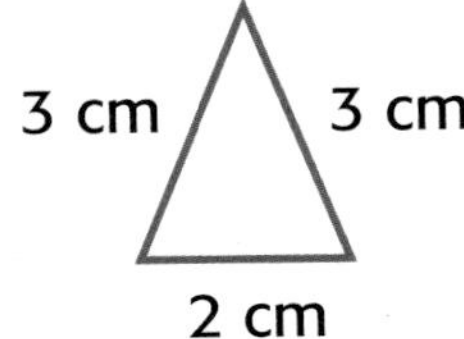

triángulo isósceles Un *triángulo* que tiene por lo menos 2 lados del mismo largo.

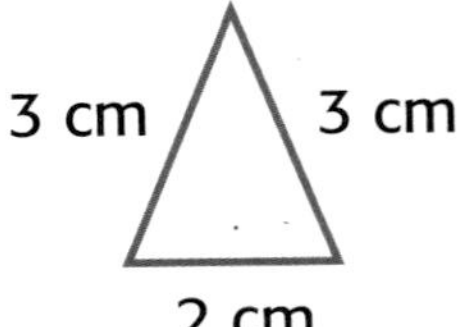

L

like denominators When two or more fractions have the same *denominator* they have like *denominators*.

denominador común El mismo *denominador* que se usa en dos o más *fracciones*.

like fractions Fractions that have the same denominator.

likely An event that will probably happen.

It is likely you will choose a red cube.

line (p. 356) A straight set of points that extend in opposite directions without ending.

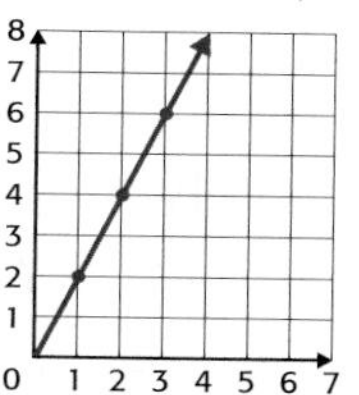

line graph A graph that uses points connected by *line segments* to represent data.

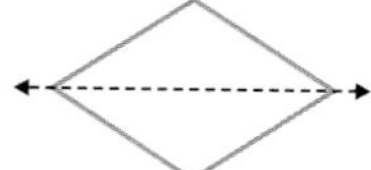

line of symmetry (p. 380) A *line* on which a figure can be folded so that its two halves match exactly.

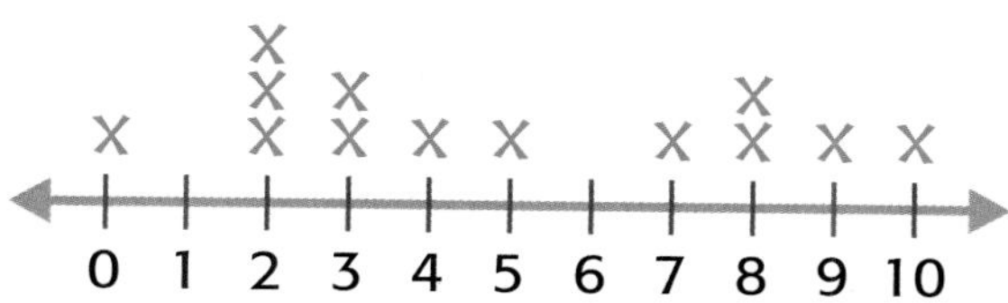

line plot A graph that uses columns of Xs above a *number line* to show frequency of data.

fracciones semejantes Fracciones que tienen el mismo denominador.

posible Un evento que probablemente sucederá.

Es posible que elijas un cubo rojo.

recta Conjunto de puntos dispuestos rectamente en direcciones opuestas y sin fin.

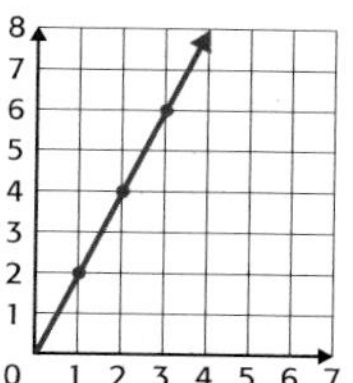

gráfica lineal Gráfica que usa puntos unidos por *segmentos de recta* para representar datos.

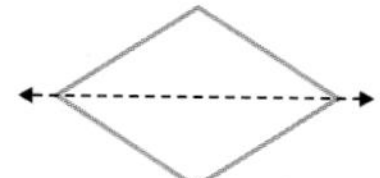

eje de simetría *Recta* sobre la cual se puede doblar una figura de manera que sus mitades se correspondan exactamente.

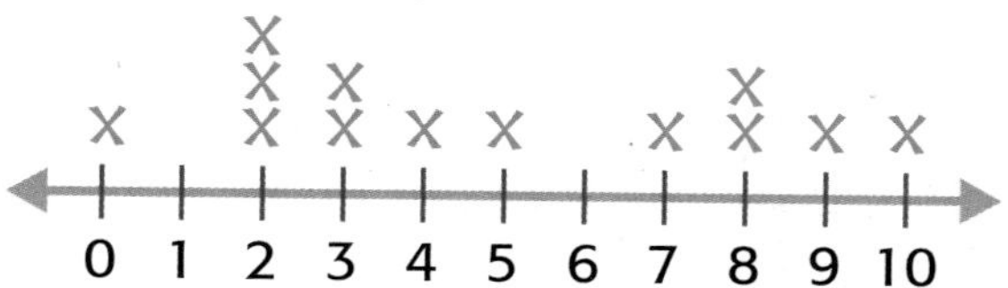

esquema lineal Gráfica que usa columnas de X sobre una *recta numérica* para representar frecuencias de datos.

line segment (p. 356) A part of a *line* between two *endpoints*. The length of the line segment can be measured.

line symmetry (p. 380) A figure has *line symmetry* if it can be folded so that the two parts of the figure match, or are *congruent.*

segmento de recta Parte de una *recta* entre dos *extremos*. La longitud de un segmento de recta se puede medir.

simetría lineal Una figura tiene *simetria lineal* si puede doblarse de modo que las dos partes de la figura correspondan o sean *congruentes*.

M

median The middle number in a group of numbers arranged in numerical order.
The median of 3, 5, 6, 7, and 8 is 6.

minuend (p. 71) The first number in a subtraction sentence from which a second number is to be subtracted.

8 − 3 = 5
(8: minuend; 3: subtrahend; 5: difference)

mixed number (p. 516) A number that has a *whole number* part and a *fraction* part.

$6\frac{3}{4}$

mode The number(s) that occurs most often in a set of numbers.

7, 4, 7, 10, 7, and 2
The mode is 7.

multiple (p. 167) A multiple of a number is the *product* of that number and any whole number.
15 is a multiple of 5 because $3 \times 5 = 15$.

multiply (multiplication) (p. 135) An operation on two numbers to find their *product*. It can be thought of as repeated *addition*.

mediana El número central de un grupo de números ordenados numéricamente.
La mediana de 3, 5, 6, 7, y 8 es 6.

minuendo El primer número en un enunciado de sustracción del cual se restará un segundo número

8 − 3 = 5
(8: minuendo; 3: sustraendo; 5: diferencia)

número mixto Número compuesto por una *parte entera* y una parte *fraccionaria*.

$6\frac{3}{4}$

moda Número o números que ocurre(n) con mayor frecuencia en un conjunto de números.
7, 4, 7, 10, 7, y 2
La moda es 7.

múltiplo Un múltiplo de un número es el *producto* de ese número y cualquier otro número entero.
15 es múltiplo de 5 porque $3 \times 5 = 15$.

multiplicar (multiplicación) Operación en dos números para calcular su *producto*. También se puede interpretar como una *adición* repetida.

N

negative number Numbers less than zero.

número negativo Números menores que cero.

net (p. 316) A flat pattern that can be folded to make a three-dimensional figure.

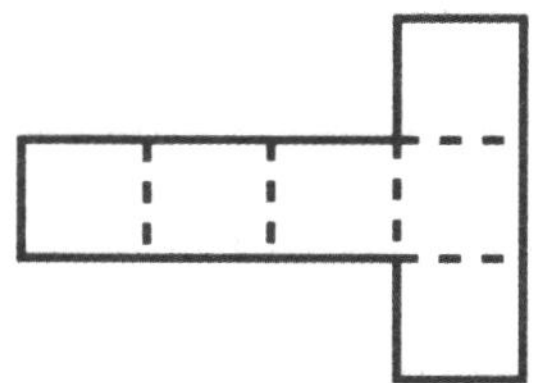

red Patrón llano que se puede doblar para formar una figura tridimensional.

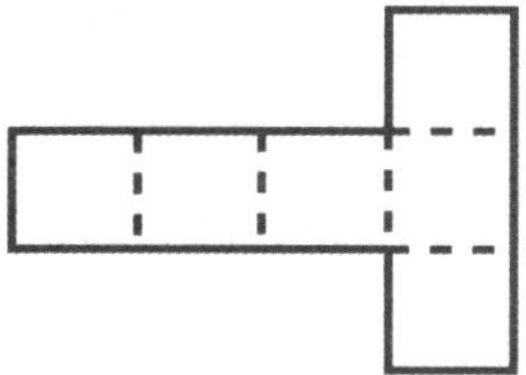

number line (p. 28) A line with numbers on it in order at regular intervals.

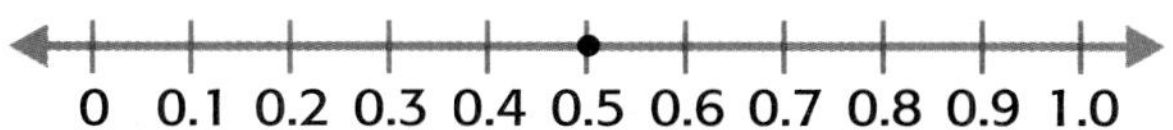

recta numérica Recta que representa números como puntos.

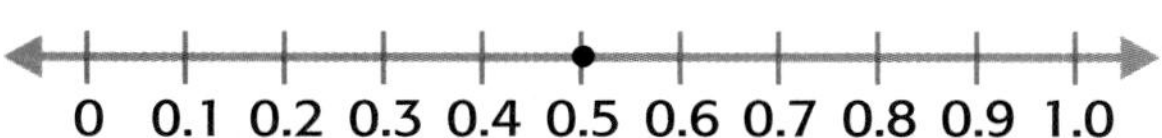

numerator (p. 493) The number above the bar in a *fraction*; the part of the fraction that tells how many of the equal parts are being used.

numerador El número que está encima de la barra de *fracción*; la parte de la fracción que te indica cuántas partes iguales están siendo usadas.

O

obtuse angle (p. 325) An *angle* that measures greater than 90° but less than 180°.

ángulo obtuso *Ángulo* que mide más de 90° pero menos de 180°.

obtuse triangle (p. 329) A *triangle* with one *obtuse angle*.

triángulo obtusángulo *Triángulo* con un *ángulo obtuso*.

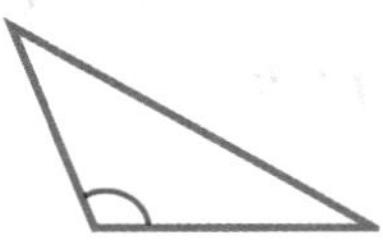

octagon (p. 318) A *polygon* with 8 sides.

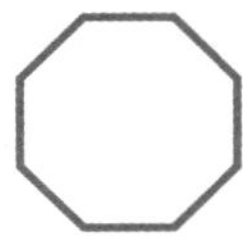

octágono *Polígono* de 8 lados.

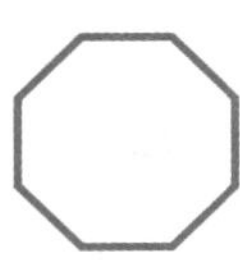

operation A mathematical process such as addition (+), subtraction (–), multiplication (×), or division (÷).

operación Proceso matemático como la adición (+), la sustracción (–), la multiplicación (×) o la división (÷).

order of operations Rules that tell what order to follow use in evaluating an expression:
(1) Do the operations in parentheses first.
(2) Multiply and divide in order from left to right.
(3) Add and subtract in order from left to right.

orden de las operaciones Reglas que te indican qué orden seguir cuando evalúas una expresión:
(1) Evalúa primero las operaciones dentro de los paréntesis ( ).
(2) Multiplica o divide en orden de izquierda a derecha.
(3) Suma o resta en orden de izquierda a derecha.

ordered pair (p. 362) A pair of numbers that are the *coordinates* of a point in a coordinate plane or grid in this order (horizontal coordinate, vertical coordinate).

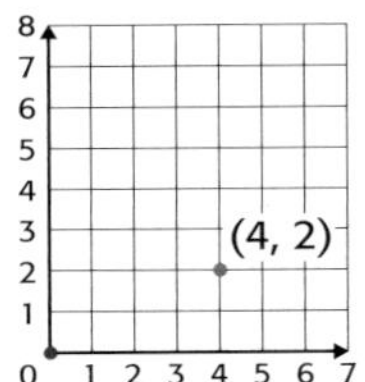

par ordenado Par de números que son *coordenadas* de un punto en un plano de coordenadas o cuadriculado, en este orden (coordenada horizontal, coordenada vertical).

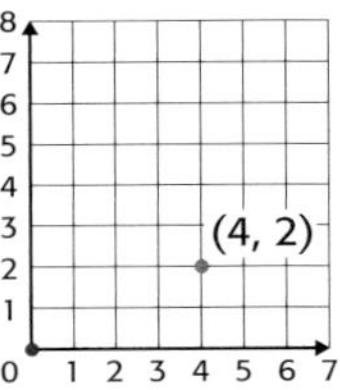

origin (p. 362) The point (0, 0) on a *coordinate graph* where the vertical axis meets the horizontal axis.

origen El punto (0, 0) en una *gráfica de coordenadas* donde el eje vertical interseca el eje horizontal, (0, 0).

outcome (p. 114) A possible result of an experiment.

resultado Resultado posible de un experimento.

outlier A number in a set of data that is much larger or much smaller than most of the other numbers in the set.

valor atípico Número en un conjunto de datos que es mucho mayor o mucho menor que la mayoría de los otros números del conjunto.

P

parallel lines (p. 357) Lines that are the same distance apart. Parallel lines do not meet.

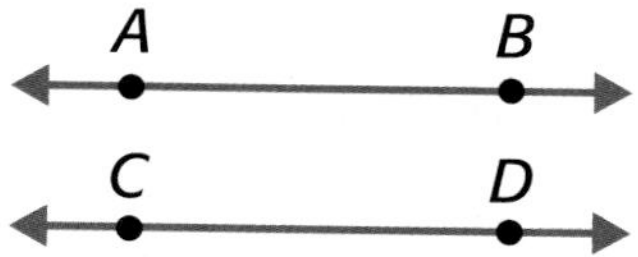

parallelogram (p. 332) A quadrilateral with four sides in which each pair of opposite sides are parallel and equal in length.

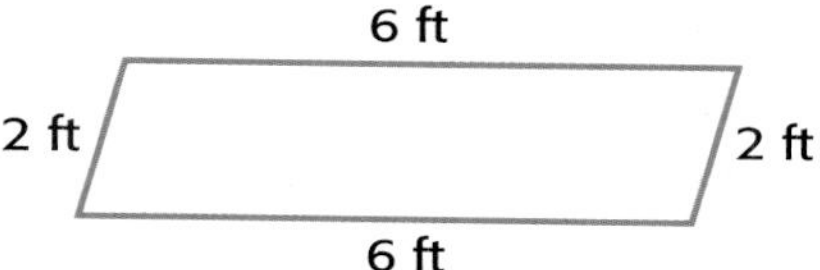

pentagon (p. 318) A *polygon* with five sides.

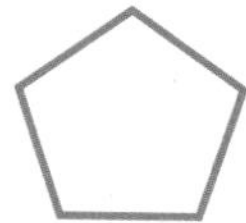

perimeter (p. 410) The distance around a shape or region.

period (p. 17) The name given to each group of three digits on a place-value chart.

perpendicular lines (p. 357) *Lines* that meet or cross each other to form *right angles*.

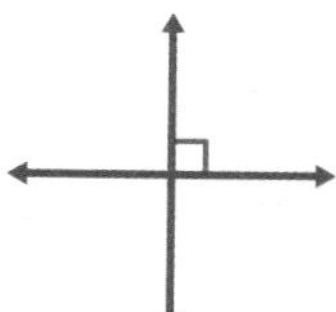

place value (p. 17) The value given to a *digit* by its position in a number.

plane figure (p. 318) A two-dimensional figure that lies entirely within one plane such as a triangle or square.

rectas paralelas Rectas separadas por la misma distancia. Las rectas paralelas no se intersecan.

paralelogramo Cuadrilátero de cuatro lados en el cual cada par de lados opuestos son paralelos y de la misma longitud.

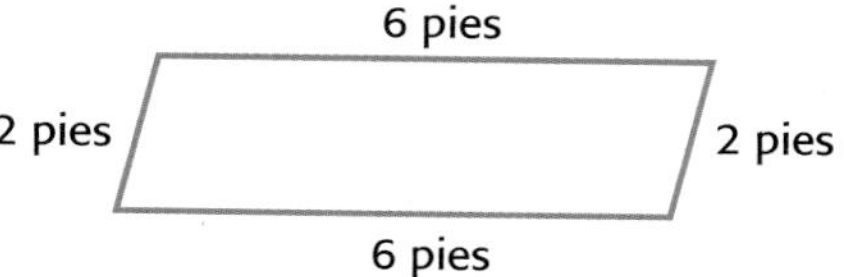

pentágono *Polígono* de cinco lados.

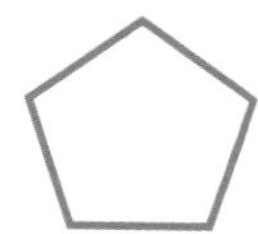

perímetro Distancia alrededor de una figura o región.

período Nombre dado a cada grupo de tres dígitos en una tabla de valores de posición.

rectas perpendiculares *Rectas* que se intersecan o cruzan formando *ángulos rectos*.

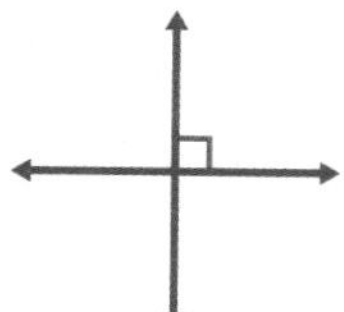

valor de posición El valor dado a un *dígito* según su posición en un número.

figura plana Figura bidimensional que yace completamente en un plano como un triángulo o un cuadrado.

polygon (p. 318) A closed *plane figure* formed using *line segments* that meet only at their *endpoints*.

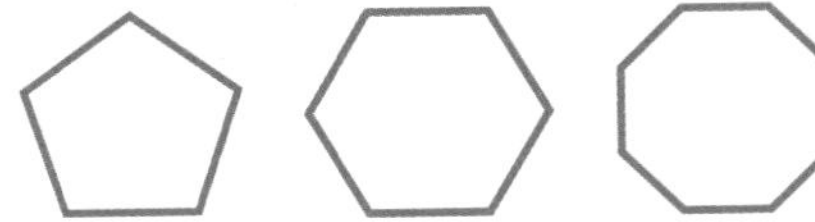

positive number Numbers that are greater than zero.

prime number A whole number with exactly two *factors,* 1 and itself.

7, 13, and 19

probability (p. 120) A number between 0 and 1 that measures the likelihood of an event happening.

product (p. 135) The answer or result of a multiplication problem. It also refers to expressing a number as the product of its factors.

pyramid (p. 315) A three-dimensional figure with a *polygon* as a base and triangular shaped *faces* that share a common *vertex*.

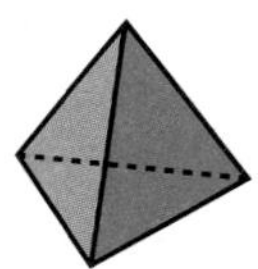

polígono *Figura plana* cerrada formada por *segmentos de recta* que sólo se unen en sus *extremos*.

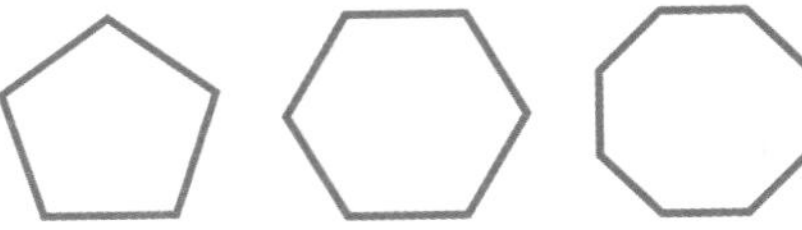

número positivo Números mayores que cero.

número primo Número entero que tiene exactamente dos *factores*, 1 y sí mismo.

7, 13, y 19

probabilidad Número entre 0 y 1 que mide la posibilidad de que ocurra un evento.

producto Repuesta o resultado de un problema de multiplicación. También se refiere a la expresión de un número como el producto de sus factores.

pirámide Figura sólida con un *polígono* como base y *caras* triangulares que comparten un *vértice* común.

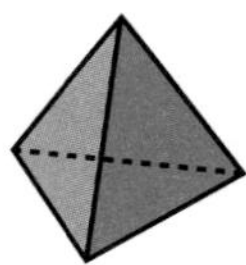

Q

quadrilateral (p. 318) A shape that has 4 sides and 4 *angles*.

square, rectangle, and parallelogram

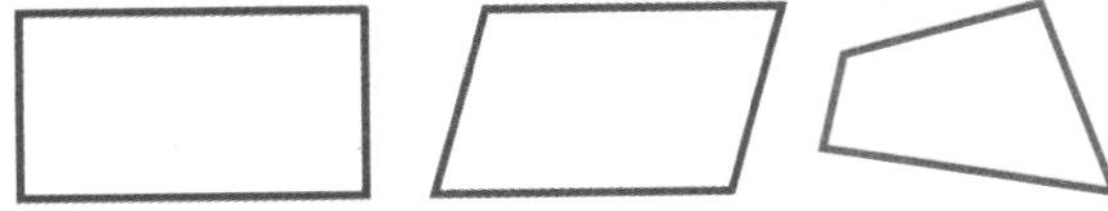

quotient (p. 136) The result of a *division* problem.

cuadrilátero Figura que tiene 4 lados y 4 *ángulos*.

cuadrado, rectángulo y paralelogramo

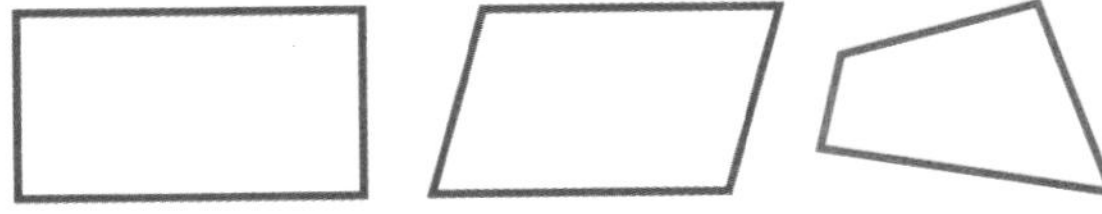

cociente Respuesta o resultado de un problema de *división*.

R

ray (p. 356) A part of a *line* that has one *endpoint* and extends in one direction without ending.

rayo Parte de una *recta* que tiene un *extremo* y que se extiende en una dirección.

rectangle (p. 332) A *quadrilateral* with four *right angles*; opposite sides are equal and *parallel*.

rectángulo *Cuadrilátero* con cuatro *ángulo rectos*; los lados opuestos son iguales y *paralelos*.

rectangular prism (p. 315) A three-dimensional figure with six faces that are rectangles.

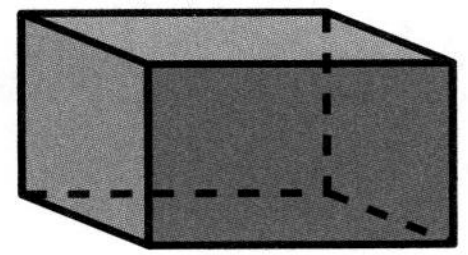

prisma rectangular Figura tridimensional de seis caras rectangulares.

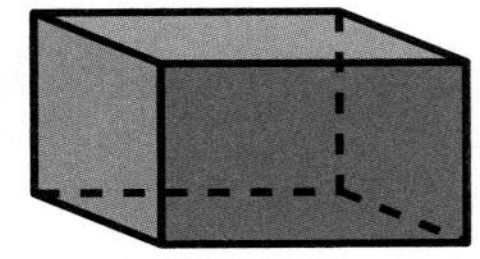

reflection (p. 368) A type of transformation that flips a figure.

reflexión Tipo de transformación en que seleda vuelta a una figura.

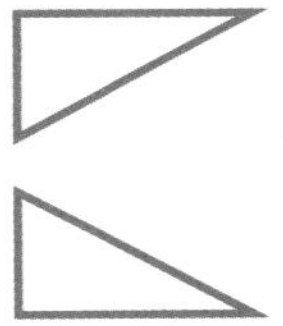

remainder (p. 267) The number that is left after one whole number is divided by another.

residuo Número que queda después de dividir un número entero entre otro número entero.

rhombus (p. 332) A *parallelogram* with four *congruent* sides.

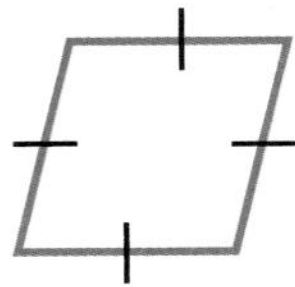

rombo *Paralelogramo* con cuatro lados *congruentes*.

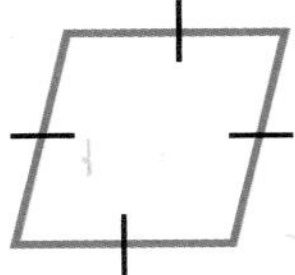

right angle (p. 325) An *angle* with a measure of 90°.

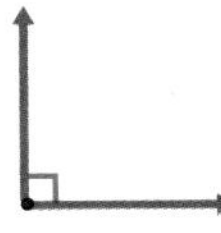

ángulo recto *Ángulo* que mide 90°.

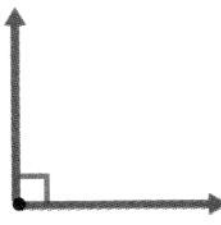

Glossary/Glosario

right triangle (p. 329) A *triangle* with one *right angle*.

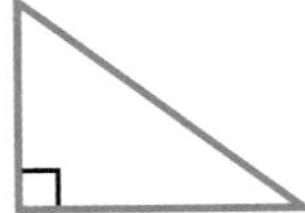

triángulo rectángulo *Triángulo* con un *ángulo recto*.

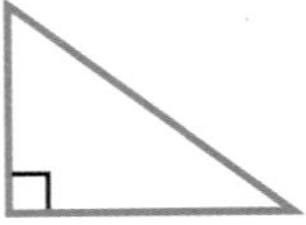

rotation (p. 368) A type of transformation in which a figure is turned about a central point.

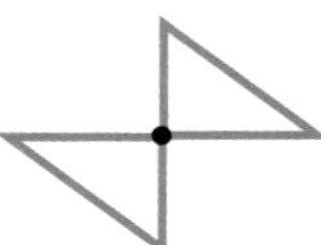

rotación Tipo de tranformación en que se hace girar una figura alrededor de un punto central.

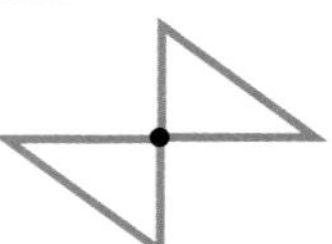

round (p. 36) To change the value of a number to one that is easier to work with. To find the nearest value of a number based on a given *place value*.

redondear Cambiar el valor de un número a uno con el cual es más fácil trabajar. Calcular el valor más cercano a un número basado en un *valor de posición* dado.

S

scalene triangle (p. 328) A *triangle* with no *congruent* sides.

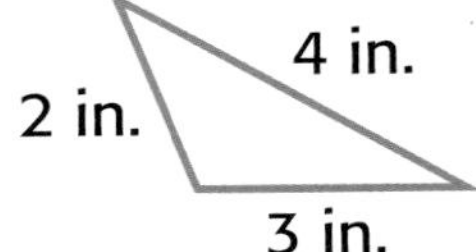

triángulo escaleno *Triángulo* sin lados *congruentes*.

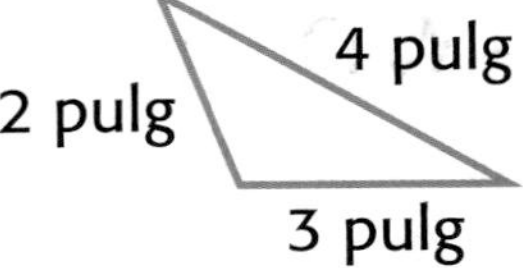

simplest form A *fraction* in which the *numerator* and the *denominator* have no common factor greater than 1.

forma reducida *Fracción* en la cual el *numerador* y el *denominador* no tienen un factor común mayor que 1.

solid figure (p. 315) A solid figure has three dimensions: length, width, and height.

figura sólida Figura sólida de tres dimensiones: largo, ancho y alto.

sphere (p. 315) A three-dimensional figure that is set of all points that are the same distance from a given point, called the center.

esfera Figura tridimensional formada por el conjunto de todos los puntos equidistantes de un punto dado llamado centro.

square A rectangle with four *congruent* sides.

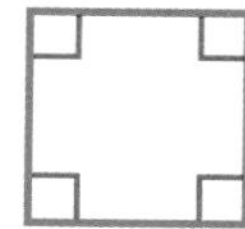

square unit (p. 414) A unit for measuring area.

standard form/standard notation (p. 18) The usual way of writing a number that shows only its *digits*, no words.

537 89 1642

subtract (subtraction) (p. 70) An operation on two numbers that tells the difference, when some or all are taken away. Subtraction is also used to compare two numbers.

$14 - 8 = 6$

subtrahend (p. 71) A number that is subtracted from another number.

$14 - 5 = 9$

↑ subtrahend

sum (p. 55) The answer to an addition problem.

survey (p. 95) A method of collecting *data*.

cuadrado Rectángulo de cuatro lados *congruentes*.

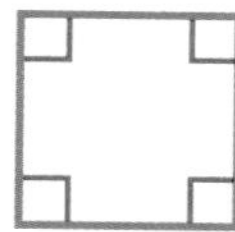

unidad cuadrada Unidad para medir el área.

forma estándar/notación estandard Manera habitual de escribir un número que sólo muestra sus *dígitos*, sin palabras.

537 89 1642

restar (sustracción) Operación en dos números que indica la diferencia, cuando algunos o todos son eliminados. La sustracción también se usa para comparar dos números.

$14 - 8 = 6$

sustraendo Un número que se sustrae de otro número.

$14 - 5 = 9$

↑ sustraendo

suma Respuesta o resultado de un problema de adición.

encuesta Método para reunir *datos*.

T

tally chart (p. 95) A way to keep track of *data* using tally marks to record the number of responses or occurrences.

What is Your Favorite Color?	
Color	**Tally**
Blue	~~||||~~ |||
Green	||||

tabla de conteo Manera de llevar la cuenta de los *datos* usando marcas de conteo para anotar el número de respuestas o sucesos.

¿Cuál es tu color favorito?	
Color	**Conteo**
Azul	~~||||~~ |||
Verde	||||

tally mark(s) (p. 95) A mark made to keep track and display *data* recorded from a survey.

marca(s) de conteo Marca que se hace para llevar un registro y representar *datos* reunidos de una encuesta.

tenth (p. 533) One of ten equal parts or $\frac{1}{10}$.

décima Una de diez partes iguales ó $\frac{1}{10}$.

translation (p. 368) A type of transformation in which a figure is slid vertically, horizontally, or both.

traslación Tipo de transformación en que una figura se desliza en sentido vertical, en sentido horizontal o en ambos sentidos.

trapezoid (p. 332) A *quadrilateral* with exactly one pair of *parallel* sides.

trapecio *Cuadrilátero* con exactamente un par de lados *paralelos*.

tree diagram (p. 117) **a.** A diagram of all the possible *outcomes* of an event or series of events or experiments.
b. A diagram of all the possible combinations of two or more objects or events being put together.

diagrama de árbol **a.** Diagrama de todos los *resultados* posibles de un evento o series de eventos o experimentos.
b. Diagrama de todas las combinaciones posibles de dos o más objetos o eventos que se combinan.

triangle (p. 318) A *polygon* with three sides and three *angles*.

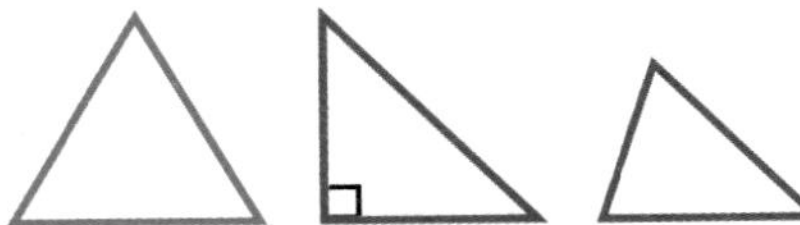

triángulo *Polígono* con tres lados y tres *ángulos*.

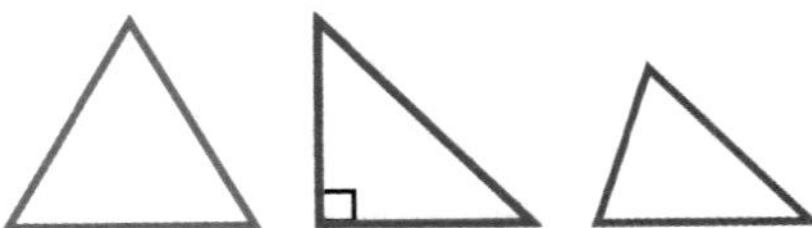

triangular prism (p. 315) A prism whose bases are triangular with *parallelograms* for sides.

prisma triangular Prisma cuyas bases son triangulares con *paralelogramos* como lados.

Glossary/Glosario

triangular pyramid (p. 315) A pyramid whose base is a *triangle*.

pirámide triangular Pirámide cuya base es un *triángulo*.

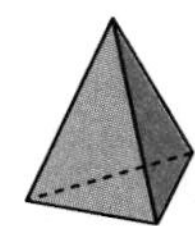

V

variable A letter or symbol used to represent an unknown quantity.

vertex (p. 315) The point where two rays meet in an *angle*.

variable Letra o símbolo que se usa para representar una cantidad desconocida.

vértice **a.** Punto de una figura bidimensional o tridimensional donde concurren dos o más de sus aristas. **b.** Extremo común de los lados de un ángulo.

X

***x*-axis** (p. 362) The horizontal axis (↔) in a coordinate graph.

***x*-coordinate** (p. 362) The first number in an *ordered pair* that indicates how far to the left or the right of the *y*-axis a point is. In (2, 3), 2 is the *x*-coordinate.

eje *x* El eje horizontal (↔) en una gráfica de coordenadas.

coordenada *x* El primer número en un *par ordenado* que indica la distancia a la izquierda o a la derecha del eje *x* a la cual se encuentra un punto. En (2, 3), 2 es la coordenada *x*.

Y

***y*-axis** (p. 362) The vertical axis (↕) in a coordinate graph.

***y*-coordinate** (p. 362) The second number in an *ordered pair* that indicates how far above or below the *x*-axis a point is. In (2, 3), 3 is the *y*-coordinate.

eje *y* El eje vertical (↕) en una gráfica de coordenadas.

coordenada *y* El segundo número en un *par ordenado* que indica la distancia hacia arriba o hacia abajo del eje *x* a la cual se encuentra un punto. En (2, 3), 3 es la coordenada *y*.

Z

Zero Property of Multiplication (p. 140) The property that states any number multiplied by zero is zero.

$0 \times 5 = 0$ $5 \times 0 = 0$

propiedad del producto nulo de la multiplicación Propiedad que establece que cualquier número multiplicado por cero es igual a cero.

$0 \times 5 = 0$ $5 \times 0 = 0$

Acknowledgements

United States coin images from the United States Mint; **iv** Doug Martin; **v** (br)courtesy Dinah Zike, (others)Doug Martin; **vi** (tc)courtesy Tita Alarcon, (others)Fulton Davenport; **vii** (cl)Carolyn Elender, (c)Elizabeth Firmin Birdwell, (others)Fulton Davenport; **viii** (tc)courtesy Ty Jones, (others)(bl)courtesy Alice Watkins, (others)Fulton Davenport; **x–xi** Lynn Stone/Animals Animals; **xii–xiii** Jeff Rotman/Getty Images; **xiv–xv** Denis Scot/CORBIS; **xvi–xvii** G. Grob/zefa/CORBIS; **xviii–xix** Ralph A. Clevenger/CORBIS; **xx–xxi** Michael Freeman/CORBIS; **xxii–xxiii** Photodisc/Getty Images; **xxv** Darrell Gulin/The Image Bank/Getty Images; **xxvi–xxvii** Getty Images; **xxviii–xxix** Guillen Photography/Alamy Images; **1** Lynn Stone /Animals Animals; **2** Richard Cummins/CORBIS; **3** Jill Stephenson/Alamy Images; **4** Arthur Morris/CORBIS; **5** (t)LYNN STONE /Animals Animals, (b)Roy Ooms; **6** Elizabeth Kreutz/NewSport/CORBIS; **7** Iain Crockart/Photographer's Choice RF/Getty Images; **8** Mary Clark/Alamy Images; **9** (l to r, t to b)Getty Images, CORBIS, S. Wanke/PhotoLink/Getty Images, Getty Images(5)Bonnie Kamin/PhotoEdit, (6)age fotostock/SuperStock; **10** Guillen Photography/Alamy Images; **11** (t)Envision/CORBIS, (b)Hisham F Ibrahim/Getty Images; **12 13** Getty Images; **14–15** Isidor Stankov/iStockphoto; **19** Elizabeth DeLaney/Index Stock Imagery; **20** Ed-Imaging; **23** Claver Carroll/CORBIS; **24** (t)Brand X/SuperStock, (b)Pixtal/SuperStock; **26** Paul Seheult/Eye Ubiquitous/CORBIS; **28** Jeff Dunn/Index Stock Imagery; **32** (l)Ingram Publishing/Alamy Images, (r)G.K. Vikki Hart/Getty Images; **35** Ed-Imaging; **36** C. Borland/PhotoLink/Getty Images; **39** (l)Ed-Imaging, (r)Ryan McVay/Getty Images; **40** Ed-Imaging; **42** (inset)J.Berndes/A.B./Zefa/CORBIS; **42–43** Stuart Westmorland/Getty Images; **52–53** The McGraw-Hill Companies; **54** (l)CORBIS, (r)C Squared Studios/Getty Images; **57** Ed-Imaging; **58** (t)Image Source/Jupiter Images, (b)Index Stock Imagery; **60** Ralf-Finn Hestoft/CORBIS; **62** Gary Rhijnsburger/Masterfile; **65** (t)Brand X Pictures/Alamy Images, (b)2006 Photos To Go; **66** Getty Images; **70** Ed-Imaging; **73** Photos To Go; **74** Raymond Forbes/agefotostock; **75 76** Ed-Imaging; **77** Getty Images; **78–79** Jeff Rotman/Getty Images; **79** (inset)Paul Springett/Alamy Images; **81** George Doyle & Ciaran Griffin/Stockdisc/Getty Images; **82** (t)CORBIS, (bl br)Ed-Imaging; **83** CORBIS; **92–93** Kwame Zikomo/SuperStock; **94** George D. Lepp/CORBIS; **96** G.K. Vikki Hart/Getty Images; **98** Oliver Benn/Royal Philharmonic Orchestra; **99** C Squared Studios/Getty Images; **107 108 110** Ed-Imaging; **111** (t tc c)The McGraw-Hill Companies, (b)Ryan McVay/Getty Images; **112** (inset) Stockdisc/Getty Images; **112–113** Tony Craddock/Getty Images; **116** David Young-Wolff/PhotoEdit; **118** Getty Images; **122** (t)A&P/Alamy Images, (b)CORBIS; **132–133** Denis Scot/CORBIS; **137** The McGraw-Hill Companies; **139** Steve Kaufman/CORBIS; **141** C Squared Studios/Getty Images; **142** BananaStock/Alamy Images; **144** Lon C. Diehl/PhotoEdit; **150** Getty Images; **152** Brian Hagiwara/PictureArts/CORBIS; **154** (l)Bettmann/CORBIS, (c)John Van Hasselt/CORBIS Sygma, (r)Webster & Stevens Collection/Museum of History and Industry, Seattle/CORBIS; **154–155** Tracy Hebden/Alamy Images; **155** (l)SuperStock, (r)Rachel Epstein/PhotoEdit; **156** Tetra Images/Alamy Images; **157** D. Hurst/Alamy Images; **158** Kevin Schafer/zefa/CORBIS; **160** Thinkstock Images/Jupiter Images; **162 164 165** Ed-Imaging; **166** Dennis Macdonald/PhotoEdit; **167** Mark Richards/PhotoEdit; **168** StockTrek/Getty Images; **169** Ed-Imaging; **171** Getty Images; **180–181** Digital Vision/PunchStock; **183** Don Smetzer/PhotoEdit; **188** Stockdisc/Jupiter Images; **190** (l)Ed-Imaging, (r)William Howard/Getty Images; **192** Ed-Imaging; **202–203** Roine Magnusson/Getty Images; **203** (inset)Joe McDonald/CORBIS; **204** Jim Cummins/CORBIS; **205** Getty Images; **206** C.C. Lockwood /Animals Animals; **207 208** Ed-Imaging; **210** Michael Newman/PhotoEdit; **216** Getty Images; **219** (l)C Squared Studios/Getty Images, (r)The McGraw-Hill Companies; **224–225** Denis Scott/CORBIS; **227** G. Grob/zefa/CORBIS; **228** Getty Images; **229** CORBIS; **230** (t)G.K. Vikki Hart/Getty Images, (c)C Squared Studios/Getty Images; **232** Ren Long/AP Images; **235 240** Ed-Imaging; **242** Richard Hutchings/PhotoEdit; **244** Age Fotostock/SuperStock; **245** Ed-Imaging; **246** (inset)Daniel A. Bedell /Animals Animals; **246–247** David Tipling/Lonely Planet Images; **248** Cooperphoto/CORBIS; **249** Robert Lubeck /Animals Animals; **252** Getty Images; **253** (l)Ryan McVay/Getty Images, (r)Michael Houghton/StudiOhio; **254** C Squared Studios/Getty Images; **264–265** Donovan Reese/Getty Images; **267** Ed-Imaging; **269** Craig Lovell/CORBIS; **271** (t)Geoff Dann/Getty Images, (c)Patti Murray/Animals Animals, (bl)Ed-Imaging, (bc)G.K. Vikki Hart/Getty Images, (br)Macmillan McGraw-Hill Companies; **277** Ryan McVay/Getty Images; **279** Stockbyte/Getty Images; **280** John Elk/Bruce Coleman; **282** CORBIS; **283** Tony Freeman/PhotoEdit, Inc.; **284** MMH DIL; **285 286** Ed-Imaging; **292** CORBIS; **295** Ed-Imaging; **296–297** Mauritius/SuperStock; **298** SuperStock, Inc./SuperStock; **299** Neal Mishler/Getty Images; **304** (l)G.K. Vikki Hart/Getty Images, (r)Getty Images; **308** C Squared Studios/Getty Images; **312–313** Masterfile; **314** Getty Images; **315** (t)G.K. Hart/Vikki Hart/Getty Images, (b)Thomas Northcut/Getty Images; **316** The McGraw-Hill Companies/Ken Karp; **317** (l)C Squared Studios/Getty Images, (c)Brand X Pictures/Getty Images, (r)Stockdisc/PunchStock; **318** (t)S. Wanke/PhotoLink/Getty Images, (cl)Getty Images, (cr)CORBIS, (b)Comstock Images/Alamy Images; **319** Getty Images; **320** (tl)C Squared Studios/Getty Images, (tr)Ryan McVay/Getty Images, (b)Bridgeman-Giraudon/Art Resource, NY; **321** Ed-Imaging; **326** Jacques Cornell/The McGraw-Hill Companies; **327** Photos.com; **328** David Young-Wolff/PhotoEdit; **329** Miles Ertman/Masterfile; **332** Werner H. Mueller/CORBIS; **333** (t)Alan King/Alamy Images, (c)courtesy George Hart/Corbis, (bl)Image Source/Alamy Images, (br)Creatas/SuperStock, (inset)Purestock/Jupiter Images; **334** (tl)Jorg Greuel/Getty Images, (tr)Burke/Triolo/Brand X Pictures/Jupiter Images, (bl)Thomas Northcut, (bc)DK Limited/CORBIS, (br)Purestock/Alamy Images; **335 336** Ed-Imaging; **338–339** Visions of America, LLC/Alamy Images; **339** (l)Mary Ann Sullivan/Bluffton University, (r)Visions of America, LCC/Alamy Images; **341** CORBIS; **348–349** Aartifacts Images/Getty Images; **355** (l)Creatas/SuperStock, (r)Jeff Greenberg/PhotoEdit; **356** Corbis; **358** (t)Brand X/ImageState, (c)C Squared Studios/Getty Images, (cr)Getty Images; **360** Rob Gage/Getty Images; **363** Getty Images; **365** Photos.com; **372 373** Getty Images; **375** Photos.com; **376** (tl)Ralph A. Clevenger/CORBIS, (tr)Ryan McVay/Getty Images, (bl)rubberball/Jupiter Images, (br)Ed-Imaging; **378–379** Getty Images; **379** (inset)Dennis di Cicco/CORBIS; **380** Darrell Gulin/CORBIS; **381** Comstock/Alamy Images; **382** (l to r)Colin Keates, Getty Images; Getty Images(4)Gallo Images/Getty Images; **383** Ed-Imaging; **386** Getty Images; **392–393** Bob Krist/CORBIS; **394** (l)Design Pics Inc./Alamy Images, (r)Creatas Images; **395** PhotoLink/Getty Images; **396** Photos to Go; **397** (t)Chris Newbert/Minden Pictures, (b)The McGraw-Hill Companies; **398** (l r)C Squared Studios/Getty Images, (t)GK Hart/Vikki Hart; **399** (tl)Photos.com, (tr)Getty Images, (cl)Jeffrey Coolidge/CORBIS, (cr)The McGraw-Hill Companies, (bl)Siede Preis/Getty Images, (br)Photos to Go; **400** STACY GOLD/National Geographic Society Images; **402** C Squared Studios/Getty Images; **403** Getty Images; **405** Photos.com; **406** D. Hurst/Alamy Images; **407** (t)Jeffrey Coolidge/CORBIS, (cl)Hans Christoph Kappel/npl/Minden Pictures, (cr)W.A.N.T. PHOTOGRAPHY/Animals Animals, (bl)Comstock Images, (br)McGraw-Hill Companies Inc./Ken Cavanagh Photographer; **408** (t)David Young-Wolff/Photo Edit, (br)CORBIS, (bl)Lon C. Diehl/PhotoEdit; **409** Getty Images; **412** Michael Freeman/CORBIS; **413** (t)Getty Images, (b)The McGraw-Hill Companies; **417 418 420** Ed-Imaging; **421** agefotostock/SuperStock; **425** Ed-Imaging; **426–427** Patrick Ray Dunn/Alamy Images; **429** (t)Getty Images, (b)C Squared Studios/Getty Images; **431** (tl)Getty Images, (tr)Photos.com, (b)CORBIS; **435** (t)C Squared Studios/Getty Images, (c)USDA Natural Resources Convservation Service, (b)The McGraw-Hill Companies; **438–439** Jessie Cohen/epa/CORBIS; **442** (b)GK Hart/Vikki Hart/The Image Bank/Getty Images; (Others) Ed-Imaging **443** (t)Burke/Triolo Productions, (cl, c)Photos.com, (cr)CORBIS, (bl, br)Colin Young-Wolff/Photo Edit; **444** (l to r, t to b)Jeff Greenberg/PhotoEdit, Image Source, Burke/Triolo, The McGraw-Hill Companies, Spencer Grant/PhotoEdit, Burke/Triolo Productions/Brand X/Corbis, Getty Images; **445** The McGraw-Hill Companies; **446** Ed-Imaging; **448** (t)Rachel Epstein/PhotoEdit, (bl)Michael Newman/PhotoEdit, (br)Ed-Imaging; **449** (l to r, t to b)Comstock/Jupiter Images, Douglas Fisher/Alamy Images, Dynamic Graphics Value/SuperStock, Elizabeth Whiting & Associates/CORBIS, DK Limited/Corbis; **450** (tl)Joson/zefa/CORBIS, (tr)David Young-Wolff/PhotoEdit, (cl)Lawrence Manning CORBIS, (cr)McGraw-Hill Companies, Inc./Jacques Cornell photographer, (bl)Amy Etra/PhotoEdit, (br)Lawrence Manning CORBIS; **451** (l)Getty Images, (r)Andrea Rugg/Beateworks/CORBIS; **452** (t)Lew Robertson, (c b)Ed-Imaging; **454** (t)Rachel Epstein/Photoedit, (r)Image Source **454** (c)Maximilian Stock Ltd/photocuisine/CORBIS, (cr)Paul Gapper/worldphotos.org/Alamy Images, (bl)Caren Alpert, (br)Rachel Epstein/Photo Edit; **455** (tl)C Squared Studios/Getty Images, (tr)Thinkstock/Alamy Images, (bl)PunchStock, (br)Corbis/Jupiter Images; **456** (tl)Lake County Museum/CORBIS, (tc)CORBIS, (tr)Getty Images, (cl)David Stares/Alamy Images, (c)G.K. Vikki Hart/Getty Images, (cr)Jeffrey Coolidge/CORBIS, (b)Lynn Stone /Animals Animals; **457** (l to r, t to b)Michael Matisse/Getty Images, Photodisc/Getty Images, Envision/CORBIS, Russell Illig, G.K. & Vikki Hart/Getty Images; **458** Photodisc/Getty Images; **459** G.K. & Vikki Hart/Getty Images; **460** Envision/CORBIS; **462** Design Pics; **463** (tl)C Squared Studios/Getty Images, (tr)G.K. Vikki Hart/Getty Images, (bl)The McGraw-Hill Companies, (br)Photos to Go; **464** Ed-Imaging; **465** (tr)Big Cheese Photo, (c)Ron Chapple/Jupiter Images, (bl)Photodisc, (br)CORBIS; **466** (tl)Monotype, LLC, (tc)Dave Mager, (tr b)C Squared Studios/Getty Images, (cl)ThinkStock LLC, (c)Image Farm Inc./Alamy Images, (cr)Charlie Roy/Jupiter Images; **467** Ed-Imaging; **468** The McGraw-Hill Companies; **471** (bl)Stockdisc/PunchStock, (br)Photos.com; **472** (c)Iconotec/Alamy Images, (bl)Mark Cassino/SuperStock, (br)Jupiter Images; **472–473** Renee Morris/Alamy Images; **474** Ed-Imaging; **475 476** Photos to Go; **479** (t tl)Ed-Imaging, (bl br)G.K. Vikki Hart/Getty Images; **482** (l to r, t to b)Colin Young-Wolff/Photo Edit, Judith Collins/Alamy Images, Jan Tadeusz/Alamy Images, Purestock, Jeffrey Coolidge/Getty Images, Joe Schmelzer/Beateworks/CORBIS; **483** Rick Gayle Studio/CORBIS; **484** (t)Ed-Imaging, (cl)D. Hurst/Alamy Images, (c)Stockdisc Classic/Alamy Images, (cr)G.K. Vikki Hart/Getty Images, (bl)Ann Cutting, (br)Siede Preis; **485** (l)Siede Preis/Getty Images, (r)Getty Images; **487** (l to r, t to b)The McGraw-Hill Companies Inc.The McGraw-Hill Companies Inc., Brand X Pictures/Alamy Images, Jose Fuste Raga/CORBISBrand X Pictures/Punchstock, Mitch Diamond, Darren Bennett/Animals Animals; **490–491** (inset)C Squared Studios/Getty Images, Siede Preis/Getty Images; **496** The McGraw-Hill Companies; **497** (l to r, t to b)Don Farrall/Getty Images, (Others)Stockdisc/PunchStock; **498** Photodisc/Getty Images; **499** (l)Ed-Imaging, (r)Getty Images; **500** Stockdisc/PunchStock; **501** (tr)C Squared Studios/Getty Images, (bl)Koopman/CORBI, (br)Ton Kinsbergen/Beateworks/CORBIS; **507** (t)Getty Images, (bl br)Ed-Imaging; **508** Ed-Imaging; **513** Getty Images; **514–515** The McGraw-Hill Companies, Inc.; **519** (l)Punchstock, (r)Getty Images; **520** Ed-Imaging; **524** The McGraw-Hill Companies; **530–531** CORBIS; **535** MedioImages/SuperStock; **538** David Muench/CORBIS; **539** Martin Harvey/CORBIS; **540** Kennan Ward/CORBIS; **541** (l)Ed-Imaging, (r)Getty Images; **542 550** Ed-imaging; **551** Michael Houghton/StudiOhio; **552** Greg Probst/CORBIS; **556–557** Digital Vision/Getty Images; **558** Stockdisc Classic/Alamy Images; **560** (l)Ed-Imaging, (r)Brad Wilson/Getty Images; **561** Ed-Imaging; **570–571** Robert Lubeck /Animals Animals; **573** Lee Canfield/SuperStock; **575** Ed-Imaging; **578** Mauritius/SuperStock; **580** CORBIS; **581** G.K. Vikki Hart/Getty Images; **582** Ed-Imaging; **584** BigStockPhoto.com; **585** David Hosking/Alamy Images; **586** Getty Images; **588–589** Donald Miralle/Getty Images; **589** (l)Empics/SportsChrome, (r)Rob Tringali/SportsChrome; **590** Getty Images; **591** Ken Karp/The McGraw-Hill Companies; **592** Ed-Imaging; **593** Bob Krist/CORBIS; **594** Bettmann/CORBIS; **595** John Cancalosi/Peter Arnold, inc.; **597** (l)Image Source/Getty Images, (r)CORBIS; **606** (t)Getty Images, (c)Punchstock, (b)Bob Daemmrich/PhotoEdit; **607** Tim Fuller; **608** BananaStock/Alamy Images; **610** (t)Food Image Source/O'Gara/Bissell/StockFood, (b)Index Open; **611** Photos.com; **612** Sindre Ellingsen/Alamy Images; **614** Laurie Rubin/Getty Images; **R0** Ed-Imaging; **R25** (t)Photos to Go, (c)Comstock Images/Alamy; **R27** (t)Nancy R. Cohen/Getty Images, (b)gds/zefa/CORBIS; **R31** (b)Creatas/PunchStock, (bl)Getty Images, (br)CORBIS; **R32** (tl)The McGraw-Hill Companies, (tr cl cr)Getty Images, (bl)D. Hurst/Alamy, (br)C Squared Studios/Getty Images; **R33** (tl)G.K. Vikki Hart/Getty Images, (bl)C Squared Studios/Getty Images, (br)Photos.com; **R35** (tl bl)The McGraw-Hill Companies, (tc)Ingram Publishing/Superstock, (tr)C Squared Studios/Getty Images, (bc)CORBIS, (br)Photos.com; **R36** (t tcl tcr bl)Photos.com, (cl)Stockdisc/PunchStock, (cr)Getty Images, (br)Photos to Go; **R37** (tl tr)Getty Images, (bl)G.K. Vikki Hart/Getty Images, (br)Photos.com; **R33** (tl)C Squared Studios/Getty Images; **TX1** Ed-Imaging

McGraw-Hill would like to acknowledge the artists and agencies who contributed to illustrating this program: **Cover** Jim Talbot represented by Mendola Artists; Argosy Publishing; Keith Batcheller, Gary Ciccarelli, Shawn McKelvey, Mark Snyder represented by AA Reps. Inc.

Acknowledgements

Index

Index

M

Index

T

W

Index

Mathematics Chart

Measurement Conversions

LENGTH

Metric	Customary
1 kilometer = 1000 meters	1 mile = 1760 yards
1 meter = 100 centimeters	1 mile = 5280 feet
1 centimeter = 10 millimeters	1 yard = 3 feet
	1 foot = 12 inches

CAPACITY AND VOLUME

Metric	Customary
1 liter = 1000 milliliters	1 gallon = 4 quarts
	1 gallon = 128 ounces
	1 quart = 2 pints
	1 pint = 2 cups
	1 cup = 8 ounces

MASS AND WEIGHT

Metric	Customary
1 kilogram = 1000 grams	1 ton = 2000 pounds
1 gram = 1000 milligrams	1 pound = 16 ounces

TIME

1 year = 365 days

1 year = 12 months

1 year = 52 weeks

1 week = 7 days

1 day = 24 hours

1 hour = 60 minutes

1 minute = 60 seconds

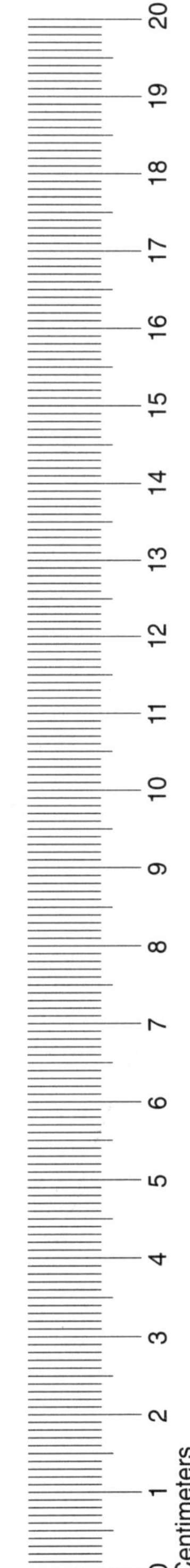

Mathematics Chart

Formulas

Perimeter	square	$P = 4s$
	rectangle	$P = 2\ell + 2w$ or $P = 2(\ell + w)$
Area	rectangle	$A = \ell w$ or $A = bh$

Inches

0 1 2 3 4 5 6